DATABASE
MANAGEMENT SYSTEM

Dr. (Prof.) Rajendra Prasad Mahapatra
BE, ME, PhD
Associate Dean
Professor
Department of Computer Science & Engineering
SRM University NCR Campus
Ghaziabad (U.P.)

Govind Verma
M-Tech
(OCA and OCP Certified)
Assistant Professor
Department of Computer Science & Engineering
SRM University NCR Campus
Ghaziabad (U.P.)

KHANNA BOOK PUBLISHING CO. (P) LTD.
Publisher of Engineering and Computer Books
4C/4344, Ansari Road, Darya Ganj, New Delhi-110002
Phone : 011-23244447-48 **Mobile:** +91-9910909320
E-mail : contact@khannabooks.com
Website : www.khannabooks.com

Dear Readers,

To prevent the piracy, this book is secured with HIGH SECURITY HOLOGRAM on the front title cover. In case you don't find the hologram on the front cover title, please write us to at contact@khannabooks.com or whatsapp us at +91-99109 09320 and avail special gift voucher for yourself.

Specimen of Hologram on front Cover title:

Moreover, there is a SPECIAL DISCOUNT COUPON for you with EVERY HOLOGRAM.

How to avail this SPECIAL DISCOUNT:

Step 1: Scratch the hologram
Step 2: Under the scratch area, your "coupon code" is available
Step 3: Logon to www.khannabooks.com
Step 4: Use your "coupon code" in the shopping cart and get your copy at a special discount
Step 5: Enjoy your reading!

Thanks,
Khanna Publishing House

ISBN: 978-93-82609-14-8

Database Management System
by **RP Mahapatra, Govind Verma**

First Edition: 2013
Reprint: 2024, 2025, 2026

To view complete list of books, please scan the QR Code:

Published by:
Khanna Book Publishing Co. (P) Ltd.
CIN: U22110DL1998PTC095547

Visit us at: www.khannabooks.com
Write us at: contact@khannabooks.com

Printed in Bharat.

In Memory of

My Parents and brothers

And

My Family with my loving son

SAI

Rajendra Prasad Mahapatra

In Memory of

My Parents and brothers

And

My Family with my loving Nephew HARSH

Govind Verma

PREFACE

This book fundamental concepts necessary for designing, using and implementing database systems and applications. This book assumes no previous knowledge of databases or database technology and the concepts are built from grounds-up basic concepts to advanced techniques and technologies. This is. The book is self-contained and has a flexible organization to suit the needs of individual course.

Some of the books cover the topics in great depth and detail while others cover only the most important topics. Obviously no single book on this subject can meet everyone's needs, but many lie to either end of spectrum to be really helpful. At the low end there are the superficial ones that leave the readers confused or unsatisfied. Those at the high end cover the subject with such thoroughness as to be overwhelming.

The present edition is primarily intended to serve the need to students preparing for B. Tech, M. Tech and MCA courses. This book is an outgrowth of our teaching experience. In our academic interaction with teachers and students, we found that they face considerable difficulties in using the available books in this growing academic discipline. The authors simply presented the subjects matter in their own style and make the subject easier by giving a number of questions and summary given at the end of the chapter.

Dr. (Prof.) Rajendra Prasad Mahapatra
Govind Verma

PREFACE

This book fundamental concepts necessary for designing, using and implementing database systems and applications. This book assumes no previous knowledge of databases or database technology and the concepts are built from ground-up basic concepts to advanced techniques and technologies. This is. The book is self-contained and has a flexible organisation to suit the needs of individual course.

Some of the books cover the topics in great depth and detail while others cover only the most important topics. Obviously no single book on this subject can meet everyone's needs, but many lie to either end of spectrum to be really helpful. At the low end there are the superficial ones that leave the readers confused or unsatisfied. Those at the high end cover the subject with such thoroughness as to be overwhelming.

The present edition is primarily intended to serve the need to students preparing for B. Tech, M. Tech and MCA courses. This book is an outgrowth of our teaching experience. In our academic interaction with teachers and students, we found that they face considerable difficulties in using the available books in this growing academic discipline. The authors simply presented the subjects matter in their own style and make the subject easier by giving a number of questions and summary given at the end of the chapter.

Dr. (Prof.) Rajendra Prasad Mahapatra
Govind Verma

ACKNOWLEDGEMENTS

We are very much grateful to our reserved Chancellor Dr. T.R. Pachamuthu SRM UNIVERSITY and Chairman Mr. Ravi Pachamoothoo SRM UNIVERSITY for his encouragement in continuing our effort in bringing out this book.

Our sincere thanks our Director Dr. Prof. Manoj Kumar Pandey, SRM UNIVSERITY NCR Campus, Ghaziabad and Administrative Officer Dr. S. Vishwanathan SRM University NCR Campus Ghaziabad for their kind co-operation.

We thank our family members for their moral support to bring out this book.

Dr. (Prof.) Rajendra Prasad Mahapatra
Govind Verma

CONTENTS

PART 1: INTRODUCTION

PART 2: DATABASE DESIGN AND DATA MODELING

PART 3: DATABASE QUERY LANGUAGES

PART 4: DATABASE STORAGE AND FILE

9. Record Storage and File Structure

PART 5: DATABASE IMPLEMENTATION

PART 6: TYPES OF DATABASES

PART 7: DATABASE APPLICATIONS

CHAPTER 1

INTRODUCTION

1.1 INFORMATION PROCESSING

Information is the backbone of any organization. In a world that focuses on achievement and advantage, information is the critical factor that enables managers and organizations to gain a competitive edge. It is the most critical resource of an organization. It is the most critical resource of an organization. Information is nothing but refined data. According to Burch and Grudnitski, "information is data that have been put into a meaningful and useful context and communicated to recipient who uses it make decisions". Information involves the communication and reception of intelligence or knowledge. Information apprises and notifies surprises and stimulates, reduces uncertainty, reveals additional alternatives or helps in eliminating irrelevant or poor ones, influence individuals and stimulates them to action.

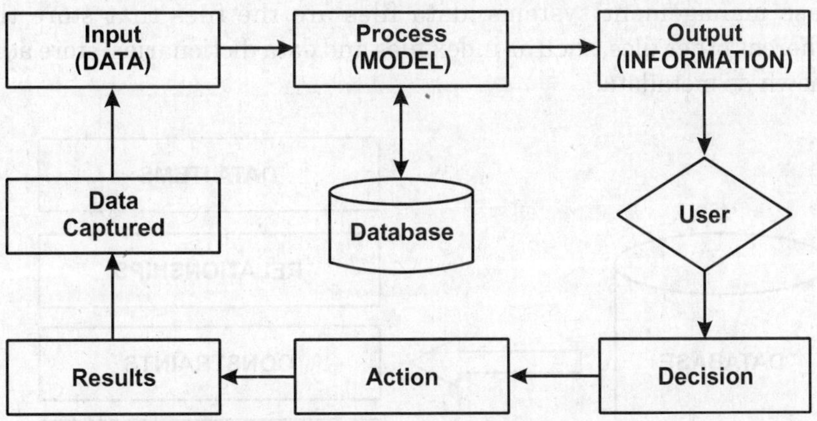

Figure 1.1 Information cycle

Information consists of data, images, text, documents and voice, often inextricably intertwined, but always organized in a meaningful context. The term data will be used throughout this text to encompass all the components of information. But it is important to remember that information is more than one data. This is explained in Figure 1.1 Notice that the data that is being processed or refined can be input, stored or both. Another point to remember is the cycle of information.

Data are processed through models to create information. The recipient receives the information and then makes a decision and takes an action. This triggers other action or events, which in turn will generate large amounts of scattered data, that are captured and serve as input and the cycle starts all over again.

1.2 COMPONENTS AND ORGANIZATION OF A DATABASE

Before we attempt to define what a database management system is, we must have a clear understanding of what the DBMS is managing the database. A database consists of four elements as shown in Figure 1.2(a):

1. Data
2. Relationships
3. Constraints
4. Schema

Data are binary computer representations of stored logical entities. They are distinct pieces of information, usually formatted in a special way. Software is divided into two general categories–data and programs. A program is a collection of instructions for manipulating data. Data can exist in a variety of forms-as numbers or text on pieces of paper, as bits and bytes stored in electronic memory, or as facts stored in a person's mind.

In database management systems, data files are the files that store the database information, whereas other files, such as index files and data dictionaries, store administrative information known as metadata.

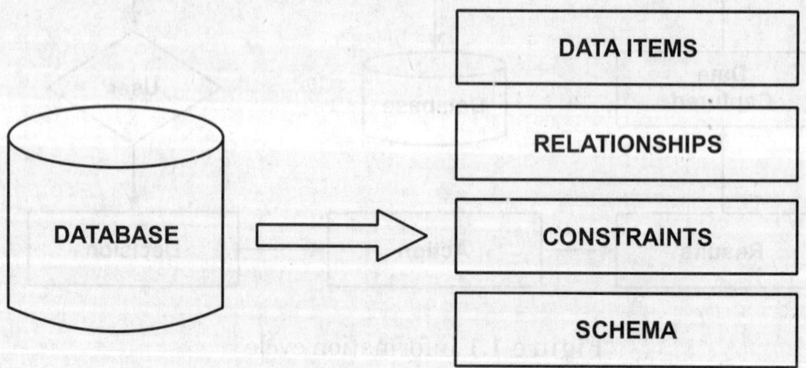

Figure 1.2 (*a*) Components of a Database

Relationship represent a correspondence between the various data elements **constraints** are predicates that define correct states. **Schema** describes the organization of data and relationships within the database.

The schema defines various views of the database for the use of the various system components of the database management system and for the application security (see Figure 1.2(b)). A schema separates the physical aspects of data storage from the logical aspects of data representation.

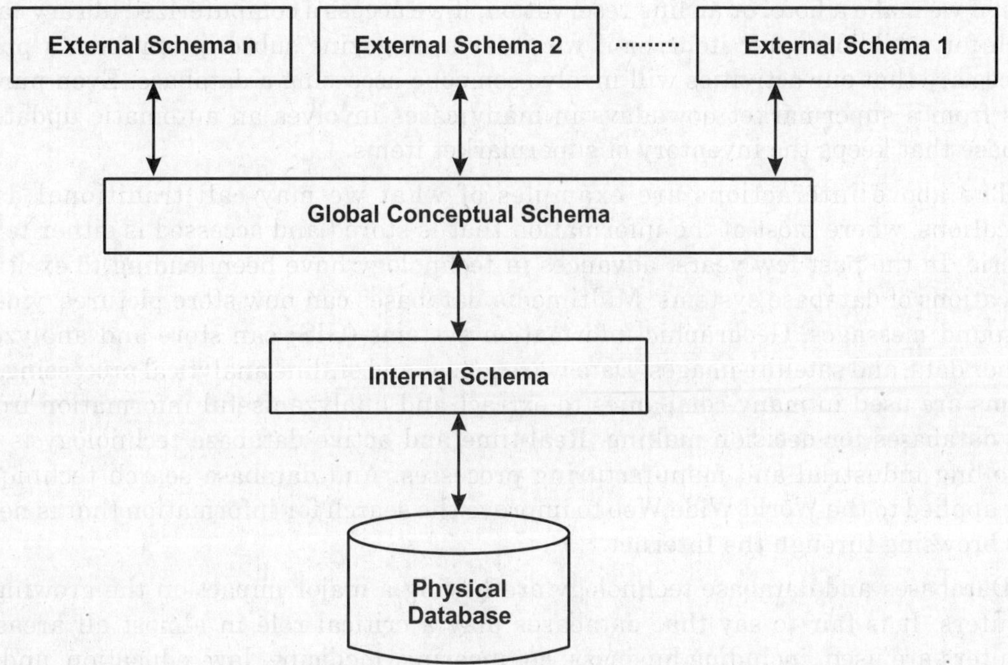

Figure 1.2 (*b*) Organization of a Database

The **internal schema** defines how and where data are organized in physical data storage. The **conceptual schema** defines the stored data structures in terms of the database model used. The **external schema** defines a view or views of the database for particular users. A database management system provides services for accessing the database while maintaining the required correctness and consistency of the stored data.

A collection of data designed to be used by different people is called a database. It is a collection of interrelated data stored together with controlled redundancy to serve one or more applications in an optimal fashion. The data are stored in such a fashion that they are independent of the programs of people using the data. A common and controlled approach is used in adding new data and modifying and retrieving existing data within the database.

A database is organized in such a way that a computer program can quickly select desired pieces of data. You can think of a database as an electronic filing system. Traditional databases are organized by fields, records and files. A field is a single piece of information; a record is one complete set of fields; and a file is a collection of records. For example, a telephone book is analogous to a file. It contains a list of records, each of which consists of three fields: name, address and telephone number. To access information from a database, you need a database management system.

1.3 DATABASES AND DATABASE USERS

Databases and database systems have become an essential component of everyday life in modern society. In the course of a day, most of us encounter several activities that involve some interaction with a database. For example, if we go to the bank to deposit or withdraw funds; if we make a hotel or airline reservation; if we access a computerized library catalog to search for a bibliographic item; or if we order a magazine subscription from a publisher, chances are that our activities will involve someone accessing a database. Even purchasing items from a supermarket nowadays in many cases involves an automatic update of the database that keeps the inventory of supermarket items.

The above interactions are examples of what we may call traditional database applications, where most of the information that is stored and accessed is either textual or numeric. In the past few years, advances in technology have been leading to exciting new applications of database systems. Multimedia databases can now store pictures, video clips, and sound messages. Geographic information systems (GIS) can store and analyze maps, weather data, and satellite images. Data warehouses and on-line analytical processing (OLAP) systems are used in many companies to extract and analyze useful information from very large databases for decision making. Real-time and active database technology is used in controlling industrial and manufacturing processes. And database search techniques are being applied to the World Wide Web to improve the search for information that is needed by users browsing through the Internet.

Databases and database technology are having a major impact on the growing use of computers. It is fair to say that databases play a critical role in almost all areas where computers are used, including business, engineering, medicine, law, education, and library science, to name a few. The word database is in such common use that we must begin by defining a database. Our initial definition is quite general.

A database is a collection of related data. By data, we mean known facts that can be recorded and that have implicit meaning. For example, consider the names, telephone numbers, and addresses of the people you know. You may have recorded this data in an indexed address book, or you may have stored it on a hard drive, using a personal computer and software such as Microsoft ACCESS, or EXCEL. This is a collection of related data with an implicit meaning is a database.

The preceding definition of database is quite general; for example, we may consider the collection of words that make up this page of text to be related data and hence to constitute a database. However, the common use of the term database is usually more restricted. A database has the following implicit properties:

- A database represents some aspect of the real world, sometimes called the mini-World or the Universe of Discourse (UoD) .Changes to the mini-world are reflected in the database.
- A database is a logically coherent collection of data with some inherent meaning. A random assortment of data cannot correctly be referred to as a database.
- A database is designed, built, and populated with data for a specific purpose. It has an intended group of users and some preconceived applications in which these users are interested.

A database management system (DBMS) is a collection of programs that enables users to create and maintain a database. In another word's the DBMS consists of a collection of interrelated data and a set of programs to access those data. The collection of data usually referred to as the database. The DBMS is hence a general-purpose software system that facilitates the processes of defining, constructing, and manipulating databases for various applications. Defining a database involves specifying the data types, structures, and constraints for the data to be stored in the database. Constructing the database is the process of storing the data itself on some storage medium that is controlled by the DBMS. Manipulating a database includes such functions as querying the database to retrieve specific data, updating the database to reflect changes in the miniworld, and generating reports from the data.

It is not necessary to use general-purpose DBMS software to implement a computerized database. We could write our own set of programs to create and maintain the database, in effect creating our own special-purpose DBMS software. In either case—whether we use a general-purpose DBMS or not—we usually have to employ a considerable amount of software to manipulate the database. We will call the database and DBMS software together a database system. (see Figure1.3)

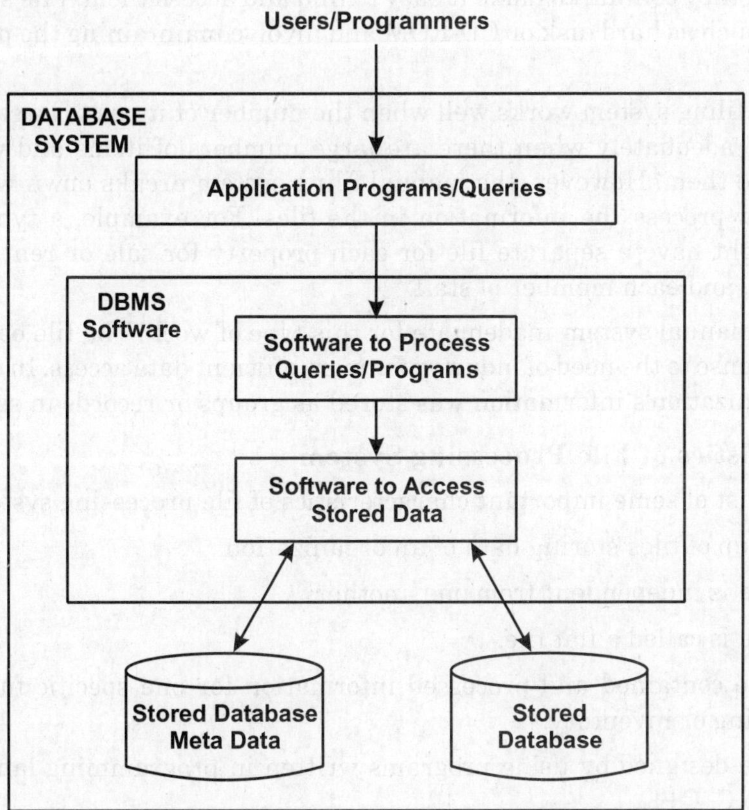

Figure 1.3 A Simplified database system environment

1.4 DATABASE AND COMPUTERS

Computerized database is more suited than manual database because of the following reasons:

- Computer has a large storage capacity. It can store thousands of records at a time.
- It has high speed, within no time it searches any desired information, arrange the data in alphabetical order, do calculations on the data and make repetitions and so on.
- Computer is more accurate.
- Data in computers can be stored in the form of a file, records and fields.
- There are two approaches for storing data in computers such as File based approach and Database approach.

1.5 FILE SYSTEM

File processing system was an early attempt to computerize the manual filing system that we are all familiar system. A file system is a method for storing and organizing computer files and the data they contain to make it easy to find and access them. File systems may use a storage device such as hard disk or CD-ROM and involve maintaining the physical location of the files.

The manual filing system works well when the number of items to be stored is small. It even works quite adequately when there are large numbers of items and we have only to store and retrieve them. However, the manual filing system breaks down when we have to cross-reference or process the information in the files. For example, a typical real estate agent's office might have a separate file for each property for sale or rent, each potential buyer and renter, and each member of staff.

Clearly the manual system inadequate for this type of work. The file based system was developed in response to the need of industry for more efficient data access. In early processing systems, an organization's information was stored as groups or records in separate files.

1.5.1 Characteristics of File Processing System

Here is the list of some important characteristics of file processing system:

- It is group of files storing data of an organization.
- Each file is independent from one another.
- Each file is called a flat file.
- Each file contained and processed information for one specific function, such as accounting or inventory.
- Files are designed by using programs written in programming languages such as COBOL, C, C++.
- The physical implementation and access procedures are written into database application; therefore, physical changes resulted in intensive rework on the part of the programmer.
- As system became more complex, file processing system offered little flexibility, presented many limitations, and were difficult to maintain.

The **File processing system** is supported by a conventional operating system. The system stores permanent records in various ûles, and it needs different application programs to extract records from, and add records to, the appropriate ûles. Before database management systems (DBMSs) came along, organizations usually stored information in such systems. Keeping organizational information in a ûle processing system has a number of major disadvantages.

1.5.2 Disadvantages of File Processing System'

- **Data redundancy and inconsistency**

  Since the files and application programs are created by different programmers over a long period, the various files are likely to have different formats and the programs may be written in several programming languages. Moreover, the same information may be duplicated in several places. For example, the address and telephone number of a particular customer may appear in a file that consists of savings account records and in a file that consists of checking account records. The Data redundancy leads to higher storage and access cost. In addition, it may lead to data inconsistency; that is, the various copies of the same data may no longer agree. For example, a changed customer address may be reflected in savings account records but not elsewhere in the system.

- **Data isolation**

  To make decision, a user might need data from two separate files. First, the files were evaluated by analysis and programmers to determine the specific data required from each file and the relationships between the data and then applications could be written in a programming language to process and extract the needed data. Imagine the work involved if data from several files was needed.

- **Integrity problems**

  The data values stored in the database must satisfy certain types of consistency constraints. For example, the balance of a bank account may never fall below a prescribed amount (say, ₹. 2500). Developers enforce these constraints in the system by adding appropriate code in the various application programs. However, when new constraints are added, it is difficult to change the programs to enforce them. The problem is compounded when constraints involve several data items from different files.

- **Atomicity problems**

  A computer system, like any other mechanical or electrical device, is subject to failure. In many applications, it is crucial that, if a failure occurs, the data be restored to the consistent state that existed prior to the failure. Consider a program to transfer ₹.5000 from account A to account B. If a system failure occurs during the execution of the program, it is possible that the ₹ . 5000 was removed from account A but was not credited to account B, resulting in an inconsistent database state. Clearly, it is essential to database consistency that either both the credit and debit occur, or that neither occur. That is, the funds transfer must be atomic it must happen in its entirety or not at all. It is difficult to ensure atomicity in a conventional file-processing system.

- **Security problems**

  Not every user of the database system should be able to access all the data. For example, in a banking system, payroll personnel need to see only that part of the database that has information about the various bank employees. They do not need access to information about customer accounts. But, since application programs are added to the system in an ad hoc manner, it is difficult to enforce such integrity constraints.

- **Difficulty in representing data from the user's view**

  To create useful applications for the user, often data from various files must be combined. In file processing it was difficult to determine relationship between isolated data in order to meet user requirements.

- **Data Inflexibility**

  Program data interdependency and data isolation, limited the flexibility of the file processing systems in providing users with ad hoc information requests.

1.6 DATABASE APPROACH

The database is a shared collection of logically related data, designed to meet the information needs of an organization. A database is a computer based record keeping system whose over all purpose is to record and maintain information. The database is single, large repository of data, which can be used simultaneously by many departments and users. Instead of disconnected files with redundant data, all data items are integrated with minimum amount of duplication. The database is no longer owned by one department but is a shared corporate resource. The database holds not only the organization's operational data but also a description of this data. For this reason, a database is also defined as a self describing collection of interrelated records. The description of the data is known as the Data Dictionary or Meta data. it is self describing nature of a database that provide program data independence.

Characteristics of data in a Database :

The data in a database should have the following:

- **Shared**- Data in a database are shared among different users and applications.
- **Persistence**- Data in a database exist permanently in the sense the data can live beyond the scope of the process that created it.
- **Validity/Integrity/Correctness**- Data should be correct with respect to the real world entity that they represent.
- **Security**- Data should be presented from unauthorized access.
- **Consistency**- Whenever more than one data element in a database represents related real world values, the values should be consistent with respect to the relationship.

- **Non-consistency-** No two data items in a database should represent the same real entity.
- **Independence-** The three levels in the schema (Internal, conceptual and external) should be independent of each other so that the changes in the schema at one level should not affect the other levels

Comparison of file management system with database management system :

Here is the comparison in tabular form between traditional file processing and database management system

File Management e.g c++ or COBOL program	***Database Management e.g Oracle or Sybase***
Small system	Large System
Relatively Cheap	Relatively expensive
Few files	Many files
Files and Files	Files and table
Simple structure	Complex structure
Redundant data	Reduced redundancy
Chance and inconsistency	Consistent
Isolated data	Data can be shared
Little Preliminary design	Vast preliminary design
Integrity left to application programmer	Rigorous inbuilt integrity checking
No Security	Rigorous security
Simple, primitive backup/recovery	Complex & sophisticated backup recovery
Often single user	Multiple users

1.7 ADVANTAGES OF USING A DBMS

In this section we discuss some of the advantages of using a DBMS and the capabilities that a good DBMS should possess. The DBA must utilize these capabilities to accomplish a variety of objectives related to the design, administration, and use of a large multi-user database.

1.7.1 Controlling Redundancy

In file system, each application has its own private files, which cannot be shared between multiple applications. This can often lead to considerable redundancy in the stored data, which results in wastage of storage space. By having centralized database most of this can be avoided. It is not possible that all redundancy should be eliminated. Sometimes there are sound business and technical reasons for maintaining multiple copies of the same data. In a database system, however this redundancy can be controlled.

1.7.2 Restricting Unauthorized Access

When multiple users share a database, it is likely that some users will not be authorized to access all information in the database. For example, financial data is often considered confidential, and hence only authorized persons are allowed to access such data. In addition, some users may be permitted only to retrieve data, whereas others are allowed both to retrieve and to update. Hence, the type of access operation retrieval or update must also be controlled. Typically, users or user groups are given account numbers protected by passwords, which they can use to gain access to the database. A DBMS should provide a security and authorization subsystem, which the DBA uses to create accounts and to specify account restrictions. The DBMS should then enforce these restrictions automatically.

Notice that we can apply similar controls to the DBMS software. For example, only the DBA's staff may be allowed to use certain privileged software, such as the software for creating new accounts. Similarly, parametric users may be allowed to access the database only through the canned transactions developed for their use.

1.7.3 Providing Persistent Storage for Program Objects

Databases can be used to provide persistent storage for program objects and data structures. This is one of the main reasons for the emergence of the object-oriented database systems. Programming languages typically have complex data structures, such as record types in PASCAL or class definitions in C++. The values of program variables are discarded once a program terminates, unless the programmer explicitly stores them in permanent files, which often involves converting these complex structures into a format suitable for file storage. When the need arises to read this data once more, the programmer must convert from the file format to the program variable structure. Object-oriented database systems are compatible with programming languages such as C++ and JAVA, and the DBMS software automatically performs any necessary conversions. Hence, a complex object in C++ can be stored permanently in an object-oriented DBMS, such as Object Store. Such an object is said to be persistent, since it survives the termination of program execution and can later be directly retrieved by another C++ program.

The persistent storage of program objects and data structures is an important function of database systems. Traditional database systems often suffered from the so-called impedance mismatch problem, since the data structures provided by the DBMS were incompatible with the programming language's data structures. Object-oriented database systems typically offer data structure compatibility with one or more object-oriented programming languages.

1.7.4 Permitting Inferencing and Actions Using Rules

Some database systems provide capabilities for defining deduction rules for inferencing new information from the stored database facts. Such systems are called deductive database systems. For example, there may be complex rules in the mini world application for determining when a student is on probation. These can be specified declaratively as rules, which when compiled and maintained by the DBMS can determine all students on probation. In a traditional DBMS, an explicit procedural program code would have to be written to support such applications. But if the mini world rules change, it is generally more convenient to change the declared deduction rules than to recode procedural programs. More powerful functionality is provided by active database systems, which provide active rules that can automatically initiate actions.

1.7.5 Providing Multiple User Interfaces

Because many types of users with varying levels of technical knowledge use a database, a DBMS should provide a variety of user interfaces. These include query languages for casual users; programming language interfaces for application programmers; forms and command codes for parametric users; and menu-driven interfaces and natural language interfaces for stand-alone users. Both forms-style interfaces and menu-driven interfaces are commonly known as graphical user interfaces (GUIs). Many specialized languages and environments exist for specifying GUIs. Capabilities for providing World Wide Web access to a database or web-enabling a database are also becoming increasingly common.

1.7.6 Representing Complex Relationships among Data

A database may include numerous varieties of data that are interrelated in many ways. A DBMS must have the capability to represent a variety of complex relationships among the data, to define new relationship as they arise, and to retrieve and update related data easily and efficiently.

1.7.7 Enforcing Integrity Constraints

Most database applications have certain integrity constraints that must hold for the data. A DBMS should provide capabilities for defining and enforcing these constraints. The simplest type of integrity constraint involves specifying a data type for each data item. Integrity of data means that data in database is always accurate, such that incorrect information cannot be stored in database. In order to maintain the integrity of data, some integrity constraints are enforced on the database. DBMS should provide capabilities for defining and enforcing the constraints.

1.7.8 Solving enterprise requirement than individual requirement

Since many types of users with varying level of technical knowledge use a database, a DBMS should provide a variety of user interface. The overall requirements of the enterprise are more important than individual user requirement. So the DBA can structure the database system to provide an overall service that is best for the enterprise".

For Example: A representation can be chosen for the data in storage that gives fast access for the most important application at the cost of poor performance in some other application. But the file system favors the individual requirements than the enterprise requirement.

1.7.9 Providing Backup and Recovery

A DBMS must provide facilities for recovering from hardware or software failures. The backup and recovery subsystem of the DBMS is responsible for recovery. For example, if the computer system fails in the middle of a complex update program, the recovery subsystem is responsible for making sure that the database is restored to the state it was in before the program started executing. Alternatively, the recovery subsystem could ensure that the program is resumed from the point at which it was interrupted so that its full effect is recorded in the database.

1.8 DISADVANTAGE OF DBMS

The disadvantages of the database approach are summarized as follows:

1.8.1 Complexity

The provision of the functionality that is expected of a good DBMS makes the DBMS an extremely complex piece of software. Database designers, developers, database administrators and end-users must understand this functionality to take full advantage of it. Failure to understand the system can lead to bad design decisions, which can have serious consequence for an organization.

1.8.2 Size

The complexity and breadth of functionality makes the DBMS an extremely large piece of software, occupying many megabytes of disk space and requiring substantial amounts of memory to run efficiently.

1.8.3. Performance

Typically, a file based system i.e. written for a specific application, such an invoicing. As result, performance is generally very good. However, the DBMS is written to be more general, to cater than just one. The effect is that some applications may not run as fast as they used to.

1.8.4. Higher impact of a failure

The centralization of resources increases the vulnerability of the system. Since all users and application rely on the availability of the DBMS, the failure of any component can bring operations to a halt.

1.8.5. Cost of DBMS

The cost of DBMS varies significantly, depending on the environment and functionality provided. There is also the recurrent annual maintenance cost

1.8.6. Additional hardware costs

The disk storage requirement for the DBMS and the database may necessitate the purchase of additional storage space. Furthermore, to achieve the required performance it may be necessary to purchase a larger machine, perhaps even a machine dedicated to running the DBMS. The procurement of additional hardware results in further expenditure.

1.8.7. Cost of conversion

In some situations, the cost of DBMS and extra hardware may be significant compared with the cost of converting existing applications to run on the new DBMS and hardware. This cost also includes the cost of training staff to use these new systems and possibly the employment of specialist staff to help with conversion and running of the system. The cost is one of the main reasons why some organizations feel tied to their current systems and cannot switch to modern database technology.

SUMMARY

This chapter we defined a database as a collection or related data, where data means recorded facts. A typical database represents some aspect of the real world and is used for specific purposes by one or more groups of users. The related information when placed in an organized form makes a database. The organization of data/organization is necessary because unorganized information has no meaning. The data is the name given to basic facts and entities such as names and numbers, and information is data that has been converted into a more useful or intelligible form. A database consists of four elements data, relationship, constraints and schema. The DBMS is now the underlying framework of the information system and has fundamentally changed the way that many organizations operate. The predecessor to the DBMS was the file-based system, which is a collection of application programs that perform services for the end-users, usually the production of reports. Each program defines and manages its own data. Although the file based system was a great improvement on the manual filing system, it still has significant problems, mainly the amount of data redundancy present and program-data dependence. The database approach emerged to resolve the problems with the file based approach. A database collection of logically related data and a description of this data, designed to meet the information needs an organization. A DBMS is a software system that enables users to define, create, maintain and control access to the database, and some advantages of the database approach include control of data redundancy, data consistency, sharing data and improved backup and security. Some disadvantages include complexity, cost reduced performance and higher impact of a failure.

EXERCISES

1. What is the difference between Data and Information?
2. What are the problems of manual database and what is the solution of that Problems?
3. What is file based approach of database? Explain its limitations.
4. What are the components of DBMS environment?
5. Describe the organization of a database.
6. What are the characteristics of data in a database?
7. What is a Database Management System?
8. What are relationships between in a database?
9. Explain the advantages and disadvantages of DBMS.
10. Compare file management system and database management system.

■

CHAPTER 2

DATABASE ARCHITECTURE

2.1 INTRODUCTION

The two main purposes of data modeling are to assist in the understanding of the meaning semantics of the data and to facilitate communication about the information requirements. The architecture of DBMS packages has evolved from the early monolithic systems, where the whole DBMS software package is one tightly integrated system, to the modern DBMS packages that are modular in design, with client-server system architecture. This evolution mirrors the trends in computing, where the large centralized mainframe computers are being replaced by hundreds of distributed workstations and personal computers connected via communications networks. In basic client-server architecture, the system functionality is distributed between two types of modules. A client module is typically designed so that it will run on a user workstation or personal computer. Typically, application programs and user interfaces that access the database run in the client module. Hence, the client module handles user interaction and provides the user-friendly interfaces such as forms or menu-based GUIs (graphical user interfaces). The other kind of module, called a server module, typically handles data storage, access, search, and other functions.

A database is a collection of data designed to be used by different people. It is a collection of interrelated data stored together with controlled redundancy to serve one or more applications in an optimal fashion. The data are stored in such a fashion that they are independent of the programs of people using the data. A common and controlled approach is used in adding new data and modifying and retrieving exiting data within the database.

Because DBMS is generic and is intended to support a wide variety of database applications. The database designer provides the names of the entities and their attributes in a machines-readable script called conceptual schema. The DBMS compiles the schema into a compact form for reference by other parts of the system and stored it in the data dictionary. This data dictionary is then available to resolve reference to table and attribute names that arise when the database users request the database services.

As mentioned earlier, database users can be individuals dealing with an interactive interface or other computer programs requesting services with calls to procedure provided by DBMS. Although there are some differences between these two, the DBMS should provide as much uniformity as possible to its users. The user interface module of the DBMS responds to the service requests using data dictionary to confirm the existence and compatibility of the data elements mentioned in the requests. A second module processes the storage and retrieval requests, performs query optimizations and carries out the data operations need to responds to request. The DBMS passes the requested data items and any error messages back to the user through the user interface module.

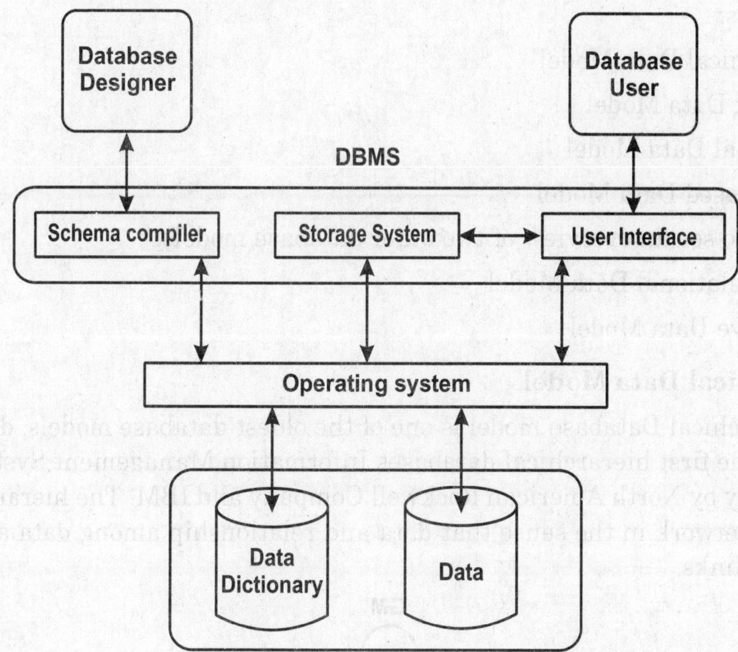

Figure 2.1 Database Environment

2.2 DATA MODEL

The relationship between the data elements can be expressed in many different ways. A DBMS can take any one of the several approaches to manage the data. Each approach constitutes a database model. A database model is an organizing principle that specifies particular mechanisms for data storage and retrieval. The model explains, in terms of services available to an interfacing application, how to access a data element when other related data elements are known. Underlying the structure of a database is the data model: a collection of conceptual tools for describing data, data relationship, data semantics, and consistency constraints, provides the necessary means to achieve this abstraction. By structure of a database we mean the data types, relationships, and constraints that should hold on the data. Most data models also include a set of basic operations for specifying retrievals and updates on the database.

Many data models have been proposed, and we can categorize them according to the types of concepts they use to describe the database structure. High-level or conceptual data models provide concepts that are close to the way many users perceive data, whereas low-level or physical data models provide concepts that describe the details of how data is stored in the computer. Concepts provided by low- level data models are generally meant for computer specialists, not for typical end users. Between these two extremes is a class of representational (or implementation) data models, which provide concepts that may be understood by end users but that are not too far removed from the way data is organized within the computer. Representational data models hide some details of data storage but can be implemented on a computer system in a direct way. In this chapter we will discuss in some detail different database models:

1. Hierarchical Data Model
2. Network Data Model
3. Relational Data Model
4. Object based Data Model

We will also see an overview of two other database models:

1. Object relational Data Model
2. Deductive Data Model

2.2.1 Hierarchical Data Model

The hierarchical Database model is one of the oldest database models, dating from late 1950s. One of the first hierarchical databases Information Management System (IMS), was developed jointly by North American Rockwell Company and IBM. The hierarchical model is similar to the network in the sense that data and relationship among data are represented by records and links.

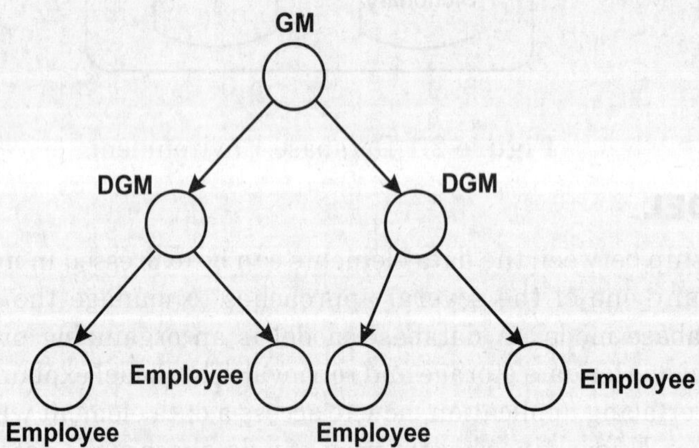

Figure: 2.2.1 Hierarchical Data Model

The hierarchical model organizes data elements as tabular rows, one for each instance of an entity. Consider a company's organizational structure. At the top we have a General Manager (GM). Under him we have several Deputy General Manager (DGMs). Each DGM looks after a couple of departments and each department will have a manager and many employees in show Figure 2.1.1. When represented in hierarchical model, there will be separate rows for representing the GM, each DGM, each department; each Manager and each Employee. The row position implies a relationship to other rows. A given employee belongs to the department that is closest above it in the list and the list and the department belongs to the manager that is immediately above it in the list and so on. The hierarchical model represents relationship with the notion of 'logical adjacency' or more accurately with 'logical proximity' in a linearized tree.

Advantage :

The hierarchical model had many advantage over the file system it replaced. It can be said that the advantages and feature of the hierarchical database systems was the reason for the development of the database models that followed it. The main advantages of this database model are:

- Simplicity
- Data Security
- Data Integrity
- Efficiency

Disadvantage :

The main disadvantages of the hierarchical database model are:

- Implementation Complexity
- Database Management Problems
- Lack of structural independence
- Programming Complexity
- Implementation Limitation

2.2.2 Network Data Model

Data in the network model are represented by collections of records, and relationships among data are represented by links, which can be viewed as pointers. The records in the database are organized as collections of arbitrary graphs. Figure 2.2.2 presents a sample network database model.

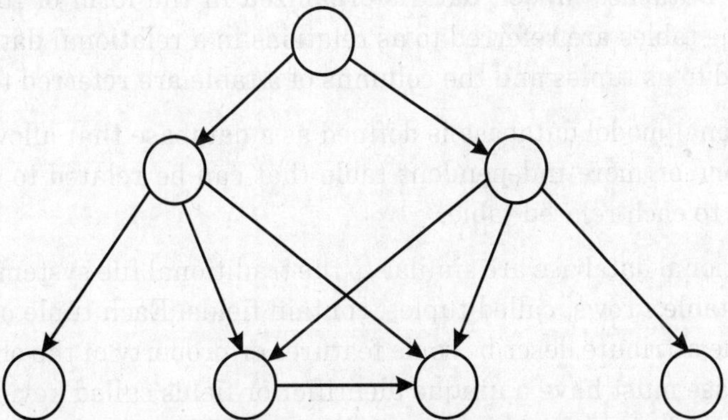

Figure 2.2.2 Network Data Model

The Network Model replaces the hierarchical tree with a graph thus allowing more general connections among the nodes. The main difference of the network model from the hierarchical model it its ability to handle many-to-many relationship. The network model was evolved to specifically handle non-hierarchical relationship. In network database terminology, a relationship is a set. Each set is made of at least two types of records: an owner record (equivalent to the parent in the hierarchical model) and a member record (similar to the child record in the hierarchical model). The difference between the hierarchical model and the network model is that the network model allows a records to appear as member in more than facilitating many-to-many relationship.

Advantages :

The network model retains almost all the advantages of the hierarchical model while eliminating some of its shortcomings. The main advantages of the network model are:

- Conceptual simplicity
- Capability to handle more relationship types
- Ease of data access
- Data Integrity
- Data Independence
- Database Standards

Disadvantages :

Even through the network database model was significantly better than the hierarchical model, it also had many drawbacks. Some of them are:

- System Complexity
- Absence of structural independence

2.2.3 Relational Model

In a Relational Database Model, data is organized in the form of rows and columns similar to a table. The tables are referred to as relations in a relational data model. Rows of the table are referred to as tuples and the columns of a table are referred to as attributes.

Note : A relational model database is defined as a database that allows you to group its data items into one or more independent table that can be related to one another by using fields common to each related table.

Tables in a relational database are similar to the traditional file system with its records, fields and files. The table's rows, called tuples, contain fields. Each tuple or row has values for the attributes. The attribute describe some features or property of the objects. Each table in a relational database must have a unique identifier or fields called key. A key consists of one there is no way to relative him unique record from a table.

The full two dimensional table represents a file or relation for example, in Table 2.2.3 there is an Employee-Service relation that describes the entity Employee by attributes Emp_code, Name and Years of service.

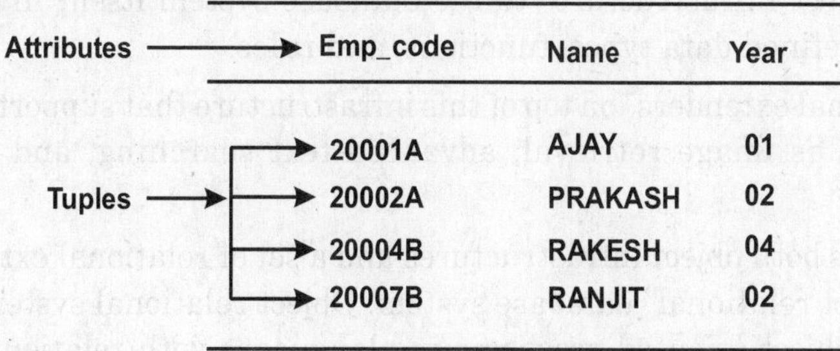

Table 2.2.3 Employee-Service relation

Advantages :

The major advantages of the relational model are:

- Structural independence
- Conceptual simplicity
- Design, implementation, maintenance and usage ease
- Ad-hoc query capability

Disadvantages :

The relational model's disadvantages are very minor compared to the advantage and their capabilities for through the shortcomings. Also the drawbacks of the relational database systems could be avoided if proper corrective measures are taken. The drawbacks are not because of the shortcomings model, but in way it is being implemented. Some of the disadvantages are:

- Hardware overheads
- Ease of design can lead to bed design
- Information islands phenomenon

2.2.4 Object Relational Model

Relational database management is one of the most successful technologies in computer science. A lot of money is spent each year on relational database systems and applications, and much of the world's business data is stored in relational form. Until recently most of individual data items, database systems supported a set of predefined data types such as integers, real numbers, and character strings. The operations defined over these data types, such as arithmetic and comparison, were also simple predefined.

Allowing users to define their own data types and functions and allowing users to define rules that govern the behavior of active data, are both ways of increasing the value of stored data by increasing its semantic content. The trend toward increasing the semantic content of stored data is the most important trend in database management today. In order to accommodate and facilitate this trend, relational database systems are being enhanced in two ways:

1. By adding an "object infrastructure" to the database system itself, in the form of support for user-defined data types, functions, and rules.
2. By adding "relational extenders" on top of this infrastructure that support specialized applications such as image retrieval, advanced text searching, and geographic applications.

A system that includes both object infrastructures and a set of relational extenders that exploit it is called an "object relational" database system. Object relational systems combine the advantage of modern object-oriented programming languages with relational database features such as multiple views of data and a high-level, nonprocedural query language. An object –relational system is a good long-term investment, because its extenders provide the capabilities you need to manage today's specialized objects, and it object infrastructure gives you the ability to define new types, functions and rules to deal with the evolving needs of your business. Some of the object-relational system available in the market are IBM's DB2 universal servers, Oracle Corporations Oracle8, Microsoft Corporations SQL Server 7 so on.

2.2.5 Deductive/inference Model

Deductive model also know as inferential model, stores as little data as possible but compensate by maintaining rules that allow new data combinations to be created when needed. Suppose that database stores that facts of the form DistBook (D,B). Meaning that distributer 'D' is distributing the book 'B'. For example DistBook(SoundMart, CountDown 2000) can appear in the database meaning that the book 'CountDown 2000'is being distributed by the distributer with name 'SoundMart'. A distributer can distribute more than one book and one book can be distributed by many distributers. So you can form another relationship where two books distributed by the same distributer and which can be represented as SameDist(X,Y), meaning books X and Y are distributed by same distributer. Although the database explicitly stores the DistBook(D,B) facts. It does not store the SameDist(X, Y) facts. Instead it stores a rule stating that SameDist (X,Y) fact, say SameDist(CountDown 2000, SQL Handbook), can be deduced from the exiting facts say DistBook(SoundMart, CountDown 2000) and DistBook(SoundMart, SQL HandBook). Such inference rules indirectly capture relationship groupings. The database thus stores certain elementary facts –axioms –from which other facts can be derived as and when needed using the rules.

2.3 STANDARDIZATION OF DBMS THREE LEVEL ARCHITECTURE OF DBMS

An early proposal for a standard terminology and general architecture for database systems was produced in 1971 by the DBTG (DATABASE TASK GROUP) appointed by the Conference of Data System and Languages (CODASYL, 1971). The DBTG recognized the need for a two level approach with a system view called the schema and user views called subschema.

A database system is a collection of interrelated files and a set of programs that allow users to access and modify these files. A major purpose of a database system is to provide users with an abstract view of the data. That is, the system hides certain details of how the data are stored and maintained.

Objective of the three level architecture

The objective of the three level architecture is to separate each user's view of the database from the way the database is physically represented. There are several reasons why this separation is desirable:

- Each user should be able to access the same data, but have a different customized view of the data. Each user should be able to change the way he or she views the data, and this change should not affect other users.
- Users should not have to deal directly with physical database storage details, such as indexing or hashing. In other words a user's interaction with the database should be independent of storage considerations.
- The Database Administrator (DBA) should be able to change the database storage structures without affecting the user's views.
- The internal structure of the database should be unaffected by changes to the physical aspects of storage, such as the change over to a new storage device.
- The DBA should be able to change to conceptual structure of the database without affecting all users.

What is Schema?

The term schema shows an overall structure (organization) of all data items including their records types stored in a database. The first thing we must do to set up a database is to define its structure namely the schema definitions. This is done by identifying the characteristics of each field contained in a database.

While defining the schema of a database, one should also consider future needs of all types of users. That is all possible fields that may be needed in the near future should be included in the database structure at the time of defining it. Although it is possible to modify the database structure at any time, but making such a modification is time consuming. Hence, it is always better to design a database very carefully in the beginning itself and minimize the need to modify it letter.

What is Subschema?

The overall design of a database is known as the schema of a database. The term SubSchema refers to an application programmer's view of the data items and record types which the user would use. Many subschemas can be derived from one schema. The subschema is also referred to as logical view.

Types of Schema

There are three different types of schema in the database corresponding to each data view of database. In other words, the data views at each of three levels are described by schema. A schema is defined as an outline or a plan that describes the records the relationships exiting at the particular level. The External view is described by means of a schema called external schema that correspond to different views of the data. Similarly the conceptual view is defined by conceptual schema, which describes all the entities, attributes and relationship together with integrity constraints. Internal view is defined by internal schema, which is a complete description of the internal model, containing definition of stored records, the methods of representation, the data fields, and the indexes used.

There is only one conceptual schema and the internal schema per database. The schema also describes the way in which data elements at one level can be mapped to the corresponding data elements in the next level.

Thus, we can say that schema establish correspondence between the records and relationships in the two levels. In a relationship defines the tables, the fields in each table, and the relationships between fields and tables. Schemas are generally stored in a data dictionary.

Instances and Schemas

Databases change over time as information is inserted and deleted. The collection of information stored in the database at a particular moment is called an instance of the database. The overall design of the database is called the database schema. Schemas are changed infrequently, if at all. The concept of database schemas and instances can be understood by analogy to a program written in a programming language. A database schema corresponds to the variable declarations (along with associated type definitions) in a program. Each variable has a particular value at a given instant. The values of the variables in a program at a point in time correspond to an instance of a database schema. Database systems have several schemas, partitioned according to the levels of abstraction. The physical schema describes the database design at the physical level, while the logical schema describes the database design at the logical level. A database may also have several schemas at the view level, sometimes called sub-schemas, that describe different views of the database. Of these, the logical schema is by far the most important, in terms of its effect on application programs, since programmers construct applications by using the logical schema. The physical schema is hidden beneath the logical schema, and can usually be changed easily without affecting application programs. Application programs are said to exhibit physical data independence if they do not depend on the physical schema, and thus need not be rewritten if the physical schema changes.

The Three-Schema Architecture

The American National standards Institute (ANSI) standards planning and requirements committee (SPARC) produced a similar terminology and architecture in 1975 (ANSI). ANSI-SPARC recognized the need for a three level approach with a system catalog.

The goal of the three-schema architecture, illustrated in Figure 2.3(a) is to separate the user applications and the physical database. In this architecture, schemas can be defined at the following three levels:

(1) The internal level has an internal schema, which describes the physical storage structure of the database. The internal schema uses a physical data model and describes the complete details of data storage and access paths for the database.

(2) The conceptual level has a conceptual schema, which describes the structure of the whole database for a community of users. The conceptual schema hides the details of physical storage structures and concentrates on describing entities, data types, relationships, user operations, and constraints. A high-level data model or an implementation data model can be used at this level.

(3) The external or view level includes a number of external schemas or user views. Each external schema describes the part of the database that a particular user group is interested in and hides the rest of the database from that user group. A high-level data model or an implementation data model can be used at this level.

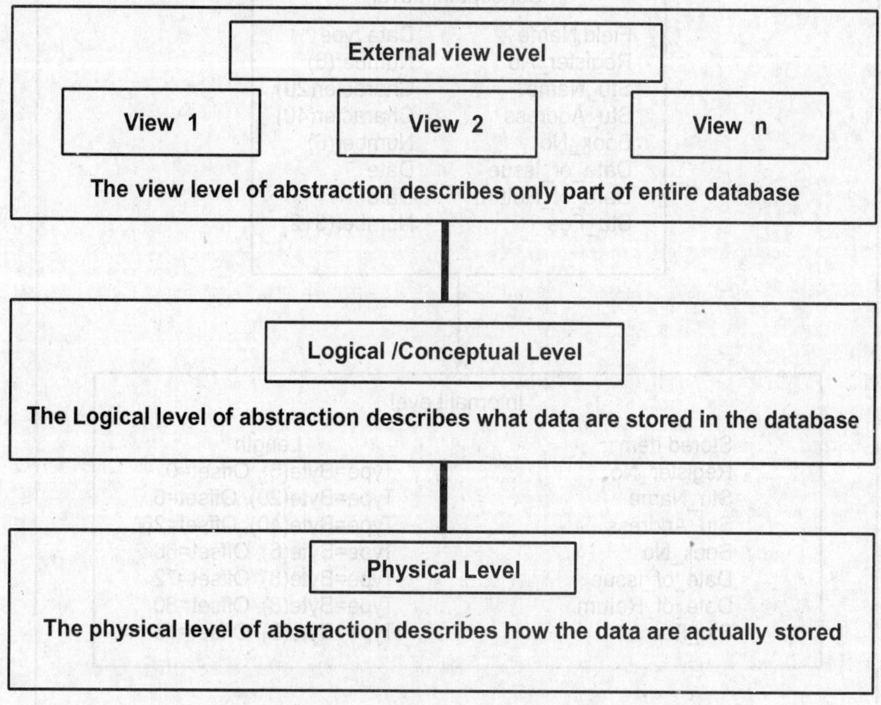

Figure 2.3 (*a*) Three Level Architecture

To understand the difference between the three levels, consider again the database schema that describes college database system. If user1 is a library clerk, the external view would contain only the student and book information. If user2 is account office clerk then he/she may be interested in students detail and fee detail.

Figure 2.3(b), shows specific information actually available at each regarding a particular user.

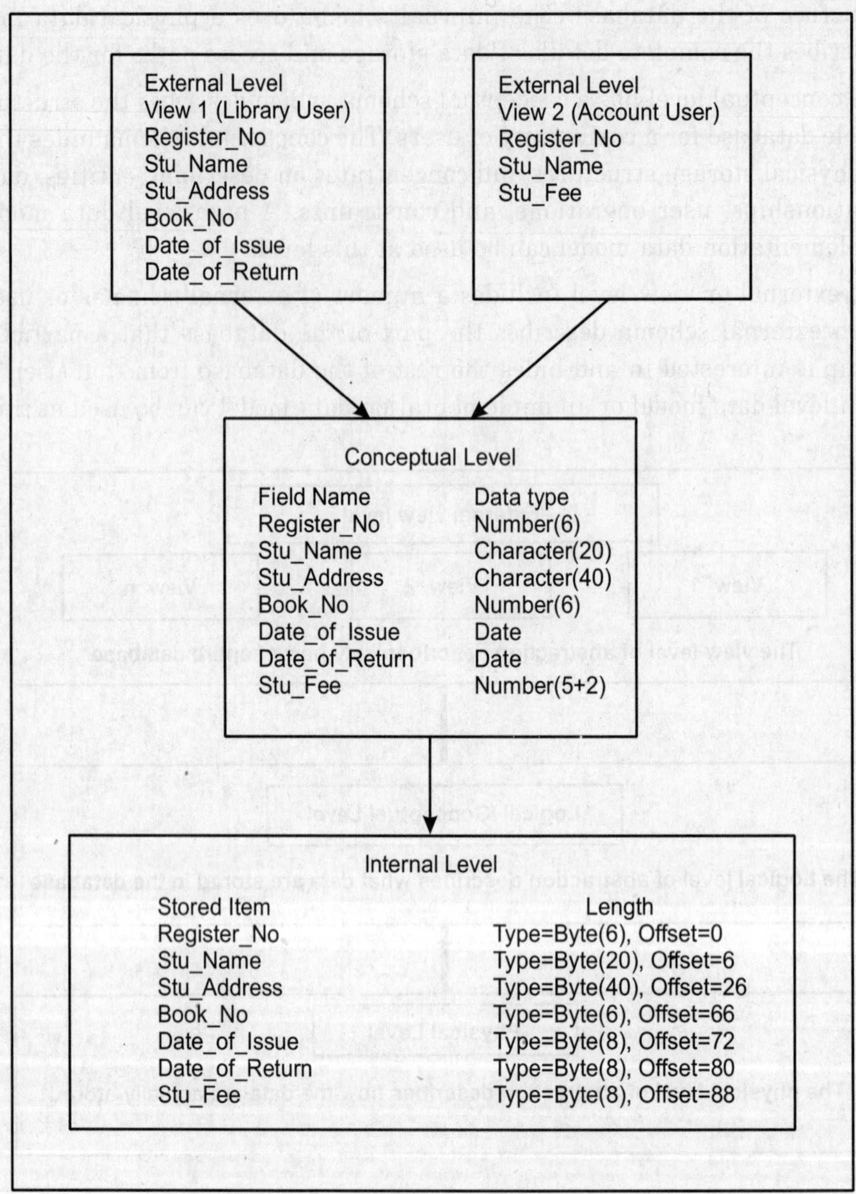

Figure 2.3 (*b*) Example of Three Level Architecture

2.4 DATABASE LANGUAGES

A database system provides a data definition language to specify the database schema and a data manipulation language to express database queries and updates. In practice, the data definition and data manipulation languages are not two separate languages; instead they simply form parts of a single database language, such as the widely used SQL language.

2.4.1 Data Defnition Language

A database schema is specified by a set of definitions expressed by a special language called a data definition language (DDL). The result of compilation of DDL statements is a set of tables that is stored in a special file called data dictionary, data directory.

A data dictionary is a file that contains metadata-that is, data about data. This file is consulted before actual data are read or modified in the database system.

For instance, the following statement in the SQL language define the account table:

```
create table account
(account_number varchar(10),
coustomer_name char(20),
amount number(20));
```

Execution of the above DDL statement creates the account table. In addition, it updates a special set of tables called the data dictionary or data directory.

The storage structure and access methods used by the database system are specified by set of definitions in a special type of DDL called a data storage and definition language. The result of compilation of these definitions is a set of instructions to specify the implementation details of the database schemas-details are usually hidden from the users. We specify a database schema by a set of definitions expressed by a special language called a data definition language (DDL).

2.4.2 Data Manipulation Language

The levels of abstraction that we discussed in section 2.3 apply not only to the definition or structuring of data, but also to manipulation of data. By data manipulation, we mean

- The retrieval of information stored in the database
- The insertion of new information into the database
- The deletion of information from the database
- The modification of information stored in the database

At the physical level, we must define algorithms that allow efficient access to data. At higher levels of abstraction, we emphasize ease of use. The goal is to provide efficient human interaction with the system.

A data-manipulation language (DML) is a language that enables users to access or manipulate data as organized by the appropriate data model. There are basically two types:

- **Procedural DMLs** require a user to specify what data are needed and how to get those data.
- **Declarative DMLs** (also referred to as nonprocedural DMLs) require a user to specify what data are needed without specifying how to get those data.

Declarative DMLs are usually easier to learn and use than are procedural DMLs. However, since a user does not have to specify how to get the data, the database system has to Figure out an efficient means of accessing data. The DML component of the SQL language is nonprocedural.

A query is a statement requesting the retrieval of information. The portion of a DML that involves information retrieval is called a query language. Although technically incorrect, it is common practice to use the terms query language and data manipulation language synonymously.

This query in the SQL language ûnds the name of the customer whose customer_id is 00A2012NO13:

```
select customer_name
from customer
where customer_id = 00A2012NO13
```

The query specifies that those rows from the table customer where the customer_id is 00A2012NO13 must be retrieved and the customer_name attribute of these rows must be displayed.

2.5 DATABASE USERS AND USER ADMINISTRATORS

A primary goal of a database system is to retrieve information from and store new information in the database. People who work with a database can be categorized as database users or database administrators.

2.5.1 Database Users and User Interfaces

There are four different types of database-system users, differentiated by the way they expect to interact with the system. Different types of user interfaces have been designed for the different types of users.

Naive users are unsophisticated users who interact with the system by invoking one of the application programs that have been written previously. For example, a bank teller who needs to transfer ₹ 5000 from account A to account B invokes a program called transfer. This program asks the teller for the amount of money to be transferred, the account from which the money is to be transferred, and the account to which the money is to be transferred. As another example, consider a user who wishes to find her account balance over the World Wide Web. Such a user may access a form, where she enters her account number. An application program at the Web server then retrieves the account balance, using the given account number, and passes this information back to the user. The typical user interface for naive users is a forms interface, where the users can fill in appropriate fields of the form. Naive users may also simply read reports generated from the database

Application programmers are computer professionals who write application programs. Application programmers can choose from many tools to develop user interfaces. Rapid application development (RAD) tools are tools that enable an application programmer to construct forms and reports without writing a program. There are also special types of programming languages that combine imperative control structures (for example, for loops, while loops and if-then-else statements) with statements of the data manipulation language.

These languages, sometimes called fourth-generation languages, often include special features to facilitate the generation of forms and the display of data on the screen. Most major commercial database systems include a fourth- generation language.

Sophisticated users interact with the system without writing programs. In- stead, they form their requests in a database query language. They submit each such query to a query processor, whose function is to break down DML statements into instructions that the storage manager understands. Analysts who submit queries to explore data in the database fall in this category.

Online analytical processing (OLAP) tools simplify analysts tasks by letting them view summaries of data in different ways. For instance, an analyst can see total sales by region (for example, North, South, East, and West), or by product, or by a combination of region and product (that is, total sales of each product in each region). The tools also permit the analyst to select specific regions, look at data in more detail (for example, sales by city within a region) or look at the data in less detail (for example, aggregate products together by category). Another class of tools for analysts is data mining tools, which help them find certain kinds of patterns in data. We study OLAP tools and data mining in Chapter 27.

Specialized users are sophisticated users who write specialized database applications that do not fit into the traditional data-processing framework. Among these applications are computer-aided design systems, knowledge-base and expert systems, systems that store data with complex data types (for example, graphics data and audio data), and environment-modeling systems.

2.5.2 Database Administrator

One of the main reasons for using DBMSs is to have central control of both the data and the programs that access those data. A person who has such central control over the system is called a database administrator (DBA). The functions of a DBA include:

- **Schema definition:** The DBA creates the original database schema by executing a set of data definition statements in the DDL compiler to a set of tables that is stored permanently in the data dictionary.
- **Storage structure and access method definition:** The DBA creates appropriates storage structures and access methods by writing a set of definitions. Which is translated by the data storage and data definition language compiler.
- **Schema and physical organization modification:** The DBA carries out changes to the schema and physical organization to reflect the changing needs of the organization, or to alter the physical organization to improve performance.
- **Granting of authorization for data access:** By granting different types of authorization, the database administrator can regulate which parts of the data base various users can access. The authorization information is kept in a special system structure that the database system consults whenever some- one attempts to access the data in the system.
- **Integrity constraint specification:** The data values stored in the database must satisfy certain consistency constraints. For example, perhaps the number of hours

an employee may in 1 week may not exceed a specified limit (say, 80 hours). Such a constraint must be specified explicitly by the database administrator. The integrity constraints are kept in a special system structure that is consulted by the database system whenever an update takes place in the system.

2.6 TRANSACTION MANAGEMENT

Often, several operations on the database form a single logical unit of work. An example is a funds transfer, in which one account (say A) is debited and another account (say B) is credited. Clearly, it is essential that either both the credit and debit occur, or that neither occur. That is, the funds transfer must happen in its entirety or not at all. This all-or-none requirement is called atomicity. In addition, it is essential that the execution of the funds transfer preserve the consistency of the database. That is, the value of the sum A + B must be preserved. This correctness requirement is called consistency. Finally, after the successful execution of a funds transfer, the new values of accounts A and B must persist, despite the possibility of system failure. This persistence requirement is called durability.

A transaction is a collection of operations that performs a single logical function in a database application. Each transaction is a unit of both atomicity and consistency. Thus, we require that transactions do not violate any database-consistency constraints. That is, if the database was consistent when a transaction started, the database must be consistent when the transaction successfully terminates. However, during the execution of a transaction, it may be necessary temporarily to allow inconsistency, since either the debit of A or the credit of B must be done before the other. This temporary inconsistency, although necessary, may lead to difficulty if a failure occurs.

It is the programmer's responsibility to define properly the various transactions, so that each preserves the consistency of the database. For example, the transaction to transfer funds from account A to account B could be defined to be composed of two separate programs: one that debits account A, and another that credits account B. The execution of these two programs one after the other will indeed preserve consistency. However, each program by itself does not transform the database from a consistent state to a new consistent state. Thus, those programs are not transactions.

Ensuring the atomicity and durability properties is the responsibility of the data- base system itself-specifically, of the transaction-management component. In the absence of failures, all transactions complete successfully, and atomicity is achieved easily. However, because of various types of failure, a transaction may not always complete its execution successfully. If we are to ensure the atomicity property, a failed transaction must have no effect on the state of the database. Thus, the database must be restored to the state in which it was before the transaction in question started executing. The database system must therefore perform failure recovery, that is, detect system failures and restore the database to the state that existed prior to the occurrence of the failure.

Finally, when several transactions update the database concurrently, the consistency of data may no longer be preserved, even though each individual transaction is correct. It is the responsibility of the concurrency-control manager to control the interaction among the concurrent transactions, to ensure the consistency of the database. Database systems designed for use on small personal computers may not have all these features. For example, many small systems allow only one user to access the database at a time. Others do not offer backup and recovery, leaving that to the user. These restrictions allow for a smaller data manager, with fewer requirements for physical resources-especially main memory. Although such a low-cost, low-feature approach is adequate for small personal databases, it is inadequate for a medium- to Large-scale enterprise.

2.7 DATABASE SYSTEM STRUCTURE

A typical structure of a DBMS with its components and relationship between them is shown in Figure 2.7. The DBMS software is partitioned into several modules. Each module or components is assigned a specific operation to perform. Some of the functions of the DBMS are supported by operating system to provide basic services and DBMS is built on top of it. The physical data and system catalog are stored on a physical disk. Access to the disk is controlled primarily by OS, which schedules disk input/output. Therefore, while designing a DBMS its interface with the OS must be taken into account.

A database system is partitioned into modules that deal with each of the responsibilities of the overall system. The functional components of a database system can be broadly divided into the query processor, database manager and data manager components.

2.7.1 Query Processor

The query processor transforms user queries into a series of low-level instructions. It is used to interpret the on-line user's query and convert it into an efficient series of operations in a form capable of being sent to the run time data manager for execution. The query processor uses the data dictionary to find the structure of the relevant portion of the database and uses this information in modifying the query and preparing and optimal plan to access the database.

2.7.2 Run Time Database Manager

Run time database manager is the central software component of the DBMS, which interfaces with user-submitted application programs and queries. It handles database access at run time. It converts operations in user's queries coming directly via the query processor or indirectly via an application program from the user's logical view to a physical file system. It accepts queries and examines the external and conceptual schemas to determine what conceptual records are required to satisfy the user's request. It enforces constraints to maintain the consistency and integrity of the data, as well as its security. It also performs backing and recovery operations. Run time database manager is sometimes referred to as the database control system and has the following components.

- **Authorization control** – The authorization control module checks the authorization of users in terms of various privileges to users.
- **Command processor** – The command processor processes the queries passed by authorization control module.
- **Integrity checker** – It checks the integrity constraints so that only valid data can be entered into the database.
- **Query optimizer** – The query optimizers determine an optimal strategy for the query execution.

- **Transaction manager** – The transaction manager ensures that the transaction properties should be maintained by the system.
- **Scheduler** – It provides an environment in which multiple users can work on same piece of data at the same time in order words it supports concurrency.

2.7.3 Data Manager

The data manager is responsible for the actual handling of data in the database. It provides recovery to the system which that system should be able to recover the data some failure. It includes recovery manager and buffer manager. The buffer manager is responsible for the transfer of data between the main memory and secondary storage (such as disk or tape). It is also referred as the cache manager.

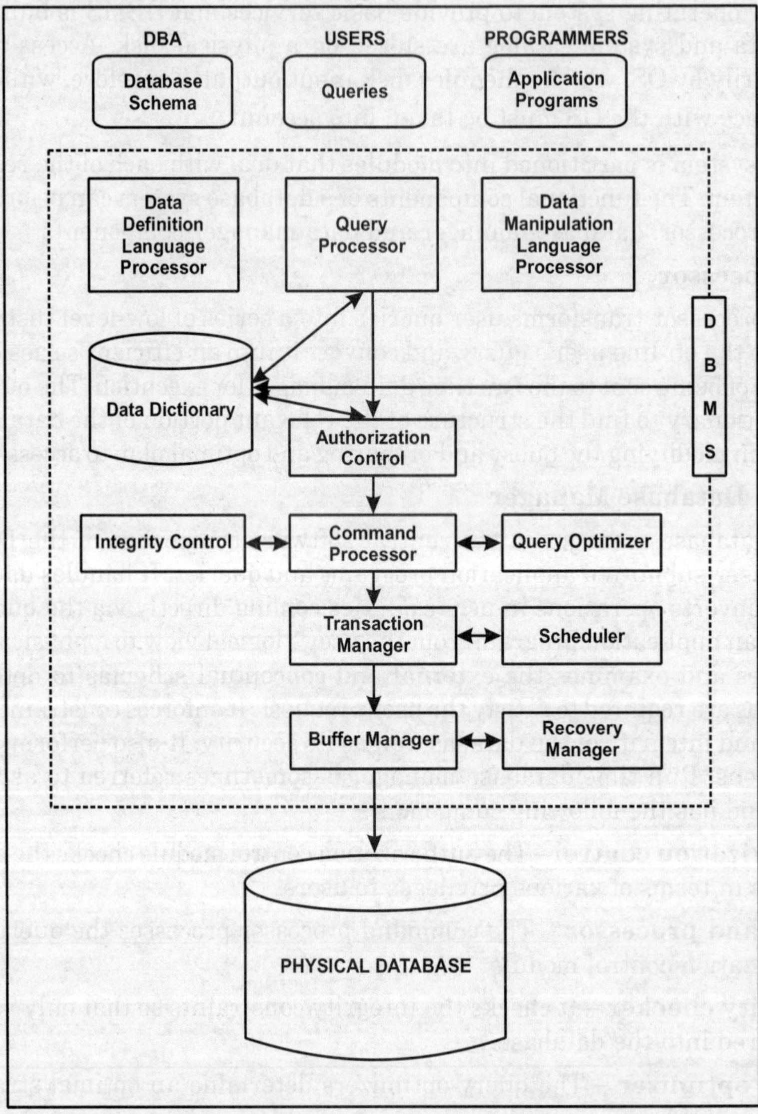

Figure 2.7 Structure and Components of DBMS

Execution Process of a DBMS

As shown in Figure 2.7, conceptually, following logical steps are followed while executing users to request to access the database system.

- Users issue a query using particular database language, for example, SQL commands.
- The passes query is presented to a query optimizer, which uses information about how the data is stored to produce an efficient execution plan for the evaluating the query.
- The DBMS accepts the users SQL commands and analyses them.
- The DBMS produces query evaluation plans that is the external schema for the user, the corresponding external/conceptual mapping, the conceptual schema, the conceptual/internal mapping, and the storage structure definition. Thus, an evaluation plan is a blueprint for evaluating a query.
- The DBMS executes these plans against the physical database and returns the answers to the user.

Using components such as transaction manager, buffer manager and recovery manager, the DBMS supports concurrency and recovery.

2.8 APPLICATION ARCHITECTURES

Most users of a database system today are not present at the site of the database system, but connect to it through a network. We can therefore differentiate between client machines, on which remote database users work, and server machines, on which the database system runs. Database applications are usually partitioned into two or three parts, as in Figure 2.8. In two-tier architecture, the application is partitioned into a component that resides at the client machine, which invokes database system functionality at the server machine through query language statements. Application program interface standards like ODBC and JDBC are used for interaction between the client and the server.

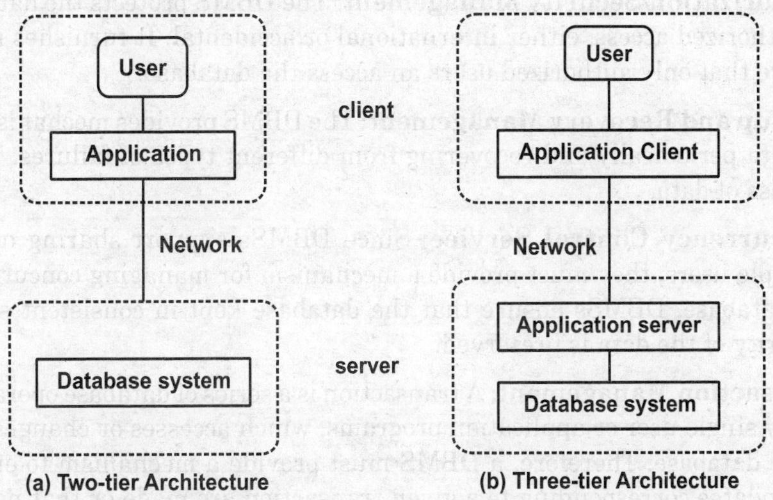

Figure 2.8 Two-tier and Three-tier Architectures

In contrast, in three-tier architecture, the client machine acts as merely a front end and does not contain any direct database calls. Instead, the client end communicates with an application server, usually through a forms interface. The application server in turn communicates with a database system to access data. The business logic of the application, which says what actions to carry out under what conditions, is embedded in the application server, instead of being distributed across multiple clients. Three-tier applications are more appropriate for large applications, and for applications that run on the World Wide Web.

2.9 FUNCTIONS AND SERVICE OF DBMS

A DBMS performs several important functions that guarantee integrity and consistency of data in the database. Most of these functions are transparent to end-users. There are the following important functions and service provided by a DBMS:

1. **Data Storage Management:** It provides a mechanism for management of permanent storage of the data. The internal schema defines how the data should be stored by the storage management mechanism and the storage manager interface with the operating system to access the physical storage.
2. **Data Manipulation Management:** A DBMS furnishes users with the ability to retrieve, update and delete exiting data in the database.
3. **Data Definition Services:** The DBMS accepts the data definitions such as external schema, the conceptual schema, and all the associated mappings in source form.
4. **Data Dictionary/System Catalog Management:** The DBMS provides a data dictionary or system catalog function in which descriptions of data items are stored and which is accessible to users.
5. **Database Communications Interface:** The end-user's requests for database access are transmitted to DBMS in the form of communication messages.
6. **Authorization/Security Management**: The DBMS protects the database against unauthorized access, either international or accidental. It furnishes mechanism to ensure that only authorized users an access the database.
7. **Backup and Recovery Management:** The DBMS provides mechanism for backing up data periodically and recovering from different types of failures. This prevents the loss of data.
8. **Concurrency Control Service:** Since DBMSs support sharing of data among multiple users, they must provide a mechanism for managing concurrent access to the database. DBMSs ensure that the database kept in consistent state and that integrity of the data is preserved.
9. **Transaction Management:** A transaction is a series of database operations, carried out by single user or application programs, which accesses or changes the contents of the database. Therefore, a DBMS must provide a mechanism to ensure that all the updates corresponding to a given transaction are made or that none of them is made.

10. **Database Access and Application Programming Interface:** All DBMS provide interface to enable applications to use DBMS services. They provide data access via structured query language (SQL). The DBMS query language contains three components: (a) a data definition language (DDL), (b) a data manipulation language (DML) and (C) a data control language.

SUMMARY

A database-management system (DBMS) consists of a collection of interrelated data and a collection of programs to access that data. The data describe one particular enterprise. The primary goal of a DBMS is to provide an environment that is both convenient and efficient for people to use in retrieving and storing information.

Database systems are ubiquitous today, and most people interact, either directly or indirectly, with databases many times every day. Database systems are designed to store large bodies of information. The management of data involves both the definition of structures for the storage of information and the provision of mechanisms for the manipulation of information. In addition, the database system must provide for the safety of the information stored, in the face of system crashes or attempts at unauthorized access. If data are to be shared among several users, the system must avoid possible anomalous results.

A major purpose of a database system is to provide users with an abstract view of the data. That is, the system hides certain details of how the data are stored and maintained. It does so by defining three levels of abstraction at which it may be viewed the physical level, the logical level, and the view level.

Underlying the structure of a database is the data model: a collection of conceptual tools for describing data, data relationships, data semantics, and data constraints. The entity-relationship (E-R) data model is a widely used data model, and it provides a convenient graphical representation to view data, relationships and constraints. The relational data model is widely used to store data in databases. Other data models are the object-oriented model, the object relational model, and semi structured data models.

The overall design of the database is called the database schema. A database schema is specified by a set of definitions that are expressed using a data definition language (DDL). A data-manipulation language (DML) is a language that enables users to access or manipulate data. Nonprocedural DMLs, which require a user to specify only what data are needed, without specifying exactly how to get those data, are widely used today.

Database users can be categorized into several classes, and each class of users usually uses a different type of interface to the database. A database system has several subsystems. The transaction manager subsystem is responsible for ensuring that the database remains in a consistent (correct) state despite system failures. The transaction manager also ensures that concurrent transaction executions proceed without conflicting. The query processor subsystem compiles and executes DDL and DML statements. The storage manager subsystem provides the interface between the low level data stored in the database and the application programs and queries submitted to the system.

Database applications are typically broken up into a front-end part that runs at client machines and a part that runs at the back end. In two-tier architectures, the front-end directly communicates with a database running at the back end. In three-tier architectures, the back end part is itself broken up into an application server and a database server.

Functions and services of a single user DBMS include data storage, retrieval, and update; a user-accessible catalog; transaction support; concurrency control and recovery services; authorization services; support for data communication; integrity services; services to promote data independence; utility services.

EXERCISES

1. What is the database? Explain with database environment.
2. Describe the organization of a database.
3. What are relationships in a database?
4. What is the database schema?
5. What is the difference between internal and external schema?
6. What is a database management system?
7. What are different types of database management systems?
8. Define the database model.
9. What are the advantages and disadvantages of the hierarchical database model?
10. Explain the network database model.
11. Explain the relational database model.
12. Explain three level architecture. What are its objectives?
13. Explain the difference between physical and logical schema.
14. Explain the object oriented database model.
15. What are five main functions of a database administrator?

16. List five responsibilities of the database manager. For each responsibility, explain the problems that would arise if the responsibility were not discharge.
17. List seven programming languages that are procedural and two that are nonprocedural. Which group is easier to learn and use? Explain your answer.
18. What is the DBMS? Explain with structure and components of a DBMS.
19. Explain and details with functions and services of DBMS.
20. Explain the difference between the transaction management and storage management.
21. What is the data dictionary? Explain its importance.
22. How user requests for required data is handled by DBMS? Explain with example.
23. What is the role mapping?
24. Explain the different types of database users.
25. What are the role of DBA, Data manager, File Manager and Disk Manager?

■

CHAPTER 3

ENTITY RELATIONSHIP MODEL

3.1 INTRODUCTION

The Entity-Relationship (E-R) data model perceives the real world as consisting of basic objects, called entities, and relationships among these objects. It was developed to facilitate database design by allowing specification of an enfterprise schema, which represents the overall logical structure of a database. The E-R data model is one of several semantic data models; the semantic aspect of the model lies in its representation of the meaning of the data. The E-R model is very useful in mapping the meanings and interactions of real-world enterprises onto a conceptual schema. Because of this usefulness, many database-design tools draw on concepts from the E-R model.

The ER model in important primarily for its role in database design. It provides useful concepts that allow us to move from an informal description of what users want from their database to a more detailed and precise, description that can be implemented in a DBMS. The database design process can be divided into six steps.

1. **Requirement Analysis:** The very first step in designing a database application is to understand what data to be stored in the database, what applications must be built on top of it, and what operations are most frequent and subject to performance requirements.
2. **Conceptual Database Design:** The information gathered in the requirements analysis step is used to develop a high level description of the data to be stored in the database, along with the constraints that are known to hold over this data.
3. **Logical Database Design:** We must be chosen a DBMS to implement our database design, and convert the conceptual database design into a database schema in the data model of the chosen DBMS. We will only consider relational DBMSs, and therefore, the task in the logical design step is to convert an ER schema into a relational database.
4. **Schema Refinement:** The fourth step in database design is to analyze the collection of relations in our relational database schema to identify potential problems and to refine it. In contrast to the requirements analysis and conceptual design steps, which are essentially subjective, schema refinement can be guided by some elegant and powerful theory.

5. **Physical Database Design:** In this step we must typical expected workloads that our database must support and further refine the database design to ensure that it meets desired performance criteria. This step may simply involve building indexes on some tables and clustering some tables, or it may involve a substantial redesign of parts of the database schema obtained from the earlier design steps.

6. **Security Design:** In this step, we identify different user group and different roles played by various users. For each role and user group, we must identify the parts of the database that they must be able to access and the parts of the database that they should not be allowed to access, and take steps to ensure that they can access only the necessary parts.

3.2 E-R MODEL

The Entity-Relationship model is a high level conceptual data model developed by Chen in 1976 to facilitate database design. A conceptual data model is a set of concepts that describe the structure of a database and the associated retrieval and update transactions on the database. The main purpose of developing a high level data model is to support a user's perception of data and to conceal the more technical aspects associated with database design. Furthermore, a conceptual data model is independent of the particular DBMS and hardware platform that is used to implement the database. A basic component of the model is the Entity-Relationship diagram, which is used to visually represent data objects. For the database designer, the utility of the ER-Model is:

- It maps well to the relational model. The constructs used in the ER model can easily be transformed into relational tables.
- It is simple and easy to understand with a minimum of training. Therefore, the model can be used by the database designer to communicate the design to the end user.
- In addition, the model can be used as a design plan by the database developer to implement a data model in specific database management software.

Components of an E-R Model

In this section we will make ourselves familiar with the components of the E-R model and their representation in the E-R diagrams. E-R model forms the basis of the (ERDs) Entity Relationship Diagrams. The ERD represents the conceptual view of the database. The ERDs represents four components Entity, Attributes, Relationship and Key attributes.

3.2.1 Entity

The fundamental item in any data model is the entity. An entity is viewed as the atomic real world item. An entity is an instance of an entity type that is uniquely identifiable. Each uniquely identifiable of an entity type is also referred to as an entity occurrence or entity instance. An entity is a **"thing"** or **"object"** in the real world that is distinguishable from all other objects. For example, each person in an enterprise is an entity. An entity has a set of properties, and the values for some set of properties may uniquely identify an entity. For instance, a person may have a person-id property whose value uniquely identifies that person.

An entity is a class of persons, places, object, events or concepts about which we need to collect and store data. Each entity is distinguishable from the other entities. Categories of different entities include:

- Persons
- Places
- Objects
- Events
- Concepts

Persons : Employee, Customer, Student, Supplier etc.
Places : Branch, Office, Building, Room etc.
Objects : Book, Machine, Vehicle etc.
Events : Sale, Reservation, Registration, Order etc.
Concepts : Qualification, Account, Course, Stocks etc.

The instance of an entity is a single occurrence of that entity. For example, the entity EMPLOYEE may have multiple instances or occurrence such as Prakash, Ajay, Mohan, Ankit etc. In data modeling, we do not concern over selves with individual instances because we recognize that each instances is described by similar data items.

3.2.2 Entity Set

An entity set is a set of entities of the same type that share the same property i.e. the entities which share common properties or attributes. For example, the set of all employee of an organization can be called as the entity set Employee. Similarly, the set of all persons who are customers at a given bank can be called as the entity set Customer.

3.2.3 Attributes

An entity is represented by a set of attributes. Attributes are descriptive properties possessed by each member of an entity set. The designation of an attribute for an entity set expresses that the database stores similar information concerning each entity in the entity set; however, each entity may have its own value for each attribute. Possible attributes of the customer entity set are student_id, student_name, student_street, and student_city. In real life, there would be further attributes, such as street number, apartment number, state, postal code, and country, but we omit them to keep our examples simple. Possible attributes of the library entity set are book_number and book_name.

A Database thus includes a collection of entity sets each of which contains any number of entities of the same type. Table 3.2.3(a) and table 3.2.3(b), shows part of a College database which consists of a two entity sets Student and Library

student_id	student_name	student_street	student_city
009A2010	Abhishek	Sadar Bazar	Lucknow
023A2010	Amit	Lodhi Road	New Delhi
036A2010	Aparajita	Allam Road	Meerut
055A2010	Debasish	Nai Sadak	Bhubaneshwar

Table 3.2.3(a) Student

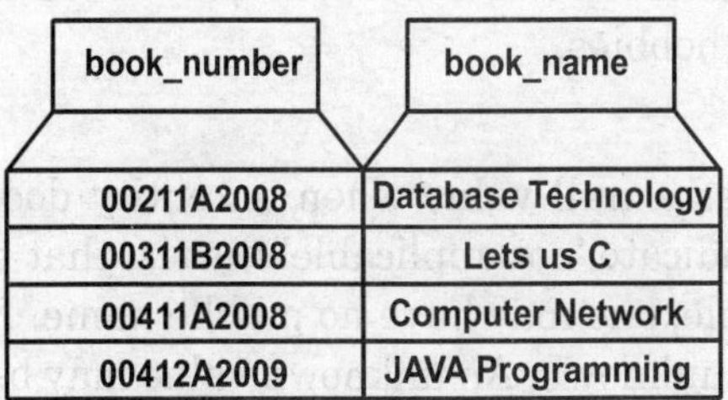

book_number	book_name
00211A2008	Database Technology
00311B2008	Lets us C
00411A2008	Computer Network
00412A2009	JAVA Programming

Table 3.2.3 (b) Library

An attribute, as used in the E-R Model, can be characterized by following attribute types.

- Simple
- Composite
- Single-values
- Multi-values
- Null
- Derived

- **Simple Attributes**

  A simple attributes is an attributes composed of a single component with an independent existence. Simple attributes cannot be further subdivided. Example of simple attributes includes Age, Sex, Salary, etc. simple attributes are sometime called atomic attributes.

- **Composite Attribute**

  An attributes composed of multiple components, each with an independent existence is called a Composite Attributes. Some attributes can be further divided to yield smaller components with an independence existence of their own. For example, the Name attributes can be composed of components like First Name, Middle Name and Last Name and so on.

- **Single-Valued Attributes**

  A single-valued attribute is one that holds a single value for a single entity. The majority of attributes are single-valued for a particular entity. For example, the Classroom entity has as single value for the Room_number attribute and therefore the Room_number attribute is referred to as being single-valued.

- **Multi-Valued Attribute**

  A Multi-valued attribute is one that holds multiple values for a single entity. Some attributes have multiple values for a particular entity. For example, a student can have multiple values for the Hobby attribute, such as reading, music, playing, and movies and so on. A multi-valued attribute may have set of numbers with upper and lower limits. For Example, the Hobby attribute of a student may between one and five values. In other words, a student may have a minimum of one hobby and maximum of five hobbies.

- **Null Attribute**

  An attribute takes a null value when an entity does not have a value for it. The null value may indicate 'not applicable' that is, that the value does not exist for the entity. For example, one may have no middle name. Null can also designate that an attribute value is unknown. An unknown value may be either missing (the value does exist, but we do not have that information) or not known (we do not know whether or not the value actually exists). For instance, if the name value for a particular customer is null, we assume that the value is missing, since every customer must have a name. A null value for the apartment-number attribute could mean that the address does not include an apartment number (not applicable), that an apartment number exists but we do not know what it is (missing), or that we do not know whether or not an apartment number is part of the customer's address (unknown).

- **Derived Attribute**

  A derived attribute is one that represents a value that is derivable from the value of a related attribute or set of attributes, not necessarily in the same entity. Some attributes may be related for a particular entity. For example the Age attribute can be derived from the date_of_birth attribute and therefore they are related. We refer the Age Attribute as a derived attribute, the value of which is derived from the date_of_birth attribute.

3.3 RELATIONSHIP, RELATIONSHIP SET, RELATIONSHIP TYPES AND STRUCTURAL CONSTRAINTS

Relationship

A relationship is an association among several entities. A relationship set is a set of relationship of the same type. For example, consider two entity sets Customer and account. We define the relationship CustAcct to denote the association between customers and their accounts. This is binary relationship set. Going back to our formal definition, the relationship set CustAcct is a subset of all the possible customer and account pairings. This is a binary relationship. Occasionally there are relationships involving more than two entity sets.

3.3.1 Relationship Types, Sets and Instances

A relationship type R among n entity types $E_1, E_2, \ldots, E_n$ defines a set of associations or a relationship set—among entities from these types. As for entity types and entity sets, a relationship type and its corresponding relationship set are customarily referred to by the same name R. Mathematically, the relationship set R is a set of **relationship instances** r_i, where each r_i associates n individual entities $(e_1, e_2, \ldots, e_n)$, and each entity e_j in r_i is a member of entity type E_j, $1 \leq j \leq n$. Hence, a relationship type is a mathematical relation on $E_1, E_2, \ldots, E_n$; alternatively it can be defined as a subset of the Cartesian product $E_1 \times E_2 \times \ldots \times E_n$. Each of the entity types $E_1, E_2, \ldots, E_n$ is said to participate in the relationship type R; similarly, each of the individual entities $e_1, e_2, \ldots, e_n$ is said to participate in the relationship instance $r_i = (e_1, e_2, \ldots, e_n)$.

Informally, each relationship instance r_i in R is an association of entities, where the association includes exactly one entity from each participating entity type. Each such relationship instance r_i represents the fact that the entities participating in r_i are related in some way in the corresponding mini-world situation. For example, consider a relationship type WORKS_FOR between the two entity types EMPLOYEE and DEPARTMENT, which associates each employee with the department the employee works for. Each relationship instance in the relationship set WORKS_FOR associates one employee entity and one department entity. Figure 3.3.1 illustrates this example, where each relationship instance r_i is shown connected to the employee and department entities that participate in r_i. In the mini-world represented by Figure 3.3,1 employee's e_1, e_3, and e_6 work for department d_1; e_2 and e_4 work for d_2; and e_5 and e_7 work for department d_3.

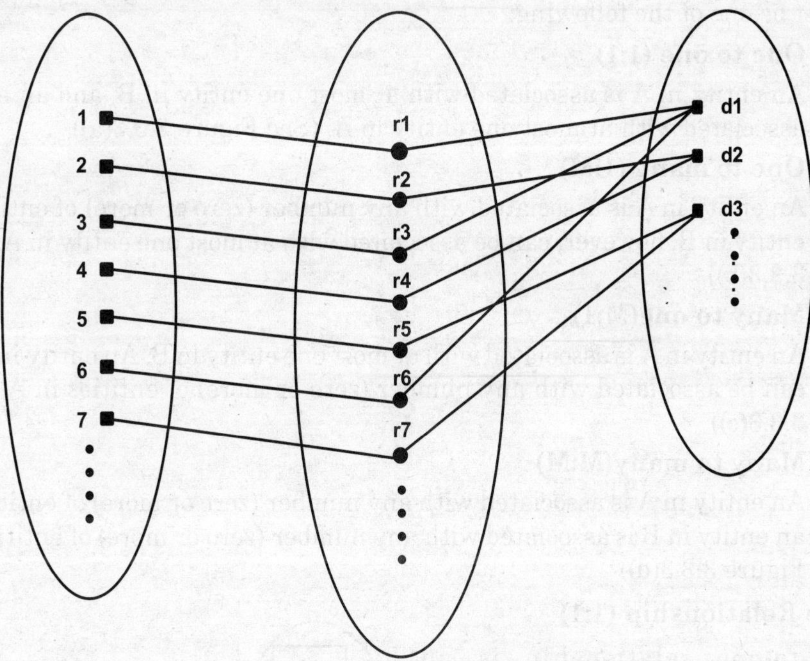

Figure 3.3.1 Some instances in the WORK_FOR relationship set, which represents a relationship type

3.3.2 Degree

The degree of a relationship is the number of entities associated with the relationship. The n-ary relationship is the general form for degree n. special cases are the binary and ternary, where the degree is 2 and 3 respectively. Binary relationships, the association between two entities are the most common type in the real world. A recursive binary relationship occurs when an entity is related to itself. An example might be "some employees are married to other employees'. A ternary relationship involves three entities and is used when a binary relationship is inadequate. Many modeling approaches recognize only binary relationships. Ternary or n-ary relationships are decomposed into two or more binary relationship

3.3.3 Mapping Constraints

An E-R enterprise schema may define certain constraints to which the contents of a database must conform. In this section, we examine mapping cardinalities and participation constraints, which are two of the most important types of constraints.

1. **Mapping Cardinalities**

   Mapping cardinalities, or cardinality ratios, express the number of entities to which another entity can be associated via a relationship set. Mapping cardinalities are most useful in describing binary relationship sets, although they can contribute to the description of relationship sets that involve more than two entity sets. In this section, we shall concentrate on only binary relationship sets.

   For a binary relationship set R between entity sets A and B, the mapping cardinality must be one of the following:

   - **One to one (1:1)**

     An entity in A is associated with at most one entity in B, and an entity in B is associated with at most one entity in A. (See Figure 3.3.3(a))

   - **One to many (1:M)**

     An entity in A is associated with any number (zero or more) of entities in B. An entity in B, however, can be associated with at most one entity in A. (See Figure 3.3.3(b))

   - **Many to one(M:1)**

     An entity in A is associated with at most one entity in B. An entity in B, however, can be associated with any number (zero or more) of entities in A. (See Figure 3.3.3(c))

   - **Many to many(M:M)**

     An entity in A is associated with any number (zero or more) of entities in B, and an entity in B is associated with any number (zero or more) of entities in A. (See Figure 3.3.3(d))

One-to-One Relationship (1:1)

A one-to-one relationship is an association only between two entities. For example, in a university each department has only one head of department. Moreover, one faculty member cannot head more than one department. This shows one-to-one relationship between department and person as head.

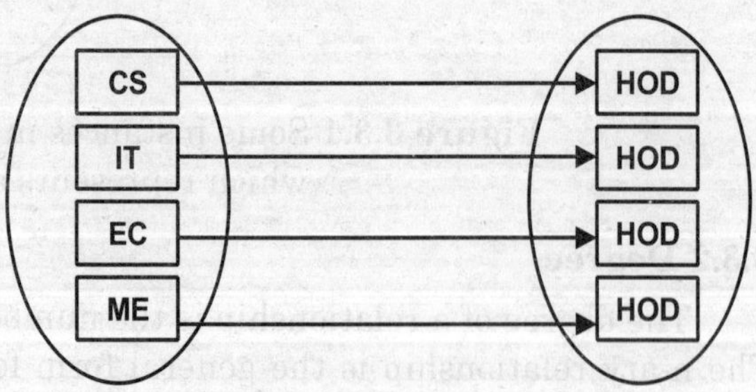

Figure 3.3.3(a) Relationship Example

One-to-Many Relationship (1:M)

One to many relationship exists when one entity is related to more than one entity. For example two entity set namely courses and teacher. If we assume that more than one subject or course is taught by one teacher, then the relationship is one-to-many between Teacher and Courses.

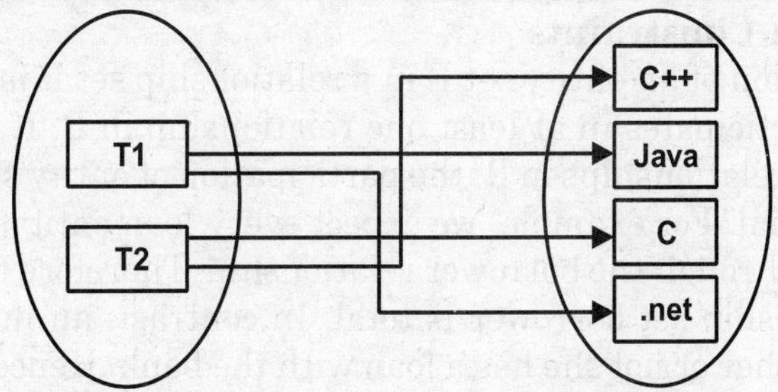

Figure 3.3.3(b) 1:M Relationship Example

Many-to-One Relationship (M:1)

A many to one relationship is when for one instance of entity A is associated with at most one instance of entity B, but for one instance of entity B, there may be any number of instance of entity A. For example many employees one department.

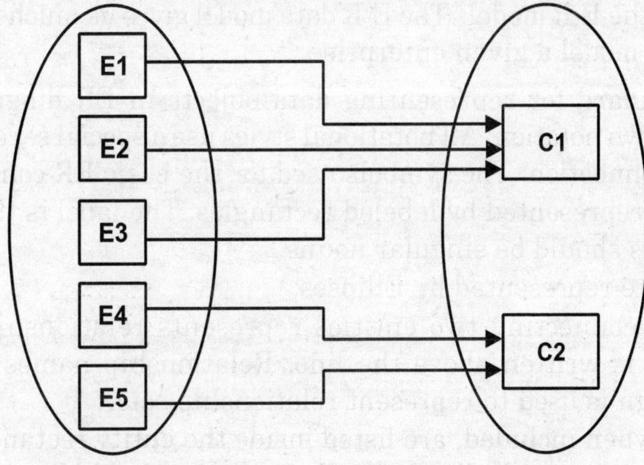

Figure 3.3.3(c) M:1 Relationship Example

Many-to-Many Relationship (M:M)

A many to many relationship describes entity that may have many relationship among each other. For example, one customer may many items and one item may be bought by many customers.

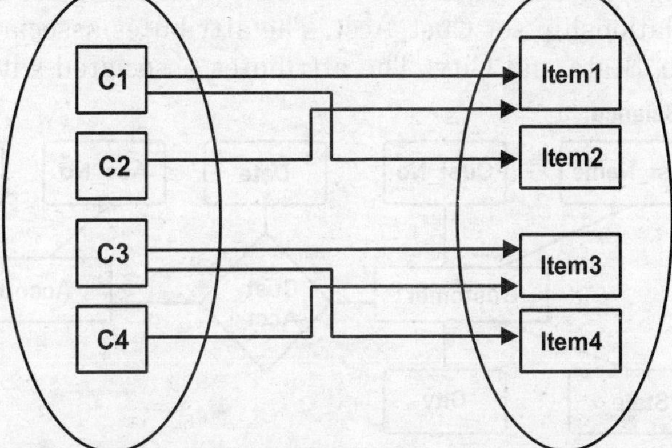

Figure 3.3.3(d) M:M Relationship Example

2. **Participation Constraints**

The participation of an entity set E in a relationship set R is said to be total if every entity in E participates in at least one relationship in R. If only some entities in E participate in relationships in R, the participation of entity set E in relationship R is said to be partial. For example, we expect every loan entity to be related to at least one customer through the borrower relationship. Therefore the participation of loan in the relationship set borrower is total. In contrast, an individual can be a bank customer whether or not she has a loan with the bank. Hence, it is possible that only some of the customer entities are related to the loan entity set through the borrower relationship, and the participation of customer in the borrower relationship set is therefore partial.

3.4 E-R DIAGRAM

The overall logical structure of a database can be expressed graphically by an E-R Diagram. E-R diagrams are simple and clear qualities that may well account in large part for the widespread use of the E-R model. The E-R data model gives us much flexibility in designing a database schema to model a given enterprise.

There is no standard for representing data objects in ER diagrams. Each modeling methodology uses its own notation. All notational styles use a special set of symbols to represent the cardinality of a connection. The symbols used for the basic ER construct are:

- Entities are represented by labeled rectangles. The label is the name of the entity. Entity names should be singular nouns.
- Attributes are represented by Ellipses.
- A solid line connecting two entities represents relationships. The name of the relationship is written above the line. Relationship names should be verbs and diamonds sign is used to represent relationship sets.
- Attributes, when included, are listed inside the entity rectangle. Attributes, which are identifiers, are underlined. Attribute names should be singular nouns.
- Multi-valued attributes are represented by double ellipses.
- Directed line is used to indicate one occurrence and undirected line is used to indicate many occurrences in relation.

For Example Consider the entity relationship diagram shown in Figure 3.4(a). The diagram as seen in Figure 3.4(a) consists of two entity sets. Customer and Account and relates through a binary relationship set Cust_Acct. The attributes associated with Customer are Cust_Name,Cust_No, State and City. The attributes associated with Account are Acc_No and Balance.

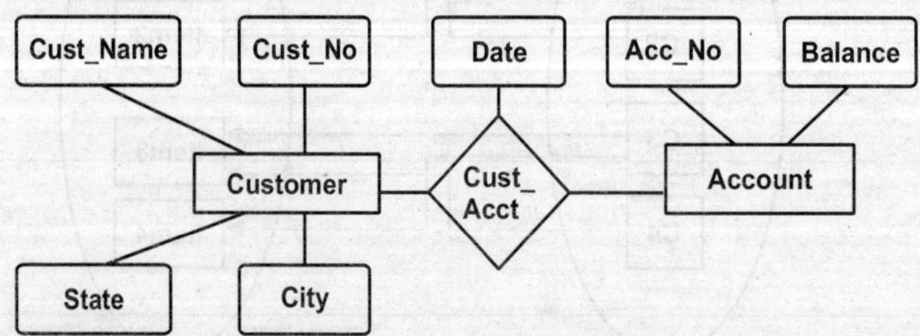

Figure 3.4(a) Entity-Relationship diagram for customer account

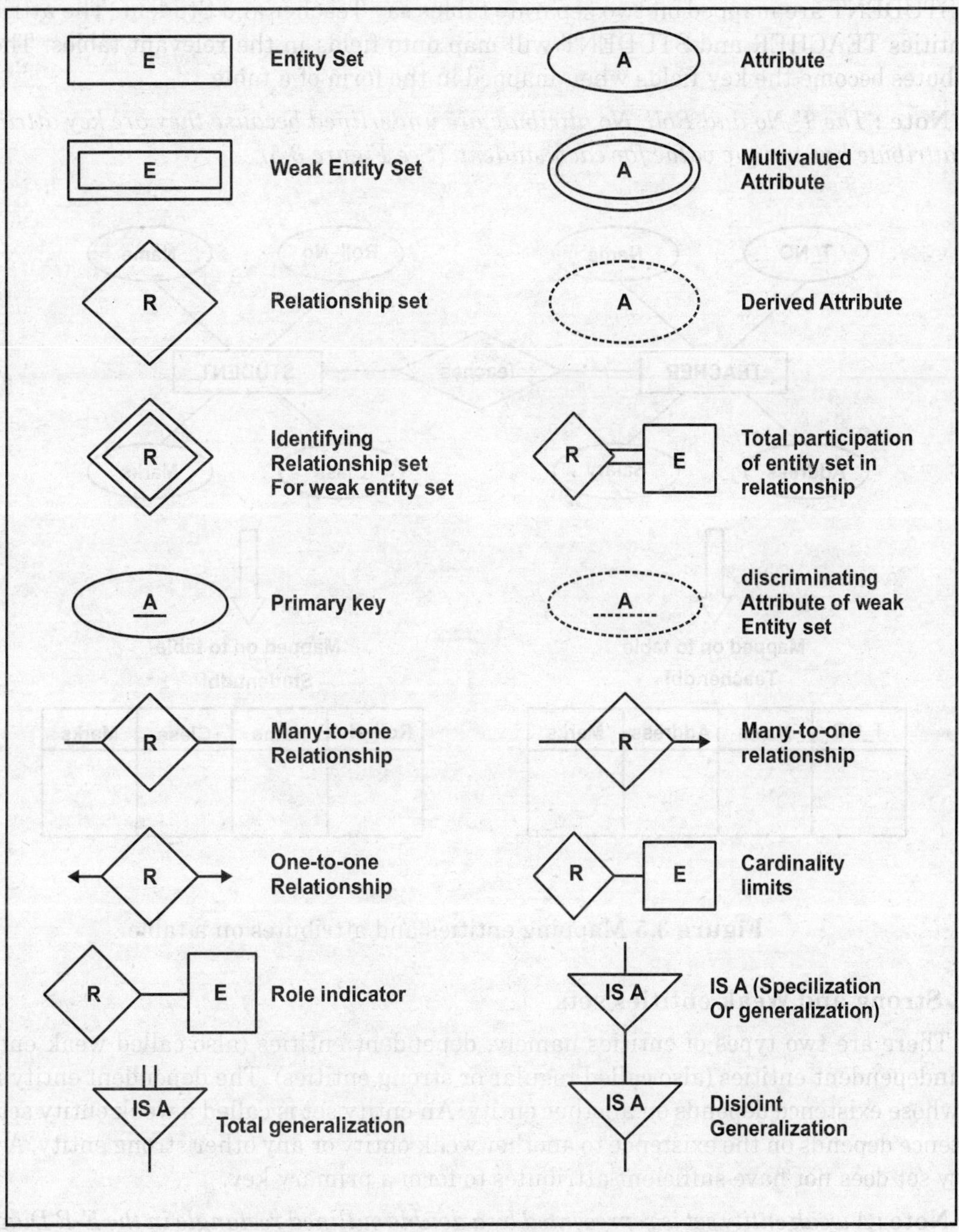

Figure 3.4(b) Symbols used in ER Diagram

3.5 DATABASE DESIGN USING E-R MODEL

A database which conforms to an E-R diagram can be represented by a set of tables. For each entity set and for each relationship set in the database, there is a unique table which is assigned the name of corresponding entity set or relationship set. Each table has a number of columns which are given unique names. For example, in Figure 3.5, the entities TEACHER and STUDENT are mapped on two separate tables say Teacher and Student. The attributes of entities TEACHER and STUDENT will map onto fields in the relevant tables. The key attributes become the key fields when mapped in the form of a table.

Note : *The T_No and Roll_No attribute are underlined because they are key attributes. Key attribute has unique value for each student. (See Figure 3.5)*

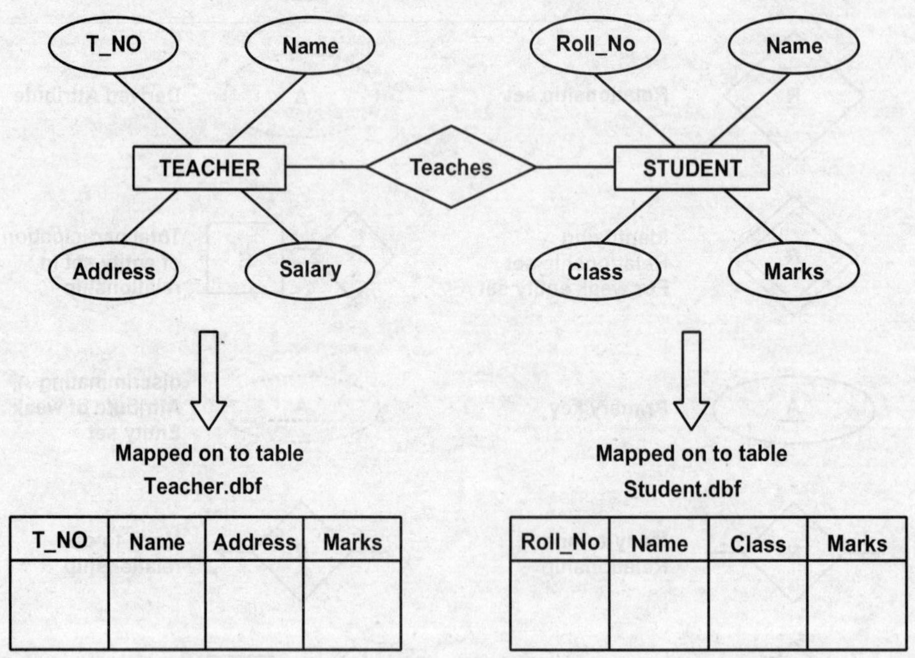

T_NO	Name	Address	Marks

Roll_No	Name	Class	Marks

Figure 3.5 Mapping entities and attributes on a table

3.5.1 Strong and Weak entities sets

There are two types of entities namely, dependent entities (also called weak entities) and independent entities (also called regular or strong entities). The dependent entity is the one whose existence depends on another entity. An entity set is called a weak entity set if its existence depends on the existence to another weak entity or any other strong entity. A weak entity set does not have sufficient attributes to form a primary key.

Note : *A weak entity set is represented by a double outlined rectangle in the E-R Diagram.*

Consider an entity type marks which represents the marks obtained by a student. Now the existence of marks depends upon the existence of entity type student (see Figure 3.5.1(a)

Note : *Every weak entity set can be converted to a strong entity set by adding appropriate attributes.*

Let us take a real life situation to understand types of entity. Suppose, a student say "Rashi" can have many instances of marks say Eng_marks, Sci_marks, SST_marks etc. related to it. If the instance "Rashi" is deleted, then all the entity marks dependent upon "Rashi" will also be removed.

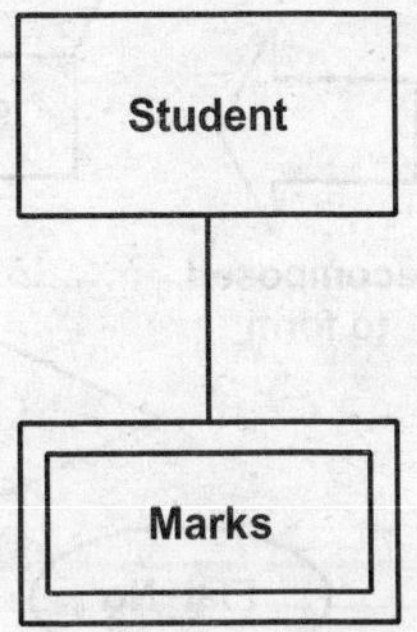

Figure 3.5.1(a) Marks is dependent (weak) entity that is dependent on entity Student

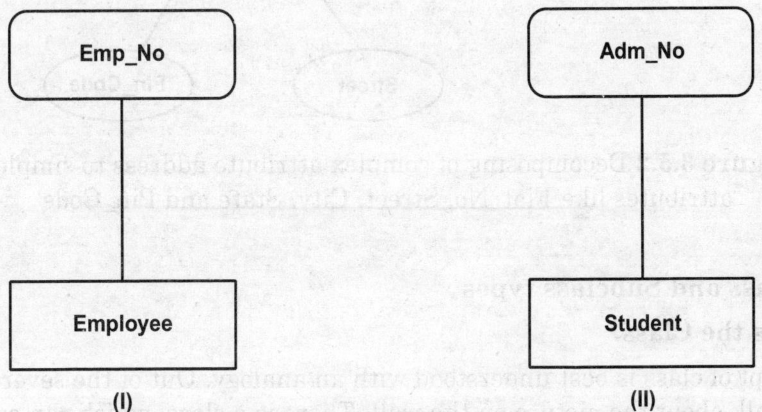

Figure 3.5.1(b) Example of Strong entities

An entity set which has a primary key is termed as a strong entity set. For example is Figure 3.5.1(b), the entities Employee and Student are strong entities, because they have the primary keys Emp_No and Adm_No.

Note : *that Emp_No and Adm_No are the primary keys in Figure 3.5.1(I) and (II)*

3.5.2 How to Draw E-R Diagram

While designing database using E-R Diagrams, you should use the following guidelines

- Do not introduce unwanted attributes
- Merge the entities with common attributes or purposes
- Decompose complex entities to simplify them, do it by decomposing complex attributes into sub-attributes (see Figure 3.5.2)

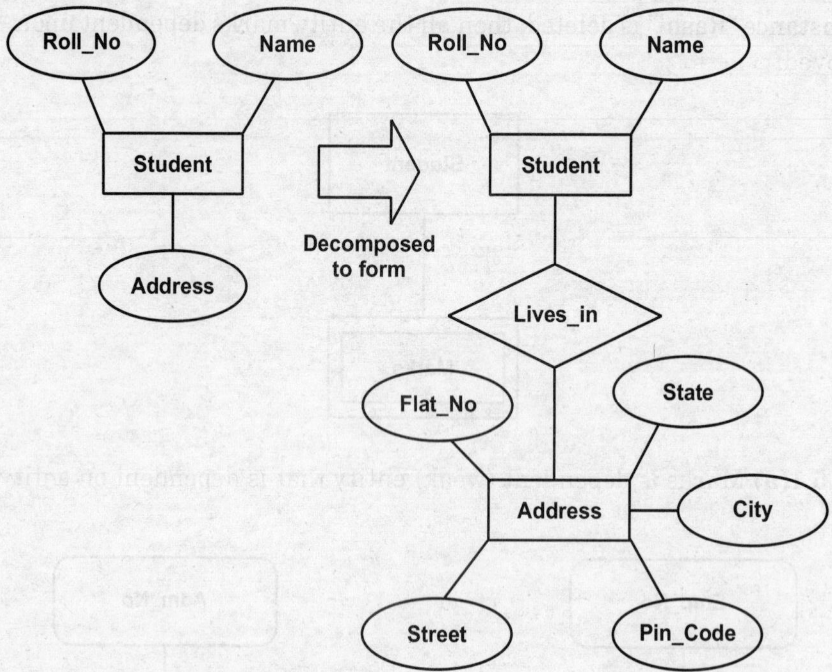

Figure 3.5.2 Decomposing of complex attribute address to simpler attributes like Flat_No, Street, City, State and Pin_Code

3.5.3 Superclass and Subclass types

3.5.3.1 What is the Class?

The concept of class is best understood with an analogy. Out of the several objects in a room, lets us talk about the picture on the wall. There is a class, which can call the class of "Pictures" of which the picture on the wall is an instance (meaning an occurrence or example). The picture in the room belongs to the class of pictures, which consists of all pictures in the world.

A Set of objects that share a common structure and a common behavior is called Class

3.5.3.2 What is an Object?

Putting it in the layman language, an object is something that has a fixed shape or well defined boundary. If you look at your computer desk, you would notice several objects of varying descriptions. They may be connected to or related to adjacent objects. For example, a keyboard may be attached parts of PC are distinct objects.

In the ordinary sense, an object is something which is capable of being seen, touched or sensed.

3.5.3.3 What is an Inheritance?

Inheritance means the methods and/or attributes defined in an object class which can be inherited or reused by another object class. A class **supertype** is an object whose instances store attributes that are common to one or more class subtype of the object. A class **subtype** is an object class whose instances inherit some common attributes from a class supertype and then add other attributes that are unique to an instance of the subtype.

Inheritance is always transitive i.e. can be transferred. A class can inherit features from superclasses many levels away. For example, if cat is a subclass of class Mammal and class Mammal is in turn a subclass of class Animal, then cat will inherit attributes both from Mammal and from Animal (see Figure 3.5.3.3).

Inheritance means that the behavior and data associated with child classes are always an extension of the properties associated with parent classes. A class and other properties as well

The class, whose objects store attributes which are common to its subclasses, is known as the supertype class. For example, a class shopkeeper is a supertype. Its objects store such attributes which are common to all shopkeepers like bakers, grocers, stationers, toy store owners etc. These shopkeeper belongs to the supertype class, shopkeeper. Thus we can expect a florist to accept money for the sale of flowers because florist object is a subclass of shopkeeper class. Such an activity is not unique to florists, but is common to all shopkeepers.

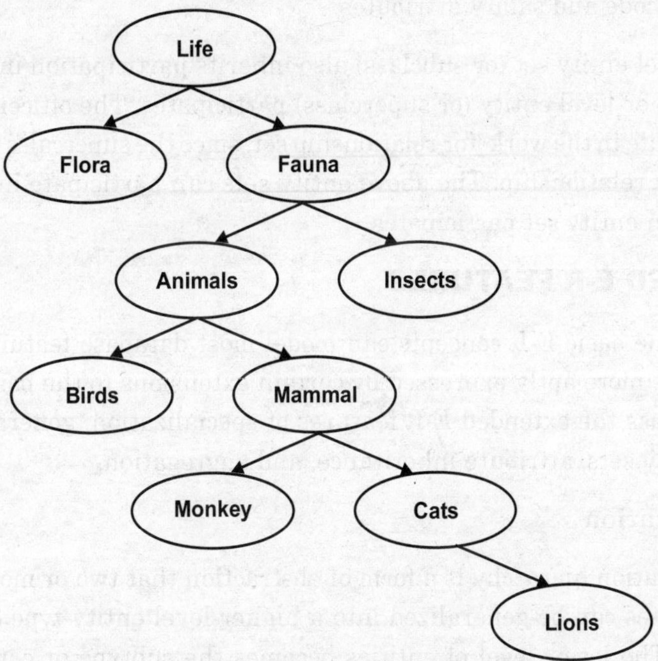

Figure 3.5.3.3 Hierarchy of life forms

The class subtype is the class which inherits qualities from a supertype class and also adds on its own qualities. For example, the florist inherits all the qualities that a shopkeeper should have. In addition he also has its own qualities like he sells flowers etc.

Similarly, in terms of the hierarchy shown in Figure 3.5.3.3, we only need to define the distinguishing features of the cat family, provided the superclass of mammal is well defined.Thus, we only need to define that members of cat family have claws, eat meat and so on. Characteristics of mammals and animals are automatically included.

The concept of inheritance is also known as generalization/specialization. Supertype class is known as the **Generalization** class and the subtype class is known as the **Specialization** class. For example, further as chair, table and cupboards are specialization classes. Generalization/Specialization is a technique where in the attributes and behaviors that are common to several types of object classes are grouped into their own class, called a super type. The attributes and methods of the supertype object class are then inherited by those object classes.

3.5.4 Attributes inheritance

Attributes inheritance is the property of the higher and lower-level entities created by specialization and generalization. The attributes of the higher-level entity sets are inherited by the lower-level entity sets. For example, customer and employee inherit the attributes of person. So the, customer is described by his or her name, locality, city and customer_id attributes. In the same way employee is described by his or her name, locality, city and additional emp_code and salary attributes.

A lower-level entity set (or subclass) also inherits participation in the relationship sets in which its higher-level entity (or superclass) participates. The officer and secretary entity sets can participate in the work_for relationship set, since the supercalss employee participates in the works_for relationship. The above entity sets can participate in any relationships in which the person entity set participates.

3.6 EXTENDED E-R FEATURES

Although the basic E-R concepts can model most database features, some aspects of a database may be more aptly expressed by certain extensions to the basic E-R model. In this section, we discuss the extended E-R features of specialization, generalization, higher- and lower-level entity sets, attribute inheritance, and aggregation.

3.6.1 Generalization

A generalization hierarchy is a form of abstraction that two or more entities that share common attributes can be generalized into a higher-level entity type called a supertype or generic entity. The lower level of entities becomes the subtype or categories, to the super type, subtypes are dependent entities. Generalization is used to emphasize the similarities among lower-level entity sets and to hide difference. It makes ER diagram simpler because shared attributes are not repeated. Generalization is denoted through a triangle component labeled 'IS A' as shown in Figure 3.6.1.

Generalization is the result of taking the union of several lower level entity sets to produce higher level entity set.

In Figure 3.6.1 Account is the higher-level entity set and saving account and current account are lower level entity sets. Higher and lower level entity sets may also be designated by the term superclass and subclass respectively. The Account entity set is the superclass of saving account and current account subclasses.

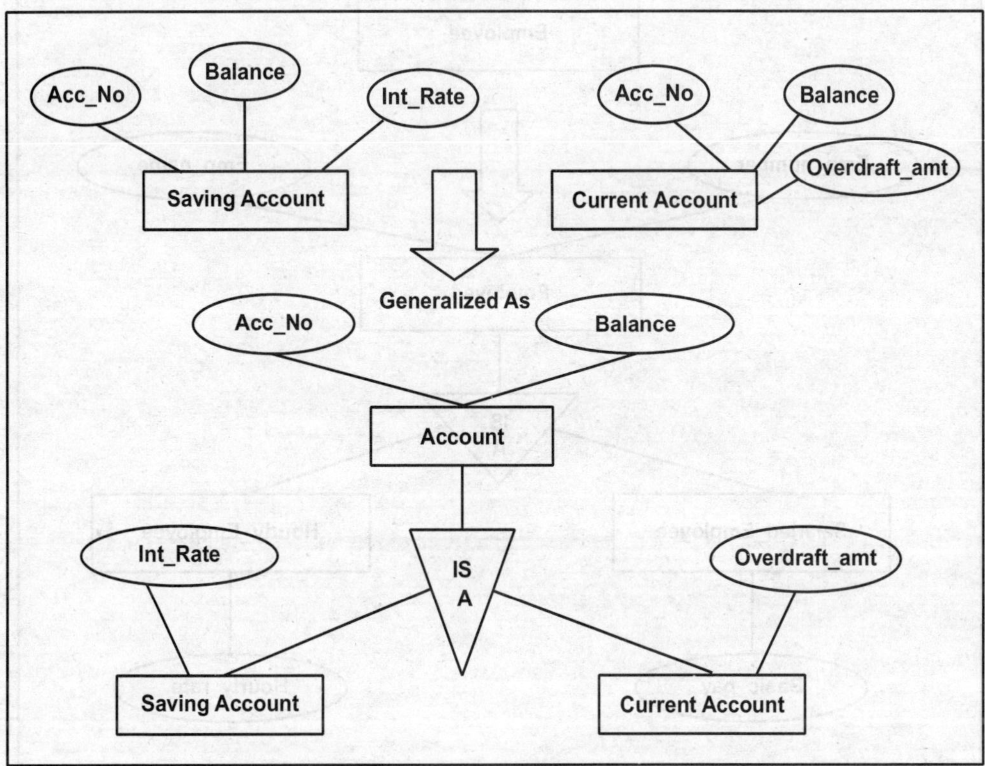

Figure 3.6.1 Representing Generalization

3.6.2 Specialization

Specialization is the process of taking subsets of a higher-level entity set to form lower level entity sets. It is a process of defining a set of subclass of an entity type, which is called as superclass of the specialization. The process of defining subclass is based on the basis of some distinguish characteristics of the entities in the super class.

For example, specialization of the Employee entity type may yield the set of subclass namely Salaried_Employee and Hourly_Employee on the method of pay as shown in Figure 3.6.2.

Specialization is the result of taking subsets of a higher level entity set to form lower level entity sets.

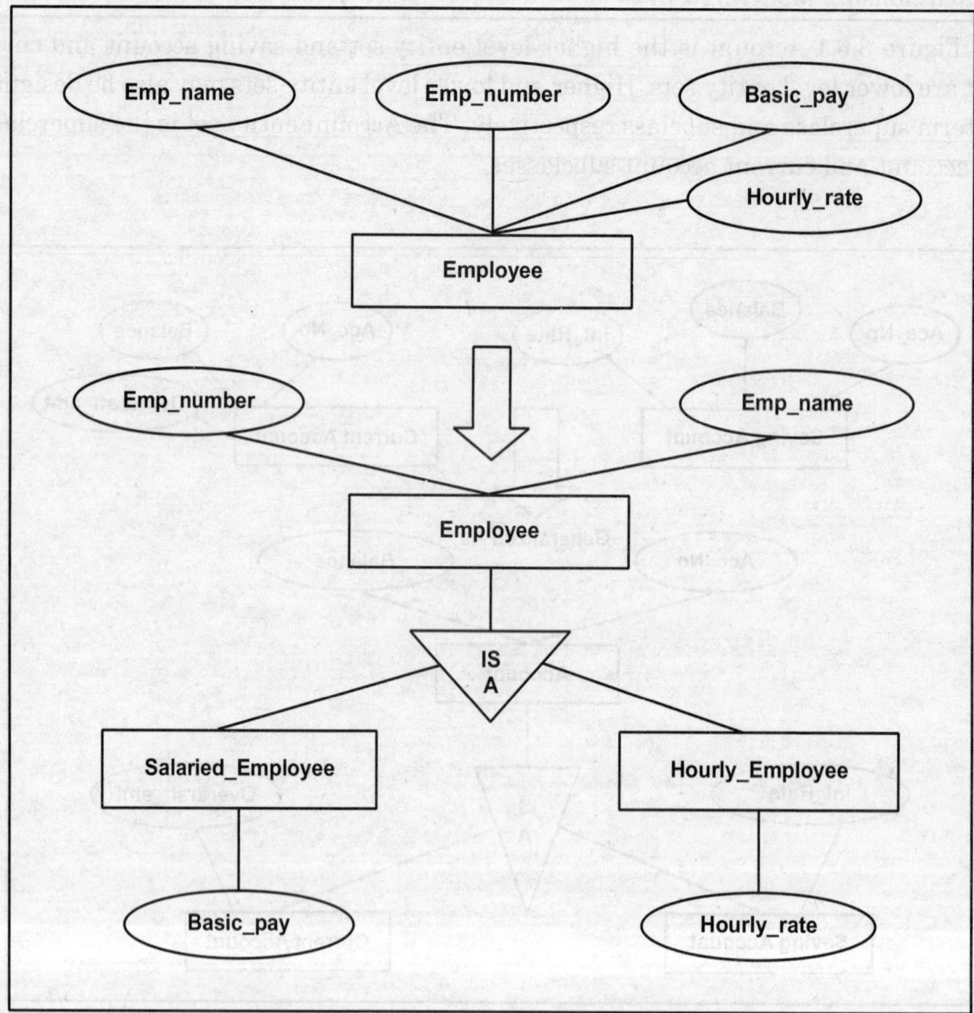

Figure 3.6.2 Representing Specialization

Difference between Generalization and Specialization

Generalization proceeds from the recognition that a number of entities set share some common features, which are described by the same, attributes and participate in the same relationship sets. Generalization is used to emphasize the similarities among lower-level entity set and to hide differences.

Specialization is the process of taking subsets of a higher-level entity set to form lower-level entity sets. Specialization emphasizes difference among entities within the set by creating distinct lower-level entity sets. These lower-level entity sets may have attributes, or may participate in relationships, that do not apply to all entities in the higher-level entity set.

3.6.3 Aggregation

Aggregation is the process of compiling information on an object, thereby abstracting a higher level object. One limitation of the E-R model is that it cannot express relationship within relationships. To illustrate the need for such a construct, consider the ternary relationship Work_on, between an employee, branch and job as shown in Figure 3.6.3(a)

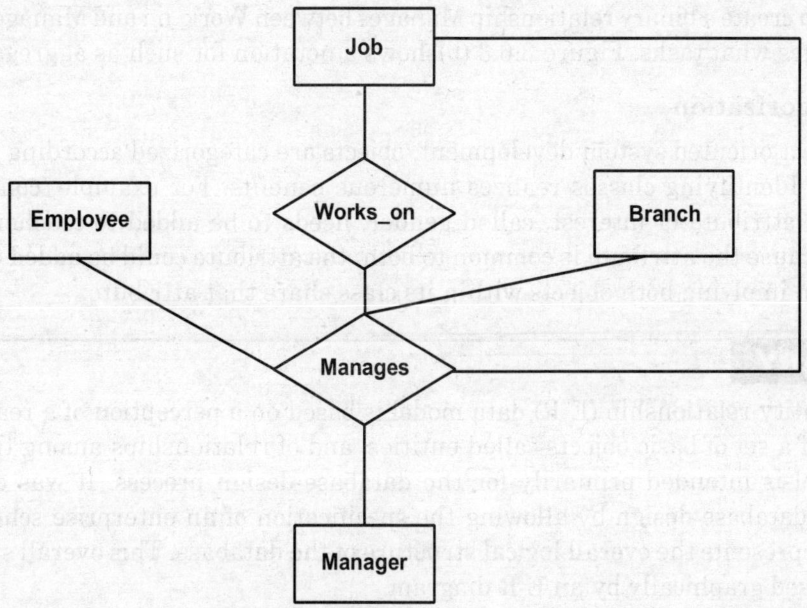

Figure 3.6.3(a) E-R diagrams with redundant relationship

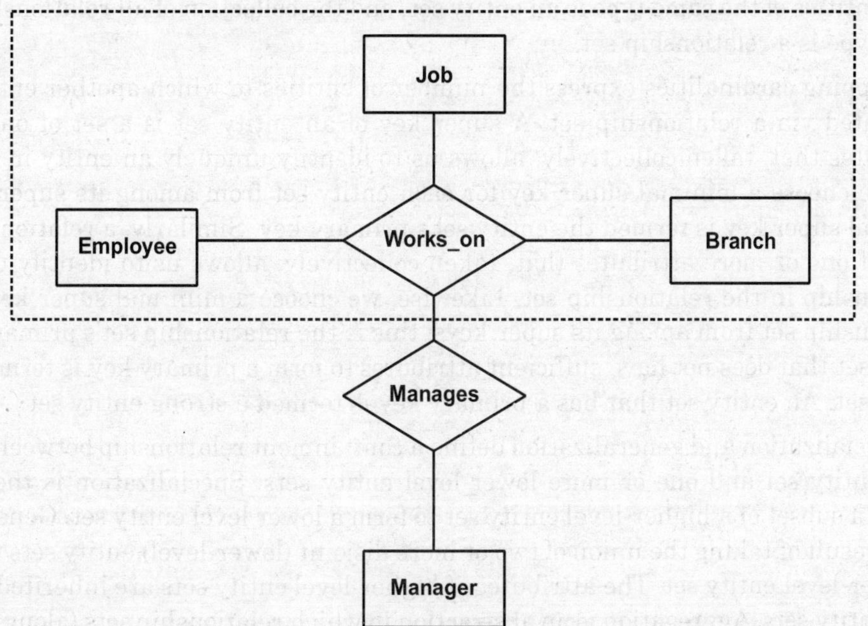

Figure 3.6.3(b) E-R diagram with Aggregation

The best way to model a situation shown in Figure 3.6.3(a) is the use of aggregation. Thus, the relationship Work_on relating the entity sets Employee, Branch and Job is a higher level entity set. Such as entity set is treated in the same manner as in any other entity set. We can then create a binary relationship Manages between Work_on and Manager to represent who manages what tasks. Figure 3.6.3 (b)shows a notation for such as aggregation.

3.6.4 Categorization

In object oriented system development, objects are categorized according to classes and subclasses. Identifying classes realizes numerous benefits. For example, consider the fact that a new attribute of interest, called gender, needs to be added to teacher and student objects. Because the attribute is common to both, the attribute could be added once, with the class person implying both objects within its class share that attribute.

SUMMARY

The entity-relationship (E-R) data model is based on a perception of a real world that consists of a set of basic objects called entities, and of relationships among these objects. The model is intended primarily for the database-design process. It was developed to facilitate database design by allowing the specification of an enterprise schema. Such a schema represents the overall logical structure of the database. This overall structure can be expressed graphically by an E-R diagram.

An entity is an object that exists in the real world and is distinguishable from other objects. We express the distinction by associating with each entity a set of attributes that describes the object. A relationship is an association among several entities. The collection of all entities of the same type is an entity set, and the collection of all relationships of the same type is a relationship set.

Mapping cardinalities express the number of entities to which another entity can be associated via a relationship set. A super key of an entity set is a set of one or more attributes that, taken collectively, allows us to identify uniquely an entity in the entity set. We choose a minimal super key for each entity set from among its super keys; the minimal super key is termed the entity set's primary key. Similarly, a relationship set is a set of one or more attributes that, taken collectively, allows us to identify uniquely a relationship in the relationship set. Likewise, we choose a mini mal super key for each relationship set from among its super keys; this is the relationship set's primary key. An entity set that does not have sufficient attributes to form a primary key is termed a weak entity set. An entity set that has a primary key is termed a strong entity set.

Specialization and generalization define a containment relationship between a higher-level entity set and one or more lower-level entity sets. Specialization is the result of taking a subset of a higher-level entity set to form a lower level entity set. Generalization is the result of taking the union of two or more disjoint (lower-level) entity sets to produce a higher-level entity set. The attributes of higher-level entity sets are inherited by lower-level entity sets. Aggregation is an abstraction in which relationship sets (along with their associated entity sets) are treated as higher-level entity sets, and can participate in relationships.

EXERCISES

1. What is the role of ER model and what are its different components?
2. What is meant by ER diagram? How can it be used for modeling?
3. Define attributes. Explain different types of attributes with example of each.
4. Explain the types of entities and categories of relationships.
5. Give an example of each of the following relationships:
   - One to one
   - One to many
   - Many to one
   - Many to many
6. Compare the connectivity and cardinality of a relationship.
7. Explain super class and sub class with an example.
8. What is attribute inheritance? How does it help in developing a system?
9. What do you mean by specialization? Explain giving examples.
10. Explain the distinction between specialization and generalization concepts.
11. Identify the different types of entities and relationship in an education system.
12. What is meant by the aggregation? Explain.
13. Explain ER modeling symbol.
14. Explain class and object with an example of each.
15. Develop an ER diagram for library management system.
16. What are the different symbols used for designing an ER diagram and explain their usage.
17. Identify the different types of entities and relationship in hospital system.
18. Discuss the steps for designing an ER diagram.
19. Develop an ER diagram for sales and purchase management system.
20. Illustrate the concepts of strong and weak entity sets in detail.
21. What are the different types of entities and relationship in railway reservation system?
22. Design an ER diagram for airline reservation system consisting of flights, aircraft, airports, fares, reservation, tickets, pilot, crew and passengers. Clearly highlight the entities, the relationships, the primary keys and the mapping constraints.
23. Design a generalization-specialization hierarchy for a motor vehicle sales company. The company sells motorcycles, passenger cars, vans and buses. Justify your placement of attributes at each level of the hierarchy. Explain why they should not be placed at a higher or lower level.

■

CHAPTER 4

RELATIONAL ALGEBRA AND RELATIONAL CALCULUS

4.1 INTRODUCTION

A data model should define the database structure and constraints. In addition to that, a data model should provide a set of operations to manipulate data. **Relational algebra** constitutes a basic set of operations for manipulating relational data. These operations enable the users to perform basic retrieval operations. The result of a retrieval operation on a table (or relation) is another relation. Thus the relational algebraic operations produce new relations, which can be further manipulated using the same **relational algebraic operations**. For example, a SELECT operation on a relation (table) produces another relation (table) and we can be perform another SELECT operation on that table too, which will produce another table and so on. A sequence of relational algebraic expression. The result of the relational algebraic expression too is a relation.

Relational algebra is a procedural language. It specifies the operations to be performed operations on exiting relations to derive result relations. It also defines the complete scheme for each of the result relations. The relational algebraic operations can be divided into **basic set oriented operations** and **relational oriented operations.**

In relational algebra each operation takes one or more relations as its operand (s) and another relation as its result. Consider an example of mathematical algebra as shown below:

$$\mathbf{4 + 5 = 9}$$

Here 4 and 5 are operands and + is an arithmetic operator which gives 9 as the result. Similarly, in relational algebra, **R1 + R2 = R3**

Here **R1**, And **R2** are relations (operands) and + is relational operator which gives **R3** as a resultant relation.

Translating SQL into Relational Algebra

In order to implement a DBMS, there must exist a set of rules which state how the database system will behave. The DBMS must take whatever SQL statements the user type in and translate them into relational algebra operations before applying them to the database. This transformation is shown in the following example:

SELECT and PROJECT can be combined together. For example, to get a list of Register numbers for Students in department number 1.

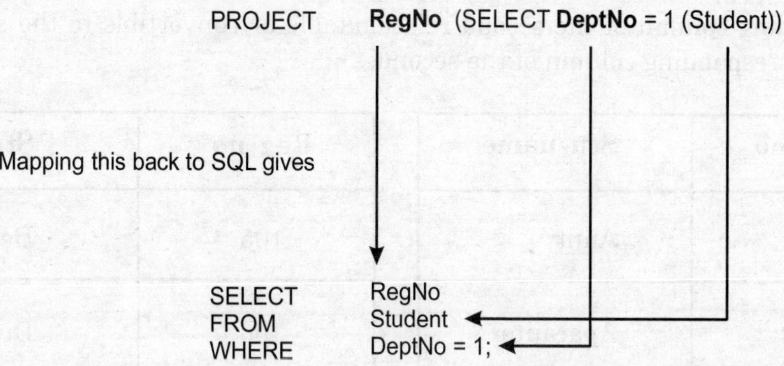

4.2 RELATIONAL ALGEBRAIC OPERATIONS

The relational algebraic operations are divided into groups. The first group includes the set operations (from the mathematic set theory). Since each relation is defined as a set of tuples the set operations are applicable to the relational data model. Set operations include the following:

- UNION
- INTERSECTION
- SET DIFFERENCE
- CARTESIAN PRODUCT

The second group of relational algebraic operations is developed specifically for the relational databases. Some of the operations in this category are:

- SELECT
- PROJECT
- RENAME
- JOIN
- DIVISION

4.2.1 Set oriented Operation

As we have seen the basic relational algebraic operations are the four set operations- UNION, INTERSECTION, SET DIFFERENCE and CARTESIAN PRODUCT. Three of these operations- UNION, INTERSECTION and SET DIFFERENCE require that the tables (relations) involved be union compatible. The CARTESIAN PRODUCT can be defined on any two relations. Two relations are said to be union compatible if the following conditions are satisfied:

- The two relations/tables must contain the same number of columns (have the same degree).
- Each column of the first relation/table must be either the same data type as the corresponding column of the second relation/table or convertible to the same data type as corresponding column of the second.

Reg_no	Stu_name
101	Amit
102	Aparajita
103	Ashish
104	Bhoomika
105	Debasis
106	Divij

Table (*a*) : CLASS (C)

Reg_no	Stu_name
105	Debasis
106	Divij
107	Harsh
108	Rahul

Table (*b*) : LIBRARY (L)

Table 4.2.1(*a*) Relation C and L

Now consider the two relations CLASS and LIBRARY. The class and library contains the entire list of Reg_No and Stu_Name. For simplicity we will call the class relation as C and the library relation as L. The two relations, as we can see, are union compatible.

UNION

In mathematical set theory, the union of the two sets is the set of all elements belonging to both sets. The set, which results from the union, must not, of course, contain duplicate elements. It is denoted by ∪. Thus the union of sets:

$$X = \{ 1,2,3,4,5 \}$$

And

$$Y = \{4,5,6,7,8 \}$$

Would be the set X UNION Y = { 1,2,3,4,5,6,7,8 }

For example : The result of this operation denoted by C ∪ L (where C and L are two compatible relations), is the relation that includes all tuples that are either in C or in L or in both C and L. Duplicate tuples would be eliminated, by using set union.

Reg_no	Stu_name
101	Amit
102	Aparajita
103	Ashish
104	Bhoomika
105	Debasis
106	Divij
107	Harsh
108	Rahul

Table (c): C ∪ L

Table 4.2.1(b) Result of union operation

INTERSECTION

In mathematical an intersection of two sets produces a set, which contains all the elements that are common to both sets. It is denoted by ∩. Thus the intersection of the two sets:

$$X = \{1,2,3,4,5\}$$

And

$$Y = \{4,5,6,7,8\}$$

Would be the set X INTERSECTION Y = {4,5}.

For example: The result of the intersection operation is a relation that includes all tuples that are in both C and L. the intersection operation is denoted by C ∩ L.

Reg_no	Stu_name
105	Debasis
106	Divij

Table (d): C ∩ L

Table 4.2.1(c) Result of intersection operation

SET DIFFERENCE

In mathematical, the difference between two sets X and Y produces a set, which contains all the members of one set, which are not in the order. It is denoted by "–". The order in which the difference is taken is obviously, significant. Thus the difference between the two sets:

X = {1,2,3,4,5}

Minus

Y = {4,5,6,7,8}

Would be **X** DIFFERENCE **Y** = {1,2,3} and between

Y = {4,5,6,7,8}

Minus

X = {1,2,3,4,5}

Would be **Y** DIFFRENCE **X** {6,7,8}

For example : The result of the difference operation is the relation that contains all tuples in C but not in L. The difference operation is denoted by C – L, L – C.

Reg_no	Stu_name
101	Amit
102	Aparajita
103	Ashish
104	Bhoomika

Table (e): C – L

Reg_no	Stu_name
107	Harsh
108	Rahul

Table (f): L – C

Table 4.2.1(d) Result of difference operation

The difference operation is not commutative. This means that X – Y is not the same as Y – X or in other words X – Y ≠ Y – X.

CARTESIAN PRODUCT

In mathematics, the Cartesian product of two sets is the set of all ordered pairs of elements such that the first element in each pair belongs to the first set and second element in each pair belongs to the second set. It is denoted by cross (X). It is for example, given two sets:

X = {1,2,3}

And Y = {4,5,6}

The Cartesian product X Cartesian product Y is the set:

{(1,4),(1,5),(1,6),(2,4),(2,5),(2,6),(3,4),(3,5)(3,6)}

For example : The Cartesian product is also known as cross product or cross join. Suppose two relation X and A. The Cartesian product is denoted by X × A and returns on tuples whose schema contains all fields of X (in the same order they appear in X) followed by all fields of A (in the same order as they appear is A). The result contains one tuple (r,s) (the concatenation of tuples r and s) for each pair of tuples where r belongs to s (r ∈ s) and s belongs to s (s ∈ r).

Reg_no	Stu_name
201	Abhishek
202	Ankit
203	Sonam
204	Anubha

Table (g): CLASS (C)

Subject
MPCS0203
CNCS0207

Table (h): Assignment (A)

The operation X × Y gives the resulting combinations as follows:

C × A

Reg_no	Stu_name	Subject
201	Abhishek	MPCS0203
201	Abhishek	CNCS0207
202	Ankit	MPCS0203
202	Ankit	CNCS0207
203	Sonam	MPCS0203
203	Sonam	CNCS0207
204	Anubha	MPCS0203
204	Anubha	CNCS0207

Table (i): C x A

Table 4.2.1(e) Cartesian product of relations C and A

4.2.2 Relational algebraic operations

The select, project and rename operations are unary operations, because they operate on one relation.

SELECT (σ)

The select operation is used to select a subset of the tuples from a relation that satisfies a selection condition. One can consider the select operation to be filter that keeps only those tuples that satisfy a qualifying condition. The select operation can also be visualized as a horizontal partition of the relation into two sets of tuples-those tuples that satisfy the condition and are selected, and those tuples that do not satisfy the condition and are discarded.

The select operation extracts specific tuples from a relation. We can use lower Greek letter (σ) to denote selection. Suppose you want to see tuples which have Branch_name = "Modinagar" from Account table. In such case, we can specify this condition with a select operation.

$$\sigma_{\text{Branch\_name = " Modinagar"}}(\text{Account})$$

The conditions are specified as mentioned below:

Account(Branch_name, Account_number, Customer_name, Balance)
In general select operations is denoted by

$$\sigma_{\text{<selection condition>}}(\text{<relation name>})$$

Where the symbol σ (sigma) is used to denote the select operator, and the selection condition is a Boolean expression specified on the attributes of relation. We can also find tuples in which the balance amount is say more than ₹ 10000/- by writing the following:

$$\sigma_{\text{Balance } > 10000}(\text{Account})$$

in general, we allow comparisons using relational operators (=, ≠, <, ≤, >, ≥) in a selection predicate. Futhermore, we can combine several predicates into a larger predicate by using the logical connection namely AND (Λ), OR (V) and NOT (¬) operators.

Consider another example. Suppose we want tuples which contain the faculty name " Gopal" who teaches DBMS, from relation (table) Teacher, then we may write the query as follows:

$$\sigma_{\text{Name = "Gopal"} \wedge \text{ Course = "DBMS"}}(\text{Teacher})$$

σ (sigma) is the selection operation symbol and Λ is logical operator AND.

PROJECT (∏)

If we think of a relation as a table, the select operation selects some of the rows from the table while discarding other rows. The project operation, on the other hand, select certain columns from the table and discards the other columns. If we are interested in only certain attributes of a relation, we use the project operation to project the relation over these attributes only. Therefore, the result of the project operation can be visualized as a vertical partition of a relation into two relations: one has the needed columns (attributes) and contains the result of the operation and the other contains the discarded columns. Projection id denoted by Greek letter pi (π).

Note : The select operation selects specific rows from a table discarding other rows. The
project operation, on the other hand, selects certain columns from the table and discards the other columns.

Suppose we want to know the customer names and their bank balance amounts from Account relation, then we may write the query:

$$\pi \text{Customer\_name, Balance}^{\text{(Account)}}$$

The general form of the project operation is:

$$\pi\text{<attribute list> (relation name).}$$

Composition of relational operations

Suppose we want to print the names and addresses of those faculty members who are teaching "DBMS" course then we can write the following query:

$$\pi_{\text{Name, Address}}(\sigma_{\text{Course = "DBMS"}}(\text{Teacher}))$$

RENAME

There are several ways in which one can use the select or project operations to get the desired results. One can write the operations as a single relational algebraic expression by nesting the operations or one can apply one operation at a time and create intermediate result relations. In the case where intermediate result relations are created, we must name the relations that hold the intermediate results. For example:

Book-Schema (Title, Author, Year, Price)

We want to retrieve the Title, Author and Year of all the books priced above ₹ 400. We can write a single relational algebraic expression as follows:

$$\pi_{\text{Title, Author, Year}}(\sigma_{\text{Price > 400}}(\text{Book}))$$

Alternatively, we can explicitly show the sequence of operations giving a name to each intermediate relation.

$$^{\text{Book400}\leftarrow\sigma}\text{Price > 400}^{\text{(Book)}}$$

$$^{\text{Result400}\leftarrow\pi}\text{Title, Author, Year}^{\text{(Book)}}$$

It is often simpler to break down complex sequence of operations by specifying intermediate result relations. It improves the readability and facilities better understanding. We can rename the intermediate result relations and also the attributes in the intermediate result relations. Renaming is very useful in the case or operations like union and join.

If no renaming is applied, the names of the attributes in the resulting relation of a select operation are the same as those in the original relation and in the same order. For the project operation with no renaming, the resulting relation has the same attribute names as those in the project attribute list and in the same order in which they appear in the list. To rename a relation or the attributes in a relation, simply list the new names in parentheses as shown below.

- $^{Book400 \leftarrow \sigma}$Price > 400$^{(Book)}$ –Here the relation is named Book400.
- $^{R400(BName,\ AName,\ PYear) \leftarrow \pi}$Title, Author, Year$^{(Book)}$- Here the attributes Title, Author and Year are renamed as BName, AName and PYear.

It is also possible to define a rename operation. That is, you can rename either the relation or the attributes or both. The general rename operation when applied to a relation can take any of the following forms:

- $\rho_{S(\text{new attribute names})}{}^{(R)}$
- $\rho_{S}{}^{(R)}$
- $\rho_{(\text{new attribute names})}{}^{(R)}$

The symbol ρ (rho) is used to denote the rename operator. S is the new relation and R is the original relation. The first expression renames both the relation and its attributes, the second renames the relation only and the third renames only attributes. This is shown in the following examples where a relation Book which has the attributes Title, Author, Year and Price is renamed.

- $\rho_{\text{Temp(BName, AName, PYear, RPrice)}}{}^{(Book)}$ – Here both the relation name and the attribute names are renamed.
- $\rho_{\text{Temp}}{}^{(Book)}$ – Here only the relation name is renamed.
- $\rho_{\text{(BName, AName, PYear, PPrice)}}{}^{(Book)}$- in this case only the attribute names are renamed.

JOIN

The join operation (denoted by ⋈) is used to combine related tuples from two relations (tables) into single tuples. The join operation is very important for any relational database with more than a single as it allows us to process more than one table at a time. A join operation matches data from or more tables, based on the values of one or more columns in each table. The join operation allows the processing of relationship between the operand relations.

For example

Using the relations mentioned below, suppose we want to retrieve the names of those employees who work in department 10, then we will use the following query.

Emp_no	Emp_name	Project
201	Vikas	AX10
202	Punit	AX10
203	Prabhash	AX11
204	Omprakash	AX10

Employee

Emp_no	Dept_no
201	10
202	20
203	10
204	30

Department

$$\pi_{(Employee.Emp\_name)}(Employee \bowtie_{Dept\_no} Department)$$

Equi Join

When two table are joined together using equality of values in one or more columns, they make an equi join. In equi join, the comparison operator (=) is only used. The result of an equi join will always have one or more pairs of attributes that have identical values in every tuple.

Theta Join

A general join condition is of the form:

<Condition> AND <Condition> AND............AND <Condition>

Where each condition is of the form Ai θ Bi. Here, Ai is an attribute of relation X. Bi is an attribute of relation Y. Here Ai and Bi have the same domain. The greek letter θ (theta) is one of the comparison operators $(=, <, \leq, >, \geq, \neq)$. A join operation is called a Theta Join. By theta join, tuples whose join attributes are null do not appear in the result.

Natural Join

In the natural join also, the comparison operator is always the equality operator =, but only the equi join contains two identical columns from the relation being joined. It is of course always possible to eliminate one of those two columns via the project operation (Π). An equi join with one of the two identical columns eliminated is called a natural join. Thus, natural join will also give a new table that does not have any duplicate columns.

Outer Join

The outer-join operation is an extension of the join operation to deal with missing information. Suppose that we have the relations with the following schemas, which contain data on full-time employees:

Employee (employee-name, street, city)

ft-works (employee-name, branch-name, salary)

employee-name	*street*	*city*
Anand	Indrapur	Varanasi
Jasjeet	Nai sadak	Jammu
Jaswinder	Shiv Marg	Delhi
Shivam	Puri Road	Bhubaneshwar

employee-name	*branch-name*	*salary*
Anand	CSE Dept	15000
Jasjeet	CSE Dept	13000
Kunal	ECE Dept	17000
Shivam	ECE Dept	20000

Figure 4.2.2(a) The employee and ft-works relations

Consider the Employee and ft-works relations in Figure 4.2.2(a). Suppose that we want to generate a single relation with all the information (street, city, branch name, and salary) about full-time employees. A possible approach would be to use the natural join operation as follows:

$$\text{Employee} \bowtie \text{ft-works}$$

The result of this expression appears in Figure 4.2.2(b). Notice that we have lost the street and city information about Jaswinder, since the tuple describing Jaswinder is absent from the ft-works relation; similarly, we have lost the branch name and salary information about Kunal, since the tuple describing Kunal is absent from the employee relation.

We can use the outer-join operation to avoid this loss of information. There are actually three forms of the operation: left outer join, denoted ⟕; right outer join, denoted ⟖; and full outer join, denoted ⟗. All three forms of outer join compute the join, and add extra tuples to the result of the join. The results of the expressions.

employee-name	***street***	***city***	***branch-name***	***salary***
Anand	Indrapur	Varanasi	CSE Dept	15000
Jasjeet	Nai sadak	Jammu	CSE Dept	13000
Shivam	Puri Road	Bhubaneshwar	ECE Dept	20000

Figure 4.2.2(b) The result of employee ⋈ ft-works.

employee-name	***street***	***city***	***branch-name***	***salary***
Anand	Indrapur	Varanasi	CSE Dept	15000
Jasjeet	Nai sadak	Jammu	CSE Dept	13000
Shivam	Puri Road	Bhubaneswar	ECE Dept	20000
Jaswinder	Shiv Marg	Delhi	**Null**	**Null**

Figure 4.2.2(c) Result of employee ⟕ ft-works.

employee ft-works, employee ft-works, and employee ft-works appear in Figures 4.2.2(c), 4.2.2(d), and 4.2.2(e), respectively.

The left outer join (⟕) takes all tuples in the left relation that did not match with any tuple in the right relation, pads the tuples with null values for all other attributes from the right relation, and adds them to the result of the natural join. In Figure 4.2.2(c), tuple (Jaswinder, Shiv Marg, Delhi , Null, Null) is such a tuple. All information from the left relation is present in the result of the left outer join.

The right outer join (⟖) is symmetric with the left outer join: It pads tuples from the right relation that did not match any from the left relation with nulls and adds them to the result of the natural join. In Figure 4.2.2(d), tuple (Kunal, null, null, ECE Dept, 17000) is such a tuple. Thus, all information from the right relation is present in the result of the right outer join.

The full outer join (⟗) does both of those operations, padding tuples from the left relation that did not match any from the right relation, as well as tuples from the right relation that did not match any from the left relation, and adding them to the result of the join. Figure 4.2.2(e) shows the result of a full outer join.

Since outer join operations may generate results containing null values, we need to specify how the different relational-algebra operations deal with null values.

It is interesting to note that the outer join operations can be expressed by the basic relational-algebra operations. For instance, the left outer join operation, r⟕s, can be written as

$$(r \bowtie s) \cup (r - \Pi R(r \bowtie s)) \times \{(null, \ldots, null)\}$$

where the constant relation {(null, . . . , null)} is on the schema S – R.

employee-name	***street***	***city***	***branch-name***	***salary***
Anand	Indrapur	Varanasi	CSE Dept	15000
Jasjeet	Nai sadak	Jammu	CSE Dept	13000
Shivam	Puri Road	Bhubaneshwar	ECE Dept	20000
Kunal	**Null**	**Null**	ECE Dept	17000

Figure 4.2.2(d) Result of employee⟖ft-works.

employee-name	***street***	***city***	***branch-name***	***salary***
Anand	Indrapur	Varanasi	CSE Dept	15000
Jasjeet	Nai sadak	Jammu	CSE Dept	13000
Shivam	Puri Road	Bhubaneshwar	ECE Dept	20000
Jaswinder	Shiv Marg	Delhi	**Null**	**Null**
Kunal	**Null**	**Null**	ECE Dept	17000

Figure 4.2.2(e) Result of employee⟗ft-works.

DIVISION

The division operator divides a dividend relation A of degree (means number of columns in a relation) m+n by a divisor relation B of degree n, and produces a resultant relation of degree m.

Relation A

Sno	Pno
S1	P1
S1	P2
S1	P3
S1	P4
S1	P5
S1	P6
S2	P1
S2	P2
S3	P2
S4	P2
S4	P4
S4	P5

Relation B

CASE-I

Pno
P1

CASE-II

Pno
P2
P3

CASE-III

Pno
P1
P2
P3
P4
P5

A devide by B

CASE-I

S.No.
S1
S2

CASE-II

S.No.
S1
S4

CASE-III

Pno
S1

In this example dividend relation A has two attributes of Sno, Pno (of degree 2) and division relation B has only one attribute Pno (of degree 1). Then A divide by B gives a resultant relation of degree 1. It means it has only one attribute of Sno.

$$\frac{A}{B} = \frac{SNO*PNO}{PNO} = SNO$$

The resultant relation has those tuples that are common values of those attributes, which appears in the resultant attribute sno.

For example, in CASE II,

P2 has Snos. → S1, S2, S3, S4

P4 has Snos.' → S1, S4

S1, S4 are the common supplier who supply both P2 and P4. So the resultant relation has tuples S1 and S4.

In CASE III

There is only supplier S1 who supply all the parts from P1 to P6.

4.3 RELATIONAL CALCULUS

Relational calculus is collective term for tuple calculus and domain calculus. The queries in the relational algebra are procedural. The relational database management systems free the user from the details of how to obtain information from the database. The users need only to specify what information they need and the RDBMS will decide how to get it.

In relational calculus, a query is expressed as a formula consisting of a number of variables and an expression involving these variables. The formula describes the properties of the result relation to be obtained. There is no mechanism to specify how the formula should be evaluated. It is up to the RDBMS to transform these non-procedural queries into equivalent, efficient procedural queries. In relational tuple calculus, the variables represent the tuples from specified relations. In domain calculus the variables represent the values drawn from specified domains.

Relational calculus is a formal query language where the queries are expressed as a variables and formulas on these variables. Such formulas specify the properties of the required result relation without specifying the method of evaluating it. Thus a relational calculus expression specifies what is to be retrieved rather than how to retrieve it. Therefore relational calculus is considered to be a non-procedural language. This is where relational calculus differs from relational algebra, which is a procedural language, where we must write a sequence of operations to specify a retrieval request.

It is possible to specify in relational calculus any retrieval that can be specified in the relational algebra and vice versa. In other word the expressive powers of both the languages are identical. This has led to the development of the concept of a relationally complete language. A relational query language is considered relationally complete, if we can express any query that can be expressed in relational calculus in that query language.

The relational calculus is not related to differential and integral calculus in mathematics, but takes it names from a branch of symbolic logic called predicate calculus. When applied to databases, it is in two forms: **tuple relational calculus**, as originally proposed by Codd (1972), and **domain relational calculus,** as proposed by Lacroix and Pirotte (1977). In first order or predicate calculus, a predicate is a truth-valued function with arguments. When we substitute values for arguments, the function yields an expression, called a proposition, which can be either true or false.

4.3.1 Tuple relational calculus

The tuple relational calculus is based on specifying a number of tuple variables. Each such tuple variable normally ranges over a particular database solution. This means that the variable may take any identical tuple from that relation as its value. A simple tuple relational calculus query is of the form {t | COND(t)}. Where 't' is a tuple variable and COND(t) is a conditional expression involving 't'. The result of such a query is a relation that contains all the tuples (rows) that satify COND(t).

For example, the relational calculus query {t | Book{t} and t.Price > 200} will get you all the books whose price is greater than ₹ 200. In the above example, the condition 'Book(t)' specifies that the range relation of the tuple variable 't' is Book. Each Book tuple 't' that satisfies the condition 't.price > 200' will retrieved. Note that 't.Price' reference the attribute Price of the tuple variable 't'.

The query {t | Book(t) and t.Price > 200} retrieves all attribute values for each selected Book tuple. To retrieves only some of the attribute (say Title, Author and Price) we can modify the query as follows:

{t.Title, t.Author, t.Price | Book(t) and t.Price> 200}

Thus in a tuple calculus expression we need to specify the following information:

- **For each tuple variable 't' the range relation 'R' of 't'.** This value is specified by a condition of the from R(t).
- **A condition to select the required tuples from the relation.** Tuple variables range over their respective range relations and the condition is evaluated for every possible combination of tuples to identify the selected combinations for which the condition evaluates to TRUE.
- **A set of attributes to be retrieved. This set is called the requested attributes.** The values of these attributes are retrieved for each selected combination of tuples. If the requested attributes list is not specified, then all the attributes of the selected tuples are retrieved.

Thus to retrieve the details of all books (Title and Author name) which were published by 'Tata McGraw' and whose price is greater than ₹ 200 we will write the query as follows:

{t.Ttile, t.Author | Book(t) and t.Publisher = 'Tata McGraw' and t.Price> 200}

Expressions and formulas

A general expression of the tuple relational calculus is of the following form:

$$\{ t_1.A_1, t_2.A_2, \ldots\ldots\ldots t_n.A_n \mid COND\ (t_1, t_2, \ldots\ t_n, t_{n+1}, t_{n+2}, \ldots\ t_{n+m})\}$$

Where $t_1, t_2, \ldots t_n, t_{n+1}, t_{n+2}, \ldots\ t_{n+m}$ are tuple variables, each A_i is an attribute of the relation on which t_i ranges and COND is a condition or formula of the tuple relational calculus. A formula is made up of predicate calculus atoms that can be one of the following:

1. An atom of the from $R(t_i)$. where R is a relation and t_i is a tuple variable. This atom identifies the range of the tuple variable t_i as the relation whose name is R.
2. An atom of the form t_i.A <comparison operator > t_j.B, where t_i and t_j are tuple variables and the <comparison operator> is any one of the following $=, \neq, <, \leq, >$ or $\geq$. A is an attribute of the relation on which t_i ranges and B is an attribute of the relation on which t_j ranges.
3. An atom of the form t_i.A<comparison operator> c or c <comparison operator> t_j.B, where t_i and t_j are tuple variable and the <comparison operator> is any one of the

following: =, ≠, <, ≤, > or ≥: A is an attribute of the relation on which t_i ranges, B is an attribute of the relation on which t_j ranges and 'c' is a constant value.

Each of the preceding atoms evaluates to either TRUE or FALSE for a specific combination of tuples and this is called the truth value of an atom. In general, a tuple variable ranges over all possible tuples in the 'universe'. For atoms of type1, if the tuple variable is assigned to a tuple that is a number of the specified relation R, the atom is TRUE: otherwise it is FALSE. In atoms of types 2 and 3, if the tuple variables are assigned to tuples such that the values of the specified attributes of the tuples satisfy the condition, then the atom is TRUE.

A formula or condition consists of one or more atoms connected via the logical operators AND, OR and NOT. A formula is defined as follows:

1. Every atom is a formula.
2. If F_1 and F_2 are formulas, so are (F_1 AND F_2), (F_1 OR F_2), NOT(F_1) and NOT(F_2).
   - (F_1 AND F_2) is TRUE if both F_1 and F_2 are TRUE otherwise it is FALSE.
   - (F_1 OR F_2) is FALSE if both F_1 and F_2 are FALSE otherwise it is TRUE.
   - NOT(F_1) is TRUE if F_1 is FALSE and it is FALSE if F_1 is TRUE.
   - NOT(F_2) is TRUE if F_2 is FALSE and it is FALSE if F_2 is TRUE

Existential and Universal Quantifiers

Two special symbols called quantifiers can appear in formulas Universal quantifier (∀) and Existential quantifier (∃). Truth values for formulas with quantifiers are described below:

If F is a formula, so is (∃t) (F), where't' is a tuple variable. The formula (∃t) (F) is TRUE if the formula F evaluates to TRUE for some (at least one) tuples assigned to free occurrences of 't' in F; otherwise (∃t) (t) is FALSE.

If F is a formula, so is (∀t) (F), where't' is a tuple variable. The formula (∀t) is TRUE if the formula F evaluates to TRUE for every tuple assigned to free occurrence of 't' in F; otherwise (∀t)(F) is FALSE.

The (∃) quantifier is called an existential quantifier because a formula (∃t) (F) is true if there exits some tuple that makes 'F' TRUE. For the universal quantifier (∀t) (F) is TRUE if every possible tuple that can be assigned to free occurrences of 't' in F is substituted for 't' and F is TRUE in every such substitution. It is called the universal or 'for all' quantifier because every tuple in the 'universe' of tuples must make F TRUE to make the quantified formula TRUE.

Consider 4 relations EMPLOYEE, DEPENDENT, DEPARTMENT, and SALAY. The EMPLOYEE relation consists of attributes like EMPNO, NAME, DEPTNO, DOB, CITY and PHONE. The DEPENDENT relation has attributes like ENO, NAME, RELATIONSHIP and DOB. The DEPARTMENT relation consists of attributes like DNO, DNAME and MANAGER. The SALARY relation consists of ENO, BASIC, HRA, TA, DEDUCTIONS, TAX and PAY. Now we will see some examples where these quantifiers are used:

1. **Get the name and city of all employees working for the 'Accounting' department.**

   {e.NAME, e.CITY | EMPLOYEE(e) and (∃d)
   (DEPARTMENT)(d) and d.DNAME= 'Accounting' and d.DNO=e.DEPTNO)}

2. **Get the name, department name of all employees whose pay is greater than ₹ 10000.**

   {e.NAME, d.NAME | EMPLOYEE(e) and
   DEPARTMENT (d) and d.DNO=e.DEPTNO) and
   (∃s) (SALARY (s) and s.ENO = e.EMPNO and s.PAY > 10000)}

3. **Get the name of all employees who have no dependents.**

   {e.NAME | EMPLOYEE(e) and (not(∃d) DEPENDENT (d) and e.EMPNO=d.ENO)}

4. **Get the name of all employees who have no dependents** (using ∀).

   {e.NAME | EMPLOYEE(e) and ((∀d) not (DEPENDENT (d)) or not
   (e.EMPNO=d.ENO)))}

5. **Get the name of all employees who have at least one dependent.**

   {e.NAME | EMPLOYEE(e) and (∃d) (DEPENDENT (d) and d.ENO=e.EMPNO)}

4.3.2 Domain relational calculus

There in another type of relational calculus called domain relational calculus or domain calculus. QBE or Query By Example is a query language related to domain relational calculus. QBE was developed almost concurrently with SQL by M. M. Zloof IBM Research Laboratory, Yorktown Heights. The formal specification of the domain calculus was proposed after the development of the QBE system. The domain calculus differs from the tuple calculus in the type of variables used in formulas. In domain calculus the variables range over single values from domains of attributes rather than ranging over tuple. To form a relation of degree 'n' for a query result, we must have 'n' of these domain variables-one for each attribute. An expression of the domain calculus is of the following form:

$$\{x_1, x_2, \ldots\ldots, x_n \mid COND(x_1, x_2, \ldots, x_n, x_{n+1}, x_{n+2} \ldots, x_{n+m})\}$$

In the above expression $x_1, x_2, \ldots, x_n, x_{n+1}, x_{n+2} \ldots, x_{n+m}$ are domain variables that range over domains of attributes and COND is a condition or formula of the domain relational calculus. A formula is made up of atoms. The atoms of a formula can be one of the following:

- An atom of the form $R(x_1\ x_2, \ldots, x_j)$, where R is the name of the relation of degree 'j' and each xi where $1 \le i \le j$ is a domain variable. This atom states that a list of values of $<x_1\ x_2, \ldots, x_j>$ must be a tuple in the relation named R, where x_i is the value of the ith attribute value of the tuple. To make the domain calculus expression more readable, we omit the commas and write $R(x_1\ x_2\ x_3)$ instead of writing $R(x_1, x_2, x_3)$.
- An atom of the form x_i **<comparison operator>** x_j where x_i and x_j are domain variables and <comparison operator> is any one of the following: $=, \neq, <, \leq, >$ or $\geq$.

- An atom of the **x_i <comparison operator>c** or **c <comparison operator>x_j**. operator x_i and x_j are domain variables, c is a constant value and <comparison operator> is any one of the following: $=, \neq, <, \leq, >$ or $\geq$.

Atoms evaluate to either TRUE or FALSE for a specific set of values called the **truth values** of the atoms. In case 1, if the domain variable are assigned values corresponding to a tuple of the specified relation R, then the atom is TRUE. In case 2 and 3, if the domain variables are assigned values that satisfy the condition, and then the atom is TRUE.

Consider 4 relations EMPLOYEE, DEPENDENT, DEPARTMENT and SALARY. This EMPLOYEE relation consists of attributes like EMPNO, NAME, DEPTNO, DOB, CITY, and PHONE. The DEPENDENT relation has attributes like ENO, NAME, RELATIONSHIP and DOB. The DEPARTMENT relation consists of attributes like DNO, DNAME and MANAGER. The SALARY relation consists of ENO, BASIC, HRA, TA, DEDUCTIONS, TAX and PAY. Now we will see some examples where these quantifiers are used:

- **Get the name and city of the employee whose employee number is 100.**

  {ru | (∃q) (∃s) (∃t) (∃v)

  (EMPLOYEE(qrstuv) and q= 100)}

- **Get the employee number of the employee whose name is Ranjit and who lives in Delhi.**

  {q | (∃r) (∃s) (∃t) (∃v)

  (EMPLOYEE(qrstuv) and r = 'Ranjit' and u= 'Delhi')}

- **Get the name of all employees who work in the Accounting department.**

  {r | (∃s) (∃l) (∃m) EMPLOYEE(qrstuv) and DEPARTMENT(lmn) and m= 'Accounting' and l=s)}

- **Get the names of all employees who have no dependents.**

  {r | (∃q) (EMPLOYEE(qrstuv) and (not(∃l) (DEPENDENT(lmno) and q=l)))}

- **Get the name, date of birth and city of all employees who have at least one dependent.**

  {rtu | (∃q)(∃l) EMPLOYEE(qrstuv) and (DEPENDENT(lmno) and q=l)}

Well Formed Formulas

The WFFs should be those sequences of symbols that are unambiguous and make sense. This can be ensured by stating some rules for the construction WFFs.

A WFFs is constructed from conditions, Boolean operators (AND, OR, NOT), and quantifiers(∃,∀)according to rules F1-F5 motioned below:

F1. Every condition is a WFFs.

F2. If f is a WFF, then so are (f) and NOT (f).

F3. If f and g are WFF, then so are (f AND g) and (f OR g)

F4. If f is a WFF in which T occurs as a free variable then T (f) and T are WFFs.

F5. Nothing else is a WFF.

SUMMARY

The relational algebra is a (high level) procedural language; it can be used to tell the DBMS how to build a new relation from one or more relation in the database. The relational calculus is a non-procedural language it can be used to formulate the definition of a relation in terms of one or more database relations. However formally the relational algebra and relational calculus are equivalent to one another: for every expression in the algebra, there is an equivalent in the calculus (and vice versa).

The relational calculus is used to measure the selective power of relational languages. A language that can be used to produce any relation that can be derived using the relational calculus is said to be relationally complete. Most relational query language are relationally complete but have expressive power than the relational algebra or relational calculus because of additional operations such as calculated, summary, and ordering functions.

The five fundamental operations in relational algebra, selection, projection, Cartesian product, union, and set difference, perform most of the data retrieval operations that we are interested in. in addition, there are also the join, intersection, and Division operations, which can be expressed in terms of the five operations. The relational calculus is a formal non-procedural language that uses predicates. There are two forms of the relational calculus: tuple relational calculus and domain relational calculus.

In the tuple relational calculus, we are interested in finding tuples for which a predicate is true. A tuple variable is a variable that ranges over a named relation: that is variable who's only permitted values tuple of the relation. In the domain relational calculus, domain variable take their values from domains of attribute rather than tuples of relation.

EXERCISES

1. What are the major aspects in which the relational model deals?
2. What is relational algebra and what are its uses?
3. What is a relational algebraic expression and what are relational algebraic operations?
4. What are the relational algebraic operations derived from set theory?
5. What is a UNION? How is it represented? Explain with an example.
6. What is a DIFFERENCE? How is it represented? Explain with an example.
7. What is a CARTESIAN PRODUCT? How is it represented? Explain with an example.
8. What do you mean by compatibility?
9. What is a SELECT operation? How is it represented? Explain with an example.

10. What is a PROJECT operation? How is it represented? Explain with an example.
11. What is a RENAME operation? How is it represented? Explain with an example.
12. What is a DIVISION operation? How is it represented? Explain with an example.
13. What is the use of a RENAME operation?
14. Discuss the difference between the five join operations: Theta join, Equijoin, Natural join, Outer join, and Semi join. Give examples to illustrate your answer.
15. Define the basic relational algebra operations. Define the join, intersection, and division operations in terms of these five basic operations.
16. What is relational calculus?
17. What is tuple calculus?
18. What is domain calculus?
19. How does tuple relational calculus differ from domain relational calculus?
20. Define the WFFs.

■

CHAPTER 5

RELATIONAL DBMS

5.1 INTRODUCTION

The foundations of Relational Database technology was laid by Dr.E.F Codd, who in his paper 'A Relational Model of Data for large shared data bank' laid the basic principles of the RDBMS. Codd was working for IBM at their San Jose Research lab in California. He laid down certain principles of database management, referred to as relational model. These principles were soon applied to experimental systems, and a start was made on the design of a database language that would interact with such systems.

The Relational Database Management Systems, as said above, are based on relational model. The relational model, in turn, is a way of looking at data. It is a prescription for how to represent and manipulate data. The RDBMS he is a software package used to store and retrieve data that is organized in the form of tables. In other words Relational database management system stores information in rows and columns and conducts searches by using data in specified columns and rows of one table as well as to find additional data in another related table.

Two dimensional tables is a natural way to represent data to a user. A table must be set up in a way that no information about the relations among data element is lost.

A table should contain the following properties:

1. Each entry in a table should only represent one data item and no two columns headings with same name
2. In each column, the data items are of the same data type.
3. Each column is a assigned with a distinct heading.
4. All rows are distinct; duplicate rows are not allowed.
5. Both the rows and the columns can be viewed in any sequence at any time without affecting the information.

A relational database model uses a collection of tables to represent both data and the relationships among those data items. Each table has multiple columns, and each column has a unique name.

A relational database management system (RDBMS) has the following properties:

1. Stores data in the form of tables.
2. Does not require the user to understand its physical implementation
3. Provides information about its content and structure in the system table.
4. Supports the concepts of NULL values.

5.2 RDBMS TERMINOLOGIES

The relational model is an abstract theory of data that is based on the mathematical theory whose principles were laid down by Dr. Codd. The relational model of Codd used certain terms and principles, which were not familiar in the data processing circles at that time. The terms that were used to describe the database properties and functions lacked the precision necessary for the formal theory that Codd was proposing. So a new set of terminology had to be evolved. The Table 5.2 gives a list of the relational term and their corresponding informal equivalent.

Table 5.2 RDBMS Terminology

Formal Relational terms	***Informal Equivalent terms***
Relation	Table
Tuple	Row, Record
Cardinality	Number of Row
Attribute	Column, field
Degree	Number of columns
Primary Key	Unique identifier
Domain	Set of legal Values

The Relational Database Management Systems, as said above, are based on the relational model. The relational model, in turn, is a way of looking at data. It is a prescription for how to represent and manipulate data. More precisely, the relational model is concerned with three aspects of data: data structure, data integrity, and data manipulation

Properties of Relations

A relation has the following properties:

Relation: A relation is a table with columns and rows.

- The relation has a name that is distinct from all other relation names in the relational schema.
- Each cell of the relation contains exactly one atomic (single) value.

- Each attribute has a distinct name.
- The values of an attribute are all from the same domain.
- Each tuple is distinct; there are no duplicate tuples.
- The order of attributes has no significance.
- The order of tuples has no significance, theoretically. (However, in practice, the order may affect the efficiency of accessing tuples.)

5.2.1 Relation

All data and relationship are represented in a two dimensional table called a relation. For example, the table shown in Figure 5.2.1 is referred to as relation. A database constructed using relations is referred to as a relational database. Relational database is constructed from flat arrangement of data items. In Figure 5.2.1, there is an Employee Service relation that describes the entity Employee by Emp_code, Emp_name and Year Of service (Year).

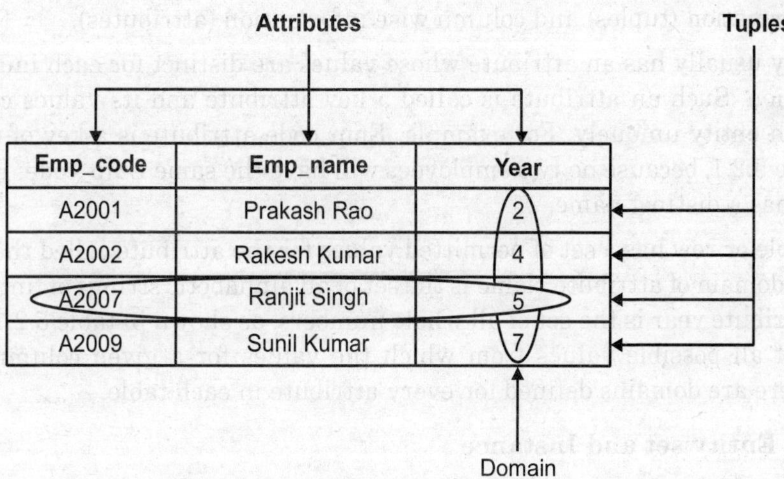

Figure 5.2.1 Employee Service Relation in table form

All relations have three components

(a) Name (b)

Degree (c)

Cardinality

- **Name**

  Name is represented by the title or entity-identifier. For example Employee Name and Years of Service relation as seen in Figure 5.2.1.

- **Degree**
- The number of columns associated with a table or relation among them is called the degree. In the table Employee Service relation, degree is 3, i.e. there are 3 attributes or fields associated with the table.

- **Cardinality**

  The number of rows in a table is called as cardinality. The number of tuples is called the cardinality of the relation and this changes as tuples are added and deleted. The cardinality is a property of the extension of the relation and is determined from the particular instance of the relation at any given moment. In the table (Employee Service relation), cardinality is 4, i.e there are 4 rows or records (tuples) associated with the table.

5.2.2 Attributes and Tuples

An attribute is a named column of a relation. In the relational model, relations are used to hold information about the object to be represented in the database. A relation is represented as a two–dimensional table in which the rows of the table correspond to individual records and the table columns corresponds to attributes. Two dimensional tables in a relational database are much like the traditional file system with its records, fields and files. Row of a relation are referred to as Tuples. In another word A relation consists of number of records or row-wise information (tuples) and column wise information (attributes).

An entity usually has an attribute whose values are distinct for each individual entity in the collection. Such an attribute is called a key attribute and its values can be used to indentify each entity uniquely. For example, Emp_code attribute is a key of the Employee entity in table 5.2.1, because no two employees will have the same Emp_code. Each attribute of a relation has a distinct name.

Each tuple or row has a set of permitted values for the attribute called the Domain. For example, the domain of attribute Name is the set of all alphabetic strings of finite length. The domain of attribute year is the set of all whole numbers, as shown in table 5.2.1. A domain is a collection of all possible values from which the values for a given column or attribute is drawn. There are domains defined for every attribute in each table.

5.2.3 Entity, Entity set and Instance

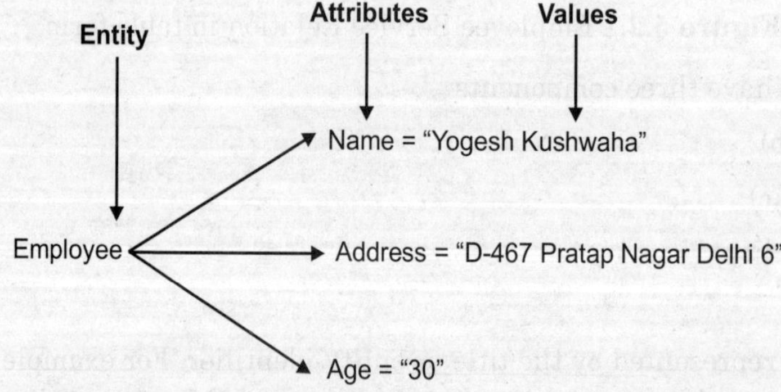

Figure 5.2.3 Entity and the values of its Attributes

An entity is an object that exists and is distinguishable from any other. In other words, an entity is a real world person, place or thing, or a conceptual (logical) person, place or thing, of significant interest to the organization and about which the organization must collect and maintain data. Each entity has particular properties called attributes that describe it. For example, an Employee entity may be described by employee's Name, Address, and Age, Figure 5.2.3 shows an entity and the values of its attributes.

For example, Employee entity has three attributes Name, Address, and Age with the values "Yogesh Kushwaha", "D-467 Pratap Nagar Delhi 6" and "30" respectively.

The collection of information stored in a database at a particular moment is called instance or occurrence of the entity.

Domain

The smallest unit of data in the relational model is the individual data value. Such values are assumed to be atomic, which means that they have no internal structure as far as the model is concerned. A domain is a set of all possible data values.

5.3 RELATIONAL DATA INTEGRITY

In the previous chapter we discussed the structural part of the relational data model. As stated earlier, a data model has two other parts: A set of integrity rules, which ensure that the data is accurate and manipulate part, defining the types of operation that are allowed on the data. In order to discuss the relational integrity rules, concept of relational keys is desired.

5.3.1 Relational Keys

There should not be any duplicate tuple within a relation. Therefore, we should identify one or more attributes (called relational keys) that uniquely identify each tuple in a relation.

5.3.2 What is Key

A database consists of tables, which consists of records, which further consist of fields. The Figure 5.3.2 provides an example of a typical table consisting of student details.

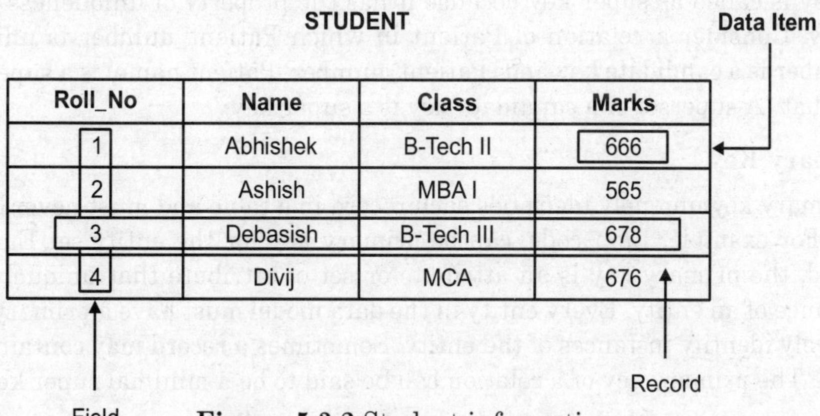

Roll_No	Name	Class	Marks
1	Abhishek	B-Tech II	666
2	Ashish	MBA I	565
3	Debasish	B-Tech III	678
4	Divij	MCA	676

Figure 5.3.2 Student information

Here, table containing five records and each containing four fields

Table Name= Student

A Row= a Records

A Column= a Fields

A Cell = A data item; particular value in a field for a particular

A table in a database may be empty, containing no records or contains many millions of them, similarly, a single records may consists of one or thousands of fields. Each field in turn contains a single data item. In order to uniquely identify each records of the table, there must be some fields or combination of fields, which should have only unique values.

For example: in order table more than one student may have the same Name, Class, Marks but they must have the different Roll_No. So, we can distinguish one record from the other with the help of Roll_No column Roll_No that is used to uniquely identify each record of the table is called as Key Fields. Key is a set of one or more columns whose combined values are unique among all occurrences in a given table. A key is the relational means of specifying uniqueness.

KEYS

A key is that data item that exclusively identifies a record. For example Student_RegNo, Account_Number, Product_code, Employee_number are used as key fields because they specifically identify a record stored in a database.

5.3.2.1 Super Key

A Super Key for an entity is a set of one or more attribute whose combined value uniquely identifies the entity in the entity set. A super key has the uniqueness property but not necessarily the irreducibility property. A candidate key is a special case of a Super key.

For Example: If Roll_No is unique in relation STUDENT then, the set of attributes (Roll_No, Name, Class) is a super key for a relation STUDENT, case set of attributes are also unique, but this combination of keys (composite key) is not having the property of irreducibility because Roll_No which is one subset of the composite key is also unique itself. Thus, this composite key is called as super key because it has the property of uniqueness but not the irreducibility. Consider a relation of Patient in which Patient_number is unique. Then, Patient_number is a candidate key and (Patient_number, Patient name) is a super key. Thus we can say that "A superset of a candidate key is a super key."

5.3.2.2 Primary Key

The primary key uniquely identifies each record in a table and must never be the same for records. For example, Emp_code, can be primary key for the entity set Employees. In another word, the primary key is an attribute or set of attribute that uniquely identify a specific instance of an entity. Every entity in the data model must have a primary key whose values uniquely identify instances of the entity. Sometimes a record may contain more than one key field. The primary key of a relation can be said to be a minimal super key.

The primary key should be chosen such that its attributes are never or very rarely changed. For instances, the address field of a person should not be part of the primary key, since it is likely to change.primary key cannot any null value because we cannot uniquely identify multiple Null values. Emp_code, on the other hand, is not changed, till he working in the organization. The primary key of any table is any candidate key of that table which the database designer arbitrarily designates as primary. The primary key may be selected for convenience, comprehension, performance, or any other reasons.

5.3.2.3 Secondary Key

A Secondary key is an attribute or combination of attribute that may not be a candidate key but classifies the entity set particular characteristic. For example, the entity set EMPLOYEE having the attribute Department, which identifies by its value which means all instance of EMPLOYEE who belong to a given department.

More than one employee may belong to a department, so the department attribute is not a candidate key for the entity set EMPLOYEE, since it cannot uniquely identify an individual employee. However, the Department attribute does identify all employees belonging to a given department. Hence, it can be considered as a secondary key.

5.3.2.4 Candidate key

A candidate key is an attribute or set of attributes that uniquely identifies a record. These attributes or combinations of attributes are called candidate keys. In such a case, one of a candidate key is chosen to be primary key. Candidate keys are those attribute of a relation, which have the properties of uniqueness and irreducibility, whose explanation is given below:

Let R be a relation. By definition, set of all attributes of R has the uniqueness property, meaning that , at any given time , no two tuples in the value of R at that time are duplicates of one another. As in the case of the STUDENT relation, for example, the subset containing just attribute Roll_No has that property.

These facts constitute the intuition behind the definition of candidate key.

Let K be a set f attribute of relation R. Then K is a candidate key for R if and only if it possesses both of the following properties:

1. **Uniqueness:** No legal value of R ever contains two distinct tuples with same value for K.
2. **Irreducibility:** No proper subset of K has the uniqueness property.

5.3.2.5 Composite Key

In many cases, as we design database, we will have tables that will use more than one column as part of the primary key. These are called composite keys or (concatenated keys). In other words, when a record cannot be uniquely identified by a single field, in such cases a composite key is used. A composite key is a group of fields that are combined together to uniquely identify a record.

5.3.2.6 Alternate Key

The alternate key of any table simply those candidate keys. Which are not currently selected as the primary key. Exactly one of those candidate keys is chosen as the primary key and the remainder, if any, are then called alternate keys. An alternate key is a function of all candidate keys minus the primary key

Example : Consider a database of students having Roll No, Name, Class and Marks as attributes having roll no and name as unique attribute for each student. Then, it will have roll no and name as unique attribute for each student. Then, it will have roll number and name as two candidate keys and programmer will preferably choose roll no as primary key and name will become alternate key. Above database has roll no, name , roll no+name, roll no+name+class, roll no+class, roll no+marks, roll no+class+marks, roll no+name+class+marks, name+class, name+marks, name+class+marks as super keys

5.3.2.7 Foreign Key

In a relation, the column whose data values correspond to the values of a key column in another relation is called a foreign key. In another word's Foreign keys are the attributes of a table, which refers to the primary key of some another table. Foreign keys permit only those values, which appears in the primary key of the table to which it refers or may be null. Foreign keys are used to link together two or more different tables which have some form of relationship with each other. The foreign key is a reference to the tuple of a table from which it was taken, this tuple being called the referenced or Target tuple. The table containing the referenced tuple will be called as Target table.

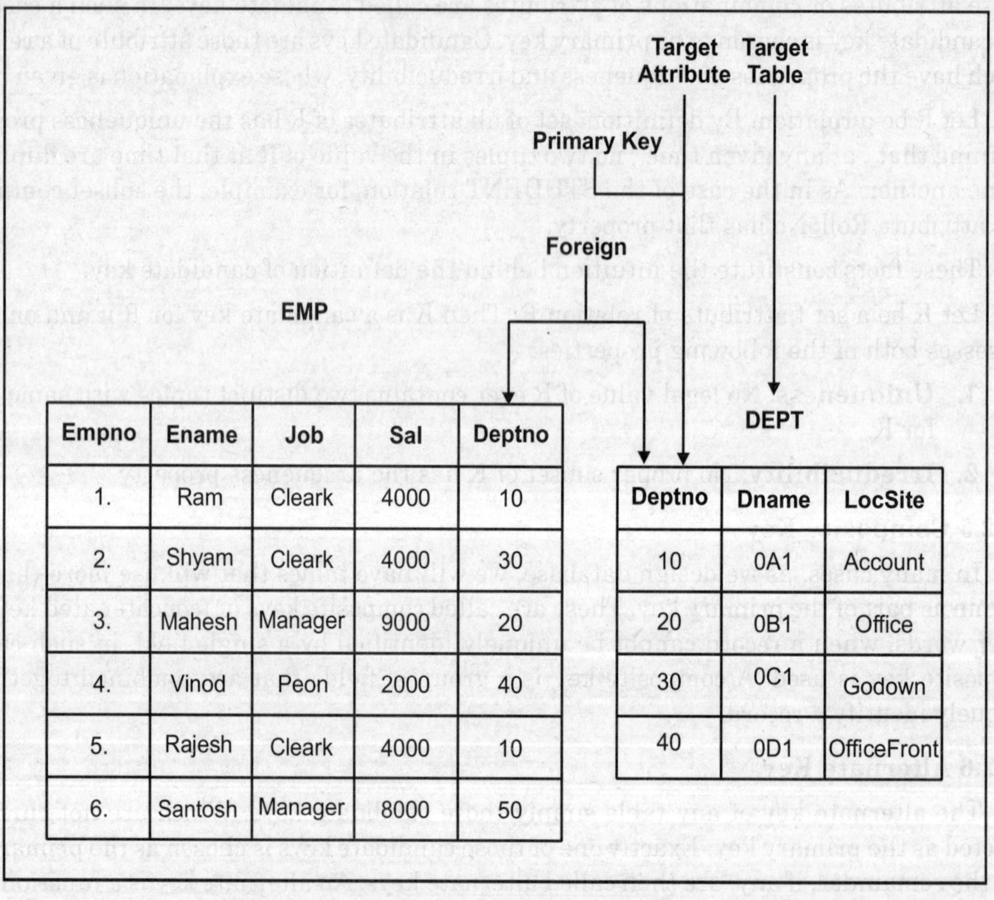

Empno	Ename	Job	Sal	Deptno
1.	Ram	Cleark	4000	10
2.	Shyam	Cleark	4000	30
3.	Mahesh	Manager	9000	20
4.	Vinod	Peon	2000	40
5.	Rajesh	Cleark	4000	10
6.	Santosh	Manager	8000	50

Deptno	Dname	LocSite
10	0A1	Account
20	0B1	Office
30	0C1	Godown
40	0D1	OfficeFront

Figure 5.3.2.7 Foreign Key

Thus, a Foreign key is an attribute that completes a relationship by identifying the parent entity. Foreign keys provide a method for method for maintaining integrity in the data (called referential integrity) and for navigating between different instances of an entity.

A foreign key must support every relationship in the model. The matter of integrity of foreign keys is referred to as Referential Integirty.

For example: Consider the below Figure 5.3.2.7, containing two tables (EMP, DEPT). if we try to insert information of employee with Deptno 50, then this is an invalid information, because there is no Deptno 50 exists in the company (as shown in table DEPT). Then, this invalid information should be prevented from insertion, which would only be possible if Deptno of EMP table refer the Deptno of DEPT table. It means that only those values are permitted in Deptno of EMP table, which appears in the Deptno attribute of the DEPT table. Thus, we can say that Deptno of EMP table is the foreign key which refers the primary key Deptno of DEPT table. Thus, we can insert the Empno 6 with any Deptno from 10, 20, 30, and 40.

Null may also be permitted in the Deptno of EMP table. Here, Deptno of DEPT table is Target attribute and DEPT is the target table.

Consider another example :

Student

Roll_No	**Name**	**Class_Code**
1	Ankit	02
2	Anil	01
3	Debashish	-

Class

Class_Code	**Name**
1	B-Tech
2	B-Tech
3	M-Tech

Here, college has three valid classes with class code 1, 2, and 3. The class_code(foreign key) of student table refers class_code of class table.

5.3.3 Domain Constraints

All the values that appear in a column of a relation (table) must be taken from the same domain. As we have seen before, a domain is a set of values that may be assigned to an attribute. A domain definition usually consists of the following components:

- Domain name
- Meaning

- Data Type
- Size or Length
- Allowable values or Allowable range (if applicable)

5.3.4 Operational Constraints

These are the constraints enforced in the database by the database by the business rules or real world limitations. For example, if the retirement age of the employees in an organization is 60, then the age column of the employee table can have a constraint "Age should be less than or equal to 60." These kinds of constraints, enforced by the business and the environment are called operational constraints.

5.3.5 Relational integrity rule

When many users enter data items into a database, it becomes important that all data items and associated among such data items are not destroyed. Hence, data insertions, updations etc. have to be carried out in such a way that database integrity is maintained. Integrity check is to be performed at the entry level itself. By checking the data 'values' conforming to certain specified rules, the names, value lying within a specified range. For example, the age of the employee should be in the range of 18 years to 70 years.

The relational model includes two general integrity rules. These integrity rules define the set of consistent database states and changes of state or both.

- **Integrity Rule 1 (Entity Integrity)**

  "If an attribute of a table is of prime attribute (unique identifier), it can not accept null values, or in other words no component of a primary key values may be null." Entity integrity ensures that instances of the entities are distinguishable and thus no prime attribute (component of a primary key) value may be null. By definition, all entities be distinguishable i.e. they must have a unique identification of some kind. Primary keys perform that unique identification function in a relational database. Hence, an identifier (Primary key value) that was completely null would be a contradiction.

  Note : If two entities are not distinguishable from each other, then definition such entities are not two entities.

- **Integrity Rule 2 (Referential Integrity)**

  "To ensure that a value that appears in one relation for a given set of attributes also appears for a certain set of attributes in another relation. Such a condition is called the referential integrity." Integrity Rule 2 is concerned with the concept of foreign key i.e. with the attributes of a relation having domains. The domain of foreign keys are those of the primary key of another relation. For example, if a base relation includes a foreign key, then it must have a primary key to match in some other relation, or contain a null value completely. (see Figure 5.3.5).

Note : The value of a primary key which appears in the base table (entity set) whenever there is a cardinality (entity relation) then the value of a primary key, which becomes a foreign key in the entity relation, the value of foreign key and primary key should be the same.

Control File	
Dept_code	**Designation**
A01	Director
B01	Manager
C01	Officer

Master File		
Emp_code	**Dept_code**	**Name**
100	A01	Vikas
102	C01	Punit
104	X01	Manoj

Figure 5.3.5 Referential Integrity

The designation code 'X01' in master file is not allowed, as it does not have a primary key match in other table, namely the control file. Employee with Emp_code 104 joins the organization, and his designation is not clearly specified at the time of data entry. Hence, the designation can be a null, so that the same can be updated later.

Note : Referential Integrity constraints are created in order to ensure that data entered into one table is matchable or compatable with corresponding data in the other related tables. Values from one column are dependent on the values of columns in other tables.

5.4 RELATIONAL DATA MANIPULATION

RDBMS is a database management system where data are organized in the form of table and all database manipulation are carried out on these tables. Users of RDBMS can create a new relation from two or more existing tables thus permitting them to manipulate data in creative ways. For example, suppose a relational DBMS maintains two relations: the Employee Service relation (Figure 5.2.1) and Employee Education relation (Figure 5.6).

A query about employees with more than two years of service in the organization and an MCA degree can be obtained by using the following procedures:

- A relationship is implied between the Employee Service relation (Figure 5.2.1) and Employee Education relation (Figure 5.6).
- A temporary table of employees who have been in the organization for more than two years is obtained from the Employee Service relation and placed in a temporary table.

Emp_code	Degree
A2001	B-TECH
A2002	MCA
A2007	M.Sc
A2009	MCA

Figure 5.6
Employee Education relation

- The information in the temporary table is taken along with the Employee Education relation to determine which employee has been in the firm for more than two years and also qualified as MCA. This result is a second temporary relation. From this second temporary relation is inferred that Rakesh Kumar and Sunil Kumar are only employees who qualify for the two conditions put together. Thus this method is very useful to manipulate several tables together to bring out information. This is the method used in RDBMS for manipulating and extracting information's.

5.5 CODD'S RULES

There are twelve rules formulated by E.F. Codd for RDBMS in 1970. If an RDBMS satisfies all these twelve rules, then full benefits of the relational database results can be obtained. The twelve rules are having the following main points.

1. Information Representation
2. Guaranteed Access
3. Systematic Treatment of Null values
4. Database Description Rule
5. Comprehensive Data Sub-Language
6. View Updating
7. High-Level Update, Insert, Delete
8. Physical Data Independence
9. Logical Data Independence
10. The Distribution Rule
11. Non Subversion
12. Integrity Rule

1. Information Representation

In the relational database model, all information should be explicitly and logically represented by entering the data values in the form of tables. The information such as view and column names should be in the table form. Data stored in data dictionary should also be in the tabular form.

2. Guaranteed Access

This rule refers to the fact that a table can be taken as a storage structure and at the intersection of each column and row there will necessarily be only one specific value of data item (or null). Every value of data item must be logically addressable by using a combination of table-name, primary-key-value and the column-name.

3. Systematic Treatment of Null values

In relational database management system null value should be supported for the representation of missing and inapplicable information only. The database management system must have a consistent method for representing null values.

For example, null values for numeric data must be distinct from zero or any other none numeric values and for character data, it must be different from a string of blanks.

4. **Database Description Rule**

The description of a database is stored and maintained in the form of tables. This allows the users with appropriate authority to query information using similar ways and using the same language. This implies that a data dictionary should be present within the RDBMS that is constructed out of tables and/or views that can be examined using the structured query language (SQL).

5. **Comprehensive Data Sub-Language**

The RDBMS must be completely manageable through its own extension of SQL. The SQL should support Data Definition, Views, Data Manipulation, Integrity Constraints and Transaction Boundary.

6. **View Updating**

Any view that can be defined using combination of data tables, and theoretically updatable, must also be capable of being updated by RDBMS.

7. **High-Level Update, Insert, Delete**

An RDBMS must do more than just be able to retrieve relational data sets. It must also be possible to insert, update and delete data items from the relational set.

8. **Physical Data Independence**

Changes made to physical storage representation or access methods do not requires changes to be made to the application programs used to manipulate data in tables.

9. **Logical Data Independence**

Application programs should not be affected by the changes made to the base tables. Changes made to tables should not require changes to be made to application programs, operating on the table.

10. **The Distribution Rule**

An RDBMS package must have distribution independence. Thus, RDBMS package must make it possible for the database to be distributed across multiple computers even though they are having heterogeneous platforms both for hardware and operating system. This is one of the most attractive aspects of the RDBMS. Database systems built on the relational framework are also well-suited for today's Client/Server database design.

11. **Non Subversion**

If the RDBMS supports facilities allowing application programs to operate on table a row at a time, then an application program using this type of database access is prevented from bypassing entity-integrity or referential-integrity constraints that may be defined for the database.

12. Integrity Rule

Integrity constraints specific to a particular relational database must be definable in SQL or some other data sub-language. These integrity constraints must be storable in the catalogue and not in the application programs.

SUMMARY

The Relational Database Management Systems, as said above, are based on relational model. The relational model, in turn, is a way of looking at data. It is a prescription for how to represent and manipulate data. The RDBMS he is a software package used to store and retrieve data that is organized in the form of tables. In other words Relational database management system stores information in rows and columns and conducts searches by using data in specified columns and rows of one table as well as to find additional data in another related table.

Relations are physically represented as tables, with the rows corresponding to individual tuples and the columns to attributes. The properties of database are: each cell contains exactly one atomic value, attribute names are distinct, attribute values come from the same domain order is immaterial, tuple order is immaterial, and there are no duplicate tuple. The degree of a relation is the number of attributes.

A super key is an attribute, or set of attributes, that identifies tuples of a relation uniquely, while a candidate key is a minimal super key. A primary key is the candidate key chosen for use in identification of tuples. A relation must always have a primary key. A foreign key is an attribute, or set of attribute, within one relation that is the candidate key of another relation. A null represents a value for an attribute that is unknown at the present time or is not applicable for this tuple.

The relational model includes two general integrity rules. These integrity rules define the set of consistent database states and changes of state or both. The first entity integrity, if an attribute of a table is of prime attribute (unique identifier), it can not accept null values, or in other words no component of a primary key values may be null, and second referential integrity, to ensure that a value that appears in one relation for a given set of attributes also appears for a certain set of attributes in another relation. Such a condition is called the referential integrity.

EXERCISES

1. What is a relational database?
2. What are the advantages and disadvantages of a relational database system?
3. Describe the evaluation of the relational database model.
4. Give the relational terminology for the commonly used database terms.
5. Explain the relational data structure.
6. What is the data value?

7. What is the domain and how is it related to a data value?
8. What do you mean by the degree of a relation?
9. Explain the following keys with example:
   - Primary key
   - Candidate key
   - Super key
   - Alternate key
   - Foreign key
10. Define entity and entity set with an example.
11. Explain the following terms
12. Entity, Tuple, Degree and Cardinality.
13. Explain the significance of primary key and foreign key in employee database.
14. What is the concept of domain? How can attribute define a domain?
15. What are the integrity rules? Explain with examples.
16. What do you mean by foreign key?
17. What is the entity integrity?
18. What is the referential integrity?
19. What are operational constraints?
20. What is the relation data manipulation?
21. What are the three characteristics of the relational data model?
22. What are the situations in which we use nulls?
23. What are Codd's rules for relational database systems?
24. What is the guaranteed access rule?

■

CHAPTER 6

DATA NORMALIZATION

6.1 INTRODUCTION

Normalization is the formal process for deciding which attributes should be grouped together in a relation. We can use commonsense to decide which field or attributes should be grouped together, but normalization provides us with a systematic and scientific process for doing this. Before proceeding with the physical design of the database, we need to validate the logical design and normalization serves as tool for validating and improving the logical design, so that the logical design satisfies certain constraints and avoids unnecessary duplication of data. In the normalization process we analyze and decompose the complex relation and transform them into smaller, simpler and well structured relations.

The process of normalization was first developed by E.F.Codd. Normalization is often performed as a series of tests on a relation to determine whether it satisfies or violates the requirements of a given normal form. Three normal forms were initially proposed, namely first, second and third normal forms. Subsequently, a stronger definition of the third normal form was introduced by R. Boyce and E.F.Codd, referred to as Boyce-Codd Normal Form (BCNF). All of these normal forms are based on functional dependencies among the attributes of a table.

Higher normal forms that go beyond BCNF were introduced later such as fourth and fifth normal forms. However these later normal forms deal with practical solutions that are very rare. Normalization is the process of building database structures to store data. We have seen the information modeling which involves analysis and identification of data that must be stored and how best to store it. This step is crucial because any application ultimately depends on its data structures.

Objective of Normalization

The objectives of the normalization process are:

- To create a formal framework for analyzing relation schemas based on their keys and on the functional dependencies among their attributes.
- To obtain powerful relational retrieval algorithms based on a collection of primitive relational operators.

- To free relational from undesirable insertion, update and deletion anomalies.
- To reduce the need for restructuring the relation as new data types are introduced.
- To carry out series of tests on individual relation schema so that the relational database can be normalized to some degree. When a test fails, the relation violating that test must be decomposed into relations that individually meet the normalization tests

Normalization is a formal process of developing data structures in a manner that eliminates redundancy and promotes integrity. Data normalization is a corner stone of the relational theory. Normalization as we have seen is accomplished in step or stages, each of which corresponds to a normal form. A normal form is a state of a table that results from applying simple rules regarding functional dependencies (or relationships between attributes) to that table. We will see an overview of the normal forms in the following section and will discuss each normal form in detail in the next sections.

1. **First Normal Form (1NF):** The multi-valued attributes (called repeating groups should be removed i.e. elimination of repeating groups.
2. **Second Normal Form (2NF):** The partial functional dependencies have to be removed, i.e. elimination of redundant data.
3. **Third Normal Form (3NF):** The transitive dependencies have to be removed, i.e. eliminates columns not dependent on key.
4. **Boyce-Codd Normal From (BCNF):** The remaining anomalies that result from functional dependencies are removed.
5. **Fourth Normal Form (4NF):** Multi-valued dependencies are removed, i.e. isolation of independent multiple relationships.
6. **Fifth Normal Form (5NF):** Any remaining anomalies are removed. In this normal form we isolate semantically related multiple relationships.

6.2 FUNCTIONAL DEPENDENCIES

Functional dependencies play an important role in differentiating good database design from not so good database design. Functional dependencies are the consequence of the interrelationships among attributes of an entity represented by a relation. Alternatively, it may be due to the relationship between entities that are also represented by a relation. Given a relation R, attributes Y of R is functionally dependent on attribute X of R if and only if each X-value in R is associated with it precisely one Y-value in R. A functional dependency is denoted by X→Y, between two sets of attributes X and Y.

To understand in a better way, let us see the database containing information concerning suppliers (S) and parts (P).The suppliers and part are uniquely identified by supplier Numbers (SNo) and Part Numbers (PNo).

	SNo	Name	Status	City
	S1	AYAY	20	BIHAR
S ⇨	S2	RANJEET	10	DELHI
	S3	AMIT	30	U.P.
	S4	PRAKASH	40	MUMBAI
	S5	RAKESH	20	ASSAM

	PNo	Name	Color	Weight/No	City
	P1	Wire	Red	20	Mumbai
P ⇨	P2	Plug	White	30	U.P.
	P3	Bolt	Green	40	Delhi
	P4	Screw	Blue	30	Goa
	P5	Handle	Red	50	Kolkata
	P6	Nut	Blue	20	Assam

In the supplier and parts database, attributes Name, Status, and City of relation S are each functionally dependent on attribute SNo, because given a particular value for SNo , there exists precisely one corresponding value for each of Name, Status and City. Symbolically we can write:

$$S.SNo \rightarrow S.Name$$

$$S.SNo \rightarrow S.Status$$

$$S.SNo \rightarrow S.City$$

The statement "S.No→S.City" is read as 'attribute S.City is functionally dependent on attribute S.SNo'. The statement "S.SNo→S.(Name, Status, City)" can be similarly interpreted if we consider the combination (Name, Status, City) as composite key of relations. Functional dependency diagrammatically as in Figure 6.2.

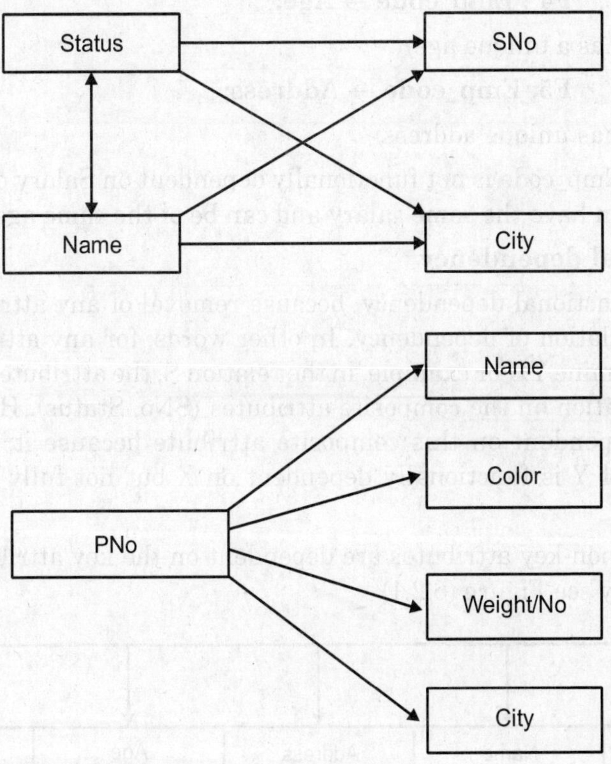

Figure 6.2 Functional dependencies in relation S and P

Note that in relation S, we have both S.SNo'!Name and Name'!S.SNo because Name is an alternate key for relation S.

Similarly, in the Student (Name, Address, Subject, Grade) relation, following functional dependencies should hold.

Name → Address

Name Subject → Grade

The underlying semantics of these two functional dependencies are that the address of a Student is unique and in each subject a student gets a unique grade. Consider an Employee database as Employee (Emp_code, Emp_Name, Dept, Salary, Age, Address) relation.

The following functional dependencies hold:

F1 : Emp_code → Emp_Name;

(each employee has a unique Emp_Code)

F2 : Emp_code → Dept;

(an employee can work in one department only)

F3 : Emp_code → Grade Age→Salary;

(Employee's salary depends on his age and grade)

F4 : Emp_code → Age;

(each employee has a unique age)

F5: Emp_code → Address;

(each employee has unique address)

In this relation Emp_code is not functionally dependent on Salary or Age because more than one employee can have the same salary and can be of the same age.

6.2.1 Full Functional dependency

X→Y is a full functional dependency, because removal of any attribute A from would result into the cancellation of dependency. In other words, for any attribute A∈ X, it does not functionally determine Y. For example, in the relation S, the attribute CITY s functionally dependent on the relation on the composite attributes (SNo, Status). However CITY is not fully functionally dependent on this composite attribute because it is also functionally dependent on SNo. (if Y is functionally dependent on X but not fully so, then X must be composite).

Note: When all non-key attributes are dependent on the key attribute, it is called full functional dependency see Figure (6.2.1)

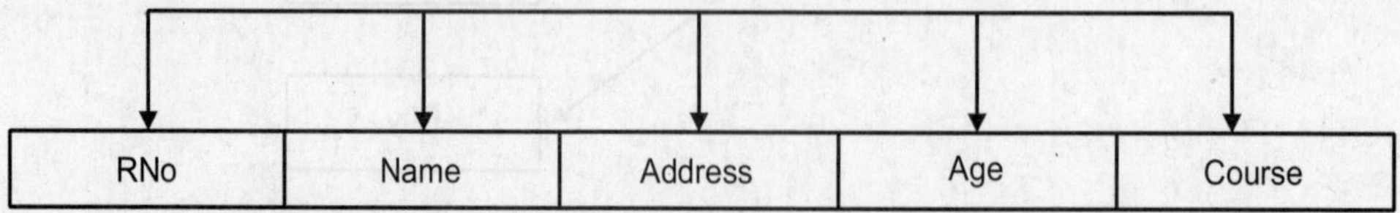

Figure 6.2.1 Concept of full functional dependency

In the above example non key attribute (Name, Address, Age and Course) are dependent on key attribute RNo. Here stands for Roll Number.

6.2.2 Partial Dependency

A functional dependency X → Y is a partial dependency if some attributes A ∈ X can be removed from X and he dependency still holds. Partial dependency in a record type occurs when some non-key attribute depends on the key attribute, and the remaining non-key attributes depends on key attribute and on one or more non-key attributes. In other words, all the non-key attributes are not dependent on the key attribute. There is a partial dependency of non-key attributes either on the key attribute or on the non-key attribute. (see Figure 6.2.2)

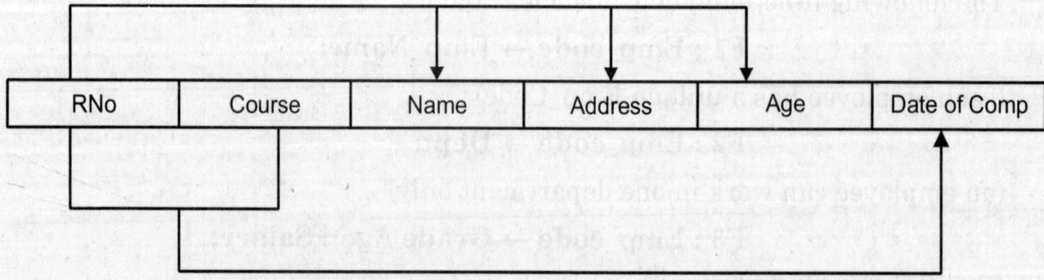

Figure 6.2.2 Concept of Partial dependency

In Figure 6.2.2, non-key attributes Name, Address and Age are dependent on RNo, and Date of Comp (Date of Completion) i.e., non-key attribute depends on RNo (Key attribute) as well as on Course (non-key attribute).

6.2.3 Transitive Dependency

A functional dependency X → Y in a relation schemas R, is a transitive dependency if there is a set of attributes Z that is neither a candidate key nor a subset key of R and both X → Y and Z → Y hold.

A general case of transitive dependencies is as follows:

A,B,C are three columns in a table

If C is related to B

If B is related to A

Then C indirectly related to A

This is the case when transitive dependency in a table exists. We can remove transitive dependency by splitting each relation into two separate tables, which are to be linked using a foreign key.

When one non-key attribute depends on other non-key attribute, it is called a transitive dependency (see Figure 6.2.3a and 6.2.3b). To calculate Distance in Figure 6.2.3a,which is a non-key attribute, we must know origin and destination which are also non-key attributes, i.e, one non-key attributes is dependent on one or more than one non-key attributes. Here distance has the transitive dependency.

As seen in Figure 6.2.3b, transitive dependency occurs because one non-key attribute is dependent on other non-key attribute is attribute is dependent on other non-key attribute is dependent on other non-key attribute i.e. if student is in Ist Year then he has been assigned hostel Block A, if he is in IInd Year, Hostel assigned is Block B IIIrd year the hostel assigned in Block C. Thus, hostel assigned to a student is dependent on the year of study in the college.

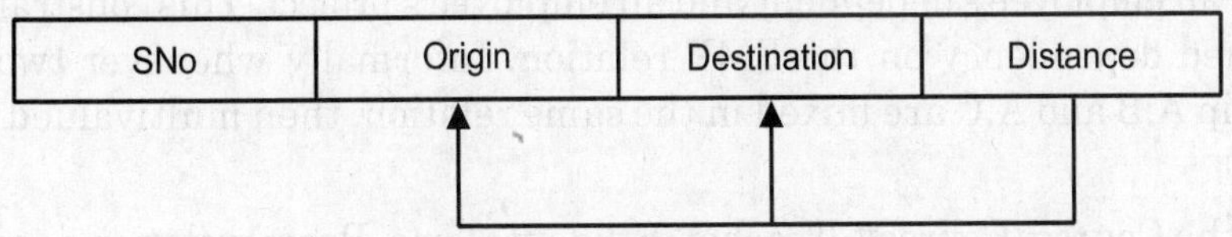

Figure 6.2.3a concept of transitive dependency

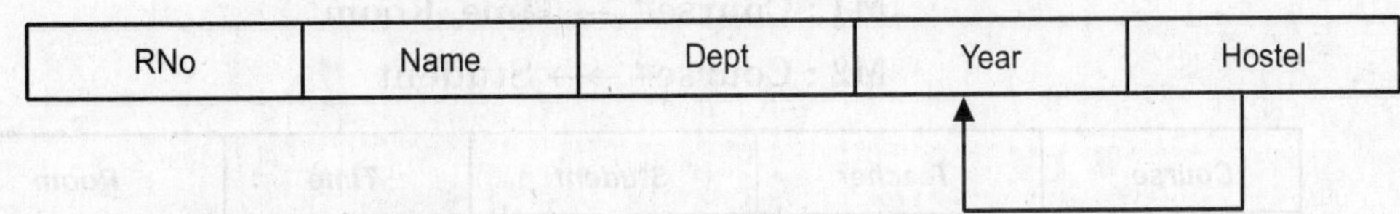

Figure 6.2.3b Concept of transitive dependency

6.2.4 Multivalued Dependency

Functional dependencies rule out certain tuples from being in a relation. If A→**B, then we** cannot have two tuples with the same A value but different B values. Multivalued dependencies, on the other hand, do not rule out the existence of certain tuples, which have multiple dependencies. Instead, they require that other tuples of a certain form be present in the relation.

Multivalued dependencies are a consequence of first normal form. First normal form does not allow an attribute in a tuple to have more than one value. If we have two or more multivalued independent attributes in the same relation schema, then we would get into a problem of having to repeat every value of one of the attribute to keep the relation instances consistent. This constraint is specified by a multivalued dependencies.

Functional dependencies are also referred to as **equality generating dependencies,** and multivalued dependencies are also referred to as **tuple generating dependencies.**

For example, consider the following relation EMP.

ENAME	PNAME	DNAME
ANAND	X1X	SANJAY
AJAY	X2X	DINESH
JAY	X3X	VIJAY
ARJUN	X4X	NARESH

A tuple in this EMP relation represents the fact that an employer whose name is ENAME works on the project whose name is PNAME and has a dependent whose name is dependent is DNAME. An employee may work on several projects and may have several dependents. Also note that the employee, projects and dependent are not directly related to one another.

To keep the tuple in the relation consistent, we must keep a tuple to represent every combination of an employee's dependent and an employee's project. This constraint is specified as a multivalued dependency on the EMP relation. Informally whenever two independent 1:N relationship A:B and A:C are mixed in the same relation, then multivalued dependencies may aries.

Consider the Course (Course#, Teacher, Student, Time, Room) relation as given in Figure 6.2.4. Consider an instance of multivalued dependencies.

M1 : Course# → Time, Room

M2 : Course# →→ Student

Course	*Teacher*	*Student*	*Time*	*Room*
CS0202	S.Kumar	Kunal	M3	003
CS0202	S.Kumar	Shivam	M3	003
MA0101	K.Bansal	Harsh	M5	002

Course	Teacher	Student	Time	Room
MA0101	K.Bansal	Shivam	M5	002
MA0101	K.Bansal	Debasish	M5	002
LE0102	A.Kumar	Sukrant	Th7	001
LE0102	A.Kumar	Kunal	Th7	001
LE0102	A.Kumar	Debasish	Th7	001
EC0204	B.Yadav	Harsh	F7	001
EC0204	B.Yadav	Shivam	F7	001
EC0204	B.Yadav	Debasish	F7	001

Figure 6.2.4 An instance of the multivalued dependencies in relation Course (Course#, Teacher, Student, Time, Room)

The meaning of these two multivalued dependencies are that the same teacher is teaching a particular course irrespective of time or room in which the course id held. Moreover, student registered for a course are not determined by the time or room where the course is held.

6.2.5 Join Dependency

Join Dependency is a constraint, similar to a functional dependency or multivalued dependency. It is satisfied if and only if the relation concerned is the join of certain number of projections. And therefore, such a constraint is called a join dependency.

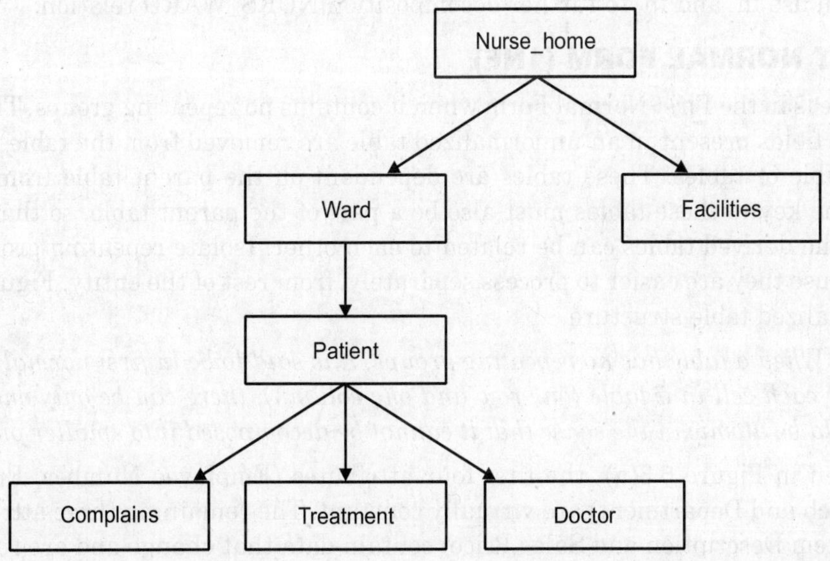

Figure 6.2.5 Hierarchical representation of a NURS_HOME database

We now consider a special class of join dependencies which help to capture data dependencies present in hierarchical data structure. For example, in the NURS_HOME database shown in Figure 6.2.5, data has an inherent hierarchical organization. It implies that information regarding wards and patients currently admitted to a ward depend only on the Nurs_home but not the facilities present in the hospital (and vice versa). Since a Nurs_home can have multiple wards, functional dependencies are not adequate to describe the data dependency among NURS_HOME and WARDS or FACILITIES. In the case, Multivalued dependencies, NURS_HOME→→WARD or NURS_HOME→→ FACILITIES hold.

Using first order hierarchical decomposition (FOHD) would enable us to represent data dependencies present in a hierarchical data structure in a more natural way. The NURS_HOME database shown in Figure 6.2.5, when decomposed, has the following representations:

fh_1 : NURS_HOME : WARD | FACILITIES

fh_2 : NURS_HOME, WARD : PATIENT

fh_3 : NURS_HOME,
WARD, PATIENT : COMPLAINTS | TREATMENT | DOCTOR

Thus we can store NURS_HOME database as the lossless join of relation.

NURS_FACILITY (NURS_HOME, FACILITY)

NURS_WARD (NURS_HOME, WARD, PATIENT, COMPLAINTS, TREATMENT, DOCTOR)

We can use fh_2 and fh_3 to further decomposition NURS_WARD relation.

6.3 FIRST NORMAL FORM (1NF)

A table is in the First Normal Form when it contains no repeating groups. The repeating columns or fields present in an unnormalized table are removed from the table and put into separate table or tables. These tables are dependent on the parent table from which it is derived. The key to these tables must also be a part of the parent table, so that the parent table and the derived tables can be related to each other. Isolate repeating groups from an entity because they are easier to process separately, from rest of the entity. Figure 6.3 shows an unnormalized table structure.

Note: *When a table has no repeating groups, it is said to be in first normal from (1NF). That is, for each cell in a table (one row and one column), there can be only one value. The value should be atomic in the sense that it cannot be decomposed into smaller pieces.*

As seen in Figure 6.3(a), the first four attributes (Employee Number, Employee Name, Store Branch and Department) are virtually constant. The remaining three attributes (Item Number, Item Description and Sales Price) contain data that change and are repeated with different sales persons. Therefore, the repeating group should be separated from the entity "saleasperson".

The normalized file is shown in Figure 6.3(b). It consists of two files:

Salesperson				Sales		
Employee Number	**Employee Number**	**Store Branch**	**Department**	**Item Number**	**Item Description**	**Sales Price (₹)**
21130680	C.Bhatia	Downtown	Hardware	TR 10	Router	500.00
				SA 1	Saw	200.00
				PT 6	Drill	100.00
				AB 16	Lawnmover	245.00
30142101	A. Bhandari	Dadeland	Home App	TT 1	Humidfier	114.00
				DS 10	Dishwasher	262.00
41984620	A.Mehta	Cutter point	Auto part	MC 16	Snow tire	200.00
				AC 146	Alternator	150.00
				BB 100	Battery	100.00
61204721	A.Banerjee	Fashion	Men's cloths	HS 10	Suit	900.00

Figure 6.3(a) Unnormalized file for sales

*= KEY

*| Employee Number	Employee Name	Store Branch	Department
21130680	C. Bhatia	Downtown	Hardware
30142101	A.Bhandari	Dadeland	Home App
41984620	A.Mehta	Cutter point	Auto part
61204721	A.Banerjee	Fashion	Men's cloths

1NF Salesperson Item Data

*| Employee Number	*| Item Number	Item Description	Sales Price (₹)
21130680	TR 10	Router	500.00
21130680	SA 1	Saw	200.00
21130680	PT 6	Drill	100.00
21130680	AB 16	Lawnmover	245.00
30142101	TT 1	Humidfier	114.00
30142101	DS 10	Dishwasher	262.00
41984620	MC 16	Snow tire	200.00
41984620	AC 146	Alternator	150.00
41984620	BB 100	Battery	100.00
61204721	HS 10	Suit	900.00

Salesperson Item File

Figure 6.3(b) First Normalization

(1) The salesperson data file with Employee Number as the **primary key.**

(2) The salesperson item with Employee Number and Item Number as new attributes. These two attributes are added to relate the records. In this file to the salesperson data file. The two attributes are used together for accessing data. Therefore, two keys are used together and such as key called a **concatenated key.**

6.4 SECOND NORMAL FORM (2NF)

A table is in the Second Normal Form if all its non-key fields are fully dependent on the whole key. This means that each field in the table must depend upon the entire key. Those that do not depend upon the combination key, are moved to another table on whose key they depend on. Structures which do not contain combination normal form. A relation in the first normal form will be in the second normal form if one following condition is satisfied:

- The primary key consists of only one attribute (field or column)
- No non-key attributes exist in the relation. In other words, all the attributes in the relation are components of the primary key.
- Every non-key attributes is functionally dependent on the full set of primary key attributes.

Second normal form (2NF) is based on the concept of full functional dependency $X \rightarrow Y$ is a full functional dependency if removal of any attribute A from X means that the dependency does not hold any more; that is for any attribute $A \in X$, $(X - \{A\})$ does not functionally determine Y. A functional dependency $X \rightarrow Y$ is a partial dependency if some $A \in X$ can be removed from X and the dependency still holds; that is, for some $A \in X$, $(X - \{A\}) \rightarrow Y$.

Rule to convert First Normal to Second Normal Form

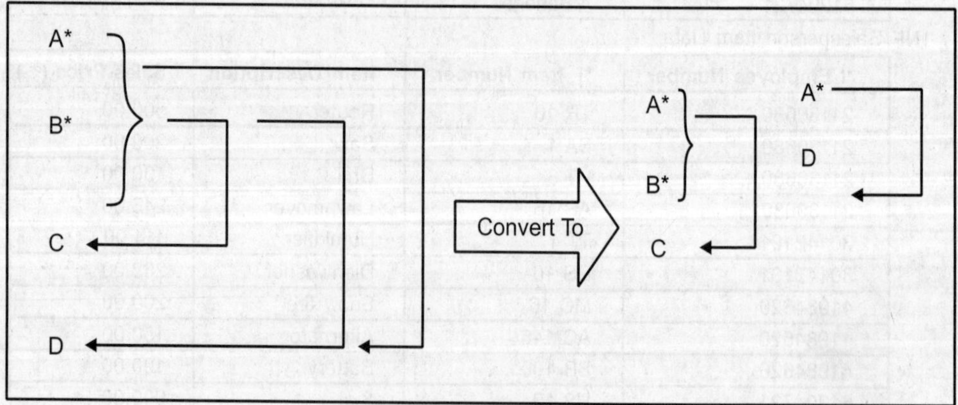

Figure 6.4(a)

Consider a relation where a primary key consists of attributes A and B. These two attributes determine all other attributes. Attribute C is fully dependent on the key. Attribute D is partially dependent on the key because we only need attribute A to functionally determine it. Attributes C and D are nonprime or non-key attributes. Here are rule is to replace the original relation by two new relations as shown in Figure 6.4(a). The first new relation has three attributes: A, B and C. The Primary key of this relation is (A, B) i.e. the primary key of the original relation. The second relation has A and D as its only two attributes. Observe that attribute A has been designated, as the primary key of the second relation and that attribute D is now fully dependent on the key. Although the Figure 6.4(a) only shows four attributes, we can generalize this procedure for any relation that we need to transform to 2NF if we assume that C stands for the collection of attributes that are fully dependent on the key and D stands for the collection of attributes that are partially dependent on the key.

Note : *A table is in Second Normal Form (2NF) if every non-key column depends on the entire key (not just part of it). This issues arises only for composite keys (with multiple columns).*

The second normalization makes sure that each non-key attribute depends on a key attribute or on a composite key. Non-key attributes that do not meet this condition are split into simpler entities. In Figure 6.4(b), each attribute in the salesperson data file depends on the primary key "Employee Number". In the salesperson item file, the attribute "Sales price" depends on a composite key (Employee Number and Item Number"). Note that sales price is firmly related to the salesperson number and item number of the sale. Also, the attribute "Item Description" tags to "Item Number", which is part of the composite key. "Item Number" is not related in any way to the "Employee Number" field. This causes several concerns. An employee transfer would make it difficult to maintain records because the sales information would be dropped when the salesperson leaves the department. This is because sales information (Item Number, Sales Price) is linked with "Employee Number" in the salesperson item file.

To solve such a problem, we create new independent tables for Item Description" and "Sales Price". In one file, we create the item description attribute with item number keys from the Salesperson item file. The remaining attributes (Employee Number, Item Number and Sales Price) become the second table or file. (see Figure 6.4(b))

- Sales items can be added without being tagged to a specific salesperson.
- If the item changes we need to change only the item file.

*= KEY

*| Employee Number	Employee Name	Store Branch	Department
21130680	C. Bhatia	Downtown	Hardware
30142101	A.Bhandari	Dadeland	Home App
41984620	A.Mehta	Cutter point	Auto part
61204721	A.Banerjee	Fashion	Men's cloths

Salesperson Data File

1NF **2NF**

*| Employee Number	*| Item Number	Sales Price (₹)
21130680	TR 10	500.00
21130680	SA 1	200.00
21130680	PT 6	100.00
21130680	AB 16	245.00
30142101	TT 1	114.00
30142101	DS 10	262.00
41984620	MC 16	200.00
41984620	AC 146	150.00
41984620	BB 100	100.00
61204721	HS 10	900.00

Salesperson Item File

*| Item Number	Item Description
TR 10	Router
SA 1	Saw
PT 6	Drill
AB 16	Lawnmover
TT 1	Humidfier
DS 10	Dishwasher
MC 16	Snow tire
AC 146	Alternator
BB 100	Battery
HS 10	Suit

Figure 6.4(b) Second Normalization

6.5 THIRD NORMAL FORM

A relation R is in Third Normal Form (3NF) if and only if the following conditions are satisfied simultaneously:

1. R is already in 2NF
2. No nonprime attribute is transitively dependent on the key.

Another way of expressing the conditions for Third Normal Form is as follows:

1. R is already in 2NF
2. No nonprime attribute functionally determine any other nonprime attribute.

These two sets of conditions are equivalent.

As these two definitions of 3NF imply, the objective of transforming relations into 3NF is to remove all transitive dependencies. So first we are going to explain the concept of transitive dependency.

Transitive Dependencies

Assume that A, B, C are set of attributes of a relation R. Further assume that the following functional dependencies are satisfied simultaneously: A→B, B→C and C→A, A→C. observe that C→B is neither prohibited nor required. If all these conditions are true, we will say that attribute C is transitively dependent on attribute A. it should be clear that these functional dependencies determine the conditions for having a transitive dependency of attribute C on A. If any of these functional dependencies are not satisfied then attribute C is not transitively dependent on attribute A.

The Figure 6.5(a) shown below summarizes these conditions. In this diagram the arrows are equivalent to the symbol "→" that we use for denoting functional dependencies. Notice that the functional dependency A→C may not be explicitly indicated but it holds true due to the Transitivity axiom. The requirements that B→A (B not functionally depends A) and C→A (C not functionally depends A) are necessary to ensure that attributes A and B are nonprime attributes.

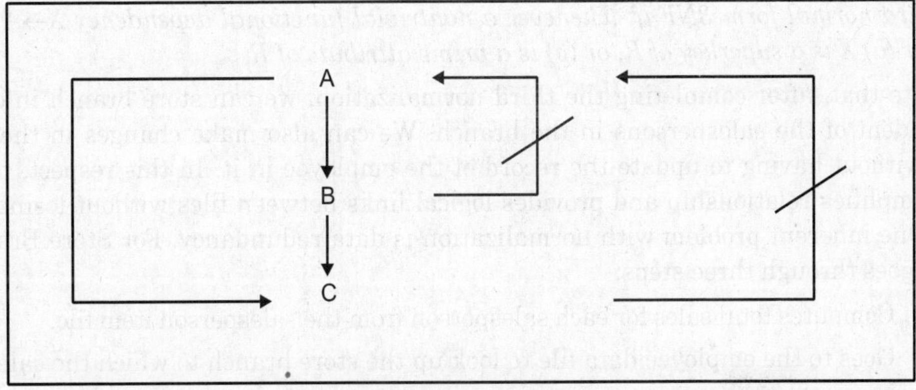

Figure 6.5(a)

Rule to Transform a Relation into Third Normal Form

To transform a 2NF relation into a 3NF we will follow the approach indicated by Figure 6.5(b). In this Figure assume that any FD not implicitly indicated does not hold. An asterisk indicates the key attribute and the arrows denote functional dependencies. The dashed line indicates that the FD A→C may not be explicitly given but it is always present because it can be derived using the difference axioms.

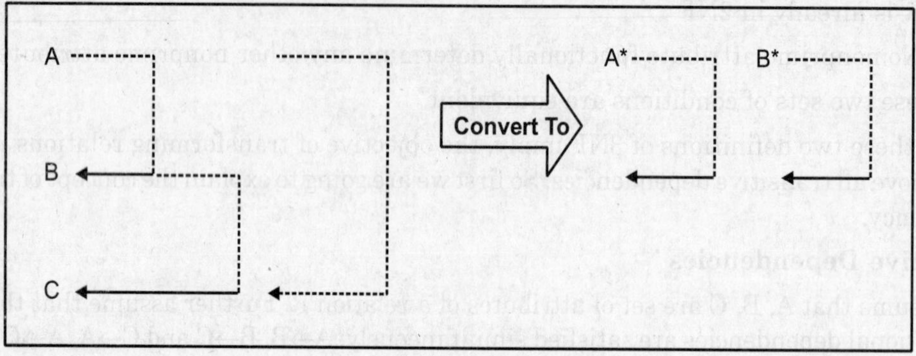

Figure 6.5(b)

For Example:

A table is said to be in the Third Normal Form, if all the non-key fields of the table are independent of all other non-key fields of the table. In Figure 6.5(c) we can observe that there is further room for improvement. In the salesperson data file, the attribute "Store branch" is tagged to the primary key "Employee Number" while the attribute "Department" which is a non-key attribute is related to "Store Branch", which is another non key attribute. Making "Store Branch" a key attribute requires isolating "Department" along with "Store Branch" and placing them in a new table as shown in Figure 6.5(c).

Note *A relation is in the third normal form if it is in second normal form and no non-prime attribute is functionally dependent on other non-prime attributes. A relation schema R is in third normal form 3NF if, whenever a nontrivial functional dependency X→A holds in R, either (a) X is a superkey of R, or (b) is a prime attribute of R.*

Note that, after completing the third normalization, we can store branch information independent of the salespersons in the branch. We can also make changes in the Depart-ment" without having to update the record of the employee in it. In this respect, normaliz-ation simplifies relationship and provides logical links between files without losing inform-ation. One inherent problem with normalization is data redundancy. For Store Branch, the system goes through three steps:

1. Computes total sales for each salesperson from the salesperson item file.
2. Goes to the employee data file to look up the store branch to which the sales person is assigned.
3. Accumulates each salesperson's sales in a specified field in the store branch file.

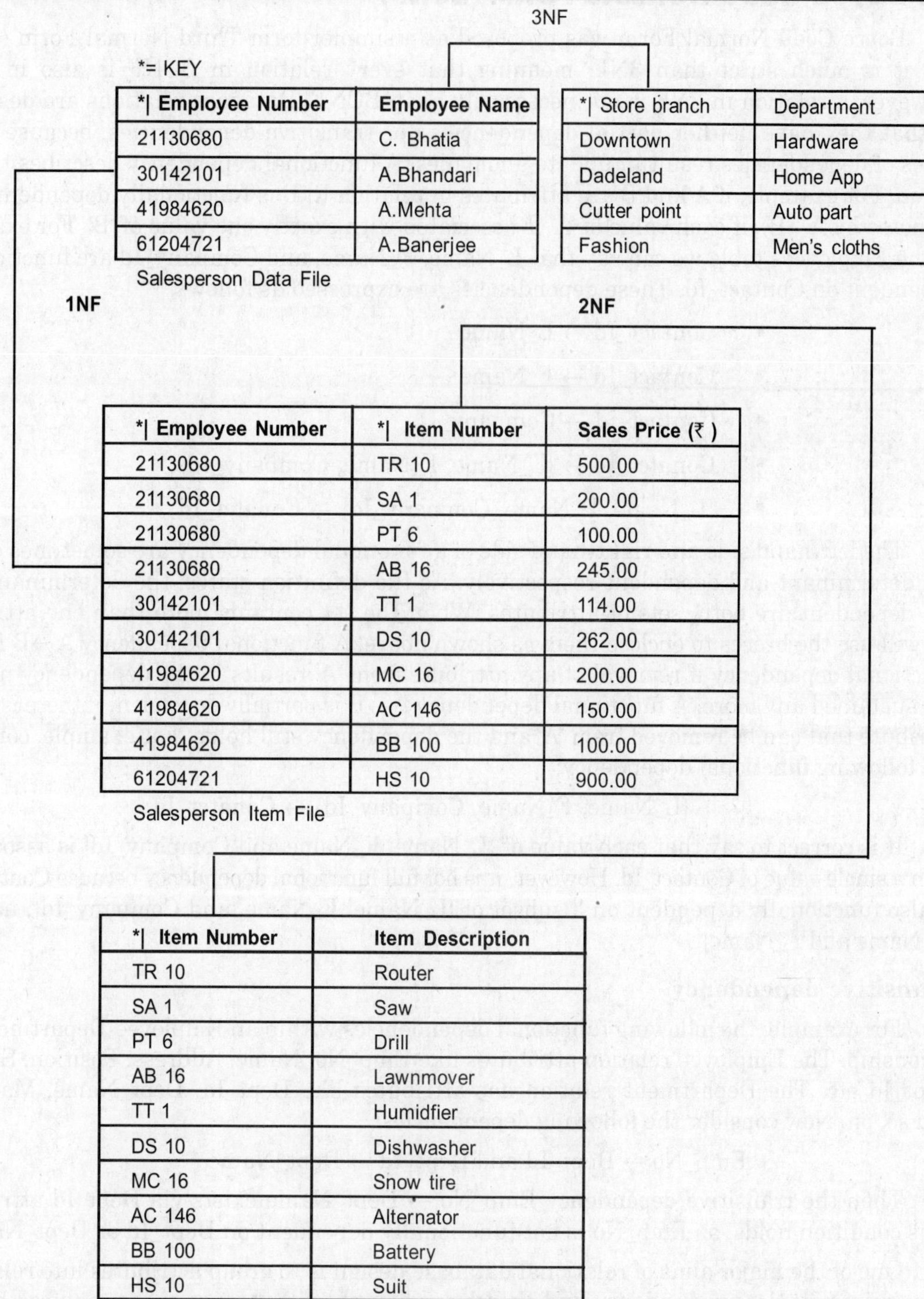

*| Employee Number	Employee Name	*| Store branch	Department
21130680	C. Bhatia	Downtown	Hardware
30142101	A.Bhandari	Dadeland	Home App
41984620	A.Mehta	Cutter point	Auto part
61204721	A.Banerjee	Fashion	Men's cloths

Salesperson Data File

*| Employee Number	*| Item Number	Sales Price (₹)
21130680	TR 10	500.00
21130680	SA 1	200.00
21130680	PT 6	100.00
21130680	AB 16	245.00
30142101	TT 1	114.00
30142101	DS 10	262.00
41984620	MC 16	200.00
41984620	AC 146	150.00
41984620	BB 100	100.00
61204721	HS 10	900.00

Salesperson Item File

*| Item Number	Item Description
TR 10	Router
SA 1	Saw
PT 6	Drill
AB 16	Lawnmover
TT 1	Humidfier
DS 10	Dishwasher
MC 16	Snow tire
AC 146	Alternator
BB 100	Battery
HS 10	Suit

Item File

Figure 6.4 Third Normalization

6.6 BOYCE CODD NORMAL FORM (BCNF)

Boyce Codd Normal Form was proposed as a simpler form Third Normal Form (3NF), but it is much strict than 3NF, meaning that every relation in BCNF is also in 3NF. However, a relation in 3NF is not necessarily be in BCNF. Database relations are designed so that they have neither partial dependencies nor transitive dependencies, because there types of dependencies result in update anomalies. A functional dependency describes the relation. For example, if A and B are attributes in relation R, B is functionally dependent on A (denoted by A→B), if each value of 'A' is associated with exactly one value of 'B'. For example in the Employees table we can say that L_Name, F_Name, and Company_Id are functionally dependent on Contact_Id. These dependencies are expressed as follows.

- Contact_Id → L_Name
- Contact_Id → F_Name
- Contact_id → Company_Id
- Conatct_Id → {L_Name, F_Name, Company_Id}
- {L_Name, F_Name, Company_Id} → Conatct_Id

The left-hand side and right-hand side of a functional dependency are sometimes called the determinant and dependent respectively. As the definition states, the determinant and the dependent are both, sets of attributes. When the set contains more than one attribute we will use the braces to enclose them as shown above. A functional dependency A→B is full functional dependency if removal of any attribute from 'A' results in the dependency not being sustained any more. A functional dependency A→B is partially dependent if there is some attribute that can be removed from 'A' and the dependency still holds. For example, consider the following functional dependency;

{L_Name, F_Name, Company_Id} → Conatct_Id

It is correct to say that each value of {L_Name, F_Name and Company_Id} is associated with a single value of Contact_Id. However, it is not full functional dependency because Contact_Id is also functionally dependent on a subset of {L_Name, F_Name, and Company_Id}, namely {L_Name and F_Name}.

Transitive dependency

For example, the following functional dependencies within an Employee-Department relationship. The Employee relation attributes like Emp_No, Name, Address, Position, Salary, Dept_Id etc. The Department relation has attributes like Dept_Id, Dept_Name, Manager and so, on. Now consider the following dependencies:

Emp_No → Dept_Id and Dept_Id → Dept_Name

Then the transitive dependency Emp_No → Dept_Name exists via Dept_Id attribute. This condition holds, as Emp_No is not functionally dependent on Dept_Id or Dept_Name.

One of the major aims of relational database design is to group attributes into relations so as minimize data redundancy and thereby reduce the file storage space required by the implemented base relations. Relations that have redundant data may have problems called update anomalies, which are classified as insertion, deletion or modification anomalies. These anomalies because, when the data in one table is deleted or updated or new data is inserted, the related data is also not correspondingly updated or deleted. Sometimes when a deletion in one table occurs, it will leave meaningless data in other tables. One of the aims of the normalization is to remove the update anomalies.

Boyce-codd normal form is based on functional dependencies that take into account all candidate keys in the relation. For a relation (table) with only one candidate key, third normal form and BCNF are equivalent. **A relation is in BCNF if and only if every determinant is a candidate key.** To test whether a relation is in BCNF, we identify all the determinants and make sure that they are candidate keys. A determinant is attribute or a group of attributes on which some other attribute is fully functionally dependent.

The difference between third normal form and BCNF is that for a functional dependency A→B, the third normal form allows this dependency in a relation if 'B' is a primary-key attribute and 'A' is not a candidate key, whereas BCNF insists that for this dependency to remain in a relation. 'A' must be a candidate key. Therefore BCNF is a stronger form of the third normal form, such that every relation is BCNF is also in third normal form. However, a relation in the third normal form is not necessarily in BCNF.

Consider a relation scheme in third normal form that has a number of overlapping composite candidate keys. In particular consider the relation GRADE (Name, Student_Id#, Course, Grade) of Figure 6.6. Here the functional dependencies are { Name Course→Grade, Student_Id# Course → Grade, Name→Student_Id#, Student_Id# → Name}. Thus, each student has a unique name and a unique student number. The relation has two candidate keys (Name, Course) and (Student_Id#, Course). Each of these keys is a composite key and contains a common attribute Course. The relation scheme satisfies the criterion of the third normal form relation, i.e., for all functional dependencies X→A in GRADE.

The problem in the relation GRADE is that it had two overlapping candidate candidate keys. In the Boyce Codd Normal Form (BCNF), which is stronger than the third normal form, the intention is to avoid the above anomalies. This is done by ensuring that for all non-trivial functional dependencies implied by the relation, determine the functional dependencies that involve a candidate keys. The relation GRADE of Table 6.6 is not in BCNF because the dependencies Student_Id# → Name and Name → Student_Id# are non-trivial and their determinates are not superkeys of GRADE.

Name	Student_Id#	Course	Grade
Abhishek	23714539	353	A
Ankit	42717390	329	A
Aparajita	23714539	328	in prog
Harsh	38815183	456	C
Ashutosh	37116259	293	B
Ashish	82317293	491	C
Chahat	82317293	353	in prog
Amit	23714539	491	C
Debasish	11011976	353	A+
Deepa	12345987	379	in prog

Figure 6.6 The Grade Relation

6.7 FOURTH NORMAL FORM (4NF)

A group of tables that satisfies the first, second and third normal forms are sufficiently well designed. However, isolating independent multiple relationships will further improve the data model when one-to-many and many-to-many relationships tables are involved. In other words, no table should contain two or more one-to-many relationships that are not directly related to the key. These kinds of relationships are called multi-valued dependencies (MVDs). Multi-valued dependencies are the result of the first normal form, which prohibited an attribute from having a set of values. If we have two or more multi-valued independent attributes in the same relation (table), we get into a situation where we have to repeat every value of one of the attributes with every value of the other attribute to keep the relation state consistent and to maintain independence among the attributes involved. This constraint is specified by a multi-valued dependency.

Consider a table (relation) Employee that has the attribute Name, Skill, Language. A row in the Employee table represents the fact that an employee works for a skill and has a language. But an employee can work in more than one skill and can have more than one language. The employee's skill and language are independent of one another. To keep the relation state consistent we must have a separate tuple to represent every combination of an employee's skill and an employee's language. This constraint is specified as a multi-valued dependency on the Employee relation. So whenever two independent one-to-many relationships (A:B and A:C) are mixed in the same relation, a multi-valued dependency arises. We will see the employee table and how the multi-valued dependency can be avoided using the fourth normal form. Given below is the Employee table and its contents:

Employee		
Name	**Skill**	**Language**

Figure 6.7(a) Employee Table

As we have seen, the above relation has two multi-valued dependencies-(Name, Skill) and (Name, Language). We resolve this by decomposing the Employee table into two tables that satisfy the fourth normal form as follows:

Skill	
Name	**Skill**

Figure 6.7(b) Skill Table

Language	
Name	**Language**

Figure 6.7(c) Language Table

6.8 FIFTH NORMAL FORM (5NF)

The fourth normal form is by no means the ultimate normal form. As we saw earlier, multi-valued dependencies help us understand and tackle some forms of repetition of information that cannot be understood in terms of functional dependencies. There are types of constraints called join dependencies that generalize multi-valued dependencies, and lead another normal form called Project-Join Normal Form (PJNF). The PJNF is called Fifth Normal Form. There is a class of even more general constraints, which leads to a normal form called **domain-key normal form.**

The chances that you will ever get to use the fifth normal form are very few, because it requires semantically related multiple relationships, which are rare. Semantically related multiple relationships are two or more relationships among tables that are related closely enough so that they can be resolved into a single relationship. Fifth normal form specifies that they remain separate.

Note *The concept of Project-Join Normal Form (PJNF) is an extension of the fourth normal form definition when join dependencies are also considered.*

A practical problem with the use of these generalized constraints is that they are not only hard to reason with, but there is also no set of sound and complete inference rules for reasoning about the constraints. Hence, PJNF and domain key normal form are used very rarely. The fifth normal form is not frequently invoked for the reason that the situation simply does not arise frequently.

6.9 DOMAIN-KEY NORMAL FORM (DKNF)

The process of normalization and the process of discovering undesirable dependencies was carried through Fifth Normal Form (5NF) as a meaningful design activity. However, it has been possible to define stricter normal form that take into account additional types of dependencies and constraints. The idea behind Domain-Key Normal Form (DKNF) is to specify the ultimate normal form that takes into account all possible types of dependencies and constraints.

The domain-key normal key does not exhibit insertion and deletion anomalies. However, unlike the other normal forms, DKNF is not defined in terms of functional dependency, multivalued dependency, or join dependency. The central requirements in DKNF are the basic concepts of domains, keys and general constraints. A domain constraint is a statement that the values of a certain attribute lie within some prescribed set of values. A key constraint is a statement that a certain attribute or attribute combination is a candidate key. A general constraint is expressed as a simple statement or predicate and specifies some special requirement. Each tuple of a relation must specify this predicate i.e. general constraint for it to be a valid tuple.

Note *A relation scheme is in DKNF, if every general constraint can be inferred from the knowledge of the attributes involved in the scheme, their underlying domains and the sets of attributes that form the keys*

An insertion anomaly in the case of DKNF occurs when a tuple is inserted in a relation and the resulting relation violates one or more general constraints. Similarly, a relation anomaly occurs when a tuple from a relation is deleted and the remaining relation violates one or more general constraints in the following example.

Example

Consider the relation scheme Transcript (SNo, Course, Grade). Suppose the attributes SNo and Course are numeric, 8 and 3 digits long, respectively. The attribute Grade is a letter grade and could be A, B, C, D, P, F. The general constraint is that for Course 000 through 900, the Grade can only be A, B, C, D, F. The domain constraints for this relation are following:

SNo is required to be 8 digits long, course is 3 digit long and Grade has to be from the set {A, B, C, D, P, F}. The key constraint for the relation is that no two tuples can exist with the same values for the key attributes, which are SNo and Course. Obviously, **SNo** Course→Grade. Finally, the general constraint can be expressed by the following:

$$\text{if Grade} > 900 \text{ then Grade} \in \{P, F\}$$
$$\text{else Grade} \in \{A, B, C, D, F\}$$

Note *The DKNF is considered to be the highest form of normalization, since all insertion and deletion anomalies are eliminated and all general constraints can verified by using only the domain constraints and key constraints.*

The problem with this relation is that a tuple such as (12345678, 991, A), which satisfies all the domain constraints and key constraints, can be inserted in the relation Transcript of Figure 6.9. However, since the tuple does not satisfy the general constraints, the relation Transcript becomes illegal after the insertion.

SNo	Course	Grade
23714539	353	A
42717390	329	A
23714539	928	P
38815183	456	F
37116259	293	B
82317293	491	C
82317293	953	F
23714539	491	C
11011978	353	A
83910827	379	P

Figure 6.9 The Transcript relation

6.10 DENORMALIZATION

No major application will run in Third Normal Form. This is probably as heretical a statement as can be made in the face of modem relational technology, but it needs to be said. Perhaps, as CPUs get faster and parallel-processing architecture is better exploited, this will no longer be true; more likely the size of major applications will also increase. Demand for information and analysis will probably continue to outpace the ability of machines to process it in a fully normalized fashion. Now, before cries for another inquisition begins this need to be explained. The issue of normalization has several components. This section does not challenge the relational model or the process of Normalization, which are an excellent and rational method of analyzing data and its fundamental relationships. This section challenges the following fallacies;

- Normalization completely rationalizes data.
- Normalization accurately maps how humans work with data.
- Normalized data is the best representation of data.
- Data stored non-redundantly will be accessed faster than data stored many times.
- Normalized tables are the best way to store data.
- Referential integrity requires fully normalized tables.

Normalization is simply a method to analyze elements of data and their relationships and the relational model is the theoretical superstructure that supports the process. Together, these provide a way of viewing the world of data. But they are not the only correct or useful ways to view the data. In fact, in a complex set of relationships, even the third normal form becomes insufficient rather quickly. Higher forms have been conceived to cope with these more difficult relations, although they are not used outside of academia. Theorists readily acknowledge that these also fail completely model reality.

Nevertheless, both the sufficiency of the relational model and the necessity of the third normal form have become so sacrosanct in some circles, that some vendors are even beginning to enforce the third normal form in their data dictionary. You won't be allowed to violate it-never mind that the application may not run! But many database vendors take a much more practical approach. They, while acknowledging the genius of the relational model, even to the degree of obeying Codd's rules, also provide tools that permit developers to use their brains and make their own decisions about Normalization, referential integrity, procedural language access, non-set-oriented processing and other heretical techniques. **In the real world, with live data, demanding users and real demands on performance and ease of use, this flexibility is fundamental to success. Normalization is analysis, not design. Design encompasses issues, particularly related to performance, ease of use, maintenance and straightforward completion of business tasks, that are unaccounted for in Normalization.**

When analyzing the data of a data of a business, normalizing the data to at least the third normal form assures that each non-key column in each table is dependent only on the whole primary key of the table. If the data relationships are complex enough, normalizing to a higher form does a fine, if not complete, job of giving you a deep understanding of data and of relations between the various elements that must be protected and sustained as the application and database are built.

For a major application, however or even a simple application where tasks do not readily map to fully normalized tables, once the analysis is complete, the design process may need to denormalize some of the tables in order to build an application that is responsive, maps to the user's tasks and will actually complete its processing in the time windows available.

Denormalization is the opposite of Normalization. It is the process of increasing redundancy in the database either convenience or to improve performance. However, proper denormalization takes place after a model has been fully normalized. Denormalization is usually done for convenience can be used to improve performance. For example in accounting packages there will be the daily transaction table, which contains the details of each and every transaction for every head of accounts. But usually there will be a monthly transaction summary, which will only have the monthly aggregate of all the transactions under each head of account. The data contained in the monthly transactions table is completely redundant; but the monthly summary information is very frequently used and calculating it each and every calculating it each and every time will slow down the application resulting in poor response times. Unfortunately, the updates to the daily transaction table are not automatically reflected in the summary table, unless database triggers are created to ensure that data integrity is maintained. So before doing a denormalization, you should make sure that the costs of maintenance do not outweigh the benefits.

It is very important to understand that the design of data structures will have a profound impact on the performance and structure of the front-end application and reports. Although it is possible to work around a poor data model with a great deal of code, it is desirable to do so. Ideally an application should start with a fully normalized data structure, which will serve as a firm foundation.

However, any recommendations attempting to produce better response will be have to differ from application to application. They will also differ over time as query optimization methods improve, and as more and more CPU power is pushed out to the peripheral devices in the computer system and network. Benchmarking your application on your system is the only way to truly optimize your database.

SUMMARY

We have seen the process and purpose of normalization and denormalization in this chapter. We have seen the different normal forms-1NF, 2NF, 3NF, 4NF, 5NF, BCNF, DKNF and so on. Normalization is a technique for producing a set of relations with desirable properties, given the data requirements of an enterprise. Normalization is a formal method that can be used to identify relations based on their keys and the functional dependencies among attributes. Relations with data redundancy suffer from update anomalies, which can be classified as insertion, deletion and modification anomalies.

One of the main concepts associated with normalization is functional dependency, which describe the relationship attributes in a relation. For example, if A and B are attributes of relation R, B is functionally dependent on A (denoted A→B), if each value of A is associated with exactly one value of B, (A and B may each consist of one or more attributes). The main characteristics of functional dependencies refers that we use for normalization have a one-to-one relationship between attribute(s) on the left and right sides of the dependency, hold for all time, and are fully functionally dependent.

Unnormalized is a table contains one or more repeating groups. The 1NF is a relation in which the intersection of each row and column contains one and only one value. The 2NF is a relation that is in First normal form and every non-primary key attribute is fully functionally dependent on the primary key. Full functional dependency indicates that if A and B are attributes of a relation, B is fully functionally dependent on A if B is functionally dependent on A but not on any proper subset of A. The 3NF is a relation that is in first and second normal form in which no non-primary key attribute is transitively dependent on the primary key. Transitive dependency is a condition where A, B and C are attributes of a relation such as that if A→B and B→C, then C is transitively dependent on A via B.

Normalization need not always improve database performance. So sometimes we will have to denormalize the tables. Denormalization is the opposite of Normalization. It is the process of increasing redundancy in the database either for convenience or to improve performance. Proper denormalization takes place after a model has been fully normalized.

EXERCISES

1. What is normalization?
2. Define normalization and why is it done?
3. What is a normal form?
4. What are different normal forms?
5. Describe the purpose of normalizing data.
6. What do you mean by functional dependency?
7. What is the transitive dependency?
8. Explain partial dependency with an example.
9. What is join dependency? Explain with an example.
10. What is the first normal form (1NF)?
11. Describe the characteristics of a table in unnormalized form and describe how such a table is converted to a first normal form relation.
12. When is the minimal normal form that a relation must satisfy? Provide a definition for this normal form.

13. Discuss the alternative ways that normalization can be used to support database design.
14. Explain second normal form (2NF).
15. What is third normal form (3NF)?
16. What is an insertion anomaly?
17. What do you mean by a deletion anomaly?
18. What is a modification anomaly?
19. Explain the Boyce-codd normal form (BCNF).
20. Explain the similarities and dissimilarities between BCNF and 3NF.
21. What is the fifth normal form (5NF)?
22. What undesirable dependencies are avoided when a relation is in 2NF?
23. What undesirable dependencies are avoided when a relation is in 3NF?
24. Explain the Domain key normal form (DKNF).
25. What is denormalization?
26. When do you perform denormalization?
27. What are the benefits of denormalization?
28. Describe the concept of transitive dependency and explain how this concept is used to define 3NF.
29. Explain why PJNF is a normal form more desirable than is 4NF.
30. Let R= (A, B, C, D, E), and let M be the following set of multivalued dependencies

$$A \rightarrow\rightarrow BC$$

$$B \rightarrow\rightarrow CD$$

$$E \rightarrow\rightarrow AD$$

List the nontrivial dependencies in M+.

■

CHAPTER 7

INTRODUCTION TO STRUCTURED QUERY LANGUAGE (SQL)

7.1 INTRODUCTION

The relational database management systems and service is one of the main branches of the IT industry where technological developments are taking place at a very rapid pace. We see hundreds of new database and related products being released every month. Major software vendors are churning out database products with more and more features with each release of their database offerings. The competition in the database market segment is so intense that survival itself is extremely difficult. Other than the database vendors there are thousands of companies who develop applications, for example ERP, E-commerce, banking, etc. which are implemented systems. In addition there are thousands of people who implement, maintain and use these systems. Databases are becoming prominent by the day. Today, almost all applications from spreadsheets and word processors to statistical analysis tools-have the capability to seamlessly integrate with the database and use it for performing tasks from statistical analysis to mail merging.

When a non-programmer site on a computer and wants to work with a database, he or she would like to use a simple high level language which can enable him/her to utilize database available on a computer completely and easily. The language should be so designated that its commands are easy to understand. Such a language initially created by IBM and modified by various other software designers is the SQL (pronounced as SEQUEL) or Structured English QUEry Language. This fourth generation language is a very simple and powerful language because it uses compact, English-like statements and performs very complex jobs to access information from a large sized database

Structured Query Language (SQL) is the standard command set used to communicate with the relational database management systems. All tasks related to relational data management-creating tables, querying the database for information, modifying the data in the database, deleting them, granting access to users, and so on–can be done using SQL. SQL is the standard language for making queries in relational database management package such as SQL server, Ingress, Sybase, Oracle etc. The standard language for accessing client/ server database is also SQL.

7.1.1 History of SQL

The SQL consists of a set of facilities for defining, accessing and managing relational database. In order to understand why SQL has become so popular and important, it is helpful to have an idea of the major developments in database technology over the past 20 and 30 years. In 1970 Edgar F. Codd, member of IBM lab in San Jose, California, published(Communications of the ACM 13, No. 6, June 1970) the classic paper, "A Relational Model of Data for Large Shared Data Banks", In which he laid down a set of abstract principles of database management, the so called relational model. The entire field of relational database management system has its origins in that paper. The Codd's paper triggered off a great deal of research and experimentation and lead to the design and prototype implementation of a variety of relational languages. A relational language is a language that realizes, In some concrete syntactic form, some or all the features of the abstract relational model. Several such languages were created in the early and mid 70s. One such language was structured English Query Language (SEQUEL), defined by Donald Chamberlain and others at the IBM San Jose Lab in 1974, and was implemented in the IBM prototype called SEQUEL-XRM in 1974-75. In 1979 SQL language was first commercially implemented by Oracle Corporation, there was no official standard until 1986. In 1986, SQL was jointly published by ANSI (American National Standards Institute) and the ISO (International Standard Organization).

The SQL'86 standard was revised in 1989 to introduce features that enforce referential integrity. By the time the 86 standards appeared, a number of products in market already used SQL, and the ISO attempted to draft a standard to which they could all conform relatively painlessly. Also with the world becoming popular, developers and users wanted to be able to interface the various database engines. As a result there arose a demand for standardization of SQL features. To address these need, ISO developed SQL'92 standard. The SQL'92 release was broken into three levels for conformance testing and development. These levels were entry, intermediate and full. In SQL '92, data is organized in a much better way. Data is contained in tables, tables are grouped in to schemas and schemas are grouped into catalogs. The catalogs can be further grouped into clusters. Some of the features which are new in SQL'92 standard are:

- Schema definition statements
- Temporary tables
- Built-in join operators
- Read-only, scrollable and dynamic cursors
- Standardized connection procedure
- Standardized error codes and diagnostics
- Altering and dropping objects

7.1.2 Characteristics of SQL

1: SQL is oriented specifically around relational databases.

2: SQL commands can operate on several groups to table as single objects. Also it processes any quantity of information, retrieved from these tables, as a single unit.

3: SQL allows use of temporary tables. Temporary tables are used for storing intermediate results. They are useful only for the duration the program is in execution terminates.

4: SQL is well suited to a client server environment, where the DBMSs resides on a server and services the client's requests. Features such as connection management, locking schemes and error diagnostics enable clients to communicate with a variety of DBMS packages.

5: SQL provides a flexible transaction management. A transaction is a group of SQL statement that succeeds or fail as a group. That is, if any one of the SQL statement fails, the whole transaction is aborted.

6: SQL allows users to create domains as object in a schema. The users can then declare table columns to be domains rather than that of data types.

7: SQL allows one to specify constraints. Constraints are rules for restricting the values that can be placed in the table column.

8: Privileges can be granted or denied using SQL commands. Privileges are the rights to perform actions on database objects.

7.1.3 Advantage of SQL

SQL has several simple to use commands activities. SQL is a high level language that provides a greater degree of abstraction than procedural language. It is so fashioned that the programmer can specify what data is needed but need specify how to retrieve it. SQL is coded without embedded data navigational instructions. This will be taken care of by the DBMS

1: Creating or Defining, deleting, and modifying table structure.

2: Defining the relationship between two or more tables.

3: Inserting data into tables.

4: Extracting data in meaningful ways, based on table's defined relationships.

5: Updating data. This includes maintaining data in a database, and manipulating the stored values to keep the information current.

6: Controlling a database. This includes system security and authorization which must be controlled and maintained.

7: The language while being simple and easy to learn can handle complex situations.

8: SQL as a language is independent of the way it is implemented internally.

7.2 SQL BASIC STRUCTURE

7.2.1 Types of SQL Commands

SQL is a simple and powerful language used to create, access, and manipulate data and structure in the database. SQL is like plain English, easy to understand and write. Oracle divides SQL statement into various categories, which are:

- Data Definition Language
- Data Manipulation Language
- Data Control Language
- Data Query Language
- Data Administration Language
- Data Transaction Language

- **Data Definition Language (DDL)**

  Data definition language is used to create, alter and delete database objects. The commands used are CREATE, ALTER and DROP. The principle logical data definition statements are CREATE TABLE, CREATE VIEW, CREATE INDEX, ALTER TABLE, DROP TABLE, DROP VIEW and DROP INDEX.

- **Data Manipulation Language (DML)**

  Data manipulation language commands let users insert, modify and delete the data in the database. SQL provides three data manipulation statements-INSERT, UPDATE, DELETE.

- **Data Control Language (DCL)**

  The data control language consists of commands that control the user access to the database objects. Thus DCL is mainly related to the security issues that are determining who has access to the database objects and what operations they can perform on them. The task of the DCL is to prevent unauthorized access to data. The Database Administrator (DBA) has the power to give and task the privileges to a specific user, thus giving or denying access to the data. The DCL commands are GRANT and REVOKE.

- **Data Query Language (DQL)**

  This is one of the most commonly used SQL statements. This SQL statement enables the users to query one or more tables to get the information they want. SQL has only one data query statement-SELECT

- **Data Administration Statements (DAS)**

  Data administration commands allow the user to perform audits and analysis on operations within the database. They are also used to analyze the performance of the system. Two data administration commands are START AUDIT and START AUDIT. One thing to be remembered here is that, data administration is totally different from administration. Database administration is the overall administration of the database and data administration is only a subset of that.

- **Transaction Control Statements (TCS)**

  Transaction controls statements are statements, which manage all the changes made by the DML statements commit data. Some of the transaction control statements are COMMIT, ROLLBACK, SAVEPOINT and SET TRANSACTION.

7.2.2 SQL Data types and Literals

Every field or column in a table is given a data type when a table is defined. These data type describe the kind of information which can be stored in a column. Since relational-database systems are based on the relationship between pieces of information, various types of data must be clearly distinguished from one another, so that are appropriate processes and comparisons can be applied. In SQL, this is done by assigning each field a data type that indicates the kind of values the field will contain. All the values in a given field must be of the same type. Some of the common data types that we shall be using in this chapter are:

- CHAR
- VARCHAR2
- NUMBER
- DATE
- LONG

- **CHAR(size)**

  A column defined with a CHAR data type is allowed to store all type of characters which include letters – both uppercase and lowercase letters such as A, B, ...,Z and a, b,....,z, special characters- like @, #, *, &, ₹ etc. and numbers that are perceived by the systems as letters. However, you cannot perform any mathematical operations on these numbers. This means that such numbers are accepted and manipulated as characters only.

  Size written in brackets after the word CHAR determine the length of data that can be stored, i.e., the number of characters that can be stored in the field. Note that default size is 1 and maximum size is 255.

- **VARCHAR2(size)**

  It is similar to CHAR but can but store sized string having a maximum length determined by size. Maximum value the size can have is 2000 characters.

- **NUMBER(p, s)**

  This data type is used to store numbers fixed or floating point. The precision(p) determines the length of the data while(s), the scale , determine the number of places after the decimal. The NUMBER data type is used to store number can be specified either to store integers or decimals with the addition of a parenthetical precision indicator.

  For example, if you had a column defined to be data type NUMBER (10,3), the number 546.3832 would be stored as 546.383, because after the decimal point we can store 3 digits. It can store a number of 10 digits including a decimal point for example a maximum number of 999999.999 can be stored with data type of NUMBER (10,3).

- **DATE(DD-MON-YY)**

  This data type stores date values in a special format internal to Oracle. It offers a great deal of flexibility to users who want to perform date manipulation operations.

There are also numerous functions that handle date operations more complex than simple arithmetic. Another nice feature of Oracle's method for date storage is that it is inherently millennium complaint. The default format in which date is stored id DD-MON-YY. If we want to store date in other format then we have to use the appropriate functions.

- **LONG**

  LONG data type stores variable length character strings containing upto 2 gigabytes size. But use of LONG data type has got the following limitations:

  - A table cannot have more than one LONG type of data field.
  - It cannot be indexed.
  - It cannot be used with SQL functions
  - It cannot appear in WHERE, GROUP BY, ORDER BY clauses.

The different data types available in ORACLE are:

DATA TYPES	DESCRIPTION
VARCHAR2	Contains variable length text strings of up to 2,000 bytes
CHAR	Contains fixed text strings of up to 255 bytes
NUMBER	Contains numeric data
DATE	Contains date data
RAW	Contains binary data of up to 255 bytes
LONG	Contains text data of up to 2 gigabytes
LONG RAW	Contains binary data up to 2 gigabytes
ROWID	Contains disk location for table rows
BLOB	Large binary object
CLOB	Large character-based object
NCLOB	Large single- or multi-byte character- based object
BFILE	Large external file

7.2.3 SQL Clauses

SQL has one basic statement for retrieving information from a database: the SELECT statement. This is process is called as Query. The queries are SQL can be very complex. We will start with simple queries, and progress to more complex ones in a step-by-step manner. The basic form of the SELECT statement, sometimes called a mapping or a select-from-where block, is formed of the three clauses SELECT, FROM and WHERE and has the following form:

SELECT <attribute list>
FROM <table list>
WHERE <condition>;

Where

- SELECT : specifies which columns are to appear in the output
- FROM : specifies the table or tables to be used
- WHERE : filters the rows subject to some condition

In SQL, the basic logical comparison operators for comparing attribute values with one another and with literal constant are =, <, <=, >, >=, and <>. These correspond to the relational algebra operators =, <, ≤, >, ≥ and < > respectively, and to the C/C++ programming language operators =, <, <=, >, >= and !=. The main difference is the not equal operator. SQL many additional comparison operators that we will present gradually as needed.

7.3 INVOKING OF SQL* PLUS

Oracle provides an interactive SQL tool called SQL*PLUS, which allows the users to enter SQL sentences and pass them to Oracle Engine for execution. SQL*PLUS is a character based interactive tool that runs in a GUI environment. It is loaded on the client machine. This is the first tool to be used by most programmers when they place their first step into ORACLE world.

Steps in invoking SQL*PLUS

- Start your Operating System normally.

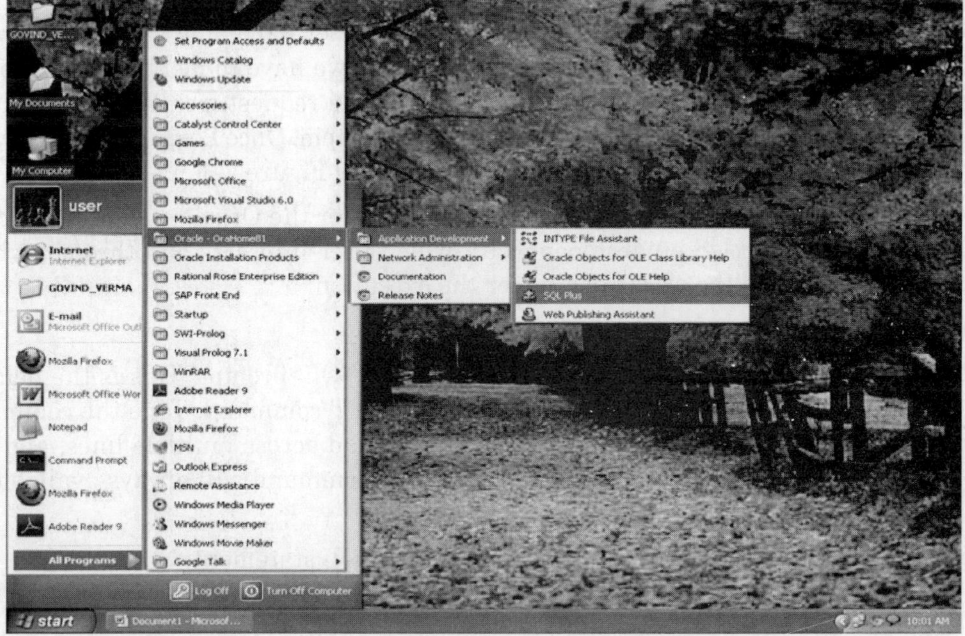

Figure 7.3(a) Starting of SQL from Operating System

- Click on the START button as shown in diagram given below and click on the Program. It displays the list of programs. Click on ORACLE for Win95 and then select SQL*PLUS.
- You are promoted for your oracle Login-id and password screen so that user may get connected to Oracle.

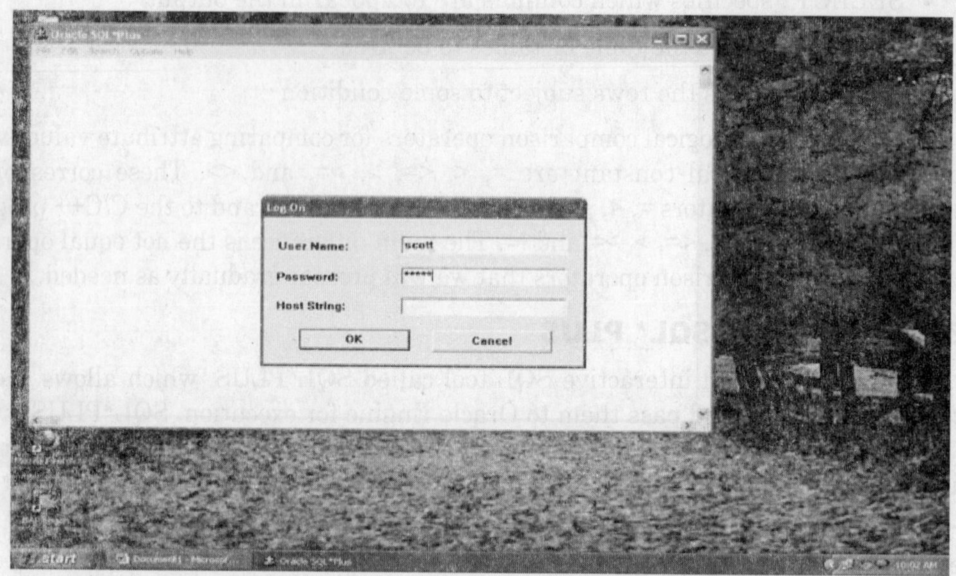

Figure 7.3 (b) First screen for authentication of valid user of Database

In the user name you have to mention authenticated user name and valid password in Password field where as in the third option of Host String we have to mention the name of the database server(If available) who is going to handle the request from this client. Host String is optional and is not required in case of standalone system. Once Login-id and password are entered, an SQL> prompt appears as shown in following Figure 7.3(c).

At this point in time, requesting user is connected either the Oracle engine. The above Figure shows the SQL *PLUS environment with which user interacts and through which user can give its queries to the oracle engine for the execution.

Writing an SQL statement

Once you are connected to SQL *PLUS, you get the SQL>prompt. This is the default prompt, which can be changed using the SET SQLPROMPT command. Type the command you wish to enter at this prompt. A command can be spread across multiple lines, and the commands are case-insensitive. The previously executed command will always available in the SQL buffer. The buffer can be edited or saved to a file.

A few simple rules guide the construction of a valid SQL statement:

- SQL statements may be on one or many lines.
- Command words cannot be split across lines.

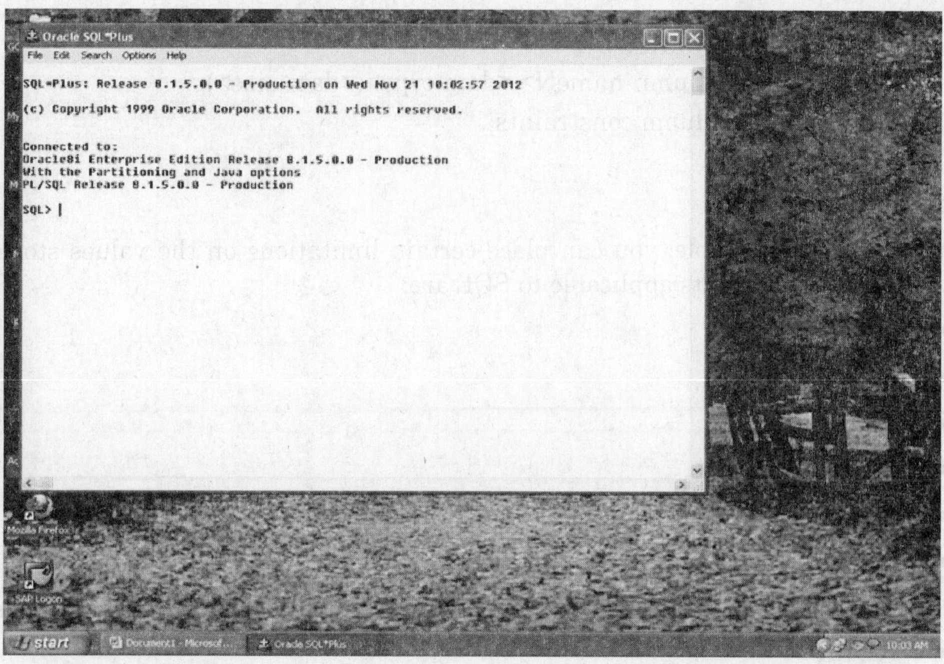

Figure 7.3 (c) Screen of SQL* PLUS where SQL queries can be entered

- An SQL command is entered at the SQL prompt, and subsequent lines are numbered. This is the SQL buffer.
- Only one line is current at any time in buffer, which can be executed in a number of ways:
- Place a semicolon (;) at the end of the last clause.
- Place a semicolon (;) or forward slash (/) on the line in the buffer.
- Place a forward slash (/) at the SQL prompt.
- Issue an R [un] command at the SQL prompt.

7.4 SQL COMMANDS

CREATE TABLE command

Tables are defined with the CREATE TABLE command. Create table command basically defines a table name describing a set of named columns in a specified order. It also defines the data types and sizes of the columns. Each table must have at least one column.

The syntax of the Create table command is as follows:

```
create table <table-name>
        (
                <column-name1> <data-type>(<data-size>)
                [column constraints],
                <column-name2> <data-type>(<data-size>)
                [column constraints],
```

....

....

<column-nameN> <data-type>(<data-size>)

[column constraints],

);

Integrity constraints

While creating a table, you can place certain limitations on the values stored in the table. Different constraints applicable to SQL are:

- NOT NULL
- UNIQUE
- PRIMARY KEY
- CHECK
- DEFAULT
- REFERENCE

All the above mentioned constraints are further elaborated in the following sub-sections.

- **NULL**

  A NOT NULL constraint prevents a column from accepting null values. If you try to insert a null value in such a column, it will be a rejected. Note that NULL value does not mean a zero value. It just means absence of any data, in that column.

- **UNIQUE**

  UNIQUE constraint ensures that values entered into a column are all different, i.e., unique. A column with this constraint will not accept any duplicate values.

- **PRIMARY KEY**

  In order to declare a column as primary key of the table, use the PRIMARY KEY constraint. There can be only one primary key in table.

- **CHECK**

  CHECK constraint is used to control the values entered into a field. A condition is specified along with the CHECK constraint which must be satisfied by all the values being entered into a column. Otherwise the value will be rejected.

  For example, CHECK (SALARY <= 100000)

  If the value of salary entered is more than 100000, then it will be rejected. Here salary is the column name.

- **DEFAULT**

  DEFAULT constraint is used to assign default values to a column, before any value is assigned to it. For example SALARY DEFAULT 0 will assign the default value of the salary as 0.0. Even if the user does not enter any value into the SALARY column. Here SALARY is the column name.

- **REFERENCES**

  A foreign key has values which form the primary key in another table. The two tables thus get related by using the foreign key. Columns which are chosen as a foreign key should not have values other than that present in the primary key of a related table. This referential integrity is implemented using the REFERENCES constraint. REFERENCES constraint is followed by the name of the related table and its primary key.

For example, to relate a column DEPT_CODE with DEPT_NO column in another table DEPARTMENT we will use the REFERENCES constraint as:

DEPT_CODE REFERENCES DEPARTMENT(DEPT_NO)

ON DELETE CASCADE OPTION

This option is used along with the REFERENCES constraint. If you use this option then whenever a parent row is deleted then all the corresponding child rows are also deleted from the related child table.

A column can have more than one constraints each separated by space.

In order to learn SQL commands, we will create two tables, EMPLOYEE and DEPARTMENT, with structures as given in table 7.4(a) and 7.4(b), respectively. Since the DEPT_CODE field of the EMPLOYEE table is dependent on the DEPARTMENT table, we will have first the DEPARTMENT table.

Table 7.4(a) The EMPLOYEE (Entity) table structure

Attribute Name	Data Type(size)	Description
EMP_ID	NUMBER(10)	Unique code assigned to each employee
EMP_NAME	VARCHAR2(20)	Name of the Employee
EMP_DESIG	CAHR(10)	Designation of the employee
DOJ	DATE	Date of joining of the employee
SALARY	NUMBER(7,2)	Salary of the employee
DEPT_CODE	NUMBER(2)	Code of the department in which the employee is working

Table 7.4(b) The DEPARTMENT (Entity) table structure

Attribute Name	Data Type(size)	Description
DEPT_CODE	NUMBER(2)	Unique code assigned to each department
DEPT_NAME	VARCHAR2(20)	Name of the department
FLOOR	NUMBER(4)	Location of the department

Type the following SQL statement, after the SQL> prompt, in the SQL *PLUS window. It will create the DEPARTMENT table

```
SQL> CREATE TABLE DEPARTMENT
(
    DEPT_CODE   NUMBER(2)   PRIMARY KEY,
    DEPT_NAME   VARCHAR2(20) NOT NULL,
    UNIQUE  CHECK (DEPT_NAME IN
    ('ACCOUNTS', 'RESEARCH', 'SALES',
    'OPERATIONS', 'MAINTENANCE')),
    FLOOR   NUMBER(4) NOT NULL);
Table created.
```

Similarly create the EMPLOYEE table using the following SQL statements.

```
SQL> CREATE TABLE EMPLOYEE
(
    EMP_ID NUMBER(10)  PRIMARY KEY,
    EMP_NAME  VARCHAR2(20)  NOT NULL,
    EMP_DESIGN  CHAR(10)   NOT NULL,
    DOJ   DATE NOT NULL,
    SALARY NUMBER(7,2) DEFAULT 0,
    DEPT_CODE NUMBER(2) REFERENCES
    DEPARTMENT (DEPT_CODE)
);
Table created.
```

DESCRIBE COMMAND

You can view the structure of the tables using the DESC <table name>; statement. (Description of the table)

SQL> DESC EMPLOYEE;

Name	Null?	Type
EMP_ID	NOT NULL	NUMBER(10)
EMP_NAME	NOT NULL	VARCHAR2(20)
EMP_DESIG	NOT NULL	CHAR(10)
DOJ	NOT NULL	DATE
SALARY		NUMBER(7,2)
DEPT_CODE		NUMBER(2)

INSERT COMMAND

After creating the tables, namely EMPLOYEE and DEPARTMENT, we shall insert data values into them using SQL command. The values to be inserted into the table DEPARTMENT and EMPLOYEE are given in tables 7.4(c) and 7.4(d) respectively.

Table 7.4(c) The DEPARTMENT

DEPT_CODE	DEPT_NAME	FLOOR
10	Accounts	1
20	Research	2
30	Sales	3
40	Operations	4

INSERT INTO command adds (appends) new rows (records) to a table. The syntax of INSERT INTO is

INSERT INTO <table name> VALUES (<value1>, <values2>,....., <valueN>);

For example, to add rows (records) to the DEPARTMENT table created earlier in this chapter, type the following statement in the SQL *PLUS window.

SQL> INSERT INTO DEPARTMENT VALUES(10, 'Accounts', 1);

1 row created

Likewise add the remaining records given in table 7.5(c) into a DEPARTMENT table.

SQL> INSERT INTO DEPARTMENT VALUES(20, 'Research', 2);

1 row created.

SQL> INSERT INTO DEPARTMENT VALUES (30, 'Sales', 3);

1 row created.

SQL> INSERT INTO DEPARTMENT VALUES(40, 'Operations', 4);

1 row created.

To add a record into the EMPLOYEE table type the following SQL statement:

SQL> INSERT INTO EMPLOYEE VALUES(101, 'Gopal', 'Manager', '01-JAN-2011', 30000, 20);

1 row created.

Table 7.4(d) The EMPLOYEE

EMP_ID	EMP_NAME	EMP_DESIG	DOJ	SALRY	DEPT_CODE
101	Gopal	Manager	01-JAN-2011	30000	20

Points to Remember

- Character data will be enclosed with in quotes.

- Column values for date type of column are provided within single quote, ORACLE internally converts the character field to date type field.
- NULL values are given as NULL, without any quote.
- If data is not available for all the columns, then the column list must be included following the table name as shown below:

  INSERT INTO command can also be used to insert only particular values into a table. For example, to insert only the employee id, name, designation and salary into the Employee table, type the following:
- SQL> INSERT INTO EMPLOYEE (EMP_ID, EMP_NAME, EMP_DESIG, SALARY) VALUES(102, 'Sachi', 'Receptionist', 30000);

Inserting through parameter substitution

Parameter substitution provides an easier way to enter the data into a table. The '&' symbol is used as the substitution operator. When a substitution operator is used, SQL*PLUS prompts for the value of the variable, accept it and then substitutes it in place of the variable.

For examples

```
SQL> SQL> INSERT INTO EMPLOYEE VALUES(&EMP_ID', '&EMP_NAME',
'&EMP_DESIG', '&DOJ', &SALARY, &DEPT_CODE);
Enter value for emp_id:: 102
Enter value for emp_name:: ranjeet
Enter value for emp_desig:: manager
Enter value for doj::12-jan-2012
Enter value for salary:: 30000
Enter value for dept_code:: 30
1 row created.
SQL>/
Enter value for emp_id:: 103
Enter value for emp_name:: kunal
Enter value for emp_desig:: salesman
Enter value for doj::10-feb-2012
Enter value for salary:: 20000
Enter value for dept_code:: 40
1 row created.
SQL>/
so on.
```

ALTER TABLE COMMAND

Modifying the Structure of the table

The structure of a table can be modified by using the ALTER TABLE command. ALTER TABLE allows changing the structure of an existing table. With ALTER TABLE it is possible to add or delete columns, create or destroy indexes, change the data type of existing columns and change their size.

Adding new Columns

ADD keyword is used to add columns or constraints to the table. For example, the following statement will add a new column PHONE to the Employee table. The PHONE column will store the phone numbers of the Employees.

Syntax:

ALTER TABLE<table-name>

ADD<new column-name> <data-type>(<data-size>);

For example:

SQL> ALTER TABLE EMPLOYEE

ADD PHONE NUMBER(20)

Table Altered.

More than one new column are add in table:

Syntax:

ALTER TABLE<table-name>

ADD(<new column-name> <datatype>(<data-size>),

<new column-name> <datatype><(data-size>));

SQL> ALTER TABLE EMPLOYEE

ADD(PHONE NUMBER(20),

ADDRESS VARCHAR2(30));

Table Altered.

Modifying Existing Columns

The MODIFY option can change the data type, column width. For example to change the column width of EMP_NAME of EMPLOYEE table, we can use the following statement.

Syntax:

ALTER TABLE <table-name>

MODIFY<column-name><new-data-type>(<new-size>);

For example

SQL>ALTER TABLE EMPLOYEE

MODIFY EMP_NAME CHAR(25);

Table Altered.

Dropping a column from a table

To remove the PHONE column on the table, DROP option can be used. For example, the following statement will remove the phone column.

Syntax:

ALTER TABLE <table-name> DROP COLUMN <column-name>;

For example

SQL> ALTER TABLE EMPLOYEE DROP COLUMN ADDRESS;

Table dropped.

Restrictions on the ALTER TABLE

The following tasks cannot be performed when using the ALTER TABLE clause:

- Change the name of the table.
- Change the name of column
- Decrease the size of a column if table data exists.

SELECT COMMAND

The SELECT statement is the most commonly used statement in SQL and is used to retrieve information already stored in the database. To retrieve data, you can either select all the column values or name specific columns in the SELECT clause to retrieve data.

Syntax of Select Statement

```
SELECT * |{[DISTINCT] column| expression [alias] ,......}
FROM <table-name>
    [where <condition>]
    [group by <column-name (s)>]
[having<condition>]
[order by <expression>];
```

In the syntax:

SELECT	is a list of one or more columns
*	selects all columns
DISTINCT	suppresses duplicates
column | expression	selects the named column or the expression
alias	gives selected columns different headings
FROM table	specifies the table containing the columns
Where	Filter the rows retrieved
GROUP BY	Determine the basis for grouping rows.
HAVING	Filtered the records that GROUP by returns.
ORDER BY	Sort the table (ascending/descending) order

Note: *Throughout this course, the words keyword, clause, and statement are used as follows:*

- A *keyword* refers to an individual SQL element.

  For example, SELECT and FROM are keywords.
- A *clause* is a part of a SQL statement.

  For example, SELECT emp_id, emp_name, ... is a clause.
- A *statement* is a combination of two or more clauses.

  For example, SELECT * FROM employees is a SQL statement.

ALL Rows and All Columns

The SELECT is the most powerful query command in SQL. Most of the query operations can be performed using this SELECT command. Suppose you want to retrieve all the data stored in DEPARTMENT table, and then type the following statement.

SELECT <Column Name1> to <Column NameN> from <table-name>;

Note: *Here, Column Name1 to Column Name N represents table name.*

Syntax:

SELECT * FROM <table-name>

For example: Display all the details related to the Department table.

SQL> SELECT * FROM DEPARTMENT;

OUTPUT

DEPT_CODE	DEPT_NAME	FLOOR
10	Accounts	1
20	Research	2
30	Sales	3
40	Operations	4
50	Maintenance	5

5 rows selected.

Filtering Table Data

While viewing data from a table it is rare that all the data from the table will be required each time, Hence, SQL provides a method of filtering table data that is not required.

The ways of Filtering table data are:

- Selected columns and all the rows
- Selected rows and all columns
- Selected columns and selected rows

Selected columns and all rows

The retrieval of specific columns from a table can be done as shown below:

Syntax:

SELECT <ColumnName1>, <ColumnName2> from <table-name>;

For example

Display the DEPT_CODE and DEPT_FLOOR of the department table.

SQL> SELECT DEPT_CODE, DEPT_FLOOR FROM DEPARTMENT;

OUTPUT

DEPT_CODE	FLOOR
10	1
20	2
30	3
40	4
50	5

5 rows selected.

Selected rows and all columns

If information of a particular client is to be retrieved from a table, its retrieval must be based on a specific condition. The Selected statement used until now displayed all rows. This is because there was no condition set informed Oracle about how to choose a specific set of rows (or a specific row) from any table. Oracle provides the option of using a **WHERE Clause** in an SQL query to apply a filter on the rows retrieved.

When a where clause is added to the SQL query, the Oracle engine compares each record in the table, with the condition specified in the where clause. The Oracle engine displays only those records that satisfy the specified condition.

Syntax:

SELECT * FROM <table-name> where<condition>;

Where, <Condition> is always quantified as <column-name= value>

For example

Display the department details of the department named Accounts

SQL> SELECT * FROM DEPARTMENT WHERE DEPT_NAME = 'Accounts';

OUTPUT

DEPT_CODE	DEPT_NAME	FLOOR
10	Accounts	1

Selected columns and selected rows

To view a specific set of rows and columns from a table the syntax will be as follows:

Syntax:

SELECT <ColumnName1>, <ColumnName2> from <table-name>

Where <condition>;

For example

Display the EMP_NAME and SALRY of the DEPT_CODE is 20 from employee table.

SQL> SELECT EMP_NAME, SALARY, DEPT_CODE

FROM EMPLOYEE

WHERE DEPT_CODE=20;

Here the display of rows will restricted to those rows where the condition (DEPT_CODE=20) is satisfied.

OUTPUT

EMP_NAME	SALRY	DEPT_CODE
Gopal	30000	20

All comparison operators, namely >, <, =, >=, <=, <> (not equals) are supported by SQL. Moreover, SQL also supports Boolean operators NOT, AND and OR. The order of evaluation of different operators can be carried out carried out by using parentheses.

For example, type the following command to extract records (rows) of these Salesman who are earning a basic salary less than or equal to (<=) 20000. The following statement will extract such records.

SQL>SELECT EMP_ID, EMP_NAME, EMP_DESIG, SALARY

FROM EMPLOYEE

WHERE SALARY <= 20000 AND

EMP_DESIG = 'Salesman';

OUTPUT

EMP_ID	EMP_NAME	EMP_DESIG	SALRY
106	Ashish Jha	Salesman	20000

Special operators available in SQL namely, IN, NOT IN, BETWEEN, NOT BETWEEN and LIKE can also be used in place of relational operators as well as AND, OR, NOT logical operators.

IN OPERATORS

- List the name of the Employees who belongs to DEPT_CODE 10, 20.

SQL> SELECT EMP_ID, EMP_NAME, DEPT_CODE

FORM EMPLOYEE

WHERE DEPT_CODE IN (10, 20);

EMP_ID	EMP_NAME	DEPT_CODE
101	Gopal	20
103	Sneha	10
107	Shekhar	20
108	Prabhash	20
109	Jai Prakash	10

BETWEEN OPERATORS

- List the EMP_ID, EMP_NAME, and SALARY of the Employees, whose salary is between 15000 and 30000.

  SQL> SELECT EMP_ID, EMP_NAME, SALARY FROM EMPLOYEE

  WHERE SALARY BETWEEN 15000 AND 30000;

  OUTPUT

EMP_ID	EMP_NAME	SALRY
101	Gopal	30000
103	Sneha	25000
107	Shekhar	15000
108	Prabhash	27000
109	Jai Prakash	29000
110	Prakash	16000
111	Neha	23000

LIKE OPERATORS

- The LIKE operator is used only with CHAR and VARCHAR2 to match a pattern.

  '%' represents a sequence of zero or more characters

  '_' stands for any single character

  Both '%' and '_' are used with the LIKE operator to specify a pattern.

Example:

List the Employees whose names start with an 'S' (not "s")

SQL>SELECT EMP_NAME FROM EMPLOYEE WHERE EMP_NAME LIKE 'S%';

Here, the LIKE operator will match the EMP_NAME column with an 'S' followed by any number of characters.

OUTPUT

EMP_NAME
SNEHA
SHEKHAR
SACHI

List the Employees names ending with an 'S'.

SQL>SELECT EMP_NAME FROM EMPLOYEE WHERE EMP_NAME LIKE '%S';

OUTPUT

EMP_NAME
VIKAS

List the names of Employees whose names have exactly 5 characters.

SQL>SELECT EMP_NAME FROM EMPLOYEE WHERE EMP_NAME LIKE '_____';
('_'5 underscores)

OUTPUT

EMP_NAME
GOPAL
SNEHA
VIKAS

List the Employees names having U as the second character:

SQL>SELECT EMP_NAME FROM EMPLOYEE WHERE EMP_NAME LIKE '_U%';

OUTPUT

EMP_NAME
PUNIT

List the Employee names having two A in their name.

SQL>SELECT EMP_NAME FROM EMPLOYEE WHERE EMP_NAME LIKE '%A%A% ';

OUTPUT

EMP_NAME
AMAN

AND, OR, NOT OPERATORS

We have seen that we can create compound search conditions by combining together conditional expressions using AND, OR and NOT. AND and OR can be used to combine more than one conational expression. We have also seen that parenthesis can be used to enforce the desired order of evolution. Given below is an example of a complex SELECT statement.

For example, to list the names of the Employees who joined after 1st January 2011 and before 31st December 2011 meaning who joined during the year 2011, we will use the following statement:

```
SQL> SELECT EMP_NAME FROM EMPLOYEE
        WHERE DOJ BETWEEN '01-JAN-2011' AND '31-DEC-2011';
```

Combinations of logical operators

```
SQL>SELECT *
FROM BOOK
WHERE (YEAR = 2012 OR PRICE>300)
AND PUBLISHER IN ("Mc Graw Hills", "Dells Books")
OR AUTHOR LIKE "C%"
AND NOT ID = "A002"
```

When more than search conditions are combined with AND, OR and NOT, according to the standard, NOT has the highest precedence followed by AND followed by OR. The truth tables for evaluating the conditional expressions are given below:

True	AND	True	=	True
True	AND	False	=	False
False	AND	True	=	False
False	AND	False	=	False
True	OR	True	=	True
True	OR	False	=	True
False	OR	True	=	True
False	OR	False	=	False
NOT		True	=	False
NOT		False	=	True

Eliminating duplicate rows when using a select statement

The DISTINCT keyword followed by the SELECT keyword ensures that the resulting rows are unique. Uniqueness is verified against the complete row, not the first column.

Syntax:

SELECT DISTINCT column-name(s) FROM table-name;

If you need to find the unique departments and salaries from EMPLOYEE table then, issue the following query:

SQL> SELECT DISTINCT DEPT_CODE, SALARY FROM EMPLOYEE;

DEPT_CODE	SALARY
10	30000
10	20000
20	25000
20	24000
20	22000
30	44000
30	45000
40	19000
40	18000
40	17000
40	16000

ORDER BY

In general, the rows displayed from a query do not have any specific order either ascending or descending. But if you want them to be shown in ascending or descending order in a particular fields, then you can control this order for the selected rows. This is done by adding the clause ORDER BY to the SELECT command.

Syntax

SELECT <column-name (s)>

FROM <table-name>

WHERE <condition>

ORDER BY <column to de ordered>

[<ASC/DESC>]

Using the command, order by will be sort the rows as specified. For example, the clause ASC sorts and displays in the ascending order. Even if you do not specify the ASC clause still the sorting of the rows would be in the ascending order by default. In other words, SQL will automatically order the output rows from lowest to highest order, unless you specify the clause DESC. The order DESC sorts and displays rows in descending order of the specified attribute or column.

For example, if you want the list of all Employees with salary more than 25000 and also if want to display the result in the ascending order of Name then type the following SQL statement:

```
SQL> SELECT EMP_ID, EMP_NAME, EMP_DESIG, SALARY
FROM EMPLOYEE
WHERE SALARY > 25000
ORDER BY EMP_NAME;
```

OUTPUT

EMP_ID	EMP_NAME	EMP_DESIG	SALARY
106	Ashish	Salesman	26000
103	Bikas	Engineer	27000
106	Punit	Area Manager	28000
109	Vikas	As. Engineer	32000
110	Yogesh	Manager	40000

If you want to show the Employee names in the descending order, then type of following:

```
SQL> SELECT EMP_ID, EMP_NAME, EMP_DESIG, SALARY
FROM EMPLOYEE
WHERE SALARY > 25000
ORDER BY EMP_NAME DESC;
```

GROUP BY

Assume that you want to know the total salary offered to each Department (i.e. Accounts, Research, Sales and Operations) which are groups in the EMPLOYEE table, then the clause GROUP BY can be used. The GROUP BY clause allows you to form groups based on the given conditions.

The syntax for using Group By command is:

```
SELECT <column>, function (<column>)
FROM <table>
GROUP BY <column>;
```

The SQL statement to query the total Basic salary offered in each department in the EMPLOYEE table would be:

```
SELECT DEPT_CODE, SUM(SALARY)
FROM EMPLOYEE
GROUP BY DEPT_CODE;
```

OUTPUT

DEPT_CODE	SUM (SALARY)
10	90000
20	85000
30	95000

GROUP BY is not the same as ORDER BY. It does not rearrange the output to display it in the order of the product code. If you want the output to be in a particular order, you need to specify ORDER BY clause as well.

HAVING

You might not always want or need to see all the sub-groups in a table in a single report. Suppose you want to see the list of only those departments where the total salary is greater than 80000. In such a case, you cannot use the aggregate functions namely SUM, etc. in the WHERE clause.

It means you could not do something like the following:

```
SQL>SELECT DEPT_CODE, SUM(SALARY)
FROM EMPLOYEE
WHERE SUM(SALARY) > 80000
GROUP BY DEPT_CODE;
```

This command would be rejected. To see the total salary over 80000, you have to see the HAVING clause. The HAVING clause defines criteria used to eliminate certain groups from the output, just as the WHERE clause does for individual rows. The correct command would thus be:

```
SQL>SELECT DEPT_CODE, SUM(SALARY)
FROM EMPLOYEE
GROUP BY DEPT_CODE
HAVING SUM(SALARY) > 80000;
```

OUTPUT

DEPT_CODE	SUM (SALARY)
20	85000
30	95000

HAVING and WHERE clauses work in a similar manner. The difference is that clause WHERE works on rows, while clause HAVING works on groups. Expressions in HAVING clause must be single_value per group.

UPDATE COMMNAD

Updating the contents of a Table

The UPDATE command is used to change or modify data values in a table.

The verb update in SQL is used to either update:

- All the rows from a table

  OR

- A select set of rows from a table

Updating All Rows

The UPDATE statement updates columns in the existing table's rows with new values. The **SET** clause indicates which column data should be modified and the new values that they should hold. The **WHERE** clause, if given, specifies which rows should be updated. Otherwise, **all** table rows are updated.

Syntax:

```
UPDATE<table-name>
SET<ColumnName1>=<Expression1>, <ColumnName2>=<Expression2>;
```

Example:

```
SQL> UPDATE EMPLOYEE
SET SALARY= SALARY + 2000
WHERE EMP_DESIG = 'Engineer';
```

DELETE COMMAND

Deleting Row(s) From a Table

Deleting Command is used to delete rows from a table. The entire row is deleted from the table. Specific columns cannot be deleted from a table before Oracle 10g.

Syntax:

```
DELETE FROM <table name>[WHERE <condition>]
```

Where clause allows a set of rows to be deleted from a table by specifying the condition(s).

Examples:

- **Delete all records from employees**

  SQL> DELETE employees;

- **Delete the records of IT from departments**

  SQL> DELETE FROM departments WHERE department_name= 'IT';

- **DELETE the records of employees who belong to 'SALES' department**

  SQL> DELETE employees WHERE department_id IN (select department_id from departments where department_name='SALES');

USING SET OPERATORS

Set operators can be used to select data from multiple tables. Set operators basically combine the result of two queries into one. These queries are known as compound queries. All set operator have equal precedence; when multiple set operators are present in the same query. They are evaluated from left to right unless specified otherwise with parentheses. The data types of the resulting columns should match in both queries. Oracle has four set operators, which are show below

ORACLE SET OPERATORS

Operator	Description
UNION	Returns all unique rows selected by either query.
UNION ALL	Returns all rows, including duplicates selected by either query
INTERSECT	Returns rows selected from both queries
MINUS	Returns unique rows selected by the first query but not the rows selected by the second query

UNOIN OPERATOR

The union operator merges the output of two or more queries in a single set of rows or columns. It eliminates the duplicates values between two or more queries.

Syntax:

SELECT<statement1>

UNION

SELECT<statement2>

[ORDER BY clause];

Here the statement 1 and 2 are valid SELECT statements and the ORDER BY clause is optional. Both the queries are executed independently, but the output of both the queries is merged. There can be more than two queries also. It must be kept in mind the individual queries should not contain the order by clause.

Example:

- Display the different jobs in department 20 and 30.

```
SQL>SELECT job from emp where deptno=20
UNION
SELECT job emp where deptno=30;
```

OUTPUT

JOB
ANALYST
CLERK
MANAGER
SALESMAN

NOTE: The data type and number of columns retrieved by the queries should be same. The name of the corresponding columns can be different.

UNION ALL OPERATOR

The union all operator merges the output of two or more queries in a single set of rows or columns. It does not eliminate the duplicate values between two or more queries.

Syntax:

SELECT<statement1>
UNION ALL
SELECT<statement2>
[ORDER BY clause];

Here the statement 1 and 2 are valid SELECT statements and the ORDER BY clause is optional. Both the queries are executed independently, but the output of both the queries is merged. There can be more than two queries also. It must be kept in mind the individual queries should not contain the order by clause.

Example:

- Display the different jobs in departments 20 and 30 (with UNION ALL).

```
SQL> SELECT job from emp where deptno=20
UNION ALL
SELECT job from emp where deptno =30
```

OUTPUT

JOB
CLERK
MANAGER
ANALYST
CLERK
ANALYST
SALESMAN
SALESMAN
SALESMAN
MANAGER
SALESMAN
CLERK

INTERSECT Operator

Another operator, which can be used to get the combined output of multiple queries, is the Intersect operator. It gives only those rows as output from both queries, which have common records among them.

Syntax:

SELECT<statement1>

INTERSECT

SELECT<statement2>

[ORDER BY clause];

Here the statement 1 and 2 are valid SELECT statements and the ORDER BY clause is optional. Both the queries are executed independently, but the output of both the queries is merged together. There can be more than two queries also. It must be kept in mind the individual queries should not contain the order by clause. Only the final result can contain the order by clause. It must be taken care the number, sequence and data type of the columns retrieved should be same in all the intersected queries.

Example

- List the jobs common to department 20 and 30.

  SQL>SELECT job from emp where deptno=20

  INTERSECT

  SELECT job from emp where deptno=30

  OUTPUT

JOB
CLERK
MANAGER

MINUS Operator

The minus operator returns the rows, which are unique to the first query. It must be remembered that in case of A-B is different from B-A. That is why the minus operator does not follow the property of communicative unlike UNION and INTERSECT operators.

Syntax:

SELECT<statement1>

MINUS

SELECT<statement2>

[ORDER BY clause];

Example

- List the jobs, which are common to department 20 only

  SQL> SELECT job from emp where deptno=20

```
MINUS
SELECT job from emp where deptno=30
MINUS
SELECT job from emp where deptno=10;
```

The output is

JOB
ANALYST

RENAME COMMAND

Renaming Tables

Oracle allows **renaming of tables**. The rename operation is done **atomically**, which means that **no other** thread can access **any of the tables** while the rename process is running.

Syntax:

RENAME <table-name> to <new-table-name>

Example: Changes the name of depart to department table.

SQL> RENAME Depart TO Department;

OUTPUT:

Table Renamed;

Note: To rename a table the ALTER and DROP privileges on the original table, and the CREATE and INSERT privileges on the new table are required.

TRUNCATING TABLES

TRUNCATE TABLE empties a table completely. Logically, this is equivalent to a DELETE statement that deletes all rows, but there are practical differences under some circumstances.

TRUNCATE TABLE differs from **DELETE** in the following ways.

- Truncate operations drop and recreate the table, which is much faster than deleting rows one by one.
- Truncate operations are not transaction safe (i.e. an error will occur if an active transaction or an active table lock exists)
- The numbers of deleted rows are not returned.

Syntax:

TRUNCATE TABLE<table-name>;

Example: Truncate the table Employees

SQL> Truncate Table Employees;

OUTPUT:

Table Truncated.

7.5 FUNCTIONS IN SQL*PLUS

Functions are program that take zero or more arguments and return a single value. Oracle has built a number of functions into SQL, and these functions can be called from SQL or PL/SQL statements (detail in next chapters).

Need of functions

Functions can be used for the following purposes:

- To perform data calculations.
- To make modification of data.
- To manipulate data for desired output.
- To converting data values from one type to another.

Classes of functions

There are two significant classes of functions:

- Single-row functions
- Group functions (also known as aggregate functions)

Single-row functions know how many arguments they will have to process before data is fetched from the tables. Group functions don't know how many arguments they will have to process until all the data is extracted and grouped into categories.

7.5.1 Single Row Functions

Single row functions act on each row returned by the query. It result one result per row.

Classification of Single Row Functions

Single Row Functions can be classified into the following categories:

1. **Character**
2. **Number**
3. **Date**
4. **Conversion**
5. **General**

Single-Row Character Functions

Single-row character functions operate on character data. Most have one or more character arguments, and most return character values.

ASCII(<c1>)

Where c1 is a character string. This function returns the ASCII decimal equivalent of the first character in c1. See also CHR() for the inverse operation.

```
SQL>SELECT ASCII ('A') Big_A, ASCII('z') Little_Z FROM dual;
```

The output is:

BIG_A	LITTLE_Z
65	122

CHR(x)

This function gives the result as a character corresponding to the value x in the character set.

SQL > SELECT CHR(97) first, chr(99) second from dual;

The output is:

FIRST	SECOND
a	B

CONCAT(<c1>,<c2>)

Where c1 and c2 are character strings. This function returns c2 appended to c1. If c1 is NULL, then c2 is returned . if c2 is NULL. Then c2 is returned. If c2 is NULL, then c1 is returned. If both c1 and c2 are NULL, then NULL is returned. CONACT returns the same results as using the concatenation operator: c1 | | c2.

SQL>SELECT CONCAT ('SRM','UNIVERSITY') UniversityName FROM dual;

The output is:

UNIVERITYNAME
SRM UNIVERSITY

INITCAP (<c1>)

Where c1 is a character string. This function returns c1 with the first character of each word in uppercase and all others in lowercase.

SQL>SELECT INITCAP ('aman', 'kunal', 'deepak') name FROM dual;

The output is:

NAME
Aman, Kunal, Deepak

LENGTH (<c>)

Where c is a character string. This function returns the numeric length in characters of c. if c is NULL, a NULL is returned.

SQL>SELECT LENGTH ('srm university') name FROM dual;

The output is:

NAME
14

LOWER (<c>)

Where c is a character string. This function returns the character string c with all characters in lowercase. It frequently appears in WHERE clauses. See also UPPER.

SQL>select lower(dname) from dept;

The output is:

lower(dname)
accounting
research
sales
operations

LPAD(<c1>,<i>[,<c2>])

Where c1 and c2 are character strings and i is an integer. This function returns the character string c1 expanded in length to i characters using c2 to fill in space as needed on the left-hand side of c1. If c1 is over i characters, it is truncated to i characters.c2 defaults to a single space. See also RPAD.

Example:

SQL> select lpad(dname,12,' '),lpad(dname,12,'*') from dept;

The output is:

lpad(dname, 12,' ')	lpad(dname,12,'*')
ACCOUNTING	**ACCOUNTING
RESEARCH	***RESEARCH
SALES	******SALES
OPERATIONS	**OPERATIONS

LTRIM(<c1>,<c2>)

Where c1 and c2 is a character string. This function returns c1 without any leading characters that appears in c2. If no c2 characters are leading characters in c1, then c1 is returned unchanged. C2 defaults to a single space. See also RTRIM.

SQL> SELECT LTRIM ('srm','s') FROM dual;

The output is:

LT
rm

RPAD (<c1>,<i>[,<c2>])

Where c1 and c2 are characters strings and I is an integer. This fuction returns the character string c1 expanded in length to I characters using c2 to fill in space as needed on the right-hand side of c1. If c1 is over I characters, it is truncated to I characters. C2 defaults to a single space. See also LPAD.

SQL>SELECT RPAD (table_name,38, '.'), num_rows FROM user_tables;

The output is:

RPAD(TABLE_NAME,38, '.')	NUM_ROWS
TEMP_ERRORS......................................9	
CUSTOMERS..................................367,296	

RTRIM(<c1>,<c2>)

Where c1 and c2 are character strings. This function returns c1 without any trailing characters that appear in c1. If no c2 characters are trailing characters in c1, then c1 is returned unchanged. C2 defaults to a single space. See also LTRIM.

SQL> SELECT RTRIM ('Mississippi', 'ip') FROM dual;

The output is:

RTRIM
Mississ

REPLACE (<c1>,<c2>[,<c3>])

Where c1, c2 and c3 are all characters string. This function returns c1 with all occurrences of c2 replaced with c3. C3 defaults to NULL. If c3 is NULL, all occurrences of c2 are removed. If c2 is NULL, then c1 is returned unchanged. If c1 is NULL, then NULL is returned.

SQL>SELECT REPLACE ('uptown', 'up', 'down') FROM dual;

The output is:

REPLACE
downtown

SUBSTR(<c1>,<i>[,<j>])

Where c1 is a character string and both i and j are integers. This function returns the portion of c1 that is j characters long, beginning at position i. if j is negative, the position is counted backwards (that is, right to left). This function returns NULL if i is 0 or negative. J defaults to 1.

SQL>SELECT SUBSTR ('Message',1,4) from dual;

The output is:

SUBS
Mess

TRANSLATE(<c1>,<c2>,<c3>)

Where c1, c2 and c3 area all character string. This function returns c1 with all occurrences of character in c2 replaced with the position ally corresponding character in c3. A NULL is returned if any of c1, c2, or c3 is NULL. If c3 has fewer characters than c2. Then the unmatched characters in c2 are removed from c1. If c2 has fewer characters than c3, then the unmatched characters in c3 are ignored.

SQL>SELECT TRANSLATE ('fumble', 'uf', 'aR') test FROM dual ;

The output is:

TEST
Ramble

TRIM(string[,char(s)])

It removes all the blank spaces from the left as well as right side of the string if no char is specified. If we give a char, then it removes the leading and trailing occurrences of that character from the string. This is new to 8i.

SQL>SELECT TRIM(' space padded ') trimmed FROM dual;

The output is:

TRIMMED
space padded

UPPER (<c>)

Where c is a character string. This function returns the character string c with all characters in uppercase. UPPER frequently appears in WHERE clauses.

Example:

SQL>select upper(dname) from dept ;

The output is:

UPPER(DNAME)
ACCOUNTING
RESEARCH
SALES
OPERATIONS

Character Function Summary

Function	Description
ASCII	Returns the ASCII decimal equivalent of a character
CHR	Returns the character given the decimal equivalent
CONCAT	Concatenates two string; same as the operator ||
INITCAP	Returns the string with the first letter of each word in uppercase
LENGTH	Returns the length of a string in characters
LOWER	Converts string to all lowercase
LPAD	Left-fills a string to a set length using a specified character
LTRIM	Strips leading characters from a string
RPAD	Right-fills a string to a set length using a specified character
RTRIM	Strips trailing characters from a string
REPLACE	Performs substring search and replace
SUBSTR	Returns a section of the specified string, specified by numeric character positions
TRANSLATE	Performs character search and replace
TRIM	Strings leading, trailing, or both leading and trailing characters from a string
UPPER	Converts string to all uppercase

Single-Row Numeric Functions

Single-row numeric functions operate on numeric data and perform some kind of mathematical or arithmetic manipulation. All have numeric arguments and returns numeric values.

ABS(<n>)

Where n is a number. This function returns the absolute of n.

SQL>SELECT ABS(-52) negative, ABS(52) positive FROM dual;

The output is:

NEGATIVE	POSITIVE
52	52

CEIL(<n>)

Where n is a number. This function returns the smallest integer that is greater than or equal to n. CEIL rounds up to a whole number. See also FLOOR.

SQL>SELECT CEIL (9.8), CEIL(-32.85), CEIL(0) FROM dual;

The output is:

CEIL (9.8)	CEIL(-32.85)	CEIL(0)
10	-32	0

COS (<n>)

It returns trigonometric cosine of the number n.

SQL>SELECT COS(45) FROM DUAL;

The output is:

COS(45)
.52532199

EXP(<n>)

Where n is a number. This function returns e (the base of natural algorithms) raised to the nth power.

SQL>SELECT EXP(1) "e" FROM dual;

The output is:

e
2.71828183

FLOOR (<n>)

Where n is a number. This function returns the largest integer that is less than or equal to n. FLOOR round down to a whole number. See also CEIL.

SQL>SEELCT FLOOR(9.8), FLOOR (-32.85), FLOOR(137) FROM dual;

The output is:

FLOOR(9.8)	FLOOR(-32.85)	FLOOR(137)
9	33	137

LOG(<n1>, <n2>)

Where n1 and n2 are numbers. This function returns the logarithm base nl of n2.

SQL>SELECT LOG(8,64), LOG(3,27), LOG(2,1024) FROM dual;

The output is:

LOG(8,64)	LOG(3,27)	LOG(2,1024)
2	3	10

MOD(<n1>, <n2>)

Where n1 and n2 are numbers. This function returns n1 modulo n2 or the remainder of n1 divided by n2. If n1 is negative, the result is negative. The sign of n2 has no effect on the result. This behavior differs from the mathematical definition of the modulus operation.

SQL>SELECT MOD(14,5), MOD(8,2.5), MOD(-64,7) FROM dual;

The output is:

MOD(14,5)	MOD(8,2.5)	MOD(– 64,7)
4	.5	–1

POWER(<n1>, <n2>)

Where n1 and n2 are numbers. This function returns n1 to the n2th power.

SQL>SELECT POWER(2, 10), POWER(3,3), POWER(5,3) FROM dual;

The output is:

POWER(2,10)	POWER(3,3)	POWER(5,3)
1024	27	125

ROUND(<n1>, <n2>)

Where n1 and n2 are numbers. This function returns n1 rounded to n2 digits of precision to the right of the decimal. If n2 is negative, n1is rounded to left of the decimal. This function is similar to TRUNC().

SQL>SELECT ROUND(12345,-2), ROUND(12345.54321,2) from dual;

The output is:

ROUND(12345, - 2)	ROUND(12345.54321,2)
12300	12345.54

SIGN(<n>)

Where n is a number. This function returns -1 if n is negative, 1 if n is positive, and 0 if n is O.

SQL>SELECT SIGN(-2.3), SIGN(O), SIGN(47) FROM dual;

The output is:

SIGN(- 2.3)	SIGN(O)	SIGN(47)
-1	0	1

SQRT(<n>)

Where n is a number. This function returns the square root of n.

SQL>SELECT SQRT(64), SQRT(49), SQRT(5) FROM dual;

The output is:

SQRT(64)	SQRT(49)	SQRT(5)
8	7	2.23606798

TRUNC(<n>)

Where n1 is a number and n2 is an integer. This function returns n1 truncated to n2 digits of precision to the right of the decimal. If n2 is negative, n1 is truncated to left of the decimal. See also ROUND.

SQL>SELECT TRUNC(123.456,2) pos, TRUNC(123.456,-I) neg FROM dual;

The output is:

POS	NEG
123.45	120

Numeric Function Summary

Function	Description
ABS	Returns the absolute value
CEIL	Returns the next higher integer
COS	Returns the cosine
EXP	Returns the base of natural logarithms raised to a power
FLOOR	Returns the next smaller integer
LN	Returns the natural logarithm
LOG	Returns the logarithm
MOD	Returns modulo (remainder) of a division operation
POWER	Returns a number raised to an arbitrary power
ROUND	Rounds a number
SIGN	Returns an indicator of sign: negative, positive. or zero
SIN	Returns the sine
SQRT	Returns the square root of a number
TRUNC	Truncates a number

Single-Row Date Functions

Single-row date functions operate on date data type.

ADD_MONTHS(<d>, <i>)

Where d is a date and i is an integer. This function returns the data d plus i months. If i is a decimal number, the database will implicitly convert it to an integer by truncating the decimal portion (for example, 3.9 becomes 3).

SQL> SELECT SYSDATE, ADD_MONTHS(SYSDATE,3)plus_3,

ADD_MONTHS(SYSDATE,-2) rninus_2 FROM DUAL;

The output is:

SYSDATE	PLUS	MINUS
01-JAN-98	01-APR-98	01-NOV-97

LAST_DAY(<d>)

Where d is a date. This function returns the last day of the month for the date d.

SQL>SELECT SYSDATE, LAST_DAY(SYSDATE)+ IFROM dual;

The output is:

SYSTEM	LAST_DAY(SY
23-NOV-1999	01-DEC-1999

MONTHS_BETWEEN(<.d1>, <d2>)

Where d1 and d2 are both dates. This function returns the number of months that d2 is later then d1. A whole number is returned if dl and d2 are the same day of the month or if both dates are the last day of a month.

SQL>SELECTMONTHS_BETWEEN (' 19-Dec-1999', '19-Mar-2000') FROM dual;

The output is:

MONTHS_BETWEEN('19-DEC-1999', '19-MAR-2000')
3

NEXT _DAY(<d>, <dow>)

Where d is a date and dow is a text string containing the full or abbreviated day of the week in the session's language. This function returns the next dow following d. The time portion of the return date is the same as the time portion of d.

SQL> SELECT NEXT_DAY('01-Jan-2004','Monday') "1st Monday" FROM dual;

The output is:

1st Monda
05-JAN-04

ROUND(<d>[, <fmt>])

Where d is a date and fmt is a character string containing a date-format string.

SQL> SELECT SYSDATE, ROUND(SYSDATE, 'MM') FROM dual;

The output is:

SYSDATE	ROUND(SYS
16-JAN-98	01-FEB-98

SYSDATE

This function takes no arguments and returns the current date and time to the second level.

SQL>SELECT SYSDATE FROM dual;

The output is:

SYSDATE
24-Nov-1999 09:26:01

Date Function Summary

Function	Description
ADD_MONTHS	Adds a number of months to a date
LAST_DAY	Returns the last day of a month
MONTHS_BETWEEN	Returns the number of months between two dates
NEXT_DAY	Returns the next day of a week following a given date
ROUND	Rounds a date/time
SYSDATE	Returns the current date/time

Single-Row Conversion Functions

Single-row conversion functions operate on multiple data types. The TO_CHAR and TO_NUMBER functions have a significant number of formatting codes that can be used to display date and number data in different ways of representations.

To_char(number | date,fmt)

This function converts a number or date value to a varchar2 character string with format model fmt. It facilitates the retrieval of data in a format different from the default format (DD-MON- YY) when using for dates. With the help of this function part of the date i.e the date, month or year can also be extracted. While using this function to convert dates following guidelines must be followed:

- The format model must be enclosed in single quotation marks and is case sensitive
- The format model can include any valid date format element be sure to separate the date value from the format model by the comma
- The names of days and months in the output are automatically padded with blanks
- You can resize the display width of the resulting character field with the SQL * Plus column command.

SQL>Select sysdate, to_char(sysdate, 'DAY') from dual;

The output is:

SYSDATE	TO_CHAR(S
07-JULY-03	MONDAY

SQL>Select to_char(sal, ₹ 99,999') salary from emp where ename = 'JASJEET' ;

The output is:

SALARY
(₹3,000)

Example:

To display current time in three different columns in form of hour, minutes and second.

SQL> SELECT TO_CHAR(SYSDATE,'HH') HOUR, TO_CHAR(SYSDATE,'MI') MIN,TO_CHAR(SYSDATE,'SS') SEC FROM DUAL;

The output is:

HO	MI	SE
03	01	16

To_date(char[, 'fmt'])

This function converts a character value into a date value where char stand for the value to be inserted in the date column and fmt is the date format in which char is specified.

SQL>Select to_date('07-july-03','RM') from dual;

The output is:

to_date('07 -july-03'), 'RM'
7

To _number(text\date)

This function which converts text or date information into a number.

SQL>SELECT TO_NUMBER('49583') FROM DUAL;

The output is:

TO_NUMBER('49583')
49583

7.5.2 Group Functions in SQL

Group functions, sometimes-called aggregate functions, return a value based on a number of inputs. The exact number of input is not determined until the query is executed and all rows are fetched. This differs from single-row functions, in which the number of inputs is known at parse time before the query is executed. Because of this difference, group functions have slightly different requirements and behavior from single-row functions. Group functions do not process NULL values and do not return a NULL value.

Aggregate Functions

The aggregate functions produce a single value for an entire group or table.

Aggregate Functions	Description
COUNT	Determine the number of rows or non NULL column values
SUM	Determines the sum of all selected columns
MAX	Determines the largest of all selected values of a column
MIN	Determines the smallest of all selected values of a column
AVG	Determines the average of all selected values of a column

In all the above functions, NULLs are ignored.

Aggregate functions are used to produce summarized results. They operate on sets of rows. They return results based on groups of rows. By default all rows in a table are treated as one group. The GROUP BY clause of the SELECT statement is used to divide rows into smaller groups (discussed in next section).

COUNT

Count function determines the number of rows or non-NULL column values.

The syntax is

COUNT (*1 [Distinct] 1 ALL| column name)

If * is passed, then the total number of rows is returned.

Examples:

- List the number of employees working with the company:

  SQL>Select COUNT(*) FROM emp;

  The output is:

COUNT(*)
14

- List the number of jobs available in the emptable .

  SQL>SELECT COUNT (DISTINCT JOB) FROM emp;

  The output is:

COUNT(DISTINCTJOB)
5

With the COUNT function, a column name can also be specified. In this case, the NULL values will be ignored.

SUM

The sum function returns the sum of values for the selected list of columns.

The syntax is

SUM([DISTINCTIALL] column name)

Example:

- List the total salaries payable to employees.

  SQL>SELECT SUM(sal) FROM emp;

  The output is:

SUM(SAL)
29025

MAX

Max function returns the maximum value of the selected list of item. Note that DISTINCT and ALL have no effect, since the maximum value would be same in either case.

The syntax is:

MAX(column name)

- List the maximum salary of employee working as a salesman.

  SQL>SELECT MAX(sal) FROM emp WHERE job='SALESMAN';

  The output is:

MAX(SAL)
1600

MIN

This function returns the minimum value of the selected list of items.

The syntax is

MIN(Column name)

Example:

- List the minimum salary from emp table.

  SQL>SELECT MIN(sal) FROM emp;

  The output is:

MIN(SAL)
800

AVG

This function returns the average of column values.

The syntax is:

AVG(DISTINCTIALL] Column name)

Example:

- List the average salary and number of employees working in the department 20.

  SQL>SELECT AVG(sal), COUNT(*) FROM emp WHERE deptno=20);

 The output is:

AVG(SAL)	COUNT(*)
2175	5

7.6 JOINING OF TABLES FOR MULTIPLE TABLE QUERIES

In Relational Database Management Systems, data stored in different tables is related. We can use the power of SQL to relate the information and query data. A SELECT statement has a mandatory SELECT clause and FROM clause. The SELECT clause can have a list of columns, expressions, functions, and so on. The FROM clause tells you which table(s) to look in for the required information. So far, we have seen only one table in the FROM clause, now we will learn how to retrieve data from more than one table. In order to query data from more than one table, we need to identify a common column that relates the two tables. In the WHERE clause, we define the relationship between the tables listed in the FROM clause using comparison operators.

When data from more than one table in the database is required, a join condition is used. Rows in one table can be joined to rows in another table according to common values existing in corresponding columns, that is, usually primary and foreign key columns. A simple join condition in the WHERE clause. Oracle performs a join whenever multiple tables appear in the queries FROM clause. The query's SELECT clause can have the columns or expressions from any or all of these tables.

Syntax of Join:

SELECT table 1.column, table 2.column FROM table 1: table 2
WHERE table 1. column l=table 2. column 2;

In the syntax:

table 1.column, table 2.column	denotes the table and column from which data is retrieved
table 1.column 1= table2.column2	is the condition that joins (or relates) the tables together

Points to Note:

- Write the join condition in the WHERE clause.
- Prefix the column name with the table name when the same column name appears in more than one table.

Here, all the examples are based on the EMP and DEPT tables, whose data shown below:

SQL>SELECT * FROM dept;

OUTPUT

DEPTNO	DNAME	LOC
10	ACCOUNTING	NEW YORK
20	RESEARCH	DALLAS
30	SALES	CHICAGO
40	OPERATIONS	BOSTON
50	PAYROLL	DALLAS

SQL>SELECT * FROM emp;

OUTPUT

EMPNO	ENAME	SALARY	COMM	DEPTNO
7566	JONES	2975		20
7654	MARTIN	1250	1400	30
7698	K_BLAKE	2850		30
7788	SCOTT	3000		20
7839	A_EDWARD	5000	50000	10
7844	TURNER	1500	0	30
7845	FORD	3000		20

How would we list the department name location for each employee, along with his or her salary? The department name and location are in the DEPT table; the employee name and salary are in the EMP table. So, to list the information together in one query, we need to do a join. The DEPTNO column is common to both tables; use this column to relate the rows.

To get the required information following query is used:

SQL>SELECT dname, loc, ename, sal FROM dept, emp

WHERE dept.deptno = emp.deptno;

OUTPUT

DNAME	LOC	ENAME	SALARY
RESEARCH	DALLAS	JONES	2975
SALES	CHICAGO	MARTIN	1250
SALES	CHICAGO	K_BLAKE	2850
RESEARCH	DALLAS	SCOTT	3000
ACCOUNTING	NEW YORK	A_EDWARD	5000
SALES	CHICAGO	TURNER	1500
RESEARCH	DALLAS	FORD	3000

7 rows selected.

Here data is selected from two tables: EMP and DEPT. The department number (DEPTNO) is the column on which join is established. Notice that in the WHERE clause, the column names are qualified by the table name; this is required to avoid ambiguity, because the column names are the same in both tables. If the column names are different in each table, you need not qualify the column names. Just as we can provide column alias names, we can alias table names, also. Aliases improve the readability of the code, and they can be short names that are easy to type and use as references. The table alias name is given next to the table name.

The following example uses alias names d and e for DEPT and EMP tables and uses them to qualify the column names:

```
SQL> SELECT d.name, d.loc, e.ename  e.sal
FROM dept d, emp e
WHERE d.deptno = e.deptno
ORDER BY d.dname;
```

Note: Once table alias names are defined; you cannot use the table name to qualify a column. You should use the alias name to qualify the column.

To execute a join of three or more tables, Oracle takes these steps:

- Oracle joins two of the based tables on the join conditions, comparing their columns
- Oracle joins the result to another table, based on join conditions.
- Oracle continues this process until all tables are joined into the result.

The Join query also contain in the WHERE clause to restrict rows based on column in one table. Here's example:

```
SQL> SELECT d.dname, d.loe, e.ename, e.sal
FROM dept d, emp e
WHERE e.deptno = d.deptno and eomm IS NOT NULL
```

OUTPUT

DNAME	LOC	ENAME	SAL
SALES	CHICAGO	ALLEN	1600
SALES	CHICAGO	WARD	1250
SALES	CHICAGO	MARTIN	1250
SALES	CHICAGO	TURNER	1500

Cartesian product

A Cartesian join occurs when data is selected from two or more tables and there is no common relation specified in the WHERE clause. If we do not specify a join condition for the tables listed in the FROM clause, Oracle joins each row from the first table to every row in the second table. If the first table has three rows and the second table has four rows, the result will have 12 rows. Suppose we add another table with two rows without specifying a join condition; the result will have 24 rows. We should avoid Cartesian joins; for the most part, they happen when there are many tables in the FROM clause and developers forget to include the join condition.

Example:

SQL>Select ename, dname FROM emp, dept;

The above query displays employee name and department name from EMP and DEPT tables. Because no WHERE clause has been specified, all rows(14 rows) from EMP table are joined with all (4 rows) in the DEPT table, there by generating 56 rows in the output as shown below:

EMP (14 Rows)

EMPNO	ENAME	DEPTNO
7839	KING	10
7634	BLAKE	30
.....	......	.....
7934	MILLER	10

DEPT (4 rows)

DEPTNO	DNAME	LOC
10	ACCOUNTING	NEW YORK
20	RESEARCH	DALLAS
30	SALES	CHICAGO
40	OPERATIONS	BOSTON

ENAME	DNAME
KING	ACCOUNTING
BLAKE	ACCOUNTING
.....	.....
KING	RESEARCH

Cartesian product 14*4=56 rows selected

7.7 DESTROYING TABLES

Sometimes tables within a particular database become obsolete and need to be discarded. In such situation using a DROP TABLE statement with the table name can destroy a specific table.

Syntax:

DROP TABLE <table-name>;

Caution: if a table is dropped all records held within it are lost and cannot be recovered.

Example16. Remove the table Departments along with the data held.

SQL> DROP TABLE Departments;

OUTPUT:

Table Dropped.

SUMMARY

The relational database management systems and service is one of the main branches of the IT industry where technological developments are taking place at a very rapid pace. We see hundreds of new database and related products being released every month. Major software vendors are churning out database products with more and more features with each release of their database offerings. The competition in the database market segment is so intense that survival itself is extremely difficult. Other than the database vendors there are thousands of companies who develop applications, for example ERP. E-commerce, banking, etc. which are implemented systems. In addition there are thousands of people who implement, maintain and use these systems. Databases are becoming prominent by the day. Today, almost all applications from spreadsheets and word processors to statistical analysis tools-have the capability to seamlessly integrate with the database and use it for performing tasks from statistical analysis to mail merging.

Structured Query Language (SQL) is the standard command set used to communicate with the relational database management systems. All tasks related to relational data management-creating tables, querying the database for information, modifying the data in the database, deleting them, granting access to users, and so on–can be done using SQL. SQL is the standard language for making queries in relational database management package such as SQL server, Ingress, Sybase, Oracle etc. The standard language for accessing client/server database is also SQL.

EXERCISES

1. What are various categories in which we can divide the SQL statements?
2. What are the features of Oracle?
3. What is the importance of View and Sequence?
4. What is meant by Tree walking feature of Oracle?
5. What are different data types of Oracle?

   Solve the following on the given database:

   S(Sno, Sname, City, Status)

   P(Pno, Pname, Color, Weight)

   SP(Sno, Pno, Qty)
6. Create the above tables by identifying appropriate Primary keys and foreign keys.
7. Apply Column level constraints on City such that it may be only "Amritsar", "Delhi", "Batala" and "Qadian".
8. Apply Column level constraints such that Qty should be between 100 to 1000, Weight is NOT NULL, Sname is NOT NULL and Pname is UNIQUE.
9. Insert five records in each table.
10. Get supplier name where city is "Amritsar".

11. Get quantity supplied by "Ajay".
12. Get the supplier name and city that supply part P1.
13. Get color of parts supplied by Sl.
14. Get color of parts supplied by Ajay.
15. Get supplier name who supply at least one red part.
16. Get part name where weight>l00 and Sno="Sl".
17. Get supplier name who supply part P1with quantity> 100.
18. Get supplier name who supply pencils with quantity> 100.
19. Get supplier number who supplies maximum quantity.
20. Get supplier numbers who supply quantity greater than average quantity.
21. Get supplier name that supply maximum quantity.
22. Get total number of suppliers.
23. Get total number of parts supplied by supplier S1.
24. Count the parts having red color.
25. Count red parts supplied by Ajay.
26. Get the total quantity supplied by S1.
27. Get maximum quantity supplied by S1.
28. Get the maximum quantity supplied by Naresh.
29. Get total quantity supplied for each supplier.
30. Get total number of records supplied for each part.
31. Increase the Quantity of part PI by 10%.
32. Change the color of Red parts supplied by Ajay to Green.
33. Delete all the red parts supplied by supplier S1.
34. Delete all the entries of part PI.
35. Create view on- table S that contains Sno and Sname of suppliers Amritsar.
36. Create a sequence that has minimum value 100 and maximum 1000.
37. Use the above sequence to store quantity information.
38. Alter the structure of table S to change the width of column Sname.
39. Alter the structure of table P to apply constraint NOT NULL on column Color.
40. Drop view created above.

■

CHAPTER 8

PL/SQL

8.1 INTRODUCTION

PL/SQL stands for Procedural Language/Structured Language. PL/SQL is extension of the SQL language. We can say it is superset of the Structured Query Language specialized for use in the oracle database. Because it is Procedural language, it eliminates many restrictions of the SQL Language. With the use of SQL user can only manipulate the information stored into database. User can perform very basic operations such as selecting the information from some prefabricated tables, inserting information into those tables, updating the information stored in table and also occasionally used to delete information from these tables. PL/SQL extends SQL by adding control structures found in the other procedural languages. Procedural constructs blend seamlessly with Oracle SQL, resulting in a structured, powerful language's ease of data manipulation and the procedural language's ease of programming.

8.2 SQL VS PL/SQL

SQL	PL/SQL
1. SQL does not have any procedural capabilities. By procedural capabilities here we mean that there is no provision of conditional checking, looping and branching, which are very essential for filtration of data before entering it into database.	1. ORACLE has provided all procedural capabilities in PL/SQL to support data filtration.
2. SQL statements are passed to oracle engine (server) one at a time. Therefore each time for each statement a call is made to the server resources are opened and closed every time. And hence generating in slow processing.	2. In PL/SQL it sends the bundle of SQL statement to the oracle server in the form of BLOCK and hence calling the server resources only once for that block even one SQL statement. After processing all the statements in a block ORACLE server closes the resources results in faster execution of SQL statements in a PL/SQL block.

SQL	PL/SQL
3. In SQL there is no provision of handling errors and exceptions. Which means that if any SQL statement fails to execute, then oracle gives its own error code which may not be user friendly.	3. Whereas in PL/SQL we can program the block of statements to handle the errors in such a way that if any of the statement fails to execute then we can display user-friendly appropriate messages.
4. SQL does not support PL/SQL statement.	4. PL/SQL supports SQL statements in its block.
5. We cannot store the intermediate results of a query in variable.	5. PL/SQL supports declaring the variables so as to store intermediate results of query for later use. These variables can be used anywhere in any other SQL statement of same PL/SQL block.

8.3 ARCHITECTURE OF PL/SQL

The PL/SQL engine executes the PL/SQL Blocks. The PL/SQL engine executes only the procedural statements and sends the SQL statement to the SQL statement executer in the Oracle Server. The PL/SQL engine resides in the Oracle Server. The Call to the Oracle engine needs to be made only nce to execute any number of SQL statements, if these SQL sentences are bumble inside a PL/SQL block.

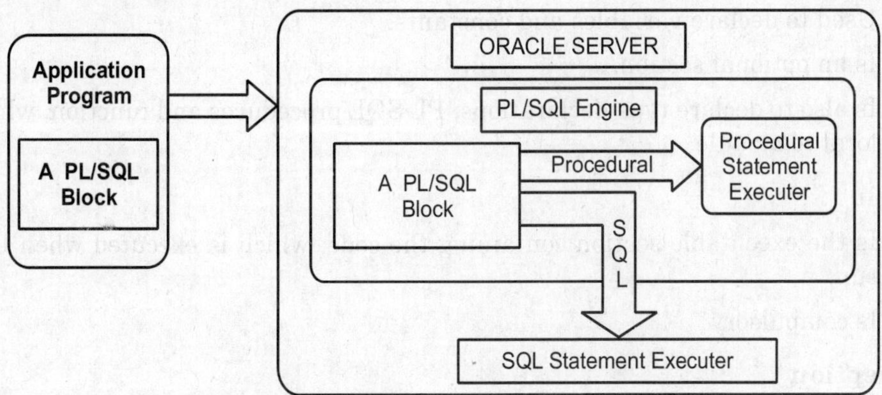

Figure 8.3 Architecture of PL/SQL

Since the oracle engine is called only once for each block, resulting increased speed of processing as compared to call for each SQL sentence.

8.4 ADVANTAGES OF PL/SQL

PL/SQL is completely portable, high performance transaction processing language, which offers the following advantages.

1: Supports the declaration and manipulation of object types and collections.

2: Allows the calling of external functions and procedure.

3: Contains new libraries of built-in packages. A package is a file that group functions, cursors, stored procedures, and variables in one place.

4: **Triggers:** A triggers is a PL/SQL program that is stored in the database and executed immediately before or after the INSERT, UPDATE and DELETE commands.

5: **Cursors:** Oracle uses workspaces to execute the SQL commands. Through PL/SQL cursors, it is possible to name the workspace and access its information.

6: **Support for PL/SQL:** PL/SQL allows us to use all the SQL data manipulation commands, transaction control commands, SQL functions (except group functions), operators and pseudocolumns, thus allowing us to manipulate data values in a table flexibly and effectively.

8.5 STRUCTURE OF PL/SQL LANGUAGE

PL/SQL is a block structured language with procedural techniques with features like logic building, looping, error handling mechanisms, data-types, variables, subroutines, procedural constructs. Block is smallest piece of PL/SQL code which groups logically related declaration and statements. Declarations are local to the blocks and ease to exist when block completes.

PL/SQL block consists of three sections:

Declare

- Used to declare variables and constants.
- Is an optional section.
- Is also to declare type declarations, PL/SQL procedures and function, which are local to module

Begin

- Is the executable section containing the code, which is executed when block is run.
- Is compulsory

Exception

- Handles exceptions occurring during processing.
- Used to place predefined Error-handles or user defined exceptions.
- Code contained in this section is executed only when an error occurs..
- Is an optional section

A PL/SQL statement is terminated with the END statement and a semicolon. Every PL/SQL program must consist of at least one block, which may contain any number of nested sub/blocks. Blocks can be nested in executable and exception-handling parts of a PL/SQL block or subprogram but not in declarative part.

```
Declare
        -Declare variable and columns
Begin
        -Process SQL statement
Exception
        -Error handlers
End;
```

8.6 PL/SQL LANGUAGE ELEMENTS

The PL/SQL essential language elements can be grouped as follows:

- Operators, indicators and punctuation
- Identifiers
- Literals
- Comments
- Expressions and comparisons
- Data types and Declarations

8.6.1 Operators, Indicators and Punctuation

In PL/SQL, these symbols are divided into a few groups:

Arithmetic Operators

Used to perform arithmetic operations.

Examples: +, -, *, /, ** (Raises the first operand to the exponent of the second)

Expression Operators

Used to create assignment, range and string catenation expressions.

Examples : = (Assignment operator, A: =3)

.. (range operator, 1 .... 4)

|| (Concatenates two or more strings, 'SRM' || 'university')

8.6.2 Identifiers

Identifiers are named conventions used for variables, constants and oracle objects like tables, procedure, functions, packages, trigger and cursors etc.

8.6.3 Literals

It specifies an exact value in a program. It is an explicit numeric, character, string or Boolean value not represented by an identifier. Literals are used to initialize constants, variables and other data values.

Examples: 10,-19, 9.99 (Numeric literals)

'a', 'A' '?', ' ',')' (Character literals)

'abc', 'jack', 'jill', '1234' (String literals)

TRUE and FALSE (Boolean literals)

8.6.4 Comments

Comments can be single line or multiple lines.

Single line comment:

Begins with - can appear within a statement, at end of line.

Example :

a number;-variable declaration

Multi line comment

Begin with /* and end with a an asterisk-slash (*/).

Example:

/* statements to select rate and quantity into

variables and calculate value */

8.6.5 Expressions and Comparisons

Expressions are constructed using operands and operators. An operand is a variable, constant, literal or function call that contributes a value to an expression.

Operator Precedence

The operations within an expression are done in an order which depends on operator precedence. Operators with higher precedence are applied first, and those with same precedence are applied in no particular order. Parenthesis can be used to control the order of evaluation.

Table shows Operator Precedence:

Operator	Operation
**, NOT	Exponentiation, logical negation
+ –	Identity, negation
–, /	Multiplication, division
+, –, II	Addition, subtraction, concatenation
=,!=,<,>,<=,>=,IS,NULL,LIKE, IKE, BETWEEN, IN AND OR	Conjunction Inclusion

8.6.6 Data Types and Declaration

Every constant and variable has a data type, which specifies a storage format, constraints, and valid range of values.

Some commonly used data types of PL/SQL are:

- NUMBER
- CHAR
- VARCHAR
- DATE
- BOOLEAN
- LONG
- LONG RAW
- LOB
- **Number Type**

  We can use the NUMBER data type to store fixed-point or floating-point numbers of virtually any size.

  The syntax follows

  <variable_name> NUMBER [(precision, scale)];

  To declare fixed-point numbers, for which you must specify scale, use the following form:

  NUMBER (precision, scale)

  To declare floating-point numbers, for which you cannot specify precision or scale because the decimal point can "float" to any position, use the following form:

  NUMBER

  To declare integers, which have no decimal point, use this form:

  NUMBER (precision) – same as NUMBER (precision, 0)

- **Character Types**

  Character types allow you to store alphanumeric data, represent words, texts, and manipulate character strings.

- **CHAR**

  We can use the CHAR data type to store fixed-length character data. The CHAR data type take an optional parameter that lets you specify a maximum length up to 32767 bytes.

  The syntax follows:

  <variable_name> CHAR [(maximum_length)];

  We cannot use a constant or variable to specify the maximum length; you must use an integer literal in the range 1....32767.

  If you do not specify a maximum length, it defaults to 1.

- **VARCHAR2**

  Used to store variable length character data i.e. it stores a string up to the length of the variable unlike CHAR data type, which stores sting variable up to the maximum length of the variable. The maximum length can be specified up to 32767 bytes. For example: if data type of address field is declared as VARCHAR(40) and address information of a particular record complete in 20 characters, then remaining 20 characters space is not padded with blank characters and memory space of 20 characters is used for some other purposes and not wasted as padded with blank characters.

- **LONG**

The LONG data type used to store variable-length character strings. The LONG data type is like the VARCHAR2 datatype, except that the maximum length of a LONG value is 32760 bytes.

Syntax: <variable_name> LONG (maximum_length) ;

LONG columns can store text, arrays of characters, or even short documents.

- **BOOLEAN**

The BOOLEAN data type used to store the logical values TRUE and FALSE and the non-value NULL, which stands for a missing, inapplicable, or unknown value.

Syntax: <variable_name> BOOLEAN;

- **DATE**

The DATE data type used to store fixed-length date/time values. DATE values include the time of day in seconds since midnight. The default might be 'DD-MON- YY', which includes a two-digit number for the day of the month, an abbreviation of the month name, and the last two digits of the year.

Syntax: <variable_name> DATE;

- **RAW**

The RAW data type used to store binary data or byte strings. For example, a RAW variable might store a sequence of graphics characters or a digitized picture. Raw data is like VARCHAR2 data, except that PL/SQL does not interpret raw data.

Syntax: <variable_name> RAW (maximum_length);

The maximum width of a RAW database column is 2000 bytes.

- **LONG RAW**

We can use the LONG RAW data type to store binary data or byte strings. LONG RAW data is like LONG data, except that LONG RAW data is not interpreted by PL/SQL. The maximum length of a LONG RAW value is 32760 bytes.

- **LOB Types**

The LOB (large object) data types BFILE, BLOB, CLOB, and NCLOB allow to store blocks of unstructured data (such as text, graphic images, video clips, and sound waveforms) up to four gigabytes in size. And, they allow efficient, random, piece-wise access to the data.

8.7 VARIABLES AND CONSTANT

The PL/SQL language allows the declaration of variables and constants, which can be used in the SQL commands contained in the PL/SQL block. All the variables and constants used must be declared.

Variables

We can declare variables in the declaration section part and use elsewhere in the body of a PL/SQL block. The following example shows how to declare a variable

Example:

```
age number (4) ;
```

A variable named age has been declared with a width of 4 bytes. Similarly we can declare a variable of Boolean data type. Example

```
Done Boolean;
```

Variable Value Assignment

There are two ways to assign values to a variable. These are:

- With the use of assignment operator
- With the use of SELECT INTO clause to get value from the database item

With the use of Assignment Operator

In this the assignment operator " : = " used to assign a value to a variable. As shown below:

```
a : = b * c ;
increase : = sal * 1.5 ;
OK : = false ;
```

We can also use substitute variables for the assignment to variables. Substitute variables are those whose values are entered at run time during execution of the PL/SQL block. There is no need to declare the substitutable variables as shown below:

```
a.:=&enter_nurnber;
```

Here, enter number is a substitute variable whose values is entered during execution, and substituted at the place of &enter_number as shown below:

Enter the value of enter_ number: 3

Then, 3 is substituted at the place of &enter_number

```
a:=3;
```

Commonly, we can use the same substitute variable name as main variable name, as shown below:

```
a: =&a;
b:=&b;
```

With the use of SELECT INTO Clause

The second way to assign values to variables is to use the SELECT command to assign the contents of the fields of a table to a variable:

```
SELECT sal INTO s FROM emp where empno = 100;
```

In this case, variable's' will get the value from sal column of emp table for empno 100.

Note: *Select statement must return a single record; if it returns no record or more than one record then an error is raised.*

Example:

Write a PL/SQL code to calculate total sal of emp having empno 100. Table emp1 having following columns

empno, ename, bp, da, hra, total.

Solution:

```
DECLARE
E NUMBER (3);
D NUMBER (3);
H NUMBER (3);
B NUMBER (3);
T NUMBER (3);
BEGIN
        SELECT BP, DA, HRA INTO B, D, H FROM EMP1 WHERE EMPNO=100;
        T=B+D+H;
        UPDATE EMP1 SET TOTAL=T WHERE EMPNO=100;
END;
```

Constant Declaration

It may be useful for you to declare constants in the declaration section of the PL/SQL blocks developed as well. Constants are named elements whose values do not change. For example, pi can be declared as a constant whose value 3.14 is never changed in the PL/SQL block.

The declaration of a constant is similar to that of declaration of a variable. We can declare constants in the declaration section and use it elsewhere in the executable part. To declare the constant we must make use of the keyword constant. This keyword must precede the data type as shown below.

pi constant number : = 3.14;

In the above example, we have assigned to the constant named pi. After this, no more assignment to the constant is allowed, i.e. 3.14 will be the initial and final value to the constant All the declaration must end with a semicolon (;).

8.7.1 Variable Attributes

Attributes allow us to refer to data types and objects from the database. PL/SQL variables and constants can have attributes. The following are the types of attributes, which are supported by PL/SQL.

- %TYPE
- %ROWTYPE

%TYPE

In general, the variables that deal with table columns should have the same data type and length as the column itself. %type attribute is used when declaring variables that refer to the database columns. When using the %type keyword, all you need to know is the name of the column and the table to which the variable will correspond.

Example:

```
DECLARE
eno emp.empno%type; - eno of same data type and width as empno of  emp table
salaryemp.sal%type;
BEGIN
.......
.......
END;
```

The advantages of using %TYPE are as follows:

- We need not know the exact data type of the column empno and sal.
- If the database definition of empno and sal is changed, then, the data type of eno and salary changes accordingly at run time.

%ROWTYPE

%rowtype attribute provides a record type that represents a row in a table. For example, if the EMPLOYEE table contains four columns-EMPID, LASTNAME, FIRSTNAME, and SALARY-and you want to manipulate the values in each column of a row using only one referenced variable, the variable can be declared with the %rowtype keyword. Compare the use of %rowtype to manual record declaration:

```
DECLARE
        my_employee employee%ROWTYPE;
 BEGIN
 ...........
 END;
```

To refer empid of employee table we have to use my_employee.empid, similarly for lastname we have to use my _employee.lastname.

The other way is:

```
DECLARE
    my_empid employee.empid%TYPE,
    my_lastname employee.lastname%TYPE,
    my_firstname employee.firstname%TYPE,
    my_salaryemployee.salary%TYPE;
BEGIN
........
END;
```

Example:

Write a PL/SQL code to calculate total sal of emp having empno 100. Table emp1 having following columns

empno, ename, bp, da, hra, total. Use %TYPE and %ROWTYPE for variable declaration.

Solution:

```
DECLARE
B EMP1.BP%TYPE;
D EMP1.DA%TYPE;
    H EMP1. HRA%TYPE;
    T EMP1. TOTAL%TYPE;
BEGIN
SELECT BP, DA, HRA INTO B, D, H FROM EMP1 WHERE EMPNO=100;
T:=B+D+H;
UPDATE EMP1 SET TOTAL=T WHERE EMPNO=100;
END;
```

With the use of %ROWTYPE:

```
DECLARE
    REC EMP1%ROWTYPE;
BEGIN
SELECT * INTO REC FROM EMP WHERE EMPNO=100;
REC.TOTAL:=REC.BP+REC.HRA+REC.DA;
    UPDATE EMP1 SET TOTAL=REC.TOTAL WHERE EMPNO=100;
END;
```

8.8 DISPLAYING USER MESSAGE ON THE SCREEN

PL/SQL requires a method through which messages can be displayed to the user on the monitor.

DBMS_OUTPUT is a package that includes a number of procedure and functions that accumulate information in a buffer so that it can be retrieved later. These functions can also be used to display messages to the user.

PUT_LINE is a procedure used to display message to the user on monitor. It accepts a single parameter of character data type. If used to display a message, it is the message 'string'.

Example:

```
DBMS_OUTPUT.PUT_LINE('ENTER THE NUMBER');
DBMS_OUTPUT.PUT_LINE('Result of Sum operation is:' ||sum);
```

To display messages to the user the SERVEROUTPUT should be set to ON. SERVEROUTPUT is a SQL *PLUS environment parameter that displays the information passed as a parameter to the PUT_LINE function.

Syntax

```
SET SERVEROUTPUT [ON/OFF];
```

8.9 CONTROL STATEMENT

We can change the logical flow of statements within the PL/SQL block with a number of control structures.

Control structures can be:

- Conditional Control
- Iterative Control
- Sequential Control

- **Conditional Control**

  It allows testing the truth of a condition and executing sections of program depending on the condition that may be true or false.

- **Iterative Control**

  It allows executing a section of program repeatedly as long as a specified condition remains true.

- **Sequential Control**

  It allows ordering the sequence of processing sections of program.

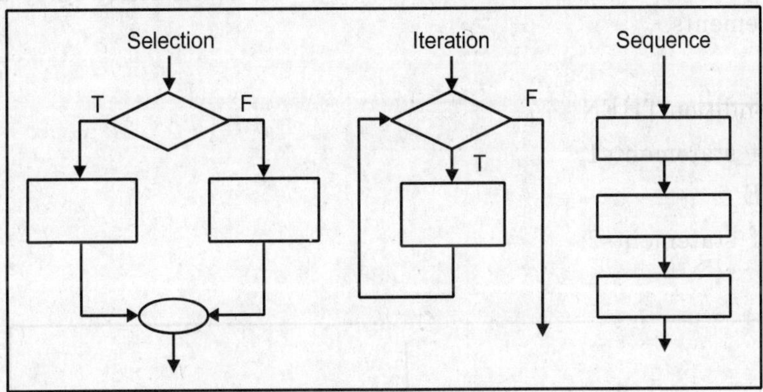

Figure 8.9 Control Structures

8.10 CONDITIONAL CONTROL

There are following conditional control statements:

- IF-THEN STATEMENT
- IF- THEN - ELSE STATEMENT
- IF-THEN-ELSIF STATEMENT (LADDER IF)

8.10.1 IF Statements

It is used to take alternative actions depending on circumstances. It executes a sequence of statements conditionally.

There are three forms of IF statements: IF-THEN, IF-THEN-ELSE, and IF-THEN-ELSIF.

8.10.2 IF-THEN

The simplest form of IF statement associates a condition with a sequence of statements enclosed by the keywords THEN and END IF (not ENDIF), as follows:

Syntax:

```
IF condition THEN
        sequence_of_statements;
END IF;
```

The sequence of statements is executed only if the condition yields TRUE. In either case, control passes to the next statement.

Example:

```
IF a > b THEN
        dbms_output.put_line('a is greater');
END IF;
```

8.10.3 IF-THEN-ELSE

The second form of IF statement adds the keyword ELSE followed by an alternative sequence of statements.

Syntax

```
        IF condition THEN
sequence_of_statements1;
        ELSE
sequence_of_statements2;
END IF;
```

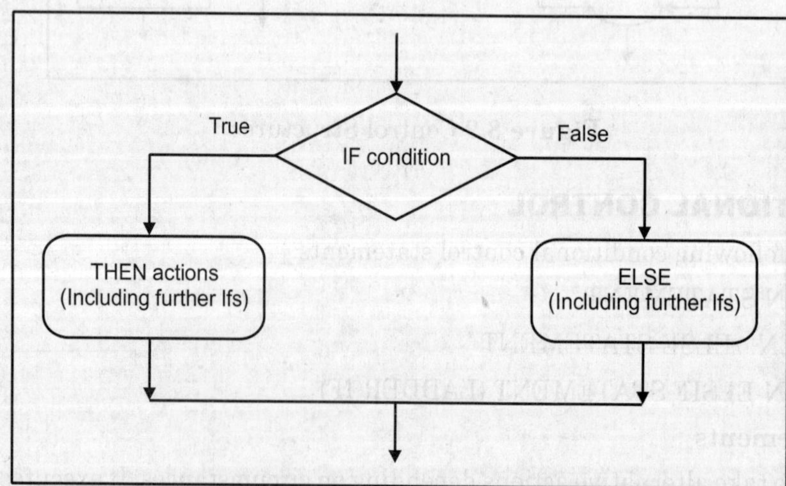

Figure 8.10.3 IF-THEN-ELSE Structure

The sequence of statements in the ELSE clause is executed only if the condition yields FALSE or NULL. Thus, the ELSE clause-ensures that a sequence of statements is executed.

Example:

To illustration of If-ELSE construct PL/SQL block to find greater of two numbers. User will enter any two numbers and IF statement will check for the greater among the entered number.

Solution:

```
DECLARE
    A NUMBER := &ENTER_A;
    B NUMBER := &ENTER _B;
BEGIN
    IF A > B THEN
        DBMS_OUTPUT. PUT_LINE (‘ A IS GREATER’);
ELSE
        DBMS_OUTPUT.PUT_LINE(‘ B IS GREATER’);
    END IF;
END;
```

The THEN and ELSE clauses can include IF statements. That is, IF statements can be nested, as the following example shows:

Example:

To illustration of Nested If-Else construct PL/SQL block to find greatest of three numbers.

Solution:

```
DECLARE
    A NUMBER := &ENTER_A;
    B NUMBER := &ENTER_B;
    C NUMBER := &ENTER_C;
BEGIN
    IF A>B THEN
        IF A>C THEN
            DBMS_OUTPUT. PUT_LINE ( ‘A IS GREATEST’ ) ;
    ELSE
            DBMS_OUTPUT. PUT_LINE ( ‘C IS GREATEST’ ) ;
        END IF;
    ELSE
        IF B>C THEN
            DBMS_OUTPUT. PUT_LINE ( ‘B IS GREATEST’ ) ;
    ELSE
            DBMS_OUTPUT. PUT_LINE ( ‘C IS GREATEST’ ) ;
        END IF;
    END IF;
END;
```

8.10.4 IF - THEN-ELSIF

Sometimes we want to select an action from several mutually exclusive alternatives. The third form of IF statement uses the keyword ELSIF (not ELSEIF) to introduce additional conditions, as follows:

Syntax:

```
IF condition1 THEN
        Sequence_of_statements1;
ELSIF condition2 THEN
        sequence_of_statements2;
ELSE
        sequence_of_statements3;
END IF;
```

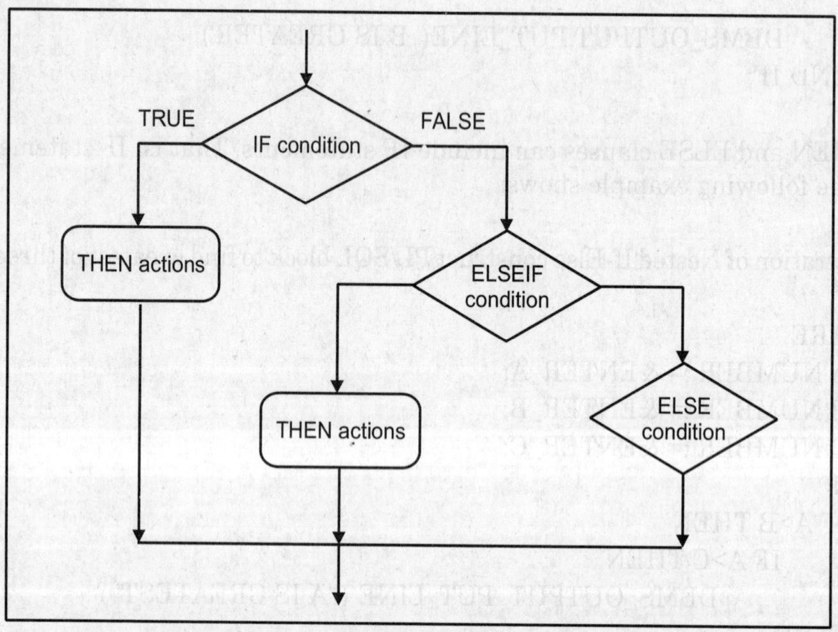

Figure 8.10.4 IF-THEN-ELSEIF Structure

If the first condition yields FALSE or NULL, the ELSIF clause tests another condition. An IF statement can have any number of ELSIF clauses; the final ELSE clause is optional. Conditions are evaluated one by one from top to bottom.

If any condition yields TRUE, its associated sequence of statements is executed and control passes to the next statement. If all Conditions yield FALSE or NULL, the sequence in the ELSE clause is executed. Consider the following example:

Example:

To illustration IF-THEN-ELSIF a PL/SQL block to calculate addition, subtraction, multiplication and division of two numbers according to user choice.

Solution:

```
DECLARE
        A NUMBER: =&A;
        B NUMBER: =&B;
        C NUMBER;
        X NUMBER;
BEGIN
        X:=&ENTER_CHOICE;
        IF X=l THEN
                C:=A+B;
                ELSIF X=2 THEN
                C:=A-B;
                        ELSIF X=2 THEN
                C: =A-B;
                        ELSIF X=3 THEN
                C: =A*B;
                        ELSIF X=4 THEN
                C:=A/B;
ELSE
        DBMS_OUTPUT. PUT_LINE ( 'NOT A VALID OPTION' ) ;
END IF;
        DBMS_OUTPUT. PUT_LINE ( 'RESULT IS' | | C);
END;
```

Description of the PL/SQL block code:

If the value of X is 1 then addition is performed, if the value of x is 2 then subtraction is performed, for X=3 multiplication is performed and for X=4 division operation is performed, otherwise not a valid option message is displayed. Instead of using four IF statements, this operation is performed with a single IF THEN ELSIF statement.

8.11 ITERATIVE CONTROL

A sequence of statements can be executed any number of times using the LOOP constructs. The LOOP command initializes a group of commands indefinitely, or until a condition forces a "break" in the LOOP and detours the execution of the program to another place. The command is used with the EXIT command, which is responsible for interrupting the LOOP execution. The LOOPS can be broadly classified into:

- Simple Loop Statement
- While Loop Statement
- For Loop Statement

8.11.1 Simple LOOP Statement

The simplest form of LOOP statement is the basic (or infinite) loop, which encloses a sequence of statements between the keywords LOOP and END LOOP, as follows:

```
LOOP
    sequence_of_statements;
END LOOP
```

With each iteration of the loop, the sequence of statements is executed, and then control resumes at the top of the loop. If further processing is undesirable or impossible, you can use an EXIT statement to complete the loop.

There are two forms of EXIT statements:

- EXIT
- EXIT-WHEN

EXIT Statement

The EXIT statement forces a loop to complete unconditionally. When an EXIT statement is encountered, the loop completes immediately and control passes to the next statement.

Example:

```
LOOP
    ......
    IF credit_rating  <3 THEN
    .......
    EXIT; - exit loop immediately
END IF;
END LOOP;
- control resumes here
```

EXIT· WHEN Statement

The EXIT-WHEN statement allows a loop to complete conditionally. When the EXIT statement is encountered, the condition in the WHEN clause is evaluated. If the condition yields TRUE, the loop completes and control passes to the next statement after the loop.

An example follows:

```
LOOP
    EXIT WHEN c>5; - exit loop if condition is true
    ........
END LOOP;
```

Until the condition yields TRUE, the loop cannot complete. So, statements within the loop must change the value of the condition. The EXIT-WHEN statement replaces a simple IF statement. For example, compare the following statements:

```
IF c > 5 THEN | EXIT WHEN c > 5;
    EXIT;  |
END IF;       |
```

These statements are logically equivalent, but the EXIT-WHEN statement is easier to read and understand.

Example:

To illustrate a LOOP-EXIT a PL/SQL block to print the numbers from 1 to N

Solution:

```
DECLARE
    VAR1 NUMBER :=1;
    N NUMBER: =&ENTER_N;
BEGIN
    LOOP
        DBMS_OUTPUT. PUT_LINE ( VAR1) ;
        VAR1 : = VAR1+1;
        EXIT WHEN VAR1 > N ;
    END LOOP;
END;
```

8.11.2 WHILE-LOOP Statement

The WHILE-LOOP statement associates a condition with a sequence of statements enclosed by the keywords LOOP and END LOOP, as follows:

Syntax:

```
WHILE condition LOOP
    Sequence_of_statements;
END LOOP;
```

Before each iteration of the loop, the condition is evaluated. If the condition yields TRUE, the sequence of statements is executed, then control resumes at the top of the loop. If the condition yields FALSE or NULL, the loop is bypassed and control passes to the next statement. An example follows:

```
WHILE  i <= 10 LOOP
    a:= n*i;
    i:=i+1;
END LOOP;
```

The number of iterations depends on the condition and is unknown until the loop completes. Since the condition is tested at the top of the loop, the sequence might execute zero times. In the last example, if the initial value of i is greater than 10, the condition yields

FALSE and the loop is bypassed. To ensure that a WHILE loop executes at least once, use an initialized Boolean variable. A statement inside the loop must assign a new value to the Boolean variable. Otherwise, you have an infinite loop.

Example:

To illustration a PL/SQL block to print the desired multiplication table.

Solution:

```
DECLARE
    TABLE_OF NUMBER :=&ENTER_TABLEOF
    COUNT NUMBER: = 1;
    RESULT NUMBER;
BEGIN
    WHILE COUNT ¢= 10
    LOOP
        RESULT := TABLE_OF * COUNT;
        DBMS_OUTPUT. PUT_LINE (TABLE_OF | | '*' | | COUNT | | '='
        | | RESULT);
        COUNT := COUNT +1 ;
        END LOOP;
END;
```

Example:

To illustration of WHILE LOOP with the use of SQL statements PL/SQL block to calculate the SIMPLE INTEREST for same PRINCIPAL and TIME but with different RATE OF INTEREST starting from 5% and to store each result in a Simple_Interest table with following structure: (Principal, Rate, Time, Si).

Solution:

```
DECLARE
    PRINCIPAL NUMBER:= &ENTER_P;
    RATE_OF_INT NUMBER := 5 ;
    TIME_IN_YEAR NUMBER := 2;
    SIMPLE_INT NUMBER (6,2);
BEGIN
    WHILE RATE_OF_INT < =15
    LOOP
        SIMPLE_INT := (PRINCIPAL*RATE_OF_INT*TIME_IN_YEAR)/100;
        INSERT INTO SIMPLE_INTEREST(PRINCIPAL,RATE,TIME,SI)
        VALUES (PRINCIPAL,RATE_OF_INT,TIME_IN_YEAR,SIMPLE_INT) ;
        RATE_OF_INT := RATE_OF_INT + 1 ;
    END LOOP;
END;
```

8.11.3 FOR-LOOP Statement

Whereas the number of iterations through a WHILE loop is unknown until the loop completes, the number of iterations through a FOR loop is known before the loop is entered. FOR loops iterate over a specified range of integers. The range is part of an iteration scheme, which is enclosed by the keywords FOR and LOOP. A double dot (..) serves as the range operator. The syntax follows:

Syntax:

```
FOR counter IN [REVERSE) lower_bound .. higher_bound LOOP
    sequence_of_statements;
END LOOP;
```

The range is evaluated when the FOR loop is first entered and is never re-evaluated. As the next example shows, the sequence of statements is executed once for each integer in the range. After each iteration, the loop counter is incremented.

```
FOR i IN 1 .. 3 LOOP - assign the values 1,2,3 to I
    sequence_of_statements; - executes three times
END LOOP;
```

The following example shows that if the lower bound equals the higher bound, the sequence of statements is executed once:

```
FOR i IN 3 .. 3 LOOP - assign the value 3 to i
    sequence_of_statements; - executes one time
END LOOP;
```

FOR-LOOP in Reverse Order

By default, iteration proceeds upward from the lower bound to the higher bound. However, if you use the keyword REVERSE, iteration proceeds downward from the higher bound to the lower bound, as the below example shows. After each iteration, the loop counter is decremented.

```
FOR i IN REVERSE 1 .. 3 LOOP - assign the values 3,2,1 to i
    sequence_of_statements; - executes three times
END LOOP;
```

PL/SQL has no such structure, but you can easily build one. Consider the following example:

```
FOR j IN 5 .. 15 LOOP          - assign values 5,6,7, ... to j
    IF MOD (j, 5) = 0 THEN     - pass multiples of 5
    sequence_of_statements;    -j has values 5,10,15
    END IF;
END LOOP;
```

This loop is logically equivalent to one, which has step value of 5. Within the sequence of statements, the loop counter has only the values 5, 10, and 15.

Scope Rules

The loop counter is defined only within the loop. You cannot reference it outside the loop. After the loop is exited, the loop counter is undefined, as the following example shows:

```
FOR ctr IN 1 .. 10 LOOP
.....
END LOOP;
Sum: = ctr - 1; - illegal
```

We need not explicitly declare the loop counter because it is implicitly declared as a local variable of type INTEGER.

Using the EXIT Statement

The EXIT statement allows a FOR loop to complete prematurely. For example, the following loop normally executes ten times, but as soon as the b becomes greater than 999, the loop completes no matter how many times it has executed:

```
FOR i IN 1 ..... 10 LOOP
    b:=a*i;
EXIT WHEN b>999;
.......
END LOOP;
```

8.12 Sequential Control

GOTO statement and NULL are commonly used to change the sequence of statements.

8.12.1 GOTO Statement

The GOTO statement branches to a label unconditionally. The label must be unique within its scope and must precede an executable statement or a PL/SQL block. When executed, the GOTO statement transfers control to the labeled statement or block. In the following example, you go to an executable statement farther down in a sequence of statements:

```
BEGIN
    ........
GOTO insert_row;
    .........
    «insert_row»
    INSERT INTO emp VALUES ...
END;
```

The GOTO statement must be followed by an executable statement.

For example:

```
LOOP
.......;...
..... 
IF A>B then
Go to <<abc>>;
END IF;
.....
....
<<abc> - it is illegal because it does not precede the executable statement.
END LOOP:
End;
```

8.12.2 NULL Statement

The NULL statement explicitly specifies inaction; it does nothing other than pass control to the next statement.

Uses of NULL Statement:

It can improve readability.

```
    IF A>B THEN
    DBMS_OUTPUT. PUTLINE (A) ;
ELSE
NULL;
END IF;
```

The solution of illegal use of GOTO statement is with the NULL statement as shown below:

```
LOOP
.... . ,....
    IF A>B THEN
        GO TO<<ABC>>;
END IF;
<<abc>> /* It is correct now because it is followed by an executable statement
        NULL without changing the meaning of the block.*/
    NULL;
END LOOP;
```

8.13 Overview of Error Handling

There are numbers of reasons due to which run time errors may be raised during the execution of a PL/SQL block. Although you cannot anticipate all possible errors, you can plan to handle certain kinds of errors meaningful to your PL/SQL program. With PL/SQL, a mechanism called exception handling lets you "bulletproof' your program so that it can continue operating in the presence of errors.

When an error occurs, an exception is raised; normal execution is stopped and control is transferred to an exception-handling section of PL/SQL program. A specific section can be defined in the program to handle exceptions. Separate subroutines called exception handlers can be created to perform all exception processing. Once an exception is raised and control is transferred to the exception part of a program, it cannot return to the execution part of the program.

8.13.1 Trapping an Exception

If the exception is raised in the executable section of the block, processing branches to the corresponding exception handler in the exception section of the block. If PL/SQL successfully handles the exception, then the exception does not propagate to the enclosing block or environment.

8.13.2 Propagating an Exception

If the exception is raised in the executable section of the block and there is no corresponding exception handler, the PL/SQL block terminates with failure and the exception is propagated to the calling environment.

8.14 Advantage of Exceptions

Using exceptions for error handling has several advantages. These are:

- With exception handling no need to check errors after each SQL command. So, errors processing is not mixed with normal processing. Without exception handling, every time you issue a command, you must check for execution errors, as follows:

```
BEGIN
        SELECT ...
                - check for 'no data found' error
        SELECT ...
                - check for 'no data found' error
        SELECT ...
                - check for 'no data found' error
```

In this case error processing is not clearly separated from normal processing. With exceptions, you can handle errors conveniently without the need to code multiple checks, as follows:

```
BEGIN
    SELECT...
    SELECT...
    SELECT...
EXCEPTION
    WHEN NO_DATA_FOUND THEN - catches all 'no data found' errors
END;
```

So, exception provides the mechanism to handle multiple errors, without inter-mixing the error checks with normal code.

- Exceptions improve readability by letting you isolate error-handling routines.
- Exceptions also improve reliability. You need not worry about checking for an error at every point it might occur. Just add an exception handler to your PL/SQL block. If the exception is ever raised in that block (or any sub-block), you can be sure it will be handled.
- All error conditions can be captured with OTHERS clause in the exception handler, which provides a mechanism to process all expected errors as well as those unforeseen.

8.15 Exception Types

There are two types of exceptions:

- Implicitly raised exceptions
- Explicitly raised exceptions

8.15.1 Implicitly Raised Exceptions

PL/SQL provides a predefined set of exceptions that are implicitly raised (automatically raised) by the system at run time in case an error is encountered in PL/SQL.

There are two types of implicitly raised exceptions:

- Predefined oracle server
- Non-predefined oracle server

8.15.2 Explicitly Raised Exceptions

User can also define their own set of user-defined exceptions and explicitly raise them on encountering an error condition.

Exception	Description	Directions for Handling
1. Predefined Oracle Server error (implicitly raised)	1. One of approximately 20 errors that occur most often in PL/SQL code.	1. Don not declare and allow the Oracle Server to raise them implicitly.
2. Non-predefined Oracle Server error (Implicitly raised)	2. Any other standard Oracle Server error.	2. Declare within the declarative section and allow the Oracle Server to raise them implicitly.
3. User-defined error (Explicitly raised)	3. A condition that the developer determines is abnormal.	3. Declare within the declarative section and raise explicitly.

8.16 TRAPPING PREDEFINED ORACLE SERVER ERRORS

PL/SQL has a set of exceptions that are predefined for the common Oracle system errors. Predefined exceptions are used to detect and handle Oracle system errors that occur internally at program run time.

An internal exception is raised implicitly whenever your PL/SQL program violates an Oracle rule or exceeds a system-dependent limit. Every Oracle error has a number, but exceptions must be handled by name. So, PL/SQL predefines some common Oracle errors as exceptions. For example, PL/SQL raises the predefined exception NO_DATA_FOUND if a SELECT INTO statement returns no rows.

Syntax

```
EXCEPTION
WHEN exception1 [OR exception2 ........] THEN
         statement1;
         statement2;
........... .
[WHEN exception3 [OR exception4 .....] THEN
         statement1;
            statement2;
            . ....... . . ]
[WHEN OTHERS THEN
            statement1;
            statement2;
```

In the Syntax

Exception	It is the standard name of a predefined exception or the name of a user defined exception exception declared within the declarative section
Statement	It is one more PL/SQL or SQL statements
Others	It is an optional exception handling clause that traps unspecified exceptions

WHEN OTHERS Exception Handler

The exception-handling section traps only those exceptions specified; any other exceptions are not trapped unless you use the OTHERS exception handler. This traps any exception not yet handled. For this reason, OTHERS is the last exception handler defined. The OTHERS handler traps all exceptions not already trapped.

List of some Predefined Exceptions

Exception	***Error***	***Raised if***
CORSOR_ALREADY_OPEN	ORA-06511	At attempt is made to OPEN an already open cursor. A Cursor must be CLOSE before it can reopen it.
DUP_VAL_ON_INDEX	ORA-00001	Attempt is made to INSERT or UPDATE duplicate values in a UNIQUE database column.

Exception	*Error*	*Raised if*
INVALID_CURSOR	ORA_01001	An illegal cursor operation such as closing an unopened cursor.
INVALID_NUMBER	ORA-01722	The conversion of a character string to a number fails in a SQL statement.
LOGIN_DENIED	ORA_01017	An attempt is made to log on to oracle with an invalid username/password
NO_DATA_FOUND	ORA-01403	SELECT INTO returns no rows, or you refer to an uninitialized row in a PL/SQL table.
NOT_LOGGED_ON	ORA-01012	PL/SQL program issues a database call without being logged on to oracle.
TOO_MANY_ROWS	ORA-01422	A SELECT INTO returns more than one row.
VALUE_ERROR	ORA-06502	The conversion of a character string to a number fails in a procedural statement, or an arithmetic conversion, truncation, or constraints error occurs.
ZERO_DIVIDE	ORA-01476	An attempt is made to divide a number by zero.

Example:

To show use of inbuilt exceptions.

```
DECLARE
    item_code NUMBER;
BEGIN
    SELECT code INTO item_code From try
    WHERE
EXCEPTION
    WHEN TOO_MANY_ROWS THEN
    DBMS_OUTPUT.PUT_LINE('TOO MANY ROWS');
    WHEN NO_DATA_FOUND THEN
    DBMS_OUTPUT.PUT_LINE('NO DATA FOUND');
END;
```

8.17 TRAPPING OF NON-PREDEFINED ORACLE SERVER ERRORS OR USER DEFINED SYSTEM

PL/SQL provides a limited set of predefined exceptions for the internal oracle system errors, but it provides a mechanism to declare user-defined exceptions to handle the other unnamed Oracle System errors. An exception variable can be defined and linked to the error using the PRAGMA EXCEPTION_INIT statement in a block's declarative section.

Syntax

PRAGMA EXCEPTION_INIT (exception_name, error_number) ;

PRAGMA is the keyword that signifies that the statement is a compiler directive, which is processed at compile time and not at run time. Rather, it directs the PL/SQL compiler to associate an exception name with an Oracle system error number.

Steps to Trapping a Non-predefined Oracle Server Exception

1. Declare the name for the exception within the declarative section.
   Syntax
   exception EXCEPTION;
   Here, exception is the name of the exception.
2. Associate the declared exception with the standard Oracle Server error number using the PRAGMA EXCEPTION_INIT statement.
   Syntax
   PRAGMA EXCEPTION_INIT(exception, error_number);
   Here: exception is the previously declared exception.
   error_number is a standard Oracle Server error number.
3. Reference the declared exception within the corresponding exception-handling routine.

   Example

   To show use of User Defined System Exceptions

```
DECLARE
      large_value EXCEPTION;
      PRAGMA EXCEPTION_INIT(LARGE_VALUE,-01438);
BEGIN
      INSERT INTO try VALUES (8, 'STEEL TABLE CHAIR' ,12);
EXCEPTION
      WHEN large_value THEN
      DBMS_OUTPUT.PUT_LINE('VALUE TOO BIG');
END;
```

Description: The insert statement tries to insert code, description and chair into the table try. If any of the values specified is larger than column width user-defined exception LARGE VALUE will be invoked. (01438 is the error number for the error 'inserted value too large for column').

8.18 TRAPPING USER DEFINED EXCEPTIONS

User defined exceptions are used to handle error conditions specific to a application program. For example in case of Library system the date of issue of a book cannot be more than date of return, if that happens then an error must be raised explicitly by the application programmer and that facility is developed with the help of User defined exceptions. Unlike predefined exceptions, user-defined exceptions must be declared and must be raised explicitly by RAISE statements.

Steps to Trap User-defined Exceptions

1. Declare the name for the user-defined exception within the declarative section.

   Syntax

   exception_name EXCEPTION;

   Here: exception_name is the name of the exception

2. Use the RAISE statement to raise the exception explicitly within the executable section.

   Syntax

   RAISE exception_name;

   Here: exception_name is the previously declared exception.

3. Reference the declared exception within the corresponding exception handling routine.

Declaring User-Defined Exceptions

Exceptions can be declared only in the declarative part of a PL/SQL block, subprogram, or package. You declare an exception by introducing its name, followed by the keyword EXCEPTION.

Syntax

<exception_name> EXCEPTION;

In the following example, you declare an exception named past due:

```
DECLARE
    past_due EXCEPTION;
```

Exception and variable declarations are similar. But remember, an exception is an error condition, not a data item. Unlike variables, exceptions cannot appear in assignment statements or SQL statements. However, the same scope rules apply to variables and exceptions.

Raising User-Defined Exceptions

User-defined exceptions must be explicitly raised when associated error condition is detected. During program execution checking can be done for error conditions specified as EXCEPTION in the DECLARE section of PUSQL program. If an error condition is encountered, the defined exception is explicitly raised by calling the RAISE statement. RAISE statement for a given exception can be placed anywhere within the scope of that exception.

Example:

In the following example, user defined exception is raised when an item become out of stock.

```
DECLARE
        out_of_stock EXCEPTION;
        number_on_hand NUMBER(4);
BEGIN
        ..........
        ..........
        IF number_on_hand < 1 THEN
        RAISE out_of_stock;
        END IF;
        ..........
EXCEPTION
        WHEN   out_of_stock THEN
                -handle the error
END;
```

We can also raise a predefined exception explicitly as shown below.

```
DECLARE
        acct_type INTEGER;
        ..........
BEGIN
        ...........
        ...........
        IF acct_type NOT IN (1, 2, 3) THEN
                RAISE INVALID_NUMBER; - raise predefined exception
        END IF;
        ..........
EXCEPTION
        WHEN INVALID_NUMBER THEN
        ROLLBACK;
        ...........
END;
```

8.19 INTRODUCTION TO CURSOR

The oracle Engine uses a work area to execute SQL statements and store information. A cursor is a PUSQL construct that allows us to name these work areas, and to access their stored information. The data that is stored in the cursor is called the Active Data Set.

Example:

When a user fires a select statement as:

SELECT empno, ename, job, sal FROM emp WHERE deptno = 10;

All the rows returned by the query are stored in the cursor at the Server and will be as displayed at the client end.

Types of Cursors : There are two types of cursors:

- Implicit Cursor
- Explicit Cursor
- **Implicit Cursors**

  Implicit Cursors are declared by PUSQL implicitly for all SQL statements. They are opened and managed by Oracle engine internally. So there is no need to open and manage by the users, these are operations, which are performed automatically.
- **Explicit-Cursor**

  Explicit cursors are user-defined cursors for processing of multiple records returned by a query. Explicit Cursors are declared explicitly, along with other identifiers to be used in a block, and manipulated through specific statements within the block's executable actions. These are user-defined cursors, defined in the DECLARE section of the- PUSQL block. The user-defined cursor needs to be opened, before the reading of the- rows can be done, after which the cursor is closed. Cursor marks the current position in an active set.

8.19.1 General Cursor Attributes

Whenever any cursor is opened and used, the oracle engine creates a set of four system variables, which keeps track of the current status of a cursor. These cursor variables can be accessed and used in a PUSQL block. Both Implicit and Explicit cursor have four attributes.

They are described as:

Attributes	Description
%ISOPEN	It returns TRUE if cursor is open, FALSE otherwise.
%FOUND	It returns TRUE if record was fetched successfully from the opened cursor, and FALSE otherwise.
%NOTFOUND	It returns TRUE if record was not fetched successfully and FALSE otherwise.
%ROWCOUNT	It returns number of records processed from cursor.

8.20 IMPLICIT CURSOR HANDLING

Implicit Cursors named "SQL" are declared by PL/SQL implicitly for all SQL statements. Implicit cursors attributes can be used to access information about the status of last insert, update, delete or single-row select statements. This can be done by preceding the implicit cursor attribute with the cursor name (i.e. SQL). The value of the cursor attributes always refers to the most recently executed SQL statement, wherever the statement appears.

Implicit Cursor Attributes

Attributes	Description
SQL%ISOPEN	It is always FALSE because Oracle automatically closes an Implicit cursor after executing its SOL statement.
SQL%FOUND	It is TRUE if the most recently executed DML statement was successful.
SQL%NOTFOUND	It is TRUE if the most recently executed DML statement was not successful.
SQL %ROWCOUNT	It returns the number of rows affected by an INSERT. UPDATE. DELETE. or single row SELECT statement.

Implicit Cursor attributes are used in procedural statement but not in SQL statements.

Use of SQL%NOTFOUND Attribute

SQL%NOTFOUND evaluates to TRUE if an INSERT, UPDATE, or DELETE affected no rows or a SELECT INTO returned no rows. Otherwise%SQLNOTFOUND evaluates to FALSE.

Example:

Consider a PL/SQL code to display a message to check whether the record is deleted or not.

Solution:

```
BEGIN
    DELETE EMP WHERE EMPNO=&EMPNO;
    IF SQL%NOTFOUND THEN
    DBMS_OUTPUT.PUT_LINE('RECORD NOT DELETED');
ELSE
    DBMS_OUTPUT.PUT_LINE('RECORD DELETED');
END IF;
END;
```

8.21 Explicit Cursor Handling

The following steps are involved in using an explicit cursor and manipulating data in its active set:

- Declare a cursor mapped to a SQL select statement that retrieves data for processing.
- Open the cursor.

- Fetch data from the cursor one row at a time into memory variables.
- Process the data held in the memory variables as required using a loop.
- Exit from the loop after processing is complete.
- Close the cursor.

Cursor Declaration

During declaration of a cursor, cursor name is given and also defines the structure of the query to be performed within it. The CURSOR statement is used to declare explicit cursor.

Syntax:

```
CURSOR <cursor-name> IS <select statement>;
```

Whereas <select statement> includes most of the usual clauses, but INTO clause is not allowed.

Opening a Cursor

Here query execution is done. It also binds any variables that are referenced. After opening the cursor the rows returned by the query are available for fetching.

Syntax:

```
OPEN <cursor-name>;
```

This statement is used within the executable actions of the block. It also establishes an active set of rows. When cursor is opened it point to the first row in the active set.

Fetching of Individual Rows

After the cursor is opened the current row is loaded into variables. The current row is the row at which the cursor is currently pointing. The retrieval of data into PL/SQL variables is done through FETCH statement.

Syntax:

```
FETCH <cursor-name> INTO <variables>;
```

For each column value returned by the query associated with the cursor, there must be a corresponding variable in the INTO list. Also their data types must be compatible. Each FETCH causes the cursor to move its pointer to the next row in the active set, and hence each FETCH will access a different row returned by the query.

Closing a Cursor

It explicitly closes the cursor, allowing it to be reopened, if required. This means that an active set can be re-established several times.

Syntax:

```
Close <cursor-name>;
```

By closing a cursor a working set of rows are released produced by last opening of the cursor. It is then possible to reopen the cursor, this establishing a fresh working set.

Explicit Cursor Attributes

Each cursor that the user defines has four attributes. These are:

Attributes	Description
%ISOPEN	Evaluates to TRUE, if the cursor is opened, otherwise evaluates to FALSE.
%FOUND	Evaluates to TRUE when last fetch succeeded.
%NOTFOUND	Evaluates to TRUE, if the last fetch failed, i.e. no more rows are left.
%ROWCOUNT	Returns the number of rows fetched

There are four attributes of explicit cursor for obtaining status information about a cursor. When appended to the cursor name these attributes let the user access useful information about the execution of a multi row query.

Example:

Consider a PUSQL code to display the empno, ename, job of employees of department number 10.

Solution:

```
DECLARE
    CURSOR C1 IS SELECT EMPNO, ENAME, JOB FROM EMP
    WHERE
    DEPTNO=10;
    REC C1%ROWTYPE; /*rec is a row type variable for cursor c1 record, containing
    empno, ename and job*/
BEGIN
    OPEN C1;
    LOOP
    FETCH C1 INTO REC;
    EXIT WHEN C1%NOTFOUND;
    DBMS_OUTPUT.PUT_LINE('EMPNO' || REC.EMPNO);
    DBMS_OUTPUT.PUT_LINE('ENAME' | REC.ENAME);
    DBMS_OUTPUT.PUT_LINE('JOB' || REC.JOB);
    END LOOP;
    CLOSE C1;
END;
```

Example:

Consider a PUSQL code to display the employee number and name of top 5 highest paid

Solution:

```
DECLARE
    EMPNAME EMP.ENAME%TYPE;
    EMPSAL EMP.SAL%TYPE;
    CURSOR TEMP1 IS SELECT ENAME, SAL FROM EMP ORDER BY SAL DESC;
BEGIN
    OPEN TEMP1;
    LOOP
        FETCH TEMP1 INTO EMPNAME, EMPSAL;
        EXIT WHEN TEMP1%ROWCOUNT>5 OR TEMP1%NOTFOUND;
        DBMS_OUTPUT.PUT_LINE(EMPNAME || EMPSAL);
        END LOOP;
    CLOSE TEMP1;
END;
```

8.22 CURSOR FOR LOOP

The Cursor FOR Loop implicitly declares its loop index as a record of type %ROWTYPE, opens a cursor, repeatedly fetches rows of the values from the active set into fields in the record, and then closes the cursor when all rows have been processed or when the EXIT command is encountered.

The syntax for the FOR Loop is:

```
FOR <variable name> IN <cursor_name> LOOP
    <statements>;
END LOOP;
```

It is a machine defined loop exit i.e. when all the values in the FOR construct are exhausted looping stops.

A cursor for loop automatically does the following:

- Implicitly declares its loop index or variable_name as a %rowtype record.
- Opens a cursor.
- Fetches a row from the cursor for each loop iteration.
- Closes the cursor when all rows have been processed.

Example:

Consider a PUSQL code to display the empno, ename, job of employees of department number 10 with CURSOR FOR Loop statement.

Solution:

```
DECLARE
    CURSOR C1 IS SELECT EMPNO, ENAME, JOB FROM EMP WHERE
    DEPTNO=10;
BEGIN
    FOR REC IN C1 LOOP
    DBMS_OUTPUT.PUT_LINE('EMPNO' | | REC.EMPNO);
    DBMS_OUTPUT.PUT_LINE('ENAME'| | REC.ENAME);
    DBMS_OUTPUT.PUT_LINE('JOB'| | REC.JOB);
    END LOOP;
END;
```

8.23 SUB-PROGRAM

Subprograms are named PL/SQL blocks that can take parameters and can be invoked. Subprograms allow decomposition of a program into logical units. These logical units can be used as building blocks to create complete application programs.

Types of Subprograms

PL/SQL has two types of subprograms:

- **Procedures**
- **Functions**

Generally, we use a procedure-to perform an action and a function to compute a value. Like unnamed or anonymous PL/SQL blocks, subprograms have a declarative part, an executable part, and an optional exception-handling part. Anonymous block provide specific operation but cannot accept or return values as in procedures or functions.

Subprograms may be further classified as local and stored type.

Local Subprograms

Such procedures and functions are local to the PL/SQL module, which contain it. They can be created in the declarative section of PL/SQL module, local to the module. The local module can be called anywhere in the module's execution section.

Stored Subprograms

A stored procedure or function is a named PL/SQL code block that have been compiled and stored in one of the Oracle engine's system tables. Stored Procedures and Functions are stored in the Oracle database. They are invoked or called by any the PL/SQL block that appear within an application. Before the procedure or function is stored, the Oracle engine parses and compiles the procedure or function. The Oracle engine compiles the PL/SQL code block.

Note : If an error occurs during the compilation of the procedure or function, an invalid procedure or function is created. The Oracle engine displays a message after creation that the procedure or function was created with compilation errors. It does not display the errors. These errors can be viewed using the select statement:

```
SELECT *FROM user_errors;
or
show errors;
```

8.24 ADVANTAGES OF SUB-PROGRAM

- **Extensibility:** Allows creation of new program modules without affecting existing program modules.
- **Modularity:** Allows breaking a program down into manageable, well-defined logic modules. Each unit provides specific services in a program. This supports top-down design and the stepwise refinement approach to problem solving.
- **Reusability:** Allows creation of subprograms that can be used by many applications.
- **Maintainability:** modularity and reusability lead to easier maintenance and enhancement.
- **Abstraction:** Subprograms provides abstraction, because during use of subprograms, we must know what they do, not how they work. Therefore, we can design applications from the top down without worrying about implementation details.
- **Dummy Subprograms (Stubs):** It allows deferring the definition of procedures and functions until we test and debug the main program

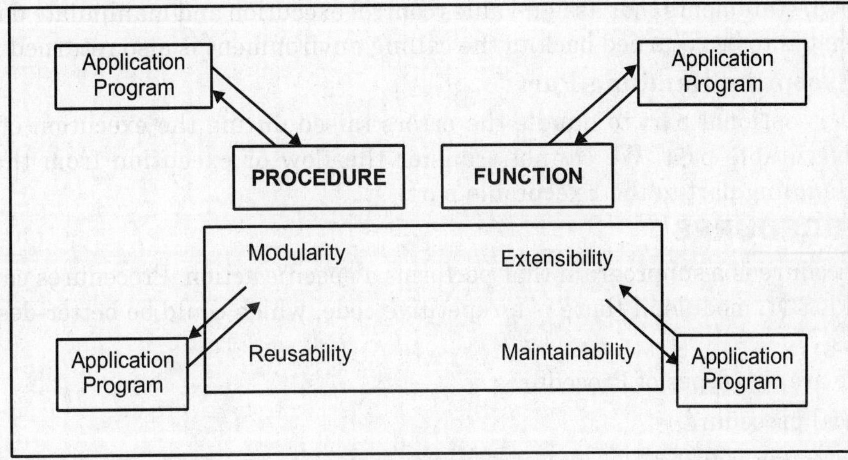

Figure 8.24

8.25 DIFFERENCE BETWEEN PROCEDURE AND FUNCTION

The comparison between procedure and function is indicated in the following table:

Procedure	Function
1. A procedure is a subprogram that can accept parameters, perform an action and return parameters.	1. A function is a subprogram that can accept parameters, compute a value and return that value to caller.
2. A procedure may not return no value.	2. A function must return only one value
3. A procedure cannot return a value as direct output.	3. A function can return a value as direct output of the function call.
4. Generally, we use a procedure to perform an action.	4. Generally, we use a function to compute a value.

Procedures and functions both have a declarative part, an executable part and an exception-handling part.

8.26 PARTS OF FUNCTIONS AND PROCEDURES

Procedure and Functions are made up of:

- A declarative parts
- An executable part, and
- An optional exception-handing part

- **Declarative Part**

  The declarative part is used to declare constants, variables, exceptions and subprograms. These objects are local to the procedure or function. The objects become invalid once the user exits from the procedure or the function.

- **Executable Part**

  It is a compulsory part, which is used to perform actions. Variables declared are put to use in this block. The executable part is a PL/SQL block consisting of SQL and PL/SQL statements that assign values control execution and manipulate data. The data that is to be returned back to the calling environment is also returned from here.

- **Exception Handling Part**

  It is optional part to handle the errors raised during the execution of code in the executable part. We cannot transfer the flow or execution from the Exception Handling part to the Executable part.

8.27 PROCEDURES

A procedure is a subprogram that performs a specific action. Procedures can be created within a PL/SQL module, if there is a repetitive code, which could be better-designed using procedures.

There are two types of Procedures:

- Local procedure
- Stored procedure

- **Stored Procedure**

  To create procedures and store them permanently in an Oracle database, we use the CREATE PROCEDURE statement, which we can execute interactively from SQL*Plus.

  Syntax:

```
CREATE OR REPLACE PROCEDURE procedurename
        (argument {IN, OUT, IN OUT} datatype,.....) {IS | AS}
        [local declarations] ;
BEGIN
        PL/SQL subprogram body;
        [EXCEPTION
        Exception PL/SQL block;]
END;
```

Argument Modes

Argument modes are used to define the behavior of formal parameters. There are three argument modes IN, OUT and IN OUT to be used with any subprograms.

Comparison of different arguments:

IN	OUT	IN OUT
1. It is the default.	1. It must be specified.	1. It must be specified.
2. It passes values to a subprogram.	2. It returns values to the caller.	2. It passes initial values to a subprogram and returns updated values to the caller.
3. It is a formal parameter acts like a constant.	3. It is a formal parameter acts like an uninitialized variable.	3. It is a formal parameter acts like an initialized variable.
4. It is a formal parameter cannot be assigned a value.	4. It is a formal parameter cannot be used in an expression and must be assigned a value.	4. It is a formal parameter should be assigned a value.
5. It can be a constant, variable or expression.	5. It must be a variable.	5. It must be a variable.

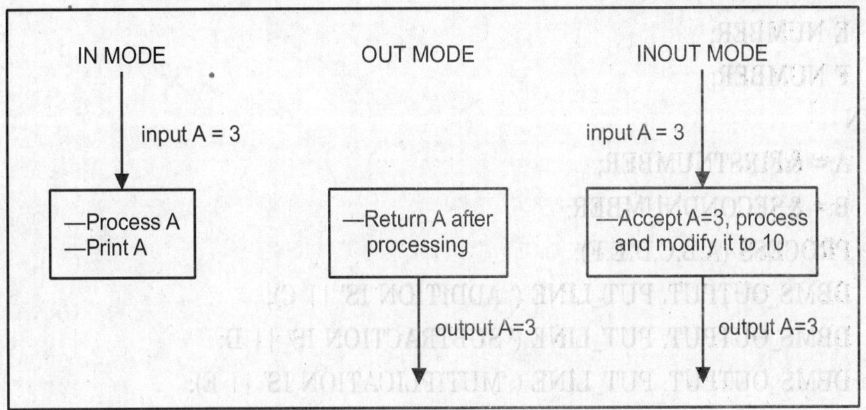

Figure 8.27 To show use of Arguments

Calling a Procedure

A stored procedure is called as a PL/SQL statement. A stored procedure can be called from any PL/SQL program by giving their names followed by parameters as shown in next example.

Example:

A Stored procedure that accepts two numbers and return addition, subtraction, multiplication and division of two numbers or in other words a stored procedure to return multiple values through arguments.

Solution:

```
CREATE OR REPLACE PROCEDURE PROCESS( A IN NUMBER, B IN NUMBER, C
OUT NUMBER, D OUT NUMBER, E OUT NUMBER, F OUT NUMBER ) IS
BEGIN
    C:=A+B;
    D:=A-B;
    E:=A*B;
    F:= A/B;
END;
```

Example:

A PL/SQL code to call the procedure PROCESS created in example

Solution:

```
DECLARE
    A NUMBER;
    B NUMBER;
    C NUMBER;
    D NUMBER;
    E NUMBER;
    F NUMBER;
BEGIN
    A:= &FIRSTNUMBER;
    B:= &SECONDNUMBER;
    PROCESS (A,B,C,D,E,F);
    DBMS_OUTPUT. PUT_LINE (' ADDITION IS' || C);
    DBMS_OUTPUT. PUT_LINE (' SUBTRACTION IS' || D;
    DBMS_OUTPUT. PUT_LINE ( 'MUTIPLICATION IS' || E);
    DBMS_OUTPUT. PUT_LINE ( 'DIVISION IS' || F) ;
END;
```

8.28 ACTUAL VERSUS FORMAL PARAMETERS

Subprograms pass information using parameters. There are two types of parameters.

- Formal Parameters
- Actual Parameters

Formal Parameters are declared in the parameter list of procedure or function definition.

For example, the following procedure declares two formal parameters named emp_id and increase:

```
PROCEDURE raise_salary (emp_id NUMBER, increase NUMBER) IS
```

Actual Parameters are referenced in a procedure or function call.

For example, the following procedure call lists two actual parameters named emp_num and amount:

```
raise_salary (emp_num, amount);
```

8.29 FUNCTIONS

A function is a subprogram that computes a value. Functions and procedures are structured alike, except that functions have a RETURN clause.

There are two types of functions:

- **Local function**
- **Stored function**

Syntax for Stored Function

```
CREATE OR REPLACE FUNCTION function_name
    (argument IN DATATYPE, ... )
    RETURN datatype {IS | AS}
    [local declarations]
BEGIN
    PL/SQL subprogram body;
    [EXCEPTION
    exception PL/SQL block;]
END;
```

RETURN Statement

The RETURN statement immediately completes the execution of a subprogram and returns control to the caller. Execution then resumes with the statement following the subprogram call. (Do not confuse the RETURN statement with the RETURN clause, which specifies the datatype of the result value in a function specification.)

A subprogram can contain several RETURN statements. Executing any of them completes the subprogram immediately. In procedures, a RETURN statement cannot contain an expression. The statement simply returns control to the caller before the normal end of the procedure is reached. However, in functions, a RETURN statement must contain an expression, which is evaluated when the RETURN statement is executed. The resulting value is assigned to the function identifier, which acts like a variable of the type specified in the RETURN clause. A function must contain at least one RETURN statement. Otherwise, PL/SQL raises the predefined exception PROGRAM_ERROR at run time.

Example:

Create a Stored function that accepts two numbers and return addition of passed values.

Solution:

```
CREATE OR REPLACE FUNCTION ADDN( A IN NUMBER, B IN NUMBER)
    RETURN NUMBER IS
    C NUMBER;
BEGIN
    C:=A+B;
    RETURN (C);
END;
```

Note: The information about all the stored procedure and functions can be obtained by using the USER_OBJECTS internal table, which has the following structure:

Name	**Null**	**Type**
OBJECT_NAME		VARCHAR2(128)
SUBJECT_NAME		VARCHAR2(30)
OBJECT_ID		NUMBER
DATA_OBJECT_I0		NUMBER
OBJECT_TYPE		VARCHAR2(19)
CREATED		DATE
LAST _DOL_TIME		DATE
TIMESTAMP		VARCHAR2(19)
STATUS		VARCHAR2(7)
TEMPORARY		VARCHAR2(1)
GENERATED		VARCHAR2(1)
SECONDARY		VARCHAR2(1)

In order to see the details of all the stored functions we can issue the following query on USER_OBJECTS table:

```
SQL>SELECT OBJECT_NAME, OBJECT_TYPE, STATUS FROM USER_OBJECTS WHERE
OBJECT_TYPE = 'PROCEDURE';
```

The output is:

OBJECT_NAME	**OBJECT_TYPE**	**STATUS**
CHECK_UPDATE	PROCEDURE	VALID

In order to see the source code of the stored subprogram we can use USER_SOURCE, which contain the following information:

Name	Null?	Type
NAME	NOT NULL	VARCHAR2(30)
TYPE		VARCHAR2(12)
LINE	NOT NULL	NUMBER
TEXT		VARCHAR2(4000)

8.30 PACKAGE

Packages are groups of procedures, functions, variables, constants, cursors, exceptions and SQL statements grouped together into a single unit. The tool used to create a package is SQL *Plus. A package once written and debugged is compiled and stored in Oracle's system tables held in an Oracle Database. All users who have executed permissions on the Oracle Database can use the package. Unlike the stored programs the package itself cannot be called.

Components of an Oracle Package

A package has usually two components:

- Package specification
- Package body

- **Package Specifications**

  A package's specification declares the memory variables, constants, exceptions, cursors and subprograms that are available for use.

  Syntax:

  ```
  CREATE OR REPLACE PACKAGE package_name AS
  FUNCTION function_name (list of arguments) RETURN data type;
  PROCEDURE procedure_name (list of arguments) ;
  End package_name;
  ```

- **Package Body**

  The body of a package contains the definition of public objects that are declared in the specification. It implements the specifications. Unlike package specification, the package body can contain subprogram bodies.

  Syntax:

  ```
  CREATE OR REPLACE PACKAGE BODY package_name AS
          FUNCTION function_name (list of arguments) RETURN data type
          {IS | AS}
          [local declaration of function]
  ```

```
BEGIN
-code of function
[EXCEPTION
-exception handler of function]
END function_name;
PROCEDURE procedure_name (list of arguments) {IS | AS}
[local declaration of procedure]
BEGIN
-code of procedure
[EXCEPTION
-exception handler of procedure]
END procedure_name;
[ .... similarly other functions and procedures]
END package_name;
```

Steps to Create Packages

The first step to create a package is to create its specification. The specification declares the objects that are contained in the body of the package. A package is created using Oracle's SQL *Plus interactive tool. After the specification is created, the body of the package to be created. The body of the package is a collection of detailed definitions of the objects that were declared in the specification.

Referencing Package Contents

The package contents can be referenced from database triggers, stored subprograms or PL/SQL blocks. To reference a package's subprogram and objects, we must use dot notation.

Syntax for Dot Notation

```
Package_name.type_name
Package_name.object_name
Package_name. subprogram_name
```

In this syntax

Package_name is the name of the declared package.

Type_name is the name of the type that is user defined, such as record.

Object_name is the name of the constant or variable that is declared by the user.

Sub_program is the name of the procedure or function contained in the package body.

For example to reference a procedure addn in package bank we can use: Bank.addn(list_of_arguments):

8.31 ADVANTAGES OF PACKGES

Packages offer the following advantages:

- **Modularity**
  Packages encapsulate related types, objects, procedures, functions, variables, constants, cursors and exceptions together in a named PL/SQL module.
- **Easier Application Design**
  A package specification can be coded and complied without its body which increases the designer productivity.
- **Information Hiding**
  By hiding implementation details in package body, better security is provided to the system. It also allows granting of privileges efficiently.
- **Added Functionality**
  A package's public variables and cursors persist for the duration of the session. Therefore all cursors and procedures that execute in this environment can share them.
- **Better Performance**
  Packages improve performance by loading multiple objects into memory at once. Therefore, subsequent calls to related subprograms in the package require no Input/ Output.

Example

Create a package specification for the Insert Oper, Retrieve, Update_Oper and Delete_Oper whose description is given below:

- **Insert_Oper:** Procedure to insert record in emp table, values are passed to procedure as input arguments.
- **Retrieve**: Procedure to retrieve record on the basis of empno. Here empno is passed to procedure as input argument and returns name and salary as output argument.
- **Update_Oper:** Function to return number of record updated, we supply value of deptno and increased amount and it will add the amount to salary for all the employees in that department.
- **Delete_Oper:** Function to delete the record of employee on the basis of empno passed to the function and it return 'Y' and 'N' according the result.

Solution:

```
CREATE OR REPLACE PACKAGE OPERATION AS
PROCEDURE INSERT_OPER(ENO NUMBER, NAME VARCHAR, JOB
VARCHAR,SAL
NUMBER, DNO NUMBER) ;
PROCEDURE RETRIEVE (ENO IN NUMBER, NAME OUT VARCHAR, SAL OUT
NUMBER) ;
FUNCTION UPDATE_OPER(DNO NUMBER,AMOUNT NUMBER) RETURN
NUMBER;
FUNCTION DELETE_OPER(ENO NUMBER) RETURN CHAR;
END;
```

Example:

Create a package body for the Insert_Oper, Retrieve, Update_Oper and Delete_Oper as described above.

Solution:

```
CREATE OR REPLACE PACKAGE BODY OPERATION IS
        PROCEDURE INSERT_OPER(ENO NUMBER, NAME VARCHAR, JOB
                VARCHAR,SAL
        NUMBER, DNO NUMBER) AS
        BEGIN
        INSERT INTO EMP (EMPNO, ENAME,JOB,SAL,DEPTNO) VALUES (ENO,
        NAME, JOB,SAL, DNO);
END INSERT_OPER;
PROCEDURE RETRIEVE (ENO IN NUMBER, NAME OUT VARCHAR, SAL OUT
NUMBER) IS
BEGIN
        SELECT ENAME, SAL INTO NAME, SAL FROM EMP WHERE EMPNO=ENO;
        END RETRIEVE;
FUNCTION UPDATE_OPER(DNO NUMBER, AMOUNT NUMBER)
RETURN NUMBER IS
        N NUMBER;
BEGIN
        UPDATE EMP SET SAL=SAL+AMOUNT WHERE DEPTNO=DNO;
        N:=SQL%ROWCOUNT;
        RETURN(N) ;
END UPDATE_OPER;
FUNCTION DELETE_OPER(ENO NUMBER) RETURN CHAR IS
BEGIN
        DELETE EMP WHERE EMPNO=ENO;
        IF SQL%FOUND THEN
        RETURN ( 'Y');
        ELSE
                RETURN ('N' ) ;
                END IF;
                END DELETE_OPER;
                END OPERATION;
```

Example :

A PL/SQL code to call Insert_Oper procedure to insert a record in emp table.

Solution :

```
DECLARE
        ENO NUMBER;
        NAME VARCHAR(20) ;
        JOB VARCHAR (20) ;
        SAL NUMBER;
        DNO NUMBER;
BEGIN
        ENO:=&EMPLOYEE_NUMBER;
        NAME:=&EMPLOYEE_NAME;
        JOB:=&EMPLOYEE_JOB;
        SAL:=&EMPLOYEE_SALARY;
        DNO:=&EMPLOYEE_DEPTNO;
        OPERATION.INSERT_OPER(ENO, NAME, JOB, SAL, DNO);
END;
```

Example :

A PL/SQL code to call retrieve procedure to retrieve a record in emp table.

Solution :

```
DECLARE
        EMPNO NUMBER;
        NAME VARCHAR(20);
        SAL NUMBER;
BEGIN
        EMPNO:=&EMPNO_TO_SEARCH;
        OPERATION. RETRIEVE (ENO, NAME, SAL);
        DBMS_OUTPUT.PUT_LINE(ENO || NAME || SAL);
END;
```

Example:

A PL/SQL code to call update_oper function to get number of record updated.

Solution:

```
DECLARE
        DEPTNO NUMBER;
        AMOUNT NUMBER;
        REC_NO NUMBER;
BEGIN
        DEPTNO:=&DEPTNO_TO_UPDATE;
        AMOUNT:=&AMOUNT_TO_INCREASE;
        REC_NO:=OPERATION.UPDATE_OPER(DEPTNO,AMOUNT)
        DBMS_OUTPUT. PUT_LINE (REC_NO || 'RECORD UPDATED');
END;
```

Example:

A PL/SQL code to call delete_oper function to get 'Y' or 'N' according to success of dclctc operation.

Solution :

```
DECLARE
        EMPNO_TO_DELETE NUMBER;
        RESULT CHAR;
BEGIN
        EMPNO_TO_DELETE:=&EMPNO_TO_DELETE;
        RESULT: =OPERATION. DELETE_OPER (EMPNO_TO_DELETE);
        DBMS_OUTPUT.PUT_LINE('RECORD DELETED:' | | RESULT);
END;
```

Alterations to an Existing Package

To recompile a package, use the ALTER PACKAGE command with the compile keyword. It eliminates the need for any implicit run time recompilation and prevents any associated runtime compilation errors and performance overhead. It is Common to explicitly compile a package after modifications to the package. Recompiling a package recompiles all objects defined within the package. Recompiling does not change the definition of the package or any of its objects.

Syntax

ALTER PACKAGE package_name COMPILE PACKAGE;

To recompile just the body of a package use the following syntax:

Syntax:

ALTER PACKAGE package_name COMPILE BODY;

8.32 DROPPING A PROCEDURE/ FUNCTION/PACKAGE

To drop a procedure, DROP PROCEDURE command is used. For this user must either own the procedure or have DROP ANY PROCEDURE system privilege?

Syntax:

DROP PROCEDURE procedure_name;

Example:

DROP PROCEDURE process;

To drop a function, DROP FUNCTION command is used. For this user must either own the function or have DROP ANY FUNCTION system privilege.

Syntax:

DROP FUNCTION function_name;

Example:

DROP FUNCTION addn;

To drop a package, DROP PACKAGE command is used. For this user must either own the package or have DROP ANY PACKAGE system privilege.

Syntax:

DROP PACKAGE package_name;

Example:

DROP PACKAGE operation;

8.33 INTRODUCTION TO TRIGGERS

A database trigger is a stored procedure that is fired when an INSERT, UPDATE, or DELETE statements is issued against the associate table. The name trigger is appropriate, as these are triggered (fired) whenever the above-mentioned commands are executed. A trigger defines an action the database should take when some database related event occurs. A trigger can include SQL and PL/SQL statements to execute it as a unit and it can invoke other stored procedures. Triggers may use to provide referential integrity, to enforce complex business rules, or to audit changes to data.

The code within a trigger, called the trigger body is made up of PL/SQL blocks.

A trigger is automatically executed without any action required by the user. A stored procedure on other hand needs to be explicitly invoked. This is the main difference between a trigger and a stored procedure.

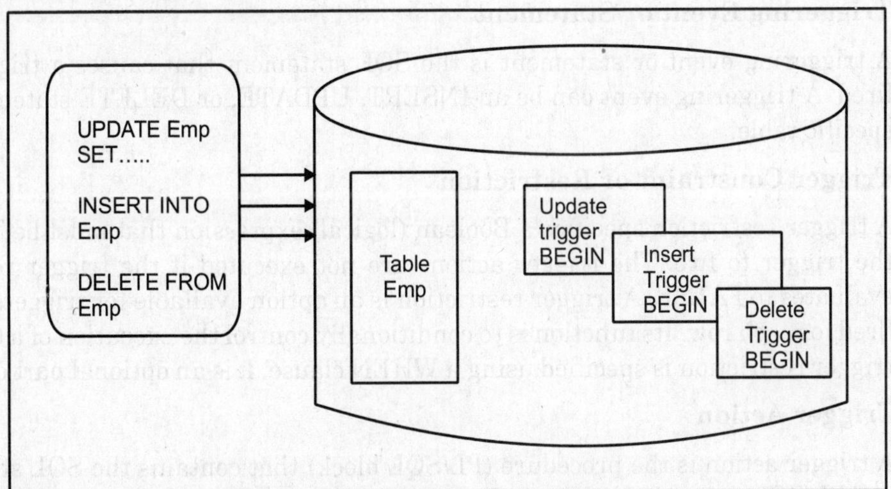

Figure 8.33 TO Show working of Trigger

8.34 USE OF DATABASE TRIGGERS

Database triggers can be used for the following purposes:

- To derive column values automatically.
- To enforce complex integrity constraints.

- To enforce complex business rules.
- To customize complex security authorizations.
- To maintain replicate tables.
- To audit data modifications.

8.35 DATABASE TRIGGER V/S PROCEDURE

Here is the comparison between database Triggers and Procedures:

Trigger	Procedure
Triggers do not accept parameters	Procedures can accept parameters
A trigger is automatically executed without any action required by the user.	A stored procedure on other hand needs to be explicitly invoked.

8.36 PARTS OF A TRIGGER

A database trigger has three parts:

- Triggering event or Statement.
- Trigger constraint (Optional)
- Trigger action

- **Triggering Event or Statement**

  A triggering event or statement is the SQL statement that causes a trigger to be fired. A triggering event can be an INSERT, UPDATE, or DELETE statement for a specific table.

- **Trigger Constraint or Restriction**

  A trigger restriction specifies a Boolean (logical) expression that must be TRUE for the trigger to fire. The trigger actions are not executed if the trigger restriction evaluates to FALSE. A trigger restriction is an option available for triggers that are fired for each row. Its function is to conditionally control the execution of a trigger. A trigger restriction is specified using a WHEN clause. It is an optional part of trigger.

- **Trigger Action**

  A trigger action is the procedure (PL/SQL block) that contains the SQL statements and PL/SQL code to be executed when a triggering statement is issued and the trigger restriction evaluates to TRUE.

8.37 TYPES OF TRIGGERS

A trigger's type is defined by the type of triggering transaction and by the level at which the trigger is executed. Oracle has the following types of triggers depending on the different applications:

- Row Level Triggers
- Statement Level Triggers
- Before Triggers
- After Triggers

Here is a brief description about above triggers:

- **Row Level Triggers**

  Row level triggers execute once for each row in a transaction. The commands of row level triggers are executed on all rows that are affected by the command that enables the trigger. For example, if an UPDATE statement updates multiple rows of a table, a row trigger is fired once for each row affected by the UPDATE statement. If the triggering statement affects no rows, the trigger is not executed at all. Row level triggers are created using the FOR EACH ROW clause in the CREATE TRIGGER command.

- **Application**

  Consider a case where our requirement is to prevent updation of empno 100 record. Then whenever UPDATE statement update records, there must be PL/SQL block that will be fired automatically by UPDATE statement to check that it must not be 100, so we have to use Row level Triggers for that type of applications.

- **Statement Level Triggers**

  Statement level triggers are triggered only once for each transaction. For example when an UPDATE command update 15 rows, the commands contained in the trigger are executed only once, and not with every processed row. Statement level trigger are the default types of trigger created via the CREATE TRIGGER command.

- **Application**

  Consider a case where our requirement is to prevent the DELETE operation during Sunday. For this whenever DELETE statement deletes records, there must be PLI SQL block that will be fired only once by DELETE statement to check that day must not be Sunday by referencing system date, so we have to use Statement level Trigger which fires only once for above application.

- **Before and After Trigger**

  Since triggers are executed by events, they may be set to occur immediately before or after those events. When a trigger is defined, you can specify whether the trigger must occur before or after the triggering event i.e. INSERT, UPDATE, or DELETE commands.

BEFORE trigger execute the trigger action before the triggering statement. These types of triggers are commonly used in the following situation:

- BEFORE triggers are used when the trigger action should determine whether or not the triggering statement should be allowed to complete. By using a BEFORE trigger, you can eliminate unnecessary processing of the triggering statement. For example: To prevent deletion on Sunday, for this we have to use statement level before trigger on DELETE statement.

- BEFORE triggers are used to derive specific column values before completing Database a triggering INSERT or UPDATE statement.

AFTER trigger executes the trigger action after the triggering statement is executed. AFTER triggers are used when you want the triggering statement to complete before executing the trigger action. For example: To perform cascade delete operation, it means that user delete the record from one table and the corresponding records in other tables are deleted automatically by a trigger which fired after the execution of DELETE statement issued by the user.

When combining the different types of triggering actions, there are mainly 12 possible valid trigger types available to us. The possible configurations are:

- BEFORE INSERT row
- BEFORE INSERT statement
- AFTER INSERT row
- AFTER INSERT statement
- BEFORE UPDATE row
- BEFORE UPDATE statement
- AFTER UPDATE row
- AFTER UPDATE statement
- BEFORE DELETE row
- BEFORE DELETE statement
- AFTER DELETE row
- AFTER DELETE statement

Here is the list of the triggering actions with their explanations and relative restrictions.

Name	Statement Level	Row Level
BEFORE option	Oracle fires the trigger only once, before executing the triggering statement	Oracle fires the trigger before modifying each row affected by the triggering statement
AFTER option	Oracle fires the trigger only once, after executing the triggering statement	Oracle fires the trigger after modifying each row affected by the triggering statement

8.38 SYNTAX FOR CREATING A TRIGGER

```
CREATE [OR REPLACE] TRIGGER trigger_name        ⎤
{BEFORE | AFTER}                                ⎥
{| DELETE | [OR] INSERT |                       ⎥ Triggering event
[OR] UPDATE [OF column_name,.......]            ⎥
ON table_name                                   ⎦

[REFERENCING {OLD AS old, NEW AS new}]          ⎤
[FOR EACH ROW [WHEN condition]                  ⎥ Triggering restriction
                                                ⎦
DECLARE                                         ⎤
Variable declaration;                           ⎥
Constant declaration;                           ⎥
BEGIN                                           ⎥ Triggering Action
        PL/SQL subprogram body;                 ⎥
[EXCEPTION                                      ⎥
        Exception PL/SQL blocks;]               ⎦
END;
```

Here

REFERENCING : Specified correlation names. The user could use the Correlation names in the PL/SQL block and WHEN clause of a row triggers to refer specifically to old and new values of the current now. The default correlation names are OLD and NEW. If the row is associated with a table named OLD or NEW, this clause can be used to specify different names to avoid confusion between the table name and the correlation name.

WHEN : Specifies the trigger restriction. This condition has to be satisfied to fire the trigger. This condition can be specified for the ROW TRIGGER.

Note : If an error occurs during the compilation of trigger, an invalid trigger is created. The Oracle engine displays a message after creation that the trigger was created with compilation errors. It does not display the errors. These errors can be viewed using the following commands:

```
SELECT *FROM user_errors;
Or
Show errors;
```

8.39 APPLICATIONS USING DATABASE TRIGGERS

Here are some examples to design application with the use of triggers:

Example:

To create a trigger for the emp table, which makes the entry in ENAME column in uppercase

Solution:

```
CREATE OR REPLECE TRIGGER upper_trigger
BEFORE INSERT OR UPDATE OF ename ON emp
FOR EACH ROW
BEGIN
:new.ename : = UPER (:new.ename);
END;
```

Description : The above example also illustrates the use of the new keyword, which refers to the new **value of the column and the old keyword, which refers to the old values of the column. When** referencing the new and old keywords in the PL/SQL blocks, they are preceded by column(:)

8.40 ERROR HANDLING IN TRIGGERS

The oracle engine provides a procedure named raise_application_error that allows programmers to issue user_defined error messages.

Syntax :

RAISE_APPLICATION_ERROR (error_number, message);

Here

Error_number	It is a negativè integer in the range-20000 to 20999
Message	It is a character string up to 2048 bytes in length

This procedure terminates procedure execution, rolls back any effects of the procedure, and returns a user-specified error number and message. Following example makes use of the RAISE_APPLICATION_ERROR

Example:

To create a trigger so that no operation can be performed on emp table on Sunday.

Solution:

```
CREATE OR REPLACE TRIGGER EMP_SUNDAY
BEFORE INSERT OR UPDATE OR DELETE ON EMP
BEGIN
IF RTRIM (UPPER (TO_CHAR (SYSDATE, 'DAY')) ) = 'SUNDAY' THEN
RAISE_AFPLICATION_ERROR(-20022, 'NO OPERATION CAN BE
PERFORMED ON SUNDAY');
END IF;
END;
```

Dropping Triggers

Triggers may be dropped via the drop trigger command. In order to drop a trigger, you must either own the trigger or have the DROP ANY TRIGGER system privilege.

Syntax:

```
DROP TRIGGER trigger_name;
```

Example:

```
DROP  TRIGGER emp_update;
```

SUMMARY

SQL can be implemented in two ways. It can be used interactively to define database objects and query and update operations. It can also embedded in a programming language (also called the host language). So we can say that SQL is a dual mode language- it is an interactive language used for ad hoc queries and updates and a programmatic database language used by application programs for database access.

Commercial SQL implementations take one of the two basic techniques for including SQL in a programming language-embedded SQL and application program interface. In the embedded SQL approach, the SQL statements are embedded directly into the program's source code, along with other programming language statements. Special delimiters specify the beginning and end of the SQL statements in the program. The embedded SQL statements are thus used in the application to perform the data access and manipulation tasks. A special SQL precompiler accepts the combined source code-code containing the programming language statements and the embedded SQL statements-and compiles it to convert it into the executable form. This compilation process is slightly different from the compilation of a program, which does not have embedded SQL statements. In the application program interface approach, the program communicates with the RDBMS using a set of functions called the Application Program Interface (API). The program passes the SQL statements to the RDBMS using API calls and uses API calls to retrieve the results. In this method, the precompiled is not required.

We saw how the relational database management system process and SQL statements. We saw different steps in query processing. We saw the advantages of embedding SQL in application programs. But there are some applications-usually general purpose applications, such as ad hoc query utilities or database design tools-for which it is simply not possible to provide all the information needed to do the compilation prior to run time. So the application developers need to find an alternative. They must generate the necessary SQL statements dynamically (i.e., during run time), compile such statements dynamically by invoking the SQL compiler at run time on an as and when needed basis and execute the newly compiled statement to get the results. These types of SQLs are called dynamic SQLs. We saw how the dynamic SQLs work and the how to write dynamic SQL programs

EXERCISES

1. What is the importance of error handling? How are errors handled in PL/SQL?
2. What are advantages of Exceptions?
3. What are different types of Exceptions? Explain each with examples.
4. What are implicitly raised exceptions? Name some predefined exceptions and their importance?
5. How can we trap the Non-Predefined Oracle Server errors? Explain with suitable examples.
6. How can we trap the user defined Exceptions?
7. What are Error Trapping Functions? Explain its importance.
8. How can we handle the exceptions raised in declarations?
9. How can we handle the exceptions raised in handlers?
10. What is the importance of Cursor? What are its types?
11. What is the Cursor attributes? Explain the importance of each.
12. How can we handle the implicit cursors?
13. What are the steps to be followed to handle the user defined cursors?
14. What is the importance of Cursor or Loop? How it simplifies the operations? Explain with suitable examples.
15. How can we pass the parameters to a cursor? Explain with examples.
16. What is meant by Subprogram? What are its types?
17. What is the difference between local and stored subprograms?
18. What are the advantages of Subprograms?
19. What is the difference between function and procedure?.
20. What is syntax to create local procedure? Explain with example.
21. What is syntax to create stored procedure? Explain with example.
22. How we can a procedure? Explain with examples.
23. What are different modes of arguments? Compare each mode.
24. What is difference between actual and formal arguments?
25. What is the importance of functions? What is the syntax to create local and stored functions?
26. What is the importance of Return statement?
27. What does Package Object mean? What is its importance?

28. What are the advantages of Packages?
29. What does trigger mean? What are its uses and explain its working?
30. Compare Database trigger and procedure.
31. What are the parts of Trigger? Explain the importance of each part.
32. What are the types of Triggers? Explain each type.
33. What are applications where we can use row level triggers?
34. What are applications where we can use statement level triggers?
35. What are applications where we can use before type triggers?
36. What are applications where we can use after type triggers?
37. What is Instead of trigger?
38. What is the syntax to create a Trigger?
39. How can we issue user defined error message during firing of a trigger?
40. How can we enable/disable a trigger?
41. How can we alter the existing trigger?
42. How can we drop a trigger?

CHAPTER 9

RECORD STORAGE AND FILE STRUCTURE

9.1 INTRODUCTION

The computer's ability to store and retrieve data is at the core of almost every business application- whether in inventory management. Word processing or management decision making. The efficiency of computer systems in information processing greatly depends on how it stores data and how fast it can retrieve the data. For example, if data are stored sequentially on a magnetic tape, they are ideal for using in batch processing applications, but they cannot be used in an on-line application or in a spreadsheet application for decision-making. Because data storage and retrieval are closely related to what can done with data, it is important to know how data are stored and retrieved.

The collection of data that makes up a computerized database must be stored physically on some computer storage medium. The DBMS software can then retrieve, update, and process this data as needed. Computer storage media form a storage hierarchy that includes two main categories:

Primary storage: This category includes storage media that can be operated on directly by the computer central processing unit (CPU), such as the computer main memory and smaller but faster cache memories. Primary storage usually provides fast access to data but is of limited storage capacity.

Secondary storage: This category includes magnetic disks, optical disks, and tapes. These devices usually have a larger capacity, cost less, and provide slower access to data than do primary storage devices. Data in secondary storage cannot be processed directly by the CPU; it must first be copied into primary storage.

9.2 MEMORY HIERARCHIES AND STORAGE DEVICES

In a modern computer system data resides and is transported throughout a hierarchy of storage media. The highest-speed memory is the most expensive and is therefore available with the least capacity. The lowest-speed memory is tape storage, which is essentially available in indefinite storage capacity.

At the primary storage level, the memory hierarchy includes at the most expensive end cache memory, which is a static RAM (Random Access Memory). Cache memory is typically used by the CPU to speed up execution of programs. The next level of primary storage is DRAM (Dynamic RAM), which provides the main work area for the CPU for keeping programs and data and is popularly called main memory. The advantage of DRAM is its low cost, which continues to decrease; the drawback is its volatility and lower speed compared with static RAM. At the secondary storage level, the hierarchy includes magnetic disks, as well as mass storage in the form of CD-ROM (Compact Disk– Read-Only Memory) devices, and finally tapes at the least expensive end of the hierarchy. The storage capacity is measured in kilobytes (KB or 1000 bytes), megabytes (MB or 1 million bytes), gigabytes (GB or 1 billion bytes), and even terabytes (1000 GB).

Several types of data storage exits in most computer systems. These storage media are classified by the speed with which data can be accessed, by the cost per unit of data to buy the medium, and by the medium's reliability. Among the media typically available are these:

- **Cache:** The cache is the fastest and most costly form of storage. Cache memory is small; its use is managed by the computer system hardware. We shall not be concerned about managing cache storage in the database system.
- **Main memory:** The storage medium used for data that are available to be operated on is main memory. The general purpose machine instructions operate on main memory. Although main memory may contain many megabytes of data or even gigabytes of data in large server systems, it is generally too small for storing the entire database. The contents of main memory are usually lost if a power failure or system crash occurs.
- **Flash memory:** Also known as electrically erasable programmable read-only memory (EEPROM), flash memory differs from main memory in that data survive power failure. Reading data from flash memory takes less than 100 nanoseconds (a nanosecond is 1 ⁄ 1000 of a microsecond), which is roughly as fast as reading data from main memory. However, writing data to flash memory is more complicated — data can be written once, which takes about 4 to 10 microseconds, but cannot be overwritten directly. To overwrite memory that has been written already, we have to erase an entire bank of memory at once; it is then ready to be written again. A drawback of flash memory is that it can support only a limited number of erase cycles, ranging from 10,000 to 1 million. Flash memory has found popularity as a replacement for magnetic disks for storing small volumes of data (5 to 10 megabytes) in low-cost computer systems, such as computer systems that are embedded in other devices, in hand-held computers, and in other digital electronic devices such as digital cameras.
- **Magnetic disk storage:** The primary medium for the long-term on-line storage of data is the magnetic disk. Usually, the entire database is stored on magnetic disk. The system must move the data from disk to main memory so that they can be accessed. After the system has performed the designated operations, the data that have been modified must be written to disk. The size of magnetic disks currently ranges from a few gigabytes to 80 gigabytes. Both the lower and upper end of this range has been growing at about 50 percent per year, and we can expect much larger capacity disks every year. Disk storage survives power failures and system crashes. Disk Storage devices themselves may sometimes fail and thus destroy data, but such failures usually occurs much less frequently than do system crashes.

- **Optical storage:** The most popular forms of optical storage are the compact disk (CD), which can hold about 640 megabytes of data, and the digital video disk (DVD) which can hold 4.7 or 8.5 gigabytes of data per side of the disk (or up to 17 gigabytes on a two sided disk). Data are stored optically on a disk, and are read by a laser. The optical disks used in read-only compact disks (CD-ROM) or read-only digital video disk (DVD-ROM) cannot be written, but are supplied with data prerecorded.

  There are "record-once" versions of compact disk (called CD-R) and digital video disk (called DVD-R), which can be written only once; such disks are also called write-once, read-many (WORM) disks. There are also "multiple-write" versions of compact disk (called CD-RW) and digital video disk (DVD-RW and DVD-RAM), which can be written multiple times. Recordable compact disks are magnetic – optical storage devices that use optical means to read magnetically encoded data. Such disks are useful for archival storage of data as well as distribution of data. Jukebox systems contain a few drives and numerous disks that can be loaded into one of the drives automatically (by a robot arm) on demand.

- **Tape storage:** Tape storage is used primarily for backup and archival data. Although magnetic tape is much cheaper than disks, access to data is much slower, because the tape must be accessed sequentially from the beginning. For this reason, tape storage is referred to as sequential access storage. In contrast, disk storage is referred to as direct-access storage because it is possible to read data from any location on disk. Tapes have a high capacity (40 gigabyte to 300 gigabytes tapes are currently available), and can be removed from the tape drive, so they are well suited to cheap archival storage. Tape jukeboxes are used to hold exceptionally large collections of data, such as remote-sensing data from satellites, which could include as much as 12 terabytes (10^{12} bytes) in the near future

The various storage media can be organized in a hierarchy (Figure 9.2) according to their speed and their cost. The higher levels are expensive, but are fast. As we move down the hierarchy, the cost per bit decreases, whereas the access time increases. This trade-off is reasonable; if a given storage system were both faster and less expensive than another — other properties being the same — then there would be no reason to use the slower, more expensive memory. In fact, many early storage devices, including paper tape and core memories, are relegated to museums now that magnetic tape and semiconductor memory have become faster and cheaper. Magnetic tapes them- selves were used to store active data back when disks were expensive and had low storage capacity.

Today, almost all active data are stored on disks, except in rare cases where they are stored on tape or in optical jukeboxes. The fastest storage media-for example, cache and main memory-are referred to as primary storage. The media in the next level in the hierarchy-for example, magnetic disks-are referred to as secondary storage, or online storage. The media in the lowest level in the hierarchy-for example, magnetic tape and optical-disk jukeboxes are referred to as tertiary storage, or offline storage.

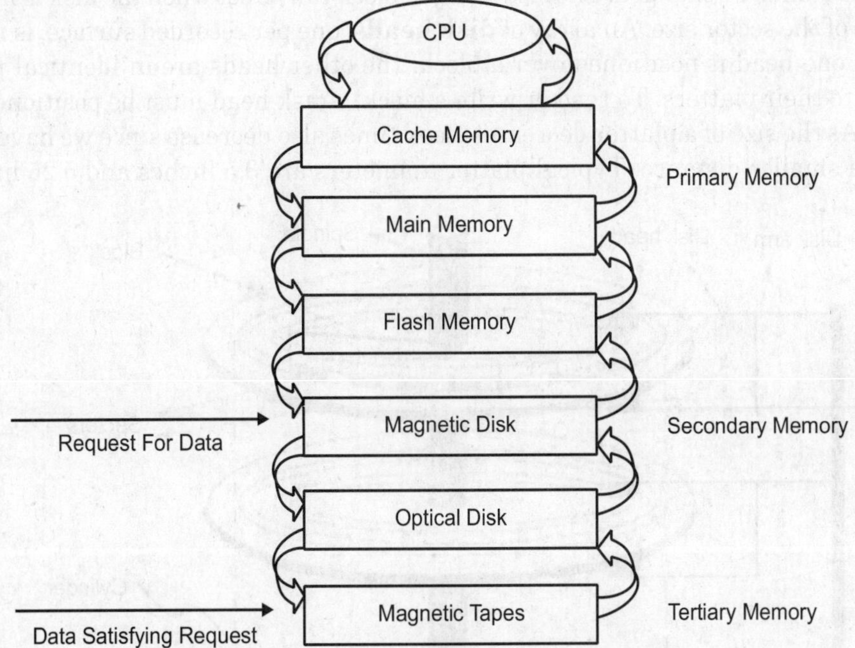

Figure 9.2 Memory Hierarchy

In addition to the speed and cost of the various storage systems, there is also the issue of storage volatility. Volatile storage loses its contents when the power to the device is removed. In the hierarchy shown in Figure 9.2, the storage systems from main memory up are volatile, whereas the storage systems below main memory are nonvolatile. In the absence of expensive battery and generator backup systems, data must be written to nonvolatile storage for safekeeping.

9.3 MAGNETIC DISK

Magnetic disks provide the bulk of secondary storage for modern computer systems. The storage capacity of a single disk ranges from 10 megabytes to 10 gigabytes. A typical large commercial database may require hundreds of disks.

Magnetic disks support direct access to a desired location and are widely used for database applications. A DBMS provides seamless access to data on disk; applications need not worry about whether data is in main memory or disk. To understand how disks work, consider Figure 9.3, which shows the structure of a disk in simplified form.

Data is stored on disk in units called **disk blocks**. A disk block is a contiguous sequence of bytes and is the unit in which data is written to a disk and read from a disk. Blocks are arranged in concentric rings called **tracks**, on one or more **platters**. Tracks can be recorded on one or both surfaces of a platter; we refer to platters as single-sided or double-sided accordingly. The set of all tracks with the same diameter is called a **cylinder**, because the space occupied by these tracks is shaped like a cylinder; a cylinder contains one track per platter surface. Each track is divided into arcs called **sectors**, whose size is a characteristic of the disk and cannot be changed. The size of a disk block can be set when the disk is initialized as a multiple of the sector size. An array of **disk heads**, one per recorded surface, is moved as a unit; when one head is positioned over a block, the other heads are in identical positions with respect to their platters. To read or write a block, a disk head must be positioned on top of the block. As the size of a platter decreases, seek times also decrease since we have to move a disk head a smaller distance. Typical platter diameters are 3.5 inches and 5.25 inches.

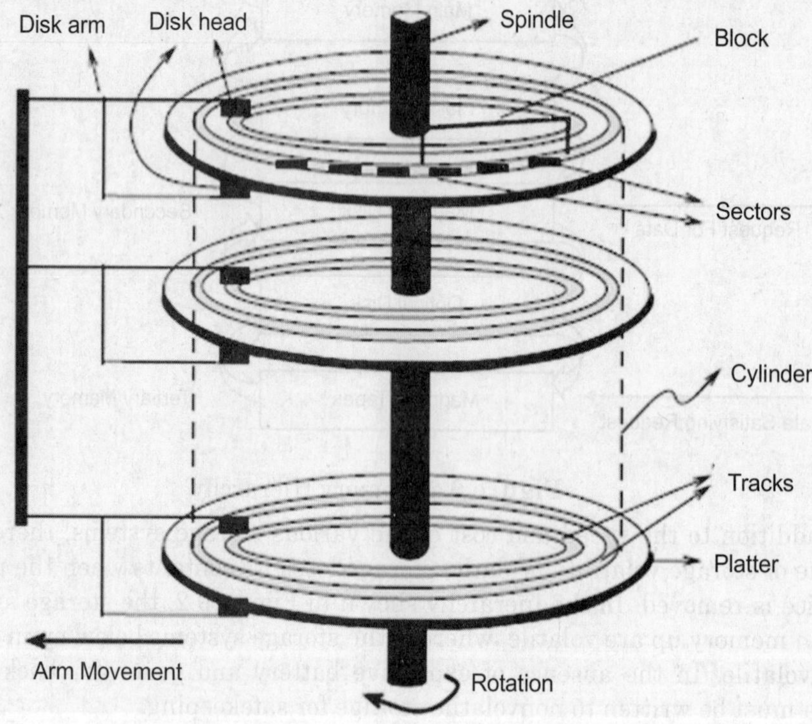

Figure 9.3 Moving head Disk Mechanism

Current systems typically allow at most one disk head to read or write at any one time. All the disk heads cannot read or write in parallel this technique would increase data transfer rates by a factor equal to the number of disk heads, and considerably speed up sequential scans. The reason they cannot is that it is very difficult to ensure that all the heads are perfectly aligned on the corresponding tracks. Current approaches are both expensive and more prone to faults as compared to disks with a single active head. In practice very few commercial products support this capability, and then only in a limited way; for example, two disk heads may be able to operate in parallel.

A **disk controller** interfaces a disk drive to the computer. It implements commands to read or write a sector by moving the arm assembly and transferring data to and from the disk surfaces. A **checksum** is computed for when data is written to a sector and stored with the sector. The checksum is computed again when the data on the sector is read back. If the sector is corrupted or the read is faulty for some reason, it is very unlikely that the checksum computed when the sector is read matches the checksum computed when the sector was written. The controller computes checksums and if it detects an error, it tries to read the sector again. (Of course, it signals a failure if the sector is corrupted and read fails repeatedly.)

While direct access to any desired location in main memory takes approximately the same time, determining the time to access a location on disk is more complicated. The time to access a disk block has several components. **Seek time** is the time taken to move the disk heads to the track on which a desired block is located. **Rotational delay** is the waiting time for the desired block to rotate under the disk head; it is the time required for half a rotation on average and is usually less than seek time. **Transfer time** is the time to actually read or write the data in the block once the head is positioned, that is, the time for the disk to rotate over the block.

9.3.1 Performance Implications of Disk Structure

1. Data must be in memory for the DBMS to operate on it.
2. The unit for data transfer between disk and main memory is a block; if a single item on a block is needed, the entire block is transferred. Reading or writing a disk block is called an I/O (for input/output) operation.
3. The time to read or write a block varies, depending on the location of the data:

   access time = seek time + rotational delay + transfer time

These observations imply that the time taken for database operations is affected significantly by how data is stored on disks. The time for moving blocks to or from disk usually dominates the time taken for database operations. To minimize this time, it is necessary to locate data records strategically on disk, because of the geometry and mechanics of disks. In essence, if two records are frequently used together, we should place them close together. The 'closest' that two records can be on a disk is to be on the same block. In decreasing order of closeness, they could be on the same track, the same cylinder, or an adjacent cylinder.

Two records on the same block are obviously as close together as possible, because they are read or written as part of the same block. As the platter spins, other blocks on the track being read or written rotate under the active head. In current disk designs, all the data on a track can be read or written in one revolution. After a track is read or written, another disk head becomes active, and another track in the same cylinder is read or written. This process continues until all tracks in the current cylinder are read or written, and then the arm assembly moves (in or out) to an adjacent cylinder. Thus, we have a natural notion of 'closeness' for blocks, which we can extend to a notion of next and previous blocks

9.4 RAID

The data storage requirements of some applications (in particular Web, database, and multimedia data applications) have been growing so fast that a large number of disks are needed to store data for such applications, even though disk drive capacities have been growing very fast.

Having a large number of disks in a system presents opportunities for improving the rate at which data can be read or written, if the disks are operated in parallel. Parallelism can also be used to perform several independent reads or writes in parallel. Furthermore, this setup offers the potential for improving the reliability of data storage, because redundant information can be stored on multiple disks. Thus, failure of one disk does not lead to loss of data.

A variety of disk-organization techniques, collectively called **redundant arrays of independent disks (RAID),** have been proposed to achieve improved performance and reliability issues. In the past, RAIDs composed to small cheap disks were viewed as a cost-effective alternative to large, expensive disks; today, large are used rarely, and RAIDs are used for their higher reliability and higher data transfer rate, rather than for economic reasons. Hence, the I in RAID now stand for **independent,** instead of **inexpensive.**

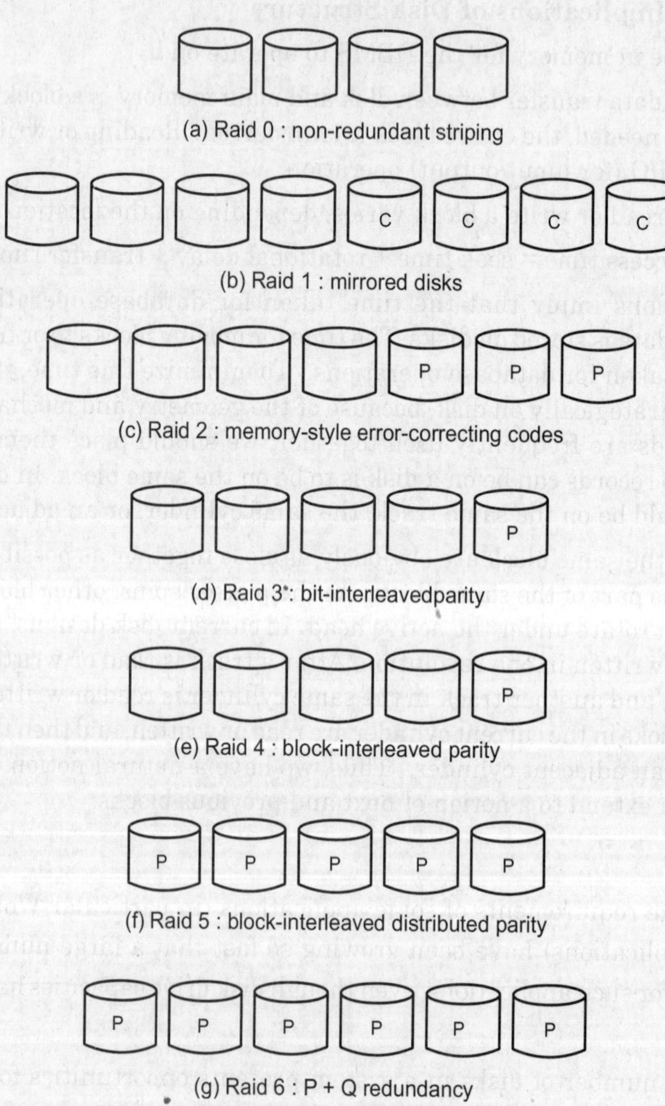

Figure 9.4 RAID levels

Disks are potential bottlenecks for system performance and storage system reliability. Even though disk performance has been improving continuously, microprocessor performance has advanced much more rapidly. The performance of microprocessors has improved at about 50 percent or more per year, but disk access times have improved at a rate of about 10 percent per year and disk transfer rates at a rate of about 20 percent per year. In addition, since disks contain mechanical elements, they have much higher failure rates than electronic parts of a computer system. If a disk fails, all the data stored on it is lost.

A **disk array** is an arrangement of several disks, organized so as to increase performance and improve reliability of the resulting storage system. Performance is increased through data striping. Data striping distributes data over several disks to give the impression of having a single large, very fast disk. Reliability is improved through **redundancy**. Instead of having a single copy of the data, redundant information is maintained. The redundant information is carefully organized so that in case of a disk failure, it can be used to reconstruct the contents of the failed disk. Disk arrays that implement a combination of data striping and redundancy are called redundant arrays of independent disks. Several RAID organizations, referred to as RAID levels, have been proposed. Each RAID level represents a different trade-off between reliability and performance.

In the remainder of this section, we will first discuss data striping and redundancy and then introduce the RAID levels that have become industry standards.

9.4.1 Data Striping

A disk array gives the user the abstraction of having a single, very large disk. If the user issues an I/O request, we first identify the set of physical disk blocks that store the data requested. These disk blocks may reside on a single disk in the array or may be distributed over several disks in the array. Then the set of blocks is retrieved from the disk(s) involved. Thus, how we distribute the data over the disks in the array influences how many disks are involved when an I/O request is processed. In **data striping**, the data is segmented into equal-size partitions that are distributed over multiple disks. The size of a partition is called the **striping unit**. The partitions are usually distributed using a round robin algorithm: If the disk array consists of D disks, then partition i is written onto disk i mod D.

As an example, consider a striping unit of a bit. Since any D successive data bits are spread over all D data disks in the array, all I/O requests involve all disks in the array. Since the smallest unit of transfer from a disk is a block, each I/O request involves transfer of at least D blocks. Since we can read the D blocks from the D disks in parallel, the transfer rate of each request is D times the transfer rate of a single disk; each request uses the aggregated bandwidth of all disks in the array. But the disk access time of the array is basically the access time of a single disk since all disk heads have to move for all requests. Therefore, for a disk array with a striping unit of a single bit, the number of requests per time unit that the array can process and the average response time for each individual request are similar to that of a single disk.

As another example, consider a striping unit of a disk block. In this case, I/O requests of the size of a disk block are processed by one disk in the array. If there are many I/O requests of the size of a disk block and the requested blocks reside on different disks, we can process all requests in parallel and thus reduce the average response time of an I/O request. Since we distributed the striping partitions round-robin, large requests of the size of many contiguous blocks involve all disks. We can process the request by all disks in parallel and thus increase the transfer rate to the aggregated bandwidth of all D disks.

9.4.2 Redundancy

While having more disks increases storage system performance, it also lowers overall storage system reliability. Assume that the **mean-time-to-failure,** or MTTF, of a single disk is 50, 000 hours (about 5.7 years). Then, the MTTF of an array of 100 disks is only 50, 000/100 = 500 hours or about 21 days, assuming that failures occur independently and that the failure probability of a disk does not change over time. (Actually, disks have a higher failure probability early and late in their lifetimes. Early failures are often due to undetected manufacturing defects; late failures occur since the disk wears out. Failures do not occur independently either: consider a fire in the building, an earthquake, or purchase of a set of disks that come from a 'bad' manufacturing batch.)

Reliability of a disk array can be increased by storing redundant information. If a disk failure occurs, the redundant information is used to reconstruct the data on the failed disk. Redundancy can immensely increase the MTTF of a disk array. When incorporating redundancy into a disk array design, we have to make two choices. First, we have to decide where to store the redundant information. We can either store the redundant information on a small number of **check disks** or we can distribute the redundant information uniformly over all disks.

The second choice we have to make is how to compute the redundant information. Most disk arrays store parity information: In the **parity scheme**, an extra check disk contains information that can be used to recover from failure of any one disk in the array. Assume that we have a disk array with D disks and consider the first bit on each data disk. Suppose that i of the D data bits are one. The first bit on the check disk is set to one if i is odd, otherwise it is set to zero. This bit on the check disk is called the parity of the data bits. The check disk contains parity information for each set of corresponding D data bits.

To recover the value of the first bit of a failed disk we first count the number of bits that are one on the D–1 non failed disks; let this number be j. If j is odd and the parity bit is one, or if j is even and the parity bit is zero, then the value of the bit on the failed disk must have been zero. Otherwise, the value of the bit on the failed disk must have been one. Thus, with parity we can recover from failure of any one disk. Reconstruction of the lost information involves reading all data disks and the check disk.

For example, with an additional 10 disks with redundant information, the MTTF of our example storage system with 100 data disks can be increased to more than 250 years! What is more important, a large MTTF implies a small failure probability during the actual usage time of the storage system, which is usually much smaller than the reported lifetime or the MTTF. (Who actually uses 10-year-old disks?)

In a RAID system, the disk array is partitioned into **reliability groups**, where a reliability group consists of a set of data disks and a set of check disks. A common redundancy scheme (see box) is applied to each group. The number of check disks depends on the RAID level chosen. In the remainder of this section, we assume for ease of explanation that there is only one reliability group. The reader should keep in mind that actual RAID implementations consist of several reliability groups, and that the number of groups plays a role in the overall reliability of the resulting storage system.

9.4.3 Levels of Redundancy

Throughout the discussion of the different RAID levels, we consider sample data that would just fit on four disks. That is, without any RAID technology our storage system would consist of exactly four data disks. Depending on the RAID level chosen, the number of additional disks varies from zero to four.

- **Level 0: Non-redundant**

  A RAID Level 0 system uses data striping to increase the maximum bandwidth available. No redundant information is maintained. While being the solution with the lowest cost, reliability is a problem, since the MTTF decreases linearly with the number of disk drives in the array. RAID Level 0 has the best write performance of all RAID levels, because absence of redundant information implies that no redundant information needs to be updated! Interestingly, RAID Level 0 does not have the best read performance of all RAID levels, since systems with redundancy have a choice of scheduling disk accesses as explained in the next section. In our example, the RAID Level 0 solution consists of only four data disks. Independent of the number of data disks, the effective space utilization for a RAID Level 0 system is always 100 percent.

- **Level 1: Mirrored**

  A RAID Level 1 system is the most expensive solution. Instead of having one copy of the data, two identical copies of the data on two different disks are maintained. This type of redundancy is often called mirroring. Every write of a disk block involves a write on both disks. These writes may not be performed simultaneously, since a global system failure (e.g., due to a power outage) could occur while writing the blocks and then leave both copies in an inconsistent state. Therefore, we always write a block on one disk first and then write the other copy on the mirror disk. Since two copies of each block exist on different disks, we can distribute reads between the two disks and allow parallel reads of different disk blocks that conceptually reside on the same disk. A read of a block can be scheduled to the disk that has the smaller expected access time. RAID Level 1 does not stripe the data over different disks, thus the transfer rate for a single request is comparable to the transfer rate of a single disk.

  In our example, we need four data and four check disks with mirrored data for a RAID Level 1 implementation. The effective space utilization is 50 percent, independent of the number of data disks.

- **Level 0+1: Striping and Mirroring**

  RAID Level 0+1, sometimes also referred to as RAID level 10, combines striping and mirroring. Thus, as in RAID Level 1, read requests of the size of a disk block can be scheduled both to a disk or its mirror image. In addition, read requests of the size of several contiguous blocks benefit from the aggregated bandwidth of all disks. The cost for writes is analogous to RAID Level 1.

As in RAID Level 1, our example with four data disks requires four check disks and the effective space utilization is always 50 percent.

- **Level 2: Error-Correcting Codes**

In RAID Level 2 the striping unit is a single bit. The redundancy scheme used is Hamming code. In our example with four data disks, only three check disks are needed. In general, the number of check disks grows logarithmically with the number of data disks. Striping at the bit level has the implication that in a disk array with D data disks, the smallest unit of transfer for a read is a set of D blocks. Thus, Level 2 is good for workloads with many large requests since for each request the aggregated bandwidth of all data disks is used. But RAID Level 2 is bad for small requests of the size of an individual block for the same reason. (See the example in Section 9.3.1.) A write of a block involves reading D blocks into main memory, modifying D + C blocks and writing D + C blocks to disk, where C is the number of check disks. This sequence of steps is called a read-modify-write cycle.

For a RAID Level 2 implementation with four data disks, three check disks are needed. Thus, in our example the effective space utilization is about 57 percent. The effective space utilization increases with the number of data disks. For example, in a setup with 10 data disks, four check disks are needed and the effective space utilization is 71 percent. In a setup with 25 data disks, five check disks are required and the effective space utilization grows to 83 percent.

- **Level 3: Bit-Interleaved Parity**

While the redundancy schema used in RAID Level 2 improves in terms of cost upon RAID Level 1, it keeps more redundant information than is necessary. Hamming code, as used in RAID Level 2, has the advantage of being able to identify which disk has failed. But disk controllers can easily detect which disk has failed. Thus, the check disks do not need to contain information to identify the failed disk. Information to recover the lost data is sufficient. Instead of using several disks to store Hamming code,

RAID Level 3 has a single check disk with parity information. Thus, the reliability overhead for RAID Level 3 is a single disk, the lowest overhead possible. The performance characteristics of RAID Level 2 and RAID Level 3 are very similar. RAID Level 3 can also process only one I/O at a time, the minimum transfer unit is D blocks, and a write requires a read-modify-write cycle.

- **Level 4: Block-Interleaved Parity**

RAID Level 4 has a striping unit of a disk block, instead of a single bit as in RAID Level 3. Block-level striping has the advantage that read requests of the size of a disk block can be served entirely by the disk where the requested block resides. Large read requests of several disk blocks can still utilize the aggregated bandwidth of the D disks. The write of a single block still requires á read-modify-write cycle, but only one data disk and the check disk are involved. The parity on the check disk can be updated without reading all D disk blocks, because the new parity can be obtained by noticing the differences between the old data block and the new data block and then applying the difference to the parity block on the check disk:

NewParity = (OldData XOR NewData) XOR OldParity

The read-modify-write cycle involves reading of the old data block and the old parity block, modifying the two blocks, and writing them back to disk, resulting in four disk accesses per write. Since the check disk is involved in each write, it can easily become the bottleneck. RAID Level 3 and 4 configurations with four data disks require just a single check disk. Thus, in our example, the effective space utilization is 80 percent. The effective space utilization increases with the number of data disks, since always only one check disk is necessary.

- **Level 5: Block-Interleaved Distributed Parity**

  RAID Level 5 improves upon Level 4 by distributing the parity blocks uniformly over all disks, instead of storing them on a single check disk. This distribution has two advantages. First, several write requests can potentially be processed in parallel, since the bottleneck of a unique check disk has been eliminated. Second, read requests have a higher level of parallelism. Since the data is distributed over all disks, read requests involve all disks, whereas in systems with a dedicated check disk the check disk never participates in reads.

  A RAID Level 5 system has the best performance of all RAID levels with redundancy for small and large read and large write requests. Small writes still require a read-modify-write cycle and are thus less efficient than in RAID Level 1. In our example, the corresponding RAID Level 5 system has 5 disks overall and thus the effective space utilization is the same as in RAID levels 3 and 4.

- **Level 6: P+Q Redundancy**

  The motivation for RAID Level 6 is the observation that recovery from failure of a single disk is not sufficient in very large disk arrays. First, in large disk arrays, a second disk might fail before replacement of an already failed disk could take place. In addition, the probability of a disk failure during recovery of a failed disk is not negligible.

  A RAID Level 6 system uses Reed-Solomon codes to be able to recover from up to two simultaneous disk failures. RAID Level 6 requires (conceptually) two check disks, but it also uniformly distributes redundant information at the block level as in RAID Level 5. Thus, the performance characteristics for small and large read requests and for large write requests are analogous to RAID Level 5. For small writes, the read-modify-write procedure involves six instead of four disks as compared to RAID Level 5, since two blocks with redundant information need to be updated. For a RAID Level 6 system with storage capacity equal to four data disks, six disks are required. Thus, in our example, the effective space utilization is 66 percent.

9.4.4 Choice of RAID Levels

If data loss is not an issue, RAID Level 0 improves overall system performance at the lowest cost. RAID Level 0+1 is superior to RAID Level 1. The main application areas for

RAID Level 0+1 systems are small storage subsystems where the cost of mirroring is moderate. Sometimes RAID Level 0+1 is used for applications that have a high percentage of writes in their workload, since RAID Level 0+1 provides the best write performance. RAID levels 2 and 4 are always inferior to RAID levels 3 and 5, respectively. RAID Level 3 is appropriate for workloads consisting mainly of large transfer requests of several contiguous blocks. The performance of a RAID Level 3 system is bad for workloads with many small requests of a single disk block. RAID Level 5 is a good general-purpose solution. It provides high performance for large requests as well as for small requests. RAID Level 6 is appropriate if a higher level of reliability is required.

9.5 TERTIARY STORAGE

In a large database system, some of the data may have to reside on tertiary storage. The two most common tertiary storage media are optical disks and magnetic tapes.

9.5.1 Optical Disks

Compact disks are a popular medium for distributing software, multimedia data such as audio and images, and other electronically published information. They have a fairly large capacity (640 megabytes), and they are cheap to mass-produce. Digital video disks (DVDs)

the DVD-5 format can store 4.7 gigabytes of data (in one recording layer), while disks in the DVD-9 format can store 8.5 gigabytes of data (in two recording layers). Recording on both

sided versions of DVD-5 and DVD-9, can store 9.4 gigabytes and 17 gigabytes respectively.

CD and DVD drives have much longer seek times (100 milliseconds is common) than do

than those of magnetic disks, although the faster CD and DVD drives have rotation speeds of about 3000 rotations per minute, which is comparable to speeds of lower-end magnetic-disk drives. Rotational speeds of CD drives originally corresponded to the audio CD standards, and the speeds of DVD drives originally corresponded to the DVD video standards, but current-generation drives rotate at many times the standard rate.

Data transfer rates are somewhat less than for magnetic disks. Current CD drives read at around 3 to 6 megabytes per second, and current DVD drives read at 8 to 15 megabytes per second. Like magnetic disk drives, optical disks store more data in outside tracks and less data in inner tracks. The transfer rate of optical drives is characterized as n×, which means the drive supports transfers at n times the standard rate; rates of around 50× for CD and 12× for DVD are now common.

The record-once versions of optical disks (CD-R, and increasingly, DVD-R) are popular for distribution of data and particularly for archival storage of data because they have a high capacity, have a longer lifetime than magnetic disks, and can be removed and stored at a remote location. Since they cannot be overwritten, they can be used to store information that should not be modified, such as audit trails. The multiple-write versions (CD-RW, DVD-RW, and DVD-RAM) are also used for archival purposes. Jukeboxes are devices that store a large number of optical disks (up to several hundred) and load them automatically on demand to one of a small number (usually, 1 to10) of drives. The aggregate storage capacity system can be many terabytes. When a disk is accessed, it is loaded by a mechanical arm from a rack onto a drive (any disk that was already in the drive must first be placed back on the rack). The disk load/unload time is usually of the order of a few seconds, very much slower than disk access times.

9.5.2 Magnetic Tapes

Although magnetic tapes are relatively permanent, and can hold large volumes of data, they are slow in comparison to magnetic and optical disks. Even more important, magnetic tapes are limited to sequential access. Thus, they cannot provide random access for secondary-storage requirements, although historically, prior to the use of magnetic disks, tapes were used as a secondary-storage medium. Tapes are used mainly for backup, for storage of infrequently used information, and as an offline medium for transferring information from one system to another. Tapes are also used for storing large volumes of data, such as video or image data that either do not need to be accessible quickly or are so voluminous that magnetic disk storage would be too expensive.

A tape is kept in a spool, and is wound or rewound past a read write head. Moving to the correct spot on a tape can take seconds or even minutes, rather than milliseconds; once positioned, however, tape drives can write data at densities and speeds approaching those of disk drives. Capacities vary, depending on the length and width of the tape and on the density at which the head can read and write. The market is currently fragmented among a wide variety of tape formats. Currently available tape capacities range from a few gigabytes [with the Digital Audio Tape (DAT) format], 10 to 40 gigabytes [with the Digital Linear Tape (DLT) format], 100 gigabytes and higher (with the Ultrium format), to 330 gigabytes (with Ampex helical scan tape formats). Data transfer rates are of the order of a few to tens of megabytes per second.

Tape devices are quite reliable, and good tape drive systems perform a read of the just-written data to ensure that it has been recorded correctly. Tapes, however, have limits on the number of times that they can be read or written reliably. Some tape formats (such as the Accelis format) support faster seek times (of the order of tens of seconds), which is important for applications that need quick access to very large amounts of data, larger than what would fit economically on a disk drive. Most other tape formats provide larger capacities, at the cost of slower access; such formats are ideal for data backup, where fast seeks are not important. Tape jukeboxes, like optical disk jukeboxes, hold large numbers of tapes, with a few drives onto which the tapes can be mounted; they are used for storing large volumes of data, ranging up to many terabytes (1012 bytes), with access times on the order of seconds to a few minutes. Applications that need such enormous data storage include imaging systems that gather data by remote sensing satellites and large video libraries for television broadcasters.

9.6 DISK SPACE MANAGEMENT

The lowest level of software in the DBMS architecture discussed in Section 1.8, called the disk space manager, manages space on disk. Abstractly, the disk space manager supports the concept of a page as a unit of data, and provides commands to allocate or deallocate a page and read or write a page. The size of a page is chosen to be the size of a disk block and pages are stored as disk blocks so that reading or writing a page can be done in one disk I/O.

It is often useful to allocate a sequence of pages as a contiguous sequence of blocks to hold data that is frequently accessed in sequential order. This capability is essential for exploiting the advantages of sequentially accessing disk blocks, which we discussed earlier in this chapter. Such a capability, if desired, must be provided by the disk space manager to higher-level layers of the DBMS. Thus, the disk space manager hides details of the underlying hardware (and possibly the operating system) and allows higher levels of the software to think of the data as a collection of pages.

9.6.1 Keeping track of free blocks

A database grows and shrinks as records are inserted and deleted over time. The disk space manager keeps track of which disk blocks are in use, in addition to keeping track of which pages are on which disk blocks. Although it is likely that blocks are initially allocated sequentially on disk, subsequent allocations and deallocations could in general create 'holes'.

One way to keep track of block usage is to maintain a list of free blocks. As blocks are deallocated (by the higher-level software that requests and uses these blocks), we can add them to the free list for future use. A pointer to the first block on the free block list is stored in a known location on disk.

A second way is to maintain a bitmap with one bit for each disk block, which indicates whether a block is in use or not. A bitmap also allows very fast identification and allocation of contiguous areas on disk. This is difficult to accomplish with a linked list approach.

9.6.2 Using OS File Systems to Manage Disk space

Operating systems also manage space on disk. Typically, an operating system supports the abstraction of a file as a sequence of bytes. The OS manages space on the disk and translates requests such as "Read byte i of file f" into corresponding low-level instructions: "Read block m of track t of cylinder c of disk d." A database disk space manager could be built using OS files. For example, the entire database could reside initialized. The disk space manager is then responsible for managing the space in these OS files.

Many database systems do not rely on the OS file system and instead do their own disk management, either from scratch or by extending OS facilities. The reasons are practical as well as technical. One practical reason is that a DBMS vendor who wishes to support several OS platforms cannot assume features specific to any OS, for portability, and would therefore try to make the DBMS code as self-contained as possible. A technical reason is that on a 32-bit system, the largest file size is 4 GB, whereas a DBMS may want to access a single file larger than that. A related problem is that typical OS files cannot span disk devices, which is often desirable or even necessary in a DBMS. Additional technical reasons why a DBMS does not rely on the OS file system are outlined in Section 9.6.2.

9.7 BUFFER MANAGER

To understand the role of the buffer manager, consider a simple example. Suppose that the database contains 1,000,000 pages, but only 1,000 pages of main memory are available for holding data. Consider a query that requires a scan of the entire file. Because all the data cannot be brought into main memory at one time, the DBMS must bring pages into main memory as they are needed and, in the process, decide what existing page in main memory to replace to make space for the new page. The policy used to decide which page to replace is called the **replacement policy.**

In terms of the DBMS architecture presented in Section 1.8, the **buffer manager** is the software layer that is responsible for bringing pages from disk to main memory as needed. The buffer manager manages the available main memory by partitioning it into a collection of pages, which we collectively refer to as the **buffer pool.** The main memory pages in the buffer pool are called **frames;** it is convenient to think of them as slots that can hold a page (that usually resides on disk or other secondary storage media).

Higher levels of the DBMS code can be written without worrying about whether data pages are in memory or not; they ask the buffer manager for the page, and it is brought into a frame in the buffer pool if it is not already there. Of course, the higher-level code that requests a page must also release the page when it is no longer needed, by informing the buffer manager, so that the frame containing the page can be reused. The higher-level code must also inform the buffer manager if it modifies the requested page; the buffer manager then makes sure that the change is propagated to the copy of the page on disk. Buffer management is illustrated in Figure 9.7.

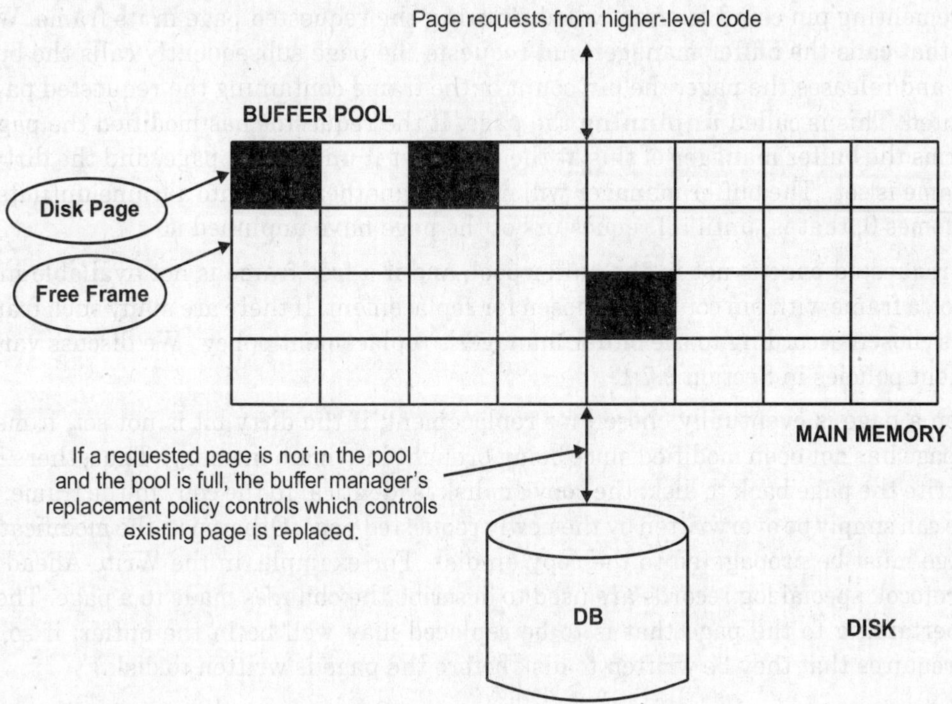

Figure 9.7 The Buffer Pool

In addition to the buffer pool itself, the buffer manager maintains some bookkeeping information, and two variables for each frame in the pool: **pin_count** and **dirty.** The number of times that the page currently in a given frame has been requested but not released—the number of current users of the page—is recorded in the pin count variable for that frame. The

Boolean variable dirty indicates whether the page has been modified since it was brought into the buffer pool from disk.

Initially, the pin count for every frame is set to 0, and the dirty bits are turned off. When a page is requested the buffer manager does the following:

1. Checks the buffer pool to see if some frame contains the requested page, and if so increments the pin_count of that frame. If the page is not in the pool, the buffer manager brings it in as follows:
   - Chooses a frame for replacement, using the replacement policy, and increments its **pin_count.**
   - If the **dirty** bit for the replacement frame is on, writes the page it contains to disk (that is, the disk copy of the page is overwritten with the contents of the frame).
   - Reads the requested page into the replacement frame.
2. Returns the (main memory) address of the frame containing the requested page to the requestor.

Incrementing pin count is often called **pinning** the requested page in its frame. When the code that calls the buffer manager and requests the page subsequently calls the buffer manager and releases the page, the pin count of the frame containing the requested page is decremented. This is called **unpinning** the page. If the requestor has modified the page, it also informs the buffer manager of this at the time that it unpins the page, and the dirty bit for the frame is set. The buffer manager will not read another page into a frame until its pin count becomes 0, that is, until all requestors of the page have unpinned it.

If a requested page is not in the buffer pool, and if a free frame is not available in the buffer pool, a frame with pin count 0 is chosen for replacement. If there are many such frames, a frame is chosen according to the buffer manager's replacement policy. We discuss various replacement policies in Section 9.7.1.

When a page is eventually chosen for replacement, if the dirty bit is not set, it means that the page has not been modified since being brought into main memory. Thus, there is no need to write the page back to disk; the copy on disk is identical to the copy in the frame, and the frame can simply be overwritten by the newly requested page. Otherwise, the modifications to the page must be propagated to the copy on disk. For example, in the Write-Ahead Log (WAL) protocol, special log records are used to describe the changes made to a page. The log records pertaining to the page that is to be replaced may well be in the buffer; if so, the protocol requires that they be written to disk before the page is written to disk.)

If there is no page in the buffer pool with pin count 0 and a page that is not in the pool is requested, the buffer manager must wait until some page is released before responding to the page request. In practice, the transaction requesting the page may simply be aborted in this situation! So pages should be released by the code that calls the buffer manager to request the page, as soon as possible.

A good question to ask at this point is "What if a page is requested by several different transactions?" That is, what if the page is requested by programs executing independently on behalf of different users? There is the potential for such programs to make conflicting changes to the page. The locking protocol (enforced by higher-level DBMS code, in particular the transaction manager) ensures that each transaction obtains a shared or exclusive lock before requesting a page to read or modify. Two different transactions cannot hold an exclusive lock on the same page at the same time; this is how conflicting changes are prevented. The buffer manager simply assumes that the appropriate lock has been obtained before a page is requested.

9.7.1 Buffer Replacement Policies

The policy that is used to choose an unpinned page for replacement can affect the time taken for database operations considerably. Many alternative policies exist, and each is suitable in different situations.

The best known replacement policy is **least recently used (LRU).** This can be implemented in the buffer manager using a queue of pointers to frames with pin_count 0. A frame is added to the end of the queue when it becomes a candidate for replacement (that is, when the pin_count goes to 0). The page chosen for replacement is the one in the frame at the head of the queue.

A variant of LRU, called **clock replacement**, has similar behavior but less overhead. The idea is to choose a page for replacement using a current variable that takes on values 1 through N, where N is the number of buffer frames, in circular order. We can think of the frames being arranged in a circle, like a clock's face, and current as a clock hand moving across the face. In order to approximate LRU behavior, each frame also has an associated referenced bit, which is turned on when the page pin count goes to 0.

The current frame is considered for replacement. If the frame is not chosen for replacement, current is incremented and the next frame is considered; this process is repeated until some frame is chosen. If the current frame has pin count greater than 0, then it is not a candidate for replacement and current is incremented. If the current frame has the referenced bit turned on, the clock algorithm turns the referenced bit off and increments current—this way, a recently referenced page is less likely to be replaced. If the current frame has pin count 0 and its referenced bit is off, then the page in it is chosen for replacement. If all frames are pinned in some sweep of the clock hand (that is, the value of current is incremented until it repeats), this means that no page in the buffer pool is a replacement candidate.

The LRU and clock policies are not always the best replacement strategies for a database system, particularly if many user requests require sequential scans of the data. Consider the following illustrative situation. Suppose the buffer pool has 10 frames, and the file to be scanned has 10 or fewer pages. Assuming, for simplicity, that there are no competing requests for pages, only the first scan of the file does any I/O. Page requests in subsequent scans will always find the desired page in the buffer pool. On the other hand, suppose that the file to be scanned has 11 pages (which is one more than the number of available pages in the buffer pool). Using LRU, every scan of the file will result in reading every page of the file! In this situation, called **sequential flooding,** LRU is the worst possible replacement strategy.

Other replacement policies include **first in first out** (FIFO) and **most recently used** (MRU), which also entail overhead similar to LRU, and **random,** among others. The details of these policies should be evident from their names and the preceding discussion of LRU and clock.

9.7.2 Buffer Management in DBMS versus OS

Obvious similarities exist between virtual memory in operating systems and buffer management in database management systems. In both cases the goal is to provide access to more data than will fit in main memory, and the basic idea is to bring in pages from disk to main memory as needed, replacing pages that are no longer needed in main memory. Why can't we build a DBMS using the virtual memory capability of an OS? A DBMS can often predict the order in which pages will be accessed, or page reference patterns, much more accurately than is typical in an OS environment, and it is desirable to utilize this property. Further, a DBMS needs more control over when a page is written to disk than an OS typically provides.

A DBMS can often predict reference patterns because most page references are generated by higher-level operations (such as sequential scans or particular implementations of various relational algebra operators) with a known pattern of page accesses. This ability to predict reference patterns allows for a better choice of pages to replace and makes the idea of specialized buffer replacement policies more attractive in the DBMS environment.

Even more important, being able to predict reference patterns enables the use of a simple and very effective strategy called **prefetching of pages**. The buffer manager can anticipate the next several page requests and fetch the corresponding pages into memory before the pages are requested. This strategy has two benefits. First, the pages are available in the buffer pool when they are requested. Second, reading in a contiguous block of pages is much faster than reading the same pages at different times in response to distinct requests. (Review the discussion of disk geometry to appreciate why this is so.) If the pages to be prefetched are not contiguous, recognizing that several pages need to be fetched can nonetheless lead to faster I/O because an order of retrieval can be chosen for these pages that minimizes seek times and rotational delays.

Incidentally, note that the I/O can typically be done concurrently with CPU computation. Once the prefetch request is issued to the disk, the disk is responsible for reading the requested pages into memory pages and the CPU can continue to do other work.

A DBMS also requires the ability to explicitly **force** a page to disk, that is, to ensure that the copy of the page on disk is updated with the copy in memory. As a related point, a DBMS must be able to ensure that certain pages in the buffer pool are written to disk before certain other pages are written, in order to implement the WAL protocol for crash recovery, as we saw in Section 1.7. Virtual memory implementations in operating systems cannot be relied upon to provide such control over when pages are written to disk; the OS command to write a page to disk may be implemented by essentially recording the write request, and deferring the actual modification of the disk copy. If the system crashes in the interim, the effects can be catastrophic for a DBMS.

9.8 FILES AND FILE ORGANIZATION

File organization, i.e. how data is arranged together in the form of a file, deals with the arrangement of data items in secondary storage devices like like magnetic disk. That is, the file organization deals with what lies below internal level. DBMS architecture has two levels, namely, the External and the internal levels. This would depend upon the user interface. However, the internal level of the DBMS architecture deals with physical storage of data items or how records are stored and manipulated on the storage media. We shall learn in this section, about the internal level of the DBMS architecture including the physical storage of data on the magnetic storage device. Physical storage level involves the methods of storing records. But the users operate on the external records which in shown in the User Interface Level. The User Interface Level refers to the external level and the stored record interface refers to the Internal Level (see Figure 9.8(a)). DBMS software package is responsible for converting the external records into internal or stored records. The conversion method used is related to Access Method. DBMS relies completely on the operating system to provide the access method function.

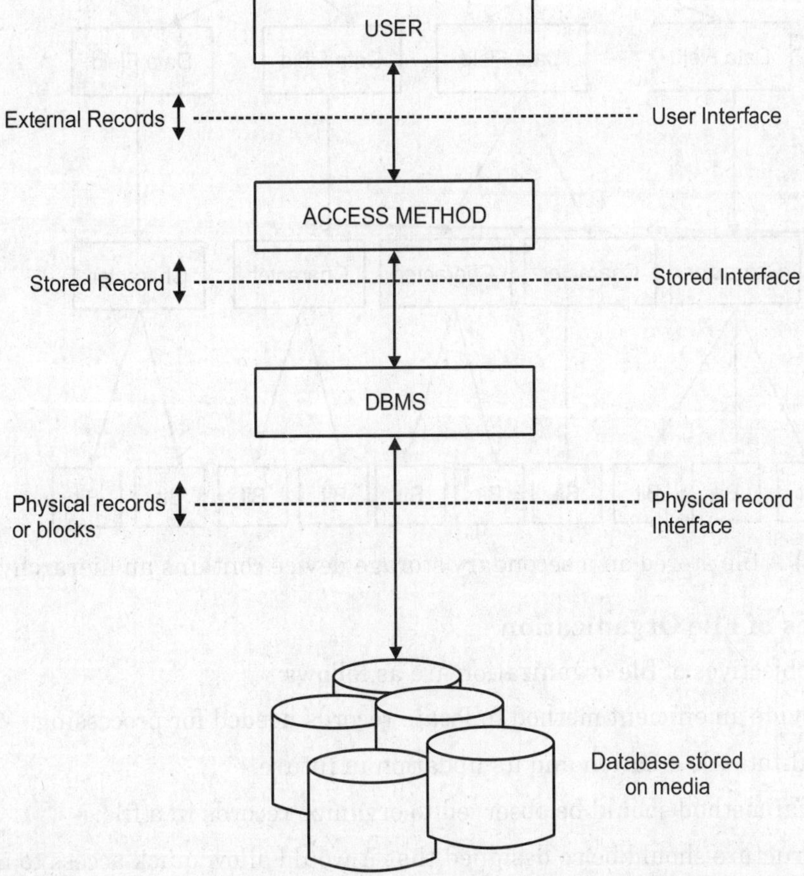

Figure 9.8(a) Connection of an external record to a physical record

Computer files are similar to ordinary files (containing papers belonging to the same subject). Both types of files stores information at a central location and both contain the basic unit of information as a record. A single record contains information about a single entity. For example, the record of the one employee, one inventory part number or one current account. A typical file structure stored on a secondary storage device in show in Figure 9.8(b).

As seen in Figure 9.8(b), data in the secondary storage device is stored in a hierarchical structure, starting with bits that form characters, and these in turn form data fields. Data fields when grouped together form records. The records grouped together would form a file.

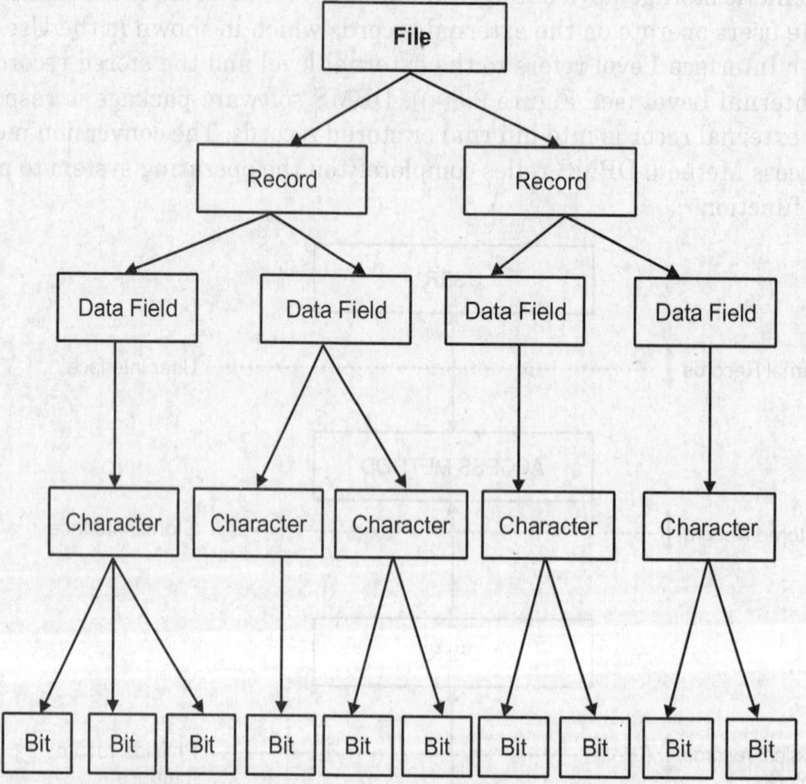

Figure 9.8(b) A file stored on a secondary storage device contains an hierarchy of data

9.8.1 Objectives of File Organization

The main objectives of file organization are as follows:

- To provide an efficient method to locate records needed for processing.
- To facilitate file creation and its updation in future.
- A logical method should be observed to organize records in a file.
- File structure should be so designed that it would allow quick access to needed data items.
- Means of adding or deleting data items or records from files must be present.

9.8.2 File Storage Organization

When data are stored on secondary storage devices, the method of file organization chosen will determine how the data can be accessed. In turn, this will affect the types of applications that can use the data, as well as the time and cost necessary to do so. The organization of data in a file is influenced by a number of factors, but most important factor among them is the time required to access a record and transfer the data to the primary storage or to write a record or to modify a record. These times vary significantly between the tape and disk storage media. Given the significant difference in these times, an important factor in information system file design is a physical organization that will support the kind of record access needed at the same time be efficient in terms of access times. The following five operations are required for the processing of records in files.

- File Creation
- Record Location (Finding the record)
- Record Creation
- Record Deletion
- Record Modification

Each file organization is more efficient in some operations than others. The storage device and the operations that are to be performed will influence the choice of the file organization. The two forms of file organization are sequential and direct. The direct file organization is again subdivided into different categories like hashed, indexed and so on.

9.8.2.1 Sequential File Organization

A sequential file a file in which the records are stored in some order, say the student file contains records of student in the ascending order of roll number of students. It is not necessary that all the records of a sequential file should be in physical adjacent positions. On a magnetic tape, the records are written one after the other along the length of the tape. In case of magnetic disks, the records of a sequential file may not be in contiguous locations. The sequential order may be given with the help of pointers on each record as shown in Figure 9.8.2.1.

1001 Rec.1	1002 Rec.2	1003 Rec.3	1004 Rec.4	1005 Rec.5	1006 Rec.6

A sequential file on tape

1001 Rec.1	1002 Rec.2		1004 Rec.3	1005 Rec.4	1006 Rec.5

1015 Rec.1	1017 Rec.2

A sequential file on disk

Figure 9.8.2.1 Sequential file Organization

When records are stored on tape, the file must be processed sequentially. When a sequential file is stored on disk, however, it may not necessarily be processed in this way all of the time. When using sequential access to reach a particular records, all the records preceding it must first be processed. What this means is that if a record is stored toward the end of a sequential file, and if this record must be retrieved, then each of the records preceding it must be processed first. This can be slow. But if the entire file-or an appreciable portion of the file must be processed together, in sequential order, then sequential organization may be very efficient. Processing data using sequential access is referred to as **sequential file processing.**

Advantages of Sequential file

The main advantages of sequential file organization are:

1. File design is simple.
2. Location of records requires only the record key.
3. When the activity rate is high, simplicity of the accessing method makes processing efficient.
4. Low cost file media such as magnetic tapes can be used for storing data

Disadvantages of Sequential file

The Main drawbacks of sequential file organization are:

1. Updating requires that all transaction records are sorted in the record key sequence.
2. A new master file, physically separate and exclusive, is always created as a result of sequential updating.
3. Addition and deletion of records is not simple.

9.8.2.2 Direct File Organization

A sequential file is not suitable for on-line enquiry. Suppose a customer at a bank wishes to know the balance amount in his savings account. If the customer file is organized sequentially, the record of this customer has to be obtained by searching sequentially from the beginning. There is no way of picking out the particular record without traversing the file from the beginning and this may take a long time. Hence, in such situations, random access or direct access file organization provides a means of accessing records speedily.

In random access or direct access method of file organization, each record has its own address on the file. With the help of this physical address, the record can be directly accessed for reading or writing. The records need not be in any sequence within the file and also need not be in adjacent locations on the storage medium. Such a file cannot be created on magnetic tape medium. Random (or direct) files are created only on magnetic disks. Since every record can be independently accessed, every transaction can be manipulated individually.

How Direct Accessing to done?

It is not necessary for the user to know where the record is kept on the disk. He identifies the record only by its key (say the account number of the customer at the bank). The operating system finds the address of the record from this key using some address-generating functions. The same address is generated while writing the record whenever it is accessed. The address-generator should not only generate unique addresses for each record but also reserve enough space for the records that may be added in future. This leads to wastage of space on the disk. There are many ways of minimizing this wastage and optimizing the available space on the disk.

Advantages of Direct Access File

The advantages of direct access file organization are:

1. Immediate access to records is possible.
2. Up-to-date information will always be available on the file.
3. Several files can be simultaneously updated.
4. Addition and deletion of records is not very complex.
5. No new master file is created for updating a random access file.

Disadvantages of Direct Access File

The disadvantages of direct access file organization are:

1. Less efficient in the use of storage space.
2. Uses a relatively expensive medium.
3. Not well suited for batch processing.
4. Data security is less due to direct access facility.

9.8.2.3 Indexed Sequential files

Some files may be required to support both batch and on-line activities. For example, a stock file may be updated periodically by batch processing and at the same time may have to provide current information about stock availability on-line. They can be thus, organized as indexed sequential files. Indexed sequential file combines the advantages of sequential and direct file organizations.

An indexed sequential file is basically a sequential file organized serially on key fields. In addition, an index is maintained which speeds up the access of isolated records. Just as you may use indexes to locate information in a book, similarly an index is provided for the file. The file is divided into a number of blocks and the highest key in each block in indexed (Table 9.8.2.3). Indexed sequential files are also known as **Indexed Sequential Access Method** (ISAM) files.

Table 9.8.2.3

KEY	Starting address of the block
125	12
860	19
1420	24
1600	42
1829	49
2225	159
2890	165
3200	807

Within each block the record is searched sequentially. This method is much faster than searching the entire file sequentially. It is also possible to have more than one level of indexing to make the search process faster. Applications involving sequential file processing can thus be carried out speedily and easily.

Advantages of ISAM files

The main advantage of indexed sequential file organization is that it is suitable for both sequential and on-line or direct access processing.

Disadvantages of ISAM files

The main disadvantages of this organization are:

1. Less efficient in the use of storage space.
2. Additions and deletions of records are more complex as they affect both the index and the record number in the file.

Implicit Indexes

The index file can be simplified if instead of **key address** pair we only store the address part. But then we have to store the addresses of every possible key in the key range, including addresses of records not present in the files. The addresses of non-existent records indicate their absence from the file.

When key address pairs are stored in an index file, it is called **Explicit Index.** When only addresses of every possible key are stored in the index file, it is called **Implicit Index.**

Figure 9.8.2.3 (a) shows explicit indexing and 9.8.2.3 (b)shows implicit indexing. Note that in the explicit indexing, record E is not present. In the implicit index at this position the address given is -5000 which is an impossible address. Rest of the addresses (for which records are present) are given as in explicit indexing.

Keys	Address
A	12
B	19
C	24
D	42
F	49
G	159
H	165
J	807

(a) Explicit Index

Index Entries
12
19
24
42
-5000
49
159
165
-5000
807

(b)Implicit Index

Figure 9.8.2.3 (a) Explicit Index (b) Implicit Index

9.8.2.4 Heap File Organization

Heap file organization is the simplest and most basic type of file organization. In heap file organization, new records are placed in a file in the order in which they are created. That is new records are stored at the end of the file. In heap file organization, there is no ordering of records and a single file is used for every relation.

Inserting Records into a Heap

Inserting a new record into a heap file is very easy following are the steps to be followed for insertion:

- The last block of the file is copied into a buffer memory.
- The new record is added at the end of this last block.
- This block is then rewritten as the last block in the file

Searching for a New Record

Searching for a record in a heap file a difficult process. A linear search of the whole file is required for locating a record. That is, if the file contains n blocks, searching a record involves on an average n/2 blocks.

Deleting a Record

To locate a record from a heap file, following steps are carried out:

Locate the block containing the record to be deleted, by searching it linearly from the beginning.

Copy the needed block into a buffer memory.

Delete the record from the block and then rewrite the block into the permanent storage.

Deleting records using the above methods leaves a lot of unused space in the file. An alternate method of deletion is to use a bit called **deletion marker** stored with each record. A record is deleted by setting the deletion marker to 1. If the record is a valid record, value of the deletion marker is 0.

To read the records stored in heap file in a sorted manner, we create a sorted copy of the file. A heap tree can be used for sorting heap file.

9.8.2.4.1 Heap Tree

A heap tree is a special case of tree data structure that is formed of nodes. The node which has no parent but itself be the parent of zero or more child nodes is called the root node. A node that does not have any child nodes is called a leaf node. The nodes which are neither leaf nodes nor the root from the internal nodes. Figure 9.8.2.4.1(a) show a tree structure. Here A is the root node. E, J, C, G, H and K are the leaf nodes. B, D and I are the internal nodes. B, C and D are the child nodes of A.

Heap tree is binary tree such that the value at a node N is greater than or equal to the value at each of the children of node N. Figure 9.8.2.4.1(b) shows a heap tree H. The largest element in H appears at the top or root of the heap tree. This means that the largest element forms the root of the binary tree. Figure 9.8.2.4.1(b) also shows the array built from this tree. Note that the nodes of heap tree H that are on the same level, appear one after the other in the array.

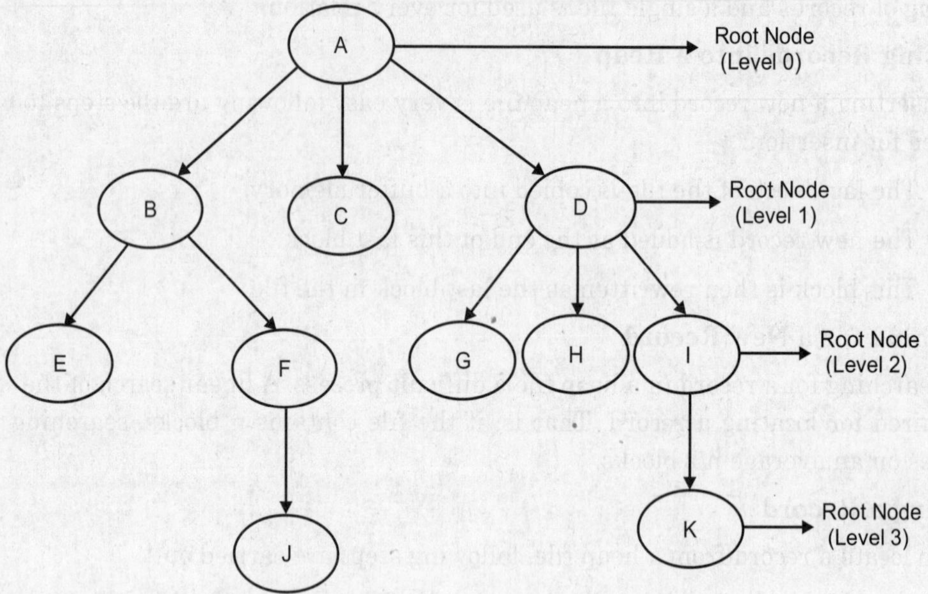

Figure 9.8.2.4.1(a) A Tree Structure

1.

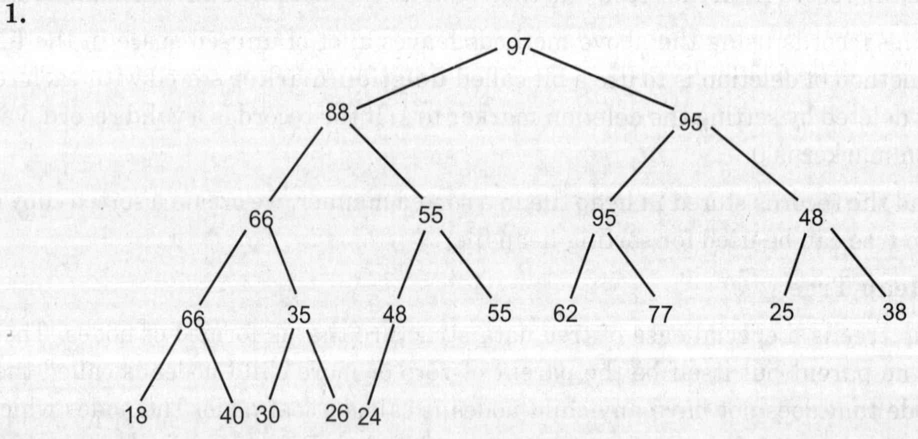

2.

97	88	95	66	55	95	48	66	35	48	55	62	77	25	38	18	40	30	26	24

Figure 9.8.2.4.1(b) (1) A Heap Tree (2) Array representation of the heap tree

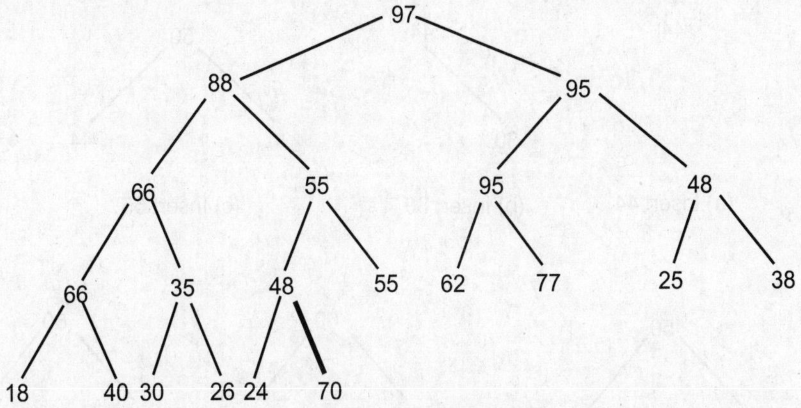

Figure 9.8.2.4.1(c) Inserting a new block 70 in a Heap tree

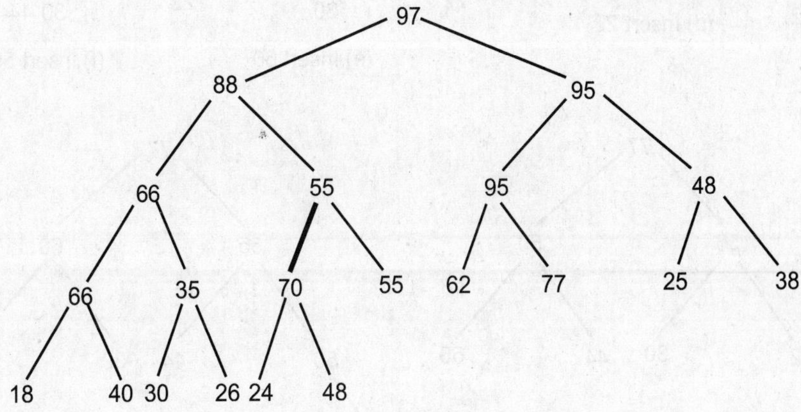

Figure 9.8.2.4.1(d) Placing 70 as it is larger than 48 in the heap tree

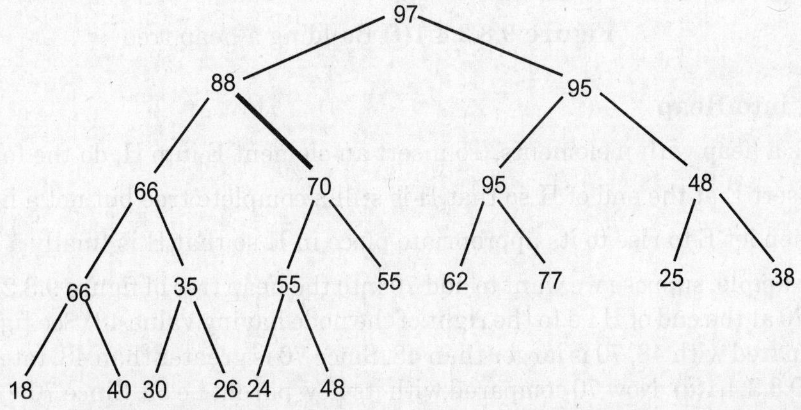

Figure 9.8.2.4.1(e) Placing 70 as it larger than 55 in the Heap tree

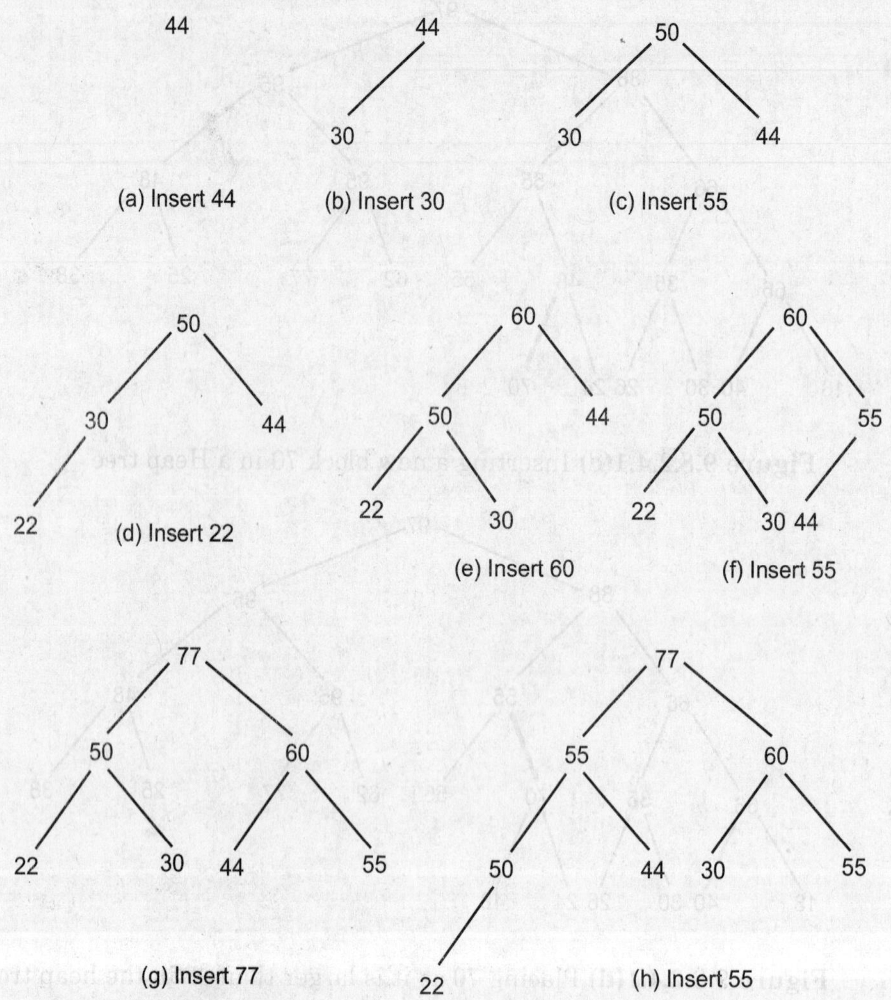

Figure 9.8.2.4.1(f) Building a heap tree

Inserting into Heap

If H is a heap with n elements. To insert an element E into H, do the following:

(a) Insert E at the end of H so that H is still a complete tree but not a heap tree.

(b) Then let E to rise to its appropriate place in H so that H is finally a heap tree.

For example, suppose we want to add 70 into the heap tree of figure 9.8.2.4.1(b). First we will store 70 at the end of H i.e to the right of the node having value 48 (See figure 9.8.2.4.1(c). When compared with 48, 70 is larger than 48. Since 70 is greater than 48, interchange 70 and 48 Figure 9.8.2.4.1(d). Now 70 compared with its new parent i.e 55. Since 70 > 55, interchange 70 and 55. The path will now look like the one seen in Figure 9.8.2.4.1(e). Now compare 70 with its new parent i.e. 88. Since 70 < 88, 70 has reached in its appropriate place.

Building a Heap Tree

Suppose we want to build a heap tree H using the following list of numbers:

44, 30, 50, 22, 60, 55, 77, 55

The heap tree H can be constructed by inserting the above mentioned numbers are after the other into an empty heap using the methods are seen in Figure 9.8.2.4.1(f). The Figure shows the different steps in building H.

Deleting from Heap Tree

To delete an element E from a heap H, do the following:

(a) Assign the element E to some variable say TEMP.

(b) Replace the deleted element E by the last node L of H so that H is still a completed tree but not necessarily a heap tree.

(c) Let L sink to its appropriate position in the heap so that H is finally a heap.

For example, suppose from the heap tree shown in Figure 9.8.2.4.1(e), we want to delete element 88. For this, we will do the following:

- In the Heap tree of Figure 9.8.2.4.1(e), 48 is the last node (L). The element E to be deleted is 88. First of the all E is deleted from the tree and stored in TEMP. Thereafter, E is replaced with L as seen in Figure 9.8.2.4.1(g).
- The tree shown in Figure 9.8.2.4.1(g) is a complete binary tree but it is not a Heap tree.
- Compare 48 with its new children which are 66 and 70. Since 48 is less than the larger child that is 70, interchange 48 and 70. The tree will now look like as seen in Figure 9.8.2.4.1(h).
- Now compare 48 with its new children which are 55 and 55. Since 48 is less than both, interchange 48 and 55. Since there are no more children of 48, 48 have reached it correct position (Figure 9.8.2.4.1(i).

Sorting using Heap Tree

If an array A contains n elements and this array is to be sorted, then we can use Heap tree to sort out the numbers. The method using Heap tree is as follows:

- Build a heap H out of the element of A.
- Repeatedly delete the root element of H. Store these deleted elements in that very order into a new array, say, B.
- B will now contain n elements in the descending order

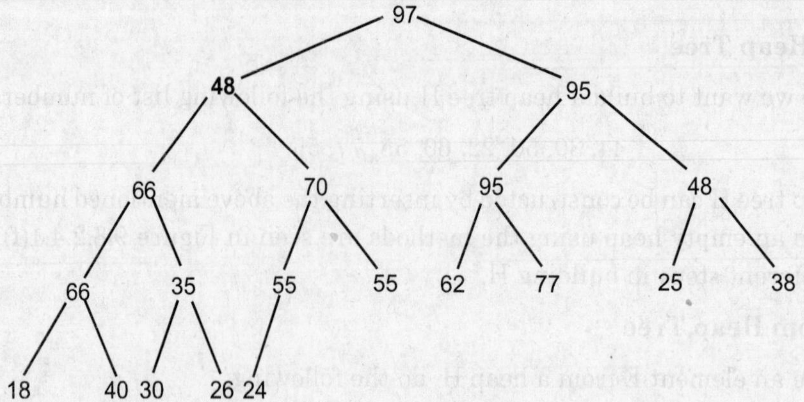

Figure 9.8.2.4.1(g) 48 replace the number 88 which is to be removed from Heap tree

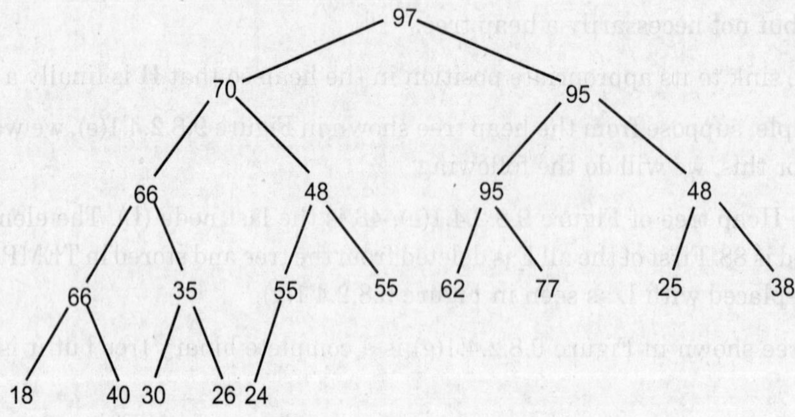

Figure 9.8.2.4.1(h) 70 being larger than 48, replace 48 by 70

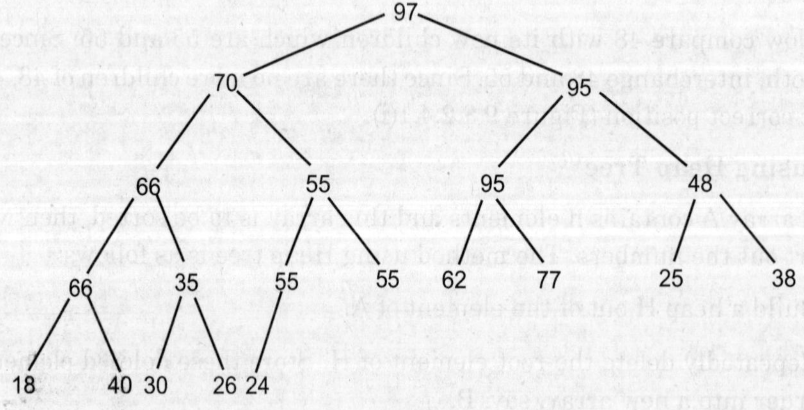

Figure 9.8.2.4.1(i) Heap tree after deleting 88

9.9 RECORD TYPES

We have seen that data is stored as records and each record is a collection of values and each value is formed by one or more bytes corresponding to a specific field in the record. Thus we can say that the records describe the entities and their attributes. Consider the example of a book that is being captured in a file. A BOOK record represents a book entity and each field value of the record specifies and attribute of the book entity like BOOK_ID, TITLE, PUBLISHER, PRICE and so on.

A collection of field names and their corresponding data types constitutes a record type definition or record format definition. The data type associated with each field specifies the type of values that a field can take. The common data type include, character (fixed-length or varying length), numeric (number, long etc.), Boolean (having 1 or 0 or TRUE or FALSE values only), Date, Time and so on. The number of bytes required for each data type is fixed for each computer system. Files could be made of records, all of which are of the same length-**fixed-length records**-or they can contain records, which are of different sizes-**variable-length records**.

9.9.1 Fixed Length Records

Consider the following BOOK record format definition (here we use COBOL for defining the record):

```
01 BOOK-RECORD.
        05 BOOK_ID          PIC X(10).
        05 TITTLE           PIC X(60).
        05 AUTHOR-NAME      PIC X(30).
```

The above record contain 3 fields has a total length of 100 (10+60+30) bytes. The above is an example of a record format definition. We have seen that a file is made up of a number of records, each record contains a number of fields and each field contains specific number of bytes. The total number of bytes that makes up the record is called the **record length**. For example, the length of BOOK record that we have just seen is 100 bytes. The following record layout (Figure 9.9.1(a)) shows a set of fixed length records:

1234567890	Modern Database Management	McFadden
1234567891	Database Solution	Connolly
1234567892	Database	Johnson
1234567893	An Introduction to Database Systems	Date
1234567894	Database Systems Handbook	Fortier
1234567895	Fundamental of Database Systems	Elmasri
1234567896	Database System Concepts	Korth
1234567897	Database Systems	Rob
1234567898	Database Management Systems	Post

Figure 9.9.1(a) A set of Fixed-Length Records

So in the case of the above records, the first record will be sorted in the first 100 bytes, the second will be stored in the next 100 bytes and so on. But there are some drawbacks for this arrangement. One, it is difficult to delete a record from this structure. The space occupied by the record that is deleted must be filled with some other record or there must be a way to mark the record as deleted. If the space is left unused or if the record is not removed, but marked as deleted, the space will be wasted.

Another problem is that if the block size is not a multiple of the record length, then some of the records will have to cross the boundary or some of the space will have to be wasted. So if the records are written on two blocks, two block accesses will be required to read or write such as a record. If the block is not fully written, then there will be wastage of storage space.

When a record is deleted from a fixed length setup, we can move the record after that to the space that was occupied by the deleted record, then move the next record to the position of the record that is just moved and so on until every record after the deleted record has been moved forward as shown in Figure 9.9.1(b), where the third record have been deleted.

As you can see, all the records from the fourth record have to be moved ahead to reorganize the file. The above method of handling the record deletion involves moving a large number of records, if there are many records in the file and if the deleted record is in the beginning of the file. A way to avoid this large number of record movements is to the last records to the position of the deleted record as shown in Figure 9.9.1(c).

1234567890	Modern Database Management	McFadden
1234567891	Database Solution	Connolly
1234567893	An Introduction to Database Systems	Date
1234567894	Database Systems Handbook	Fortier
1234567895	Fundamental of Database Systems	Elmasri
1234567896	Database System Concepts	Korth
1234567897	Database Systems	Rob

Figure 9.9.1(b) Third record deleted and all the other records moved

1234567890	Modern Database Management	McFadden
1234567891	Database Solution	Connolly
1234567898	Database Management Systems	Post
1234567893	An Introduction to Database Systems	Date
1234567894	Database Systems Handbook	Fortier
1234567895	Fundamental of Database Systems	Elmasri
1234567896	Database System Concepts	Korth
1234567897	Database Systems	Rob

Figure 9.9.1(c) Third record deleted and the last record moved to the position of the deleted record

It is not a good idea to move records to the space that is left vacant by the deleted records as it involved additional block accesses. Also record insertions are normally more when compared to deletions. So it is a perfectly acceptable solution to leaves open the space occupied by the deleted records and wait for a subsequent insertion before reusing the space. So in this case, the records will not be moved, but the vacant space will be filled when a new record is added to the file.

Since we have found that the more efficient method of file handling is to delete the records, leave the space open and then insert the new records to those vacant positions as and when new records are inserted to the file. So we need to have a method to find these vacant spaces when a record is to be inserted. At the beginning of each file, a certain number of bytes (called file header) are allocated for storing information about the file. One way to find the position of the vacant record is to store the address of the deleted records in the file header. We can then store the address of the next available record in the first record. So the header will point to the first available vacant position, the first vacant position will point to the next available vacant position and so on. Thus the deleted records along with the file header will form a linked list called a free tree. Figure 9.9.1(d) shows such an arrangement.

Header			
Record 0	1234567890	Modern Database Management	McFadden
Record 1	1234567891	Database Solutions	Connolly
Record 2			
Record 3	1234567893	An Introduction to Database Systems	Date
Record 4			
Record 5	1234567895	Fundamentals of Database Systems	Elmasri
Record 6			
Record 7	1234567897	Database Systems	Rob
Record 8			

Figure 9.9.1(d) File after the deletion of records 2, 4, 6 and 8

When a new record is to be inserted, it is inserted in the position indicated by the header. The header pointer is updated to the next available record. Figure 9.9.1(e) shows, the file of Figure 9.9.1(d) after a record is inserted. When there are no free spaces available, the new record is added to end of the file.

Header			
Record 0	1234567890	Modern Database Management	McFadden
Record 1	1234567891	Database Solutions	Connolly
Record 2	1234567899	Distributed Database	Govind
Record 3	1234567893	An Introduction to Database Systems	Date
Record 4			
Record 5	1234567895	Fundamentals of Database Systems	Elmasri
Record 6			
Record 7	1234567897	Database Systems	Rob
Record 8			

Figure 9.9.1(e) Changing the address information after record insertion

The main problem in using pointers to point to the vacant spaces is that is involves complex programming. If a record that contains a pointer is moved or deleted, then the pointers become incorrect and needs reorganization. Such incorrect pointers are **dangling pointers.** To avoid dangling pointers, the records that contain pointers should not be moved or deleted. Such records are termed as **pinned records.**

9.9.2 Variable Length Records

As we have before, files could also be made of records, which are different sizes. These records are called variable-length records. A file may contain variable-length records in any following situations:

- Records having variable length fields
- Records having repeating fields
- Records having optional fields
- File containing records of different record types

9.9.2.1 Records having variable length ÿelds

The file records are of the same record type, but one or more fields are varying length, variable-length fields. Consider the following example. Here we have modified the BOOK record to make TITLE and AUTHOR as variable length fields. Here it should be noted that COBOL string or character data types are fixed length. So we use the syntax of Pro*COBOL for this example. How Pro*COBOL implements variable length fields is beyond the scope of this discussion.

Just remember that a variable length field is a field whose maximum allowed length would be specified. When the actual length of the value is less the maximum length, the field will take only the actual required space. In the case of fixed length fields, even if the actual value is less than the specified length, the remaining length will be filled the spaces or null values. So **PIC X(60) VARYING** means that is an alphanumeric field whose maximum length is 60 bytes.

```
01 BOOK-RECORD.
      05 BOOK-ID             PIC X(10).
      05 TITLE               PIC X(60) VARYING.
      05 AUTHOR-NAME         PIC X(30) VARYING.
```

In the above record format definition, we can see the record is a variable-length record whose maximum length is 100 bytes. But whenever, the length of the value in any of the two fields-TITLE and AUTHOR-is less than 60 or 30 bytes respectively, the length of the record will be reduced accordingly. The record layout in Figure 9.9.2.1 shows this arrangement:

1234567890	Modern Database Management	McFadden
1234567891	Database Solution	Connoly
1234567892	Database	Johnson
1234567893	An introduction to Database systems	Date
1234567894	Database Systems Handbook	Fortier
1234567895	Fundamentals of Database Systems	Elmasri
1234567896	Database System Concept	Korth
1234567897	Database Systems	Rob
1234567898	Database Management Systems	Post

Figure 9.9.2.1 Records having variable length fields

9.9.2.2 Records having repeating fields

The file records contain fields that may have multiple values for the same record. A field that contains multiple values for the same group is called a repeating field and the group of values for the field is called a repeating group. Here again we have modified the BOOK record. A book can have more than one author; we will modify the record format definition to handle this situation.

```
01 BOOK-RECORD.
      05 BOOK-ID                PIC X(10).
      05 TITLE                  PIC X(60).
      05 NUMBER-OF-AUTHORS      PIC 9(1).
      05 AUTHOR-NAME            PIC X(60)
   OCCURS 1 TO 9 TIMES DEPENDING ON NUMBER-OF-AUTHORS.
```

Here the record length varies depending on the number of authors. If there is only one author the record length will be 131 bytes (10+60+1+60). If there are 2 authors the record length will be 191, and if there are 3 authors the record length will be 251 and so on. This is shown in Figure 9.9.2.2.

1234567890	Modern Database Management	3	McFadden	Hoffe	Prescott
1234567891	Database Solution	2	Connoly	Begg	
1234567892	Database	1	Johnson		
1234567893	An introduction to Database Systems	1	Date		
1234567894	Database Systems Handbook	1	Fortier		
1234567895	Fundamentals of Database System	2	Elmasri	Navathe	
1234567896	Database System Concept	3	Korth	Silberschtz	Sudarshan
1234567897	Database Systems	2	Rob	Coronol	
1234567898	Database Management Systems	1	Post		

Figure 9.9.2.2 Records Having Repeating Fields

9.9.2.3 Records having optional fields

Some files contain records for which some of the fields are optional or other words, some of the fields will not have values in all the records. These records-records with optional fields-can be formatted in many different ways. If the total number of fields in each record is large, but the actual number of fields that actually appear in each record is small (for example, there are 50 fields in a record and out of the 50, if fields are optional), then we can prefix the field value with the field names rather than just storing the field values. So only the values that are present in each record will be stored. Thus we will include in each record a sequence of **'field-name, field-value'** pairs instead of just the field values. For example, TITLE= Database Solutions, instead of just Database Solutions. Another method is to assign a field position (1 for the first field, 2 for the second field and so on) to each field and then include in each record a sequence of **'field-position, field-value'** pairs instead of just the field values. For example, 2=Database Solutions, instead of just Database Solutions.

9.9.2.4 Records having optional fields

The file contains records of different record types (mixed file) and hence the varying size. This would happen if the records of different types were placed together on disk blocks. For a file that contains records of different types, each record needs to be preceded by a record type indicator. Processing of these records is much more complex than processing fixed-length records or processing of varying-length records of the same type.

9.9.2.5 Implementation of variable length records

Since the file contains records of varying lengths, it is not possible to find the record from the record length a in the case of fixed-length records. For example, in the case of a file containing fixed-length records (each record of size 50 bytes). We can find the position of any record relative to the position of the first record. If the first record occupies the space 1 to 50 bytes, we know that the second record will be in the position of 51 to 100 bytes and so on.

Since the length of each record is not known in the case of variable length records, it is not possible to find the position of a record by the above method.

A simple solution to this problem is to attach and end-of-record symbol to the end of each record. Some times when the field sizes are different we need to use end-of-field symbols along with the end-of-record symbols in the case of variable-length records. The Figure 9.9.2.5 shows the use of end-of-field and end-or-record symbols in files having variable-length records.

An alternative method is to store the length of each record, at the beginning of the record. This type of record representation has some disadvantage. First, it is not easy to reuse the space occupied by a deleted record as the deleted that is deleted and that need to be inserted will be of different lengths. So either the new record needs to be stored in fragments (if the new record is longer than the deleted one) or there will be wastage of storage space (if the new record is shorter than the deleted one).

Another problem is that, if the varying length record needs to grow (as in the case of records with repeating fields), there is no space. The record has to be moved and rewritten. This movement of records is inefficient and costly.

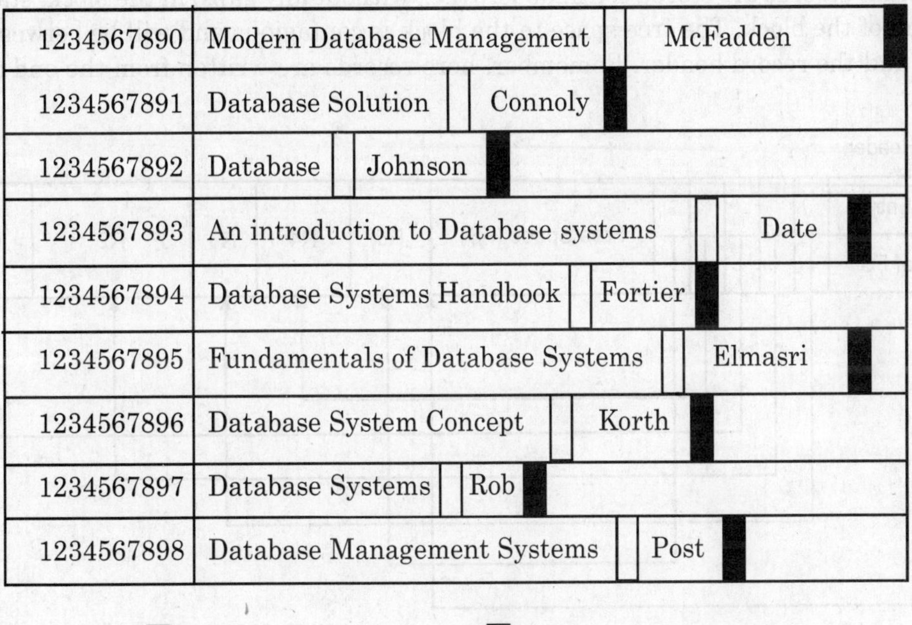

Figure 9.9.2.5 Storing Variable-length Records

A third method of storing the variable length records is shown in Figure 9.9.2.5(a) In this method, a header file that contains the following information is stored at the beginning of each block:

- The number of record entries in the header

- The end of free space in the block
- The location and size of each record in the block

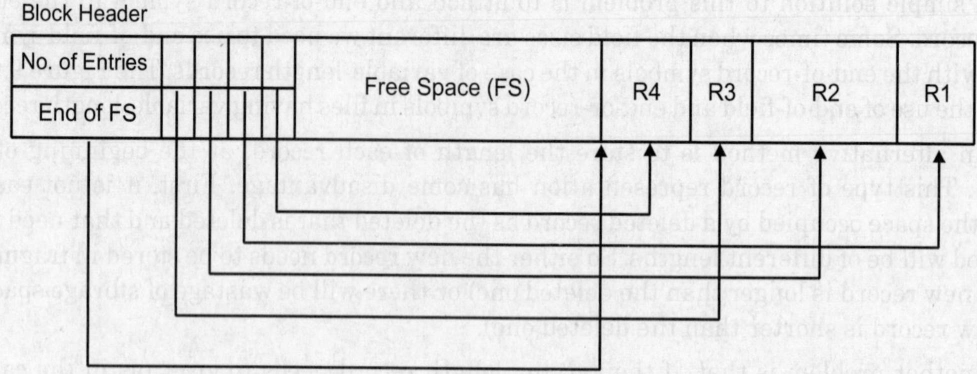

Figure 9.9.2.5(a) Storing variable-length records using Block Headers

The actual records are stored contiguously (i.e., without any gaps) in the block, starting from the end of the block. The free space in the block is contagious and will be between the last record and the record header. Remember, here records are written from the end of the block.

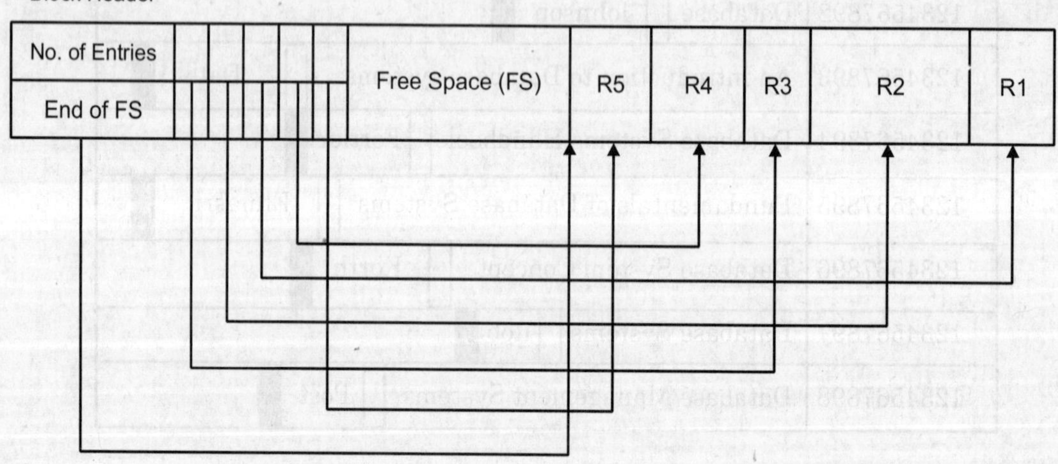

Figure 9.8.2.5(b) Adding a record to the file of Figure 9.9.2.2

When a record is added, it is written after the last record (in the free space), the number of record entries in the header is updated and an entry containing its size and location is added to the header. This is shown in Figure 9.9.2.5(b).

When a record is added, it is written after the last record (in the free space), the number of record entries in the header is updated and an entry containing its size and location is added to the header. This is shown in Figure 9.9.2.5(c).

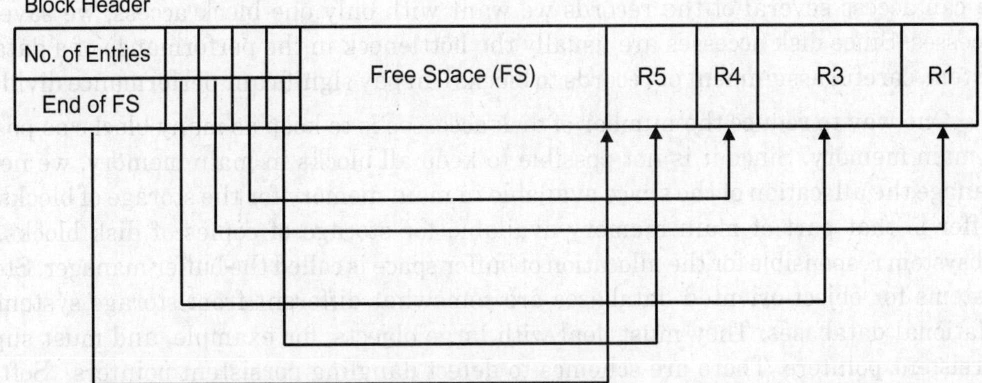

Figure 9.9.2.5(c) Deleting a record from the file of Figure 9.9.2.5

Sometimes variable-length records are stored in a file system by using fixed length records. Here the maximum possible length for the record is reserved for each record. Records shorter than the maximum length will leave unused space, which is filled with null characters or end-of-record symbols. Here the problem is that if most of the records in the file have sizes much shorter than the maximum length of the record, then a lot of space will go wasted. So this method is used only if most of the records in the file have sizes close the maximum size.

SUMMARY

Several types of data storage exist in most computer systems. They are classified by the speed with which they can access data, by their cost per unit of data to buy the memory, and by their reliability. Among the media available are cache, main memory, flash memory, magnetic disks, optical disks, and magnetic tapes. Two factors determine the reliability of storage media: whether a power failure or system crash causes data to be lost, and what the likelihood is of physical failure of the storage devise. We can reduce the likelihood of physical failure by retaining multiple copies of data. For disks, we can use mirroring. Or we can use more sophisticated methods based on redundant arrays of independent disks (RAIDs). By striping data across disks, these methods offer high throughput rates on large accesses; by introducing redundancy across disks, they improve reliability greatly. Several different RAID organizations are possible, each with different cost, performance and reliability characteristics. RAID level 1 (mirroring) and RAID level 5 are the most commonly used.

We can organize a file logically as a sequence of records mapped onto disk blocks. One approach to mapping the database to files is to use several files, and to store records of only one fixed length in any given file. An alternative is to structure files so that they can accommodate multiple lengths for records.

There are different techniques for implementing variable-length records, including the slotted-page method, the pointer method, and the reserved-space method. Since data are transferred between disk storage and main memory in units of a block, it is worthwhile to assign file records to blocks in such a way that a single block contains related records. If we can access several of the records we want with only one block access, we save disk accesses. Since disk accesses are usually the bottleneck in the performance of a database system, careful assignment of records to blocks can pay significant performance dividends.

One way to reduce the number of disk accesses is to keep as many blocks as possible in main memory. Since it is not possible to keep all blocks in main memory, we need to manage the allocation of the space available in main memory for the storage of blocks. The buffer is that part of main memory available for storage of copies of disk blocks. The subsystem responsible for the allocation of buffer space is called the buffer manager. Storage systems for object-oriented databases are somewhat different from storage systems for relational databases: They must deal with large objects, for example, and must support persistent pointers. There are schemes to detect dangling persistent pointers. Software and hardware based swizzling schemes permit efficient dereferencing of persistent pointers. The hardware-based schemes use the virtual memory-management support implemented in hardware, and made accessible to user programs by many current generation operating systems.

EXERCISES

1. What is the most important difference between a disk and a tape?
2. What are file, records, and data items?
3. Explain and details with RAID models.
4. What is the sequential file organization?
5. What is direct file organization?
6. Explain the terms seek time, rotational delay, and transfer time.
7. When does a buffer manager write a page to disk?
8. What does it mean to say that a page is pinned in the buffer pool? Who is responsible for pinning pages? Who is responsible for unpinning pages?
9. What happens if there is a page request when all pages in the buffer pool are dirty?
10. What are the different types of records?
11. How are fixed length records?
12. How are fixed length stored and manipulated in a file?
13. What are pinned records?
14. What are the different types of variable length records?
15. How is variable length records implemented?

■

CHAPTER 10

INDEXING AND HASHING

10.1 INTRODUCTION

All files are organized using two constructs to link or connect one piece of data with another sequential storage or pointers. In the case of sequential storage one field or record is stored right after another fields or record. Even though sequential storage is easy to implement and use, most of time it is not the easiest way to organize data. A pointer is a fields or record. In most cases, a pointer contains the address (or locations) of the associated data. We will see the use of pointers with respect to indexing and hashing in this chapter.

A file organization is a technique for physically arranging the records of a file on secondary storage devices. When choosing the file organization, you should consider the following factors.

- Speed of data retrieval
- Speed of processing data
- Speed of update operations
- Storage space usage efficiency
- Failure and data loss protection
- Reorganization needs (Frequency)
- Scalability (capability to grow, as more records are added to the file)
- Security

In the real life scenario many of these objective conflict and you must select a file organization that provides a reasonable balance among the criteria within the resources available. We have seen the different file organizations in the last chapter. But we will briefly describe them in this chapter for the sake of completeness. The basic file organization methods are sequential, indexed and hashed.

In a sequential file organization, the records in the file are stored in sequence according to a primary key value. To locate a particular record, a program must scan the file from the beginning until the desired record is located. A common example of a sequential file is the alphabetical list of persons in the white pages of a telephone directory. In an indexed file organization, the records are stored either sequentially or non-sequentially and an index is created that allows the applications to locate the individual records using index. In the indexed file organization, if the records are stored sequentially based on the primary key value, then that file organization is called an indexed sequential organization. An indexed sequential organization is a nice compromise between purely sequential file organization and an indexed non-sequentially file organization. In the case of sequential file organization the records can be stored sequentially, whereas in the case of indexed non-sequential organization the records can be stored randomly anywhere in the disk. Indexed sequential organization in comparison with indexed non-sequential organization, allows more efficient use of space and faster sequential data processing without any compromise in the record accessing speed.

In index can point to a record or to another index. Or in other words, indexes can be built on top of indexes creating a hierarchical set of indexes. An index also is a file and if it is very large, its efficiency decreases. So we can improve the efficiency of a large index by indexing the index. So each index in the top index file will have pointers to another index file and each entry in that index file will have pointers to another index file or a record. This arrangement is shown in Figure 10.1.

The general structure of a hierarchical index like the one in Figure 10.1 is called a tree. This tree will have the root node (the top most index file) at the top and the leaf nodes (the records) at the bottom. The performance of a tree of index entries is influenced by the tree structure used. The most common of type of tree used by access methods and database management systems to store indexes is a balanced tree or B-tree and the most popular form of the B-tree is the B^+-tree. In a B-tree all the leaves (which usually contain data records or pointers to records) are stored at the same distance from the root. We will see more about B-tree later in this chapter.

In a hashed file organization, the address of each record is determined using a hashing algorithm. A hashing algorithm, as we have seen is a routine that converts a primary key value into a record address. Although there are several variations of hashed files, in most cases the records are located non-sequentially as dictated by the hashing algorithm. Thus with a hashed file organization sequential file processing in impractical.

We have seen an overview of the various file organizations. Now we will study indexing and hashing in detail.

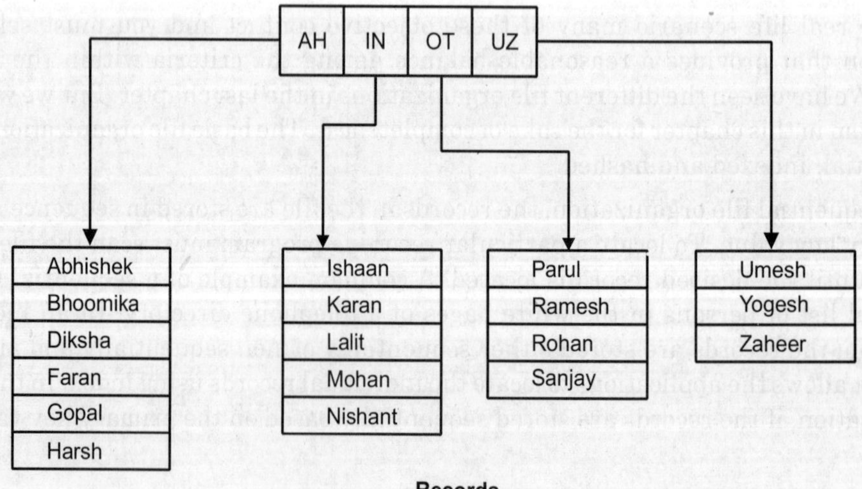

File 10.1 Index organization

10.2 INDEXING

An index for a file system works in the same way as the catalog in a library. A library will have its books cataloged in many different ways- by author, by subject, by title and so on. When we want to look for a books are sorted on the basis of author names). The catalog will have the information about the book and using the catalog we can locate the book among the thousands of books in the library. The problem with catalogs is that as the number of books grows, the size of the catalog also grows and if the library is maintaining multiple catalogs(by author, by subject, by title, etc.), then managing and maintaining all the catalogs will become a very tedious job. In real world databases with millions of records, indexes like the book catalog will be too large to be handled efficiently. So we will have to look for more sophisticated indexing technique. We will see them in details later in this chapter.

Basically there are two types of indexes-ordered indexes and hashed indexes.

- **Ordered indices** - Such indices are based on a sorted ordering of the values.
- **Hash indices** - Such indices are based on the values being distributed uniformly across a range of bucket to which a value is assigned is determined by a function, called a hash function.

  There are several techniques for implementing ordered indexing and hashing and each technique is best suited for a particular database application. Each technique should be first evaluated before choosing one. Evaluation should be based on the following factors:

- **Access types:** The types of access that are supported efficiently. Access types can include ûnding records with a speciûed attribute value and ûnding records whose attribute values fall in a speciûed range.
- **Access time:** The time it takes to ûnd a particular data item, or set of items, using the technique in question.
- **Insertion time:** The time it takes to insert a new data item. This value includes the time it takes to ûnd the correct place to insert the new data item, as well as the time it takes to update the index structure.
- **Deletion time:** The time it takes to delete a data item. This value includes the time it takes to ûnd the item to be deleted, as well as the time it takes to update the index structure.
- **Space overhead:** The additional space occupied by an index structure. Provided that the amount of additional space is moderate, it is usually worth- while to sacriûce the space to achieve improved performance.

We often want to have more than one index for a ûle. For example, libraries maintained several card catalogs: for author, for subject, and for title. An attribute or set of attributes used to look up records in a ûle is called a search key. Note that this deûnition of key differs from that used in primary key, candidate key, and super key. This duplicate meaning for key is (unfortunately) well established in practice. Using our notion of a search key, we see that if there are several indices on a ûle, there are several search keys.

10.3. ORDERED INDEXES

In order to access the records in a file we can use an index structure. Each index structure is associated with a search key. The index stores the values of the search keys in sorted order and associates each search key with the records that contain that search key. For example, if Author_Name is a search key, the index stores the values of the author names sorted in the alphabetical order and associates the records (the books details) that contain the author name with each author name. The records in the indexed file (as we have seen before) can themselves be stored in some sorted order. In the file containing the records is sequentially ordered, the index whose search key specifies the sequential order of the file is called the **Primary Index.** Primary Indexes are also known as **clustering indexes.** The search key of a primary index is usually the primary key (but it is not a perquisite). Indexes whose search key specifies an order that is different from the sequential order of the file are called **secondary indexes** or **non-clustering indexes.**

10.3.1 Primary Index

One of the oldest indexing scheme used in database systems are files with primary index on the search key. These files are called index-sequential files.

Author_Name	Subject	Price
Balaguruswamy	Programming with C+	300
Balaguruswamy	Programming with JAVA	300
Deepak Kumar	Mathematics	300
Gopal Verma	Accountant Salvations	200
Mohan Kumar	Zoology/Botany	100
Rahul Sharma	Advanced Chemistry	200
S. Sudarshan	Database Systems Concept	150
S. Sudarshan	Data Warehouses	150

Figure 10.3.1(a) List of Books

Index-sequential files are designed for applications that require both sequential processing of the entire file and also random access to individual records. Consider the list of books (given in figure 10.3.1(a)) where the books are sorted in the order of the Author _name. Figure 10.3.1(b) shows a sequential file created using the above data. In the figure the records are stored in search key order with Author_name as the search key.

Author_Name	Subject	Price
Balaguruswamy	Programming with C+	300
Balaguruswamy	Programming with JAVA	200
Deepak Kumar	Mathematics	400
Gopal Verma	Accountant Salvations	200
Mohan Kumar	Zoology/Botany	100
Rahul Sharma	Advanced Chemistry	200
S. Surdarshan	Database Systems Concept	150
S. Surdarshan	Data Warehouse	200

Figure 10.3.1(b) Sequential file of the books Details

A Primary index is an ordered file whose records are fixed length with two fields. The first field is of the same data type as the ordering key field-called the primary key-of the data file, and the second field is a pointer to a disk block (a block address). There is one index entry (or index record) in the index file for each block in the data file. Each index entry has the value of the primary key field for the first record in a block and a pointer to that block as its two field values.

We will refer to two field values of index entry i as <K(i), P(i)>.

<K(1)=(Record 1), P(1)= Address of block 1>

<K(2)=(Record 2), P(2)= Address of block 2>

<K(n)=(Record... n), P(n)= Address of block.... n>

K= Primary key

P= Block Pointer

i= No of records

10.3.1.1 Dense and Sparse Indexes

An **index record** or **index entry** consists of a search-key value, and pointers to one or more records with that value as their search-key value. The pointer to a record consists of the identifier of a disk block and an offset within the disk block to identify the record within the block.

There are two types of ordered indices that we can use:

- **Dense index**: An index record appears for every search-key value in the file. In a dense primary index, the index record contains the search-key value and a pointer to the first data record with that search-key value. The rest of the records with the same search key-value would be stored sequentially after the first record, since, because the index is a primary one, records are sorted on the same search key. Dense index implementations may store a list of pointers to all records with the same search-key value; doing so is not essential for primary indices.

- **Sparse index**: An index record appears for only some of the search-key values. As is true in dense indices, each index record contains a search-key value and a pointer to the first data record with that search-key value. To locate a record, we find the index entry with the largest search-key value that is less than or equal to the search-key value for which we are looking. We start at the record pointed to by that index entry, and follow the pointers in the file until we find the desired record.

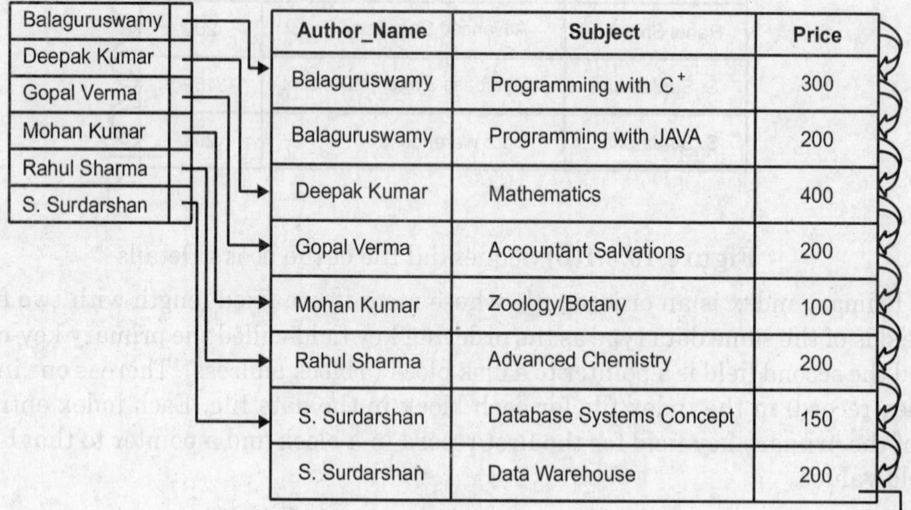

Figure 10.3.1(c) Dense Index

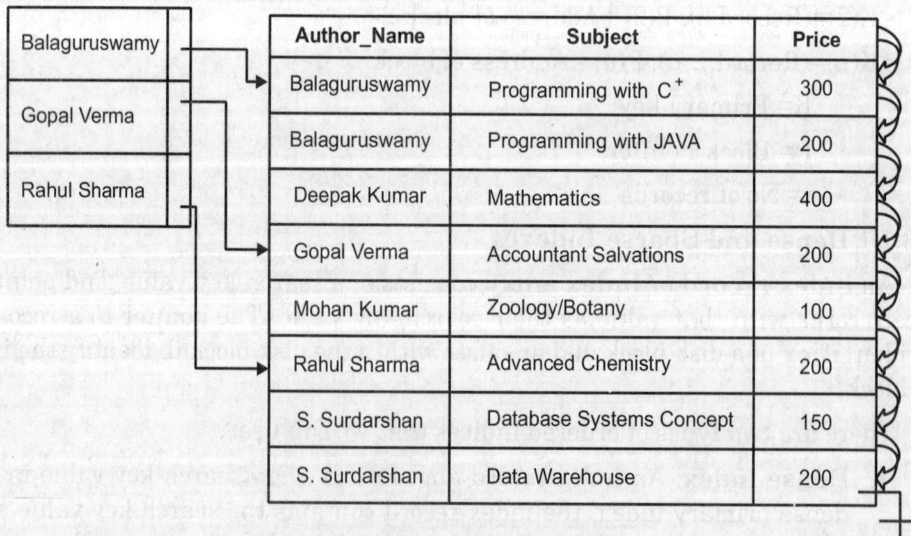

Figure 10.3.1(d) Sparse Index

The Figure 10.3.1(c) and 10.3.1(d) show dense and sparse indexes for the book file. Suppose we are looking up records for the author " S. Surdarshan". If we use the dense index in Figure 10.3.1(c), we follow the pointer directly to the first "S. Surdarshan" record and follow the pointer in that record to locate the next record in the search key (Author_Name) order. We will continue processing until we encounter a record for an author other than "S. Surdarshan". If we are using the sparse index in figure 10.3.1(d), there is no index entry for "S. Surdarshan" (In the apphabetical order) is "Gopal Verma" we follows that pointer.

We then read the book file in sequential order until we find the first "S. Surdarshan" record and begin processing at that point. Thus you can locate a record faster using a dense index than when using a sparse index. However, sparse indexes have some advantages over dense indexes. One, they require less space. Two, they impose less maintenance overhead for insertions and deletions. When choosing between dense and sparse indexes, the system designer has to make a trade-off between performance (access time) and space overhead.

10.3.1.2 Multilevel Indices

Even if we use a sparse index, the index itself may become too large for efficient processing. It is not unreasonable, in practice, to have a file with 100,000 records, with 10 records stored in each block. If we have one index record per block, the index has 10,000 records. Index records are smaller than data records, so let us assume that 100 index records fit on a block. Thus, our index occupies 100 blocks. Such large indices are stored as sequential files on disk.

If an index is sufficiently small to be kept in main memory, the search time to find an entry is low. However, if the index is so large that it must be kept on disk, a search for an entry requires several disk block reads. Binary search can be used on the index ûle to locate an entry, but the search still has a large cost. If the index occupies b blocks, binary search requires as many as [$\log_2$ (b)] blocks to be read. ([x] denotes the least integer that is greater than or equal to x; that is, we round upward.) For our 100-block index, binary search requires seven block reads. On a disk system where a block read takes 30 milliseconds, the search will take 210 milliseconds, which is long. Note that, if overflow blocks have been used, binary search will not be possible. In that case, a sequential search is typically used, and that requires b block reads, which will take even longer. Thus, the process of searching a large index may be costly.

To deal with this problem, we treat the index just as we would treat any other sequential file, and construct a sparse index on the primary index, as in Figure 10.3.1.2. To locate a record, we first use binary search on the outer index to find the record for the largest search-key value less than or equal to the one that we desire. The pointer points to a block of the inner index. We scan this block until we find the record that has the largest search-key value less than or equal to the one that we desire. The pointer in this record points to the block of the file that contains the record for which we are looking.

Using the two levels of indexing, we have read only one index block, rather than the seven we read with binary search, if we assume that the outer index is already in main memory. If our file is extremely large, even the outer index may grow too large to fit in main memory. In such a case, we can create yet another level of index. Indeed, we can repeat this process as many times as necessary. Indices with two or more levels are called multilevel indices. Searching for records with a multilevel index requires significantly fewer I/O operations than does searching for records by binary search. Each level of index could correspond to a unit of physical storage. Thus, we may have indices at the track, cylinder, and disk levels.

A typical dictionary is an example of a multilevel index in the nondatabase world. The header of each page lists

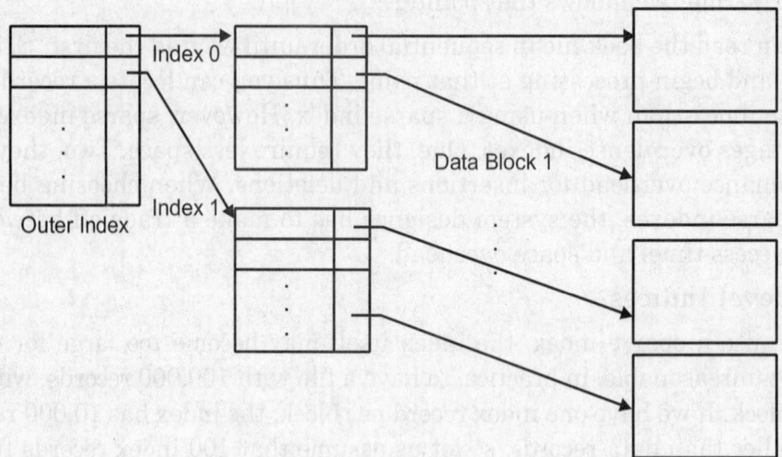

Figure 10.3.1.2 Two level sparse index

10.3.2 Secondary Indexes

A secondary index on a candidate key is similar to a dense primary index, except that the records pointed to by the successive values in the index are not stored sequentially. For example, consider the book catalog. A secondary index on price will have prices listed in the ascending order. But the records pointed by the successive values in the index are not ordered sequentially. This is shown in Figure 10.3.2 secondary indexes can be structured differently from a primary index. If the search key of the primary index is not a candidate key and if the index points to the first records with a particular value for the search key, the other records can be fetched by a sequential scan of the file (or in the other words, the file will be ordered by the search key). But if the search key of a secondary index is not a candidate key, then it is not enough to point to just the first record with each search key value, because the remaining records with the same search key value could be anywhere in the file since the records are ordered by the search key of the primary index, rather than by the search key of the secondary index. Therefore a secondary index must contain pointers to all records in the file. We achieve this by using an extra level of pointers. Thus the pointers of the secondary index do not point directly to the file, but to a bucket that contains the pointers to the file. Figure 10.3.2 shows a secondary index on the book catalog, on the non-candidate key (price).

Scanning the primary index is very efficient because the records in the file are stored physically in the same order as the index order. But it is practically impossible to store a file physically ordered both by a search key of the primary index and the search key of the secondary index as the secondary key order and the primary key order are different. For example, in the book catalog, the primary key order is the alphabetical order of the Author_Name whereas the secondary key order is the ascending order of the price.

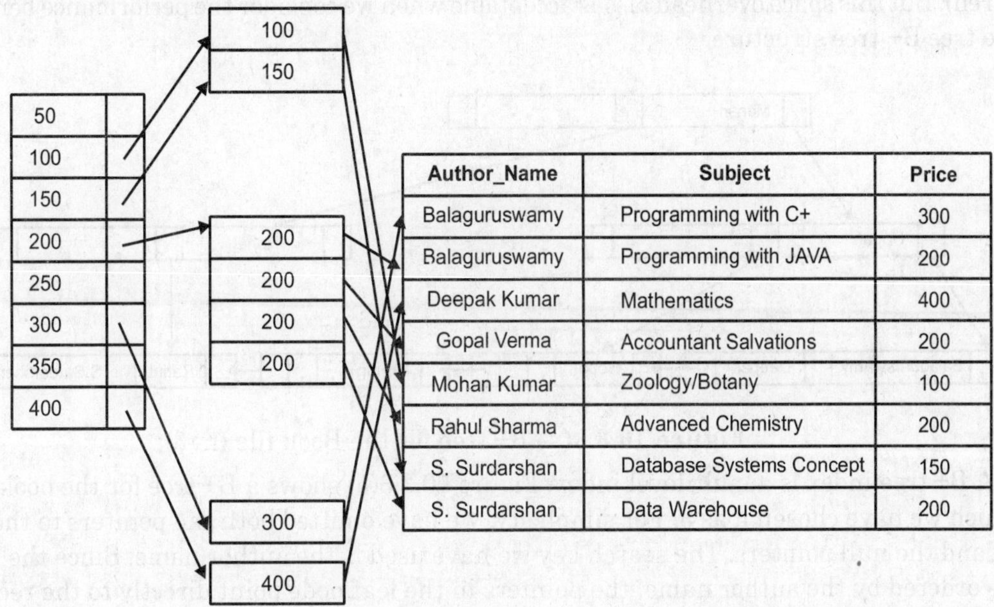

Author_Name	Subject	Price
Balaguruswamy	Programming with C+	300
Balaguruswamy	Programming with JAVA	200
Deepak Kumar	Mathematics	400
Gopal Verma	Accountant Salvations	200
Mohan Kumar	Zoology/Botany	100
Rahul Sharma	Advanced Chemistry	200
S. Surdarshan	Database Systems Concept	150
S. Surdarshan	Data Warehouse	200

Figure 10.3.2 Secondary index on the Book file on the search key price

We have seen that we can use a sparse index for the primary index, where we store only some values of search key. But this is not possible in the case of the secondary indexes. If the secondary index stores only some values of the search key, records with intermediate search key values can be anywhere in the file and it is impossible to find them without searching the entire file. So secondary indexes should be dense with an index entry for each value of the search key and a pointer to every record in the file.

Secondary indexes improve the performance of queries that use keys other than the search key of the primary index. But they impose a considerable overhead on the database maintenance. So the database designer should decide which of the secondary indexes are required based on the frequency of the queries and modifications.

10.3.3 B+ Tree Indexes

In the case of index sequential files, the performance degrades as the file grows. This is because the index lookup and the sequential scans take more time as more records are there in the file. Although this performance degradation can be overcome (to a certain extend) by reorganizing the file, frequent the reorganizations are undesirable and will add to the file maintenance overheads. One of the index structures that maintain its efficiency even with the insertion and deletion of data is the B+ tree index structure. A B+ tree index takes the form of a balanced tree in which every path from the root to the tree leaf is of the same length. Each non-leaf node in the tree has between 'n/2' and 'n' children (n/2 < = c < = n), where 'n' is fixed for a particular tree. The B+ tree structures create performance overhead on insertion and deletion and add space overhead. This performance overhead is acceptable even for files with high modification frequency, because the cost of file reorganization is eliminated. Also there will be some amount of wasted space as some nodes will be half empty (nodes with 'n/2' children). But this space overhead also is acceptable when we consider the performance benefits of the tree B+ tree structure.

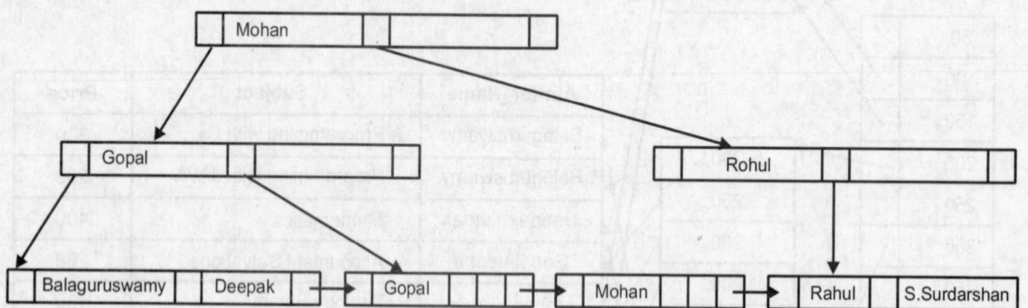

Figure 10.3.3(a) B+ tree for the Book file (n=3)

A B+ tree index is a multilevel index. Figure 10.3.3(a) shows a B+ tree for the book file, in which we have chosen n as 3. For simplicity, we have omitted both the pointers to the file itself and the null pointers. The search key we have used is the author name. Since the book file is ordered by the author name, the pointers in the leaf node point directly to the records in the file. Each node of a B+ tree contains a pointer and the associated search key value as shown in Figure 10.3.3(b).

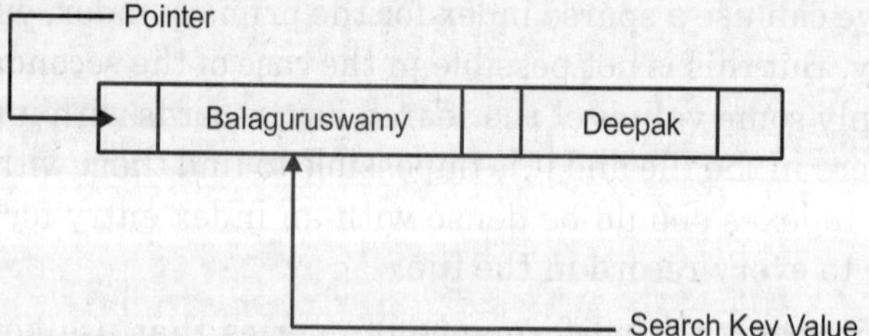

Figure 10.3.3(b) Leaf Node of a B+ tree

The pointer in the leaf node of the tree B+ tree points either to a file with the associated search key value or to a bucket of pointers. The pointers in the bucket points to a file record with the search key value of the pointer. The bucket structure is used only if the search key does not form the primary key and if the file is not sorted in the search key value order. Each leaf can hold up to n-1 values. The minimum value that a leaf can contain is (n-1)/2. The ranges of values in each leaf do not overlap. If the B+ tree index is a dense index, then every search key value should appear in some leaf node. In the Figure 10.3.3(b), there are 3 pointers and 2 search key values. The last pointer is used for a special purpose. Since there is a linear order on the leaves based on the search key values that they contain, we use the last pointer in each leaf node to chain together the leaf nodes in the search key order. This ordering allows for efficient sequential processing of the file.

The non-leaf nodes of the B+ tree form a multilevel sparse index on the leaf nodes. The structure of the non leaf node is the same as the leaf node, except that all pointers are pointers to tree nodes. A non-leaf node may hold up to 'n' pointers, but must hold at least 'n/2' pointers. The number of pointers in a node is called the **fanout** of the node.

Figure 10.3.3(c) shows a B+ tree for the book file, in which we have chosen n as 5. For simplicity, here also, we have omitted both the pointers to the file itself and the null pointers. It is always possible to construct a B+ tree for any 'n' in which the non-leaf nodes contain at least 'n/2' pointers.

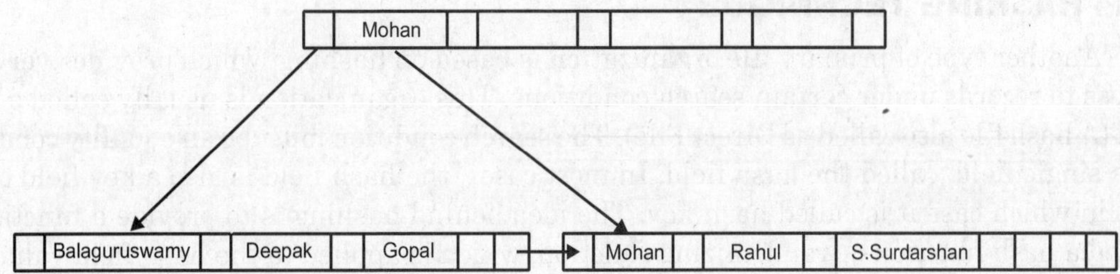

Figure 10.3.3(c) B+ tree for the Book File (n=5)

In the above example, the B+ tree is balanced. Or in other words, the length of every path from the root to a leaf node is the same. This property is a requirement for the B+ tree. As we have seen 'B' in the B+ tree stands for "balanced". It is the balance property of B+ trees that ensures good performance for lookup (querying), insertion and deletion of records.

10.3.4 B-Tree Indexes

B-tree indexes are similar to B+ tree indexes. The main difference between a B-tree index and a B+ tree index is that a B-tree eliminates the redundant storage of search key values. In the B+ tree of Figure 10.3.3(a), the search keys "Mohan", "Gopal" and "Rahul" appear twice. Every search key value appears in some leaf node and several are repeated in non-leaf nodes. A B-tree allows serach key values to appear only once. Figure 10.3.4 shows a B-tree that represents the same search keys, as does the B+ tree of Figure 10.3.3(a).

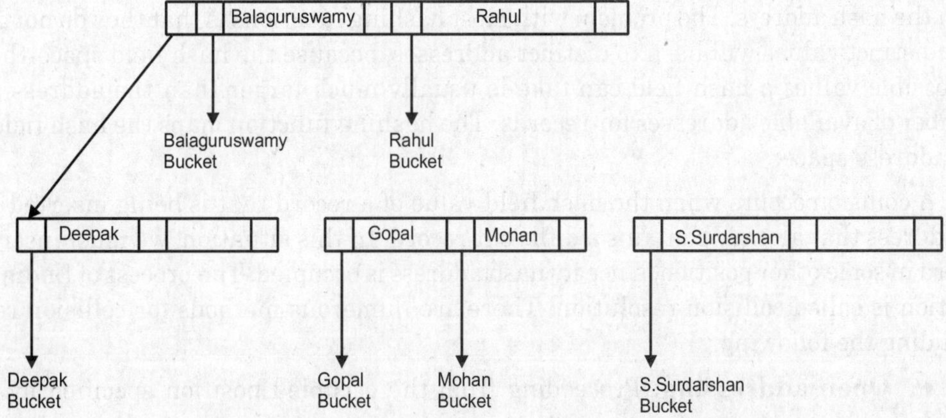

Figure 10.3.4 B-tree Equivalent of the B+ tree in Figure 10.3.3(a)

Since search key are not repeated in the B-tree, we can store the index using fewer tree nodes than in the corresponding B+ tree index. However, since the search keys that appear in the leaf nodes appear nowhere else in the B-tree, we are forced to includc an additional pointer field for search key in a non-leaf node. These additional pointers point either to file records or to buckets for the associated search key. The space advantages for B-trees are marginal for large indexes and usually do not outweigh the disadvantages of the B-tree like the difficulty in the index maintenance. Thus the structural simplicity of the B+ tree is preferred in most cases.

10.4 HASHING TECHNIQUE

Another type of primary file organization is based on hashing, which provides very fast access to records under certain search conditions. This organization is usually called a hash file. (A hash file also called as Direct File). The search condition must be an equality condition on a single field, called the hash field. In most cases, the hash field is also a key field of the file, in which case it is called hash key. The idea behind hashing is to provide a function h, called a hash function or randomizing function, which is applied to the hash field value of a record and yields the address of the disk block in which the record is stored. A search for the record within the block can be carried out in a main memory buffer. For most records, we need only a single block access to retrieve that record.

10.4.1 Internal Hashing

For internal files, hashing is typically implemented as a hash table through the use of an array of records. Suppose that the array index range is from 0 to M - 1 (Figure 10.4.1(a)); then we have M slots whose addresses correspond to the array indexes. We choose a hash function that transforms the hash field value into an integer between 0 and M - 1. One common hash function is the h(K) = K mod M function, which returns the remainder of an integer hash field value K after division by M; this value is then used for the record address.

Other hashing functions can be used. One technique, called folding, involves applying an arithmetic function such as addition or a logical function such as exclusive or to different portions of the hash field value to calculate the hash address. Another technique involves picking some digits of the hash field value-for example, the third, fifth, and eighth digits-to form the hash address. The problem with most hashing functions is that they do not guarantee that distinct values will hash to distinct addresses, because the hash field space-the number of possible values a hash field can take-is usually much larger than the address space-the number of available addresses for records. The hashing function maps the hash field space to the address space.

A collision occurs when the hash field value of a record that is being inserted hashes to an address that already contains a different record. In this situation, we must insert the new record in some other position, since its hash address is occupied. The process of finding another position is called collision resolution. There are numerous methods for collision resolution, including the following:

- **Open addressing:** Proceeding from the occupied position specified by the hash address, the program checks the subsequent positions in order until an unused (empty) position is found.

- **Chaining:** For this method, various overflow locations are kept, usually by extending the array with a number of overflow positions. In addition, a pointer field is added to each record location. A collision is resolved by placing the new record in an unused overflow location and setting the pointer of the occupied hash address location to the address of that overflow location. A linked list of overflow records for each hash address is thus maintained, as shown in Figure 10.4.1(b).
- **Multiple hashing:** The program applies a second hash function if the first results in a collision. If another collision results, the program uses open addressing or applies a third hash function and then uses open addressing if necessary.

	Name	Eno	Job	Salary
0				
1				
2				
3				
M-2				
M-1				

Figure 10.4.1(a) Array of M positions for use in internal hashing

M-2		M+1
M-1		-1
M		M+5
M+1		-1
M+2		M+4

Figure 10.4.1(b) Collision resolution by chaining records

Hash File Organization

In a hash file organization, we obtain the address of the disk block containing a desired record directly by computing a function on the search-key value of the record. In our description of hashing, we shall use the term bucket to denote a unit of storage that can store one or more records. A bucket is typically a disk block, but could be chosen to be smaller or larger than a disk block.

Formally, let K denote the set of all search-key values, and let B denote the set of all bucket addresses. A hash function h is a function from K to B. Let h denote a hash function.

To insert a record with search key Ki, we compute h(Ki), which gives the address of the bucket for that record. Assume for now that there is space in the bucket to store the record. Then, the record is stored in that bucket.

To perform a lookup on a search key value Ki, we simply compute h(Ki), then search the bucket with that address. Suppose that two search keys, K_5 and K_7, have the same hash value; that is, $h(K_5) = h(K_7)$. If we perform a lookup on K_5, the bucket $h(K_5)$ contains records with search-key values K_5 and records with search-key values K_7. Thus, we have to check the search-key value of every record in the bucket to verify that the record is one that we want.

Deletion is equally straightforward. If the search-key value of the record to be deleted is Ki, we compute h(Ki), then search the corresponding bucket for that record, and delete the record from the bucket.

10.4.2 External Hashing

Hashing for disk files is called external hashing. In the case of disks, the target address space is made of buckets. Each bucket contains multiple records. A bucket is either one disk block or a cluster (a series of contiguous blocks). The hashing function maps a key into a relative bucket number, rather than assign an absolute block address to the bucket. A table maintained in the file header converts the bucket number into the corresponding disk block address. This is shown in Figure 10.4.2.

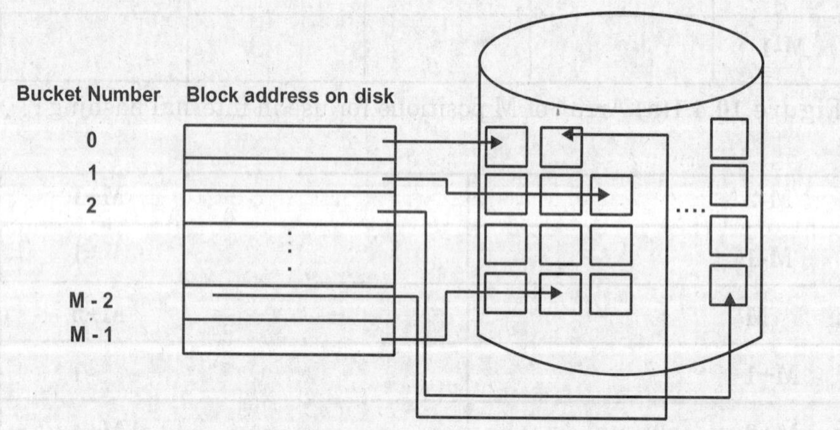

Figure 10.4.2 Matching bucket numbers to disk address

The collision problem is less severe when using buckets because more records can be assigned to a bucket without causing problems. But when the bucket is filled to its capacity and a new record is to be inserted into a bucket, we must make the necessary provisions to insert the new record. We can use a variation of the chaining technique in which a pointer is maintained in each bucket to a linked list of overflow records of the bucket. The pointers in the linked list should be record pointers, which include both a block address and a relative record position within the block. Hashing provides the fastest possible access for retrieving a record given the value of its hash field. Although most hash functions do not maintain records in the order of the hash field values, some hash functions called order-preserving hash functions maintain the records in the order of the order of the hash fields values. A simple example of an order preserving hash function is to take the first few digit of an employee number field as the hash address and keep the records sorted by employee number within each bucket. Another example is to use an integer hash key as an index to a relative file, if the hash key values fill up a particular interval. For example, if the employee number in a company are assigned as 1, 2, 3, and so on, up to the total number of employees, we can use the identify hash function that maintains order. But this technique works only if the keys are generated in order.

The hashing scheme described is called static hashing because a fixed number of buckets M is allocated. This can be a serious drawback for dynamic files. Suppose that we allocate M buckets for the address space and let m be the maximum number of records that can fit in one bucket; then at most (m * M) records will fit in the allocated space. If the number of records turns out to be substantially fewer than (m * M), we are left with a lot of unused space. On the other hand, if the number of records increases to substantially more than (m * M), numerous collisions will result and retrieval will be slowed down because of the long lists of overflow records. In either case, we may have to change the number of blocks M allocated and then use a new hashing function (based on the new value of M) to redistribute the records.

These reorganizations can be quite time consuming for large files. Newer dynamic file organizations based on hashing allow the number of buckets to vary dynamically with only localized reorganization.

When using external hashing, searching for a record given a value of some field other than the hash field is as expensive as in the case of an unordered file. Record deletion can be implemented by removing the record from its bucket. If the bucket has an overflow chain, we can move one of the overflow records into the bucket to replace the deleted record. If the record to be deleted is already in overflow, we simply remove it from the linked list. Notice that removing an overflow record implies that we should keep track of empty positions in overflow. This is done easily by maintaining a linked list of unused overflow locations.

Modifying a record's field value depends on two factors: the search condition to locate the record and the field to be modified. If the search condition is an equality comparison on the hash field, we can locate the record efficiently by using the hashing function; otherwise, we must do a linear search. A nonhash field can be modified by changing the record and rewriting it in the same bucket. Modifying the hash field means that the record can move to another bucket, which requires deletion of the old record followed by insertion of the modified record.

10.4.3 Dynamic Hashing

A major drawback of the static hashing scheme just discussed is that the hash address space is fixed. Hence, it is difficult to expand or shrink the file dynamically. The schemes described in this section attempt to remedy this situation. The first scheme-extendible hashing-stores an access structure in addition to the file, and hence is somewhat similar to indexing. The main difference is that the access structure is based on the values that result after application of the hash function to the search field. In indexing, the access structure is based on the values of the search field itself. The second technique, called linear hashing, does not require additional access structures.

These hashing schemes take advantage of the fact that the result of applying a hashing function is a nonnegative integer and hence can be represented as a binary number. The access structure is built on the binary representation of the hashing function result, which is a string of bits. We call this the hash value of a record. Records are distributed among buckets based on the values of the leading bits in their hash values.

10.4.3.1 Extendible Hashing

In extendible hashing, a type of directory—an array of 2^d bucket addresses—is maintained, where d is called the global depth of the directory. The integer value corresponding to the first (high-order) d bits of a hash value is used as an index to the array to determine a directory entry, and the address in that entry determines the bucket in which the corresponding records are stored. However, there does not have to be a distinct bucket for each of the 2^d directory locations. Several directory locations with the same first d' bits for their hash values may contain the same bucket address if all the records that hash to these locations fit in a single bucket. A local depth d'—stored with each bucket—specifies the number of bits on which the bucket contents are based. Figure 10.4.3.1 shows a directory with global depth d = 3.

The value of d can be increased or decreased by one at a time, thus doubling or halving the number of entries in the directory array. Doubling is needed if a bucket, whose local depth d' is equal to the global depth d, overflows. Halving occurs if d > d' for all the buckets after some deletions occur. Most record retrievals require two block accesses—one to the directory and the other to the bucket.

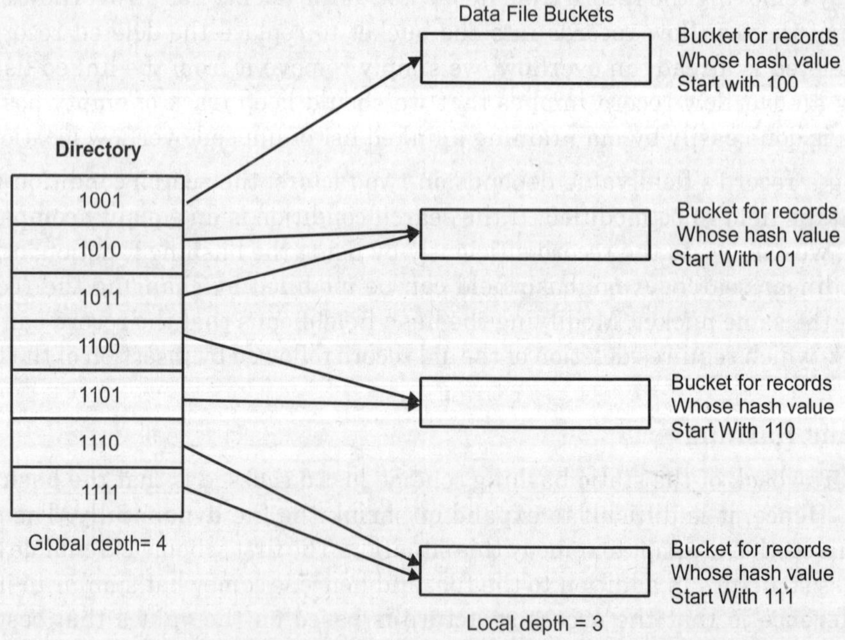

Figure 10.4.3.1 Structure of the extensible hashing Scheme

The main advantage of extendible hashing that makes it attractive is that the performance of the file does not degrade as the file grows, as opposed to static external hashing where collisions increase and the corresponding chaining cause's additional accesses. In addition, no space is allocated in extendible hashing for future growth, but additional buckets can be allocated dynamically as needed. The space overhead for the directory table is negligible. The maximum directory size is 2^k, where k is the number of bits in the hash value. Another advantage is that splitting causes minor reorganization in most cases, since only the records in one bucket are redistributed to the two new buckets. The only time reorganization is more expensive is when the directory has to be doubled (or halved). A disadvantage is that the directory must be searched before accessing the buckets themselves, resulting in two block accesses instead of one in static hashing. This performance penalty is considered minor and hence the scheme is considered quite desirable for dynamic files.

10.4.3.2 Linear Hashing

The idea behind linear hashing is to allow a hash file to expand and shrink its number of buckets dynamically without needing a directory. Suppose that the file starts with M buckets numbered 0, 1, . . ., M - 1 and uses the mod hash function h(K) = K mod M; this hash function is called the initial hash function . Overflow because of collisions is still needed and can be handled by maintaining individual overflow chains for each bucket. However, when a collision leads to an overflow record in any file bucket, the first bucket in the file—bucket 0—is split into two buckets: the original bucket 0 and a new bucket M at the end of the file. The records originally in bucket 0 are distributed between the two buckets based on a different hashing function (K) = K mod 2M. A key property of the two hash functions and is that any records that hashed to bucket 0 based on will hash to either bucket 0 or bucket M based on h_{i+1}; this is necessary for linear hashing to work.

As further collisions lead to overflow records, additional buckets are split in the linear order 1, 2, 3, ... If enough overflows occur, all the original file buckets 0, 1, . . . , M - 1 will have been split, so the file now has 2M instead of M buckets, and all buckets use the hash function h_{i+1}. Hence, the records in overflow are eventually redistributed into regular buckets, using the function h_{i+1} via a delayed split of their buckets. There is no directory; only a value n—which is initially set to 0 and is incremented by 1 whenever a split occurs—is needed to determine which buckets have been split. To retrieve a record with hash key value K, first apply the function h_i to K; if $h_i(K) < n$, then apply the function h_{i+1} on K because the bucket is already split. Initially, n = 0, indicating that the function applies to all buckets; n grows linearly as buckets are split.

When n = M after being incremented, this signifies that all the original buckets have been split and the hash function h_{i+1} applies to all records in the file. At this point, n is reset to 0 (zero), and any new collisions that cause overflow lead to the use of a new hashing function h_{i+1} (K) = K mod 4M. In general, a sequence of hashing functions h_{i+1} (K) = K mod (2^jM) is used, where j = 0, 1, 2, . . . ; a new hashing function h_{i+j+1} is needed whenever all the buckets 0, 1, . . . , (2^jM) - 1 have been split and n is reset to 0. The search for a record with hash key value K is given by Algorithm 5.3.

Splitting can be controlled by monitoring the file load factor instead of by splitting whenever an overflow occurs. In general, the file load factor *l* can be defined as *l* = r/(bfr * N), where r is the current number of file records, bfr is the maximum number of records that can fit in a bucket, and N is the current number of file buckets. Buckets that have been split can also be recombined if the load of the file falls below a certain threshold. Blocks are combined linearly, and N is decremented appropriately. The file load can be used to trigger both splits and combinations; in this manner the file load can be kept within a desired range.

ALGORITHM: The search procedure for Linear Hashing

```
if n = 0
then m←!hj (K) (* m is the hash value of record with hash key K *)
else    begin
            m →! hj (K);
            if m < n then m→!h_{j+1} (K)
            end;
Search the bucket whose hash value is m (and its overflow, if any);
```

SUMMARY

All files are organized using two constructs to link or connect one piece of data with another sequential storage or pointers. In the case of sequential storage one field or record is stored right after another fields or record. Even though sequential storage is easy to implement and use, most of time it is not the easiest way to organize data. A pointer is a fields or record. In most cases, a pointer contains the address (or locations) of the associated data. We will see the use of pointers with respect to indexing and hashing in this chapter.

There are two types of indexes-ordered and hashed indexes. An ordered index is based on a sorted ordering of the values. A hashed index is based on the values being uniformly distributed using a mathematical function called hash function. There are several techniques for implementing ordered indexing and hashing and each technique is best suited for a particular database application.

We have seen several ordered indexing and hashing schemes. We can organize files of records as ordered files, using indexed sequential organization or using B+ tree or B-tree organizations. We can also organize files using hashing.

EXERCISES

1. What is a pointer and how are they used in file organization?
2. What is a file organization?
3. What is the indexed sequential file organization?
4. What is a B+ tree index?
5. What is a B-tree index?
6. What is hashed file organization?

7. What is the indexing?
8. What is an ordered index?
9. What is the sparse and dense index?
10. What are the differences between a dense and sparse index?
11. How is B+ tree index organized?
12. What is hashing?
13. What are hash files and hash fields?
14. What is folding?
15. What is the hash function?
16. Why are buckets used in hashing?
17. What is dynamic hashing?
18. What is the extensible hashing?
19. What is linear hashing?
20. What are the advantages and disadvantages of static hashing?

CHAPTER 11

QUERY PROCESSING AND OPTIMIZATION

11.1 INTRODUCTION

We have seen the different types of queries. In this chapter we will see how these queries are processed and how they are optimized. This chapter requires basic familiarity with the concepts of relational algebra and file structures. **Query processing** refers to the range of activities involved in extracting data from the database. These activities include translation of queries expressed in high level database language into expressions that can be implemented at the physical level of the file system. The cost of processing a query is usually dominated by secondary storage access. Which is slow compared to memory access. There are many possible strategies for processing any given query, especially if the query is a complex one. The query execution cost difference between a good and a bad strategy (in terms of secondary storage or disk access) is often substantial. Hence it is worthwhile for the system to spend a substantial amount of time on the selection of a good strategy for processing a query.

A query expressed in a high level query language such as SQL must first be scanned, parsed and validated. The scanner identifies the language tokens-such as SQL keyboards, attribute names, and relation names-in the text of the query, whereas the parser checks the query syntax to determine whether it is formulated according to the syntax rules (rules of grammar) of the query language. The query must also be validated, by checking that all attribute and relation names are valid and semantically meaningful names in the schema of the particular database being queried. An internal representation of the query is then created, usually as a tree data structure called a query tree data structure called a query tree. It is also possible to represent the query using a graph data structure called a query graph. The DBMS must then devise an execution strategy for retrieving the result of the query from the database files. A query typically has many possible execution strategies, and the process of choosing a suitable one for processing a query is known as **query optimization.**

11.2 QUERY PROCESSING

Query processing is the process of transforming a query written in a high level (like SQL) into a correct and efficient execution strategy expressed in a low-level language and to execute the strategy to retrieve the required data.

Query processing is a stepwise process. The first step is to transform the query into a standard form. For example, a query expressed in QBE is translated into SQL and subsequently into a relational algebraic expression. During this transformation process, the parser checks the syntax and verifies if the relations and the attributes used in the query are defined in the database. The next step in query processing is query optimization. This is performed by transforming the query into **equivalent expressions** that are more efficient to execute. The transformation is also based on the presence (or the lack of it) of certain database structure like indexes and also on the factors like whether the files are sorted or not and so on. The transformed query is used to create a number of strategies called **access plans.** These access plans are used to evaluating the transformed query. The physical characteristics of the data and the physical storage details are taken into account in generating the access plans. The cost of each access plan is then determined and the plan with the least cost is chosen and is executed. Query processing consists of four main phases-query decomposition (query parsing and validation), optimization, code generation and query execution. This is shown in Figure 11.2.

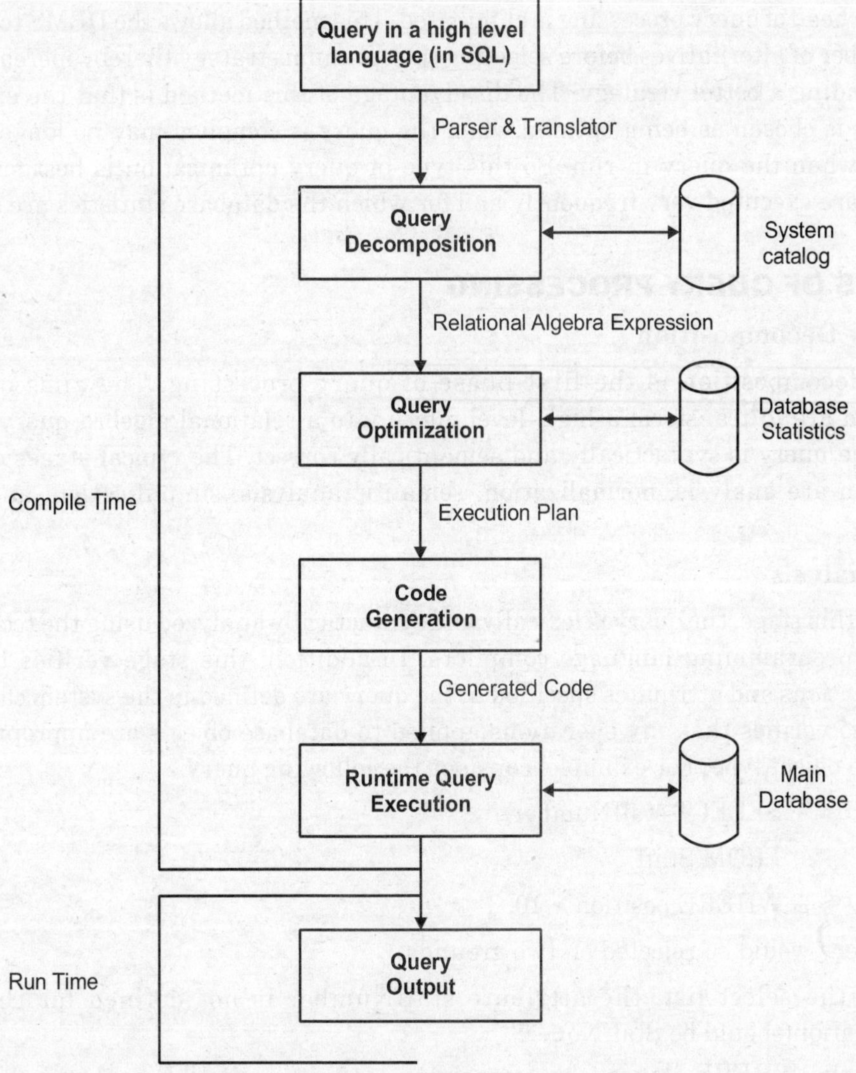

Figure 11.2 Steps of Query Processing

There are two ways in which the first three phases of query processing- decomposition, optimization and code generation-can be performed. One is to dynamically carry out decomposition and optimization. **Dynamic query optimization** is advantageous because all the information used to select the best strategy is up-to-date. The disadvantages are that the performance of the query is affected because the query has to be parsed, validated and optimized before it can be executed. In some cases, the number of execution strategies analyzed to reach the best alternative need to be reduced in order to keep the overhead costs within acceptable limits. This reduction in the number of alternatives might result in selecting a strategy that is not the best.

The second method is called **Static query optimization**. In this method the query is parsed, validated and optimized once. The advantage of static query optimization is that the run-time overhead of query processing is eliminated. This method allows the DBMS to analyze a larger number of alternatives before selecting the optimum strategy thereby increasing the chances of finding a better strategy. The disadvantage of this method is that the execution strategy that is chosen as being optimal when the query is complied may no longer be the optimal one when the query in run. So this type of query optimization is best suited for queries that are executed very frequently and for which the database statistics are static in nature.

11.3 STEPS OF QUERY PROCESSING

11.3.1 Query Decomposition

Query decomposition is the first phase of query processing. The aims of query decomposition are to transform a high–level query into a relational algebra query, and to check that the query is syntactically and semantically correct. The typical stages of query decomposition are analysis, normalization, semantic analysis, simplification, and query restructuring.

(1) Analysis

In this stage, the query is lexically and syntactically analyzed using the techniques of programming language compilers. In addition, this stage verifies that the relations and attributes specified in the query are defined in the system catalog. It also verifies that any operations applied to database objects are appropriate for the object type. For example, consider the following query:

```
SELECT staffNumber
FROM Staff
WHERE position > 10;
```

This query would be rejected on two grounds:

(1) In the select list, the attribute staffNumber is not defined for the Staff relation(should be StaffNo).

(2) In the WHERE clause, the comparison '<10' is compatible with the data type position, which is a variable character string.

Once completion of this stage, the high level query has been transformed into some internal representation that is more suitable for processing. The internal form that is typically chosen is some kind of query tree, which is constructed as follows.

- A leaf node is created for each base relation in the query.
- A non leaf node is created for each intermediate relation produced by a relational algebra operation.
- The root of the tree represents the result of the query.
- The sequence of operations is directed from the leaves to the root.

Figure 11.3.1 shows an example of a query tree for the following SQL statement

```
SELECT *
FROM Staff s, Branch b
WHERE s.branchNo = b.branchNo AND
(s.position = 'Manager' AND b.city = 'Delhi');
```

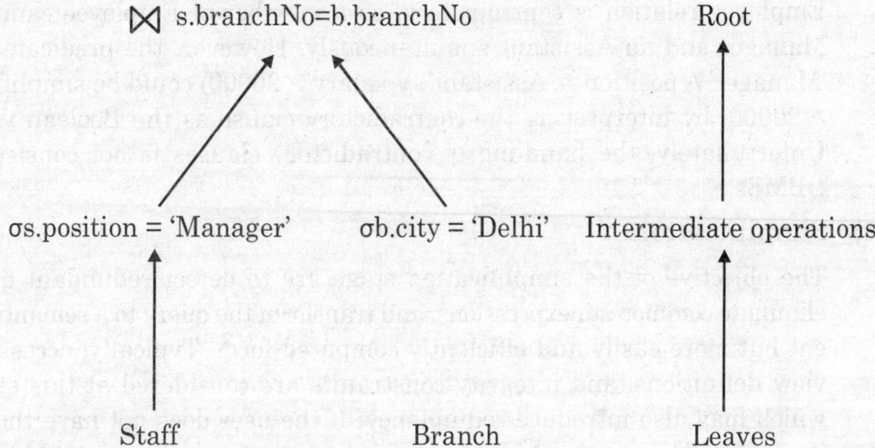

Figure 11.3.1 Example of Relational algebra tree

The above example uses relational algebra in its internal representations and this type of a query is called a Relational algebra tree.

(2) Normalization

The normalization stage of query processing converts the query into a normalized form that can be more easily manipulated. The predicate (in SQL, the WHERE condition), which may be arbitrarily complex, can be converted into one of two forms by applying a few transformation rules

- **Conjunctive normal form:** A sequence of conjuncts that are connected with the ∧ (AND) operator. Each conjunct contains one or more terms connected by the ∨ (OR) operator.

  (position = 'Manager' ∨ salary > 20000) ∧ branchNo = 'BH0012'

  A conjunctive selection contains only those tuples that satisfy all conjuncts.

- **Disjunctive normal form:** A sequence of disjuncts that are connected with the ∨ (OR) operator. Each disjuncts contains one or more terms connected by the ∨ (AND) operator. For example, we could rewrite the above conjunctive normal form as:

  (position = 'Manager' ∧ branchNo = 'BH0012') ∨ (salary > 20000 ∧ branchNo = 'BH0012')

  A disjunctive selection contains those tuples formed by the union of all tuples that satisfy the disjuncts.

(3) Semantic analysis

The objective of semantic analysis is to reject normalized queries that are incorrectly formulated or contradictory. A query is incorrectly formulated if components do not contribute to the generation of the result, which may happen is some join specifications are missing. A query is contradictory if its predicate cannot be satisfied by any tuple. For example, the predicate cannot be satisfied by any tuple. For example, the predicate (position = 'Manager' ∧ position = 'Assistant') on the Employee relation is contradictory, as a member of Employee cannot be both a Manager and an Assistant simultaneously. However, the predicate ((position = 'Manager' ∧ position = 'Assistant') ∨ salary > 20000) could be simplified to (salary > 20000) by interpreting the contradictory clause as the Boolean value FALSE. Unfortunately, the handling of contradictory clauses is not consistent between DBMSs.

(4) Simplification

The objective of the simplification stage are to detect redundant qualifications, eliminate common subexpressions, and transform the query to a semantically equivalent but more easily and efficiently computed form. Typically, access restrictions, view definitions, and integrity constraints are considered at this stage, some of which may also introduce redundancy. If the user does not have the appropriate access to all components of the query, the query must be rejected. Assuming that the user has the appropriate access privileges, an initial optimization is to apply the well known idempotency rules of boolean algebra.

CREATE VIEW Staff1 AS

SELECT staffNo, fName, lName, salary, branchNo

FROM Staff

WHERE branchNo= 'BH0012';

Now consider the following query:

SELECT *

FROM Staff1

WHERE (branchNo = 'BH0012' AND salary > 20000);

As we have seen in chapter on views, during view resolution the above query will be converted as follows:

SELECT staffNo, fName, lNmae, salary, branchNo
FROM Staff
WHERE (branchNo = 'BH0012' AND salary > 20000) AND branchNO = 'BH0012';
and the where condition reduces to (branchNo = 'BH0012' AND salary > 20000).

Integrity constraints may also be applied to help simplify queries. For example, consider the following integrity constraint, which ensures that only managers have a salary greater than ₹ 20,000.

(5) Query restructuring

In the final stage of query decomposition, the query is restructured to provide a more efficient implementation. We use transformation rules to convert one relational algebra expression into a equivalent form that is more efficient.

11.3.2 Translating SQL Queries into Relational Algebra

In practice, SQL is the query language that is used in most commercial RDBMSs. An SQL query is first translated into an equivalent extended relational algebra expression—represented as a query tree data structure—that is then optimized. Typically, SQL queries are decomposed into **query blocks,** which form the basic units that can be translated into the algebraic operators and optimized. A query block contains a single SELECT-FROM-WHERE expression, as well as GROUP BY and HAVING clauses if these are part of the block. Hence, nested queries within a query are identified as separate query blocks. Because SQL includes aggregate operators—such as MAX, MIN, SUM, AND COUNT—these operators must also be included in the extended algebra, as we discussed in Chapter 4.

Consider the following SQL query on the EMPLOYEE relation

```
SELECT LNAME, FNAME
FROM   EMPLOYEE
WHERE Salary >    (SELECT   MAX (Salary)
                   FROM     EMPLOYEE
                   WHERE    DNO=5);
```

This query includes a nested sub-query and hence would be decomposed into two blocks. The inner block is

```
(SELECT MAX (Salary)
FROM EMPLOYEE
WHERE DNo=5)
```

and the outer block is

```
SELECT Lname, Fname
FROM EMPLOYEE
WHERE  Salary > c
```

Where c represent the result returned from the inner block. The inner block could be translated into the extended relational algebra expression

$$\Pi_{Lname,\ F_{name}}(\sigma_{Salary}>c(EMPLOYEE))$$

The query optimizer would then choose an execution plan for each block. We should note that in the above example, the inner block needs to be evaluated only once to produce the maximum salary, which is then used as the constant c, by the outer block. We called this an uncorrelated nested query. It is much harder to optimize the more complex correlated nested queries, where a tuple variable from the outer block appears in the WHERE clause of the inner block.

11.3.3 Query Optimization

In this section we look at the heuristical approach to query optimization, which uses transformation rules to convert one relational algebra expression into an equivalent form that is known to be more efficient. For example, in Example 11.3.1 we observed that it was more efficient to perform the selection operation on a relation before using that relation in a join, rather than perform the join and then the selection operation. We will see in this section, that there is a transformation rule allowing the order of join and selection operations to be changed so that selection can be performed first. Having discussed what transformations are valid, and second section we present a set of heuristics that are known to produce 'good' execution strategies.

(1) Transformation Rules for the Relational Algebra Operations

By applying transformation rules, the optimizer can transform one relational algebra expression into an equivalent expression that is known to be more efficient. We will use these rules to restructure the (canonical) relational algebra tree generated during query decomposition. In listing these rules, we use thee relation R, S and T with R defined over the attributes $A = \{A_1, A_2, \ldots\ldots\ldots\ldots, A_n\}$, and S defined over $B = \{B_1, B_2, \ldots\ldots\ldots, B_n\}$; p, q and r denote predicates, and L, L_1, L_2, M, M_1, M_2 and N denote sets of attributes.

(1) Conjunctive selection operations can be cascade into individual selection operations (and vice versa).

$$\sigma p \wedge q \wedge r(R) = \sigma p(\sigma q(\sigma r(R)))$$

This transformation is sometimes referred to as cascade of selection.

For example:

$$\sigma_{branchNo} = \text{'BH0012'} \wedge {}_{salary} > 15000(Staff) = \sigma_{branchNo} = \text{'BH0012'}\ (\sigma_{salary} > 15000(Staff))$$

(2) Commutativity of Selection operations.

$$\sigma_p(\sigma_q(R)) = \sigma_q(\sigma_p(R))$$

For example:

$$\sigma_{branchNo} = \text{'BH0012'}(\sigma_{salary} > 15000(Staff)) = \sigma_{salary} > 15000(\sigma_{branchNo} = \text{'BH0012'}(Staff))$$

(3) In a sequence of Projection operations, only the last in the sequence is required.

$$\Pi_L \Pi_M \cdot\ \cdot\ \cdot\ .\Pi_N(R) = \Pi_L(R)$$

For example:

$$\Pi_{lName}\Pi_{branchNo,lName}(Staff) = \Pi_{lName}(Staff)$$

(4) Commutativity of Selection and Projection.

If the predicate p provide only the attributes in the projection list, then the Selection and Projection operations commute:

$$\Pi_{Ai.......Am}(\sigma p(R)) = \sigma p(\Pi_{Ai........Am}(R))$$

Where $P \in \{A_1, A_2,.........A_m\}$

For example:

$$\Pi_{fName,\ lName}(\sigma_{lName= 'Verma'}(Staff)) = \sigma_{lName= 'Verma'}(\Pi_{fName,\ lName}(Staff))$$

(5) Commutativity of Theta join (and Cartesian product)

$$R \bowtie_p S = S \bowtie_p R$$

$$R \times S = R \times R$$

As the Equijoin and Natural join are special cases of the Theta join, then this rule also applies Join operations. For example, using the Equijoin of Staff and Branch:

$$Staff \bowtie_{Staff.branchNo = Branch.branchNo} Branch = Branch \bowtie_{Staff.branchNo= Branch.branchNo} Staff$$

(6) Commutativity of Selection and Theta join (or Cartesian Product).

If the selection predicate involves only attributes of the relations being joined, then the Selection and join (or Cartesian product) operations commute.

$$\sigma_p(R \bowtie_r S) = (\sigma_p(R)) \bowtie_r S$$

$$\sigma_p(R \times S) = (\sigma_p(R)) \times S$$

Where $p \in \{A_1, A_2.......A_n\}$

Alternatively, if the selection predicate is a conjunctive predicate of the form $(p \wedge q)$, where p involves only attributes of R, and q involves only attributes of S, then the selection and Theta join operations commute as: $\sigma_p \Pi_q(R$

$$\sigma_{p \wedge q}(R \bowtie_r S) = (\sigma_p(R)) \bowtie_r (\sigma_q(S))$$

$$\sigma_{p \wedge q}(R \times S) = (\sigma_p(R)) \times (\sigma_q(S))$$

For Example:

$$\sigma_{position= 'Manager' \wedge city= 'Delhi'}(Staff \bowtie_{Staff.branchNo = Branch.branchNo} Branch) =$$

$$(\sigma_{position = 'Manager'}(Staff)) \bowtie_{Staff.branchNo = Branch.branchNo}(\sigma_{city = 'Delhi'}(Branch))$$

(7) Commutativity of Projection and Theta join (or Cartesian product).

If the projection list is of the form $L = L_1 \cup L_2$, where L_1 involves only attributes of R, and L_2 involves only attributes of S, then provided the join condition only contains attributes of L, the Projection and Theta join operations commute as:

$$\Pi_{L1 \cup L2}(R \bowtie_r S) = (\Pi_{L1}(R)) \bowtie_r (\Pi_{L2}(S))$$

For example:

$$\Pi_{position,\ city,\ branchNo}(Staff \bowtie_{Staff.branchNo=Branch.branchNo} Branch)=$$

$$(\Pi_{position,\ branchNo}(Staff)) \bowtie_{Staff.branchNo=Branch.branchNo} (\Pi_{city,branchNo}(Branch))$$

If the join condition contains additional attributes not in L, say attributes $M = M_1 \cup M_2$ where M_1 M_1 involves only attributes of R, and M_2 involves only attributes of S, then a final Projection operation is required:

$$\Pi_{L1 \cup L2}(R \bowtie_r S) = \Pi_{L1 \cup L2}(\Pi_{L1 \cup M1}(R)) \bowtie_r (\Pi_{L2 \cup M2}(S))$$

For example:

$\Pi_{position, city}(Staff \bowtie_{Staff.branchNo=Branch.branchNo} Branch) =$

$(\Pi_{position, city}((\Pi_{position, branchNo}(Staff)) \bowtie_{Staff.branchNo=Branch.branchNo} (\Pi_{city,branchNo}(Branch)))$

(8) Commutativity of Union and Intersection (but not Set difference)

$R \cup S = S \cup R$

$R \cap S = S \cap R$

(9) Commutativity of Selection and set operations (Union, Intersection, and Set difference).

$$\sigma_p(R \cup S) = \sigma_p(S) \cup \sigma_p(R)$$

$$\sigma_p(R \cap S) = \sigma_p(S) \cap \sigma_p(R)$$

$$\sigma_p(R - S) = \sigma_p(S) - \sigma_p(R)$$

(10) Commutativity of Projection and Union.

$$\Pi_L(R \cup S) = \Pi_L(S) \cup \Pi_L(R)$$

(11) Associativity of Theta join (and Cartesian product).

Cartesian product and Natural join are always associative:

$$(R \bowtie S) \bowtie T = R \bowtie (S \bowtie T)$$

$$(R \times S) \times T = R \times (S \times T)$$

If the join condition q involves only attributes from the relations S and T, then Theta join is associative in the following manner:

$$(R \bowtie_p S) \bowtie_{q \wedge r} T = R \bowtie_{p \wedge r} (S \bowtie_q T)$$

For example:

$(Staff \bowtie_{Staff.staffNo=PropertyForRent.staffNo} PropertyForRent) \bowtie_{ownerNo=Owner.ownerNo \wedge Staff.lName=Owner.lName} Owner = Staff \bowtie_{Staff.staffNo=PropertyForRent.staffNo \wedge Staff.lName=lName} (PropertyForRent \bowtie_{ownerNo} Owner$

(12) Associativity of Union and Intersection (but not Set difference).

$$(R \cup S) \cup T = S \cup (R \cup T)$$

$$(R \cap S) \cap T = S \cap (R \cap T)$$

Heuristical Processing Strategies

Many DBMSs use heuristics to determine strategies for query processing. In this section we examine some good heuristics that could be applied during query processing.

(1) Perform Selection operations as early as possible.

Selection reduces the cardinality of the relation and reduces the subsequent processing of that relation. Therefore, we should use rule 1 to cascade the selection operations, and rules 2, 4, 6, and 9 regarding commutativity of Selection with unary and binary operations, to move the selection operations as far down the tree as possible. Keep selection predicates on the same relation together.

(2) Combine the Cartesian product with a subsequent selection operation whose predicate represents a join condition into a Join Operation.

We have already noted that we can rewrite a Selection with a Theta join predicate and Cartesian product operation as a Theta join operation:

$$\sigma_{R.a \Theta S.b(}R \text{ x } S) = R \bowtie_{R.a \Theta S.b} S$$

(3) Use associativity of binary operations to rearrange leaf nodes so that the leaf nodes with the most restrictive Selection operations are executed first.

Again, our general rule of thumb is to perform as much reduction as possible before performing binary operations. Thus, if we have two consecutive join operations to perform:

$$(R \bowtie_{R.a \Theta S.b} S) \bowtie_{S.c \Theta T.d} T$$

Then we should use rule 11 and 12 concerning associatitity of Theta join (and Union and Intersection) to reorder the operations so that the relations resulting in the smaller join is performed first, which means that the second join will also be based on a smaller first opened.

(4) Perform Projection operations as early as possible.

Again, Projection reduces the cardinality of the relation and reduces the subsequent processing of that relation. Therefore, we should use rule 3 to cascade the Projection operations, and rules 4, 7, and 10 regarding commutativity of Projection with binary operations, to more the Projection operations as far down the tree as possible. Keep projection attributes on the same relation together.

(5) Compute common expressions once.

If a common expression appears more than once in the tree, and the result it produces is not too large, store the result after it has been computed once and then reuse it when required. This is only beneficial if the size of the result from the common expression is small enough to either be stored in main memory or accessed from secondary storage at a cost less than that of recomputing it. This can be especially useful when querying views, since the same expression must be used to construct the view each time.

11.4 COST ESTIMATION FOR THE RELATIONAL ALGEBRA OPERATIONS

A query optimizer should not depend solely on heuristic rules; it should also estimate and compare the costs of executing a query using different execution strategies and should choose the strategy with the lowest cost estimate. For this approach to work, accurate cost estimates are required so that different strategies are compared fairly and realistically. In addition, we must limit the number of execution strategies to be considered; otherwise, too much time will be spent making cost estimates for the many possible execution strategies. Hence, this approach is more suitable for compiled queries where the optimization is done at compile time and the resulting execution strategy code is stored and executed directly at runtime. For interpreted queries, where the entire process shown in Figure 11.2 occurs at runtime, a full-scale optimization may slow down the response time. A more elaborate optimization is indicated for compiled queries, whereas a partial, less time-consuming optimization works best for interpreted queries.

We call this approach **cost based query optimization,** and it uses traditional optimization techniques that search the solution space to a problem for a solution that minimizes an objective (cost) function. The cost functions used in query optimization are estimates and not exact cost functions, so the optimization may select a query execution strategy that is not the optimal one.

11.4.1 Cost Components for Query Execution

The cost of executing a query includes the following components:

1. **Access cost to secondary storage:** This is the cost of searching for, reading, and writing data blocks that reside on secondary storage, mainly on disk. The cost of searching for records in a file depends on the type of access structures on that file, such as ordering, hashing, and primary or secondary indexes. In addition, factors such as whether the file blocks are allocated contiguously on the same disk cylinder or scattered on the disk affect the access cost.
2. **Storage cost:** This is the cost of storing any intermediate files that are generated by an execution strategy for the query.
3. **Computation cost:** This is the cost of performing in-memory operations on the data buffers during query execution. Such operations include searching for and sorting records, merging records for a join, and performing computations on field values.
4. **Memory usage cost:** This is the cost pertaining to the number of memory buffers needed during query execution.
5. **Communication cost:** This is the cost of shipping the query and its results from the database site to the site or terminal where the query originated.

11.4.2 Catalog Information Used in Cost Functions

To estimate the costs of various execution strategies, we must keep track of any information that is needed for the cost functions. This information may be stored in the DBMS catalog, where it is accessed by the query optimizer. First, we must know the size of each file. For a file whose records are all of the same type, the **number of records (tuples) (*r*),** the (average) **record size (*R*),** and the **number of blocks (*b*)** (or close estimates of them) are needed. The **blocking factor (*bfr*)** for the file may also be needed. We must also keep track of the **primary access method** and the **primary access attributes** for each file. The file records may be unordered, ordered by an attribute with or without a primary or clustering index, or hashed on a key attribute. Information is kept on all secondary indexes and indexing attributes. The **number of levels (*x*)** of each multilevel index (primary, secondary, or clustering) is needed for cost functions that estimate the number of block accesses that occur during query execution. In some cost functions the **number of first-level index blocks** is needed.

Another important parameter is the **number of distinct values (d)** of an attribute and its **selectivity (sl),** which is the fraction of records satisfying an equality condition on the attribute. This allows estimation of the **selection cardinality (s = sl * r)** of an attribute, which is the average number of records that will satisfy an equality selection condition on that attribute. For a key attribute, d = r, sl = 1/r and s = 1. For a **nonkey attribute,** by making an assumption that the d distinct values are uniformly distributed among the records, we estimate sl = (1/d) and so s = (r/d).

Information such as the number of index levels is easy to maintain because it does not change very often. However, other information may change frequently; for example, the number of records *r* in a file changes every time a record is inserted or deleted. The query optimizer will need reasonably close but not necessarily completely up-to-the-minute values of these parameters for use in estimating the cost of various execution strategies.

11.4.3 Algorithms for External Sorting

Sorting is one of the primary algorithms used in query processing. For example, whenever an SQL query specifies an ORDER BY-clause, the query result must be sorted. Sorting is also a key component in sort-merge algorithms used for JOIN and other operations (such as UNION and INTERSECTION), and in duplicate elimination algorithms for the PROJECT operation (when an SQL query specifies the DISTINCT option in the SELECT clause).

External sorting refers to sorting algorithms that are suitable for large files of records stored on disk that do not fit entirely in main memory, such as most database files. The typical external sorting algorithm uses a **sort-merge strategy,** which starts by sorting small subfiles—called **runs**—of the main file and then merges the sorted runs, creating larger sorted subfiles that are merged in turn. The sort-merge algorithm, like other database algorithms, requires buffer space in main memory, where the actual sorting and merging of the runs is performed. The basic algorithm consists of two phases :

(1) the sorting phase and (2) the merging phase.

In the **sorting phase,** runs (portions or pieces) of the file that can fit in the available buffer space are read into main memory, sorted using an internal sorting algorithm, and written back to disk as temporary sorted subfiles (or runs). The size of a run and **number of initial runs(n_R)** is dictated by the **number of file blocks (b)** and the **available buffer space(n_B)** . For example, if n_B = 5 blocks and the size of the file **b** = 1024 blocks, then n_R =[(b/n_B], or 205 initial runs each of size 5 blocks (except the last run which will have 4 blocks). Hence, after the sort phase, 205 sorted runs are stored as temporary subfiles on disk.

In the **merging phase,** the sorted runs are merged during one or more **passes.** The **degree of merging (d_M)** is the number of runs that can be merged together in each pass. In each pass, one buffer block is needed to hold one block from each of the runs being merged, and one block is needed for containing one block of the merge result. Hence, d_M is the smaller of (n_B - 1) and n_R, and the number of passes is [($\log_{dM}(n_R)$]. In our example, d_M= 4 (four-way merging), so the 205 initial sorted runs would be merged into 52 at the end of the first pass, which are then merged into 13, then 4, then 1 run, which means that four passes are needed. The minimum d_M of 2 gives the worst-case performance of the algorithm, which is

$$(2 * b) + (2 * (\log_2 b)))$$

The first term represents the number of block accesses for the sort phase, since each file block is accessed twice—once for reading into memory and once for writing the records back to disk after sorting. The second term represents the number of block accesses for the merge phase, assuming the worst-case d_M of 2. In general, the log is taken to the base d_M and the expression for number of block accesses becomes

$$(2 * b) + (2 * (b * (\log_{dM} n_R)))$$

11.4.4 Costs Functions for SELECT

A number of search algorithms are possible for selecting records from a file. These are also known as **file scans,** because they scan the records of a file to search for and retrieve records that satisfy a selection condition. If the search algorithm involves the use of an index, the index search is called an **index scan.** The following search methods (S1 through S6) are examples of some of the search algorithms that can be used to implement a select operation:

- **S1- Linear search (brute force):** Retrieve every record in the file, and test whether its attribute values satisfy the selection condition.
- **S2-Binary search:** If the selection condition involves an equality comparison on a key attribute on which the file is ordered, binary search—which is more efficient than linear search—can be used.
- **S-Using a primary index (or hash key):** If the selection condition involves an equality comparison on a key attribute with a primary index (or hash key).
- **S4-Using a primary index to retrieve multiple records:** If the comparison condition is >, >=,<, or <= on a key with a primary index.
- **S5-Using a clustering index to retrieve multiple index:** If the selection condition involves equality comparison on a nonkey attribute with a clustering index.
- **S6-Using a secondary (Tree) index on an equality comparison:** This search method can be used to retrieve a single record if the indexing field is a key (has unique values) or to retrieve multiple records if the indexing field is not a key. This can also be used for comparisons involving >, >=, <, or <=.

  Search methods for complex selection

  If a condition of a SELECT operation is a **conjunctive condition**—that is, if it is made up of several simple conditions connected with the AND logical connective. The DBMS can use the following additional methods to implement the operation:

- **S7-Conjunctive selection using an individual index***:* If an attribute involved in any **single simple condition** in the conjunctive condition has an access path that permits the use of one of the Methods S2 to S6, use that condition to retrieve the records and then check whether each retrieved record satisfies the remaining simple conditions in the conjunctive condition.
- **S8-Conjunctive selection using a composite index:** If two or more attributes are involved in equality conditions in the conjunctive condition and a composite index (or hash structure) exists on the combined fields.

- **S9-Conjunctive selection by intersection of record pointers:** If secondary indexes (or other access paths) are available on more than one of the fields involved in simple conditions in the conjunctive condition, and if the indexes include record pointers (rather than block pointers), then each index can be used to retrieve the **set of record pointers** that satisfy the individual condition. The **intersection** of these sets of record pointers gives the record pointers that satisfy the conjunctive condition, which are then used to retrieve those records directly. If only some of the conditions have secondary indexes, each retrieved record is further tested to determine whether it satisfies the remaining conditions.

11.4.5 Implementing the JOIN Operation

The JOIN operation is one of the most time-consuming operations in query processing. Many of the join operations encountered in queries are of the EQUIJOIN and NATURAL JOIN varieties, so we consider only these two here. For the remainder of this chapter, the term join refers to an EQUIJOIN (or NATURAL JOIN). There are many possible ways to implement a two-way join, which is a join on two files. Joins involving more than two files are called multiway joins. The number of possible ways to execute multiway joins grows very rapidly. In this section we discuss techniques for implementing only two-way joins. For example EMPLOYEE, DEPARTMENT, and PROJECT relations. The algorithms we consider are for join operations of the form

$$R \bowtie_{A=B} S$$

Where A and B are domain compatible attributes of R and S respectively. The methods we discuss can be extended to more general forms of join. We illustrate four of the most common techniques for performing such as a join, using the following example operations

$$\text{EMPLOYEE} \bowtie_{\text{Dno=Dnumber}} \text{DEPARTMENT}$$

$$\text{EMPLOYEE} \bowtie_{\text{Mgr\_ssn=Ssn}} \text{EMPLOYEE}$$

Methods for Implementing Joins

- **J1- Nested-loop join (brute force):** For each record t in R (outer loop), retrieve every record s from S (inner loop) and test whether the two records satisfy the join condition t[A] = s[B].
- **J2- Single-loop join (using an access structure to retrieve the matching records):** If an index (or hash key) exists for one of the two join attributes say, B of S—retrieve each record t in R, one at a time (single loop), and then use the access structure to retrieve directly all matching records s from S that satisfy s[B] = t[A].
- **J3- Sort merge join:** If the records of R and S are physically sorted (ordered) by value of the join attributes A and B, respectively, we can implement the join in the most efficient way possible. Both files are scanned concurrently in order of the join attributes, matching the records that have the same values for A and B. If the files are not sorted, they may be sorted first by using external sorting. In this method, pairs of file blocks are copied into memory buffers in order and the records of each file are scanned only once each for matching with the other file—unless both A and B are nonkey attributes, in which case the method needs to be modified slightly. A

variation of the sort-merge join can be used when secondary indexes exist on both join attributes. The indexes provide the ability to access (scan) the records in order of the join attributes, but the records themselves are physically scattered all over the file blocks, so this method may be quite inefficient, as every record access may involve accessing a different disk block.

- **J4- Hash Join:** The records of files R and S are both hashed to the same hash file, using the same hashing function on the join attributes A of R and B of S as hash keys. First, a single pass through the file with fewer records (say, R) hashes its records to the hash file buckets; this is called the **partitioning phase,** since the records of R are partitioned into the hash buckets. In the second phase, called the **probing phase,** a single pass through the other file (S) then hashes each of its records to probe the appropriate bucket, and that record is combined with all matching records from R in that bucket. This simplified description of hash-join assumes that the smaller of the two files fits entirely into memory buckets after the first phase.

11.4.6 Algorithms for PROJECT and set operations

A PROJECT operation $\Pi_{<\text{attribute list}>}(R)$ is straightforward to implement if <attribute list> includes a key of relation R, because in this case the result of the operation will have the same number of tuples as R, but with only the values for the attributes in <attribute list> in each tuple. If <attribute list> does not include a key of R, duplicate tuples must be eliminated. This is usually done by sorting the result of the operation and then eliminating duplicate tuples, which appear consecutively after sorting. Hashing can also be used to eliminate duplicates: as each record is hashed and inserted into a bucket of the hash file in memory, it is checked against those already in the bucket; if it is a duplicate, it is not inserted. It is useful to recall here that in SQL queries, the default is not to eliminate duplicates from the query result; only if the keyword DISTINCT is included are duplicates eliminated from the query result.

Set operations—UNION, INTERSECTION, SET DIFFERENCE, and CARTESIAN PRODUCT—are sometimes expensive to implement. In particular, the CARTESIAN PRODUCT operation R x S is quite expensive, because its result includes a record for each combination of records from R and S. In addition, the attributes of the result include all attributes of R and S. If R has n records and j attributes and S has m records and k attributes, the result relation will have n * m records and j + k attributes. Hence, it is important to avoid the CARTESIAN PRODUCT operation and to substitute other equivalent operations during query optimization.

The other three set operations—UNION, INTERSECTION, and SET DIFFERENCE — apply only to union-compatible relations, which have the same number of attributes and the same attribute domains. The customary way to implement these operations is to use variations of the sort-merge technique: the two relations are sorted on the same attributes, and, after sorting, a single scan through each relation is sufficient to produce the result. For example, we can implement the UNION operation, R ∪ S, by scanning and merging both sorted files concurrently, and whenever the same tuple exists in both relations, only one is kept in the merged result. For the INTERSECTION operation, R C S, we keep in the merged result only those tuples that appear in both relations

Hashing can also be used to implement UNION, INTERSECTION, and SET DIFFERENCE. One table is partitioned and the other is used to probe the appropriate partition. For example, to implement R D S, first hash (partition) the records of R; then, hash (probe) the records of S, but do not insert duplicate records in the buckets. To implement R C S, first partition the records of R to the hash file. Then, while hashing each record of S, probe to check if an identical record from R is found in the bucket, and if so add the record to the result file. To implement R - S, first hash the records of R to the hash file buckets. While hashing (probing) each record of S, if an identical record is found in the bucket, remove that record from the bucket.

11.5 PIPELINING

A query specified in SQL will typically be translated into a relational algebra expression that is a sequence of relational operations. If we execute a single operation at a time, we must generate temporary files on disk to hold the results of these temporary operations, creating excessive overhead. Generating and storing large temporary files on disk is time-consuming and can be unnecessary in many cases, since these files will immediately be used as input to the next operation. To reduce the number of temporary files, it is common to generate query execution code that corresponds to algorithms for combinations of operations in a query.

For example, rather than being implemented separately, a JOIN can be combined with two SELECT operations on the input files and a final PROJECT operation on the resulting file; all this is implemented by one algorithm with two input files and a single output file. Rather than creating four temporary files, we apply the algorithm directly and get just one result file. In Section 11.3.3 we discuss how heuristic relational algebra optimization can group operations together for execution. This is called **pipelining** or stream-based processing.

It is common to create the query execution code dynamically to implement multiple operations. The generated code for producing the query combines several algorithms that correspond to individual operations. As the result tuples from one operation are produced, they are provided as input for subsequent operations. For example, if a join operation follows two select operations on base relations, the tuples resulting from each select are provided as input for the join algorithm in a stream or **pipeline** as they are produced.

11.6 QUERY OPTIMIZATION IN ORACLE

We have seen query processing and query optimization in this chapter. In the following sections we will see an overview of the query optimization in oracle. This only a brief overview, the aim is to give an idea of how the query optimization works in the real world. For a detailed discussion on Oracle's query optimization refer to the Oracle manuals or books on the oracle query processor and performance tuning.

Optimization, as we have seen, is the process of choosing the most efficient way to execute an SQL statement. This is an important step in the processing of any data manipulation language (DML) statement-SELECT, INSERT, UPDATE, or DELETE. Many different ways to execute an SQL statement often exist, for example, by varying the order in which tables or indexes are accessed. The procedure oracle uses to execute a statement can greatly affect how quickly the statement executes.

The optimizer is the portion of the oracle database server that determines the most efficient way to execute any query statement. The optimizer considers several factors to make a choice between multiple alternatives. The choice is usually the best of the most efficient of the all the options. The optimizer uses two different techniques to formulate the most efficient path to execute the statements. These options are the rule-based approach and cost-based approach.

11.6.1 The Execution Plan

To execute a query, oracle may have to perform many steps. Each of these steps either retrieves rows of data physically from the database or prepares them in some way for the user issuing the statement. The combination of the steps oracle uses to execute a statement is called an execution plan.

- Rule Based: Oracle chooses an execution plan based on the access paths available and assigns a rank to these paths. Oracle always chooses the path with the lower rank over one with the higher rank.
- Cost Based: Oracle considers available access paths and determine which execution plan is most efficient based on the statistics in the data dictionary for the tables accessed by the statements and their associated clusters and indexes.

Example: SELECT ename, job, sal, dname

```
FROM emp, dept
WHERE emp.deptno = dept.deptno
AND NOT EXISTS
    (SELECT *
    FROM salgrade
    WHERE emp.sal BETWEEN lowsal AND highsal);
```

11.6.2 Steps of Execution Plan

Each step of the execution plan returns a set of rows that are either used by the next step or returned in the last step to the user or application issuing the SQL statement. A set of rows returned by a step is called a row source.

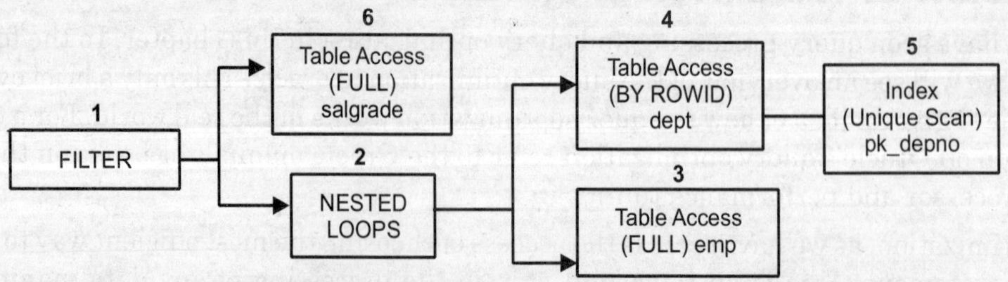

Figure 11.6.2 Graphical Representation of the Execution Plan

Figure 11.6.2 shows the flow of row sources from one step to another. The numbering of the step reflects the order in which they are displays in response to the EXPLAIN PLAN command. This generally is not the order in which the steps are executed. Each step of the execution plan either retrieves rows from the database or accepts rows from one or more row sources as input:

- Steps indicated by the shaded boxes physically retrieve data from an object in the database. Such steps are called access paths:
  1. Steps 3 and 6 read all the rows of the EMP and SALGRADE tables respectively.
  2. Steps 5 looks in the PK_DEPTNO index, each DEPTNO value returned by step 3. There it finds the ROWIDs of the associated rows in the DEPT table.
  3. Step 4 retrieves from the DEPT table the rows whose ROWIDs were returned by step 5.
- Step indicated by the a clear boxes operate on row sources:
  1. Step 2 performs a nested loops operation, accepting row sources from step 3 and 4, joining each row from step 3 step sources to its corresponding row in step 4, and returning the resulting rows to step 1.
  2. Step 1 performs a filter operation. It accepts row sources from step 2 and 6, eliminates rows from step 2 that have a corresponding row in step 6, and returns the remaining rows from step 2 to the user or application issuing the statement.

11.6.3 The Explain Plan Command

You can examine the execution plan chosen by the chosen by the optimizer for an SQL statement by using the EXPLAIN PLAN command, which causes the optimizer to choose the execution plan and then inserts data describing the plan into a database table. For example 11.6.3 shows the output table is such a description for the statement examined in the previous section:

ID	OPERATION	OPTIONS	OBJECT_NAME
0	SELECT STATEMENT		
1	FILTER		
2	NESTED LOOPS		
3	TABLE ACCESS	FULL	EMP
4	TABLE ACCESS	BY ROWID	DEPT
5	INDEX	UNIQUE SCAN	PK_DEPTNO
6	TABLE ACCESS	FULL	SALGRADE

Figure 11.6.3 Output of EXPLAIN PLAN Command

Each box in Figure 11.6.3 and each row in the output table correspond to a single step in the execution plan. For each row in the listing the value in the ID column is the value shows in the corresponding box in Figure 11.6.3. You can obtain such a listing by using the EXPLAIN PLAN command and then querying the output table.

11.6.4 Execution Plan

The steps of the execution plan are not performed in the order in which they are numbered. Rather, oracle first performs the steps that appear as leaf nodes in the tree structured graphical representation of the execution of the execution plan (step 3, 5 and 6 in figure 11.6.2). The rows returned by each step become the row sources of its parent step. Then oracle performs the parent steps. To execute the statement for Figure 11.6.2, for example, oracle performs the step in this order.

- First, oracle performs step 3, and returns the resulting rows, one by one to step 2.
- For each row returned by step 3, oracle performs these steps.
  1. Oracle performs step 5 and returns the resulting ROWID to step 4.
  2. Oracle performs step 4 and returns the resulting row to step 2.
  3. Oracle performs step 2, joining the single row from step 3 with a single row from step 4, and returning a single row to step 1.
  4. Oracle performs step 6 and returns the resulting row, if any, to step 1.
  5. Oracle performs step 1. If a row is not returned from step 6, oracle returns the row from step 2 to the user issuing the SQL statement.

11.7 COST BASED AND RULE BASED OPTIMIZATION

To create an execution plan for an SQL statement, the optimizer uses one of two approaches-cost based or rule based.

11.7.1 The Cost Based Approach

Using the cost-based approach, the optimizer determines which execution plan is not efficient by considering available access paths and factoring in information based on statistics in the data dictionary for the schema objects (tables, clusters, indexes) accessed by the statement. The cost based approach also considers hints or optimization suggestions placed in a comment in the statement. Conceptually, the cost based approach consists of these steps:

1. The optimizer generates a set of potential execution plans for the statement based on its available access paths and hints.
2. The optimizer estimates the cost of each execution plan based on the data distribution and storage characteristics and statistics for the tables, clusters and indexes in the data dictionary.
3. The optimizer compares the costs of the execution plans and chooses the one with the smallest cost.

11.7.2 Histograms

Oracle's cost based optimizer uses data value histograms to get accurate estimates of the distribution of column data. Histograms provide improved selectively estimates in the presence of data skew, resulting in optimal execution plans with non-uniform data distributions. You generates histograms by using the ANALYZE command. One of the fundamental capabilities of any cost based optimizer is determining the selectively of predicates that appear in queries. Selectivity estimates are used to decide when to use an index and the order in which to join tables. Most attributes domains (a tables columns) are not uniformly distributed. The oracle cost based optimizer uses height balanced histograms on specified attributes to describe the distributions of non-uniform domains. Consider a column C with values between 1 and 100 and a histogram with 10 buckets. If the data in C is uniformly distributed, this histogram would look like Figure 11.7.2(a), where the numbers are endpoint values

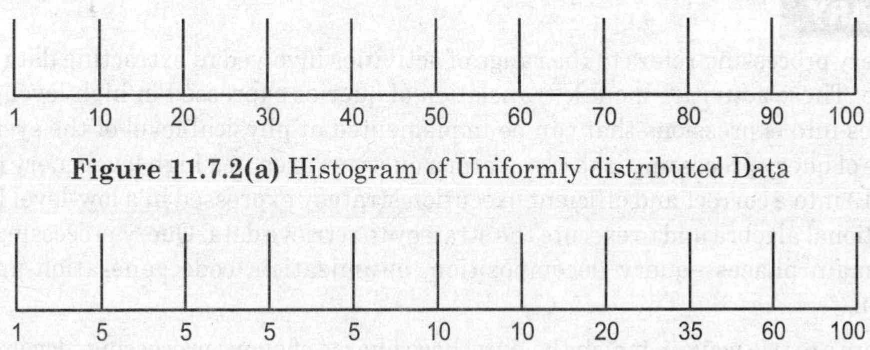

Figure 11.7.2(a) Histogram of Uniformly distributed Data

Figure 11.7.2(b) Histogram of Data that is not Uniformly Distributed

The number of rows in each bucket is one-tenth the total numbers of rows in the table. Four tenths of the rows have values between 60 and 100 in this example of uniform distribution. If the data is not uniformly distributed, the histogram might look like Figure 11.7.2(b)

11.7.3 Rule Based Approach

Using the rule based approach; the optimizer chooses an execution plan based on the access paths available and the ranks of these access paths. You can use rule based optimization to access both relational data and object types. Oracle's ranking of the access paths is heuristic. If there is more than one way to execute an SQL statement, the rule based approach always uses the operation with the lower rank. Usually operation of lower rank execute faster than those associated with constructs of higher ranks.

11.8 SEMANTIC QUERY OPTIMIZATION

A different approach to query optimization, called semantic query optimization, has been suggested. This technique, which may be used in combination with the techniques discussed previously, uses constraints specified on the database schema-such as unique attributes and other more complex constraints—in order to modify one query into another query that is more efficient to execute. We will not discuss this approach in detail but only illustrate it with a simple example. Consider the SQL query:

```
SELECT    E.Lname, M.Lname
FROM      EMPLOYEE AS E, EMPLOYEE AS M
WHERE     E.Supar_ssn=M.Ssn AND E.Salary > M.Salary
```

This query retrieves the names of employees who earn more than their supervisors. Suppose that we had a constraint on the database schema that stated that no employee can earn more than his or her direct supervisor. If the semantic query optimizer checks for the existence of this constraint, it need not execute the query at all because it knows that the result of the query will be empty. This may save considerable time if the constraint checking can be done efficiently. However, searching through many constraints to find those that are applicable to a given query and that may semantically optimize it can also be quite time-consuming. With the inclusion of active rules in database systems, semantic query optimization techniques may eventually be fully incorporated into the DBMSs of the future.

SUMMARY

Query processing refers to the range of activities involved in extracting data from the database. These activities include translation of queries expressed in high level database languages into expressions that can be implemented at physical level of the system. The objective of query processing is to transform a query written in a high level query language (like SQL) into a correct and efficient execution strategy expressed in a low-level language like relational algebra and to execute the strategy to retrieve data. Query processing consists of four main phases –query decomposition, optimization, code generation and query execution.

There are two ways in which the first three phases of query processing- decomposition, optimization and code generation-can be performed. One is to dynamically carry out decomposition and optimization. **Dynamic query optimization** is advantageous because all the information used to select the best strategy is up-to-date. The disadvantages are that the performance of the query is affected because the query has to be parsed, validated and optimized before it can be executed. In some cases, the number of execution strategies analyzed to reach the best alternative need to be reduced in order to keep the overhead costs within acceptable limits. This reduction in the number of alternatives might result in selecting a strategy that is not the best.

The second method is called **Static query optimization**. In this method the query is parsed, validated and optimized once. The advantage of static query optimization is that the run-time overhead of query processing is eliminated. This method allows the DBMS to analyze a larger number of alternatives before selecting the optimum strategy thereby increasing the chances of finding a better strategy. The disadvantage of this method is that the execution strategy that is chosen as being optimal when the query is complied may no longer be the optimal one when the query in run. So this type of query optimization is best suited for queries that are executed very frequently and for which the database statistics are static in nature.

EXERCISES

1. What is query processing?
2. What are the steps involved in query processing?
3. What is an access plan?
4. Explain the query processing process with the help of a diagram.
5. What is query decomposition?

6. What is a relational algebraic query tree?
7. How would you check the semantic correctness of a query?
8. What is heuristic query optimization?
9. What are typical phases of query processing?
10. Explain how heuristic query optimization is performed with an example.
11. What are advantages of cost based query optimization?
12. What are main cost components in executing a query?
13. What is the pipelining and what are its advantages?
14. Explain the rule based and cost based query optimization in oracle.
15. Mention the different steps followed during query optimization.
16. What is a relational algebra query tree?
17. What is a query execution plan?
18. Discuss the different algorithms for implementing each of the following relational operators and the circumstances under which each algorithms can be used: SELECT, PROJECT, JOIN, UNION, INTERSECT, SET DIFFERNCE,
19. What are the different methods used for implementing joins?
20. What are main strategies for implementing the join operation?

CHAPTER 12

DATABASE SECURITY

12.1 INTRODUCTION

Security is an important issue in database management because information stored in a database is a very valuable and many a time, very sensitive commodity. So the data in a database management systen. need to be protected from abuse- they should be protected from unauthorized access and updates. If you are using a single database and you are the only user, then the whole issue of data security boils down to keeping your machine secure form other users. But the commercial database management systems are rarely single users. Many people and application s will be concurrently accessing it to get information, many users and programs will be updating the information, and yet another group of people and application will be deleting information that has become obsolete or incorrect. How does the DBMS recognize these users? By users we mean people and application programs. How will it distinguish from the authorized users from intruders? How will it reject the request made by unauthorized users? All these are taken care by the security mechanism of the database management system.

Database security involves allowing or disallowing users from performing actions on the database and the objects within it. All database management system provides comprehensive discretionary access control. Discretionary access control regulates all users access to named objects through privileges. A privilege is permission to access a named object in a prescribed manner: for example, permission to query a table. Because privileges are granted to users at the discretion of other users, this is called discretionary security.

12.2 DATABASE SECURITY ISSUES

Database security includes policies framed to protect data, falling in the hands of unauthorized users, security also includes the techniques used to ensure that database element are not changed or deleted by viruses or by unauthorized perso. s. In short data security addresses the following issues:

12.2.1 Types of Security

Database security is a broad area that addresses many issues, including the following:

- Privacy of certain data element
- Preserving policies of the organization
- System related security level
- Maintaining integrity of database

1. **Privacy of certain data element**

   Privacy relates to the legal and ethical rights regarding the access to certain personal data items. Some critical information may be regarded as private say for example the medical records of a person. Such records not be accessed, read or modified by unauthorized persons.

2. **Preserving policies of the organization**

   Some governmental, institutional or corporate level organizations have specific policies as to what kind of information should be made public. For example a person's credit rating and medical records should never be made public.

3. **System related security level**

   The level of the system at which the security should be enforced. For example, whether a security should be enforced at the hardware level, operating system level or DBMS level.

4. **Maintaining integrity of database**

   Database items stored in the database should be valid and consistent. Besides integrity constraints in the database management system controlling access to the database can greatly help to preserve the database integrity.

12.2.2 Threats to Databases

Threats to databases results in the loss or degradation of some or all of the following commonly accepted security goals: integrity, availability, and confidentiality

- **Loss of Integrity.** Database integrity refers to the requirement that information be protected from improper modification. Modification of data includes creation, insertion, modification, changing the status of data, and deletion. Integrity is lost if unauthorized changes are made to the data by either intentional or accidental acts. If the loss of system or data integrity is not corrected, continued use of the contaminated system or corrupted data could result in the inaccuracy, fraud, or errozeous decisions
- **Loss of availability.** Database availability refers to making objects available to a human user or a program to which they have a legitimate right.
- **Loss of confidentiality.** Database confidentiality refers to the protection of data unauthorized disclosure. The impact of unauthorized disclosure of confidential information can range from violation of the Data Privacy Act to the jeopardization of national security. Unauthorized, unanticipated, or unintentional disclosure could result in loss of public confidence, embarrassment, or legal action against the organization.

  To protect database against these types of threats, it is common to implement four kinds of control measures: access control, inference control, flow control, and encryption. We discuss each of these in chapter.

  In a multiuser database system, the DBMS must provide techniques to enable certain users or user groups to access selected portions of a database without gaining access to the rest of the database. This is particularly important when a large integrated database is to be used by many different users within the same organization. For example, sensitive information such as employee salaries or performance reviews should be kept confidential from most of the database system's users. A DBMS typically includes a database security and authorization subsystem that is responsible for ensuring the security of portions of a database against unauthorized access. It is now customary to refer to two types of database security mechanisms

- **Discretionary security mechanisms:** These are used to grant privileges to users, including the capability to access specific data files, records, or fields in a specified mode (such as read, insert, delete, or update).
- **Mandatory security mechanisms:** These are used to enforce multilevel security by classifying the data and users into various security classes (or levels) and then implementing the appropriate security policy of the organization. For example, a typical security policy is to permit users at a certain classification level to see only the data items classified at the user's own (or lower) classification level.

12.2.3 Control Measure

There are four main control measures that are used to provide security of data in databases. They are as follows

- Access control
- Inference control
- Flow Control
- Data Encryption

A security problem common to all computer systems is that of preventing unauthorized persons from accessing the system itself, either to obtain information or to make malicious changes in a portion of the database. The security mechanism of a DBMS must include provisions for restricting access to the database system as a whole. This function is called **access control** and is handled by creating user accounts and passwords to control the login process by the DBMS.

Statistical database used to provide statistical information or summaries of values based on various criteria. For example, a database for population statistics may provide statistics based on age groups, income levels, size of household, education levels, and other criteria. Statistical database users such as government statisticians or market research firms are allowed to access the database to retrieve statistical information about a population but not to access the detailed confidential information on specific individuals. Security for statistical databases must ensure that information on individuals cannot be accessed. It is sometimes possible to deduce certain facts concerning individuals from queries that involve only summary statistics on groups; consequently this must not be permitted either. This problem, called **statistical database security.** The corresponding control measures are **inference control** measures.

Another security issue is that of **flow control,** which prevents information from flowing in such a way that it reaches unauthorized users. Channels that are pathways for information to flow implicitly in ways that violate the security policy of an organization are called convert channels.

A final control measure **data encryption,** which is used to protect sensitive data (such as credit card numbers) that is being transmitted via some type of communications network. Encryption can be used to provide additional protection for sensitive portions of a database as well. The data is **encoded** by using some coding algorithm. An unauthorized user who accesses encoded data will have difficulty deciphering it, but authorized users are given decoding or decrypting algorithms (or keys) to decipher the data. Encrypting techniques that are very difficult to decode without a key have been developed for military applications.

A complete discussion of security in computer systems and databases is outside the scope of this textbook. We give only a brief overview of database security techniques here. The interested reader can refer to one of the references at the end of this chapter for a more comprehensive discussion.

12.2.4 Database Security and the DBA

As we discussed in later Chapter, the database administrator (DBA) is the central authority for managing a database system. The DBA's responsibilities include granting privileges to users who need to use the system and classifying users and data in accordance with the policy of the organization. The DBA has a

DBA account in the DBMS, sometimes called a system or superuser account, which provides powerful capabilities that are not made available to regular database accounts and users (Note 1). DBA privileged commands include commands for granting and revoking privileges to individual accounts, users, or user groups and for performing the following types of actions:

1. **Account creation:** This action creates a new account and password for a user or a group of users to enable them to access the DBMS.
2. **Privilege granting:** This action permits the DBA to grant certain privileges to certain accounts.
3. **Privilege revocation:** This action permits the DBA to revoke (cancel) certain privileges that were previously given to certain accounts.
4. **Security level assignment:** This action consists of assigning user accounts to the appropriate security classification level.

   The DBA is responsible for the overall security of the database system. Action 1 in the preceding list is used to control access to the DBMS as a whole, whereas actions 2 and 3 are used to control discretionary database authorizations, and action 4 is used to control mandatory authorization.

12.2.5 Access Protection, User Accounts, and Database Audits

Whenever a person or a group of persons needs to access a database system, the individual or group must first apply for a user account. The DBA will then create a new **account number** and **password** for the user if there is a legitimate need to access the database. The user must **log in** to the DBMS by entering the account number and password whenever database access is needed. The DBMS checks that the account number and password are valid; if they are, the user is permitted to use the DBMS and to access the database. Application programs can also be considered as users and can be required to supply passwords.

It is straightforward to keep track of database users and their accounts and passwords by creating an encrypted table or file with the two fields Account Number and Password. This table can easily be maintained by the DBMS. Whenever a new account is created, a new record is inserted into the table. When an account is canceled, the corresponding record must be deleted from the table. The database system must also keep track of all operations on the database that are applied by a certain user throughout each **login session,** which consists of the sequence of database interactions that a user performs from the time of logging in to the time of logging off. When a user logs in, the DBMS can record the user's account number and associate it with the terminal from which the user logged in. All operations applied from that terminal are attributed to the user's account until the user logs off. It is particularly important to keep track of update operations that are applied to the database so that, if the database is tampered with, the DBA can find out which user did the tampering.

To keep a record of all updates applied to the database and of the particular user who applied each update, we can modify the **system log.** The **system log** includes an entry for each operation applied to the database that may be required for recovery from a transaction failure or system crash. We can expand the log entries so that they also include the account number of the user and the on-line terminal ID that applied each operation recorded in the log. If any tampering with the database is suspected, a **database audit** is performed, which consists of reviewing the log to examine all accesses and operations applied to the database during a certain time period. When an illegal or unauthorized operation is found, the DBA can determine the account number used to perform this operation. Database audits are particularly important for sensitive databases that are updated by many transactions and users, such as a banking database that is updated by many bank tellers. A database log that is used mainly for security purposes is sometimes called an **audit trail.**

12.2.6 Dimensions of Security

Database management system provides different levels of security. These are the following:

1: **Network Level Security:** Network software level security is required in case of distributed database systems. Network software have built in methods for login security controls, permitting authorized users to log in and gain access to resources on the network. Another level of security provided by network software is the rights security. Rights security controls the files, sub directories and directories, a user or a group of users can access. Another level of security is attributes security. Attribute security determines if a particular files (or directory) can be viewed, shared renamed, modified or deleted by a user or not. Therefore, even if a user or group of users have the privilege to delete a particular file, but they cannot do so, if the attribute of file does not allow.

2: **Operating system level security:** Even if you have strong DBMS software, a weak operating system may serve as a means of unauthorized deletion of database files. So, Secure OS is important.

3: **Database system level security:** Some database users may be allowed to access only a portion of the database and denied access to other portions.

4: **Program level security:** It debars unauthorized users from using particular programs that may access the database. For example, a bank clerk may be allowed to use a program that retrieves details of a customer account, but not a program that modifies the balance amount.

5: **Records Level Security:** It debars unauthorized users from accessing or updating certain records, such as records of managers in the Employee Table.

6: **Field Level Security:** It debars unauthorized users from accessing or updating data in certain fields such as salary fields

12.3 DATA SECURITY RISKS

The field of data security is teeming with mistaken beliefs that cause people to design ineffective security solution. It is a popular belief that hackers cause most security breaches, but is reality 80% of data loss is to insiders. Another popular misconception is that encryption is a panacea that makes the data secure. But encryption is only one of the approaches to securing data. Security also requires access control, data integrity, system availability, and auditing. Many people strongly believe that firewalls make the data secure. But statistics shows that more than 40% of internet breaks-ins occurs in spite of a firewall being in place. To design a security solution that will truly protect data. You must understand the security requirements relevant to your site, and the scope of current threats to your data.

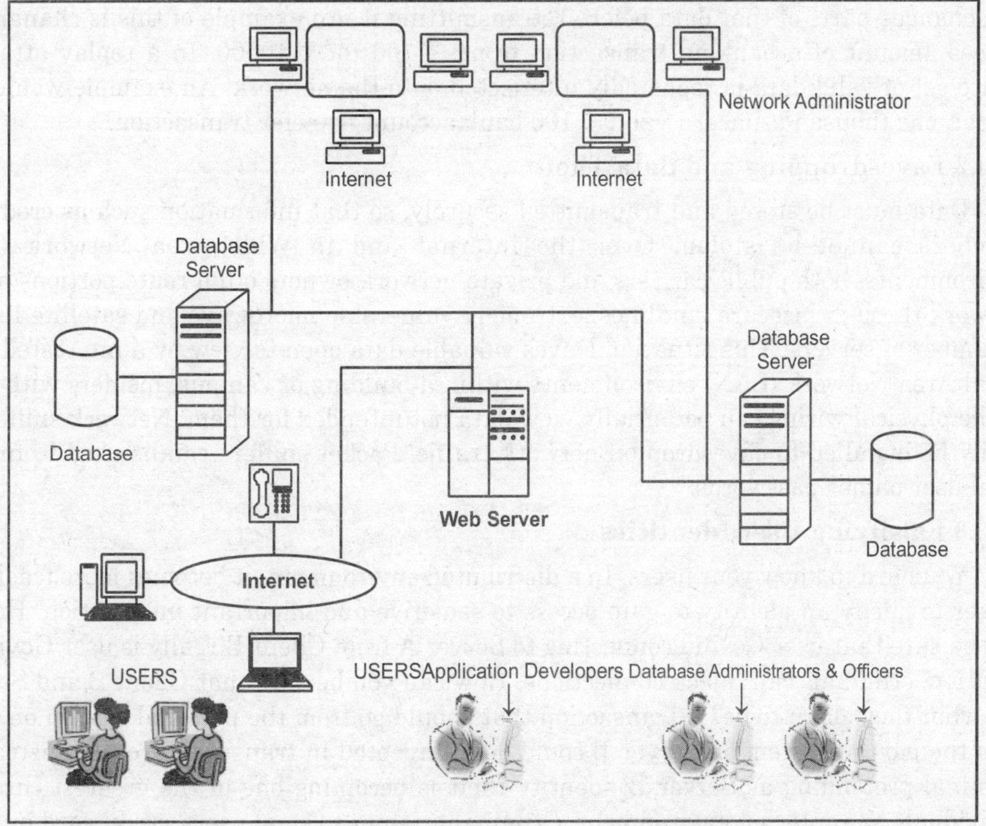

Figure 12.3 Potential Threats Points in a Database Environment

We have seen that the database security is the concern of the entire organization. The organization should identify all the risk factors and weak elements from the database security perspective and find solutions to counter and neutralize each such threat.

A threat is any situation, event or personal that will adversely affect the database security and the smooth and efficient functioning of the organization. A threat may be caused by a situation or event involving a person, action or circumstance that is likely to bring harm to the organization. The harm may be tangible, such as loss of data, damage to hardware, loss of software or intangible such as loss of customer goodwill or credibility and so on. Figure 12.3 identifies the different dimensions of database security and the various threat points in a typical database environment.

The integrity and privacy of data are at risk from unauthorized users, external sources listening in on the network, and internal users giving away the store. We will see these threat points in a little more details.

12.3.1 Data Tampering

Privacy of communication is essential to ensure that data cannot be modified or viewed in transit. Distributed environment bring with them the possibility that a malicious third party can perpetrate a computer crime by tempering with data as it moves between sites. In a data modification attack, an unauthorized party on the network intercepts data in transit and changes parts of that data before retransmitting it. An example of this is changing the rupees amount of a banking transaction from ₹ 100 to ₹ 10000. In a replay attack, an entire set of valid data is repeatedly interjected onto the network. An example would be to repeat, one thousand times, a valid ₹ 100 bank account transfer transaction.

12.3.2 Eavesdropping and data Theft

Data must be stored and transmitted securely, so that information such as credit card numbers cannot be stolen. Over the internet and in Wide Area Network (WAN) environments, both public carriers and private network owners often route portions of their network through insecure landlines, extremely vulnerable microwave and satellite links, or a number of servers. This situation leaves valuable data open to view by a interested party. Local Area Network (LAN) environments within a building or campus, insiders with access to the physical wiring can potentially view data not intended for them. Network sniffers can easily be installed to eavesdrop on network traffic. Packet sniffers can be used to find and steal user names passwords.

12.3.3 Falsifying User Identities

You need to know your users. In a distributed environment, it becomes more feasible for a user to falsify an identity to gain access to sensitive and important information. How can you be sure that user Govind connecting to Server A from Client B really is user Govind? In addition, criminals can hijack connections. How can you be sure that Client B and Server A are what they claim to be? A transaction that should go from the personal system on Server A to the payroll system on Server B could be intercepted in transit and routed instead to a terminal pretending as Server B. identity theft is becoming one of the greatest threats to individuals in a internet environment. Criminal attempt to steal users' credit card numbers, and then make purchases against the accounts. Or they steal other personal data, such as bank account numbers and driver's license numbers. And set up bogus accounts in someone else's name. Non-repudiation is another identity concern: how can a person's digital signature be protected? If hackers steal someone's digital signature, that person may be held responsible for any action performed using their private signing key.

12.3.4 Password related Threats

In large systems, users must remember multiple passwords for the different applications and services that they use. For example, a developer can have access to a development application on a workstation, as PC for sending email, and several computers or intranet sites for testing, multiple passwords in several ways:

- They may select easy-to-guess passwords, such as name, fictional character, or a word found in a dictionary, all of these passwords are vulnerable to dictionary attacks.
- They may also choose to standardize passwords so that they are the same on all machines or web sites. This results in a potentially large exposure in the event of a compromised password. They can also use passwords with slight variations that can be easily derived from known passwords.
- Users with complex passwords may write them down where as attacker can easily find them, or they may just forget them-requiring costly administration and support efforts.

All of these strategies compromise password secrecy and service availability. Moreover, administration of multiple user accounts and passwords is complex, time-consuming, and expensive.

12.3.5 Unauthorized Access to Tables and Columns

The database may contain confidential tables, or confidential columns in a table, which should not be available indiscriminately to all users authorized to access the database. It should be possible to protect data on a column level.

12.3.6 Unauthorized Access to Data Rows

Certain data rows may contain confidential information that should not be available indiscriminately to users authorized to access the table. You need granular access control-a way to enforce confidentiality on the data itself. For example, in a shared environment businesses should have access only to their own data; customers should be able to see only their own orders. If the necessary compartmentalization is enforced upon the data, rather than added by a application, then it cannot be bypassed by users, systems must therefore be flexible and should be able to support different security policies depending on whether you are dealing with customers or employees. For example, you may require stronger authentication for employees (who can see more data) than you do for customers can only see their own records.

12.3.7 Lack of Accountability

If the system administrator is unable to track users' activities, then users cannot be held responsible for their actions. There must be some reliable way (such as audit trails) to monitor who is performing what operations on the data.

12.3.8 Complex User Management Requirements

Systems must often support thousands-or hundreds of thousands-of users and therefore they must be scalable. In such large-scale environments, the burden of managing user accounts and passwords makes your system vulnerable to error and attack. You need to know who the user really is across all tiers of the application-to have reliable security. Administration of thousands, or hundreds c^f thousands of users, is difficult enough on a single system. This burden is compounded when security must be administrated on multiple systems. To meet the challenges of scale in security administration, you should be able to centrally manage users and privileges across multiple application and databases, using a directory based on industry standards. This can reduce system management costs and increase business efficiency.

12.4 DATA SECURITY REQUIREMENTS

We should use technology to ensure a secure computing environment for the organization. Although it is possible to find a technological solution for all problems, most of the security issues could be resolved using appropriate technology. The basic security standards which technology can ensure are confidentiality, integrity and availability.

12.4.1 Confidentiality

A secure system ensures the confidentiality of data. This means that it allows individuals to see only data that they are supposed to see. Confidentiality has several aspects like privacy of communications, secure storage of sensitive data, authenticated users and granular access control

- **Privacy of communications:** The DBMS should be capable of controlling the spread of confidentiality personal information such as health, employment, and credit records. It should also keep the corporate data such as trade secrets, proprietary information about products and processes, competitive analyses, as well as marketing and sales plans secure and away from the unauthorized people.
- **Secure Storage of Sensitive Data:** How can you ensure that data remains private, once it has been collected? Once confidential data has been entered, its integrity and privacy must be protected on the databases and severs wherein it resides.
- **Authenticated Users:** How can you designate the persons and organizations who have the right to see data? Authentication is a way of implementing decisions about whom to trust. Authentication methods seek to guarantee the identity of system users: that a person is who he says he is, and not an impostor.
- **Granular Access Control:** How much data should a particular user see? Access control is the ability to hide portions of database, so that access to the data does not become an all-or-nothing proposition. A clerk in the HR department might need some access to the EMPLOYEE Table- but be should not be permitted to access salary information for the entire company. The granularity of access control is the degree to which data access can be differentiated for particular tables, views, rows, and columns of a database.

12.4.2 Integrity

A secure system ensures that the data it contains is valid. Data integrity means that data is protected from deletion and corruption, both while it resides within the database, and while it is being transmitted over the network. Integrity has several aspects:

- System and object privileges control access to application tables and system commands, so that only authorized users can change data.
- Referential integrity is the ability to maintain valid relationships between values in the database, according to rules that have been defined
- A database must be protected against viruses designed to corrupt the data.
- The network traffic must be protected from deletion, corruption, and eavesdropping.

12.4.3 Availability

A secure system makes data available to authorized users, without delay. Denial-of-service attacks are attempts to authorized users' ability to access and use the system when needed. System availability has a number of aspects:

- **Resistance:** A secure system must be designed to fend off situations, or deliberate attacks, which might put it out of commission. For example, where must be facilities within the database to prohibit runaway queries. User profiles must be in place to define and limit the resources any given user may consume. In this way the system can be protected against users consuming too much memory or too many processes, thus preventing others from doing their work.
- **Scalability:** System performance must remain adequate regardless of the number of users or processes demanding service.
- **Flexibility:** Administrators must have adequate means of managing the user population. They might do this by using a directory, for example.
- **Ease of Use:** The security implementation itself must not diminish the ability of valid users to get their work done.

12.5 DATABASE USERS

Database management systems need to know whether you are a user to decide whether to allow you access data in the database or to perform update operations on the database. Different database products use different methods for user identification. Some products rely on the user's identity at the operating system level-these systems recognize anyone who can log on to the computer as an authorized user. More sophisticated database management systems have their own identification and authentication mechanisms. To be an authorized user of these systems one must have a User ID (also called Login ID or Account Name) and a password. For you to gain access to the system, you need to get the combination correct. The privileges of each user will be stored in the database and it is the function of the database management system to make sure that each user does only what he or she is supposed to do. Most multiuser database management system recognize at least two kinds of special users-a super user (also known as the database administrator or DBA) and the owners of database objects. Many database products recognize more varieties of special or privileged users. The users form a hierarchy with the ordinary user at the bottom and the super at the top. The amount of privileges each user has depends on his position in the hierarchy.

12.5.1 Types of Database Users

The types of database users and their duties and responsibilities can vary from one environment to another. A small company can have one database administrator who administers the database for application developers and users. A very large corporation will find it necessary to divide the duties of a database administrator among several people, and among several areas of specialization. The main users of a database are:

- Database Administrators
- Security Officers
- Network Administrators
- Application Developers
- Application Administrators
- Database Users

1. **Database Administrators:** Each database requires at least one database administrator (DBA) to administer it. Because a database management system can be large and can have many users, often this is not a one person job. In such cases, there is a group of DBAs who share responsibility. A database administrator's responsibilities can be include the following tasks:
   - Installing and upgrading the DBMS and application tools.
   - Allocating system storage and planning future storage requirements for the database system.
   - Creating primary database storage structures after application developers have designed an application.
   - Creating primary objects (tables, views, indexes) once application developers have designed an application.
   - Modifying the database structures, as necessary, form information given by application developers.
   - Enrolling users and maintaining system security.
   - Controlling and monitoring user access to the database.
   - Monitoring and optimizing the performance of the database.
   - Planning for backup and recovery of database information.
   - Maintaining archived data on tape.
   - Backing up and restoring the database.
   - Contacting DBMS vendor for technical support.
2. **Security Officers:** In some cases, an organization assigns one or more security officers to a database. A security officer enrolls users, controls and monitors user

access to the database and maintains system security. If a company does not have a separate security officers, then the above duties are performed by the DBA.

3. **Network Administrators:** Some organization have one or more network administrators depending on the database environment. A network administrator can perform the networking related tasks, manages the distributed database, and administer the networking products.
4. **Application Developers:** The application developers design and implement database applications. Their responsibilities include the following tasks and they perform some of these tasks in collaboration with DBAs:
   - Designing and developing the database application
   - Designing the database structure for an application
   - Estimating storage requirements for an application
   - Specifying modifications of the database structure for an application
   - Relaying the above information to a database administrator
   - Turing the application during development
   - Establishing an application's security measures during development
5. **Application Administrators:** A database system can assign one or more application administrators to administrate a particular application. Each application can have its own administrator.
6. **Database Users:** Database users interact with the database through applications or utilities. A typical user's responsibilities include the following tasks:
   - Querying the database for deletion making and other related activities
   - Perform data entry
   - Perform modifications and deletions of existing (depending on access privileges)
   - Generating reports and charts from the data

12.6 PROTECTING DATA WITHIN THE DATABASE

The data stored in a database is confidential and should not be accessible by unauthorized users or application programs (such as viruses). To prevent the database from being accessed by unauthorized users, different security measures need to be adopted. These are discussed in the following sections.

12.6.1 Database Audit

Database system keeps track of all the operations that a user performs during a **log-in session.** When a user logs in, the DBMS records the user's account number and then associates it with the terminal from which the user logged in. all operations done from that terminal are attributed to that user account number till the user **logs-off.**

If any tampering with the database is suspected, a **database audit** is performed. Database audit consists of reviewing the database accesses and operations done a user account during a certain period of time. When an illegal or unauthorized operation is found, the DBA can determine the account number which performed such as operation. A database log that is used mainly for security purposes is called an **audit trail.**

12.6.2 Authenticating Users to the Database

Identification and Authentication of a user can be done through any of the following methods:

1. **What you know:** The simplest and most common method is the usage of user's account number and password for authentication purpose. Instead of a simple password, the database system may also ask the user one or more questions. Only an authenticated user will have the right answers to such as questions.
2. **What you have:** In an another method, each user is given a badge, card or key to be used for identification purposes. A password or question answer scheme as above can be used for authentication purpose.
3. **What you are:** Special hardware or software can be used to identify a user, using some of his/her physical or physiological characteristics, such as thumb print.

12.6.3 Statistical Databases

Statistical Database are such database which store confidential information about users or organization. Examples include database storing medical records, income of individuals. Statistical database answers only statistical queries like computing total, average, etc. The goal of a statistical database is to maximize information-sharing and at the same time preserving the privacy of individuals. In order to maximize sharing, statistical database allows every to preserve privacy of individual information, only queries that involve large records are processed by statistical databases. For example, it is not possible to get a response from a database to a query that asks for the salary of an individual.

But if a malicious user has some knowledge about certain records in a database, he can still find out the salary of an individual. For example, suppose Mr. Soumyajit Sen knows that there are only two people including him in the Accounts department. He knows his own salary. He can now find out the salary of Mr. Ravindra Kumar using the following query:

```
SELECT SUM(EMP.SALARY) FROM EMP
WHERE DEPT_CODE = 101
```

Suppose answer to the above query comes to be ₹ 50,000. Then, Mr. Soumyajit Sen salary being ₹ 20000, Ravindra Kumar salary can be computed as ₹ .50000 - ₹ 20000 = ₹ 30000.

To prevent over smart users from using such as smart methods for accessing private information, one can use the following techniques:

- Rejection of these queries that involve only a small number of records in a database.
- Rejection of queries if the number of intersection records with previous queries made by the user is very large. This is to prevent such users as Mr. Soumyajit Sen. For this, the system should maintain a history of records that were used in queries asked by a particular user.

- A third method is random falsification. In this approach, a small amount of data is randomly made wrong. This result of statistical computation of such data remains correct so that normal users do not suffer.
- A random sample of data representing the entire database is selected. Then this sample data is used to respond to any query. The normal user thus will not suffer and at the same time there will not be any danger to the database.
- There can also be an audit trail of activities on the database. This trail will record the identity of the users and their interactions with the database. The very fact that this can be done will discourage users with malicious intentions.

12.6.4 Data Encryption

Confidential data may be stored in an encrypted (coded) form in a database. This encrypted data cannot be read by anyone, unless he knows how to decipher (decrypt) it. The process requires an encryption device for converting the original message into a meaningless code, as well as a decryption device for translating the code back into the original text. In business data processing, this can be accomplished by using specialized computer software.

An algorithm known as encryption algorithm can be used for encrypting the data. A good encrypting algorithm has the following features:

A. It should be very simple for authorized users to encrypt and decrypt data.

B. It is very difficult to keep the algorithm secret. Hence, the security of data should not depend on the secrecy of the algorithm, but on a parameter of the algorithm. This parameter is known as key. The key should be known only to authorized users.

C. The Key used should be very difficult for an intruder to determine.

Public key Encryption

Public-key encryption is one of the commonly used techniques for data encryption. In this technique, two separate keys are used. It uses one key for encryption, say A and another related key for decryption, say B. The encryption key is placed in a public register and is known as the **public key.** The decryption key is kept secret and is known as **private key.**

Each user, $\mathbf{U}_i$ is given a public key, $\mathbf{A}_i$ and a private key, $\mathbf{B}_i$. The public key is known to everyone. The private key is known only to the user to whom it belongs to. If a user $\mathbf{U}_1$ wants to store encrypted data, he encrypted them using public key $\mathbf{A}_1$.Decryption is done using the private key $\mathbf{B}_1$, known only to $\mathbf{U}_1$. But, if the user $\mathbf{U}_1$ wants to share this data with user $\mathbf{U}_2$, he encrypts it using $\mathbf{A}_2$. $\mathbf{U}_2$ can decrypt the data safely using his private key, $\mathbf{B}_2$.

12.7 GRANTING AND REVOKING PRIVILEGES AND ROLES

Restricting database access only to authorized users can be implemented by the access control mechanism. Access control is made available by creating user's accounts and passwords. The Database Administrator (DBA) has the responsibility of granting access permissions and user accounts to several of a database.

DBA has the following responsibilities:

A. Account Creation: Creating a new account and password for a user or a group of users.

B. Privilege Granting: Allowing a user account to have access to certain parts of database.

C. Privilege Revocation: Take away the privileges from a user account that were previously given to him

D. Security Level Assignment: Assignment user Accounts to the appropriate security level.

Whenever a user or a group of users need to access a database, they must first apply for the user account. The DBA then may or may not grant a user account and password. If these are given, the user(s) will then log in to the DBMS by providing his user account and password. The DBMS will then check the validity of user account and password. If they are valid, user is permitted to access specified portion of the database.

12.7.1 Propagation of privileges using GRANT OPTION

A user having privileges can pass on his privileges to another user by getting the Grant option. The second user can then grant the same privileges to other user. For example, when an owner A of relation R grants privilege on R to another account B, the privilege can be given with or without Grant Option. If the WITH GRANT OPTION is given, this means that B can also grant that privilege on R to other users.

Suppose that the database administrator wants to grant account S1 with the privilege of creating tables, he will give the following command:

GRANT CREATETAB TO S1

The createtab privilege gives account S1 the capability to create tables. Suppose S1 created two tables using this privilege. Now S1 wants to grant privilege of inserting and deleting tuples on these relations to user S4, then S1 can use the following command.

GRANT INSERT, DELETE ON EMP, DEPT TO S4

Since S4 was not given the grant option, S4 cannot grant these privilege to any other user. Now suppose S1 wants to grant SELECT privilege to S5 and also the privilege of propagating the SELECT privilege to other accounts, then it can give the following command:

GRANT SELECT ON EMP, DEPT TO S5
WITH GRANT OPTION

Now suppose that S1 wants to revoke the SELECT privilege on EMP from S5, and then it can give the following command.

REVOKE SELECT ON EMP FROM S5

NOTE'! Grant statement is used to grant access privileges. Revoke command is used to revoke the earlier granted privileges.

Next, suppose that S1 wants to give back to S5 a limited capability to SELECT name, designation and salary from the EMP relation, then S1 Will first create the following view:

CREATE VIEW S5EMP AS
SELECT EMP_NAME, DESIG, SALARY
FROM EMP
WHERE DEPT_CODE = 20

After creating the view, S1 can grant SELECT privilege on S5EMP as follows:

GRANT SELECT ON S5EMP TO S5

WITH GRANT OPTION

Thus, a user can propagate either whole or part of access privileges to other users. This leads to an authorization grant tree as seen Figure 12.7.1(a). All the paths in an authorization grant tree starts with DBA. This is because it is the Database Administrator who first passes access rights to other users.

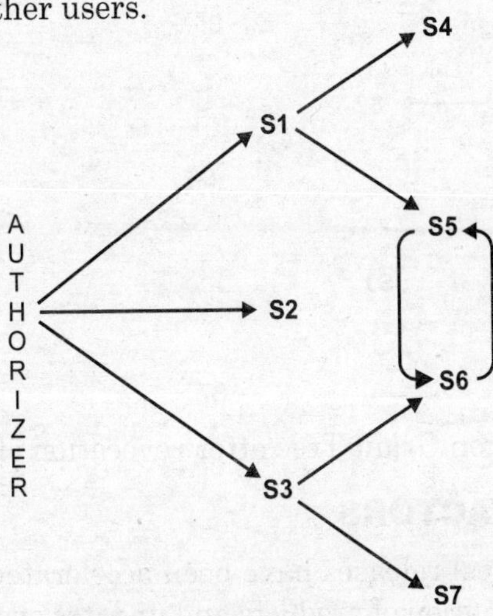

Figure 12.7.1(a) Authorization Grant Tree

When an access right is taken back from a user, all other users who were given access rights by this user also lose such privileges. For example, in Figure 12.7.1(a), S6 is granted control by both S5 and S3. But when access right was snatched away from S3, S6 retains those rights granted by S5 but loses rights granted by S5 (See Figure 12.7.1(b). Also observe that S5 loses rights granted by S6.

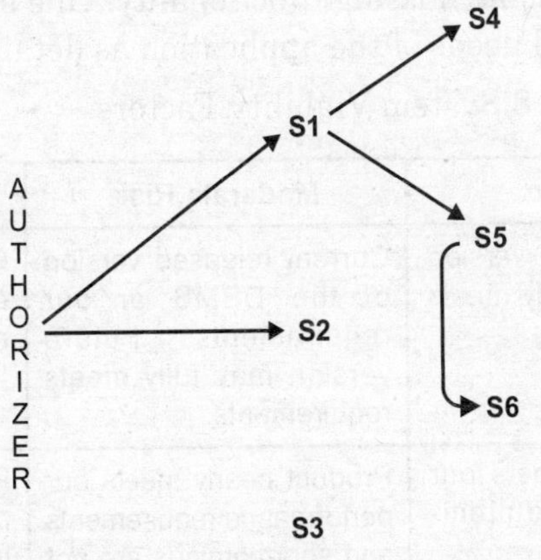

Figure 12.7.1(b) Authorization Grant Tree after revocation access rights from S3

Now if access right to S5 is snatched away by S1, then both S5 and S6 will lose their rights (See Figure 12.7.1(c))

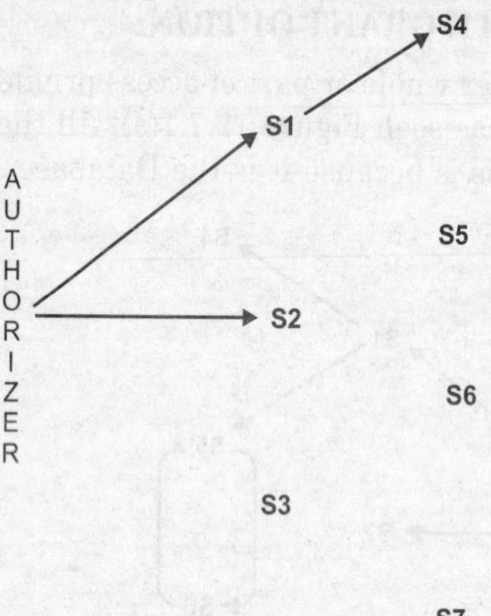

Figure 12.7.1(c) Authorization Grant Tree after revocation of access rights from S5

12.8 SYSTEM VIABILITY FACTORS

New product (DBMS packages) releases have been accelerated during the past several years, particularly with the distribution of products and updates over the internet. But, when you select a database management package for your organization, you will have to take into consideration certain factors such as the functionality, performance, platforms, security, reliability, usability, openness, documentation and cost. All these should be evaluated when selecting a DBMS product.

The functionality and cost of the product often drive the decision to purchase a particular product. It is, however, rare that a product will provide an exact match to your requirements. There will always be some missing functionality. One should therefore select a product that most meets the critical needs of the application as detailed in table 12.8.

Table 12.8 System Viability Factors

	Low Risk	**Moderate Risk**	**High Risk**
Functionality	Current released version of the DBMS fully meets our requirements.	Current released version of the DBMS or our requirements. Future version may fully meets requirements.	Current released version of the DBMS does not meet our requirements.
Performance	Product fully meets our performance requirem-ents.	Product nearly meets our performance requirements and shortcomings are not critical, will be met in future versions or with using faster hardware.	Product does not meet performance requirements in critical areas(e.g. transactions/second).

	Low Risk	Moderate Risk	High Risk
Security	Product meets security requirements for product.	Product meets most security requirements of the product-other can be handled in program or using other means	Current version of product does not handle security requirements of the projects.
Reliability	Product is stable and has proven itself over time with its customer base. Product can handle error situations gracefully and can recover fast.	Product has occasional errors but none will result in data loss or other critical problems.	Product has errors that result in data loss, work loss system crashes etc.
Usability	Product has an easy to understand interface and requires modest training. Can handle a range of users – from novice to expert.	Product requires some training to use properly.	Product has difficult user interface and requires training for users to become proficient.
Openness	Product can interface to the products from other vendors.	Product has some capabilities to interface to other products.	Product works well within its own systems and does not work well with other products.
Documentation	User manuals and support documentation are extremely high quality	User manuals and support documentation are of adequate quality	User manuals and support documentation do not exist or not easily available.

The product needs to be evaluated in terms of its ability to scale up and meet future growth needs. The DBMS product should be so robust that they work fine even in environments that demand extreme peak loads such as distributed, networked applications.

Reliability of a database system can be assessed by understanding the range of other client applications and installation, and the vendor's track record in building similar reliable products. Full reliability is rare find, therefore occasional errors and downtime may be acceptable for few database activities. That is, a less reliable DBMS tool may be accepted if it is satisfying a seldom used or low-priority system functioning. Today, due to the rush to bring many products into the market, products are not carefully tested before release. One must therefore recognize that a new product in a hot market segment will have problems, some potentially crippling the system's reliability.

Openness of a system refers to the ability of a package to interface with, make its data available, and provide programming interface to packages from other vendors. Facilities for exchanging data, such as multiple file formats enable different packages to integrate and work together as a system.

External reviews on products and vendors are available on the internet and in industry publication. These reviews should be studied to provide additional information in making a selection. It is important to note, however that many reviews of products are based on quick examinations of the products. Speaking with experienced users of the products is always the best source of information.

12.9 PRIVACY ISSUES AND PRESERVATION

Preserving data privacy is a growing challenge for database security and privacy experts. In some perspectives, to preserve data privacy we should even limit performing large-scale data mining and analysis. The most commonly used techniques to address this concern are to avoid building mammoth central warehouses as a single repository of vital information. Another possible measure is to intentionally modify or perturb data.

Of all data were available at single warehouses, violating only a single repository's security could expose all data. Avoiding central warehouses and using distributed data mining algorithms minimize the exchange of data needed to develop globally valid models. By modifying, perturbing and anonymizing data, we can be also mitigate privacy risks associated with data mining. This can be done by removing identity information from the released data and injecting noise into the data. However, using these techniques, we should pay attention to the quality of the resulting data in the database, which may undergo too many modifications. We must be able to estimate the errors may be introduced by these modifications.

Privacy is an important area of ongoing research in database management. It is complicated due to its multidisciplinary nature and the issues related to the subjectivity in the interpretation of privacy, trust and so, on. As an example, consider medical and legal records and transactions, which must maintain certain privacy requirements while they are being defined and enforced. Providing access control and privacy for mobile devices is also receiving increased attention. DBMSs need robust techniques for efficient storage of security-relevant information on small devices, as well as trust negotiation techniques where to keep information related to user identifies, profiles, credentials and permissions and how to use it for reliable user identification remains an important problem. Because large-sized streams of data are generated in such environments, efficient techniques for access control must be devised and integrated with processing techniques for continuous queries. Finally, the privacy of user location data, acquired from sensors and communication networks, must be ensured.

12.10 CHALLENGES OF DATABASE SECURITY

Considering the vast growth in volume and speed of threat to database and information assets, research efforts need to be devoted to the following issues: data, quality, intellectual property rights, and database survivability.

12.10.1 Data Quality

The database commodity needs techniques and organizational solutions to access and attest the quality of data. These techniques may include simple mechanisms such as quality stamps that are posted on web sites. We also need techniques that provide more effective integrity semantics verification and tools for the assessment of data quality, based on techniques such as records linkage. Application-level recovery techniques are also needed for automatically repairing incorrect data. The ETL (extract, transform, load) tools widely used to load data in data warehouses are presently grappling with these issues.

12.10.2 Intellectual property right

With the widespread use of the internet and intranets, legal and informational aspects of data are becoming major concerns of organizations. To address these concerns, watermarking techniques for relational data have recently been proposed. The main purpose of digital watermarking is to protect content from unauthorized duplication and distribution by enabling provable ownership of the content which the object can be altered while retaining its essential properties. However, research is needed to access the robustness of such techniques and to investigate different approaches aimed at preventing intellectual property rights violations.

12.10.3 Database Survivability

Database systems need to operate and continue their functions, even with reduced capabilities, despite disruptive events such as information warfare attacks. A DBMS, in addition to making every to prevent an attack and detecting one in the event of occurrence, should be able to do the following.

- **Confinement.** Take immediate action to eliminate the attacker's access to the system and to isolate or contain the problem to prevent further spread.
- **Damage assessment.** Determine the extent of the problem, including failed functions and corrupted data.
- **Reconfiguration.** Reconfigure to allow operation to continue in a degraded mode while recovery proceeds.
- **Repair.** Recover corrupted or lost data and repair or install failed system functions to reestablish a normal level of operation.
- **Fault treatment.** To the extent possible, identify the weakness exploited in the attack and take steps to prevents a recurrence.

The goal of the information warfare attacker is to damage the organization's operation and fulfillment of its mission through disruption of its information systems. The specific target of an attack may be the system itself or its data. While attacks that bring the system down outright are severe and dramatic, they must also be well timed to achieve the attacker's goal, since attacks will receive immediate and concentrated attention in order to bring the system back to operational condition, diagnose how the attack took place and install preventive measures.

To date, issues related to database survivability have not been sufficiently investigated. Much more research needs to be devoted to techniques and methodologies that ensure database system survivability.

12.11 DATABASE SECURITY SOLUTION

Database security is the protection of the database against intentional or unintentional threats that may be computer-based or non-computer based controls. Disasters come in all forms and the impact to your organization's bottom line, productivity and survival can be seriously damaging. As information becomes a key driver in your daily business operations, you cannot afford any unplanned downtime and data loss.

Security considerations apply to the whole enterprise-the data, the database, the DBMS, the users, the applications, the hardware and other infrastructure. So on efficient and effective database security program will ensure that database security is not compromised at any of these points. We saw the different security issues and the ways and means to solve them.

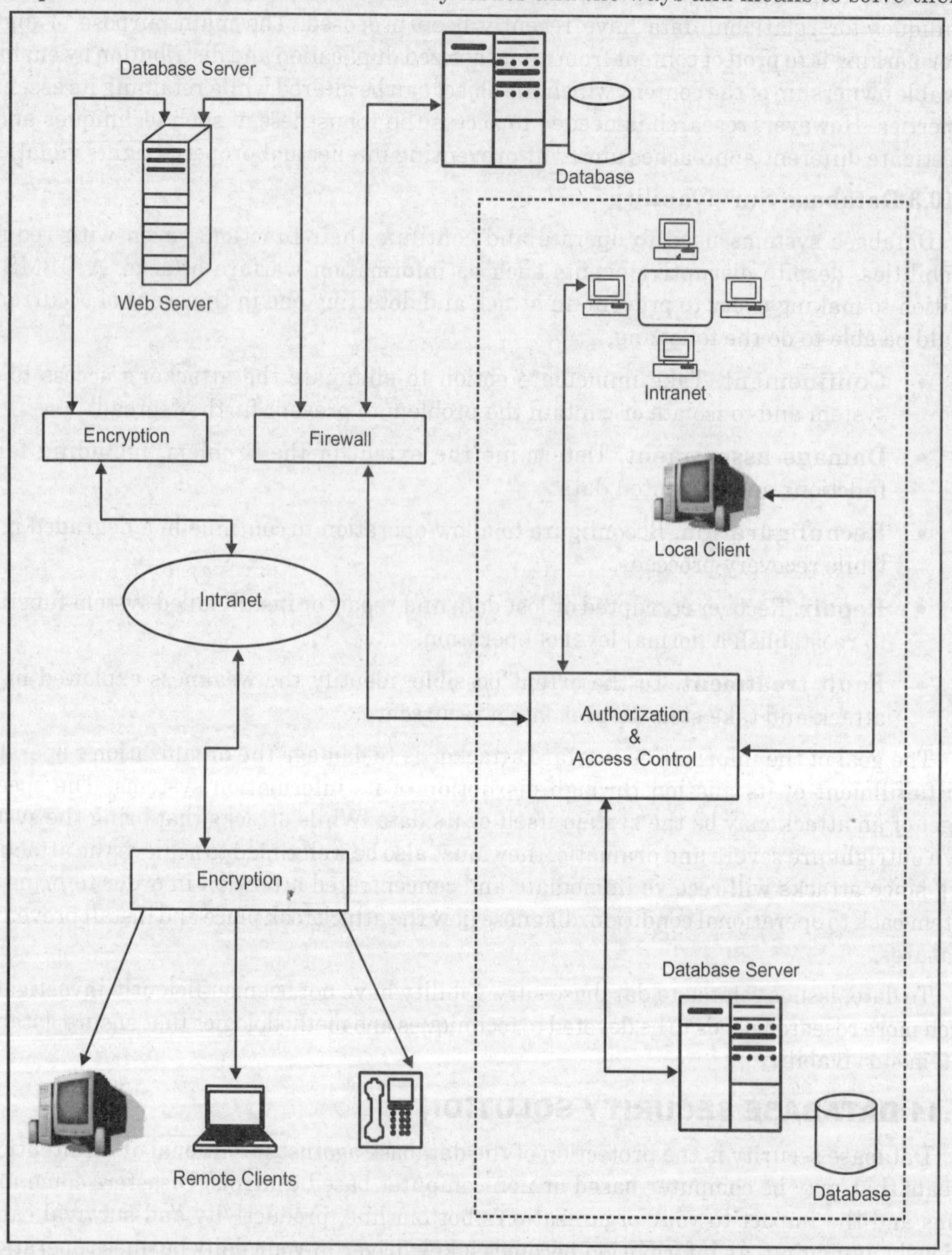

Figure 12.11 Database Security Solution-Authorization & Access Control, Encryption, Firewall etc.

The database security solutions are summarized in Figure 12.11. The figure shows a typical database environment. The intranet and the local clients are secured using **Authorization** (using passwords and other identification methods) and **Access control** (using privileges and roles).

The remote clients, the distributed databases, the web clients, etc. send the data over network after **Encrypting** the data. We have seen that we can use encryption standards like DES, 3DES, etc. The organization's database and internal database users are protected using a **Firewall.**

Authorization is the granting of a privilege to a user thus enabling the user to have legitimate access to a system. **Authorization** is the mechanism that determine s whether a user is who he or she claims to be. The two methods by which the access control is done are by using privileges and roles.

A **Privilege** is permission to access a named object in a prescribed manner. A **Role** is a mechanism that can be used to provide authorization. Roles and privileges can be granted or revoked from users other roles using the SQL commands GRANT and REVOKE.

Encryption is a technique of encoding data, so that only authorized users can understand it. A number of industry standard encryption algorithms are useful for the encryption and decryption of data on the server.

Two of the most popular encryption standards are Data Encryption Standard (DES) and Triple DES (3DES). Sensitive information that travels over an intranet or the internet can be protected by encryption.

Firewall is a single point of control on a network, used to prevent unauthorized clients from reaching the server. It acts as a filter, screening out unauthorized network users from using the intranet.

Security auditing is a means of monitoring the effectiveness of the security policies and is a critical aspect of system security. A good security policy will maintain a record of system activity to ensure that users are held accountable for their actions. Auditing helps deter unauthorized user behavior that may not otherwise be prevented.

SUMMARY

Database security is the protection of the database against intentional or unintentional threats that may be computer-based or non-computer based controls. Disasters come in all forms and the impact to your organization's bottom line, productivity and survival can be seriously damaging. As information becomes a key driver in your daily business operations, you cannot afford any unplanned downtime and data loss.

Authorization is the granting of a privilege to a user thus enabling the user to have legitimate access to a system. **Authorization** is the mechanism that determine s whether a user is who he or she claims to be. The two methods by which the access control is done are by using privileges and roles. A **Privilege** is permission to access a named object in a prescribed manner. A **Role** is a mechanism that can be used to provide authorization. Roles and privileges can be granted or revoked from users other roles using the SQL commands GRANT and REVOKE. **Encryption** is a technique of encoding data, so that only authorized users can understand it. A number of industry standard encryption algorithms are useful for the encryption and decryption of data on the server.

Security auditing is a means of monitoring the effectiveness of the security policies and is a critical aspect of system security. A good security policy will maintain a record of system activity to ensure that users are held accountable for their actions. Auditing helps deter unauthorized user behavior that may not otherwise be prevented.

EXERCISES

1. What is database security?
2. Why is database security important for an organization?
3. Give some examples of mistaken beliefs about database security?
4. Explain are potential threat points in a database system?
5. What are data security risks?
6. What do you mean by eavesdropping and data theft?
7. What are the main password related threats to the data in the database?
8. How do people gain unauthorized access to database objects?
9. How does lack of accountability affect database security?
10. What are the different dimensions of database security?
11. What are the basic data security requirements?
12. What do you mean by confidentiality of data?
13. How is confidentiality of data ensured in a database system?
14. What are the different types of database users?
15. Who is a database administrator of DBA?
16. What are the duties and responsibilities of a DBA?
17. What is the use of the GRANT command?
18. What is the use of the REVOKE command?
19. What is data encryption?
20. Why is network security important?
21. What are firewalls and what are they used for?
22. How are users authenticated to the database?
23. What is the difference between authentication, authorization and access control?
24. What is security auditing and why are they important?

CHAPTER 13

DATABASE INTEGRITY

13.1 INTRODUCTION

The term data integrity refers to the correctness and completeness of the data in a database. A relational database is a collection of related tables-tables that contain related information, tables that are connected by foreign key relationship and tables that are part of the same physical entity. When the contents of the database are modified with the INSERT, DELETE and UPDATE statements, the integrity of the data can be lost in many different ways. Some of these are given below:

- Invalid data may get added to the database. For example, placing an order for a book that does not exist.
- Changes to the database may get lost due to power failure or a system crash.
- Existing data may be modified to an incorrect value. For example, ordering a book from a distributer who does not supply it.
- Programs, which update the data, could abort halfway, leaving the database in a partly modified state.
- Parent rows could get deleted when child rows exist. For example, a department could get deleted from the department table, when there are still employees belonging to that department in the employee table.

When many users enter data items into a database it becomes very important that the values of data items and association among various data items are not disturbed. Hence, data insertions, updations etc. have to be carried out in such a way that database integrity is always maintained. In another words, Database integrity is the preservation of data correctly and implies the process of keeping the database from accidental deletion or alteration.

One of the important functions of an RDBMS is to preserve the integrity of the data contained in it. To preserve data integrity, the RDBMS imposes what is known as data integrity constraints. There are different types of integrity constraints-entity constraints, referential integrity and domain integrity etc. These constraints restrict the data values that can be inserted into the database, the value that could be deleted and values and could be modified.

For example, some columns in a table should contain a valid value. In other words, these columns cannot contain null value. The integrity constraints have mechanisms, which will ensure that such columns will contain valid value when an INSERT or UPDATE operation is performed against the table. Another situation is where a column can have values from a specified list-a domain. For example consider the 'Marital Status' column in the employee table. The possible values are married or unmarried or unknown.

The primary key value of each row in a table should be unique. It cannot contain a null because the database cannot differentiate one null from another. There will be many business rules that should be followed when inserting, modifying or deleting the data. So for the data to have any meaning, the data in the database should follow these business rules. For example, when a new employee is added to the employee table, his department ID should be present in the department table.

Another factor that causes data integrity problems is data consistency. The data in a database will be accessed by many users at the same time. There will be instances, where different users will be updating the same time. The integrity constraints have mechanisms to handle these kinds of situations.

SQL provides a variety of methods for defining the integrity constraints that are to be enforced by the SQL implementation. An integrity constraint can sometimes be a conditional expression. In some other instances they use a special syntax of their own. For example, the integrity constraint given below is a constraint, which states that the total bonus of all the employees should be less than ₹ 10,000,000.

```
CREATE ASSERTION CBNS
CHECK ((SELECT SUM(BONUS) FROM EMPLOYEE) < 10000000
```

As we have just seen, certain constraints are referred in the standard as 'assertions' and not as constraints. When a user attempts to create a new constraint, the system checks that the constraint is satisfied by all the existing data in the database. If it is not, the new constraint will not be accepted. If the constraint is satisfied by the existing data then it will be accepted and enforced from that point onwards.

All constraints have a name. if the user does not specify a name, then the system will implicitly provide an implementation-dependant name to be constraint. It is a good practice to explicitly specify the constraint name as it will help in understanding the error message that they system will provide when a constraint is violated.

13.2 TYPES OF INTEGRITY CONSTRAINTS

Integrity constraints can be classified as general constraints, domain constraints and base constraints. Base table constraints include the column constraints also. General constraints are constraints that apply to combinations of columns in combinations of base tables. Domains constraints are those constraints, which are associated with a specific domain and apply to every column that is defined on that domain. Base table constraints are constraints that are associated with some specific base table. Column constraints are specific to a column in a base table.

There are two additional features of the SQL standard that fall under the category of integrity constraints-data type checking and the CHECK option. In the case of data type checking, SQL will reject any attempt to violate the data type specification on INSERT or

UPDATE. For example, one cannot insert a character string into a numeric field. If the CHECK option is specified, SQL will reject any attempt from an INSERT or UPDATE on a view that violates the defining condition for that view.

13.3 RESTRICTIONS ON INTEGRITY CONSTRAINTS

There are certain restrictions that should be kept in mind when creating the integrity constraints. They are:

- If the constraint includes an aggregate function reference, that reference must be contained within a subquery.
- The constraints cannot include any reference to parameters or host variables, because the constraints are independent of specific applications
- The constraints cannot use any reference to any of the niladic functions like USER, CURRENT_USER, SESSION_USER, SYSTEM_USER, CURRENT_DATE, CURRENT_TIME, CURRENT_TIMESTAMP etc. The reason for this restriction is that such reference will return different values on different invocations.

13.3.1 General Constraints

A general constraint is one that applies to combinations of columns in combinations of base tables. These constraints are created using the CREATE ASSERTION statement. The syntax of the CREATE ASSERTION is given below:

```
CREATE ASSERTION name
CHECK (conditional-expression)
```

The following examples illustrate the use of the general constraints:

1. The salary should be less than ₹ 50,000

```
CHECK ASSERTION ICSAL
CHECK ((SELECT MIN (SALARY) FROM EMPLOYEE < 50000)
```

2. The basic pay should be a positive value

```
CREATE ASSERTION ICBP
CHECK (NOT EXISTS (SELECT * FROM SALARY
WHERE NOT (BASIC > 0)))
```

3. The basic pay of the employees in department D5 should be greater than 5000.

```
CREATE ASSERTION ICEMP
CHECK (NOT EXISTS (SELECT * FROM SALARY
WHERE DEPTID = 'D5'
AND BASIC > 5000))
```

4. The HRA of all employees in department D1 should be twice the basic pay.

```
CHECK ASSERTION ICHRA
CHECK (NOT EXISTS (SELECT * FORM SALARY
WHERE DEPTID = 'D1'
AND HRA = BASIC *2))
```

As we can see from the above examples, almost all the general constraints involve a conditional expression that begins with 'NOT EXISTS'. This is quite natural, because integrity constraints are usually of the from **'every x satisfies y',** which in turn usually to be expressed in SQL, as **'no x does not satisfy y'.** If the general constraints are converted into base table constraints, then the usage of the 'NOT EXISTS' operator can be avoided.

13.3.2 Domain Constraints

Domain constraints can be specified by means of the CREATE DOMAIN statement and can be added to or dropped from existing domain by means of the ALTER DOMAIN statement. The syntax of the CREATE DOMAIN statement is as follows:

```
CRAETE DOMAIN domain-name [AS] data-type
[default-definition]
[domain-constraints-definition-list]
```

The 'default definition' has the following syntax:

```
DEFAULT{literal   | niladic-function  | NULL}
```

The 'niladic-function' can be any of the following : USER, CURRENT_USER, SESSION_USER, SYSTEM_USER, CURRENT_DATE, CURRENT_TIME and CURRENT_TIMESTAMP

The 'domain-constraints-definition-list' will have the following syntax:

```
[CONSTRAINTS constraints-name] CHECK (conditional-expression)
```

The optional 'CONSTRAINTS constraints-name' defines a name for the new constraint and the 'conditional-expression' defines the constraint. If the constraint name is not specified, then as mentioned above, the constraint is given an implementation-dependent name. A given domain constraint should not be refer to a base table that includes a column that is defined on the domain to which the constraints applies. The following example is a domain definition that includes domain constraints.

```
CRAETE DOMAIN NAME CHAR(20)
DEFAULT 'General'
CONSTARINTS ICDNAME
CHECK (VALUE IN('Administration', 'Consultancy', 'Maintenance', 'General'))
```

The above CREATE DOMAIN will create a domain with a default value: 'General'. That is, if the user does not enter the value for a column based on this domain, then the value-General-will be placed in that position by default. Now suppose a user attempts to INSERT or UPDATE a value into a column defined on the above domain and if the value for that column is not in the value-list provided by the constraint, the operation will fail as it violates the constraints.

The special symbol VALUE can be placed only in a domain constraints. It stands for the scalar value in question, the value for which the constraints is to be checked. VALUE inherits its data type from the applicable domain. In the above example, the VALUE has a data type of CHAR(20). So if you want to specify that nulls are not allowed for the domain, then you should have your constraints as follows:

CRAETE DOMAIN NAME CHAR(20)
CONSTARINTS ICDNAME
CHECK (VALUE IS NOT NULL)

The ALTER DOMAIN statement allows you to modify or delete a constraint. The syntax for ALTER DOMAIN is given below:

ALTER DOMAIN domain-name
ADD domain-constraints-definition
| DROP CONSTARINT constraint-name

ADD permits new constraints to be specified for an existing domain. The new constraint does not replace any existing constraints for the domain in question, but is logically AND to them. DROP CONSTRAINT removes the named constraint. Here it should be noted that the DROP DOMAIN statement would not removes any of the constraints attached to it. It converts them into base table constraints and attaches any of the constraints attaches them to every base table includes a domain that is being dropped. So to drop or remove a domain constraint, you have to use the DROP CONSTARINT clause of the ALTER DOMAIN statement.

13.3.3 Base Table Constraints

The base table constraints are constraints associated with a specific base table. However this does not mean that such a constraint cannot refer to other base tables. In fact, many such constraints like foreign key constraints refer to other tables. Base table constraints can be initially specified by a means of the CREATE TABLE statement and can be added to or dropped from an existing base table by means of the ALTER TABLE statement. When the table is dropped using the DROP TABLE statement, the constraints associated with the table are also dropped. The syntax of the CREATE TABLE statement is as follows:

CRAETE TABLE table-name
(base-table-element-definition)

The 'base-table-element-definition' is either a column definition or a base table constraint definition. A base table constraint definition can be any of the following:

- A candidate key definition
- A foreign key definition
- A 'CHECK CONSTAINT' definition
- A Column constraint

13.3.3.1 Candidate key definition

A candidate key is a unique identifier (a column or combination of columns) of each of the table. At any time, no two rows in a table will have the same value for the candidate key column or columns. A table can have any number of candidate keys. Out of these one candidate key is designated as the primary key. The remaining candidate keys are called alternate keys. In SQL candidate key is defined as follows:

[CONSTARINT constraint-name]
{PRIMARY KEY | UNIQUE} (column-comma-list)

In the above definition, if the keyword 'PRIMARY KEY' is used, then it defines the primary key for the table. The term 'UNIQUE' is used to define the alternate keys. The 'column-comma-list' is the name of the column or columns that is to be defined as either the primary key or alternate key. The following example creates a primary key definition for the table book:

```
CRAETE TABLE BOOKS
(ISBN_NO        VARCHAR2(20)    NOT NULL,
BOOK_ID         VARCAHR2(30)    NOT NULL,
BOOK_TITLE      CHAR(20)        NOT NULL WITH DEFAULT,
AUTHOR          CHAR(20)        NOT NULL WITH DEFAULT,
PRICE           NUMBER(20)      NULL,
PRIMARY KEY (ISBN_NO),
UNIQUE (BOOK_ID));
```

A table with name BOOKS is created and the column ISBN is defined as the primary key and the column BOOK_ID is defined as an alternate key. When you define a column as either a primary key or as an alternate key, each such column is additionally assumed to be NOT NULL even if the NOT NULL is not specified explicitly. So even if you omit the NOT NULL specifications for the columns ISBN_NO and BOOK_ID it will be indirectly enforced because of the primary key and alternate key definitions.

13.3.3.2 Foreign key definition

A foreign key is a column or combination of columns in one base table whose values are required to match some candidate key (usually a primary key) value in some other base table. For example, the Department IDs in the primary key of the DEPARTMENT table. Every column in the EMPLOYEE table has a department ID column. Every value of the department ID in the EMPLOYEE table should match with a value of the department ID in the DEPARTMENT table. So we can say that the DEPTID in the EMPLOYEE table is a foreign key matching the primary (DEPTID) in the DEPARTMENT table. The following statements define the EMPLOYEE and DEAPRTEMNT tables and the primary and foreign keys for them.

```
    CREATE TABLE EMPLOYEE
    (EMP_NO         VARCHAR2(20)    NOT NULL,
    EMP_NAME        CHAR(20)        NOT NULL,
    DEPTID          CHAR(4)         NOT NULL,
    PRIMARY KEY (EMP_NO),
    FOREIGN KEY (DEPTID) REFERENCES DEPARTMENT (DEPTID));
CRAETE TABLE DEPARTMENT
(DEPTID             CHAR(4)         NOT NULL,
EMP_NAME            CHAR(30)        NOT NULL,
PRIMARY KEY (DEPTID));
```

The syntax of the foreign key definition is given below:

[CONSTARINT constraint-name]
FOREIGN KEY (column-comma-list) references-definition

Here the 'column-comma-list' is the name of the column or columns that form the foreign key and the 'references definition' take the following form:

REFERENCES base-table-name [(column-comma-list)]
[MATCH {FULL | PARTIAL}]
[ON DELETE {NO ACTION | CASCADE | SET DEFAULT | SET NULL}]
[ON UPDATE {NO ACTION | CASCADE | SET DEFAULT | SET NULL}]

The 'column-comma-list' in the FOREIGN KEY clause (not the one in the references-definition) identifies the column or column combination that constitutes the foreign key. The 'base-table-name' in the references-definition identifies that referenced column.

The 'column-comma-list' in the references-definition should be the same as the column-comma-list in a primary key or alternate key definition of the referenced table. Omitting the column-comma-list is equivalent to specifying a column-comma-list that is identical to the one in the primary key definition of the referenced table.

The optional 'MATCH' clause has no effect and can safely be ignored, if either the foreign key consists of a single column of if every component column of the foreign key has 'not null allowed' specification. But if any of these conditions are not true then MATCH will have significance. The MATCH FULL' option requires that foreign keys in a child table fully match a primary key in the parent table. With this option, no part of the foreign key can contain a NULL as primary key values cannot be null. The 'MATCH PARTIAL' option allows null values in parts of the foreign key as long as the non-null values match the corresponding parts to some primary key in the parent table.

The optional 'ON DELETE' and 'ON UPDATE' clauses denote the referential actions. The idea behind the referential actions is that it might sometime be possible to maintain referential integrity, not simply be rejecting an update that would violate it, but rather performing another compensating action in addition to the one that is requested. For example, you enforce referential integrity while deleting a column from the DEPARTMENT table by deleting all the employees of that department from the EMPLOYEE table. So instead of rejecting a DELETE on the DEPARTMENT table, since the foreign key constraints are violated, you can still maintain integrity by deleting all the related rows in the EMPLOYEE table.

The ON DELETE and ON UPDATE define the delete and update rules for the references candidate key.

- Specifying the **'ON ACTION'** option is equivalent to omitting the 'ON DELETE / UPDATE clause entirely.
- **ON DELETE CASCADE-** This option tells the RDBMS that when a parent row is deleted, all the child rows should also be automatically deleted from the child table. For example, deleting a department from the DEPARTMENT table will result in the deletion of all the employees in that from the employees in that department from the EMPLOYEE table.

- **ON DELETE CASCADE** –This option tells the RDBMS that when a primary key value is changed in the parent row, the corresponding foreign key values in all its child rows should also automatically be changed in the child table, to match the new primary key value. Changing the department ID in the DEPARTMENT table will change the ID of that department for all the employees belonging to that department in the EMPLOYEE TABLE.
- **ON DELETE SET DEFAULT**- In this case, every component of the foreign key must have a defined default value. So when the parent row is deleted, each component of the foreign key is set to the applicable default value for all child rows in the child table.
- **ON UPDATE SET DEFAULT** – When a primary key value in a parent row is updated the components of the foreign key values in all of its child rows in the child table should automatically be set to the default values.
- **ON DELETE SET NULL** – In this case, every component of the foreign key must have nulls allowed. So when the parent row is deleted, each component of the foreign key is set to NULL for the foreign key values of all the child rows in the child table.
- **ON UPDATE SET NULL**- When the parent row is updated, the components of the foreign key that correspond to the updated components of the candidate key are set to NULL in all matching rows in the child table.

Consider the CATALOG – AUTHOR – PUBLISHER – CATEGORY example. The primary key of the CATALOG table is BOOK_ID, AUTHOR table is AUTHOR_ID, PUBLISHER table is PUBLISHER_ID and that of the CATEGORY table is CATEGORY_ID. The CATALOG table has BOOK_ID, TITLE, AUTHOR_ID, PUBLISHER_ID, CATEGORY_ID, YEAR and PRICE. So AUTHOR_ID, PUBLISHER_ID and CATEGORY_ID are foreign keys for the CATALOG table. Consider the following example:

```
CREATE TABLE CATALOG
(BOOK_ID        CHAR(10)      NOT NULL,
TITLE           CHAR(30),
AUTHOR_ID       CHAR(10),
PUBLISHER_ID    CHAR(10),
CATEGORY_ID     CHAR(10),
YEAR            DATE,
PRICE           NUMBER(10,2),
PRIMARY KEY (BOOK_ID),
FOREIGN KEY (AUTHOR_ID) REFERNCES AUTHOR
                              ON DELETE CASCADE
                              ON UPDATE CASCADE,
FOREIGN KEY (PUBLISHER_ID) REFERNCES PUBLISHER
                              ON DELETE CASCADE
                              ON UPDATE CASCADE,
```

FOREIGN KEY (CATEGORY_ID) REFERNCES CATEGORY
ON DELETE CASCADE
ON UPDATE CASCADE);

The above definition of the base table CATALOG creates three foreign key constraints. An attempt to delete a specific AUTHOR_ID in the AUTHOR table will cascade to delete all books for that row from the CATALOG table as well. Same is the case with an attempt to delete a publisher from the PUBLISHER table or a category from the CATEGORY table. Similarly, an attempt to update the primary key value in a specific Author, Publisher or Category will result in the update of the foreign key value in the CATALOG table for that author, publisher or category.

You can add new constraints to a base table using the ALTER TABLE statement. The same statement can be used for removing or dropping existing constraints. The syntax of the ALTER TABLE statement is given below:

ALTER TABLE table-name
ADD base-table-constraints-definition
| DROP CONSTARINT constraint-name {RESTICT | CASCADE}

ADD permits a new constraint to be specified for an existing base table. The new constraint does not replace any existing constraints for the base table in question, but is logically AND to them. DROP CONSTRAINT removes the named constraint. RESTRICT and CASCADE have meaning only if the constraints is a candidate key definition. An attempt to drop a candidate key definition will fail if any foreign key references that candidate key, unless CASCADE is specified, which case all such foreign key definitions also will be dropped.

13.3.3.3 Column Constraints

The base table constraints apply to the entire table, whereas the column constraints apply to the single column within a single base table. The column constraint can be part of the column definition. The syntax of the column definition is given below:

column-name {data-type}
[DEFAULT {literal | niladic-function | NULL}]
[column-constraint-definition-list]

Here the **'column-constraint-definition-list'** specifies the column constraint. A column constraint definition can be any of the following:

- NOT NULL
- PRIMARY KEY OR UNIQUE
- A 'references definition'
- A 'CHECK constraint' definition

Each of these can be preceded by the optional 'CONSATRINT constraint-name' as we have seen with domain and base table constraints. We have seen the NOT NULL, PRIMARY KEY and UNIQUE definitions in the previous examples. The references-definition defines the foreign key constraints as we have seen in the previous section. One or more CHECK constraints can be associated with each table defined in a database. The CHECK constraints are specified in the CHECK clause in the CREATE TABLE statement. Once these constraints are defined, the RDBMS will automatically evaluate the check constraints expression whenever an SQL INSERT, UPDATE or DELETE statement is executed. If the evaluation of the CHECK constraint is the true, then the update is allowed otherwise the data in the table remains unchanged. The following example shows all the four cases of column constraints.

```
        CREATE TABLE EMPLOYEE
        (EMP_NO         NUMBER(10)     NOT NULL,
        EMP_ID          VARCHAR2(10),
        EMP_NAME        CHAR(20)       NOT NULL,
        DEPT_ID         CHAR(2)        NOT NULL WITH DEFAULT,
                        BONUS          NUMBER(10)   NOT NULL,
                        CHECK (BONUS BETWEEN 4000.00 AND 10000.00),
                        PRIMARY KEY (EMP_NO),
                        UNIQUE (EMP_ID),
        FOREIGN KEY (DEPT_ID) REFERENCES DEPARTMENT (DEPT_ID));
```

In the above example, a table with name EMPLOYEE is created with the following five columns:

- The first column (also third, fourth and fifth) uses the 'NOT NULL' column constraint. The 'EMP_NO NUMBER NOT NULL' is the short form of 'EMP_NO NUMBER (CHECK EMP_NO IS NOT NULL)'.
- The 'CHECK' constraint is used to enforce the condition that the bonus should be between ₹ .4000 and ₹ .10,000.
- The 'PRIMARY key' and 'UNIQUE' clauses are used to define the primary key and alternate key constraints.
- The 'FOREIGN KEY...... REFERENCES.....' option is used to define the foreign key constraint.
- Column constraints can be specified only within a column definition. Thus they must be defined when the column is defined either by means of the CREATE TABLE or ALTER TABLE statements. Once defined they logically become the base table constraints and can be dropped from an existing base table by means of the 'ALTER TABLE.......DROP CONSTRAINT...' statement or by using the DROP TABLE statement.

SUMMARY

The term data integrity refers to the correctness and completeness of the data in a database. One of the important functions of a RDBMS is to preserve the integrity of the data contained in it. To preserve data integrity, the RDBMS imposes what is known as data integrity constraints.

There are different types of types of integrity constraints-entity integrity, referential integrity, etc. These constraints restrict the data values that can be inserted into the database, the value that could be deleted and values that could be modified. Integrity constraints can be classified as general constraints and base table constraints.

Base table constraints include the column also. General constraints are constraints that apply to combinations of columns in combinations of base tables. Domain constraints are those constraints, which are associated with a specific domain and apply to every column that is defined on that domain. Base table constraints are constraints that are associated with some specific base table. Column constraints are specific to a column in a base table.

There are two additional features of the SQL standard that fall under the category of integrity constraints-data types checking and the check option. In the case of data type checking, SQL will reject any attempt to violate the data type specification on INSERT or UPDATE.

EXERCISES

1. What do you mean by data integrity?
2. What do you mean by entity integrity?
3. What do you mean by referential integrity?
4. What do you mean by the term integrity constraints?
5. What are the different types of integrity constraints?
6. What is a base table integrity constraint? Explain with an example.
7. What is a candidate key definition? Explain with an example.
8. What is a primary key definition? Explain with an example.
9. What is the column constraint? Explain with an example.
10. What is a general table integrity constraint? Explain with an example.
11. What is the syntax of the CREATE ASSERTION statement? Explain with an example.
12. What is a domain table integrity constraint? Explain with an example.
13. What is the syntax of the CREATE DOMAIN statement? Explain with an example.
14. What is the syntax of the ALTER DOMAIN statement? Explain with an example.
15. What are the restrictions on integrity constraints?

CHAPTER 14

TRANSACTION MANAGEMENT SYSTEM

14.1 INTRODUCTION

Transaction management is the ability of a database management system to manage the various transactions that occur within the system. Concurrency control is the activity of coordinating the actions of processes that operate in parallel and accesses shared data, and therefore potentially interfere with each other. Transaction management and concurrency control issues arise in the design of hardware, operating systems, real time system, communications systems, and database systems, among others.

The concept of transaction provides a mechanism for describing logical units of database processing. **Transaction processing systems** are systems with large databases and hundreds of concurrent users that are executing database transactions. Examples of such systems include systems for reservations, banking, credit card processing, stock markets, supermarket checkout, and other similar systems. They require high availability and fast response time for hundreds of concurrent users. In this chapter we present the concepts that are needed in transaction processing systems. We define the concept of a transaction, which is used to represent a logical unit of database processing that must be completed in its entirety to ensure correctness. We discuss the concurrency control problem, which occurs when multiple transactions submitted by various users interfere with one another in a way that produces incorrect results.

14.2 TRANSACTION

Usually a collection of several operations performed on the database is considered to be s single unit, from the database user's viewpoint. Nowadays, almost all the banks offer internet banking facility. You could view the account balance, the transaction, do funds transfer, pay telephone bills, electricity and water charges, request for a demand draft or cheque book, and so on. Suppose you want to pay your telephone bills using the on-line bill payment facility. You log on to the BSNL site, enter your user name and password and go to the bill information section. You will be presented with the bill details and amount that you have to pay. Choose the online payment facility by clicking on the appropriate link, the link that will connect you to your bank. The bank's payment gateways appears where you will enter your user name and password given to you by your bank and authorize a funds transfer- i.e. you instruct the bank to credit the bill amount to bill amount to the BSNL account from your account. Suppose the bill amount is ₹ .

2000 rupees. So you will instruct the bank to debit ₹ 2000 from your account and credit the same amount (₹ 2000) to the BSNL account. For you this entire process is a single operation-payment of the telephone bill. But within the database system the comprises several operations. It is essential that either all these operations occur (In which case the bill payment will be successful) or in case of a failure none of the operations should take (in which case the bill payment would be unsuccessful and you will be asked to try again). It is unacceptable if your account is debited and the BSNL account is not credited. You will lose the money and your phone will be disconnected, collections of operations that form a single logical unit of work are called **transactions.**

A database management system should ensure that the transactions are executed properly –either the entire transaction executes or none of it does. A transaction is a unit of database activities that accesses and possibly updates various data items. A transaction is usually the result of a program written in a high level manipulation language or programming language. Statements or function calls of the form "begin transaction..... transaction statement.......end transaction" usually delimit a transaction. The transaction consists of all the operations executed between the beginning and end of the transaction.

A transaction can have one of two outcomes. If it completes successfully, the transaction is said to have committed and the database reaches a new consistent state. On the other hand, if the transaction does not execute successfully, the transaction is aborted. If a transaction is aborted, the database must be restored to the consistent state it was in before the transaction started. Such as transaction is rolled back or undone. A committed transaction cannot be aborted. If we decide that the committed transaction was a mistake, we must perform another compensating transaction to reverse its effect. However, an aborted transaction that is rolled back can be restarted later and, depending on the cause of the failure, may successfully execute and commit at that time.

14.2.1 Transaction support

The DBMS has no inherent way of knowing which updates are grouped are grouped together to form a single logical transaction. It must therefore provide a method to allow the user to indicate the boundaries of a transaction. The keywords begin transaction, commit, and rollback are available in many data manipulation languages to delimit transaction. If these delimiters are not used, the entire program is usually regarded as a single transaction, with the DBMS automatically performing a commit when the program terminates correctly and a rollback if it does not. Note that in addition to the obvious states of active committed and aborted, there are two other states, partially committed- which occurs after the final statement has been executed. At this point, it may be found that the transaction has violated serializability or has violated an integrity constraint and the transaction has to be aborted. Alternatively, the system may fail and any data updated by the transaction may not have been safely recorded on secondary storage. In such cases, the transaction would go into the failed state and would have to be aborted. If the transaction has been successful, any updates can be safely recorded and the transaction can go to the committed state. Failed-which occurs if the transaction cannot be committed or the transaction is aborted while in the active state, perhaps due to the user aborting the transaction or as a result of the concurrency control protocol aborting the transaction to ensure serializability.

14.2.2 Properties of Transaction

There are properties that all transactions should posses. The four basic or so called ACID, properties of a transaction are:

- **Atomicity**- The 'all or nothing' property. A transaction is an indivisible unit that is either performed it its entirety or is not performed at all. It is the responsibility of the recovery subsystem of the DBMS to ensure atomicity.
- **Consistency** – A transaction must transform the database from one consistent state to another consistent state. It is responsibility of both the DBMS and the application developers to ensure consistency. The DBMS can ensure consistency by enforcing all the constraints that have been specified on the database schema, such as integrity and enterprise constraints. However, in itself this insufficient to ensure consistency.

  For example, suppose we have a transaction that is intended to transfer money from one bank account to another and the programmer makes an error in the transaction logic and debit one account but credits the wrong account, then the database is an inconsistent state. However, the DBMS would not have been responsible for introducing this inconsistent and would have had no ability to detect the error.
- **Isolation** - Transaction execute independently of one another. In other words, the partial effects of incomplete transactions should not be visible to other transactions. It is the responsibility of the concurrency control subsystem to ensure isolation.
- **Durability** – The effects of a successfully completed (committed) transaction re permanently recorded in the database and must not be lost because of a subsequent failure. It is the responsibility of the recovery subsystem to ensure durability

  We will consider the banking example to gain a better understanding of the ACID properties and why they are important. In previous example, we have considered only two accounts (your account and the BSNL account). But now we will consider a banking system that contains several accounts and set of transactions that accesses and updates the accounts. Access to a database is accomplished by two operations given below:
- **Read** (X) – This operation transfers the data item 'X' from the database to a local buffer belonging to the transaction that executed the read operation.
- **Write** (X) – The write operation transfers the data item 'X' from the local buffer of the transaction that executed the write operation to the database.

Now suppose that Ti is a transaction that transfers ₹ . 5000 from account UBI40145 to SBI112131. This transaction is defined as follows:

```
Ti      Read (UBI40145);
        UBI40145:= UBI40145 – 5000;
        Write (UBI40145);
        Read (SBI112131);
        SBI112131:= SBI112131 + 5000;
        Write (SBI112131);
```

14.3 TRANSACTION STATE

In the absence of failures all transactions complete successfully. A transaction may not always complete its execution successfully. Such a transaction is termed **aborted**. If we are to ensure the atomicity property, an aborted transaction must have no effect on the state of the database. Thus, any changes that the aborted transaction made to the database must be undone. Once the changes caused by an aborted transaction have been undone, we say that the transaction has been **rolled back**. It is part of the responsibility of the recovery scheme to manage transaction aborts.

A transaction that completes its execution successfully is said to be **committed**. A committed transaction that has performed updates transforms the database into a new consistent state, which must persist even if there is a system failure. Once a transaction has committed, we cannot undo its effects by aborting it. The only way to undo the effects of a committed transaction is to execute a **compensating transaction**. We need to be more precise about what we mean by **successful completion** of a transaction. We therefore establish a simple abstract transaction model. A transaction must be in one of the following states:

- **Active:** This is the initial state, the transaction stays in this state while it is executing.
- **Partially committed**: A transaction is in this state when it has executed the final statement.
- **Failed**: A transaction is in this state once the normal execution of the transaction cannot proceed.
- **Aborted**: after the transaction has been rolled back and the database has been restored to its state prior to the start of the transaction.
- **Committed**: after successful completion sate once it has been successfully executed and the database is transformed into a new consistent state.

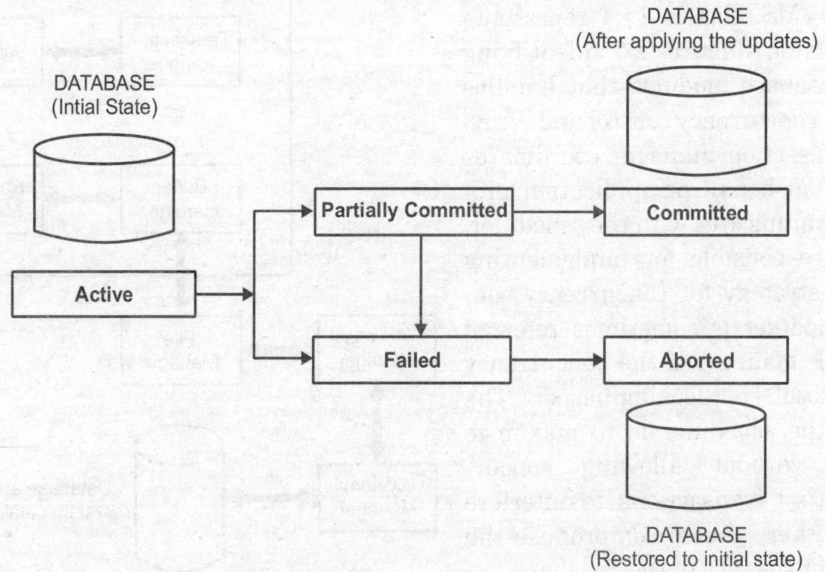

Figure 14.3 Transaction States

The state diagram corresponding to a transaction appears in Figure 14.3. We say that a transaction has committed only if it has entered the committed state. Similarly, we say that a transaction has aborted only if it has entered the aborted state. A transaction is said to have terminated if has either committed or aborted. A transaction starts in the active state. When it finishes its final statement, it enters the partially committed state. At this point, the transaction has completed its execution, but it is still possible that it may have to be aborted, since the actual output may still be temporarily residing in main memory, and thus a hardware failure may preclude its successful completion.

The database system then writes out enough information to disk that, even in the event of a failure, the updates performed by the transaction can be re-created when the system restarts after the failure. When the last of this information is written out, the transaction enters the committed state.

A transaction enters the failed state after the system determines that the transaction can no longer proceed with its normal execution (for example, because of hardware or logical errors). Such a transaction must be rolled back. Then, it enters the aborted state. At this point, the system has two options:

It can restart the transaction, but only if the transaction was aborted as a result of some hardware or software error that was not created through the internal logic of the transaction. A restarted transaction is considered to be a new transaction.

It can kill the transaction. It usually does so because of some internal logical error that can be corrected only by rewriting the application program, or because the input was bad, or because the desired data were not found in the database.

14.4 DATABASE ARCHITECTURE

In chapter 2 we presented architecture for a DBMS. Figure 14.4 represents an extract from Figure 2.7 identifying four level database modules that handles transactions, concurrency control and recovery. The transaction manager coordinates transactions on behalf of application programs. It communicates with the scheduler, the module responsible for implementing a particular strategy for concurrency control. The scheduler is sometimes referred to as the lock manager if the concurrency control protocol is locking-based. The objective of the scheduler is to maximize concurrency without allowing concurrently executing transactions to interfere with one another, and so compromise the integrity or consistency of the database.

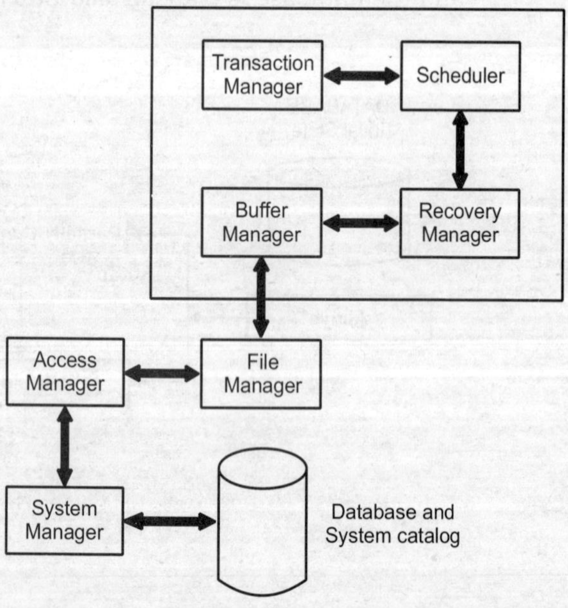

Figure 14.4 DBMS Transaction subsystems

If a failure occurs during the transaction, then the database could be inconsistent. It is the task of the recovery manager to ensure that the database is restored to the state it was in before the start of the transaction, and therefore a consistent state. Finally, the buffer manager is responsible for efficient transfer of data between disk storage and main memory.

14.5 THE NEED FOR CONCURRENCY CONTROL

Concurrency control is the process of managing simultaneous operations (queries, updates, inserts, deletes etc) on the database without having them interfere with one another. The database as a collection of data designed to be used by different people. We also saw that one of the properties of the data stored in the database is that it can be shared-data in a database can be shared among different users and applications. So one of the major objectives and advantages of a database is to enable multiple users to access shared data concurrently. If all users of the database were only reading the data then concurrent access would have been very easy as nobody is making any changes to the data in the database. But if two or more users are accessing the database simultaneously and if at least one user is updating the data, there can be interferences that might result in consistencies.

The concurrency control of managing simultaneous operations on the database without having them interfere with one another

A major objective in developing a database is to enable many users to access shared data concurrently. Concurrent access is relatively easy if all users are only reading data, as there is no way that can interfere with one another. However, when two or more users are accessing the database simultaneously and it least one is updating data, there may be interference that can result is inconsistencies.

This objective is similar to the objective of multi-user computer systems, which allow two or more programs (or transactions) to execute at the same time. For example, many systems have input/output (I/O) subsystems that can handle I/O operations independently, while the main central processing unit (CPU) performs other operations. Such systems can allow two or more transactions to execute simultaneously. The system begins executing the first transaction until it reaches an I/O operation. While the I/O is being performed, the CPU suspends the first transaction and executes commands from the second transaction. When the second transaction reaches an I/O operation, control then returns to the first transaction and its operations are resumed from the point at which it was suspended. The first transaction continues until it again reaches another I/O operation. In this way, the operations of the two transactions are **interleaved** to achieve concurrent execution. In addition, **throughput**-the amount of work that is accomplished in a given time interval-is improved as the CPU is executing other transactions instead of being in an idle state waiting for I/O operations to complete.

However, although two transactions may be perfectly correct in themselves, the interleaving of operations in this way may produce an incorrect result, thus compromising the integrity and consistency of the database. We examine three examples of potential problems caused by concurrency: the **multiple update problems**, the **uncommitted dependency problem** and the **inconsistency analysis problem.**

14.5.1 Multiple update problem

In the multiple problem, the data written by one transaction (an update operation) is being overwritten by another update transaction. This can be illustrated using our banking example. Consider our account UBI40145 that has ₹ 50000 balance in it. Suppose a transaction TR1 is withdrawing ₹ 10000 from the account while another transaction TR2 is depositing ₹ 20000 to the account. If these transactions were executed serially (one after another), the final balance would be ₹ 60000, irrespective of the order in which the transactions are preformed.

In other words, if the transactions were performed serially, then the result would be same if TR1 is performed first or TR2 is performed first-order is not important. But if the transactions are performed concurrently, then depending on how the transactions are executed the results will vary. Consider the execution of the transactions given below (Table 14.5.1):

Table 14.5.1 Multiple update problem

Sequence	TR1	TR2	Account Balance
1	Begin transaction		50000
2	Read(UBI40145)	Begin transaction	50000
3	UBI40145:=UBI40145-10000	Read(UBI40145)	50000
4	Write (UBI40145)	UBI40145:=UBI40145+20000	40000
5	Commit	Write(UBI40145)	70000
6		Commit	70000

Both transactions start nearly at the same time and both read the account balance of 50000. Both transactions perform the operations that they are supposed to perform-TR1 will reduce the amount by 10000 and will write the result to the database; TR2 will increase the amount by 20000 and will write the result to the database overwriting the previous update. Thus the account balance will gain additional 10000 producing a wrong result. If TR2 were to start execution first, the result would have been 40000 and the result would have been wrong again. This situation could be avoided by preventing TR2 from reading the value of the account balance until the update by TR2 has been completed.

14.5.2 Uncommitted dependency problem

The uncommitted dependency problem occurs when one transaction is allowed to see the intermediate results of another transaction before it is committed. An example of such a situation is shown in Table 14.5.2 Here TR1 starts execution and after the results are written to the database it aborts due to some reason. Since the transaction has aborted, the database should be restored to the original consistent state. But before the roll back is performed, transaction TR2 reads the account balance and starts executing. So instead of a balance of 70000 (since only transaction TR2 was committed). We now end up with a wrong result of 60000. This happened because the transaction TR2 was permitted to read the intermediate result of transaction TR1, i.e., before transaction TR1 was terminated (either committed or rolled back).

Table 14.5.2 Uncommitted dependency problem

Sequence	TR1	TR2	Account balance
1	Begin transaction		50000
2	Read(UBI40145)		50000
3	UBI40145:=UBI40145-10000		50000
4	Write(UBI40145)	Begin transaction	40000
5		Read(UBI40145)	40000
6	**Roll back**	UBI40145:=UBI40145+20000	50000
7		Write(UBI40145)	60000
8		Commit	60000

This problem is avoided by preventing TR2 from reading the account balance the transaction TR1 is terminated-i.e., either committed or rolled back.

14.5.3 Incorrect analysis problem

So far we have the problems arising when concurrent transactions are updating the database. But problems could arise even when a transaction is not updating the database. Transactions that read the database can also produce wrong results, if they are allowed to read the database when the database is in an inconsistent state. This problem is often referred to as dirty read or unrepeatable read. The problem of dirty read occurs when a transaction reads several values from the database while other transactions are updating those values.

Consider the case of a transaction that reads the account balances from all accounts to find the total amount in the various accounts. Suppose that there are other transactions, which are updating the account balances-either reducing the amounts (withdrawals) or increasing the amounts (deposits). So when the first transaction reads the account balances and finds the totals, it will be wrong, as it might have read the account balances before the update in the case of some accounts and after the updates in other accounts. This problem is solved by preventing the first transaction (the one that reads the balances) from reading the account balances until all the transactions that update the accounts are completed.

14.6 SERIALIZABILITY

We have seen some of the problems associated with the concurrent execution of transactions. The objective of concurrency control is to schedule or arrange the transactions in such a way as to avoid any interference. One obvious (but very inefficient) way of avoiding the interference of the transactions is to execute them one at a time- one transaction is committed before another is allowed to begin. But in a multi-user environment, where there are hundreds of users and thousands of transactions the serial execution of the transactions is not a viable option. The DBMS will have to find ways and device strategies to maximize concurrency in the system, so that many transactions can execute in parallel without interfacing with one another.

As we have seen a transaction consists of a sequence of operations consisting or read and write actions on the database followed by either a commit or abort and roll back. A schedule is a sequence of operations in each on the individual transactions. A schedule thus consists of a sequence of operations from a group transactions subject to the condition that the order or operations for each individual transaction is preserved.

A schedule where the operations of each transaction are executed consecutively without any other interference from other transactions is called a serial schedule. In a serial schedule, the transactions are performed in serial order. There is no interference between the transactions, since only one transaction is being executed at any given time. The order of execution can be important in a serial execution on the nature of the transactions involved.

For example, if in the banking, suppose there are two transactions – one transaction calculates the interest on the account and another transaction deposits some money into the account. Here the order of the execution is important, as the result will be different depending on whether the interest is calculated before or after the money is deposited into the account.

A non-serial schedule is a schedule where the operations from a group of concurrent transactions are interleaved. In the case of a non-serial schedule, the problems that we have seen earlier (multiple update, uncommitted dependency and incorrect analysis) can arise, if the schedule is not proper. Serial execution prevents the above-mentioned problems. The serial execution always leaves the database in a consistent state although different result could be produced depending on the order of execution.

The objective of serializability is to find non-serial schedule that allows transactions to execute concurrently without interfering with one another and thereby producing a database state that could be produced by a serial execution. We say that a non-serial schedule is correct if it produces the same results as some serial execution. Such a schedule is said to be serializable. To prevent inconsistency from transactions interfering with one another, it is essential to guarantee serializability of concurrent transactions. In serializability, the order of the read and write operations are important and the serializability rules are given below:

- If two transactions only read a data item, they do not conflict and the order is not important.
- If two transactions either read or write completely separate data items, they do not conflict and the execution order is not important.
- If one transaction writes a data item and another either reads or writes the same data item, the order of execution is important.

Consider the 3 schedules (see table 14.6) S1, S2 and S3. Each contains two transactions (TR1 and TR2, TR3 and TR4 & TR5 and TR6). The schedule S1 contains transactions TR1 and TR2. Since the write operation on account UBI40145 in transaction TR2 does not conflict with the read operation on account SBI112131 in TR1, we can change the order of these operations as shown in schedule S2 to produce an equivalent schedule. The first and second schedules are the same (equivalent) as the serial schedule S3.

Schedule S3 is a serial and since S1 and S2 are equivalent to S3, we can say that schedules S1 and S2 are serializable schedules. This type of serializability is known as conflict serializability. A conflict serializable schedule orders any conflicting operations in the same way as some serial execution.

Table 14.6 Equivalent Schedules

S1		S2		S3	
TR1	**TR2**	**TR3**	**TR4**	**TR5**	**TR6**
Begin Transaction		Begin Transaction		Begin Transaction	
Read (UBI40145)		Read (UBI40145)		Read (UBI40145)	
Write (UBI40145)		Write (UBI40145)		Write(UBI40145)	
	Begin Transaction		Begin Transaction	Read (SBI112131)	
	Read (UBI40145)		Read (UBI40145)	Write (SBI112131)	
	Write (UBI40145)	Read (SBI112131)		Commit	
Raed (SBI112131)			Write (UBI40145)		Begin transaction
Write (SBI112131)					Read (UBI40145)
Commit		Write(SBI112131)			Write(UBI40145)
	Read(SBI112131)	Commit			Read (SBI112131)
	Write (SBI112131)		Read(SBI112131)		Write (SBI112131)
	Commit		Write (SBI112131)		Commit
			Commit		

14.6.1 View Serializability

There exist many type of serializability that is less stringent than the conflict serializability. One such serializability is the view serializability. Two schedules consisting of some operations from a group of transactions are view equivalent if the following conditions are satisfied:

- For each data item 'X' , if transaction 'TRi' reads the initial value of 'X' in schedule S1, then transaction 'TRi' must also read the initial value of 'X' in schedule S2.
- For each read operation on data item 'X' by transaction 'TRi' in schedules S1, if the value read from 'X' has been written by transaction 'TRj' , then the transaction 'TRi' must also read the value of 'X' produced by 'TRj' in schedule S2.
- For each data item 'X', if the last write operation on 'X' was performed by transaction 'TRi' in schedule S1, the same transaction must perform the final write on data item 'X' in schedule S2.

Table 14.6.1 A view Serializable Schedule that is not Conflict Serializable

TR1	TR2	TR3
Read(UBI40145)		
	Write(UBI40145)	
Write(UBI40145)		
		Write(UBI40145)

A schedule is view serializable if it is view equivalent to a serial schedule. Every conflict serializable schedule is view serializable but all view serializable schedules are not conflict serializable. For example consider the schedule given in table 14.6.1

The transactions TR2 and TR3 perform write operations without performing a read operation. Writes of this type are called blind writes. Blinds writes appear in any view serializable schedule that is not conflict serializable.

14.7 RECOVERABILITY

We have assumed in the above discussion that all the transaction will be successfully completed. We have not considered the possibility of a transaction failure. If a transaction fails we need to undo the effect of the transaction and bring the database to the consistent state prior to the start of the transaction. So when a transaction aborts, all the transactions dependent on the aborted transaction also should be aborted and rolled back. To achieve this, we need to place certain restrictions on the type schedule permitted in the system. We will have to limit the acceptable schedules to the ones that bring are database back to a consistent state. There are three types of such schedules- recoverable schedules, non-cascading schedules and strict schedules.

14.7.1 Recoverable Schedules

Consider the schedule given in the table 14.7.1. The transaction TR1 performs only a read operation. Suppose the schedule allows the transaction TR2 to commit immediately after performing the read. In other words transaction TR2 commits before TR1.

Table 14.7.1 A non-recoverable schedule

TR1	TR2
Read (UBI40145) Write (UBI40145)	
	Read (UBI40145)
	Commit
Read (SBI112131)	
....	

Consider a situation where the transaction TR1 fails before it commits. Since TR2 has read the value written by TR1, we must abort TR2 also to ensure atomicity. But this is not possible as transaction TR2 has already been committed. Thus we have a situation where it is impossible to recover correctly from the failure of TR1. The above situation is an example of a non-recoverable schedule. **Non-recoverable** schedules are not allowed. All database management systems require that all the schedules are recoverable. A **recoverable schedule** is one where, for each pair of transactions TR1 and TR2, for TR2 to read a data item previously written by TR1, the commit operation of TR1 should appear before the commit operation of TR2.

14.7.2 Non-cascading schedules

Even if a schedule is recoverable, to recover correctly from the failure of some transactions we may have to roll back several transactions. Such situations occur if more than one transaction has read the data written by the first transaction which was aborted. Consider the example given in table 14.7.2.

Transaction TR1 writes a value that is read by transaction TR2. Transaction TR2 writes a value that is read by transaction TR3. Suppose at that point transaction TR1 fails. TR1 should be rolled back. Since TR2 is dependent on TR1 it also should be rolled back. Since TR3 is dependent on TR2 it too have to be rolled back. This phenomenon, in which a single transaction failure leads to a series of rollbacks, is called a cascading rollback. Cascading rollbacks are not desirable, as it leads to undoing a significant amount of work, it is desirable to restrict schedules to those where cascading rollbacks cannot occur. Such schedules are called non-cascading schedules. A non-cascading schedule is where, for each pair of transaction s TR1 such that TR2 reads a data item previously written by TR1, the commit operation of TR1 appears before the read operation of TR2

Table 14.7.2 A Cascading Schedule

TR1	TR2	TR3
Read (UBI40145)		
Write (UBI40145)		
......		
......	Read(SBI112131)	
......	Write (SBI112131)	Read (SBI112131)
......	....	

14.7.3 Strict Schedules

This is a more restrictive schedule than the recoverable schedules and non-cascading schedules. In this schedule, transactions cannot read or write a data item 'X' until the last transaction that wrote the data item 'X' has committed or aborted. Strict schedule simply the recovery process. In a strict schedule, the process of undoing a write operation of an aborted transaction is easy because one simply has to restore the 'before-image' of the data item. This simple procedure always works for strict schedules but may not for recoverable or non-cascading schedules.

We have seen three schedules- recoverable, cascadeless and strict. Each is characterized according to the terms recoverability, avoidance of cascading rollbacks and strictness. These properties of schedules are successfully more stringent conditions. Thus strictness implies cascading rollback avoidance and recoverability; avoidance of cascading rollback implies recoverability. But the reverse is not always true.

14.8 TRANSACTION DEFINITION IN SQL

A data manipulation language must include a construct for specifying the set of actions that constitute a transaction. The SQL standard specifies that a transaction begins implicitly. Transactions are ended by one of these SQL statements:

- **Commit work** – commits the current transaction and begins a new one.
- **Roll back work** – causes the current transaction to abort.

The keyword work is optional in both the statements. If a program terminates without either of these commands, the updates are either committed or rolled back which of the two happens is not specified by the standard and depends on the implementation.

The standard also specifies that the system must ensure both serializability and freedom from cascading rollback. The definition of serializability used by the standard is that a schedule must have the same effect as would some serial schedule. Thus, conflict and view serializability are both acceptable.

The SQL-92 standard also allows a transaction to specify that is may be executed in a manner that causes it to become nonserializable with respect to other transactions.

SUMMARY

A transaction is a unit of program execution that accesses and possibly updates various data items. Understanding the concept of a transaction is critical for understanding and implementing updates of data in a database, in such a consistent. Transactions are required to have the ACID properties: atomicity, consistency, isolation, and durability.

Serializability of schedules generated by concurrently executing transactions can be ensured through one of a variety of mechanisms called concurrency control schemes. Schedules must be recoverable, to make sure that if transaction a sees the effects of transaction **b**, and **b** then aborts, then **a** also gets aborted. Schedules should preferably be cascadeless, so that the abort of a transaction does not result in cascading aborts of other transactions. Cascadelessness is ensured by allowing transactions to only read committed data. The concurrency-control–management component of the database is responsible for handling the concurrency-control schemes. Chapter 15 describes concurrency-control schemes. The recovery-management component of a database is responsible for ensuring the atomicity and durability properties of transactions. The shadow copy scheme is used for ensuring atomicity and durability in text editors; however, it has extremely high overheads when used for database systems, and, moreover, it does not support concurrent execution. We can test a given schedule for conflict serializability by constructing a precedence graph for the schedule, and by searching for absence of cycles in the graph. However, there are more efficient concurrency control schemes for ensuring serializability.

EXERCISES

1. What is transaction management?
2. List the ACID properties. Explain the usefulness of each.
3. What is a transaction?
4. How does the DBMS ensure that the transactions are executed properly?
5. What are transaction states?
6. What are the different transaction states?
7. Explain the different transaction states with an example.
8. Why is concurrency control needed? What is its importance?
9. What is the multiple update problem? Explain with an example.
10. What is the uncommitted dependency problem? Explain with an example.
11. What is the incorrect analysis problem? Explain with an example.
12. What is a schedule?
13. What is serializability?
14. What is serial execution and serial schedule?
15. What is a non-serial schedule?
16. What is recoverability?
17. What are non-cascading schedules?
18. What is strict schedule?
19. What is a view serializable schedule?
20. What are recoverable schedules?

CHAPTER 15

CONCURRENCY CONTROL

15.1 INTRODUCTION

We saw in Chapter 14 that one of the fundamental properties of a transaction is isolation. When several transactions execute concurrently in the database, however, the isolation property may no longer be preserved. To ensure that it is, the system must control the interaction among the concurrent transactions; this control is achieved through one of a variety of mechanisms called **concurrency control** schemes. The concurrency control schemes that we discuss in this chapter are all based on the serializability property.

The transaction processing usually multiple to run concurrently. By allowing multiple transactions to run concurrently will improve the performance of the system terms of increased throughput or improved response time, but this allows causes several complications with consistency of the data. Ensuring consistency in spite of concurrent execution of transaction require extra work, which is performed by concurrency controller system of DBMS.

15.2 LOCK BASED PROTOCOLS

One way to ensure serializability is to require that data items be accessed in a mutually exclusive manner; that is, while one transaction is accessing a data item, no other transaction can modify that data item. The most common method used to implement this requirement is to allow a transaction to access a data item only if it is currently holding a lock on that item.

15.2.1 Locks

A lock is a variable associated with a data item that describes the status of the item with respect to possible operations that can be applied to it. Generally, there is one lock for each data item in the database. Locks are used as a means of synchronizing the access by concurrent transactions to the database items.

15.2.2 Share/Exclusive (for Read/Write) Locks

We should allow several transactions to access the same item A if they all access A for reading purposes only. However, if a transaction is to write an item A, it must have exclusive access to A. For this purpose, a different type of lock called a multiple mode lock is used. In this scheme there are shared/exclusive or read/write locks are used.

15.2.3 Locking Operations

There are three locking operations called read_lock(A), write_lock(A) and unlock(A) represented as lock-S(A), lock-X, unlock(A) (Here, S indicates shared lock, X indicates exclusive lock) can be performed on a data item. A lock associated with an item A, LOCK(A), now has three possible states: "read-locked", "write-locked" or "unlocked". A read-locked item is also called share-locked item because other transactions are allowed to read the item, whereas a write-locked item is called exclusive-locked, because a single transaction exclusively holds the lock on the item.

15.2.4 Compatibility of Locks

Suppose that there are A and B two different locking modes. If a transaction TR1 request a lock of mode A on item Q on which transaction TR2 currently hold a lock of mode B. If transaction TR1 can be granted lock, in spite of the presence of the mode B lock, then we say mode A is compatible with mode B. Such a function is shown in one matrix as shown below:

	S	X
S	true	false
X	false	false

Figure 15.2.4 Lock compatibility matrix comp

The graph shows that if two transactions only read the same data object they do not conflict, but if one transaction write a data object and another either read or write the same data object, then they conflict with each other. A transaction requests a shared lock on data item Q by executing the lock-S(Q) instruction. Similarly, an exclusive lock is requested through the lock-X(Q) instruction. A data item Q can be unlocked via the unlock(Q) instruction.

To access a data item, transaction TR1 must first lock that item. If the data item is already locked by another transaction in an incompatible mode, the concurrency control manger will not grant the lock until all incompatible locks held by other transactions have been released. Thus TR1 is made to wait until all incompatible locks held by the other transactions have been released.

Example:

As an illustration consider the simplified banking system. Let A and B be two accounts that accessed by transactions TR1 and TR2. Transaction TR1 transfers ₹ 50 from account B to account A and is defined as:

TR1
lock-X(B);
read(B, b);
b := b " 50;
write(b, B);
unlock(B);
lock-X(A);
read(A, a);
a := a + 50;
write(A, a);
unlock(A);

Transaction TR2 displays the total amount of money in accounts A and B that is, the sum A+B and is defined as

TR2
lock-S(A);
read(A, a);
unlock(A);
lock-S(B);
read(B, b);
unlock(B);
display(a + b);

Suppose that the values of accounts A and B are ₹ 100 and ₹ 200 respectively. If these two transactions are executed serially, either in the order TR1 and TR2 or the order TR2, TR1 then transaction TR2 will display the value ₹ 300. If however, these transactions are executed concurrently, as shown in schedule 1. In this case, transaction TR2 displays ₹ 250, which is incorrect. The reason for this mistake is that the transaction TR1 unlocked data item B too early, as a results of which TR2 shows an inconsistent state.

Schedule 1

TR1	TR2	Concurrency control manager
read(B, b)		
b:= b- 50		
write(B, b)		
unlock(B)		
	lock-S(A)	grant-S(A, TR2)
	read(A, a)	
	unlock(A)	
	lock-S(B)	grant-S(B, TR2)
	read(B, b)	
	unlock(B)	
	display(a + b)	
lock-X(A)		grant-X(A, TR2)
read(A, a)		
a:= a + 50		
write(A, a)		
unlock(A)		

15.3 SOLUTION OF INCONSISTENCY PROBLEM

Suppose now that unlocking is delayed to the end of transaction. The transaction TR3 corresponds to TR1 with unlocking delayed and is defined as:

TR3
lock-X(B);
read(B, b);
b := b " 50;
write(B, b);
lock-X(A);
read(A, a);
a:= a + 50;
write(A, a);
unlock(B);
unlock(A);

Transaction TR4 corresponds to TR2 with unlocking delayed, and is defined as

TR4
lock-S(A);
read(A, a);
lock-S(B);
read(B, b);
display(a + b);
unlock(A);
unlock(B);

You should verify that the sequence of reads and writes in schedule 1 which leads to an incorrect total of ₹ 250 being displayed, is no longer possible with TR3 and TR4 as shown in Schedule 2.

Schedule 2

TR3	TR4
lock-X(B)	
read(B)	
B := B 50	
write(B)	
	lock-S(A)
	read(A)
	lock-S(B)
	Wait...
	Wait...
lock-X(A)	
Wait...	
Wait...	

Unfortunately, the use of locking can lead to an undesirable situation. Consider the partial schedule 2. TR3 is holding an exclusive mode lock on B and TR4 is requesting a shared mode lock on B i.e. TR4 is waiting for TR3 to unlock B. Similarly, TR4 is holding a shared mode lock on A and T3 is requesting an exclusive mode lock A, thus TR3 is waiting for TR4 to unlock A.

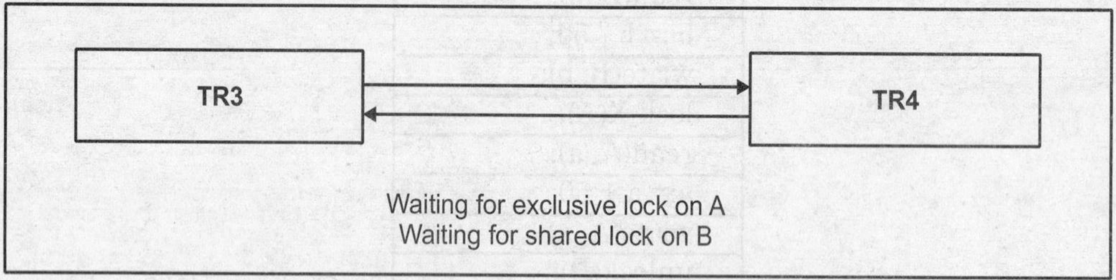

Figure 15.3(a) Representing a case of Deadlock

Thus we have arrived at a state where neither of these transactions can ever proceed with its normal execution. This situation is called **deadlock.**

TR1	TR2
lock-X(A)	
read(A, a)	lock-X(B)
a:=a-100	read(B, b)
write (A, a)	b:=b*1.06
lock-X(B)	write(B, b)
wait	Lock-X(A)
wait	Wait
.....	Wait
	......

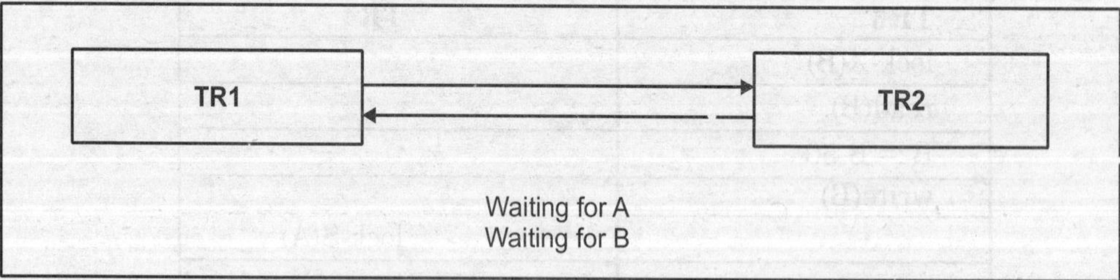

Figure 15.3(b) Representing another case of deadlock

Conclusion

Thus we can say that the solution of inconsistency leads to deadlock problem. If we do not use locking or unlock data items as soon as possible after reading or writing them, we may get inconsistent states. On the other hand, if we do not unlock a data item before requesting a lock on another data item deadlocks may occur. There are ways to avoid deadlock in some situations. Deadlocks are definitely preferable to inconsistent states, since they can be handled by rolling back of transactions, where as inconsistent states may lead to real world problems that cannot be handled by the database system.

15.4 THE TWO PHASE LOCKING PROTOCOL

A transaction follows the two phase locking protocol, if all locking operations the first unlock operations in the transaction. There are two phases in the schedule. There are:

- **Growing Phase:** During which all locks are requested.
- **Shrinking Phase:** During which all locks are released.

Initially, a transaction is in the growing phase. The transaction acquires locks as needed. Once the transaction releases a lock, it enters the shrinking phase and it issues no more lock requests.

Example:

TR3	TR4
lock-X(B);	lock-S(A);
read(B, b)	read(A);
b:=b-50	lock-S(B);
write(B, b);	read(B);
lock-X(A)	display(A+B);
read(A, a)	unlock(A);
a:=a+50;	unlock(B);
write(A, a)	
unlock(B);	
unlock(A);	

Transaction TR3 and TR4 are two phase. On the other hand transaction TR1 and TR2 are two phase as shown below.

TR1	TR2
lock-X(B);	lock-S(A);
read(B, b)	read(A, a);
b:=b-50;	unlock(A);
write(B, b);	lock-S(B);
unlock(B);	read(B, b);
lock-X(A)	unlock(B);
read(A, a);	display(a+b);
a:=a+50;	
write(A, a);	
unlock(A, a);	

Note that the unlock instructions do not need to appear at the end of the transaction. For example, in the case of instruction TR3, we could move the unlock(B) instruction to just after the lock-A(A) instruction and still retain we two-phase locking property. The point in the schedule where the transaction has obtained its final lock the end of its growing phase is called the lock point of the transaction.

Now transaction can be ordered according to their lock points.

5.4.1 Problems with two-phase locking protocols

There are two problems with two-phase locking protocols. These are:

1. Deadlock

2. Cascading Roll-Back

Deadlock

As discussed above, two phase locking does not ensure freedom from deadlock. As shown in transaction TR3 and TR4 are in two phase, but still there is problem of deadlock.

Cascading Roll-Back

As shown in partial schedule shown on next page each transaction observes two phase locking protocol.

TR5	TR6	TR7
lock-X(A)		
read(A, a)		
lock-S(B)		
read(B, b)		
write(A, a)		
unlock(A)		
	lock-X(A)	
	read(A, a)	
	write(A, a)	
	unlock(A)	
		lock-S(A)
		read(A, a)
Rollback		

Lets us consider, if transaction TR5 fails after the read(A, a) operation of transaction of TR7. Then TR5 must be rollback, which results into rollback of TR6 and TR7 also. Because, transaction TR6 and TR7 reads the value of A modified by transaction TR5. Since transaction TR5 fails and rollback, it means that transaction TR5 obtain the original value of A and cancels the modified value of A, but the other transactions TR6 and TR7 process the modified value of A and result into inconsistent state of database. In order to obtain the consistent state of database transactions TR6 and TR7, must also rollback and has to start again. It is case of dirty read.

Solutions to avoid cascading of rollbacks

There are two solutions to avoid cascading of rollback. There are:

- **Strict two phase locking protocol**
- **Rigorous two phase locking protocol**

Strict two phase locking protocol

The strict two-phase locking protocol, requires, that in addition to locking being two phases, all exclusive mode locks taken by a transaction must be held until that transaction commits. This requirement ensures that any data written by an uncommitted transaction are locked in exclusive mode until the transaction commits, preventing any other transaction from reading the data.

Rigorous two phase locking protocol

It requires all locks to be held until the transaction commits. It can be easily verified that, with rigorous two-phase locking transactions can be serialized in the order in which they commit. Most database systems implement either strict or rigorous two phase locking.

15.5 NON TWO-PHASE LOCKING PROTOCOLS

In order to develop those protocols, which are not based on two phase locking technique, one must have additional information on how each transaction will access the database. There are various models that differ amount of such information required. There are two types of protocols which are not being on two phase locking scheme:

- **Graph Based Protocol**
- **Time Stamp Based Protocol**

15.5.1 Graph Based or Tree Protocol

This protocol requires that we must have prior knowledge about the order in which the database items will be accessed. Here we introduce a Graph or Tree protocol where the data item are arranged in a tree. The nodes of the tree represent data items to be accessed and if (X,Y) in an arc of the tree, then X is called the parent of Y. If there is a directed path from X to Y, then is called ancestor of Y. Transactions access sub-tress. An entity can be accessed after all its ancestors in the sub-tree have been accessed.

Rules of Graph or Tree Protocol

The rules of tree protocol are as follows:

- No data item can be accessed unless the transaction locks it.
- A data item X can be locked by a transaction T only if T currently holds the lock on the parent of X, unless X is the root of the sub tree accessed by T.

- A transaction T after unlocking a data item cannot subsequently relock it.
- Transaction can unlock data item any time.

Figure 15.5.1 shows a set of data items organized as a tree.

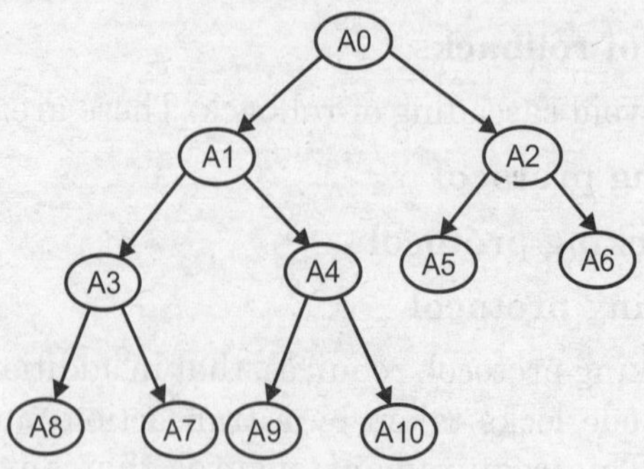

Figure 15.5.1

The following three transactions follow the tree protocol on this graph. We have shown only lock and unlock instruction.

TR1 needs exclusive lock on A0, A1, A4, A9, A2 and A5.

TR2 need exclusive lock on A1, A4, A10, A3 and A7.

TR3 need exclusive lock on A3, A7, and A8.

A schedule of transaction obeying the tree protocol on these data items is shown below.

TR1	TR2	TR3
Lock(A0)		
Lock(A1)		
Lock(A4)		
Unlock(A1)		Lock(A3)
Lock(A9)		Lock(A7)
Unlock(A4)	Lock(A1)	Lock(A8)
Unlock(A9)		Unlock(A3)
Lock(A2)	Lock(A4)	Unlock(A7)
Lock(A5)	Lock(A10)	Unlock(A8)
Unlock(A2)	Unlock(A4)	
Unlock(A5)	Lock(A3)	
Unlock(A0)	Lock(A7)	
	Unlock(A1)	
	Unlock(A10)	
	Unlock(A3)	
	Unlock(A7)	

Observe that transaction are not in two phase. Here the transaction TR1 could release a lock on the data item A1, after it has finished processing with it, thereby allowing TR3 to proceed concurrently. This cannot have in case of two phase locking protocol. But in case of tree protocol, lock is released by TR1 and TR3 can proceed resulting in increase in concurrently as compared to two phase locking protocol.

The above schedule is equivalent to a serial schedule TR1'!TR3'!TR2 or TR3'!TR1'!TR2. It can be shown that the precedence graph of a schedule based on a tree protocol cannot have a cycle. Hence the tree protocol ensures serializability.

Advantages of Graph Protocol over Two Phase Locking Protocol

- In case of Tree Protocol unlocking may occur earlier. Earlier unlock may lead to shorter waiting time and to increase in concurrency.
- This protocol is deadlock free, so on rollback required.

Disadvantages of Graph Protocol over Two Phase Locking Protocol

- In some cases a transaction may have to lock data items that are not access. For example, a transaction that needs to access data items A0 and A8 in the database graph of Figure 15.5.1 must lock not only A0 and A8 but also lock data items A3 and A1. This additional locking result in increased locking overhead, the possibility of additional waiting time, and a potential decrease in concurrency.
- In case without prior knowledge of what data items will need to be locked, transaction will have to lock the root of the tree, and that can reduce concurrency greatly.

15.5.2 Timestamp Based Protocol

This protocol require that we must have prior knowledge about the order in which the transactions will be accessed in contrast to Graph based protocol in which we require the knowledge of ordering of data items in the transactions. In order to ordering the transactions, we associate a unique fixed timestamp, denoted by TS(Ti) to each transaction like Ti. This timestamp is assigned by the database system before the transaction Ti starts execution. If a transaction Ti has been assigned timestamp TS(Ti), and a new transaction Tj enters the system, then TS(Ti)< TS(Tj).

There are two simple methods for implementing this scheme:

- Use the value of the system clock as the timestamp; that is, a transaction's timestamp is equal to the value of the clock when the transaction enters the system.
- Use a logical counter that is incremented after a new timestamp has been assigned; that is a transaction's timestamp is equal to the value of the counter when the transaction enters the system.

The timestamp of the transactions determine the serializability order. Thus, if TS(Ti)<TS(Tj), then the system must ensure that the produced schedule is equivalent to a serial schedule in which transaction Ti appears before transaction Tj.

Drawback of Timestamp

- Each value stored in the database requires two additional timestamp fields, one for the last time the fields (attribute) was read and one for the last update.
- It increases the memory requirements and the processing overhead of database.

Implementation

To implement this scheme, we associate with each data item Q two timestamp values:

- **W-timestamp(Q)** denotes the largest timestamp of any transaction that executed write(Q) successfully.
- **R-timestamp(Q)** denotes the largest timestamp of any transaction that executed read(Q) successfully.

These timestamp are updated whenever a new read(Q) or write(Q) instruction is executed

The Timestamp Ordering Protocol

The timestamp ordering protocol ensures that any conflicting read and write operations are executed in timestamp order. This protocol operates as follows.

1. Suppose that transaction Ti issues read(Q).

   (a) If TS(Ti)<W-timestamp(Q), then Ti needs to read a value of Q that was already overwritten. Hence the read operation is rejected, and Ti is rolled back.

   Example: Let us suppose that Ti has a timestamp 4.00PM and W-timestamp(Q) is 4.02PM it means that if a transaction whose timestamp is 4.00PM and want to read the data item who is already written by transaction of the timestamp 4.02PM. Thus the read request of 4.00PM transaction is rejected and TS(Ti) is rolled back.

   (b) If TS(Ti)>=W-timestamp(Q), then the read operation is executed, and R-timestamp(Q) is set to the maximum of R-timestamp(Q) i.e TS(Ti)

   Example: If a transaction of timestamp 4.05PM issue instruction to read a data item which is written by a transaction of timestamp 4.02PM, then the read operation is allowed and R-timestamp for Q data item set equal to 4.05PM because transaction of timestamp 4.05PM performs the read operation successfully.

2. Suppose that transaction Ti issues write(Q).

   (a) If TS(Ti)<R-timestamp(Q), then the value of Q that Ti is producing was needed previously and the system assumed that value would never be produced. Hence, the write operation is rejected, and Ti is rolled back.

   Example: If a transaction whose timestamp 3.58PM issue an instruction to write a data item whose R-timestamp is 4.00PM, then it means that transaction TS(Ti) want to write a data item which is successfully read by a transaction of higher timestamp then the write operation is rejected and Ti is rolled back.

   (b) If TS(Ti)<W-timestamp, then Ti attempting to write an obsolete value of Q. Hence this write operation is rejected and Ti is rolled back.

   Example: If TS(Ti) issue an instruction to write a data item with timestamp 3.58PM is successfully written by a transaction whose timestamp is 4.00PM, then it means that data item is already written by higher timestamp transaction so the write operation of transaction having 3.58PM timestamp is rejected and TS(Ti) is rolled back.

(c) Otherwise, the write operation is executed and W-timestamp(Q) is set to TS(Ti).

Example: If TS(Ti) timestamp is greater the 4.00PM and R-timestamp and W-timestamp less then TS(Ti) then the transaction can perform the write operation without any problem.

A transaction Ti, that is rolled back by the concurrency control scheme as result of either a read or writes operation being issued is assigned a new timestamp and is restarted.

To illustrate this protocol, we consider transactions TR14 and TR15. Transaction TR14 displays the contents of accounts A and B is defined as

TR14
read (B, b)
read (A, a)
display (a+b)

Transaction TR15 transfers ₹ 50 from account A to B, and then displays the contents of both:

TR15
read (B, b)
b:=b-50
write(B, b);
read(A, a)
a:=a+50;
write (A, a);
display (a+b)

Suppose that transaction TR14 starts at 1.00PM and transaction TR15 starts at 1.02PM that is TS(TR14)<TS(TR15). The schedule is us under:

TR14	TR15	Observations
read(B,b)		R-timestamp(B)=TS(TR14) that is 1.00PM
	read(B,b)	TS(TR15)>R-timestamp(B) so read operation is performed and R-timestamp(B)=TS(T15) that is 1.02PM.
	b:=b-50	
	write(B,b)	W-timestamp(B)=TS(TR15) that is 1.02PM
read(A,a)		R-timestamp(A)=TS(TR14)
	read(A,a)	TS(TR15)>R-timestamp(A) so read operation is performed and R-timestamp(A)=TS(TR15)
display(a+b)		
	a:a+50	
	write(A,a)	TS(TR15)=R-timestamp(A) so write operation is granted
	display(a+b)	

This schedule shows that both the transaction perform concurrently under timestamp schedule without giving inconsistent results.

If the order of transactions changed then we will get the inconsistent state of database and that case is not possible under timestamp locking protocol as shown below:

TR14	TR15
read(B,b)	
	read(B,b)
	b:=b-50
	write(B,b)
	read(A,a)
	a:a+50
	write(A,a)
	Display
read(A,a)	
display(A+b)	

This schedule will result in inconsistent of database, because TR14 will display 3050 and TR15 will display 3000, but this schedule is not allowed in timestamp based protocol because read(A,a) operation requested by TR14 is not be granted because TS(TR14)<W-timestamp(A) which is equal to TS(TR15). So according to protocol TR14 read operation is rejected and TR14 is roll backed. Then transaction TR14 has to restart after some time and a new timestamp is assigned to TR14. For example suppose 1.05PM i.e. TS(TR14)> TS(TR15) then the schedule is as follows.

The transaction TR14 will read the A and B modified values because R-timestamp(A), W-timestamp(A) and R-timestamp(B) and W-timestamp(B) all are equal to TS(TR15). Then will read the value of A and B only If TS(T14)>W-timestamp of A and B which become possible when it restarts, so consistency of the data is automatically maintained it means that if transaction TR14 is roll backed it starts again after some time with new timestamp and produce the consistent results.

This protocol also ensures freedom from deadlock, since no transaction ever waits.

15.5.3 Thomas Write Rule

In order to increase the concurrency and to reduce the roll backs of timestamp based protocols. Thomas purposed a new rule named as Thomas' Write Rule.

To understand the concept of Thomas write rule let us consider the following schedule:

TR1	TR2
read(A,a)	write(A,a)
write(A,a)	

Apply the timestamp ordering protocol schedule, since TR1 starts before TR2, so TS(TR1)<TS(TR2). The read(A,a) operation of TR1 succeeds, as does the write(A,a) operation of TR2. When TR1 attempts its write (A,a) operation, we find that TS(TR1)<W-timestamp(A), since W-timestamp(A)=TS(TR2). Thus the write(A,a) by TR1 is rejected and transaction TR1 must be rolled back.

Although the rollback of TR1 is required by the timestamp ordering protocol it is unnecessary. Since TR2 has already written A, the value of TR1 is attempting to write is one that will never need to be read. Any transaction Ti with TS(Ti)<TS(TR1) that attempts a read (A) will be rolled back, since TS(Ti)<W-timestamp(A) and any transaction Tj with TS(Tj)>TS(TR2) must read the value of A written by TR2, rather than the value written by TR1.

Modified Write Rule

Suppose that transaction Ti issues write(Q)

1. If TS(Ti)<R-timestamp(Q) then the value of Q that Ti is producing was previously needed and it was assumed that the value would never be produced. Hence, the write operation is rejected and Ti is rolled back. (same as timestamp based protocol)
2. If TS(Ti)<W-timestamp(Q) then Ti is attempting to write an obsolete value of Q. Hence this write operation can be ignored.
3. Otherwise, the write operation is executed and W-timestamp(Q) is set to TS(Ti). (same as timestamp based protocol)

The difference between the preceding rules and those of time-stamp based protocol lies in the second rule. The timestamp ordering protocol requires that Ti be rolled back if Ti issues write(Q) and TS(Ti)<W-timestamp(Q). However here, in this cases where TS(Ti)<W-timestamp(Q) we ignore the obsolete write. This modification to the timestamp ordering protocol is called Thomas Write Rule.

SUMMARY

The transaction processing usually multiple to run concurrently. By allowing multiple transactions to run concurrently will improve the performance of the system terms of increased throughput or improved response time, but this allows causes several complications with consistency of the data. Ensuring consistency in spite of concurrent execution of transaction require extra work, which is performed by concurrency controller system of DBMS.

The transactions can terminate successfully or unsuccessfully. A transaction that has terminated successfully is said to be committed and the transaction that has terminated unsuccessfully is said to be aborted. The actions performed by an aborted transaction must be undone. This process called rollback.

Concurrency control is needed when multiple users are allowed to access the database simultaneously. Without concurrency control there will be many problems like multiple update problem, uncommitted dependency problem, incorrect analysis problem and so on.

Serial execution means executing the transaction one after another, one at a time, with no interleaving. A schedule is the sequence of the operations of transactions. A schedule is serializable if it produces the same results as some serial schedule.

The different methods for ensuring serializability are locking, timestamp ordering and validation based protocols. The first two methods-locking and timestamp are called pessimistic methods. The validation based protocols are called optimistic protocol as they processed under the assumption that conflicts are rare.

EXERCISES

1. What are concurrency control schemes?
2. What is the locking?
3. What are different types of locks?
4. What are advantages of two phase locking? Explain with how does 2PL works.
5. What is the deadlock?
6. How are deadlock handled?
7. What is timestamp ordering protocol?
8. Explain the locking technique of concurrent execution of transaction with suitable examples.
9. What does compatibility of locks mean?
10. What are different approaches used by concurrency control algorithms?
11. Explain Two-Phase locking protocol with examples.
12. What are the problems of two-phase locking protocol and give possible solutions of those problems?
13. What is timestamp? How do timestamp do based protocols for concurrency control differ from locking based protocols?
14. Describe the basic timestamp ordering protocol for concurrency control. What is Thomas' write rule and how does this affect the basic timestamp ordering protocol?
15. Discuss the difference between pessimistic and optimistic concurrency control.

CHAPTER 16

BACKUP AND RECOVERY

16.1 INTRODUCTION

In general backup and recovery refers to the various strategies and procedure involved in protecting your database against data loss and reconstructing the data should that loss occur. The reconstructing of data is achieved through media recovery, which refers to the various operations involved in restoring, rolling forward, and rolling back a backup of database files.

A backup is a copy of data. This copy can include important parts of the database such as the control important of the database such as the control file and data files. A backup is a safeguard against unexpected data loss and application error s. If you lose the original data, then you can reconstruct it by using a backup.

Backups are divided into physical backups and logical backups. Physical backups, which are the primary concern in the backup and recovery strategy, are copies of physical database files. You can make physical backups with either and recovery manger utility of of the DBMS or operating system utilities. In contract, logical backups contain logical data (For example, tables and stored procedures) extracted with some DBMS utility (like Oracle Export utility) and stored in a binary file. You can use logical backups to supplement physical backups.

16.2 DATABASE BACKUP

Backup and recovery is very system dependant. On large system, managing a multi-gigabyte database in a complex client-server environment is a daunting task. Software and hardware components must cooperates with precise timing I order to provide information to the end-timing in order to provide information to the end user. For Example consider a simple SQL query over the network. In a split second, the SQL Command is parsed, passed from the application to the operating system, where it is broken into packages by a network layer and transmitted over Ethernet to the server. At the server, the packages are recompiled and shipped from the host network layer to the operating system, finally arriving at the server program. This is just the transmission process. Once the database server receives the request, there are still many more processes that need to happen before data is finally ready for shipping back to the client machine. Add to that the millions of electronic switches flipping continuously within the split second. What can possibly go wrong?

According to IEEE outages (failure) are classified into outage types and can be grouped into the following categories.

- Physical
- Design
- Operations
- Environmental

Physical outages are usually caused by hardware failures. These include media failure or a CPU failure. Design outages are caused by software failures. Any software bug. Whether in the operating system, database software or application software contributes to the design outage. Operation outages on the other hand are caused by human intervention. Some examples of operation outages are failures attributes due to poor DBA skills, user errors, inappropriate system setup or inadequate backup procedures. An environmental outages in due to external causes like earthquakes, power surges and abnormal and temperature conditions.

Why plans backups?

Planning and testing backup procedures for your database is the only insurance you have against failures of media, operating system, software and any other kind of failures that cause a serious crash resulting in loss of vital database files. The better a backup plan the more choices available during recovery. Furthermore, a solid plan and rigorous testing will give you peace of mind and the tools to handle database recovery. Much like earthquake and fire drills, a proper backup and recovery procedure will require discipline and practice.

Backup planning is nothing new. But it has grown complicated due to the constant adaptation to the ever-changing technology. Client-server computing is rapidly becoming the computing environment of the 90s, but for information system organization, this change has complicated systems management tasks. The DBA's self-confidence in handling down production database and the time it takes to bring the database back into action will depend on the types of backups that are available.

Importance of backups

Taking backups of any database is similar to buying insurance on your car-you won't realize the importance of it unless you get into an accident and the amount of coverage you have depends on the kind of policy that you taken. Similarly, the type and frequency of your backups determine the speed and success of the recovery. Various backup methods exist today. The DBA needs to determine what kind of backup procedures is required for his/her site.

Backups can be broadly categorized into physical and logical backups. A physical backup is a backup where the actual physical database files are copied from one location to the other (usually from disk to tape). Operating system backups is an example of physical backup. Logical backups are backups that extract the data using SQL from the database and store it in a binary file. Unlike physical backups, the logical backup utilities actually read the data in the objects using SQL and store the data in the binary file. This file is used to restore these particular database objects into the database. So the logical backup utilities allow the DBAs to back up and recover selected database objects within the database. Most DBMSs provide some sort of backup utility as part of the system. For example, the Export/Import utilities provided by Oracle can be used to take logical backups.

Transaction logs

A DBMS keeps a log of the changes made to it. This log is called the transaction log. The archive log files contain the changes made to the database. These log files becomes very useful in bringing back the system to a stable after a system crash. But keeping the logs or keeping track and recording all the changes made to the database have its own advantages and disadvantages. The advantage is that since all changes made to the database are stored in the log files. If the database files are lost due to any kind of failure including media failures, you can completely recover the database without losing any data. All committed transactions can be retrieved. The disadvantages are additional disk space required to store the archive logs. Also the DBA will have more administrative work to maintain the archive log destination and make sure that the archive log files are copied to tape.

Database recovery

Database recovery is the process of restoring a database to the correct state in the event of a failure. Database recovery is a service that is provided by the DBMS to ensure that the database is reliable and remains in consistent state in case of a failure. Recovery techniques are often intertwined with concurrency control mechanisms.

A major responsibility of the database administrator is to maintain the up time of a database, and to prepare for possibility of hardware, software, network, and process and system failure. In the event of a failure, the DBA should also be prepared to bring the database back to operation as quickly as possible and with little or no data loss. If properly planned, recovery will be a smooth operation, thereby protecting the users and the database. Recovery processes vary, depending on the type of failure that has occurred, the structures that have been affected and the type of recovery that is desired.

Data storage

In order to understand database recovery procedures, we need to have some knowledge about storage media and their access methods. Storage media can be classified as volatile or non-volatile storage media.

- **Volatile storage media**
  Data stored in volatile storage gets deleted when the power is switched off. Volatile storage media includes main memory and cache memory. These are made up of IC chips and hence data access is very fast. Data stored in volatile storage media cannot survive when system crashes. However, power failure is normally backed by uninterrupted power supply (UPS) facility.
- **Non-volatile storage media**
  Data stored in non-volatile storage media survive system crashes. It includes disks and magnetic tapes. Disks are used for online storage and tapes are used for archive storage. These are magnetic devices; hence data access would be slow. Non-volatile storage devices are subject to failures when head crashes or power supply is fluctuating.

- **Stable storage device**

  Data stored in stable storage device is never lost. Such a storage media is impossible to obtain, but techniques can be used to implement such a system where data loss is practically nil. Replicating the needed information in several nonvolatile storage media, with independent failure mechanisms is one such technique. The information stored must be updated regularly to ensure that failure at one site does not affect the normal functioning of the system.

Data access

As we saw in Chapter 9, the database system resides permanently on nonvolatile storage (usually disks), and is partitioned into fixed-length storage units called **blocks.** Blocks are the units of data transfer to and from disk, and may contain several data items. We shall assume that no data item spans two or more blocks. This assumption is realistic for most data-processing applications, such as our banking example.

Transactions input information from the disk to main memory, and then output the information back onto the disk. The input and output operations are done in block units. The blocks residing on the disk are referred to as **physical blocks;** the blocks residing temporarily in main memory are referred to as **buffer blocks**. The area of memory where blocks reside temporarily is called the disk buffer.

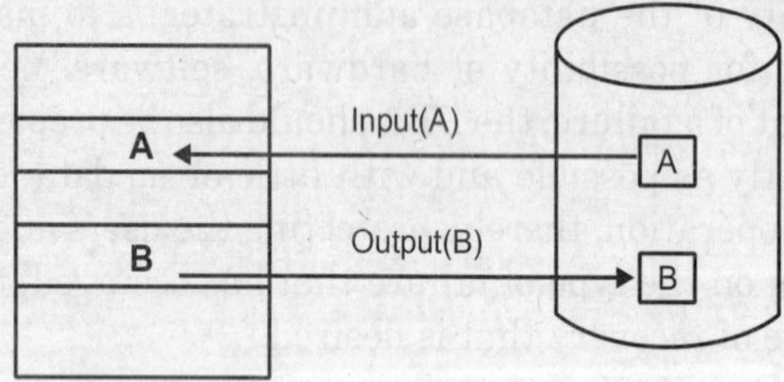

Figure 16.1 Block storage operations

Block movements between disk and main memory are initiated through the following two operations:

1. **input**(B) transfers the physical block B to main memory.
2. **output**(B) transfers the buffer block B to the disk, and replaces the appropriate physical block there.

Figure 16.1 illustrates this scheme.

Each transaction T_i has a private work area in which copies of all the data items accessed and updated by T_i are kept. The system creates this work area when the transaction is initiated; the system removes it when the transaction either commits or aborts. Each data item X kept in the work area of transaction T_i is denoted by x_i. Transaction T_i interacts with the database system by transferring data to and from its work area to the system buffer. We transfer data by these two operations:

1. **read**(X) assigns the value of data item X to the local variable x_i. It executes this operation as follows:
   (a) If block B_X on which X resides is not in main memory, it issues input(B_X).
   (b) It assigns to x_i the value of X from the buffer block.
2. **write**(X) assigns the value of local variable x_i to data item X in the buffer block. It executes this operation as follows:
   (a) If block B_X on which X resides is not in main memory, it issues input(B_X).
   (b) It assigns the value of x_i to X in buffer B_X.

Note that both operations may require the transfer of a block from disk to main memory. They do not, however, speciûcally require the transfer of a block from main memory to disk.

A buffer block is eventually written out to the disk either because the buffer manager needs the memory space for other purposes or because the database system wishes to reflect the change to B on the disk. We shall say that the database system performs a force-output of buffer B if it issues an output(B).

When a transaction needs to access a data item X for the first time, it must execute read(X). The system then performs all updates to X on x_i. After the transaction accesses X for the final time, it must execute write(X) to reflect the change to X in the database itself.

The output(B_X) operation for the buffer block B_X on which X resides does not need to take effect immediately after write(X) is executed, since the block B_X may contain other data items that are still being accessed. Thus, the actual output may take place later. Notice that, if the system crashes after the write(X) operation was executed but before output(B_X) was executed, the new value of X is never written to disk and, thus, is lost.

16.3 RECOVERY FACILITIES

A database management system should provide the following facilities to assist with the recovery:

- A **backup mechanism** that makes periodic copies of the database
- **Logging facilities** that keep track of the current state of transactions and database changes
- A **checkpoint facility** that enables updates to the database that are in progress to be made permanent.
- A **recovery manager** that allows the system to restore the database to a consistent state following a failure

  The Figure 16.3 shows a typical recovery operation

16.3.1 Backup mechanism

We had a detailed discussion of the backup mechanism in the beginning of this chapter. As we have seen, the DBMS should provide a mechanism to create backup copies of the database and the log files to be created at regular intervals without having to first stop the system. The backup copy of the database can be used to recover the database in the event that the database has been damaged or destroyed. A backup can be a complete copy of the entire database or an incremental copy. An incremental backup consists only of modification made since the last complete or incremental backup. The backups are usually stored on an offline-storage like magnetic tape.

16.3.2 Logging

To keep track of the database transaction, the DBMS maintains special files called log files or journals that contain information about all updates (insertions, modification and deletions) to the database. The log file contains information like transaction identifier, type of the log record (transaction start, insert, update, delete, commit, abort, etc), identifier of data item affected by the database action(insert, delete and update operations), before-image of the data item, after image of the data item, log management information, checkpoint records and so on.

Since the information contained in the log files are critical for the database recovery, two (sometime even three) separates copies are maintained. In the past the log files were stored on magnetic tapes. But nowadays, DBMSs are expected to recover from minor failures very quickly and so the files are stored online on a fast direct access storage device (DASD).

Since the online log files are also prone to failures, the log files are periodically archived and are stored in offline storage. These log files are called archive log files. In some database environments, where huge amount of logging information is generated every day, it is not possible to hold all this information online all the time. In such cases also, the log files are archived. Only the most recent logs are kept online (so that the database can quickly recover from minor failures). The old information is transferred to the offline-storage and in the case of major failures, where considerable portions of the log files are required for the recovery process, the log information is brought back online from the offline storage- archive logs.

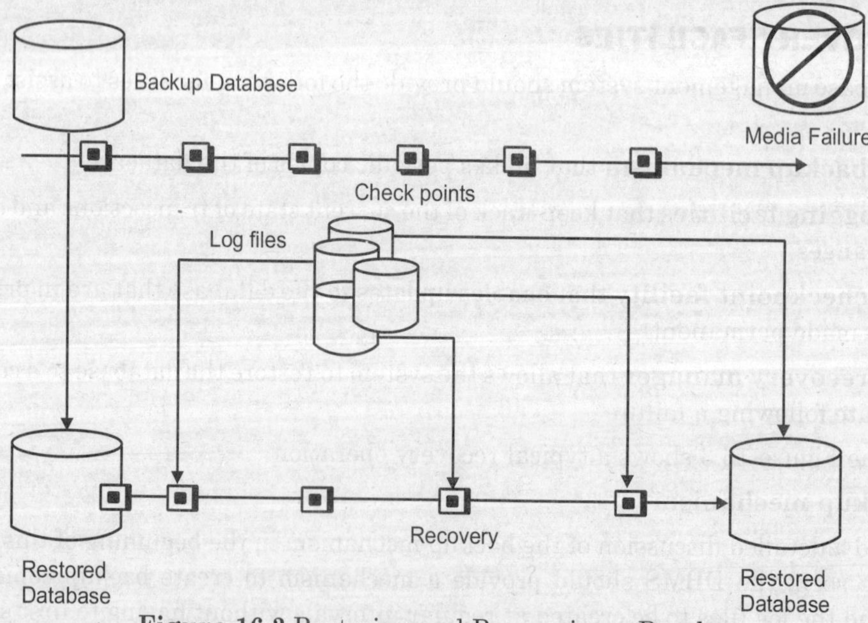

Figure 16.3 Restoring and Recovering a Database

16.3.3 Checkpointing

The log file information is used to recover the database from a failure. One problem with this situation is that we may not know how far back in the log to search and we may end up redoing transactions that have been safely written to the database. To limit the amount of search and subsequent processing that we need to carry out on the log file, we use checkpointing. A checkpoint is a point of synchronization between the database and the transaction log file. All buffers are force-written to secondary storage at the checkpoint. Checkpoints are also called syncpoints or savepoints.

Checkpoints are schedules at predetermined intervals and involves operations like written all log records in main memory to secondary storage, writing the modified blocks in the database buffers to secondary storage and writing a checkpoint record to the log file. The checkpoint record contains the identifiers of all transactions that are active at the time of the checkpoint.

If the transaction are executed serially, when a failure occurs we check the log file to find the transaction that started before the last checkpoint. All the earlier transactions would have committed previously and would have been written to the database. Therefore, we need only redo the transaction that was active at the checkpoint and any subsequent transactions for which both start and commit record appear in the log. If a transaction is active at the time of failure, the transaction must be undone. If the transactions are performed concurrently, we will have to redo all transactions that have committed since the checkpoint and undo all transactions that were active at the time of the failure.

16.4 RECOVERY TECHNIQUES

The extent of damage that has occurred to the database plays a significant role in the choice of the recovery technique that will be used. For example, if the database has been heavily damaged, then the last backup copy will have to be restored and the update operations performed on the database since the last backup have to be reapplied using the log file. If the database has not been physically damaged, but has become inconsistent, then it is enough to undo the changes that caused the inconsistency. It may also be necessary to redo some transactions to ensure that the updates they performed have reached the database. Here we do not need the backup copy of the database. We can restore the database to a consistent state by using the before and after images held in the log file.

In the case where the database is damaged, first the database is restored from the backup copy. Then the **redo logs** are applied to bring the database to the state before it crashed. In this state the database will contain the actions of the transaction that were completed and that were being executed at the time of the crash. This phase is called the roll forward phase and this will restore the database to a state at the time of the crash and the database will contain the actions of both committed and uncommitted transactions. Then the **undo logs** are used to roll back the effects of uncommitted transactions previously applied by the **roll forward** phase. After the roll forward, any changes that were not committed must be undone. The DBMS applies undo logs to roll back uncommitted changes in data blocks that were either written before the crash or introduced by redo application during cache recovery. This process is called **rollback** or transaction recovery. Figure 16.4 illustrates rolling forward and rollback, the two steps necessary to recover from any type of system failure. There are many techniques to bring back a database to a consistent state. Some of them are **deferred update, immediate update** and **shadow paging** etc.

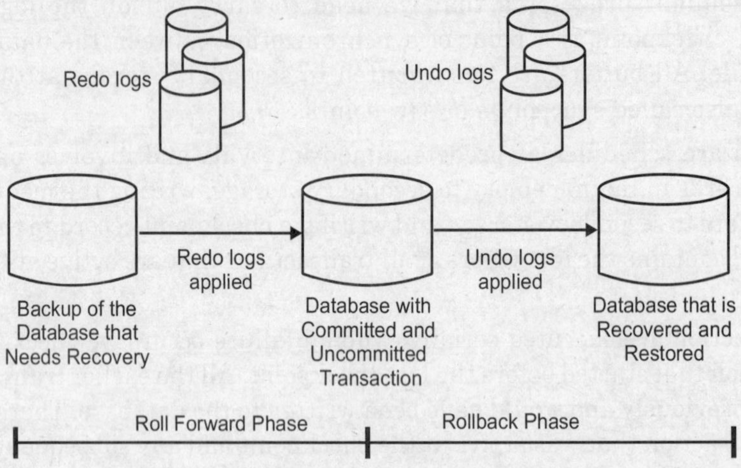

Figure 16.4 Rolling Forward and Rolling Back

16.4.1 Recovery techniques using deferred update

Using the deferred update recovery protocol, update are not written to the database until after a transaction has reached its commit point. If a transaction fails before it reaches this point, it will not have modified the database and so on undoing of changes will be necessary. However, it may be necessary to redo the updates of committed transactions as their effect may not have reached the database. In this case, we use the log file to protect against system failures in the following ways:

- When a transaction starts, write a transaction start record to the log.
- When any write operation is performed, write a log record containing all the log data specified previously (excluding the before-imaging of the update). Do not actually write the update to the database buffers or the database itself.
- When a transaction is about to commit, write a transaction commit log record, write all the logs records for the transaction to disk and then commit the transaction. Use the log records to perform the actual updates to the database.
- If a transaction aborts, ignore the log records for the transaction and do not perform the writes.

Note that we write the log records to disk before the transaction is actually committed, so that if a system failures occurs while the actual database updates are in progress, the log records will survive and the updates can be applied later. In the event of a failure, we examine the log to identify the transactions that were in progress at the time of failure. Starting at the last entry in the log file, we go back to most recent checkpoint record:

- Any transaction with transaction start and transaction commit log records should be redone. The redo procedure performs all the writes to the database using the after-image log records for the transactions, in the order in which they written to the log. If this writing has been performed already, before the failure, the write has no effect on the data item, so there is no damage done if we write the data again (that is, the operation is indepotent).
- For any transaction with transaction start and transaction abort log records, we do nothing since no actual writing was done to the database, so these transactions do not have to be undone.

16.4.2 Recovery techniques using immediate update

Using the immediate update recovery protocol, updates are applied to the database occur without waiting to reach the commit point. As well as having to redo the updates of committed transactions following a failure, it may now be necessary to undo the effects of transactions that had not committed at the time of failure. In this case, we use the log file to protect against system failures in the following way:

- When a transaction starts, write a transaction start record to the log.
- When a write operation is performed, write a record containing the necessary data to the log file.
- Once the log record is written, write the update to the database buffers.
- The updates to the database itself are written when the buffers are next flashed to secondary storage.
- When the transaction commits, write a transaction commit record to the log.

It is essential that log records (or at least certain parts of them) are written before the corresponding write to the database. This is known as the write-ahead log protocol. If updates were made to the database first, and failure occurred before the log record was written, then the recovery manager would have no way of undoing (or redoing) the operation.

If the system fails, recovery involves using the log to undo or redo transactions:

- For any transaction for which both a transaction start and transaction commit record appear in the log, we redo using the log records to write the after-image of updated fields, as described above. Note that if the new values have already been written to the database, these writes, although unnecessary, will have no effect. However, any write that did not actually reach the database will now be performed.
- For any transaction for which the log contains a transaction start record but not a transaction commit record, we need to undo that transaction. This time the log records are used to write the before-image of the affected fields and thus restore the database to its state prior to the transaction's start. The undo operations are performed in the reverse order to which they were written to the log.

16.4.3 Shadow Paging

In a single user environment, shadow paging system can be used for data recovery instead of using transaction logs. In the shadow paging scheme, a database is divided into a number of fixed-sized disk pages, say n. Thereafter, a current directory is created that will be having n entries with each entry pointing to a disk page in the database. The current directory is transferred to the main memory.

When a transaction begins executing, the current directory is copied into a shadow paging directory. The shadow directory is then saved on the disk. The transaction will be using the current directory. Hence during the transaction execution, all the modifications are made on the current directory and the shadow directory is never modified.

Note: *When a transaction performs the write operation, a new copy of the modified database page is created. This is done to ensure that the old copy of the database page is not overwritten until the transaction commits*

The current directory is modified to point to the new database page while the shadow directory continues to point to the old database page. Figure 16.4.3 illustrates the concept of shadow paging. To recover from a failure occurring during the transaction execution what we have to do is to just remove the new database pages as well as the current directory. The previous database version is safe in the old database pages pointed to by the entries in the shadow directory.

If the transaction executes successfully, the current directory is copied to a single storage. The only thing we have to do is to change the pointer entries in the shadow paging directory which can be done by just overwriting the entries in shadow directory with the current directory.

Note: *Thus the shadow paging scheme reduces the need of transporting the updated database pages from the main memory to the disk storage.*

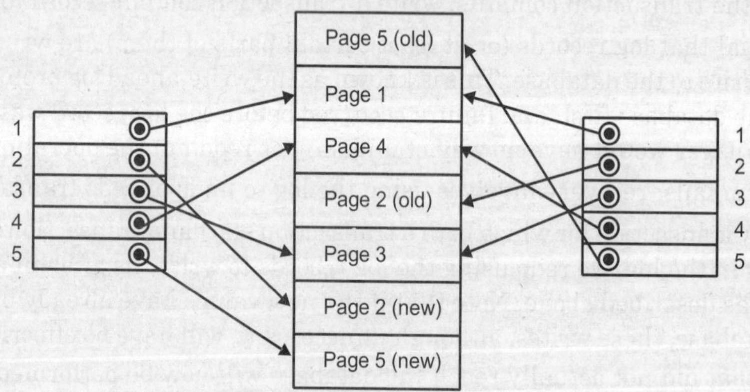

Figure 16.4.3 Shadow Paging Scheme

For example, in Figure 16.4.3, the current directory is pointing to the pages 1, 2 (new), 3, 4 and 5 (new). The new pages (2 and 5) are created as a result of changes made by the transaction. Note that the shadow directory points to the old pages (2 and 5) as well as the pages 1, 3 and 4 where there are no changes. Besides, the main memory contains both the old and the new pages. Hence, if there occurs any failure, the old pages remain intact, pointed to by the shadow directory. If the transaction commits successfully and the changes have to be written on to the stable storage, the contents of the shadow entry are overwritten by the contents of current directory. Also, the old pages (2 and 5) are removed from the memory and only the new modified pages are retained.

16.5 DETACHED TRANSACTION ACTIONS

A transaction is executed on occurrence of any of the following events:

- Some operation on the database is to be done such as insertion or deletion of a tuple, up-dation of an attribute etc.
- Another transaction raises an event in the middle of its execution such as abort or start of a transaction.
- An event raised by a clock at some particular point in time.
- An event raised because some error has occurred in the database.

If an event occurs within a centralized system, the transaction executed relative to the event can be:

- **Immediate** – in which case the transaction is executed as soon as the event occurs.
- **Deferred** – in which case the event is evaluated from within the same transaction that triggered the event.
- **Detached** – in which case the event is handled from within a different transaction other than the one in which the event took place.

Note: Detached transaction is a transaction that is evaluated as a separate transaction and that retains any transactional locks acquired in a previous activity.

There are two types of detached transaction actions:

1. **Dependent Detached Transaction Actions:** In which case the execution of the action is dependent upon committing of the transaction where the event took place.
2. **Independent Detached Transaction Action:** In which case the execution of the action is independent of the committing of the transaction where the event took place.

Out of these, the dependent detached transaction is the preferred one. This is because if the transaction, where the event took place, aborts then the dependent detached transaction will not get executed. The dependent detached transaction will only commit if the transaction where the event took place got committed successfully. Whereas an independent detached transaction is an autonomous transaction and does not depend on any other transaction for its execution, therefore may cause errors and hence not preferred.

In distributed database management systems, parts of the database reside at different sites that are connected by a communication network. Each site will be having its own recovery and transaction management techniques. Similarly, in a system that makes use of multiple database systems such as relational, object-oriented, hierarchical etc. each database system employs different recovery and transaction management techniques. In such situations, parts of transaction actions are executed at different sites or using different database system. The transaction actions executing at a particular site use the resources of that site and are under the control of a local recovery manager and local log tables. Such transaction actions are called detached transaction actions.

In addition, in distributed database management systems, there is a global recovery manager or coordinator that controls all these transaction actions as a whole and work towards maintaining the atomicity of the transaction. The protocol followed in such cases is known as the two-phase commit protocol. The two phase of the commit protocol are the following:

1. **Phase I:** The participating sites or database systems signal the coordinator that the transaction actions at their end have conducted. The global coordinator will then send a "prepare to commit" signal to each site. The participating sites will then force-write all log records and send a "ready to commit" signal to coordinator. If the participating sites cannot commit due to some reason or disk failure in between, they will send a "cannot commit" signal to the coordinator.
2. **Phase II:** Upon receiving the "ready to commit signal" from all the participants, the coordinator will send a "commit" signal to all participating sites. The sites will then write a [commit] entry in the log. If any of the participating sites had sent a "cannot commit" signal the global coordinator will send a "roll back" signal to all the sites. Each site will then undo their transaction actions, using the log.

16.6 DISASTER DATABASE MANAGEMENT SYSTEM

Disaster database management system is a new talk in the IT field. Although not yet implemented, it will contain details of all disasters that have occurred in the past, their causes and the consequences. Disasters include earthquakes, floods, fire, storms etc. which can bring the working of an organization to a halt. A disaster database may also contain the procedures or mode of investigations and trials carried out in the past. These details can aid in the study of disasters, which will in turn lead to formulation of preventive and corrective measures. The database may also store information on how each employee of an organization has to deal with potential disasters. These details can serve as an serve as an instruction booklet for the authorities and personnel concerned, if a disaster ever occurs.

For example, suppose a railway mishap occurs. Then the railway officials can quickly query the "disaster database" for the steps one is expected to follows. The database management system will list the do's and don'ts, such as inform the nearest police or military official, rush the injured to the nearest hospital, prepare a list of the number of people died or injured, inform the near and dear ones of the victims etc. All these duties, depending on the level of database system, can be done manually or automatically by the computer system if the necessary data is fed to it. The official will thus be able to take the necessary actions without errors or omissions.

SUMMARY

In general backup and recovery refers to the various strategies and procedure involved in protecting your database against data loss and reconstructing the data should that loss occur. The reconstructing of data is achieved through media recovery, which refers to the various operations involved in restoring, rolling forward, and rolling back a backup of database files.

Backups are divided into physical backups and logical backups. Physical backups, which are the primary concern in the backup and recovery strategy, are copies of physical database files. You can make physical backups with either and recovery manger utility of the DBMS or operating system utilities. In contract, logical backups contain logical data (For example, tables and stored procedures) extracted with some DBMS utility (like Oracle Export utility) and stored in a binary file. You can use logical backups to supplement physical backups.

The extent of damage that has occurred to the database plays a significant role in the choice of the recovery technique that will be used. For example, if the database has been heavily damaged, then the last backup copy will have to be restored and the update operations performed on the database since the last backup have to be reapplied using the log file. If the database has not been physically damaged, but has become inconsistent, then it is enough to undo the changes that caused the inconsistency. It may also be necessary to redo some transactions to ensure that the updates they performed have reached the database. Here we do not need the backup copy of the database. We can restore the database to a consistent state by using the before and after images held in the log file.

Disaster database management system is a new talk in the IT field. Although not yet implemented, it will contain details of all disasters that have occurred in the past, their causes and the consequences. Disasters include earthquakes, floods, fire, storms etc. which can bring the working of an organization to a halt. A disaster database may also contain the procedures or mode of investigations and trials carried out in the past. These details can aid in the study of disasters, which will in turn lead to formulation of preventive and corrective measures. The database may also store information on how each employee of an organization has to deal with potential disasters.

EXERCISES

1. What are database backup?
2. What are different types of failures?
3. Why should we plan backups?
4. What are transactions logs?
5. What is database recovery?
6. What is shadowing?
7. What is write ahead logging?
8. "Stable storage cannot be implemented" Explain why? Explain how database systems deal with such a problem.
9. Explain difference between a system crash and a disaster.
10. What are the different causes of failure of data in a database system?
11. State why planning database backup is importance and how recovery is carried out if a disaster occurs?
12. Compare are shadow paging recovery scheme with the log based recovery schemes in terms of ease of implementation and overhead cost.
13. Why do recovery routines use a log?
14. Discuss the shadow paging recovery scheme.
15. Explain the steps to be performed when a database is to be recovered from hard disk crash.

CHAPTER 17

CLIENT SERVER DATABASES

17.1 INTRODUCTION

Today, computing is no longer limited to a single place and at a central location. As need grow and corporations become larger in reach and levels of complexity, the business solution that are appropriate also change. And since IT is usually at the center of most strategic and internal business planning and implementation activities today, it is but natural that this should also undergo a commensurate change. A client/server solution is very much like a package of small but powerful systems that go to the core of any enterprise requirement, especially in the realms of distributed computing and services to go with it. Organizations going in for client/server systems are basically concerned with reducing cycle times and sharing information it improve operational efficiency. For a company that is going in for a client/ server systems there are a number of areas that need to be addressed and resolved. These may arise from external or internal factors. Today most companies need to substantiate their investment in IT infrastructure. Today each and every investment has to be justified in terms of payback period, amount of retraining, etc. A well planned client/server system is the most effective and efficient solution.

A client/server system also brings out the real inter-dependability of the organization's parts. Very often there is a large amount of data that is common in any enterprise. This may relate to marketing practices, HR policies, administrative guidelines, tax and levy structure etc. if a process can be instituted that will take care of these areas, then redundancies of workflow will be taken care of. So most companies want to go in for a centralized system, which can manage all theses. And once a proper client/server model is built, that will take care of these issues and the rest of the equation balances itself.

The problems of the LAN have led to the evaluation of the client/server model. Client/ server computing delivers and benefits of the network-computing model along with the shared data access and high performance characteristics of the host based computing model.

A client/server has three distinct components, each focusing on a specific job: a database server, a client application and a network. The Figure 17.1 shows the components of a client/ server computing model. The database server focuses on efficiently managing a resource such as a database of information. The server's primary job is to manage its resources optimally among multiple clients that concurrently request the server for the same resources. Database servers concentrate on takes such as:

- Managing a single database of information among many concurrent users.
- Controlling database access and other security requirements.
- Protecting database information with backup and recovery features.
- Centrally enforcing global integrity rules across all client applications.

A client application is the part of the system that users employ to interact with data. The client application in a client/server system focuses on jobs like:

- Presenting an interface through which the user can interact with the server to accomplish work.
- Managing the presentation logic such as pop-up lists on a entry form or bar graphs in a graphical data representation tool.
- Performing application logic such as calculating fields in a data entry form.
- Validating the data entered.
- Requesting and receiving information from a database server.

The network and communication software are the vehicles that transmit data between the clients and the server in a system. Both the clients and the server run communication software that allows them to talk across the network.

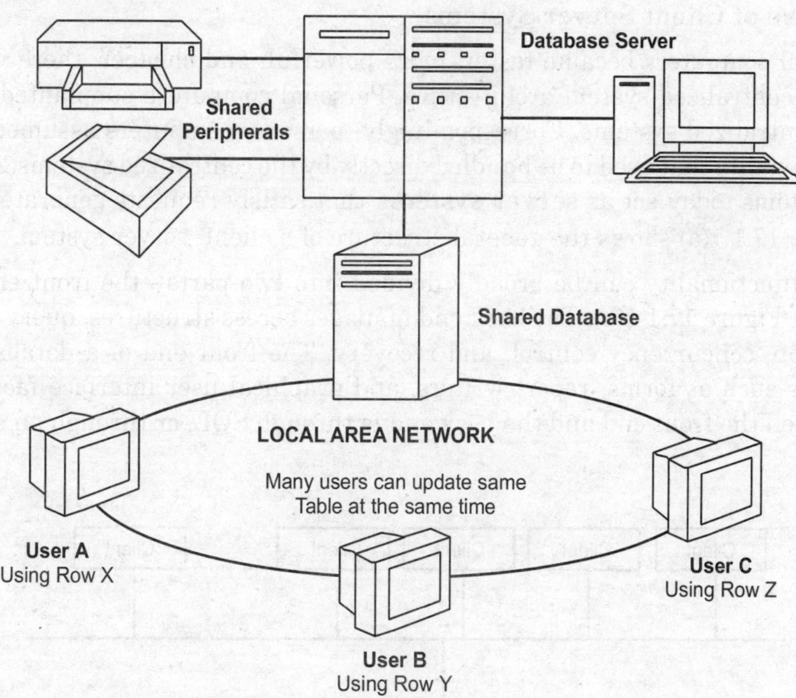

Figure 17.1 The Client/Server Computing Model

The concept of the client/server architecture is for the client and the server to communicate across the network with one or more clients accessing the server. A client/server system can deliver better performance than a fileserver system because a client's application and a database server work together to split the processing load of an application. The server manages the database among number of clients, while the clients send, receive and process the data they receive from the server. In a client/server application, the client application works with small specific data sets, such as rows in a table and not files as in a fileserver system. A database server is intelligent, locking and returning only the rows the client requests, which ensures concurrency, minimizes network traffic and improves system performance.

With the emergence of client/server technology as the predominant business-computing model, the integration of different information technologies has created a need for a new breed of powerful development tool to produce these applications. These applications are being designed to integrate with the dynamic environment of database management system technology and operating systems.

More and more sophisticated and complex systems are developed and deployed to manage and control data. These systems are being developed for personal computers and minicomputers. This means that developers have access to the systems that were once available only to the users of larger systems like mainframes. Now a stage has reached that the popularity, efficiency and ease of the use of the client/server systems is focusing the organizations that are using mainframes to restructure the IT infrastructure.

17.1.1 Structure of Client Server Systems

As personal computers became faster, more powerful, and cheaper, there was a shift away from the centralized system architecture. Personal computers supplanted terminals connected to centralized systems. Correspondingly, personal computers assumed the user-interface functionality that used to be handled directly by the centralized systems. As a result, centralized systems today act as **server systems** that satisfy requests generated by client systems. Figure 17.1.1(a) shows the general structure of a client–server system.

Database functionality can be broadly divided into two parts—the front end and the back end—as in Figure 17.1.1(b). The back end manages access structures, query evaluation and optimization, concurrency control, and recovery. The front end of a database system consists of tools such as forms, report writers, and graphical user interface facilities. The interface between the front end and the back end is through SQL, or through an application program.

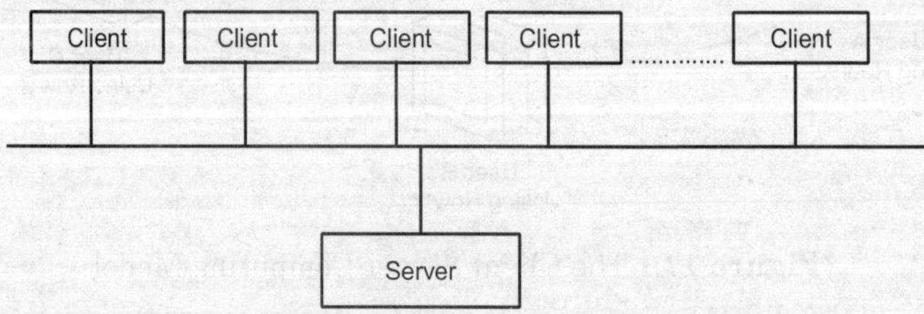

Figure 17.1.1(a) General structure of a client server system

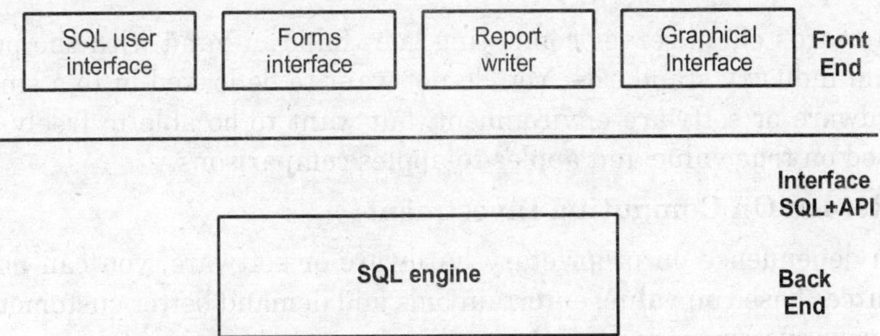

Figure 17.1.1(b) Front end and back end functionality

Client Server systems can be broadly categorized as transaction servers and data servers.

- **Transaction-server** systems, also called **query-server** systems, provide an interface to which clients can send requests to perform an action, in response to which they execute the action and send back results to the client. Usually, client machines ship transactions to the server systems, where those transactions are executed, and results are shipped back to clients that are in charge of displaying the data. Requests may be specified by using SQL, or through a specialized application program interface.
- **Data-server systems** allow clients to interact with the servers by making requests to read or update data, in units such as files or pages. For example, file servers provide a file-system interface where clients can create, update, read, and delete files. Data servers for database systems offer much more functionality; they support units of data—such as pages, tuples, or objects—that are smaller than a file. They provide indexing facilities for data, and provide transaction facilities so that the data are never left in an inconsistent state if a client machine or process fails.

17.2 BENEFITS OF CLIENT SERVER COMPUTING

Market research and investment patterns indicate that client/server computing is taking the IT industry by storm. What benefits should you expect from employing a client/server paradigm? Again, there is no universal agreement on the client/server advantages; but the most often projected benefits are:

17.2.1 Adaptability

You want the flexibility required to maintain a state-of-the-art technology environment and employ best-of-breed solutions. You want the ability to adopt the computing environment to meet the needs of an ever-changing business environment; to easily up or down size resources to match your changing business requirements.

17.2.2 Reduced Operating Costs

Computer hardware and software costs are on a continually downward spiral, which means that real computing value is ever increasing. Client/server computing offers you a way to cash in on this bonanza by replacing expensive large systems with less expensive smaller ones networked together.

17.2.3 Platform Independence

The push towards client/server computing goes hand-in-hand with the push towards open systems and industry standards. You do not want to be locked in to a single vendor's proprietary hardware or software environment, but want to be able to freely interchange components based on true value and apples-to-apples comparisons.

17.2.4 Better Return On Computing Investment

Freed from dependence on proprietary hardware or software, you can now purchase computing resources based on value, entertain bids and demand better customer service. On the other hand, your customers are also demanding improved service and faster results from you-they will not accept booking time on the mainframe well in advance, or wait long for your staff to become proficient in mainframe operating systems. Client/server computing both answers and fuels the demand for "information at our fingertips". Advances in client/server tools have led to rapid application development.

17.2.5 Improved Performance

With more processing power scattered throughout the enterprise. You expect to process information more quickly with faster response time. With open networked systems and lower components costs, you expect to be able to quickly and responses where they are needed to easily fix performance bottlenecks. With the power of all networked MIPS and advanced software architectures. You improved OLTP times.

17.2.6 Easier Data Access and Processing

The rise of client/server systems coincides with the advent of GUIs and interactivity. The major benefits of a GUI are reduced staff training costs, and the spreading of computer usage to a wider audience. Online interactive client/server systems are a major improvement is usability over older batch-oriented systems. More people are able to access more data more quickly than ever before. You want to use this to empower your team, reduce your product development cycles, improve your time to market and gain a competitive edge.

17.2.7 Decentralized Operations

Decentralizing IT operations puts computing power and data access in the hands of the users, transforming clerical workers into "knowledge workers". This increases the productivity of MIS staff by reducing trivial request and allowing them to concentrate on mission-critical applications. Client/server architectures improve the service you can offer by supplying information at the point closet to your customers.

Although, these benefits are impressive, the mainframe-computing environment provides some very real advantages that you cannot forgo in the move to client/server computing. Client/server computing must continue to ensure:

- **High Reliability-** The move towards client/server would be a non-starter if these systems could not ensure high transaction rates, timely and continuous data access, data integrity and corporate security. Mission-critical business data require highly reliable systems.
- **Protecting Existing Investment-** It is silly to throw out the baby with the bath water. Whenever possible, existing legacy systems should be leveraged rather than

scrapped. New client/server systems should adopt to technology changes and not become the legacy systems of tomorrow. This requires software systems that can access and interoperate with software running on the desktop and in glass house. This requires software systems that are open, integrated and adaptable.

17.3 APPLICATION ARCHITECTURE

Like in any other situation good application can bring a host of benefits to the application developer, the customer and the user. Some of the benefits are reduced development time, reuse of major application components across other applications, scalability of applications, ease of maintenance, improved performance etc. But the design and development of good application architecture is not an easy task. The developer, the designers, the analysis and the users will have to spend a lot of time and effort on it. But without this investment, the customer or user will have duplicate work, produce high maintenance applications that do not comply with the common standards and spend a lot of time in duplicate testing and documentation. Thus if an organization is planning to rely on the information technology for its growth, then its IT infrastructure should be based on solid foundations and the time spent on designing a good application architecture will save a lot of time, effort and money.

A client server system is best understand and perceived as a logical interconnected system that simplifies tasks in IT by decomposition. So the main trust of client/server development is the application area rather than the hardware infrastructure. Developers and system integrators will be asked to develop system that should meet the following ends:

- Make the system platform and protocol independent
- Enable connections across system and users
- Hide the process and make the application transparent
- Secure business transactions
- Ensure future growth as the user demand increases
- Enable internet and internet access

The application undertaken by the developer will seek to design an architecture that provides ease-of use with opportunities for reusability. Uniformity and homogeneity are also two very critical areas that a developer will seek to address.

We saw the benefits of a client server system. When developing a client/server application based on enterprise requirements, different types of architectures need to be considered. The most common among the client server architecture are the **Two-tiered** and **Three-tiered** architectures. A tiered architecture is when a logical section on an application can be divided into categories or tiers.

17.3.1 Two-tiered Architecture

A two-tiered architecture is the traditional client server environment that divided the application into the Graphical User Interface (client) and the Data (server). The GUI can be developed using a product like Visual Basic or PowerBuilder and the Data can be setup using a database management system. A typical two-tiered architecture is shown in Figure 17.3.1(a).

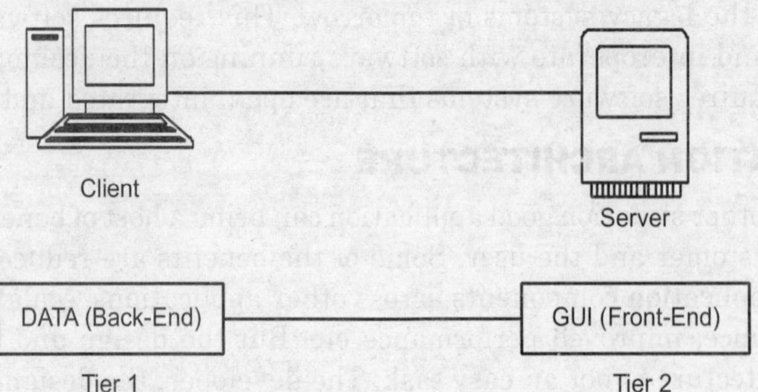

Figure 17.3.1(a) Two-tiered Architecture

The GUI is often referred to as the **'Presentation Layer'**. In the two-tiered architecture, all the pieces of the application are either on the client (tier 1) or server or server (tier 2). For example, if the application has a number of business rules that is needs to process, then those rules can either reside on the client or server. Consider a case where PowerBuilder is the client and oracle is the server. If the business rules are on the client then code is written as a part of the DataWindow or a window level function or as a user object. This is shown in Figure **17.3.1(b).**

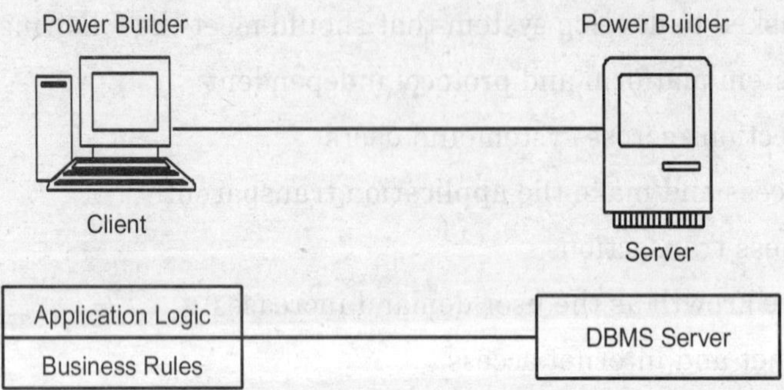

Figure 17.3.1(b) Business Rules Residing on the Client

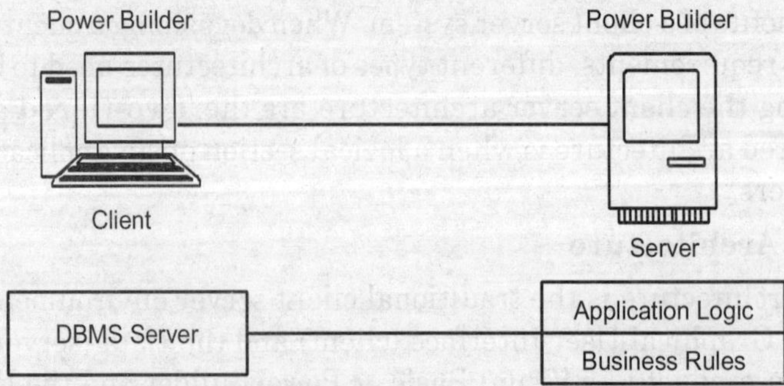

Figure 17.3.1(c) Business Rules Residing on the server

But if the business rules are on the server tied to the database management system, they can be written in the form of stored procedures, functions, triggers etc. This arrangement is shown in the Figure 17.3.1(c). Usually, in a two-tiered client server system, all the components of the application are either written on the client or the server.

There are both advantages and disadvantages for this kind of two-tiered systems. The advantages are there are only two-components, the client and the server to deal with. So in most cases there will be only two vendors, the GUI vendor (PowerSoft or MicroSoft) and the DBMS vendor (say Oracle Corp., Microsoft or Sybase). Developers do not have to learn multiple products. Development time is faster.

If the business rules are written on the DBMS, then changing the DBMS (say from Oracle to Sybase) requires the rules also to be changed. The same applies for the rules residing on the client. You cannot change Visual Basic to PowerBuilder without redoing the business rules for PowerBuilder. Another main disadvantage of a two-tiered application is the scalability of the application.

17.3.2 Three-tiered Architecture

A three tiered architecture is when an application is divided into three logical categories or tiers. Today the most widely accepted form of client server system is the three-tiered architecture. The components of this architecture are:

- The application (GUI) or User services
- Business rules or Business Services
- Data Server or Data Services

All these layers or tiers interact with one another and in the best of circumstances are independent of the individual compositions. With a three-tiered architecture, by separating the business rules of an enterprise, the investment in the business rules will not be lost as applications and application development tools are changed or if the database management system is changed. This architecture will also change the problem of scalability and reuse. In a three-tiered architecture, the business rules are designed as a separate tier such that any application or applications or any DBMS can be used as shown in Figure 17.3.2.

The manner in which a client server system is organized will lend the maximum long-term benefits to the user. In most cases, the user and the database tier are constant for a given organization. And the business tier (or business rules) is the one that usually undergoes the maximum amount of change and modification as the business grows and changes. This is called the growth of a client server system.

The three-tier architecture raises the definition of services from instructions and API calls to business services. A service is a logical business function that can be aggregated into physical code called components. The components are referred to as business objects. The collection builder's job becomes that of combining these new business components into a solution. The collection builder of business components can be thought of as a set of business service relationships. By grouping these business component in different ways, we provide different business solutions.

Business components can be called by other business components in the same tier or a higher tier. These business components can have the following three capabilities.

- **Properties** – The characteristics of the business object. For example, in a tax-calculation service the properties might include the name, permanent tax, number taxable income etc.
- **Methods** – The functionality implemented, such as compute tax rate or tax amount.
- **Event** – Notification of the occurrence of an event to the caller of the business object (client).

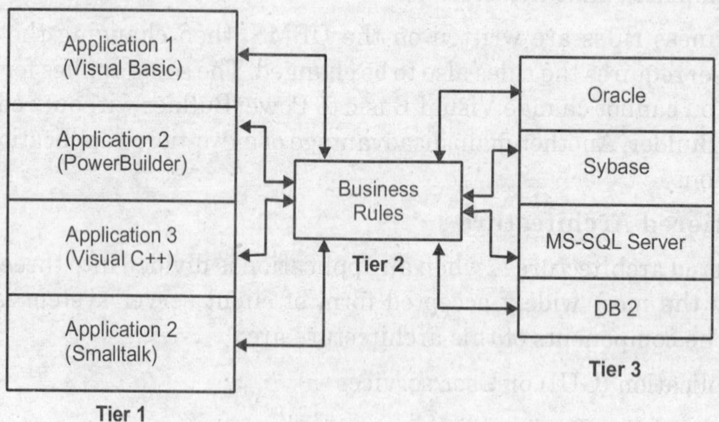

Figure 17.3.2 Three-tiered Architecture

Now we will see each of the three tiers of the three-tiered architecture, which are:

- Presentation (GUI) or User Services
- Business rules or Business Services
- Data Server or Data Services

17.3.2.1 Presentation (GUI) or User Services

In this tier, development is ideally split into two parts, divided by skills as follows:

- **Analyst & User** – Develops the GUI, graphics and massages presented to the user. This can be accomplished by prototyping, with no business object attached. This is usually called the 'stub code' since it will be completed and real business object will be engaged or substituted.
- **Solution Developer** – The solution developer creates the application specific code on the client side. He typically uses a high level language like PowerScript or VBA and essentially uses the entry points to various business services to create the flow of control required by the application.

17.3.2.2 Business rules or Business Services

The business services tier encapsulates business rules and process enabling clarity or purpose for each individual object. A collection of detailed business objects, called components are mixed with many other components at this level. Various business solutions call upon one or more of these business components, usually through the user-services tier, to provide a solution. Many business solutions can share a set of business objects.

Initially, three-tier client server development requires building business object at the business services tier. After several business solution are built, a solid set of business objects will exist that represent the user's enterprise-computing environment. Thereafter, development of new business solutions may require no new business objects or only a few.

Building business components can be a complex task requiring a thorough understanding of the user's overall business and how the various segments of the user's business would interact with a common business object. For instance, all businesses have customers and most segments of a business interact with the customer information in some way or other. So it makes a lot of sense to build a customer component that is reusable across the company. To do so and to eliminate redundant customer databases, the analyst must understand how the various departments interact with customer information, what information they manage, what information they need and what portion of the information management can be automated by this component.

17.3.2.3 Data Services Tier or Business Data

Traditionally, data business object or servers are thought of only in terms of database. The data services tier consists of data in any form. Isolating actual data from the solutions by the business-rules tier improves the reliability and accuracy because each function exists only once. The business objects tend to improve over time and everyone benefits from the improvements. Corporate policy changes can be implemented immediately and placed in effect for every business solution the next time they access the data. Putting the business rules in the code logic of the business object instead of triggers and procedure provides more complex logic functions for the resolution of a business function.

SUMMARY

Today, computing is no longer limited to a single place and at a central location. As need grow and corporations become larger in reach and levels of complexity, the business solution that are appropriate also change. And since IT is usually at the center of most strategic and internal business planning and implementation activities today, it is but natural that this should also undergo a commensurate change.

A client/server solution is very much like a package of small but powerful systems that go to the core of any enterprise requirement, especially in the realms of distributed computing and services to go with it. Organizations going in for client/server systems are basically concerned with reducing cycle times and sharing information it improve operational efficiency. As personal computers became faster, more powerful, and cheaper, there was a shift away from the centralized system architecture. Personal computers supplanted terminals connected to centralized systems. Correspondingly, personal computers assumed the user-interface functionality that used to be handled directly by the centralized systems. As a result, centralized systems today act as **server systems** that satisfy requests generated by client systems.

The most common among the client server architecture are the Two-tiered and Three-tiered architectures. A tiered architecture is when a logical section on an application can be divided into categories or tiers. Since both the architectures have pros and cons, the actual selection should be done only after examining the user's goals, the application, the size, scalability needs, growth pattern of the organization, etc.

EXERCISES

1. What is the client server computing?
2. What are the building blocks of client/server systems?
3. What are the structures of client/server systems?
4. What are benefits of client/server computing?
5. What is a two tiered architecture? Explain with the help of a diagram?
6. What are advantages and disadvantages of the three tiered architecture?
7. What do you mean by application architectures?
8. What are the different components of a three tiered client server system?
9. What are business rules and what are the functions of the business services tier?
10. What are the functions of the data services tier?

CHAPTER 18

PARALLEL DATABASES

18.1 INTRODUCTION

Parallel processing divides a large task into many smaller tasks, and executes the smaller tasks concurrently, on several nodes. As a result, the larger task completes more quickly. As node is a separate processor, often on a separate machine. Multiple processors, however, can reside on a single machine.

Some tasks can be effectively divided, and thus are good candidates for parallel processing. Other tasks, however, do not lend themselves to this approach. Parallel processing within a computer system allows database-system activities to be speeded up, allowing faster response to transactions, as well as more transactions per second. Queries can be processed in a manner that exploits the parallelism offered by the underlying computer system. The need for parallel query processing has lead to the development of parallel systems.

For example, in a bank with only one clerk, all customers must a single queue to be served. With two clerks, the task can be effectively split so that customers form two queues and are served twice as fast. This is an instance in which parallel processing is an effective solution. But consider the following situation. According to the bank procedures, only the manager of each branch can approve a loan request. A branch has only one manger and so parallel processing is not applicable here. Even if you put four or five clerks to speed up the loan approval process before it reaches the manger, all the requests must form a single queue for bank manger's approval. No amount of parallel processing can overcome this built-in bottleneck to the system. Some is the case with database transactions. Some tasks could be effectively divided, some others cannot. But in the case of the tasks, that could be divided, parallel processing time, thus improving performance. The Figure 18.1(a) and 18.1(b) contrast sequential processing of a single parallel query with parallel processing of the same query.

In sequential processing, the query is executed as a single large task. In parallel processing, the query is divided into multiple smaller tasks, and each component task is executed on a separate node. The Figure 18.1(c) and 18.1(d) contrast sequential with parallel processing of multiple independent tasks from an on-line transaction processing (OLTP) environment. In sequential processing (Figure 18.1(c)), independent tasks compete for a single resource. Only task 1 runs without having to wait. Task 2 must wait until task 1 has completed;

task 3 must wait until tasks 1 and 2 have completed, and so on. Although the figure shows the independent tasks as the same size, the size of the tasks will vary.

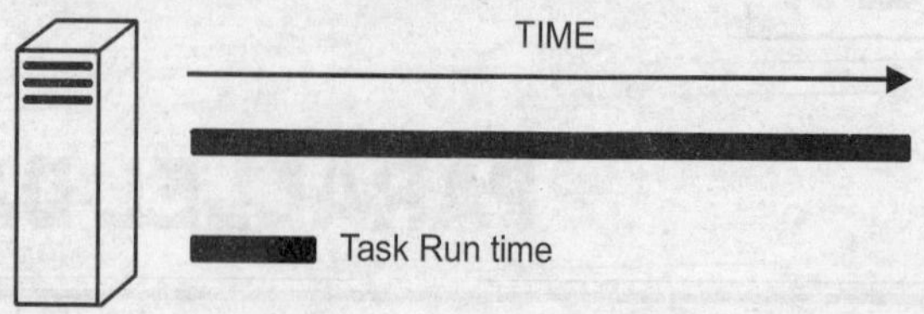

Figure 18.1(a) Sequential Processing of a Large Task

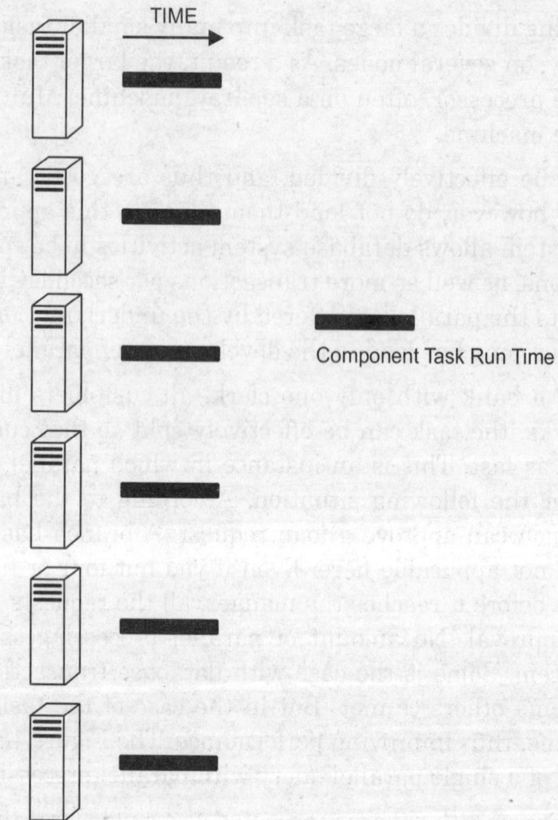

Figure 18.1(b) Parallel Processing Executing Component Tasks in parallel

Figure 18.1(d) illustrates parallel processing (for example, a parallel server on a symmetric multiprocessor), where more CPU power is assigned to the tasks. Each independent task executes immediately on its own processor: no wait time involved. So the time taken to complete the tasks is much less in parallel processing compared to sequential processing. Effective implementation of parallel involves two challenges-structuring tasks so that certain tasks can execute at the same time (in parallel) and preserving the sequencing of tasks that must be executed serially.

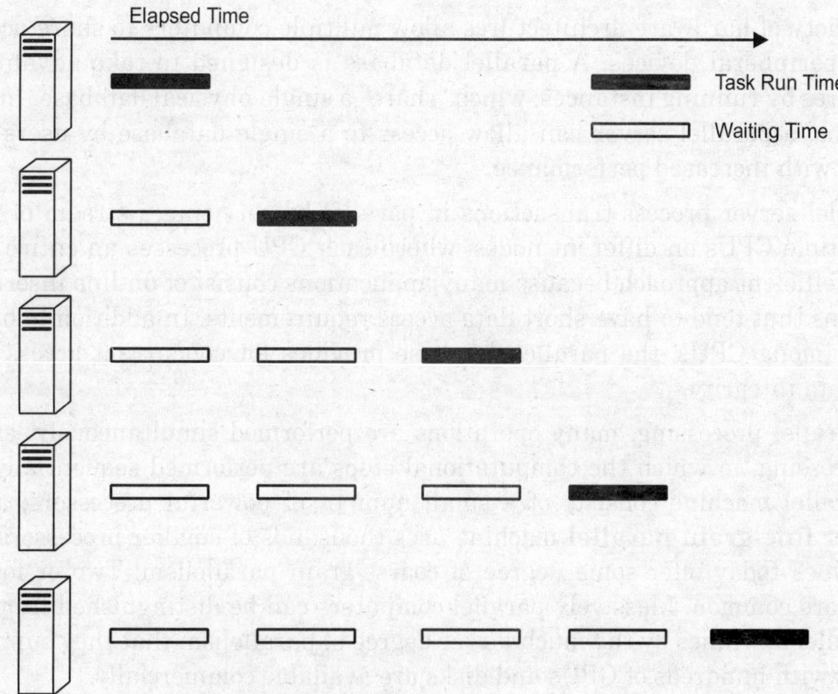

Figure 18.1(c) Sequential Processing of multiple independent Tasks

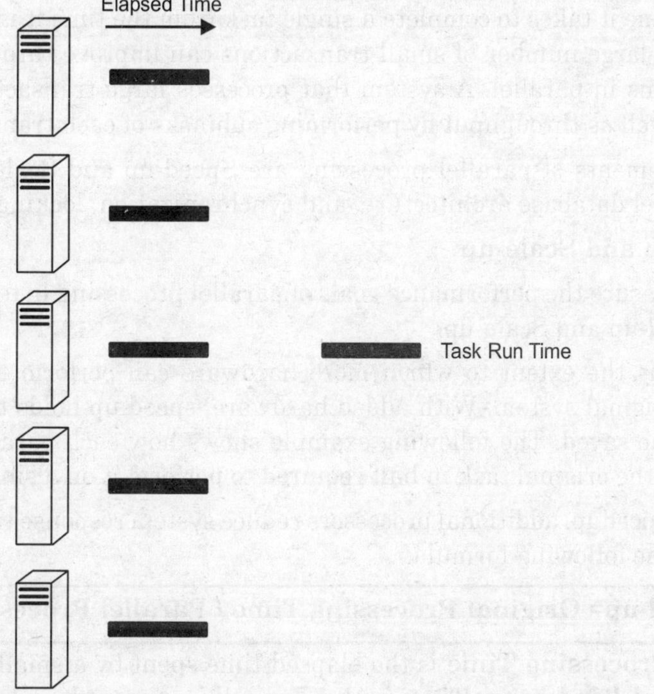

Figure 18.1(d) Parallel Processing of Multiple independent Tasks

18.2 THE KEY ELEMENTS OF PARALLEL PROCESSING

A variety of hardware architectures allow multiple computers to share access to data, software, peripheral devices. A parallel database is designed to take advantage of such architectures by running instances, which "share" a single physical database. In appropriate applications, a parallel server can allow access to a single database by users on multiple machines, with increased performance.

Parallel server process transactions in parallel by servicing a stream of transactions using multiple CPUs on different nodes, where each CPU processes an entire transaction. This is an efficient approach because many applications consist of on-line insert and update transactions that tend to have short data access requirements. In addition to balancing the workload among CPUs, the parallel database provides for concurrent access to data and protects data integrity.

In parallel processing, many operations are performed simultaneously, as opposed to serial processing, in which the computational steps are performed sequentially. A **coarse-grain** parallel machine consists of a small number of powerful processors; a **massively parallel** or **fine-grain parallel** machine uses thousands of smaller processors. Most high-end machines today offer some degree of coarse-grain parallelism: Two or four processor machines are common. Massively parallel computers can be distinguished from the coarse-grain parallel machines by the much larger degree of parallelism that they support. Parallel computers with hundreds of CPUs and disks are available commercially.

There are two main measures of performance of a database system: (1) through-put, the number of tasks that can be completed in a given time interval, and (2) response time, the amount of time it takes to complete a single task from the time it is submitted. A system that processes a large number of small transactions can improve throughput by processing many transactions in parallel. A system that processes large transactions can improve response time as well as throughput by performing subtasks of each transaction in parallel.

The key elements of parallel processing are Speed-up and Scale-up, interconnection networks, parallel database architecture, and synchronization, locking and messaging.

18.2.1 Speed-up and Scale-up

You can measure the performance goals of parallel processing in terms of two important properties-Speed-up and Scale-up.

Speed-up is the extent to which more hardware can perform the same task is less time than the original system. With added hardware, speed-up holds the task constant and measure the time saved. The following example shows how each parallel hardware system performs half of the original task in half required to perform it on a single system.

With good speedup, additional processors reduce system response time. You can measure speedup using the following formula:

Speed-up= Original Processing Time / Parallel Processing Time

Original Processing Time is the elapsed time spent by a small system on the given task and **Parallel Processing Time** is the elapsed time spent by a larger, parallel system on the given task. For example, if the original system took 100 seconds to perform a task, and two parallel systems took 50 seconds, then the value of speed-up would be equal to 2.

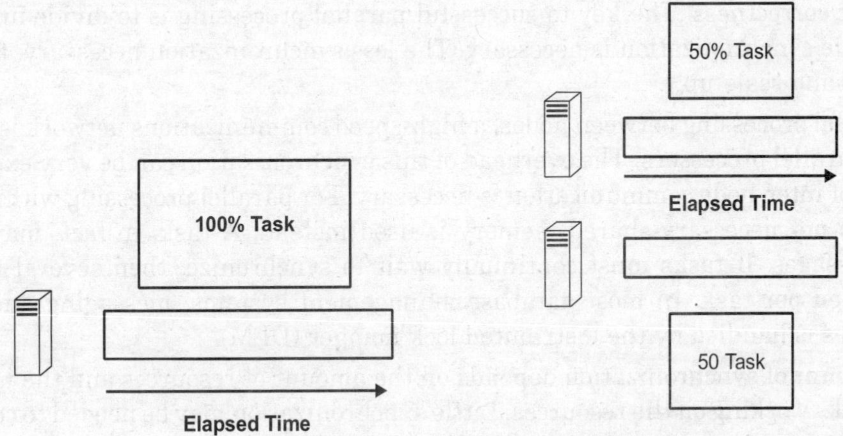

Figure 18.2.1(a) Speed-up (Reduction in processing time by 50%)

Scale-up is the ability of a system n times larger to perform a job n times larger, in the same time period as the original system. With added hardware, a formula for scale-up holds the time constant, and measures the increased size of the job, which can be done. With good scale-up, if transaction volumes grow, you can keep response time constant by adding hardware resources such as CPUs. You can measure scale-up using this formula:

Scale-up = Parallel Processing Volume / Original Processing Volume

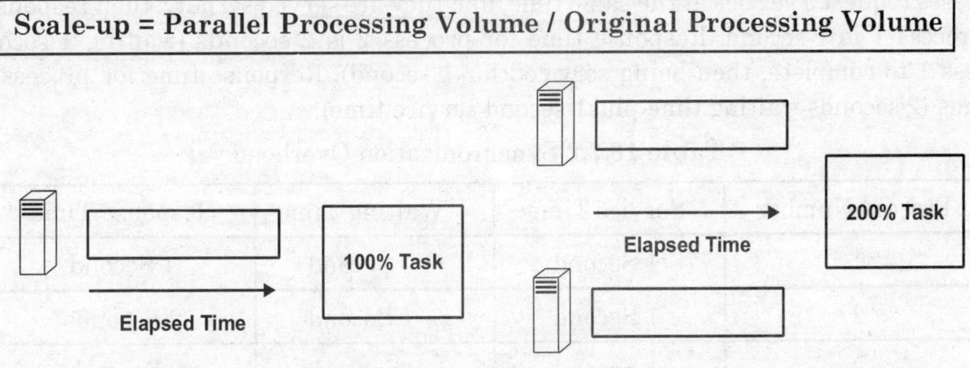

Figure 18.2.1(b) Scale-up

Original Processing Volume is the transaction volume processed in a given amount of time on a small system. **Parallel Processing Volume** is the transaction volume processed in a given amount of time on a parallel system. For example, if the original system can process 1000 transactions in a given amount of time, and the parallel system can process 2000 transactions in this amount of time, then the value of scale-up would be equal to 2. That is, 2000/1000 = 2. A value of 2 indicates the ideal of linear scale-up-when twice as much hardware can process twice the data volume in the same amount of time. For most OLTP applications, no speedup can be expected; only scale-up. The overhead due to synchronization may, in fact, cause speed-down.

18.2.2 Synchronization

Coordination of concurrent tasks is called **Synchronization.** Synchronization is necessary for correctness. The key to successful parallel processing is to divide up tasks so that very little synchronization is necessary. The less synchronization necessary, the better the speed-up and scale-up.

In parallel processing between nodes, a high-speed communications network is required among the parallel processors. The overhead of this synchronization can be very expensive if a great deal of inter-node communication is necessary. For parallel processing within a node, messaging is not necessary-shared memory is used instead. A task, in fact, may require multiple messages. If tasks must continually wait to synchronize, then several messages may be needed per task. In most database management systems, messaging and locking between nodes is handled by the distributed lock manger (DLM).

The amount of synchronization depends on the amount of resources and the number of users and tasks working on the resources. Little synchronization may be needed to coordinate a small number of concurrent tasks, but lots of synchronization may be necessary to coordinate many concurrent tasks.

A great deal of time spent in synchronization indicates high contention for resources. Too much time spent in synchronization can diminish the benefits to parallel processing. With less time spent in synchronization, better speed-up and scale-up can be achieved.

Response Time equals time spent waiting and time spent doing useful work. Table 18.2.2 illustrates how overhead increases as more concurrent processes are added. If 3 processes request a service at the same time, and they are served serially, then response time for process 1 is 1 second. Response time for process 2 is 2 seconds (waiting 1 second for process 1 to complete, then being serviced for 1 second). Response time for process 3 is 3 seconds (2 seconds waiting time plus1 second service time).

Table 18.2.2 Synchronization Overhead

Process Number	Service Time	Waiting Time	Response Time
1.	1 Second	0 Second	1 Second
2.	1 Second	1 Second	2 Seconds
3.	1 Second	2 Seconds	2 Seconds

18.2.3 Cost of Synchronization

While synchronization is a necessary element of parallel processing to preserve correctness you need to manage its cost in terms to performance and system resources. Different kinds of parallel processing software may permit synchronization to be achieved, but a given approach may or may not be cost effective.

Sometimes synchronization can be accomplished very cheaply. In other cases, however, the cost of synchronization may be too high. For example, if one table takes inserts from many nodes, a lot of synchronization is necessary. There will be high contention from the different nodes to insert into the same data block-the data block must be passed between the different nodes. This kind of synchronization can be done-but not efficiently.

18.2.4 Locking

Locks are fundamentally a way of synchronizing tasks. Many different locking mechanisms are necessary to enable the synchronization of tasks required by parallel processing. External locking facilities as well as mechanisms internal to the database are necessary.

As we have seen earlier, a distributed lock manager (DLM) is the external locking facility used by many parallel databases. A DLM is operating system software, which coordinates resources sharing between nodes running a parallel server. The instances of a parallel server use the distributed lock manager to communicate with each other and coordinate modification of database resources. Each node operates independently of other nodes, expect when contending for the same resource.

The DLM allows application to synchronize access to resources such as data, software, and peripheral devices, so that concurrent requests for the same resources are coordinated between applications running nodes. The DLM performs the following services for applications:

- Keeps track of the current "ownership" of a resource.
- Accepts lock requests for resources from application processes
- Notifies the requesting process when a lock on a resource is available
- Gets access to a resource for a process

18.2.5 Messaging

Parallel processing requires fast and efficient communication between nodes-a system with high bandwidth and low latency, which efficiently communicates with the DLM. Bandwidth is the total size of messages, which can be sent per second.

Latency is the time required to locate the first bit or character in a storage location, expressed as access time minus word time. It is the time (in seconds) it takes to place a message on the network. Latency thus indicates the number of messages, which can be put on the network per second.

A communications network with high bandwidth is like a wide highway with many lanes to accommodate heavy traffic-the number of lanes affects the speed at which traffic can move. A network with low latency is like a highway with an entrance ramp, which permits vehicles to enter without delay-the cost of getting on the highway is low. Massively Parallel Processing (MPP) is a parallel computing architecture that uses hundreds and thousands of processors. In clustering we use two or more systems that work together. The difference between MPP and clusters is that MPP uses many more processors than clustering. MPP systems characteristically use networks with high bandwidth and low latency; clusters use Ethernet connections with relatively low bandwidth and high latency.

18.3 INTERCONNECTION NETWORKS

Parallel systems consist of a set of components (processors, memory, and disks) that can communicate with each other via an interconnection network. Figure 18.3 shows three commonly used types of interconnection networks:

- **Bus.** All the system components can send data on and receive data from a single communication bus. This type of interconnection is shown in Figure 18.1a. The bus could be an Ethernet or a parallel interconnect. Bus architectures work well for small numbers of processors. However, they do not scale well with in- creasing parallelism, since the bus can handle communication from only one component at a time.
- **Mesh.** The components are nodes in a grid, and each component connects to all its adjacent components in the grid. In a two-dimensional mesh each node connects to four adjacent nodes, while in a three-dimensional mesh each node connects to six adjacent nodes. Figure 18.3b shows a two-dimensional mesh. Nodes that are not directly connected can communicate with one an-other by routing messages via a sequence of intermediate nodes that are directly connected to one another. The number of communication links grows as the number of components grows, and the communication capacity of a mesh therefore scales better with increasing parallelism.
- **Hypercube.** The components are numbered in binary, and a component is connected to another if the binary representations of their numbers differ in exactly one bit. Thus, each of the n components is connected to log(n) other components. Figure 18.3c shows a hypercube with 8 nodes. In a hypercube interconnection, a message from a component can reach any other cmponent by going through at most log(n) links. In contrast, in a mesh architecture a component may be $2(\sqrt{n} - 1)$ links away from some of the other components (or $\sqrt{n}$ links away, if the mesh interconnection wraps around at the edges of the grid). Thus communication delays in a hypercube are significantly lower than in a mesh.

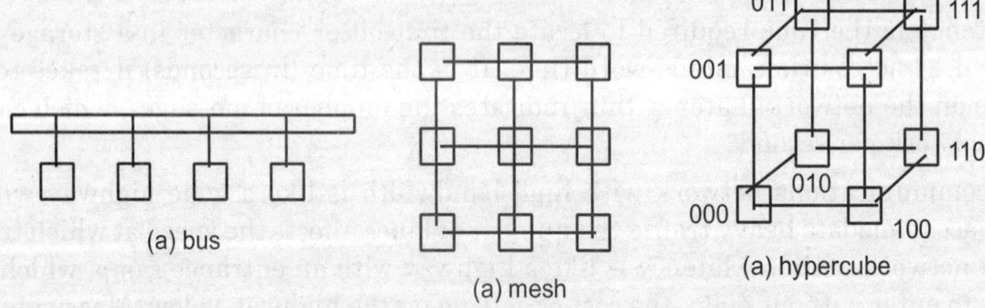

Figure 18.3 Interconnection networks

18.4 PARALLEL DATABASE ARCHITECTURES

There are several architectural models for parallel machines. Among the most prominent ones are those in Figure 18.4 (in the Figure, M denotes memory, P denotes a processor, and disks are shown as cylinders):

- **Shared memory.** All the processors share a common memory (Figure 18.4a).
- **Shared disk**. All the processors share a common set of disks (Figure 18.4b). Shared-disk systems are sometimes called clusters.

- **Shared nothing.** The processors share neither a common memory nor common disk (Figure 18.4c).
- **Hierarchical.** This model is a hybrid of the preceding three architectures (Figure18.4d).

In Sections 18.4.1 through 18.4.4, we elaborate on each of these models. Techniques used to speed up transaction processing on data-server systems, such as data and lock caching and lock de-escalation, outlined in Section 18.2.2, can also be used in shared-disk parallel databases as well as in shared-nothing parallel databases. In fact, they are very important for efficient transaction processing in such systems.

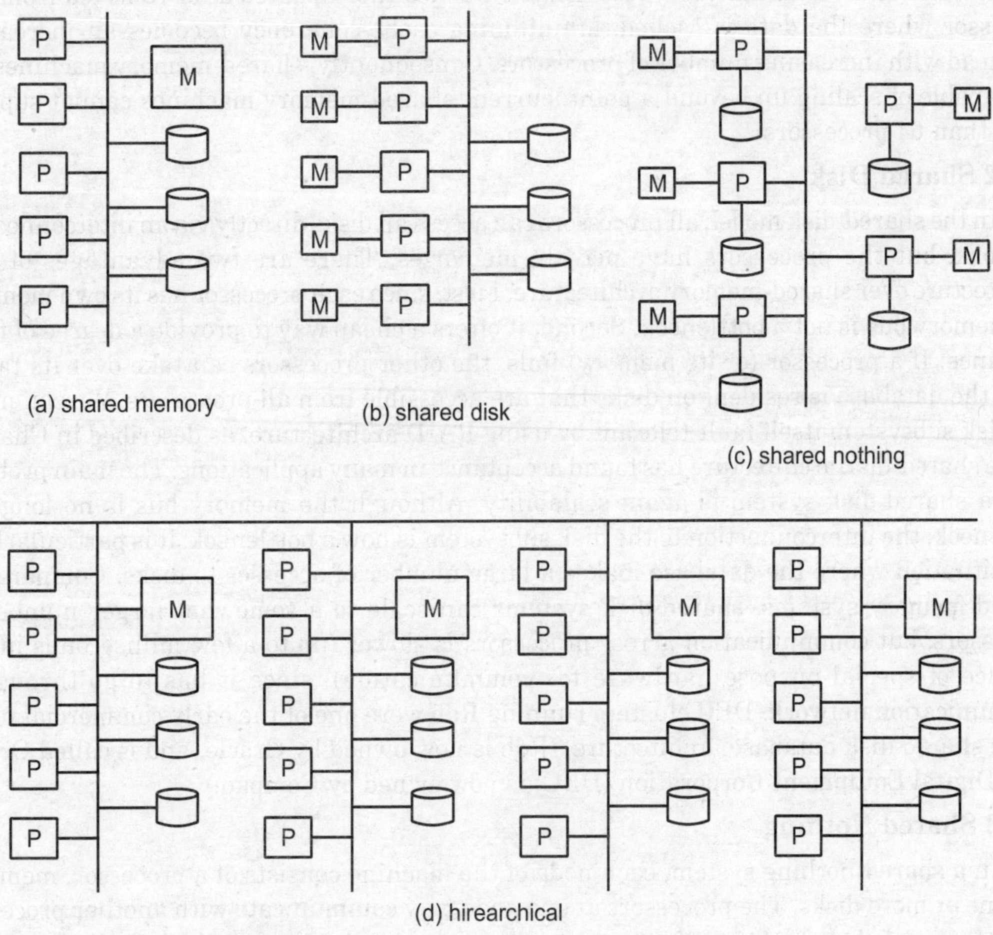

Figure 18.4 Parallel Database Architecture

18.4.1 Shared Memory

In **shared-memory** architecture, the processors and disks have access to a common memory, typically via a bus or through an interconnection network. The benefit of shared memory is extremely efficient communication between processors—data in shared memory can be accessed by any processor without being moved with software. A processor can send messages to other processors much faster by using memory writes (which usually take less than a microsecond) than by sending a message through a communication mechanism. The downside of shared-memory machines is that the architecture is not scalable beyond 32 or 64 processors because the bus or the interconnection network becomes a bottleneck (since it is shared by all processors). Adding more processors does not help after a point, since the processors will spend most of their time waiting for their turn on the bus to access memory. Shared memory architectures usually have large memory caches at each processor, so that referencing of the shared memory is avoided whenever possible. However, at least some of the data will not be in the cache, and accesses will have to go to the shared memory. Moreover, the caches need to be kept coherent; that is, if a processor performs a write to a memory location, the data in that memory location should be either updated at or removed from any processor where the data is cached. Maintaining cache-coherency becomes an increasing overhead with increasing number of processors. Consequently, shared-memory machines are not capable of scaling up beyond a point; current shared-memory machines cannot support more than 64 processors.

18.4.2 Shared Disk

In the shared-disk model, all processors can access all disks directly via an interconnection network, but the processors have private memories. There are two advantages of this architecture over shared-memory architecture. First, since each processor has its own memory, the memory bus is not a bottleneck. Second, it offers a cheap way to provide a degree of fault tolerance: If a processor (or its memory) fails, the other processors can take over its tasks, since the database is resident on disks that are accessible from all processors. We can make the disk subsystem itself fault tolerant by using RAID architecture, as described in Chapter 9. The shared-disk architecture has found acceptance in many applications. The main problem with a shared-disk system is again scalability. Although the memory bus is no longer a bottleneck, the interconnection to the disk subsystem is now a bottleneck; it is particularly so in a situation where the database makes a large number of accesses to disks. Compared to shared-memory systems, shared-disk systems can scale to a somewhat larger number of processors, but communication across processors is slower (up to a few milliseconds in the absence of special-purpose hardware for communication), since it has to go through a communication network. DEC clusters running Rdb were one of the early commercial users of the shared disk database architecture. (Rdb is now owned by Oracle, and is called Oracle Rdb. Digital Equipment Corporation (DEC) is now owned by Compaq.)

18.4.3 Shared Nothing

In a shared-nothing system, each node of the machine consists of a processor, memory, and one or more disks. The processors at one node may communicate with another processor at another node by a high-speed interconnection network. A node functions as the server for the data on the disk or disks that the node owns. Since local disk references are serviced by local disks at each processor, the shared-nothing model overcomes the disadvantage of requiring all I/O to go through a single interconnection network; only queries, accesses to nonlocal disks, and result relations pass through the network. Moreover, the interconnection networks for shared-nothing systems are usually designed to be scalable, so that their transmission capacity increases as more nodes are added. Consequently, shared-nothing architectures are more scalable and can easily support a large number of processors. The main drawbacks of shared-nothing systems are the costs of communication and of nonlocal disk access, which are higher than in a shared-memory or shared-disk architecture since sending data involves software interaction at both ends. The Teradata database machine was among the earliest commercial systems to use the shared-nothing database architecture. The Grace and the Gamma research prototypes also used shared-nothing architectures.

18.4.4 Hierarchical

The hierarchical architecture combines the characteristics of shared-memory, shared disk, and shared nothing architectures. At the top level, the system consists of nodes connected by an interconnection network, and do not share disks or memory with one another. Thus, the top level is a shared-nothing architecture. Each node of the system could actually be a shared-memory system with a few processors. Alternatively, each node could be a shared-disk system, and each of the systems sharing a set of disks could be a shared-memory system. Thus, a system could be built as a hierarchy, with shared-memory architecture with a few processors at the base, and a shared nothing architecture at the top, with possibly a shared-disk architecture in the middle. Figure 18.4(d) illustrates a hierarchical architecture with shared-memory nodes connected together in a shared-nothing architecture. Commercial parallel database systems today run on several of these architectures. Attempts to reduce the complexity of programming such systems have yielded distributed virtual-memory architectures, where logically there is a single shared memory, but physically there are multiple disjoint memory systems; the virtual memory- mapping hardware, coupled with system software, allows each processor to view the disjoint memories as a single virtual memory. Since access speeds differ, depending on whether the page is available locally or not, such an architecture is also referred to as a nonuniform memory architecture (NUMA).

18.5 BENEFITS OF PARALLEL PROCESSING

Parallel processing can benefit certain kinds of applications by providing enhanced throughput (Scale-up) and improved Response Time (Speed-up). Improved response time can be achieved either by breaking up a large task into smaller components or by reducing wait time. The table 18.5 shows which types of workload can attain speed-up with properly implemented parallel processing.

Table 18.5 Speed-up and Scale-up for different types of workload

Workload	Speed-up	Scale-up
On-line Transaction Processing	No	Yes
Decision Support Systems	Yes	Yes
Batch Processing	Possible	Yes
Parallel Query Processing	Yes	Yes

Enhanced Throughput-Scale-up

If tasks can run independently of one another, they can be distributed to different CPUs or nodes and there will be a scale-up more processes will be able to run through the database in the same amount of time.

If processes can run ten times faster, then the system can accomplish ten times more in the original amount of time. Parallel processing permits scale-up a system might maintain the same response time the data queried increases tenfold, or if more users can be served.

With a mixed workload of DSS, OLTP, and reporting applications, scale-up can be achieved by running multiple programs on different nodes. Speed-up can also be achieved if you rewrite the batch programs, splitting them into a number of parallel streams to take advantage of the multiple CPUs, which are now available.

Improved response time-Speed-up

DSS application and parallel query can attain speed-up with parallel processing: each transaction can run faster.

For OLTP applications, however, no speed-up can be expected-only scale-up. With OLTP applications each process is independent: even with parallel processing, each insert or update on an order table will still run at the same time speed. In fact, the overhead due to synchronization may cause a slight speed-down.

Speed-up can also be achieved with batch processing, but the degree of speed-up depends on the synchronization between tasks.

18.6 BENEFITS OF PARALLEL DATABASE

- **Higher Performance:** With more CPUs available to an application, higher speed-up and scale-up can be attained. The improvement in performance depends on the degree of inter-node locking and synchronization activities. Each lock operation is processor and message intensive; there can be a lot of latency. The volume of lock operations and database contention, as well as the throughput and performance of the DLM, ultimately determine the scalability of the system.
- **Higher Availability:** Nodes are isolated from each other, so a failure at one node does not bring the whole system down. The remaining nodes can recover the failed node and continue to provide data access to users. This means that data is much more available than it would be with a single node upon node failure, and amounts to significantly higher availability of the database.
- **Greater Flexibility:** A parallel server environment is extremely flexible, instances can be allocated or deallocated as necessary. When there is high demand for the database, more instances can be temporarily allocated. The instances can be deallocated and used for other purposes once they are no longer necessary.
- **More Users: Parallel** database technology can make it possible to overcome memery limits, enabling a single system to serve thousands of users.

SUMMARY

In this chapter we saw an overview of parallel processing and parallel databases. Parallel processing divides a large task into many smaller tasks, and executes the smaller tasks concurrently on several nodes. As a result, a larger task completes more quickly. A node is a separate processor, often on a separate machine. Multiple processors, however, can reside on a single machine. A parallel database is designed to take advantage of such architectures by running multiple instances, which "share" a single physical database. We saw the key concepts of both parallel processing and parallel databases. We also saw the advantages of using parallel databases.

EXERCISES

1. What is parallel processing?
2. What is the difference between sequential processing and parallel processing?
3. What are the advantages of parallel processing?
4. What is a parallel database?
5. What are the typical applications where parallel database are used?
6. What are the benefits of parallel databases?
7. What are the key elements of parallel processing?
8. What do you mean by speedup?
9. How is speedup calculated?
10. What do you mean by scale-up of a parallel processing system?
11. How is scale-up calculated?
12. What is synchronization and why is it necessary?
13. What do you mean by response time?
14. What are the costs of synchronization?
15. What is locking?
16. How is locking performed?
17. What is a distributed lock manger? What is its function?
18. What do you mean by messaging?
19. What are the benefits of parallel processing?
20. What are the benefits of parallel databases?

16. How is locking [illegible]?
17. What is [illegible]? What is [illegible]?
18. What do you mean by [illegible]?
19. What are the [illegible] of parallel databases?

CHAPTER 19

DISTRIBUTED DATABASES

19.1 INTRODUCTION

A distributed database is a database physically stored in two or more computer systems. Although geographically dispersed, a distributed database system manages and controls the entire database as a single collection of data. If redundant data is stored in separate database due to performance requirements, updates to one set of data will automatically update the additional sets in a timely manner.

A distributed system is one in which both data and transaction processing is divided between one or more computers connected by a network, each computer playing a specific role in the system. Distributed databases bring together the advantages of distributed computing and database management. A distributed computing system consists of a number of processing elements (not necessarily homogenous) that are interconnected by a computer network and that cooperate in performing certain assigned tasks. As a general goal, distributed computing systems divide a big, unmanageable problem into smaller pieces and solve it efficiently in a coordinated manner. A distributed database is a collection of multiple logically interrelated database distributed database management system is the software that manages a distributed database while making the distribution transparent to the user.

A distributed database system allows applications to access data from local and remote databases. In a homogenous distributed database system, each database in the system is by the same system is by the same vendor. In a heterogeneous distributed database system, at least one of the databases will be that of a different vendor. For example in an oracle homogenous distributed database system all the database in the system will be oracle's databases. On the other hand in a heterogeneous distributed database system there can be oracle database. Sybase database and DB2 database all in the same system. Distributed database use a client/server architecture to process information requests.

A distributed database appears to a user as a single database but is, in fact, a set of database stored on multiple computers. The data on several can be simultaneously accessed and modified using a network. Each database server in the distributed database is controlled by its local DBMS, and each cooperates to maintain the consistency of the global database. A Distributed therefore has the following characteristics:

- A collection of logically related shared data
- The data is split into a number of fragments

- Fragments may be replicated
- Fragments/replicas are allowed to sites
- The sites are linked by a communications network
- The data at each site is under the control of a DBMS
- The DBMS at each site can bundle applications autonomously
- Each DBMS participates in at least one global application

Distributed database is thus a set of databases in a distributed system that can appears to application as a single data source. Distributed processing on the other hand are the operations that occur when an application distributes its tasks among different computers in a network. For example, a database application typically distributes front-end presentation tasks to client computers and allows a back-end database server to manage shared access to a database. Consequently, a distributed database application processing system is more commonly referred to as a client/server database application system. Figure 19.1 shows the diagram of distributed database architecture.

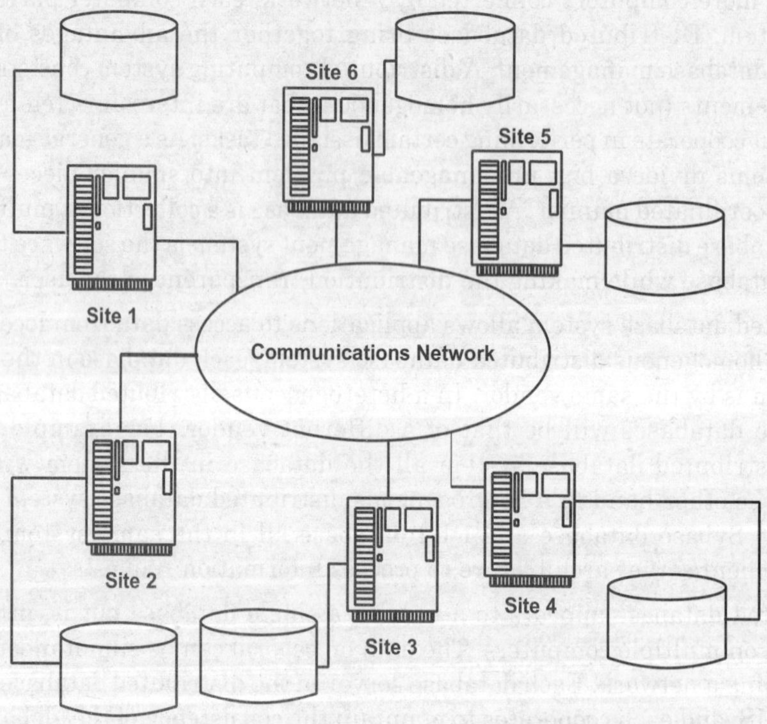

Figure 19.1 Distributed Database Architecture

There is a special kind of distributed database systems- systems that use replication. In a pure (that is, not replicated) distributed database, the system mangers a single copy of all data and supporting database objects. Typically, distributed database applications use distributed transactions to access both local and remote data and modify the global database in real-time.

The term replication refers to the operation of copying and maintaining database objects in multiple databases belonging to a distributed database. While replication relies on distributed database technology, database replication offers applications benefits that are not possible within a pure distributed database environment.

Most commonly, replication is used to improve local database performance and protect the availability of applications because alternate data access options exits. For example, an application may normally access a local database rather than a remote server to minimize network traffic and achieve maximum performance. Furthermore, the application can continue to function if the local server experiences a failure, but other servers with replicated data remain accessible.

19.2 PARALLEL VERSUS DISTRIBUTED TECHNOLOGY

Turning our attention to system architectures, there are two main types of multiprocessor system architectures that are commonplace:

- **Shared memory (tightly coupled) architecture:** Multiple processors share secondary (disk) **storage and also share primary memory.**
- **Shared disk (loosely coupled) architecture:** Multiple processors share secondary (disk) storage but each has their own primary memory.

These architectures enable processors to communicate without the overhead of exchanging messages over a network. Database management systems developed using the above types of architectures are termed parallel database management systems rather than DDBMS, since they utilize parallel processor technology. Another type of multiprocessor architecture is called shared nothing architecture. In this architecture, every processor has its own primary and secondary (disk) memory, no common memory exists, and the processors communicate over a high-speed interconnection network (bus or switch). Although the shared nothing architecture resembles a distributed database computing environment, major differences exist in the mode of operation. In shared nothing multiprocessor systems, there is symmetry and homogeneity of nodes; this is not true of the distributed database environment where heterogeneity of hardware and operating system at each node is very common.

19.3 ADVANTAGES AND DISADVANTAGES OF DISTRIBUTED DATABASE

The distribution of data and applications has potential advantages over traditional centralized database systems. Unfortunately, there are also disadvantages. In this section we review the advantages and disadvantages of the Distributed database.

Advantages

1. **Transparency**

   Ideally a distributed database should be distribution transparent. This means hiding the details of where each file is physically stored within the system. We have seen that a distributed database management system makes the distribution transparent to the user. The following types of transparencies are possible:

   - **Distribution or network transparency:** This refers to freedom for the user from the operational details of the network. Network transparency may be divided into location transparency. Location transparency refers to the fact that the command used to perform a task independent of the location of the data and location of the system where the command was issued. Naming transparency implies that once a name is specified, the named objects can be accessed unambiguously without additional specification.

- **SQL and Commit transparency:** A distributed database management system should provide query, update and transaction transparency. For example, standard SQL statement such as SELECT, INSERT, UPDATE and DELETE should work just as they do in a non-distributed database environment. The distributed database management system should guarantee that all nodes involved in a distributed transaction take the same action: they all commit or all roll back the transaction. If a network or system failure occurs during the commit of a distributed transaction, the transaction should be automatically and transparency resolved globally. Specifically, when the network or system is restored, the nodes either all commit or all roll back the transaction.
- **Replication transparency:** Replication is the process by which we store copies of the database objects at multiple sites for better availability, performance and reliability. Replication transparency makes the user unaware of the existence of the copies.
- **Fragmentation transparency:** There two types of fragmentation transparency-Horizontal and Vertical. Horizontal fragmentation distributes a relation (table) into sets of tuples (rows). Vertical fragmentation distributes a relation into sub-relations where each sub-relation is defined by a subset of columns of the original relation. A global query by the user must be transformed into several fragment queries. Fragmentation transparency makes the user unaware of the existence of fragments.

2. **Improved Reliability and Availability**

Reliability is defined as the probability that the system is up and running at a certain point in time. Availability is the probability that the system is continuously available during a time interval. When the data and the DBMS software are distributed over several locations, one location may fail while other locations continue to operate. Only the data and software of the failed location is inaccessible. This improves both reliability and availability. Further improvement is achieved by judiciously replicating data and software at more than one site. In the case of centralized systems the failure at one location makes the whole system unavailable to all users. But in a distributed database, if a location fails, some of the data might become unreachable, but users may still be able to access other parts of the database.

3. **Performance improvement**

A distributed DBMS fragments the database by keeping the data closer to where it is needed most. Data localization reduces the contention for CPU and I/O services and network traffic. When a large database is distributed over multiple sites, smaller databases exist at each site. As a result, local queries and transactions accessing data at a single site have better performance because of the smaller local database. In addition each site has a smaller number of transactions executing than if all transactions are submitted to a single centralized database. Query performance can be improved by executing multiple queries at different sites or breaking up a query into a number of subqueries that execute in parallel.

4. **Improved Scalability**

   In a distributed environment, expansion of the system in terms of adding more data, increasing database sizes or adding more processors in much easier than other systems.

5. **Site Autonomy**

   Site autonomy means that each server participating in a distributed database is administrated independently from all other databases. Although several databases can work together, each database is a separate repository of data that is managed individually. Some of the benefits of site autonomy in a distributed database include:

   - Independent failures are less likely to disrupt other nodes of the distributed database. No single database failure need halt all distributed operations or be a performance bottleneck.
   - Administrators can recover from isolated system failures independently from other nodes in the system.
   - A data dictionary exists for each local database-a global catalog is not necessary to access local data.
   - Nodes can upgrade software independently.

Disadvantages

- **Complexity**

  A distributed database that hides that distributed nature from the user and provides an acceptable level of performance, reliability and availability is inherently more complex than a centralized database. The fact that data can be replicated also adds an extra level of complexity to the distributed database. If the software does not handle data replication adequately, there will be degradation in availability, reliability and performance compared with the centralized system, and the advantages we cited above will become disadvantages.

- **Cost**

  Increased complexity means that we can expect the procurement and maintenance costs for a distributed database to be higher than those for a centralized database. Furthermore, a distributed database requires additional hardware to establish a network between sites. There are ongoing communication costs incurred with the use of this network. There are also additional labor costs to manage and maintain the local DBMSs and the underlying network.

- **Security**

  In a centralized system, access to the data can be easily controlled. However, in a distributed database not only does access to replicated data have to be controlled in multiple locations, but the network itself has to be made secure. In the past, networks were regarded as an insecure communication medium. Although this is still partially true, significant development have been made to make networks more secure.

- **Integrity control more difficult**

  Database integrity refers to the validity and consistency of stored data. Integrity is usually expressed in terms of constraints, which are consistency rules that the database is not permitted to violate. Enforcing integrity constraints generally requires access to a large amount of data that defines the constraints but which is not involved in the actual update operation itself. In a distributed database, the communication and processing costs that are required to enforce integrity constraints may be prohibitive.

- **Lack of standards**

  Although distributed database depend on effective communication, we are only now starting to see the appearance of standard communication and data access protocols. This lack of standards has significantly limited the potential of distributed database. There are also no tools or methodologies to help users convert a centralized database into a distributed database.

- **Lack of experience**

  General purpose distributed database have not been widely accepted, although many of all protocol and problems are well understood. Consequently, we do not yet have the same level of experience in industry as we have with centralized database. For a prospective adopter of this technology, this may be a significant deterrent.

- **Database design more complex**

  Besides the normal difficulties of designing a centralized database, the design of a distributed has to make account of fragmentation of data, allocation of fragments to specific sites and data replication.

19.4 ADDITIONAL FUNCTIONS OF DISTRIBUTED DATABASES

Distribution leads to increased complexity in the system design and implementation. To achieve the potential advantages listed previously, the DDBMS software must be able to provide the following functions in addition to those of a centralized DBMS:

- **Keeping track of data:** The ability to keep track of the data distribution, fragmentation, and replication by expanding the DDBMS catalog.
- **Distributed query processing:** The ability to access remote sites and transmit queries and data among the various sites via a communication network.
- **Distributed transaction management:** The ability to devise execution strategies for queries and transactions that access data from more than one site and to synchronize the access to distributed data and maintain integrity of the overall database.

- **Replicated data management:** The ability to decide which copy of a replicated data item to access and to maintain the consistency of copies of a replicated data item.
- **Distributed database recovery:** The ability to recover from individual site crashes and from new types of failures such as the failure of a communication links.
- **Security:** Distributed transactions must be executed with the proper management of the security of the data and the authorization/access privileges of users
- **Distributed directory (catalog) management:** A directory contains information (metadata) about data in the database. The directory may be global for the entire DDB, or local for each site. The placement and distribution of the directory are design and policy issues.

19.5 DISTRIBUTED DATA STORAGE

Consider a relation r that is to be stored in the database. There are several approaches to storing this relation in the distributed database:

- **Replication:** The system maintains several identical replicas (copies) of the relation, and stores each replica at a different site. The alternative to replication is to store only one copy of relation r.
- **Fragmentation:** The system partitions the relation into several fragments, and stores each fragment at a different site.
- **Fragmentation and replication:** A relation can be partitioned into several fragments and there may be several replicas of each fragment.

In the following subsections, we elaborate on each of these techniques.

19.5.1 Data Replication

If relation r is replicated, a copy of relation r is stored in two or more sites. In the most extreme case, we have full replication, in which a copy is stored in every site in the system. There are a number of advantages and disadvantages to replication.

- **Availability:** If one of the sites containing relation r fails, then the relation r can be found in another site. Thus, the system can continue to process queries involving r, despite the failure of one site.
- **Increased parallelism:** In the case where the majority of accesses to the relation r result in only the reading of the relation, then several sites can process queries involving r in parallel. The more replicas of r there are, the greater the chance that the needed data will be found in the site where the transaction is executing. Hence, data replication minimizes movement of data between sites.
- **Increased overhead on update:** The system must ensure that all replicas of a relation r are consistent; otherwise, erroneous computations may result. Thus, whenever r is updated, the update must be propagated to all sites containing replicas. The result is increased overhead. For example, in a banking system, where account information is replicated in various sites, it is necessary to ensure that the balance in a particular account agrees in all sites.

In general, replication enhances the performance of read operations and increases the availability of data to read-only transactions. However, update transactions incur greater overhead. Controlling concurrent updates by several transactions to replicated data is more complex than in centralized systems, which we saw in Chapter 15. We can simplify the management of replicas of relation r by choosing one of them as the primary copy of r. For example, in a banking system, an account can be associated with the site in which the account has been opened. Similarly, in an airline- reservation system, a flight can be associated with the site at which the flight originates. We shall examine the primary copy scheme and other options for distributed concurrency control in Section 19.8.

19.5.2 Data Fragmentation

If relation r is fragmented, r is divided into a number of fragments $r_1, r_2,..., r_n$. These fragments contain sufficient information to allow reconstruction of the original relation r. There are two different schemes for fragmenting a relation: horizontal fragmentation and vertical fragmentation. Horizontal fragmentation splits the relation by assigning each tuple of r to one or more fragments. Vertical fragmentation splits the relation by decomposing the scheme R of relation r.

We discuss the various ways for fragmenting a relation in sections 19.5.2.1 to 19.5.2.3. We shall illustrate these approaches by fragmenting the relation account, with the schema

Account-schema = (account-number, branch-name, balance)

The relation account (Account-schema) is shown in Figure 19.5.2

branch-name	**account-number**	**balance**
Delhi6	A-305	5000
Delhi6	A-226	500
AnandVihar	A-177	300
AnandVihar	A-402	10000
Delhi6	A-155	500
AnandVihar	A-408	1100
AnandVihar	A-639	750

Figure 19.5.2 Sample account relation

19.5.2.1 Horizontal Fragmentation

In horizontal fragmentation, a relation r is partitioned into a number of subsets, $r_1, r_2, . . . , r_n$. Each tuple of relation r must belong to at least one of the fragments, so that the original relation can be reconstructed, if needed. As an illustration, the account relation can be divided into several different fragments, each of which consists of tuples of accounts belonging to a particular branch. If the banking system has only two branches—Delhi6 and AnandVihar—then there are two different fragments:

$$account_1 = \sigma_{branch\text{-}name} = \text{"Delhi6" (account)}$$

$$account_2 = \sigma_{branch\text{-}name} = \text{"AnandVihar" (account)}$$

Horizontal fragmentation is usually used to keep tuples at the sites where they are used the most, to minimize data transfer.

In general, a horizontal fragment can be defined as a selection on the global relation r. That is, we use a predicate P_i to construct fragment r_i as follows:

$$r_i = \sigma P_i\,(r)$$

We reconstruct the relation r by taking the union of all fragments; that is,

$$r = r_1 \cup r_2 \cup \cdots \cup r_n$$

These two fragments are shown in Figure 19.5.2.1. Fragment account1 is stored in Delhi6 site. Fragment account2 is stored in the AnandVihar site. In our example, the fragments are disjoint. By changing the selection predicates used to construct the fragments, we can have a particular tuple of r appear in more than one of the r_i.

branch-name	account-number	balance
Delhi6	A-305	5000
Delhi6	A-226	500
Delhi6	A-155	500

$account_1$

branch-name	account-number	balance
AnandVihar	A-177	300
AnandVihar	A-402	10000
AnandVihar	A-408	1100
AnandVihar	A-639	750

$account_2$

Figure 19.5.2.1: Horizontal fragmentation of relation account

19.5.2.2 Vertical Fragmentation

In its simplest form, vertical fragmentation is the same as decomposition (see Chapter 6). Vertical fragmentation of r(R) involves the definition of several subsets of attributes R_1, R_2, . . .,R_n of the schema R so that

$$R = R_1 \cup R_2 \cup \cdots R_n$$

Each fragment r_i of r is defined by

$$r_i = \Pi_{Ri}\,(r)$$

The fragmentation should be done in such a way that we can reconstruct relation r from the fragments by taking the natural join

$$r = r_1 \bowtie r_2 \bowtie r_3 \bowtie .... \bowtie r_n$$

One way of ensuring that the relation r can be reconstructed is to include the primary-key attributes of R in each of the R_i. More generally, any superkey can be used. It is often convenient to add a special attribute, called a tuple-id, to the schema R. The tuple-id value of a tuple is a unique value that distinguishes the tuple from all other tuples. The tuple-id attribute thus serves as a candidate key for the augmented schema, and is included in each of the R_is. The physical or logical address for a tuple can be used as a tuple-id, since each tuple has a unique address.

branch-name	account-number	customer-name	balance
Delhi6	A-305	Prakash	5000
Delhi6	A-226	Jaswinder	500
AnandVihar	A-177	Jaswinder	300
AnandVihar	A-402	Shekhar	10000
Delhi6	A-155	Shekhar	500
AnandVihar	A-408	Shekhar	1100
AnandVihar	A-639	Ajay	750

Figure 19.5.2.2(a) Sample deposit relation

To illustrate vertical fragmentation, we consider for our bank database an alternative database design that includes the schema.

Deposit-schema =(branch-name, account-number, customer-name, balance)

Figure 19.5.2.2(a) shows the deposit relation for our example. In Figure 19.5.2.2(b), we show the relation deposit': the deposit relation of Figure 19.5.2.2(a) with tuple-ids added. Figure 19.5.2.2(c) shows a vertical decomposition of the schema Deposit-schema ∪ {tuple-id} into

Deposit-schema-1 (branch-name, customer-name, tuple-id)

Deposit-schema-2 (account-number, balance, tuple-id)

Two relations shown in Figure 19.5.2.2(c) result from computing

$$\text{Deposit } 1 = \Pi_{\text{Deposit-schema-1}} (\text{deposit'})$$

$$\text{Deposit } 2 = \Pi_{\text{Deposit-schema-2}} (\text{deposit'})$$

To reconstruct the original deposit relation from the fragments, we compute

$$\Pi_{\text{Deposit-schema}} (\text{deposit}_1 \bowtie \text{deposit}_2)$$

Note that the expression

$$\text{deposit}_1 \bowtie \text{deposit}_2$$

is a special form of natural join. The join attribute is tuple-id. Although the tuple-id attribute facilities the implementation of vertical partitioning, it must not be visible to users, since it is an internal artificial of the implementation, and violates data independence – which is one of the main virtues of the relational model.

branch-name	**account-number**	**customer-name**	**balance**	**tuple-id**
Delhi6	A-305	Prakash	5000	1
Delhi6	A-226	Jaswinder	500	2
AnandVihar	A-177	Jaswinder	300	3
AnandVihar	A-402	Shekhar	10000	4
Delhi6	A-155	Shekhar	500	5
AnandVihar	A-408	Shekhar	1100	6
AnandVihar	A-639	Ajay	750	7

Figure 19.5.2.2(b) The deposit relation of Figure 19.5.2.2(a) with tuple-ids

branch-name	**customer-name**	**tuple-id**
Delhi6	Prakash	1
Delhi6	Jaswinder	2
AnandVihar	Jaswinder	3
AnandVihar	Shekhar	4
Delhi6	Shekhar	5
AnandVihar	Shekhar	6
AnandVihar	Ajay	7

deposit_1

account-number	**balance**	**tuple-id**
A-305	5000	1
A-226	500	2
A-177	300	3
A-402	10000	4
A-155	500	5
A-408	1100	6
A-639	750	7

deposit_2

Figure 19.5.2.2(c) Vertical fragmentation of relation deposit

19.5.2.3 Mixed Fragmentation

The relation r is divided into a number of fragment relation $r_1, r_2, \ldots\ldots, r_n$. Each fragment is obtained as the result of application of either the horizontal-fragmentation or vertical fragmentation scheme on relation r, or on a fragment of r that was obtained previously.

As an illustration, suppose that the relation r is the deposit relation of Figure 19.4.2.2(a). This relation is divided initially into the fragments $deposit_1$ and $deposit_2$, as defined previously. We can now further divide fragment deposit1using the horizontal-fragmentation scheme, into the following two fragments:

$$deposit_{1a} = \sigma_{branch\text{-}name} = \text{"Delhi 6"} (deposit_1)$$

$$deposit_{1b} = \sigma_{branch\text{-}name} = \text{"Anand vihar"} (deposit_1)$$

Thus relation r is divided into three fragments: $deposit_{1a}$, $deposit_{1b}$ and $deposit_2$. Each of these fragments may reside in a different site.

19.5.3 Data Replication and Fragmentation

The techniques described in sections 19.4.2.1 and 19.4.2.2 for data replication and data fragmentation can be applied successively to the same relation. That is, a fragment can be replicated replicas of fragments can be fragmented further, and so, on. For example, consider a distributed system consisting of sites $S_1, S_2, \ldots\ldots, S_{10}$. We can fragment deposit into $deposit_{1a}$, $deposit_{1b}$, and $deposit_2$, for example, store a copy of $deposit_{1a}$ at site S_1, S_3, and S_7; a copy of $deposit_{1b}$ at site S_7 and S_{10}; and a copy of $deposit_2$ at sites S_2, S_8, and S_9.

19.6 DISTRIBUTED TRANSACTIONS

Access to the various data items in a distributed system is usually accomplished through transactions, which must preserve the ACID properties (Chapter 14). There are two types of transaction that we need to consider. The local transactions are those that access and update data in only one local database; the global transactions are those that access and update data in several local database.

19.6.1 System Structure

Each site has its own local transaction manager, whose function is to ensure the ACID properties of those transactions that execute at that site. The various transaction managers cooperate to execute global transactions. To understand how such a manager can be implemented, consider an abstract model of a transaction system, in which each site contains two subsystems:

- The **transaction manager** manages the execution of those transactions (or sub-transactions) that access data stored in a local site. Note that each such transaction may be either a local transaction (that is, a transaction that executes at only that site) or part of a global transaction (that is, a transaction that executes at several sites).
- The **transaction coordinator** coordinates the execution of the various transactions (both local and global) initiated at that site.

The overall system architecture appears in Figure 19.6.1

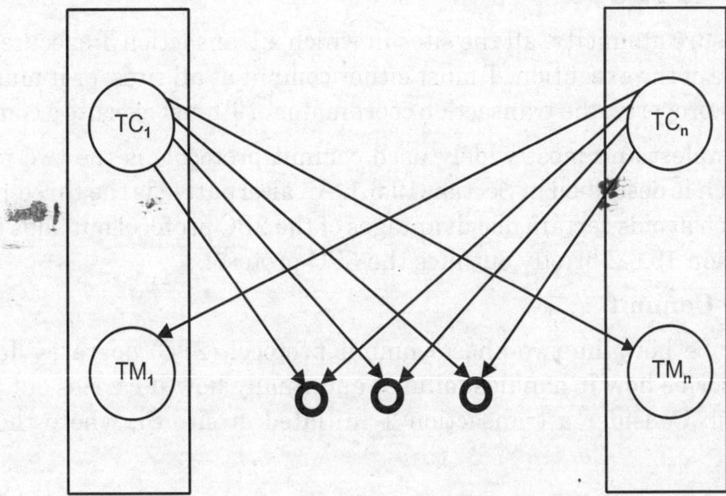

Figure 19.6.1 System Architecture

The structure of a transaction manager is similar in many respects to the structure of a centralized system. Each transaction manager is responsible for

- Maintaining a log for recovery purposes
- Participating in an appropriate concurrency-control scheme to coordinate the concurrent execution of the transactions executing at that site

The transaction coordinator subsystem is not needed in the centralized environment, since a transaction accesses data at only a single site. A transaction coordinator, as its name implies, is responsible for coordinating the execution of all the transactions initiated at that site. For each such transaction, the coordinator is responsible for

- Starting the execution of the transaction
- Breaking the transaction into a number of sub-transactions and distributing these sub-transactions to the appropriate sites for execution
- Coordinating the termination of the transaction, which may result in the transaction being committed at all sites or aborted at all sites

19.6.2 System Failure Modes

A distributed system may suffer from the same types of failure that a centralized system does (for example, software errors, hardware errors, or disk crashes). There are, however, additional types of failure with which we need to deal in a distributed environment. The basic failure types are

- Failure of a site
- Loss of messages
- Failure of a communication link
- Network partition

19.7 COMMIT PROTOCOL

If we are to ensure atomicity, all the sites in which a transaction T executed must agree on the final outcome of the execution. T must either commit at all sites, or it must abort at all sites. To ensure this property, the transaction coordinator of T must execute a commit protocol.

Among the simplest and most widely used commit protocols is the two-phase commit protocol (2PC), which is described in Section 19.6.1. An alternative is the three-phase commit protocol (3PC), which avoids certain disadvantages of the 2PC protocol but adds to complexity and overhead. Section 19.6.2 briefly outlines the 3PC protocol.

19.7.1 Two-Phase Commit

We first describe how the two-phase commit protocol (2PC) operates during normal operation, then describe how it handles failures and finally how it carries out recovery and concurrency control. Consider a transaction T initiated at site Si, where the transaction coordinator is Ci.

19.7.1.1 The Commit Protocol

When T completes its execution—that is, when all the sites at which T has executed inform Ci that T has completed—Ci starts the 2PC protocol.

- **Phase 1** Ci adds the record<prepare T> to the log, and forces the log onto stable storage. It then sends a prepare T message to all sites at which T executed. On receiving such a message, the transaction manager at that site determines whether it is willing to commit its portion of T. If the answer is no, it adds a record <no T> to the log, and then responds by sending an abort T message to Ci. If the answer is yes, it adds a record <ready T> to the log, and forces the log (with all the log records corresponding to T) onto stable storage. The transaction manager then replies with a ready T message to Ci.
- **Phase 2**. When Ci receives responses to the prepare T message from all the sites, or when a pre specified interval of time has elapsed since the prepare T.message was sent out, Ci can determine whether the transaction T can be committed or aborted. Transaction T can be committed if Ci received a ready T message from all the participating sites. Otherwise, transaction T must be aborted. Depending on the verdict, either a record <commit T> or a record <abort T> is added to the log and the log is forced onto stable storage. At this point, the fate of the transaction has been sealed. Following this point, the coordinator sends either a commit T or an abort T message to all participating sites. When a site receives that message, it records the message in the log.

A site at which T executed can unconditionally abort T at any time before it sends the message ready T to the coordinator. Once the message is sent, the transaction is said to be in the **ready state** at the site. The ready T message is, in effect, a promise by a site to follow the coordinator's order to commit T or to abort T. To make such a promise, the needed information must first be stored in stable storage. Otherwise, if the site crashes after sending ready T, it may be unable to make good on its promise. Further, locks acquired by the transaction must continue to be held till the transaction completes.

Since unanimity is required to commit a transaction, the fate of T is sealed as soon as at least one site responds abort T. Since the coordinator site *Si* is one of the sites at which T executed, the coordinator can decide unilaterally to abort T. The final verdict regarding T is determined at the time that the coordinator writes that verdict (commit or abort) to the log and forces that verdict to stable storage. In some implementations of the 2PC protocol, a site sends an acknowledge T message to the coordinator at the end of the second phase of the protocol. When the coordinator receives the acknowledge T message from all the sites, it adds the record <complete T> to the log.

19.7.2 Three-Phase Commit

The three-phase commit (3PC) protocol is an extension of the two-phase commit protocol that avoids the blocking problem under certain assumptions. In particular, it is assumed that no network partition occurs, and not more than k sites fail, where k is some predetermined number. Under these assumptions, the protocol avoids blocking by introducing an extra third phase where multiple sites are involved in the decision to commit. Instead of directly noting the commit decision in its persistent storage, the coordinator first ensures that at least k other sites know that it intended to commit the transaction. If the coordinator fails, the remaining sites first select a new coordinator. This new coordinator checks the status of the protocol from the remaining sites; if the coordinator had decided to commit, at least one of the other k sites that it informed will be up and will ensure that the commit decision is respected. The new coordinator restarts the third phase of the protocol if some site knew that the old coordinator intended to commit the transaction. Otherwise the new coordinator aborts the transaction.

While the 3PC protocol has the desirable property of not blocking unless k sites fail, it has the drawback that a partitioning of the network will appear to be the same as more than k sites failing, which would lead to blocking. The protocol also has to be carefully implemented to ensure that network partitioning (or more than k sites failing) does not result in inconsistencies, where a transaction is committed in one partition, and aborted in another. Because of its overhead, the 3PC protocol is not widely used. See the bibliographical notes for references giving more details of the 3PC protocol

19.8 CONCURRENCY CONTROL IN DISTRIBUTED DATABASES

In this section, we show how some of the concurrency control schemas discussed earlier can be modified such that they can be used in a distributed environment. We assume that each site participates in the execution of a commit protocol to ensure global transaction atomicity.

19.8.1 Locking Protocols

The various locking protocols described in Chapter 15 can be used in a distributed environment. The only change that needs to be incorporated is in the way the lock manager deals with replicated data. We present several possible schemes that are applicable to an environment where data can be replicated in several sites. As in Chapter 15, we shall assume the existence of the shared and exclusive lock modes.

19.8.1.1 Single-Lock Manager Approach

In the single lock-manager approach, the system maintains a single lock manager that resides in a single chosen site—says Si. All lock and unlock requests are made at site Si. When a transaction needs to lock a data item, it sends a lock request to Si. The lock manager determines whether the lock can be granted immediately. If the lock can be granted, the lock manager sends a message to that effect to the site at which the lock request was initiated. Otherwise, the request is delayed until it can be granted, at which time a message is sent to the site at which the lock request was initiated. The transaction can read the data item from any one of the sites at which a replica of the data item resides. In the case of a write, all the sites where a replica of the data item resides must be involved in the writing.

The scheme has these advantages:

- **Simple implementation**- This scheme requires two messages for handling lock requests, and one message for handling unlock requests.
- **Simple deadlock handling**- Since all lock and unlock requests are made at one site, the deadlock handling algorithms discussed in Chapter 15 can be applied directly to this environment.

The disadvantages of the scheme are:

- **Bottleneck** - The site *Si* becomes a bottleneck, since all requests must be processed there.
- **Vulnerability**- If the site *Si* fails, the concurrency controller is lost. Either processing must stop, or a recovery scheme must be used so that a backup site can take over lock management from *Si*,

19.8.1.2 Multiple Coordinators

A compromise between the advantages and disadvantages just noted can be achieved through a multiple coordinator approach, in which the lock manger function is distributed over several sites.

Each lock manger administers the lock and unlock requests for a subset of the data items. Each lock manager resides in a different site. This approach reduces the degree to which the coordinator is a bottleneck, but it complicates deadlock handling, since the lock and unlock requests are not made at a single

19.8.1.3 Primary Copy

When a system uses data replication, we can choose one of the replicas as the **primary copy**. Thus, for each data item Q, the primary copy of Q must reside in precisely one site, which we call the **primary site** of Q.

When a transaction needs to lock a data item Q, it requests a lock at the primary site of Q. As before, the response to the request is delayed until it can be granted. Thus, the primary copy enables concurrency control for replicated data to be handled like that for un-replicated data. This similarity allows for a simple implementation. However, if the primary site of Q fails, Q is inaccessible, even though other sites containing a replica may be accessible.

19.8.1.4 Majority Protocols

The majority protocol works this way: If data item Q is replicated in n different sites, then a lock-request message must be sent to more than one-half of the n sites in which Q is stored. Each lock manager determines whether the lock can be granted immediately (as far as it is concerned). As before, the response is delayed until the request can be granted. The transaction does not operate on Q until it has successfully obtained a lock on a majority of the replicas of Q.

This scheme deals with replicated data in a decentralized manner, thus avoiding the drawbacks of central control. However, it suffers from these disadvantages:

- **Implementation** - The majority protocol is more complicated to implement than are the previous schemes. It requires 2(n/2 + 1) messages for handling lock requests, and (n/2 + 1) messages for handling unlock requests.
- **Deadlock handling**- In addition to the problem of global deadlocks due to the use of a distributed lock-manager approach, it is possible for a deadlock to occur even if only one data item is being locked. As an illustration, consider a system with four sites and full replication. Suppose that transactions *T*1 and *T*2 wish to lock data item *Q* in exclusive mode. Transaction *T*1 may succeed in locking *Q* at sites *S*1 and *S*3, while transaction *T*2 may succeed in locking *Q* at sites *S*2 and *S*4. Each then must wait to acquire the third lock; hence, a deadlock has occurred. Luckily, we can avoid such deadlocks with relative ease, by requiring all sites to request locks on the replicas of a data item in the same predetermined order.

19.8.1.5 Timestamping

The principal idea behind the time-stamping scheme in chapter 15 is that each transaction is given a unique timestamp that the system uses in deciding the serialization order. Our first task, then, in generalizing the centralized scheme to a distributed scheme is to develop a scheme for generating unique timestamps. Then, the various protocols can operate directly to the non-replicated environment.

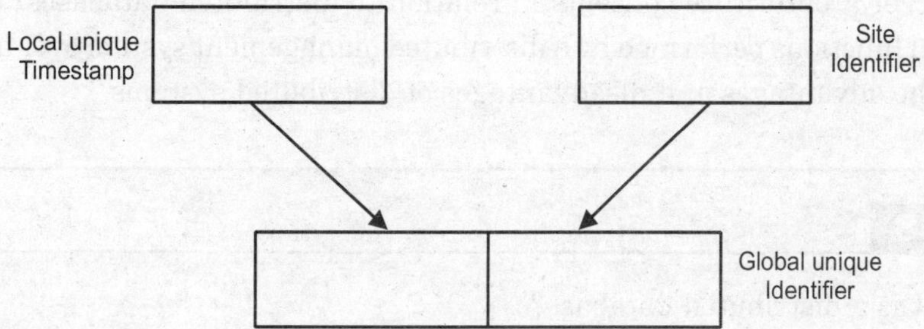

Figure 19.8.1.5 Generation of Unique Timestamp

There are two primary methods for generating unique timestamps, one centralized and one distributed. In the centralized scheme, a single site distributes the timestamps. The site can use a logical counter or its own local clock for this purpose. In the distributed scheme, each site generates a unique local timestamp by using either a logical counter or the local clock. We obtain the unique global timestamp by concatenating the unique local timestamp with the site identifier, which also must be unique (Figure 19.8.1.5). The order of concatenation is important! We use the site identifier in the least significant position to ensure that the global timestamps generated in one site are not always greater than those generated in another site. Compare this technique for generating unique timestamp with the one that we presented earlier for generating unique names.

We may still have a problem if one site generates local timestamps at a rate faster than that of the other sites. In such a case, the fast site's logical counter will be larger than that of other sites. Therefore, all timestamps generated by the fast site will be larger than those generated by other sites. What we need is a mechanism to ensure that local timestamps are generated fairly across the system. We define within each site Si a **logical clock** (LCi), which generates the unique local timestamp. The logical clock can be implemented as a counter that is incremented after a new local timestamp is generated. To ensure that the various logical clocks are synchronized, we require that a site Si advance its logical clock whenever a transaction Ti with timestamp <x,y> visits that site and x is greater than the current value of LCi. In this case, site Si advances its logical clock to the value x + 1.

If the system clock is used to generate timestamps, then timestamps will be assigned fairly, provided that no site has a system clock that runs fast or slow. Since clocks may not be perfectly accurate, a technique similar to that for logical clocks must be used to ensure that no clock gets far ahead of or behind another clock.

SUMMARY

In this chapter we got an introduction to distributed databases and distributed database management systems. A distributed database is a database physically stored in two or more computer systems. Although geographically dispersed, a distributed database system manages and controls the entire database as a collection as a collection of data. We saw the basic concepts, features and advantages of distributed databases. We also discussed the client server architecture concepts in relation to distributed databases. We also saw the additional functions performed by a distributed management system over a distributed DBMS and the advantages and disadvantages of distributed systems.

EXERCISES

1. What is a distributed database?
2. What are the components of a distributed database system? Explain with the help of a diagram.
3. What is the difference between homogenous and heterogeneous distributed database systems?
4. What do you mean by replication?

5. What are advantages of distributed systems?
6. What is fragmentation transparency?
7. What is the difference between horizontal and vertical fragmentation?
8. What is two phase commit mechanism? How does it work?
9. What are the functions of distributed database management systems?
10. What is a system structure?
11. Explain and details with commit protocol in distributed system.
12. What do you mean by primary copy?
13. What is a timestamping?
14. Explain and details with concurrency control in distributed system.
15. What are the advantages and disadvantages of distributed systems?

CHAPTER 20

SPATIAL AND MULTIMEDIA DATABASES

20.1 INTRODUCTION

Spatial database provide concepts for databases that keep track of objects in a multidimensional space. Multimedia database provide features that allow users to store and query different types of multimedia information like images, video clips, audio clips and documents. We will see an overview of these two database types in this chapter.

20.2 SPATIAL DATA

A common example of spatial data can be seen in a road map. A road map is a 2-dimentional object that contains points, lines and polygon s that can represent cities, roads and political boundaries such as states or provinces. A road map is a visualization of geographic information. The location of cities, roads and political boundaries that exist on the surface of the earth projected onto a 2-dimentional display and relative distances of the rendered objects.

The data that indicates the earth location (latitude and longitude or height and depth) of these rendered objects is the spatial data. When the map is rendered, this spatial data is used to project the locations of the objects on a 2-dimentional piece of paper. A GIS is often used to store, retrieve and render this Earth-relative spatial data. Other types of spatial data include data from computer aided design (CAD) systems. Instead of operating on objects on a geographic scale, CAD/CAM systems work on a smaller scale such as for an automobile engine or much smaller scale as for printed circuit boards.

The difference among these systems GIS and CAD/CAM are only in the scale of the data, not its complexity. They might all actually involve the same number of data points. On a geographic scale, the location of a bridge can vary by a few tenths of an inch without causing any noticeable problems to the road builders. But, if the diameter of an engine's pistons is off by a few tenths of an inch, the engine will not run. A printed circuit board is likely to have many of thousands of objects etched on its surface that are no bigger than the smallest details shown on a road builder's blueprints.

20.3 SPATIAL DATABASES

The spatial data management systems are designed to make the storage, retrieval and manipulation of spatial data easier and more natural to users such as a geographic information system (GIS). Once this data is stored in a spatial database, it can be easily and meaningfully manipulated and retrieved as it relates to all the other data stored in the database. Spatial database provide concepts for database that keep track of objects in a multi-dimensional space. For example cartographic databases that store maps include two-dimensional spatial descriptions of their objects. These databases are used in many applications, such as environmental, logistics management and war strategies. Other databases such as meteorological objects that have spatial characteristics that describes them. The spatial relationships among objects are important and they are needed when querying the databases. A spatial database can refer to an n-dimensional space for any 'n'.

The main extensions that are needed for spatial databases are models that can interpret spatial characteristics. In addition, spatial indexing and storage structures are often needed to improve performance. The basic extensions needed are include 2-D geometric concepts such as points, lines, segments, circles, polygons, arcs etc., in order to specify the spatial characteristics of objects. In addition spatial operations are needed to operate on the objects' spatial characteristics. For example, we need spatial operations to compare the distance between two objects and other such operations. We also need spatial Boolean conditions to check whether two objects spatially overlap and perform other similar operations. For example a geometric information system will contain description of the spatial positions of many types of objects. Some objects such as highways, buildings and other landmarks have static spatial characteristics. Other objects like vehicles, temporary buildings etc. have dynamic characteristics that change over time.

20.4 SPATIAL DATA MODEL

The spatial data model is a hierarchical structure consisting of elements, geometries and layers, which correspond to representations of spatial data. Layers are composed of geometries which in turn are made up of elements. For example, a point might represent a building location, a line string might be a road or flight path and a polygon could be a state, city, zoning district or city block.

20.4.1 Element

An element is the basic building block of a geometric feature for the Spatial Data Option. The supported spatial elements types are points, line strings and polygons. For example, elements might be modeled to historic markers (point clusters), roads (line strings) and country boundaries (polygons). Each coordinates in an element is stored as an X, Y pair.

Point data 1 consists of one coordinate and the sequence number is 0. Line data consists of two coordinates representing a line segment of the element, starting with sequence number 0. Polygon data consists of coordinate pair values, one vertex pair for each line segment of the polygon. The first coordinates pair (with sequence number 0), represents the first line segment, with coordinates defined in either a clockwise or counter-clockwise order around the polygon with successive sequence numbers. Each layer's geometric objects and their associated spatial index are stored in the database tables.

20.4.2 Geometry

A geometry or geometric object is the representation of a user's spatial feature, modeled as an ordered set of primitive elements. Each geometric object is required to be uniquely identified by a numeric geometric identifier (GID), associating the object with its corresponding attribute set.

A complex geometric feature such as polygon with holes would be stored as a sequence of polygon elements. In a multi-element polygonal geometry, all sub-elements are wholly contained within the outermost element, thus building a more complex geometric from simpler pieces. For example, geometry might describe the fertile land in a village. This could be represented as a polygon with holes that represent buildings or objects that prevent cultivation.

20.4.3 Layer

A layer is a heterogeneous collection of geometrics having the same attribute set. For example, one layer in a GIS might include topographical features, while another describes population density and a third describes the network of roads and bridges in the area (lines and points).

20.5 SPATIAL QUERIES

Spatial query is the process of selecting features based on their geographic (or spatial) relationship to other features. For example, you might be interested in finding out which features lie within a certain distances of other features, which are adjacent to other features, which are contained inside features or which intersect other features.

In spatial databases, you can perform spatial queries using features from different themes. The process of overlaying one theme with anther in order to determine their geographic relationships is called **spatial overlay.** In this way, you can analyze the relationships between themes. Let us imagine you are new to a city and want to find a good hotel. Where is the hotel closet to your locations? Suppose you are standing at the airport. Two of your themes (Airport and hotels) can be analyzed to determine the spatial relationship between them.

Spatial query is part of a larger process called spatial analysis. Spatial combines the various spatial querying techniques into a series of steps. Which help you solve problems such as:

- Locating areas of economic deprivation
- Analyzing the proximity or areas of long term illness to industrial regions
- Analyzing flooding patterns and determining the areas and types of land use affected
- Determining potentially hazardous areas in landslide-prone areas
- Determining the relationship between population density and number of schools

We can categories the spatial queries into the following types-Range query, nearest neighbor query and spatial joins.

20.5.1 Range Query or Proximity Query

A range query finds objects of a particular type that are within a given spatial area or within a particular distance from a given location. For example, find all schools with the

Delhi city area or find all hospitals within 2 kilometers of the accident etc. are all range queries.

20.5.2 Nearest Neighbor Query or Adjacency

Nearest neighbor query finds an object of a particular type that is closer to a given location. You can think of adjacency as a spatial case of proximity query, because you are finding features that are zero distances away from the selected features. Adjacency linear features must be connected and adjacent polygon features must share a common boundary. For example, find the school that is closest to your house, or find the hospital nearest to the accident site, etc. are nearest neighbor queries.

20.5.3 Spatial joins or Overlays

Overlays join the objects of two types based on same spatial condition, such as the objects interesting or overlapping spatially or being within a certain distance of one another. For example, find all the motels that are on the highway from Chennai to Bangalore or find all police stations within 2KM of the riot site, etc. are spatial joins.

For these and the other types of spatial queries to be answered efficiently, spatial techniques for spatial indexing are needed. One of the best-know technique is the use of R-trees and their variations. R-trees group together objects that are in close spatial physical proximity on the same leaf nodes of a tree structured index. Since a leaf node can point to only a certain number of objects, algorithms for dividing the space into rectangular subspace that include the objects are needed. Typical criteria for dividing the space include minimizing the rectangle areas, since this would lead to quicker narrowing of the search space. Problems such as having objects with overlapping spatial areas are handled in different ways by the different R-tree variations. The internal nodes or R-tree are associated with rectangles whose area covers all the rectangles in its sub-tree. Hence, R-trees can easily answer queries, such as find all objects within a given area by limiting the tree search to those sub-trees whose rectangles intersect with the area given in the query. Other spatial storage structures include quadtrees and their variations. **Quadtree** is a spatial index which recursively decomposes a data set (e.g. image) into square cells of different sizes until each cell has a homogeneous value. Quadtrees are often used for storing raster data. Raster is a cellular data structure composed of rows and columns for storing images. Groups of cells with the same value represent features. Quadtrees divide each space or subtree into equally sized areas and proceed with subdivisions of each subspace to identify the positions objects.

20.6 MULTIMEDIA DATABASES

Multimedia computing has emerged in the last few years as a major area of research. Multimedia computer systems have opened a wide range of potential applications by combining a variety of information sources, such as voice, graphics, animation, images, audio and full motion video. The fundamental characteristic of multimedia systems is that they incorporate continuous media, such as voice, video and animated graphics. This implies the need for multimedia systems to handle data with strict timing requirements and at high rate. The use of continuous media in distributed systems implies the need for continuous data transfer over relatively long periods of time (e.g. play out of video stream from a remote camera).

Additional important fundamental issues are media synchronization, very large storage requirements, and need for special indexing and retrieval techniques, tuned to multimedia data types.

Multimedia databases provide features that allow users to store and query different types of multimedia information. The multimedia information includes images (pictures, photographs, drawings, etc), video (movies, newsreels, home, videos, etc.), audio (songs, speeches, phone message, etc.) and documents (books, article, etc.). The main types of database queries are the ones that help in locating multimedia data containing certain objects in interest. For example, we might want to retrieve all photographs with the picture of a computer from our photo gallery or we might want to retrieve video clips that contain a certain person from the video database. These queries are **content-based-retrieval** because the multimedia source is being retrieved based on its content-whether it contains certain objects or not.

The multimedia database must use some model to organize and index the multimedia sources based on their contents. Identifying the contents of multimedia sources is a difficult task. There are two main approaches to this issue. In the first approach, we use a process called automatic analysis. Automatic analysis identifies certain mathematical characteristics in the content of the multimedia source. This approach uses different techniques depending on the type of the multimedia sources-audio, video, document etc. The second approach depends on manual identification of the objects and activities of interest in each multimedia source and uses this information to index the sources. This approach can be applied to all the different multimedia sources, but requires human input where a person manually scans each multimedia source to identify and catalog the objects and activities it contains so that it can be used to index these sources.

20.6.1 Multimedia Sources

The different multimedia sources are image, video, audio and document. We will see the characteristics of these sources in the next sections.

20.6.1.1 Image

An image is usually stored either in raw form as a set of pixel or cell values or in compressed form to save space. The image shape descriptor describes the shape of the image. A grid of cells represents each image. Each cell contains a pixel value that describes the cell content. In black and white images the pixels can be one bit. In gray scale and color images, the pixel is multiple bits. Because the images required large amounts of space they are stored in compressed form. Compression standards (like GIF standard) use various mathematical transformations (like Discrete Fourier Transform (DFT), Discrete Cosine Transform (DCT) and wavelet transforms) to reduce the number of cells stored but still maintain the image characteristics.

In order to identify an image is divided into homogeneous segments using a homogeneity predicate. For example, in a color image, cells image that are adjacent to one another and whose pixel values are close grouped into a segment. The homogeneity predicate defines the conditions for how to automatically group those cells. Segmentation and compression can hence identify the main characteristics of an image.

Inexpensive image-capture and storage technologies have allowed massive collections of digital images to be created. However, as a database grows, the difficulty of finding relevant images increases. Two general approaches to this problem have been developed, both of which use metadata for image retrieval:

- **Manual Identification**-Using information manually entered or included in the table design, such as titles, descriptive keywords from a limited vocabulary and predetermined classification schemes.
- **Automatic Analysis**-Using automated image feature extraction and object recognition to classify image content-that is, using capabilities unique to content-based retrieval.

You can also combine both approaches in designing a table to accommodate images-use traditional text columns to describe the semantic significance of the image (for example, that the pictured automobile won a particular award, or that its engine has six or eight cylinders), and use the **Visual Information Retrieval** types for the image, to permit content-based queries based on intrinsic attributes of the image (for example, how closely its color and shape match a picture of a specific automobile).

As an alternative to defining image-related attributes in columns separate from the image a database designer could create a specialized composite data type that combines Visual Information Retrieval and the appropriate text, numeric and date attributes.

The primary benefit of using content-based retrieval is reduced time and effort required to obtain image-based information. With frequent adding and updating of images in massive databases, it is often not practical value.

Examples of database applications where content-based retrieval is useful –where the query is semantically of the form, “find objects that look like this one”-include:

- Medical imaging
- Trademarks and copyrights
- Art galleries and museums
- Retailing
- Fashion and fabric design
- Interior design or decorating
- Low enforcement and criminal investigation

For example, a web-based interface to a retail-clothing might allow users to search by traditional categories (such as style or a price range) and also by image properties (such as color to texture). Thus, a user might ask for formal shirts in a particular price range that are off-white with pin stripes. Similarly, fashion designers could use a database with images of fabric swatches, designs, concept sketches and actual garments to facilities their creative processes.

An image database query would find images in the database that are similar to a given image. The given image could be an isolated segment that contains a pattern of interest and the query could be to find other images containing the same pattern. There are two querying techniques-distance function and transformation. In distance function approach, a distance function is used to compare the given image with the stored images and their segments. If the distance value returned is small, the probability of a match is high, indexes can be created to group together stored images that are close in the distance by having a small number of transformations that can transform one image's cells to match the other image. Transformations include rotations, translations and scaling. Transformation approach is more general, but it is more difficult and time consuming.

20.6.1.2 Video

A video source is typically represented as a sequence of frames, where each frame is a still image. However, rather than identifying the objects and activities in every individual frames, the video is divided into video segments, where each segment is made up of a sequence of contiguous frames that includes the same objects or activities. Each segment is identified by its starting and ending frame. The objects and activities identified in each video segment can be used to index the segments. An indexing technique called frame segment trees has been proposed for video indexing. The index includes objects (such as persons, buildings, vehicles, etc.) and activities (such as a batsmen executing a cover drive, a person making a speech, etc.)

20.6.1.3 Document

A text or document source is basically the full text of some article, book or magazine. These sources are typically indexed by identifying the keywords that appear in the text and their relative frequencies. However, filler words are eliminated from that process. Because there could be too many keywords, when attempting to index a collection of documents, techniques have been developed to reduce the number of keywords to those are most relevant to the collection. A technique called singular value decomposition (SVD), which is based on matrix transformations, can be used for this purpose. Singular value decomposition is a general-purpose mathematical analysis tool that has been used in a variety of information-retrieval applications. An indexing technique called telescoping vector trees (TV-trees) can then be used to group similar documents together.

20.6.1.4 Audio

Audio sources include stored recorded messages such as speeches, presentations or even surveillance recording of phone message or conversations by law enforcement authorities. Here, discrete transforms can be used to identify the main characteristics of a certain person's voice in order to have similarity based indexing and retrieval. Audio characteristic features include loudness, intensity, pitch and clarity.

We will see a multimedia database-image database-in some detail. The idea of this discussion is to give you an overview of the features, functionality and complexity involved in creating and maintaining a multimedia database.

20.6.2 Image Databases

An image database is a collection of images, together with descriptive data derived directly from those images, maintained in applications-independent form and organized for efficient storage and retrieval. An important distinction to be made here is between image data, which are the bits comprising the image itself and image metadata, which are the data that can be derived from that image. Metadata for a photograph, for example, might include the location of the scene depicted in the photograph, who took it, on what date it was taken and the items represented in the photograph, Metadata, in a sense, gets at the semantic meaning or context of the image not contained in the image pixels themselves.

20.6.2.1 Image Properties

- **Shape Descriptor** – A shape descriptor describes the region of the object of interest within an image. The simplest shape is a rectangle.
- **Property Descriptor** – A property descriptor that describes the properties of the individual pixels in the given image. e.g. RGB values of the pixel.
- **Cell** – it is impossible to associate properties with individual pixels and cells (rectangular groups of cells) are the answer. Every image 'I' has an associated pair of positive integers (m x n), called the grid resolution of the image. This divides the image into (m x n) cells of equal size called the image grid. A cell property is a triple (Name, Values, Method), where **Name** is a string denoting the property's name, **Values** is a set of values that the property may assume and **Method** is a algorithm that tells us how to compute the property involved. For example, consider the case of black and white images. A reasonable cell property in this case is (bwcolor,{b,w},bwalgo) where our property name is 'bwcolor' and the possible values are 'b' (black) and 'w' (white), respectively. Bwalgo may be an algorithm that takes a cell as input and returns either black (b) or white (w) as output, by somehow combining the black/white levels of the pixels in the cell. On the other hand, with gray-scale images (with 0 = white and 1 = black), we may have the cell property (gray level, [0.1], grayalgo) where our property name is graylevel, its possible values are real numbers in the [0.1] interval and the associated method graylgo takes a cell as input and computes its gray level.
- **Others** – Other elements of image content that may be relevant in the design of more complete tools of image searching:
  - Color: green, magenta, purple, jade etc.
  - Shape: cross, oval, half-circle etc.
  - Spatial relationships: above, left of, row, column, center etc.
  - Line: thick, straight, dotted, jagged etc.
  - Texture: coarse, grainy, spotted, smooth etc.
  - Motion (for video and animation): upward, left-right, continuous etc.
  - Volume (for 3 D objects): cube, sphere etc.

20.6.2.2 Image Data Compression

Data compression literally means making data smaller. This implies representing the same quantity of information using fewer symbols. Data decomposition means retrieving the original information from the compressed format. Data compression is often measured by the compression ratio achieved. This is the ratio of a string's uncompressed size to its compressed size. Other measures of data compression include the ratio of compressed bits to uncompressed bytes (1/8 of the compression ratio) or the parent reduction in size of the string.

Data compression allows increased storage of data. In this context the compression ratio is often the most important consideration. Data compression also allows accelerated transmission of data. In this context the speed of the compression-decomposition process is important. In general, the more time spent on compression, the larger the compression ratio will be. Unfortunately time is treated for better compression at a diminishing rate.

How much can data be compressed? Kolmogorov complexity is a measure of how much data can be compressed. It is the size of the smallest string, which represents instructions to produce the string S for a given language L. consider the following strings:

- "AAAAAAAAAAAAAAAAAAAA" (20 characters)
- "repeat 20 times: A" (18 characters)
- "20 'A' s" (7 characters)

In English, this is about as small as we can compress the string. Some of the common compression techniques are:

- Run-length Encoding
- Huffman Encoding
- Arithmetic Encoding
- Substitution Methods

Compression algorithms can also be divided into **lossless** and **lossy** techniques. **Lossless data compression** is what we generally think of when we talk about compressing our data. it is expected that after decompression the data will look exactly as it did before compression. The problem of lossless compression is that not all data can be compressed. **Lossy compression** on the other hand is willing to accept some change to the data after compression and decompression. This allows much greater compression of the data. Lossy compression is most often used when compressing multimedia.

Consider an image of 1024 x 768 pixels, each with a 24 bit value for color. If some of the pixels were to change up or down a few shades, a viewer would probably not be able to tell the difference. This is the method of compression that JPEG uses. JPEG compression allows you to select the amount of degradation you to live with in order to save space.

Now consider a backup of your operating system. Backups are also often compressed to save space. In this case, you want all your data to be restored in its original form. If one bit was changed it could be disastrous.

While some methods are better suited to lossy techniques and others are better suited to lossless techniques, many of the listed methods could be used in either manner. It is also possible to combine the ideas presented in each of the listed methods.

The JPEG algorithm is based on segmenting the image into 8 x 8 blocks, which are then decomposed into 64 orthogonal basis signals via a forward Discrete Cosine Transform (DCT). These basis signals are then uniformly quantized in accordance with 64-element quantization tables. The quantization is in effect a normalization of each element by the step size prescribed in the table. The step size is generally chosen to be the perceptual threshold and is usually based on the modulation contrast sensitivity function (or the MTF). After quantization, the DC coefficients are run length encoded as the differences between successive blocks, then each of the other coefficients are reordered according to a "zig zag" pattern and entropy coded. The standard provides for either Huffman or Arithmetic coding. The JPEG standard further defines a lossless coding scheme which is solely based on prediction and completely independent from the DCT.

20.6.2.3 Compressed Image Representations

Consider a two-dimensional image 'l' consisting of (p1 x p2) pixels. Then, typically, l(x, y) is a number denoting one or more attributes of the pixel. For example, l(x, y) may be number between 0 and 255 (inclusive), denoting an encoding of the image's RGB values.

In general, reasoning about an image by considering all the pixels is not feasible because each of p1, p2 may be 1024 or more, leading to over a million entries in the image matrix 'l'. A common approach is to transform this matrix 'l' into a compressed representation of the matrix. The creation of the compressed representation, cr(l), of image l consists of two parts:

- **Size selection** – The size (h) of the compressed image is selected by the image database designer. The larger the size, the greater is the fidelity of the representation. However, as the size increases, so does the complexity of creating an index an index for manipulating such representations, and searching this index. Thus, an appropriate trade-off needs to be made. We still assume that the selected size of cr(l) is some pair of positive integers (h1, h2).
- **Transform selection** – The user must select a transformation that is capable of converting the image into a compressed representation. In other words, we must select a transformation that, given the image 'l' and any pair of numbers, 1< = i< = h1 and 1 < = j < = h2, will determine what the value of cr(i,j) is.

20.6.2.4 Image Segmentation

Image segmentation is the process of partitioning an image into groups of connected pixels, called **regions,** with similar properties like gray levels, colors, textures, motion characteristics (motion vectors), edge continuity, etc. Regions are important for the interpretation of images because they may correspond to objects in a scene. An image may contain several objects and each object may contain several regions corresponding to different parts of an object. Due to a number factors (noise, bad illumination, 3D world etc.), segmentation is usually not perfect, image interpretation requires objects specific knowledge. There are two approaches to segmentation-Region segmentation and Edge segmentation.

- **Region Segmentation** – The pixels of the same object are grouped together and are marked to indicate that they form a region. Criteria for region segmentation: Pixels may be assigned to the same region if they have similar intensity values and they are close to one another.

- **Edge Segmentation** – Edge segmentation finds the pixels (edges) that lie on the boundary of a region. This process is called edge detection. In ideal images, a region is bounded by a closed contour. The close counters may be obtained from the regions by edge detection. The regions may be obtained from the closed contours by boundary-filling. In real images, it is rare to obtain regions from contours and vice versa.

20.6.2.5 Similarity-Based Retrieval

We have seen that we can take an image as input and return a compressed version of the image as output, using image transformations such as the DCT, the DFT, or wavelet transform. We have also seen how we can segment an image or separate the image into homogeneous regions called segments. An important question that still remains to be answered is the following: How do we determine whether the content of a segment (of a segmented image) is similar to another image (or a set of images) that we have? There are many, many cases where we have a large image database, and the user wishes to ask a query like "Here is a picture of a person. Can you tell me who it is?" There have been two broad approaches to similarity-based retrieval of images:

- **Metric approach** – In this approach, there is assumed to be a distance metric 'd' that can compare any two images. The closer two objects are in distance; the more similar they are considered to be. In this approach, the problem of similarity-based retrieval may be stated as "Given an input image 'I', find the "nearest" neighbor of 'I' in the image archive". The metric-based approach is by far most widely followed approach in the database world.
- **Transformation approach** – The metric approach assumes that the notion of similarity is "fixed", that is, in any given application only one notion of similarity is used to index the data (though different applications may use different notions of similarity). Thus, users should be able to specify what they consider to be similar, rather than the system forcing this upon them. In short, the transformational approach questions the claim that a given body of data (images, text, etc) has a single associated notion of similarity. The transformation-based approach is more general than the metric approach. It is based on the principle that given two objects o1, o2 the level of dissimilarity between o1 and o2 is propositional to the (minimum) cost of transforming object o1 into object o2, or vice versa. In the case of images, these operators may include translation, rotation and scaling (e.g. reduction and magnification). An extension operator that modifies a shape by adding a new shape to it may also be included. Likewise, an extension operator may cull out a shape from existing object. The user may choose to use only a subset of these operators. Furthermore, he may add new operators if he so wishes. Each operator has an associated cost function-the higher the cost, the less preferable it is to use the operation.

We have seen an overview of image databases, the need for compression, segmentation and image retrieval process.

SUMMARY

We have seen an overview of spatial and multimedia databases. Spatial databases provide concepts for databases that keep track of objects in a multimedia space. Multimedia databases provide feature that allows users to store and query different types of multimedia information like messages, video clips, audio clips and documents. We also saw images databases in a little more details. These two areas are still evolving and a lot of research is being done to develop more efficient and powerful spatial and multimedia databases.

EXERCISES

1. What do you mean by spatial data?
2. What are spatial databases?
3. What is a spatial data model?
4. What is geometry or geometry object?
5. What is the special query?
6. What do you mean by spatial analysis and what are its advantages?
7. What are range query?
8. What are spatial join?
9. What is an R tree?
10. What are multimedia databases?
11. What is the automatic analysis and manual identification approaches to multimedia indexing?
12. What are the properties of images?
13. Name some applications where content-based retrieval is used.
14. What is a document and how are they stored in a multimedia database?
15. What are the properties of the audio source?
16. What are images databases?
17. What is JPEG algorithm and what is it used for?
18. What are compressed images representations?
19. What is the difference between region segmentation and edge segmentation?
20. What is the difference between metric approach and transformation approach?

CHAPTER 21

MOBILE DATABASES

21.1 INTRODUCTION

People on the move, need services, information and entertainment that move with them. With access to mobile services, decisions and transaction happen here and now. Mobile services powered by Wireless Application Protocol (WAP) have been widely accepted by users. Currently there are some 50 million WAP enabled handsets in circulation worldwide and virtually every new mobile phone is likely to be WAP enabled. In the next few years, the number of WAP users across the world is estimated to grow at an exponential rate. This growth is driven by the introduction of GPRS (General Packet Radio Service), WAP 2.0, Bluetooth (a short range radio technology aimed at simplifying communications among mobile devices and between devices and the internet) and Mobile Commerce Mobile services benefit from three major factors that boost information value to end-users- personalization, time sensitivity and location awareness. Combining these elements adds even more value.

We are in the midst of a wireless and mobile revolution. In the near future, a typical computing environment business, personal, scientific or educational will provide wireless network connectivity between powerful data servers and mobile, sometime disconnected, computers and mobile, sometimes disconnected, computers and devices. This has created exciting opportunities for developing a wide range of innovative database application and systems.

However, an open question remains: what kind of system will be capable o offering scalable data services and exhibit scalable performance? Besides advances in communications and hardware, does achieving pervasive mobile computing require innovative theories and paradigms in data management or new data engineering technique? Before we start our discussion on mobile computing and mobile database we will see an overview of three technologies that play a vital role in shaping the mobile computing field. These technologies are:

- Wireless Application Protocol (WAP)
- Wireless Markup Language (WML)
- Extended Markup Language (XML)

21.1.1 Wireless Application Protocol

WAP is a secure specification that allows users to access information instantly via handheld wireless devices such as mobile phones, pagers, two way radios, smart phones and communicators. WAP support most wireless networks. These include CDPD, CDMA, GSM, PDC, PHC, TDMA, FLEX, ReFLEX, iDEN, TETRA, DECT, DataTAC, and Mobitex. WAP is supported by all operating systems. The operating systems specifically engineered for handled devices include PalmOS, EPOC, Windows CE, FLEXOS, OS/9 and JavaOS.

WAPs use micro browsers to display and access the internet. Micro browsers are browsers with small file sizes that can accommodate the low memory constraints to handheld devices and the low bandwidth constraints of a wireless-handheld network.

Although WAP supports HTML and XML the WML language is specifically devised for small screens and one-hand navigation without a keyword. WML is scalable from two-line text displays up through graphic screens found on items such as smart phones and communicators. WAP also supports WMLScript. It is similar to JavaScript. It is similar to JavaScript, but makes minimal demands on memory and CPU power because it does not contain many of the unnecessary functions found in other scripting languages.

Mobile device's properties-low arithmetic capacity, similar display, poor memory resources-made necessary to change the well known internet protocols and document types. There was a need for a new standard, so Ericsson, Motorola, Nokia and Unwired Planet founded the Wireless Application Protocol Forum-a nonprofit organization aimed to work on WAP standards. Since then, many others joined this organization (like IBM, AT&T, Alcatel).

WAP was created from different technologies. For the transport the responsibility is on the WAP protocol stack. The stack is based on a network protocol like GSM (Global System for Mobile Communications) SMS (Short Messaging Service) or USSD (Unstructured Supplementary Service Data). The only requirement for this is to be capable to work in full duplex mode and to transmit documents from one point to another. To provide security, transactions and sessions are WAP's responsibility.

The higher levels of WAP protocol stack provide features necessary for web browsing. They make less traffic on the network compared to traditional TCP/IP-HTTP combination. The next levels of WAP define the format of the document, which is treated by WAP browsers. This format is something like HTML, but it is not compatible with that. It is called WML. WML is an XML (Extensible Markup Language) application. The unconventional thing, compared to HTML, is that, within a page (called deck) there can be one or more cards. The WML browser can choose between cards and can navigate between these, without needing to download additional information from the server.

Making possible the binary encoding of XML documents communication is much more efficient like it was in traditional HTML browsers. In WML, pages can be inserted scripts, just like in case of HTML. There are WMLScripts. WMLScript is a simplified version of JavaScript. WAP deals with translating the WMLScript code to bytecode, saving up lot of space. When WAP was created it was clear that there must be some kind of connection with the existing internet content. How it is realized it is shown in Figure 21.1.1:

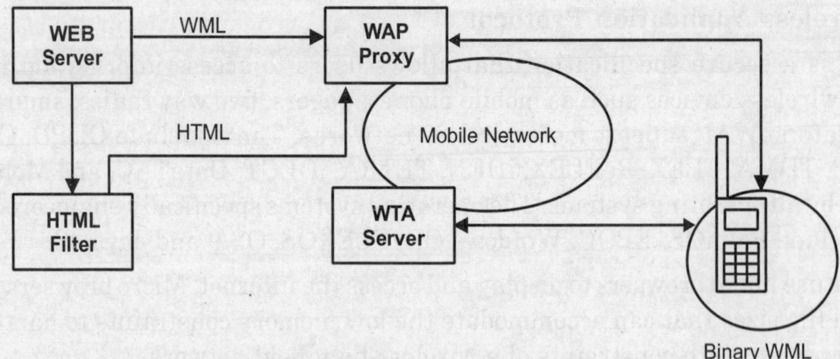

Figure 21.1.1 WAP in Action

The WTA Server or the Wireless Telephony Application Server is used to perform the normal cellular phone services. The WAP proxy has the function of converting WAP request to HTTP, thus making possible to contact traditional web servers. It also converts the web servers' response to binary WML, making it possible to WAP devices to show the content. Because WAP is an open standard with important supporters, it desirable that mobile application's market will not be restricted by compatibility problems.

21.1.1.1 WAP Architecture

The WAP standard defines two essential elements:

- An end-to-end application protocol
- An application environment based on a browser

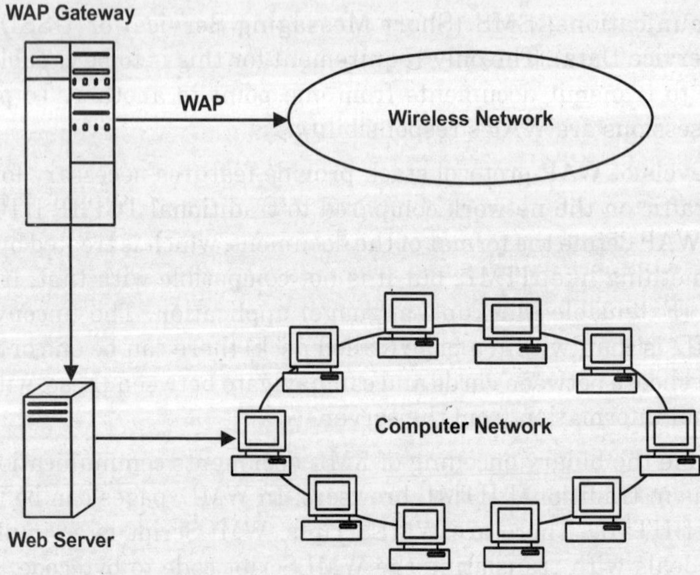

Figure 21.1.1.1 Structure of a WAP Network

The **application protocol** is a communication protocol stack that is embedded in each WAP-enabled wireless device (also known as the user agent). The server side implements the other end of the protocol, which is capable of communicating with any WAP client. The server side is known as a WAP gateway and routes requests from the client to an HTTP (or web) server. The WAP gateway can be located either in a telecom network or in a computer network (an ISP). Figure 21.1.1.1 illustrates an example of the structure of a WAP network. The client communicates with the WAP gateway in the wireless network. The WAP gateway translates WAP requests to WWW requests, so the WAP client is able to submit requests to the Web server. Also, the WAP gateways translates web responses into WAP responses or a format understand by the WAP client.

21.1.1.2 The WAP Programming Model

The WAP programming model is similar to the web programming model with matching extensions, but it accommodates the characteristics of the wireless environment.

As you can see, the WAP programming model is based heavily on the Web programming model. But how does the WAP gateway work with HTML? In some cases, the data services or content located on the web server is HTML based. Some WAP gateways could be made to convert HTML pages into a format that can be displayed on wireless devices. But because HTML was not really designed for small screens, the WAP protocol defines its own markup language, the Wireless Markup Language (WML), which adheres to the XML standard and is designed to enable powerful applications within the constraints of handheld devices. In most cases, the actual application or other content located on the web server will be native WAP created with WML or generated dynamically using java servlets or JSP.

In HTML, there are no functions to check the validity of user input or to generate messages and dialog boxes locally. To overcome this limitation, JavaScript was developed. Similarly, to overcome the same restrictions in WML, a new language known as WMLScript has been developed. The WAP programming model is shown in Figure 21.1.1.2.

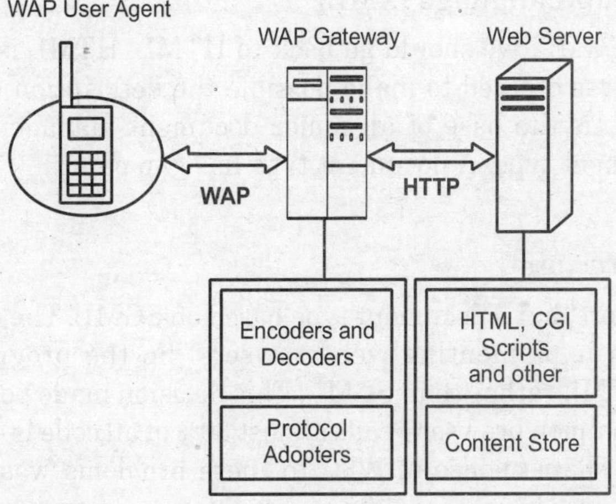

Figure 21.1.1.2 WAP Programming Model

21.1.2 Wireless Markup Language (WML)

The Wireless Markup Language (WML) is an based markup language that was designed to describe how WAP content is presented on a wireless terminal. Almost every mobile phone browser around the world supports WML differs from HTML in the following:

- WML was specifically designed for wireless terminals with a target screens that is only a few lines long and about an inch wide.
- WML in case sensitive and all tags and attributes should be in lowercase.
- Unlike HTML, WML is unforgiving of incorrectly nested tags.
- WML does not assume that a "QWERTY" keyboard or a mouse is available for user input.

Based on these differences, WML provides a smaller, telephony aware set of tags that make it more appropriate than HTML for handheld wireless terminals. Similar to HTML, through, with WML you can give the user input options and specify how the user agent should respond when, for example, the user presses a key.

WMLScript, which is based on ECMAScript (the standard for JavaScrip), is a language that you can use to provide programmable functionality to WAP applications. It is part of the WAP specification and it can be used to add script support to the client. The main difference between WMLScript and ECMAScript is complied into byte code before it is sent to the client. The main reason for this is of course to cope with the narrowband communication channels and to keep client memory requirement to a maintain.

WMLScript can be used to check the validity of user input, but most important, you can use it to generate messages and dialogs locally, so error messages and confirmations can be viewed faster, and to access facilities of the user agent-for example, it allows the programmer to make phone calls, access the SIM card, or configure the user agent after it has been deployed.

21.1.3 EXtended Markup Language (XML)

To see the basics of XML, we should go back to HTML. HTML is a simple application built on SGML. SGML was created to make possible the description of any document in a unified language. SGML is the base of all major document management systems. SGML defines markup, a document type. A document type has two parts:

- Document Tags
- The document structure

HTML is nothing more, but a document type based on SGML. The dependence on SGML gave a lot of trouble in implementing web browsers. So the programmers made their applications based on HTML rather than SGML. This decision made possible the appearance of a bunch of errors. In common browsers' code almost 30% of all code is dealing with incorrect HTML code correction. The response of W3C to these problems was that they simplified SGML. This is how XML was born.

XML has been carefully designed with the goal that every valid XML document should also be an SGML document. There are some areas of difference between XML and SGML, but these are minor, should not cause practical problems, and will almost certainly reconcile with SGML in the near future. An XML processor can read clean, valid, HTML, and with a few small changes, an HTML browser like Netscape Navigator or Microsoft Internet Explorer would be able to read XML. The biggest difference between XML and HTML is that in XML, you can define your own tags for your own purposes, and if you want, share those tags with other users. XML leaves out many features of SGML. There are a few areas where XML and SGML really differ:

- XML defines, for documents, the property of being well-formed; this does not really correspond to any SGML concept. A document that is well-formed is easy for a computer program to read and ready for network delivery. Specifically, in a well-formed document all the begin-tags and end-tags match up, empty tags use the special XML syntax (e.g. <empty/>), all the attribute values are nicely quoted (e.g. <a href= http://www.lnl.net/xml.html>) and all the entities are declared.
- XML has very specific built-in method for handling international (non ASCII) text. It is compatible with SGML, but at the moment, few SGML processors are properly internationalized.

XML is a text document is which we can define control sequences. Each control sequence can have a bunch of parameters and an end sequence. An XML document is well formed if each sequence has its matching end pair, the sequences are correctly planted one inside another and the string constants are of corresponding format.

21.2 MOBILE COMPUTING

The advancements in wireless technology have led to **mobile computing.** Mobile computing environment will provide database applications with useful aspects of wireless technology. Mobility is one of the key factors reshaping how companies and end-users conduct daily business. Constant availability is fast becoming an essential part of future competitiveness. Businesses that embrace the idea of the Mobile Information Society will reinvent themselves as real-time organization, where access and interaction can be instant. The new competitive market place is all about mobile services.

The mobile computing platform allows users to establish communication with other users and to manage their work while they are on the move. This feature is very useful for geographically dispersed organizations like courier companies, sales personnel, globe trotting executives etc. There are number of hardware and software problems that must be resolved before the full potential of mobile computing can be utilized. Some problems like data management, transaction management, recovery management etc. are same as in the case of distributed database management systems. In mobile computing these problems are more complex because of the narrow bandwidth. The current upper limits are 1Mbps for infrared communication. 2 Mbps for radio communication, 9.14 Kbps for cellular telephony. Compare this with the upper limit of Ethernet, which is 10 Mbps, that of fast Ethernet, which is 100 Mbps, and that of ATM (Asynchronous Transfer mode), which is 155 Mbps. Clearly we can see the bandwidth of mobile computing environment is narrow compared to distributed computing. Other problems that are specific to mobile computing are the relatively short active life of the power supply of the mobile units and the changing locations of required information (in the cache, in the air, or at the server). In addition to all these, mobile computing has its own architectural challenges.

Mobile applications can make your business more flexible, more customer-focused and more effective. WAP is enabling corporate mobile phone users to pick up their e-mails, synchronize calendars and access their corporate database. Already today people manage their finances smoothly with their mobile phone.

Studies indicate that the number of global mobile intranet users is estimated to grow to over 80 million in 2005. Already large number companies are extending their corporate applications to WAP-enabled phones. By going totally mobile, organizations can gain better control over the services that makes available to its employees and customers. These services can be tailor-made to match their unique needs and help them become more efficient in their everyday activities.

The general architecture of a mobile computing environment is shown in Figure 21.2. It is a distributed architecture where a number of servers-**fixed hosts** and base stations-are connected through a high-speed wired network. Fixed host are general purpose computers that are not equipped to manage mobile units but can be configured to do so. Base stations are equipped with wireless interface and can communicate with mobile units and support data access. Mobile units include laptops computers, palmtop computers, Personal Digital Assistants (PDAs), other handheld devices and WAP enabled cellular phones. Mobile units and base stations communicate through wireless channels having bandwidths (1 to 10 Mbps) significantly lower than those of the wired network (in the range of 100 Mbps). A downlink channel is used for sending data from a base station to a mobile unit and an uplink channel is used to send data from a mobile to base station. Mobile units are battery powered portable computers that move freely in a geographic mobility domain-an area that is restricted by the limited bandwidth of wireless communication channels. The mobile units should be able to move anywhere within the geographic mobility domain and should be able to access the base station.

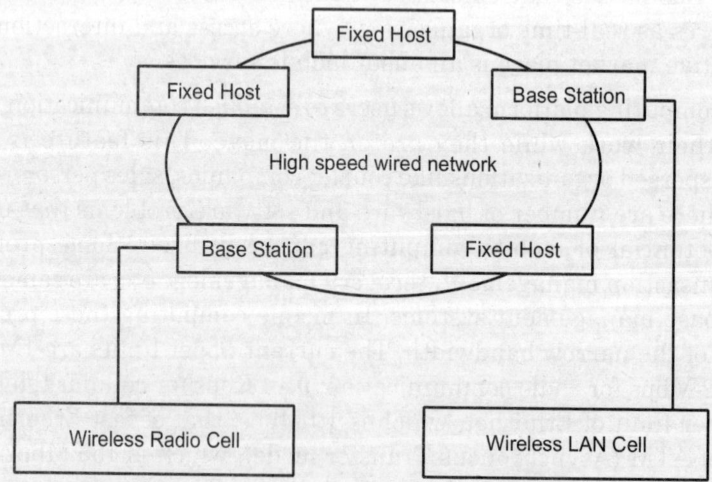

Figure 21.2 Mobile Computing Environments

In a mobile database environment, the data generally changes very rapidly. Users often query the base station and the servers to remains up-to-date. Users in a mobile environment are mobile and their exit and entry from and to a geographically mobility domain in random. The averages duration a user stays in a cell is called **residence latency.** Wireless networks differ from wired network in many ways. Database users in a wired network remain connected to the network and to a continuous power source. Thus response time is the key performance issue. But in a wireless network, both the response time and the active life of the user's power source-battery-are important.

21.3 MOBILE DATABASES

We are currently witnessing increasing demands on mobile computing to provide the types of support required by a growing number of mobile workers. Such individuals require work as if in the office but in reality they are working from remote locations including homes, clients, premises, or simply while en route to remote location. The office may accompany a remote worker in the form of a laptop, PDA (Personal Digital Assistant), or other Internet access device. With the rapid expansion of cellular, wireless and satellite communications, it will soon be possible for mobile users to access any data, anywhere, at any time. However business etiquette, practicalities, security and costs may still limit communication such that it is not possible to establish online connections for as long as users want, wherever they want. Mobile databases offer a solution for some of these restrictions.

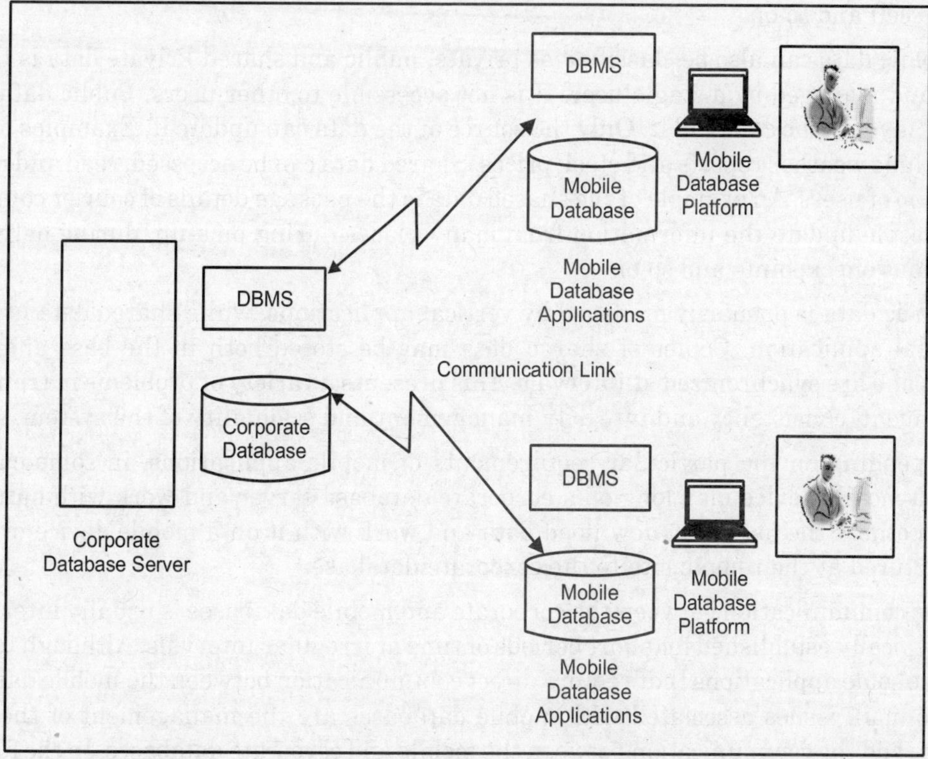

Figure 21.3 Typical architecture for mobile database environment

With mobile databases, users have access to corporate data on their laptop, PDA, or other internet access device that is required for applications at remote sites. The typical architecture for a mobile database environment is shown in Figure 21.3. The components of a mobile database environment include:

- Corporate database server and DBMS that manages and stores the corporate data and provides corporate applications.
- Remote database and DBMS that manages and stores the mobile data and provides mobile applications.
- Mobile database platform that includes laptop, PDA, or other Internet Access Devices.
- Two-way communication links between the corporate and mobile DBMS.

Applications that run on the mobile hosts have different data requirements. Users either engage in personal communications or they receive updates on frequently changing information.

Mobile applications can be classified as horizontal and vertical applications. In horizontal applications the users cooperate on performing a task and they can handle data distributed throughout the network. Two very important horizontal applications are mail-enabled applications and information services to mobile users. In vertical applications users can access data within a specific cell but not outside that cell. For example, the users can access information about the parking space availability at an airport cell, the location of hospitals within a cell and so on.

Mobile data can also be classified as private, public and shared Private data is the data owned and managed by a single user. It is not accessible to other users. Public data can be used by anyone who can read it. Only the source of the data can update it. Examples of public data include weather reports and stock prices. Shared data can be accessed, read and updated by a group of users. An example of the shared data is the package details of courier companies. Many people update the information from many places-during pick-up, during delivery, at the various checkpoints and so on.

Public data is primarily managed by vertical applications, while shared data is used by horizontal application. Copies of shared data may be stored both in the base and mobile stations and are synchronized at intervals. This presents a variety of problems in transaction management, consistency and integrity management and scalability of the system.

Depending on the particular requirements of mobile applications, in some cases the user of a mobile device may long on a corporate database server and work with data there, while in others the user may download data and work with it on a mobile device or upload data captured at the remote site to the corporate database.

The communication between the corporate and mobile databases is usually intermittent and is typically established for short periods of time at irregular intervals. Although unusual, there are some applications that require direct communication between the mobile databases. The two main issues associated with mobile databases are the management of the mobile database and the communication between the mobile and corporate databases. In the following section we identify requirements of mobile DBMSs.

21.3.1 Mobile DBMSs

All the major DBMS vendors now offer a mobile DBMS. In fact, this development partly responsible for driving the current dramatic growth in sales for the major DBMS vendors. Most vendors promote their mobile DBMS as being capable of communicating with a range of major relational DBMSs and in providing database services that require limited computing resources to match those currently provided by mobile devices. The additional functionality required of mobile DBMSs includes the ability to:

- Communicate with the centralized database server through modes such as wireless or Internet Access.
- Replicate data on the centralized database server and mobile device.
- Synchronize data on the centralized database server and mobile device.
- Capture data from various sources such as the Internet.
- Manage data on the mobile device.
- Analyze data on a mobile device.
- Create customized mobile applications.

DBMS vendors are driving the prices per user to such a level that it is now cost-effective for organizations to extend applications to mobile devices, where the applications were previously available only in-house. Currently, most mobile DBMSs only provide prepackaged SQL functions for the mobile application, rather than supporting any extensive database querying or data analysis. However, the prediction is that in the near future mobile devices will offer functionality that at least matches the functionality available at the corporate site.

21.3.2 Mobile Database Processing

Mobile database processing is a dynamic and exciting topic. Terms such as "global computing" and "anywhere access" open up the world to you. You are longer bound by the four walls of your office. Terms such as "empowered users" and "personalized data marts" imply more autonomy and independence for end users than ever before. However romantic and exciting this newfound mobility may sound, we must keep in mind that mobile database processing usually takes place in the context of a larger enterprise. In the enterprise environment, user autonomy and independence may include additional issues, complexities and problems that must be addressed in order to achieve the envisaged goals.

The most widely used example in the context of mobile databases is the travelling salesperson. Today's sales executives travel to remote locations all over the country to market and sell their products. On their notebook computers, they carry a database of all available products. The database also contains the orders they have taken or the sales they have made. From their hotel rooms every night, they dial into the base office where they download new product information and new marketing details to their personal database. They upload their sales and orders data to the office's database, from which management then calculates the salesperson's commission and reconciles stocks. These sales executives are empowered and mobile. They can roam the countryside and sell their products without having to rely on communication with the base office during office hours. In the case of insurance agents, who are not limited by a physical inventory, the scenario is quite simple. In the case of travelling salespeople who sell physical products, the problem is not so simple; they must keep closer links with their home base to ensure that they don't order or sell out-of-stock products. Some other examples of mobile database are in the transportation industry, courier industry etc.

21.4 TECHNOLOGY REQUIREMENTS

We require a broad range of technologies to implement the types of mobile databases. The technology can broadly be classified under hardware, database, replication, communication and application requirements.

21.4.1 Hardware requirements

This first requirement for mobile databases is adequate processing power, sufficiently large data storage and extended functionality on the laptop PC. One of the problems to consider is that the applications accessing the mobile database are usually running on the same machine as the database. In the mobile database context, you cannot use client/server architectures to split the processing loads to machines dedicated to the tasks for which they have been specially configured. Few people would want to drag two notebook computers around, just to be able to do client/server processing. We therefore have the client applications and the database server software running on a single machine, which places even higher demands on the processing power, parallel processing and throughput capabilities of the laptop PC.

Advance in hardware technology are making the mobile computing hardware more powerful and efficient. The size and weight of the portable devices like laptops, mobile phones, etc. are coming drastically. The processing powers of the machines, the active life of the batteries all the increasing. Few years back the laptops were bigger than our briefcases. Today, we hide a notebook with dual Pentium processors, a color screen, two 1.2GB disks, and a CD-ROM inside our briefcase. Modem speeds have also increased, but not as fast as hard disk capacity or processor speeds. The future looks very bright-the devices will become more and more powerful, will occupy less and less space, will have more powerful batteries and will cost less and less.

21.4.2 Databases requirements

For proper mobile database processing, an extended file system with some query and update capabilities is just not good enough. ANSI SQL-3 standard query and update functionality is preferable, even through many of the leading relational DBMSs still do not support all the SQL-3 standards. You require the functionality of a full-fledged DBMS. For example, you need extensive database definition capabilities-full transaction control, backup and recovery facilities, performance monitoring and tuning facilities and to a lesser extent, security definition and enforcement capabilities. Some aspects of a server based DBMS are less necessary in a example; however, as the power of mobile platforms and the demands of mobile database applications increases, these capabilities may soon be required. Another requirement is the ability to run on mobile operating systems such as PlamOS, EPOC, Windows CE, FLEXOS, OS/9, or JavaOS. Not all notebook users want to install Windows Me, Linux, or another desktop operating system.

For extensive applications you want to run against the database, you must be able to create all the database objects that you create on a state-of-the-art, multi-user, server-based database. Ideally you require a complete implementation of the relational data model. Although no major relational DBMS today meets all of E.F.Codd's rules, a mobile DBMS must at least provide the same functionality as a server-based DBMS. In addition to relational tables, this functionality includes full support for domains and the relational integrity constraints-namely the domain, key, column, referential and user-defined integrity constraints-which should all be defined declaratively. You must also be able to create, drop and maintain views, indexes, stored procedures and triggers.

The fact that mobile applications usually have a single user does not mean that you do not need full transaction control. The transaction performed by this user still must be atomic-either all the actions of a transaction must be committed to the database or none at all. Our travelling salespeople cannot place an order without ordered items. In addition, with the event-driven nature and the ad hoc flow of GUI applications, you need transaction isolation as well. The results of an incomplete transaction-a transaction still in progress-must be hidden from other transactions through proper concurrency control mechanisms, such as locking or timestamp. If our salespeople want a report of the placed orders, the report cannot include the details of an order that has not been committed yet.

Just as for any server-based database, you require the facilities to perform full and partial backups of your desktop databases and facilities to restore them, should any problems arise. The backup facilities must cater to all the problems that can happen to a database, such as machine failures, disk failures, software failures and user errors. There are three additional requirements for mobile databases. First, the backup and restore facilities must be easy to use. For example, a sales executive must be able to restore his database on the laptop to the most recent usable and correct state after he let the laptop PC's battery run out while he was busy with an uncommitted transaction on an open database. He must be able to restore his database without any assistance from the DBA at the office because the problem may occur after hours or he may not be reachable by telephone or radio. Second, the backup data should also take up as little space as possible-on a portable laptop PC, you rarely have as much disk space for all the backup data as on the database server at the office. You also usually do not have all the secondary storage devices, such as digital audiotapes and cartridge tapes that you have on your database server at the office. Finally, the backups should not take long to run, and it must be possible to schedule them at ad hoc times. It must also be easy to remember to do them the usage patterns of mobile databases are much more erratic than those of server-based databases. They also do not necessarily have scheduled downtimes-when the machine is on but the database in not being used-to allow for offline backups.

Therefore, although full function DBMSs are required on the laptop PC, these DBMSs must also be as easy to use and manage as possible. You cannot expect mobile database users to be DBAs too. Many DBMS vendors include the term "self-managing databases" in their sales and marketing literature. Although few of the mobile DBMSs satisfy this requirement at this stage, it is encouraging to see that they moving in the correct direction.

21.4.3 Replication requirements

Replication is a very important functional requirement for mobile databases. in any situation where multiple mobile databases are used or where is a "home base" database, you must have replication facilities to synchronize the data and operations between the databases.

21.4.4 Communication requirements

Mobile database applications often require special communication facilities-dual-up, satellite, radio communications, etc. We have seen that the mobile databases need to be synchronized with the host database. Replication facilities require underlying communication facilities.

Many of the mobile application users are not connected to the enterprise network for long periods of time. They are only connected for short periods of time. During the short periods of connectivity, the users want the information exchange to take place, preferably, with as little interaction as possible. In many of these cases, we must deal with unreliable communication media. Dial-up and radio links are not always as fast and reliable as we would want them. even satellite links can have intermittent failures.

There are many fast-developing technologies that are making mobile communications more feasible than in the past. Hardware improvements, such as high speed modems, cellular telephones, and other wireless links (including satellite, infrared and radio-based links), make communication to remote locations more feasible. To this we can add the improvements of the remote access software-asynchronous messaging facilities, more robust communication protocols, file transfer mechanisms, email and various other protocols that are available on the internet.

These advances make communication in the mobile database world easier and more usable for our intermittently connected users. However, some of these technologies have yet to find wide acceptance in the enterprise world in which our mobile database users often operate.

21.4.5 Application requirements

The application executed against the mobile database should be full function. People will not use the applications if they are so scaled-down that they do not help in the users' day-to-day tasks. For example, if the sales executive's personalized data mart cannot give him summary statistics about the products his clients have purchased, as well as drill-down capabilities for specific policies of interest, he will call the head office for up-to-date statistics and detailed service information before visiting a client, rather than powering up his mobile database application to retrieve information that is only half useful.

With the increasing importance of the World Wide Web, mobile database applications should be web-enabled, or at least have a browser-like look-and-feel. Users are now getting used to browser functions. The challenge for application interface designers is to provide easy-to-use natural interface that function efficiently over an intranet, or even over the internet.

Mobile applications should be lightweight and small. They should not consume exorbitant resources to run. Although you can get a laptop computer with dual Pentium processors, 64MB memory and 4GB disk space, you should keep in mind that this same machine must also run the database server software. A computer that runs both the client software and the database server needs more power than a computer that only runs the client software. You do not want to compromise on the database server's functionality, manageability and control, either. Similarly, you do not want to compromise on the replication facilities. However, not all the mobile users can afford the luxury of using the most powerful portable computer on the market.

SUMMARY

Today, people around the world are using hundreds of thousands of handheld devices from Personal Digital Assistant (PDAs) loaded with business critical data, to devices storing medical, life saving information. In fact the market for these devices is exploding. As the applications on these devices become more sophisticated, it is critical that data management solutions be able to operate within resource constrained environments. Fast access to local data on the handheld device is important to travelling executives, sales people, doctors and telecommuters all of whom require immediate results. Mobile users require solutions where both structured and unstructured information is recorded, stored and transferred across a multitude of computing equipment and devices, and across a variety of communication lines. The mobile application should be designed for the particular requirements of devices with limited processing power, limited memory and limited battery capacity. They should also be designed for wireless communication with limited bandwidth. Although these limitations are continuously relaxed due to technological advances, optimized resources utilization will always be an issue.

EXERCISES

1. What are the factors that fuel growth of WAP users?
2. What are the factors that boost the information value of mobile users?
3. What are the technologies that play a vital role in the mobile computing field?
4. What is WAP?
5. How does WAP works?
6. Describe the WAP architecture?
7. Explain the WAP programming model.
8. What is WML and what is it used for?
9. What is XML, what is it used for and what are its advantages?
10. What is mobile computing?
11. Explain the mobile computing environment with the help of a diagram.
12. What are mobile databases?
13. What are horizontal and vertical mobile applications?
14. What is the difference between private, public and shared data?
15. What is mobile database processing?
16. What are the technology requirements for mobile computing?
17. What are the requirements of mobile databases?
18. What are the hardware requirements for mobile computing?
19. What are the replication and communication requirements for mobile computing?
20. What are the application requirements for mobile computing?

CHAPTER 22

WEB DATABASES

22.1 INTRODUCTION

The internet and the World Wide Web are radically changing the access to and availability of information. This new communication medium is creating radical new ways to provide value to customers, suppliers and employees. Early web pages were static and provided rapid access to information similar to a printed page. Today, more and more web sites are highly interactive and support electronic commerce and dynamic information delivery is the database. The changes in the web technology is shown in Figure 22.1.

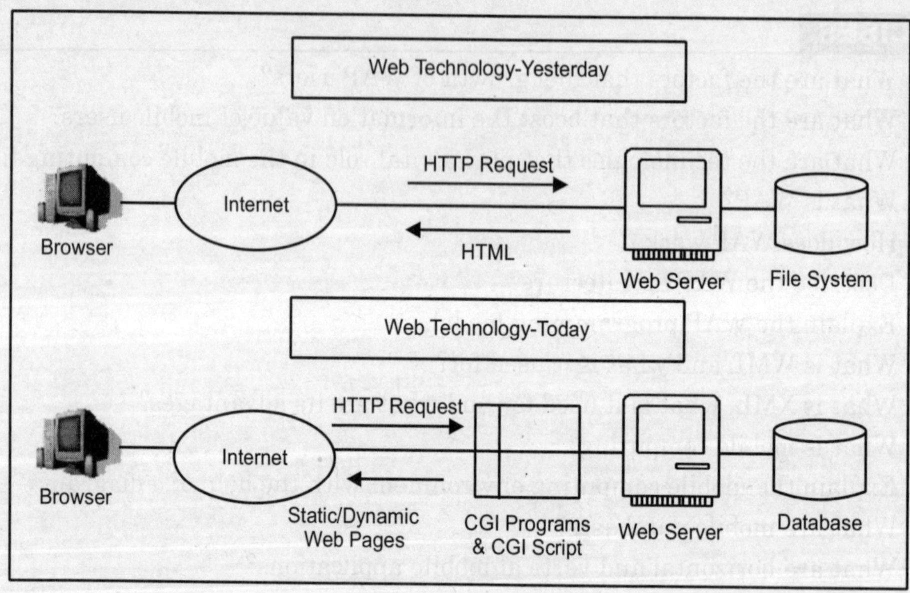

Figure 22.1 Web Technology-Yesterday and Today

The integration of database with the web provides a powerful new dimension for competitive advantage. It is also one of the most perplexing topics on the internet. Many organizations have databases that support business operations and understand the power of web-enabling this data. However, they lack the internet connectivity necessary to support web information strategies such as E-commerce, supply chain management or web publishing. The integration of database with the web or moving the information that you want to provide on the web into a database is a good decision, as databases are designed to handle the storage and retrieval of constantly updated information, they let you incorporate data that changes a lot, such as e-commerce transactions, into your web site without making the site slow.

The best solution is an SQL database or relational database. SQL is the industry standard tool for extracting information from relational databases. SQL is not very difficult to learn and implementing it pays off in the long run. Using a database as your web site's back end separates your ever-changing data from the look and feel of your site.

For such a system to work, a number of pieces of technology have to fit together. We will describe Web/Database architecture in general and then take a look at the main approaches that dominates the web today.

22.2 INTERNET AND WORLD WIDE WEB

Internet is the world's largest computer network, the network of networks, scattered all over the world. It was created nearly 25 years ago as a project for the U.S. Department of Defense. Its goal was create a method for widely separated computers to transfer data efficiently even in the event of nuclear attack. From a handful of computer users in the 1960s, today the internet has grown to thousand of regional networks that can connect millions of users. The amount of information available through the internet is staggering. The most successful attempt at presenting information available through the internet is the World Wide Web (WWW). The World Wide Web is a system, based on hypertext and HTTP, for providing, organizing and accessing a wide variety of resources (text, images and sound) that are available via the internet. You could get information about people, products, organizations, research data, electronic versions of the printed media, etc. from the internet.

Internet has grown explosively in the 1990s. The World Wide Web (WWW) has accelerated the growth of the internet by giving it an easy to use, point and click, graphical interface. Users are attracted to the WWW because it is interactive, because it is easy to use and because it combines graphics, text, sound and animation into a rich communications medium.

The WWW is the graphical internet service that provides a network of interactive document and the software to access them. It is based on documents called pages that combine text, pictures, forms, sound, animation and hypertext links called hyperlinks. To navigate the WWW users "surf" from one page to another by pointing and clicking on the hyperlinks in text or graphics. The WWW is many things to its millions of users. It is used as a market place, art gallery, library, community center, school, publishing house and whatever else its authors create. The World Wide Web, also referred to as the WWW or W3 or simply "the web" is the universe of information available via hypertext transfer protocol (HTTP), the World Wide Web and HTTP:

- Allow you to create "links" from one piece of information to another
- Can incorporate references to sounds, graphics and movies etc.
- "Understand" other internet protocols

The web presents information as a series of "documents" often referred to as web pages that are prepared using the Hypertext Markup Language (HTML). Using HTML the document's author can specially code sections of the document to "point" to other information resources. These specially coded sections are referred to as hypertext links. Users viewing the web page can select the hypertext link and retrieve or connect to the information resources that the link points to. Hypertext "links" can lead to other documents, sounds, images, databases (like library catalogs), e-mail addresses etc. the World Wide Web is non-linear – there is no top and there is no bottom. Non-linear means, you do not have to follow a hierarchical path to information resources. You can jump from one link (resource) to another; you can go directly to a resource if you know the Uniform Resource Locator (URL); you can even jump to specific parts of a document. Because the Web is not hierarchical and can handle graphics, it offers a great deal of flexibility in the way information resources can be organized, presented and described.

22.2.1 Internet Addressing

In general, internet addressing is a systematic way to identify people, computers and internet resources. On the internet, the term "address" is used loosely. Address can mean many different things from an electronic mail address to a URL.

- **IP Address** – An IP address is a unique number that identifies computers on the internet; every computer directly connected to the internet has one. An IP address consists of four numbers separated by periods. Each number must be between 0 and 255.
- **Domain Name** – Most computers on the internet have a unique domain name. special computers, called domain name servers, look up the domain and match it to the corresponding IP address so that data can be properly routed to its destination on the internet. Domain names are easier for most people to relate to then a numeric IP address.
- **URL** – URL stands for Uniform Resource Locator. URLs are used to identify specific sites and files available on the World Wide Web.

22.2.1.1 IP Address

If you want to connect to another computer, transfer files to or from another computer, you first need to know where the other computer is-you need the computer's "address." An IP (Internet Protocol) address is a unique identifier for a particular machine on a particular networks; it is part of a scheme to identify computers on the internet. IP addresses are referred to as IP numbers and internet addresses. An IP address consists of four sections separated by periods. Each section contains a number ranging from 0 to 255. Example: 202.54.1.6. These four sections represent both the machine itself, or host, and the network that the host is on. The network portion of the IP address is allocated to Internet Service Providers (ISPs) by the InterNIC, under the authority of the Internet Assigned Numbers Authority (ISNA). ISPs then assign the host portions of the IP address to the machines on the networks that they operate.

22.2.1.2 Domain Name

A domain name is a way to identify and locate computers connected to the internet. No two organizations can have the same domain name. Each domain name corresponds to numeric IP addresses. The Internet uses the numeric IP address to send data. For instance, you may be connecting to a World Wide Web server with the domain name "www.microsoft.com" , but as far as the network is concerned, you are connecting to the Web server with the IP address associated with that domain name as shown in Figure 22.2.1.2.

The Domain Name Server completes the task of matching domain names to IP addresses. Domain names, and their corresponding IP addresses, must be unique. If more than one organization on the internet had the same domain name, confusion would occur when the network tried to identify and communicate with the computers within those organizations. The Domain Name System is a collection of databases that contain information about domain names and their corresponding IP addresses. Domain Name Servers are computers that translate domain names to IP addresses. The domain names allow internet users to deal with the more intuitive domain names, rather than having to remember a series of numbers.

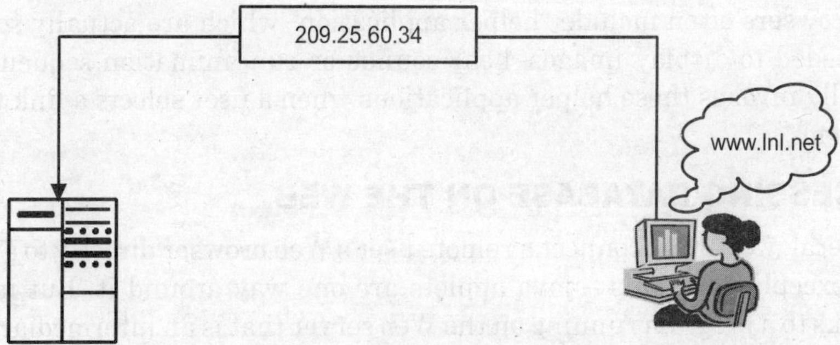

Figure 22.2.1.2 Domain Name and IP Address

22.2.1.3 Uniform Resource Locator (URL)

Information on the web is organized according to the URL or in other words, each and every resource – web pages, images, sound files, etc. - on the web have a URL. This URL provides the complete path name of the resource. The pathname consists of a string of machine and directory names separated by slashes (/) and ends with a file name. For example, the details of the books written by Govind Verma can be found at the URL http://www.InI.net/govind/book.html. A URL usually begins with a hypertext transport protocol (http://). HTTP is the set of rules, or protocol, that governs the transfer of hypertext between two or more computers. The World Wide Web encompasses the universe of information that is available via HTTP. Hypertext is text that is specially coded using a standard system called Hypertext Markup Language (HTML).

The HTML codes are used to create links. These links can be textual or graphic and when clicked on, can link the user to another resource such as other HTML documents, text files, graphics, animation and sound. HTTP is based on the client server principle. HTTP allows the browser to establish a connection to the server and make a request. The server accepts the connection initiated by the client and sends back a response. An HTTP request identifies the resources that the client is interested in and tells the server what "action" to take on the resource.

22.2.2 Web Browsers

A browser is a piece of software that acts as an interface between the user and the inner-workings of the internet, specifically the World Wide Web. Browsers are also referred to as web clients, or Universal Clients, because in the client server model, the browser functions are the client program. The browser acts on behalf of the user. The browser:

- Contacts a web server and sends a request for information
- Receives the information and then displays it on the user's computer

A browser, as mentioned above, can be graphical or text-based and can make the internet easier to use and more intuitive. A graphical browser allows the user to view images on their computer, "point-and-point" with a mouse to select hypertext links, and uses drop-down menus and toolbar buttons to navigate and access resources on the internet. The WWW incorporates hypertext, photographs, sound, video, etc. that can be fully experienced through a graphical browser. Browsers often include "helper application" which are actually software programs that are needed to display images, hear sounds or run animation sequences. The browser automatically invokes these helper applications when a user selects a link to a resource that requires them.

22.3 ACCESSING DATABASE ON THE WEB

In general, we cannot connect a remote user's Web browser directly to a database system. There are exceptions to this – java applets are one way around it. But in most cases, the browser talks to a program running on the Web server that is an intermediary to the database. This program can be a Common Gateway Interface (CGI) script, a Java servlet, or some code that lives inside an Active Server Page (ASP) or Java Server Page (JSP) document. The program retrieves the information from the database and sends it to the user as HTML pages. The user does not know whether the page is an ordinary HTML document or the output of some script that generates HTML. Figure 22.3 shows the typical interaction between a user and a Web-based database system. The different steps are explained below:

1. The user types in a URL or fills out a form or submits a search on a Web page and clicks the submit button.
2. The browser sends the user's query from the browser to the web server, which passes it on to a CGI script.
3. The CGI script loads a library that lets it talk to an SQL database server, and it uses that library to send SQL commands to the database server.
4. The database server executes the SQL commands and sends the requested information to the CGI script.
5. The CGI script generates an HTML document and writes the HTML document to the web server.
6. The web server sends the HTML page back to the remote user.

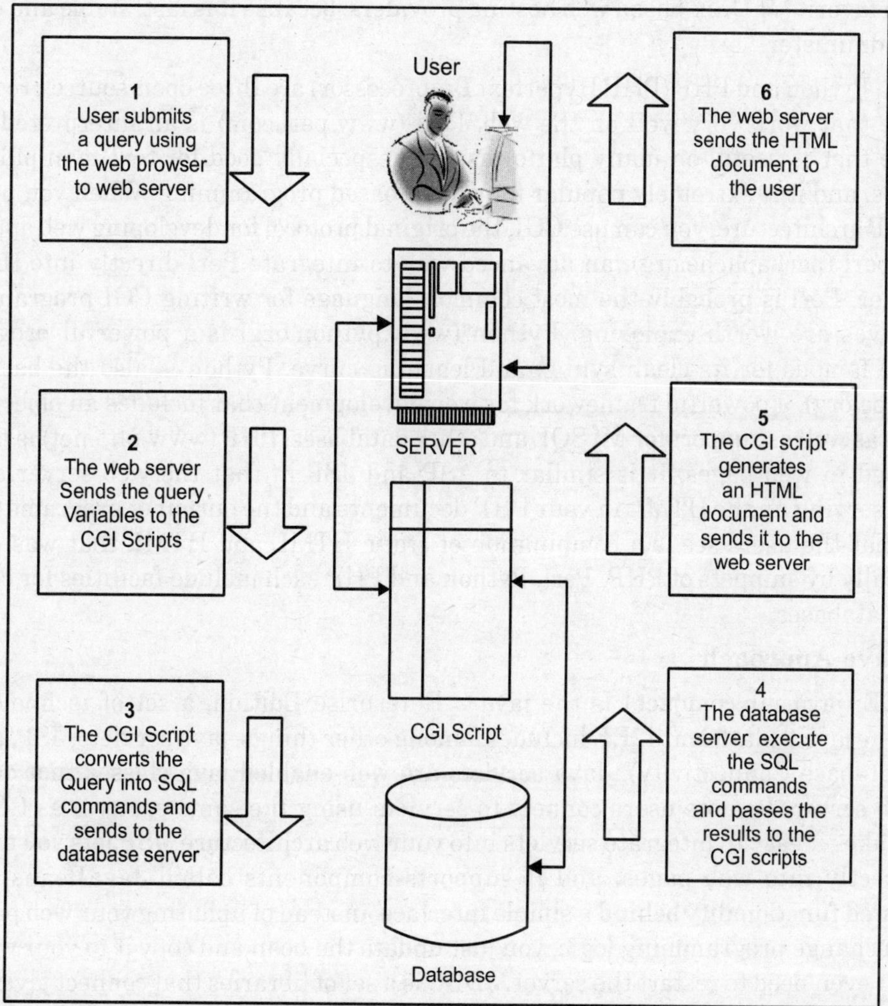

Figure 22.3 How a user exchanges information with a Web-based database

22.3.1 Open Source Approach

LAMP (www.onlamp.com) is an acronym that encompasses a variety of technology. It stands for Linux, Apache, MySQL and P*. The P* stands for the three programming languages that support web database development – Perl, Python and PHP.

Linux is one of the most popular platforms for serving web content, and this popularity has been increasing steadily. Linux is free and reliable, and it scales acceptably well for busy web sites. The Apache Web server is also free. Also as with Linux, major internet players such as IBM have taken a huge interest in Apache and have participated in its development. The Apache Foundation (www.apache.org) is composed of independent open-source developers and representatives from corporations interested in Apache's future. Its efforts have resulted in a stable web server that meets the high standards of open-source enthusiasts as we as high-end corporate users. For example, IBM's WebSphere (www.mysql.com) is the SQL quickly became a favorite of Unix-based web hosting providers, because it is fast, stable and extremely easy to administer.

Perl, Python and PHP (PHP Hypertext Preprocessor) are three open-source programming language that work very well on the web. Perl (www.perl.com) is an interpreted scripting language that is useful on many platforms. It is especially good for text manipulation and databases, and it is extremely popular for server-based programming. When you use Perl on the LAMP architecture, you can use CGI, the original protocol for developing web applications, or mod_perl (perl.apache.org), an advanced way to integrate Perl directly into the Apache web server. Perl is probably the most common language for writing CGI programs, but its alternatives are worth exploring. Python (www.python.org) is a powerful programming language famous for its clean syntax and learning curve. Python is also the basis of Zope (www.zope.org), a powerful framework for web development that includes an object-oriented database as well as support for MySQL and other databases. PHP (www.php.net) is a language you embed in web pages. It is similar to ASP and JSP in that the web server alternates between serving up the HTML in your PHP documents and the output of programs written in PHP. What the users see is a combination of static HTML and HTML that was generated dynamically by snippets of PHP. Perl, Python and PHP each include facilities for connecting to SQL databases.

22.3.2 Java Approach

J2EE (java.sun.com/j2ee) is the java 2 Enterprise Edition, a set of technology based around the java 2 platform. J2EE includes, among other things, java servlets, JSP, and JDBC (Java Database Connectivity). Java servlets are web-enabled java classes that can run on your web server. Remote users connect to servlets using the same protocol as CGI scripts, which makes it easy to integrate servlets into your web architecture. JSP lets you embed java code directly into web pages, and it supports components called JavaBeans that hide complicated functionality behind a simple interface, instead of updating your web pages every time you change programming logic, you just update the bean and copy it to your web server. You don't even need to restart the server. JDBC is a set of libraries that connect java programs (including servlets and JSPs) to SQL databases. JDBC allows access to relational databases through the execution of SQL statements.

22.3.3 Microsoft Approach

The Microsoft solution for web databases consists of Active Server Pages (ASP), ActiveX Data Objects (ADO), and Internet Information Server (IIS). But with the introduction of Microsoft's new Window technology, .NET (www.microsoft.com/net), this scenario is going to change. The .NET platform moves all windows programming to a web-centric model where applications communicate with each other using the web's HTTP and XML.

IIS is Microsoft's web server. The full version is available with Windows NT server and windows 2000. If you are running Windows 95, 98, Me, or NT Workstation, you can install Personal Web Server (PWS). Both IIS and PWS include support for ASP, which is similar to JSP and PHP. ASP documents differ from JSP and PHP in that you can write the programs in any ActiveX scripting language, including VBScript, Jscript, Perl, Python, and others, ActiveX scripting versions of Perl and Python are available from ActiveState.

ADO is a programming model that lets you interact with databases using Visual Basic, C++, Perl and other languages. ASP.NET is a more advanced version of ASP that supports the new C# language as well as VB.NET, ASP.NET improves on the original ASP implementation by first compiling all ASP.NET pages to a platform-independent Intermediate Language (IL), then compiling the IL to native x86 code with a just-in-time (JIT) compiler. As a result, ASP.NET runs much faster than its predecessor. ADO.NET is the next generation of ADO. It offers a more object-oriented programming model than ADO, and simplifies moving relational data to XML and vice versa. More information on the .NET technologies can be found at the MSDN Home page (msdn.microsoft.com/net/).

We have seen the different approaches to web database and database access. Companies like Microsoft and Netscape are releasing their own middleware products capable of multiple database connectivity. These include Internet Server API (ISAPI) from Microsoft and Netscape API (NSAPI) from Netscape. The DBMS vendors are also providing various options for making database access on the web easy. The move to integrate the databases and web are also making rapid progress. Now applications that can create database enabled web site are available in the market. We will see one such product-9i Application Server Portal – a complete solution for building, deploying and maintaining self-service, integrated web sites and portals.

SUMMARY

The internet and the World Wide Web are radically changing the access to and availability of information. This new communication medium is creating radical new ways to provide value to customers, suppliers and employees. Early web pages were static and provided rapid access to information similar to a printed page. Today, more and more web sites are highly interactive and support electronic commerce and dynamic information delivery is the database.

Internet is the world's largest computer network, the network of networks, scattered all over the world. It was created nearly 25 years ago as a project for the U.S. Department of Defense. Its goal was create a method for widely separated computers to transfer data efficiently even in the event of nuclear attack. From a handful of computer users in the 1960s, today the internet has grown to thousand of regional networks that can connect millions of users. The amount of information available through the internet is staggering. The most successful attempt at presenting information available through the internet is the World Wide Web (WWW). The World Wide Web is a system, based on hypertext and HTTP, for providing, organizing and accessing a wide variety of resources (text, images and sound) that are available via the internet. You could get information about people, products, organizations, research data, electronic versions of the printed media, etc. from the internet.

In general, we cannot connect a remote user's Web browser directly to a database system. There are exceptions to this – java applets are one way around it. But in most cases, the browser talks to a program running on the Web server that is an intermediary to the database. This program can be a Common Gateway Interface (CGI) script, a Java servlet, or some code that lives inside an Active Server Page (ASP) or Java Server Page (JSP) document.

EXERCISES

1. What are the recent advances in web technology?
2. What is the internet?
3. What is WWW?
4. What are hypertext links?
5. What is HTTP? How does it work?
6. What is ID address?
7. What is the domain name?
8. What is the use of a domain name?
9. What is a domain name server and what is it used for?
10. What is a URL?
11. What are web browsers?
12. How do you access databases on the web? Explain with the help of a diagram.
13. What is the open source approach of web technology?
14. What is the java web database approach?
15. What is Microsoft's approach to web database connectivity?

CHAPTER 23

OBJECT BASED DATABASES

23.1 INTRODUCTION

Object orientation is an approach to software construction that has shown considerable promise for solving some of the classic problems of software development. The underlying behind object technology is that all software should be constructed out of standard, reusable components wherever possible. Traditionally, software engineering and database management have existed as separate disciplines. Database technology has concentrated on the static aspects of information storage, while software engineering has modeled the dynamic aspects of software. With the arrival of the third generation of Database Management Systems, namely **Object-Oriented Database Management Systems** (OODBMSs) and Object-Relational Database Management Systems (ORDBMSs), the two disciplines have been combined to allow the concurrent modeling of both data and the processing acting upon the data.

A number of software vendors have got together to form the Object Database Management Group (ODMG) and to specify a standard for object-oriented DBMS (OODBMS). To do this, the group has specified a standard syntax and semantics for OODBMS. The intention is that this syntax and semantics should be portable across implementations of OODBMS. The first version of the ODMG standard was released in 1993 (Cattell, 1994), the second version was released in 1997 (Eaglestone and Ridley, 1998). The third and current version was launched in 2000 (Cattell, 2000). The ODMG standard can be seen to be a reaction to an attempt to develop a specification of mandatory features for OO databases published in 1990 (Atkinsonet al., 1990). The OODBMS manifesto proposes thirteen mandatory features for an OODBMS. The first eight rules detail the importance of an OODBMS conforming to OO principles. The last five rules specify that an OODBMS must support a number of classic DBMS features:

- **Complex objects** - Complex objects must be supported. It must be possible to build complex objects by applying constructors to basic objects, such as set, tuple and list.
- **Objects identity** - Object identity must be supported. All objects must have a unique identity that is independent of the values of its attributes
- **Encapsulation** - Encapsulation must be supported. Strictly speaking, encapsulation requires that programmers only have access to objects through their defined interfaces. In many practical DBMS the enforcement of encapsulation is not as important as the need for ad-hoc query

- **Object classes** - The construct of object classes must be supported. The schema in an OODBMS must comprise a set of classes
- **Inheritance** - Inheritance of methods and attributes must be supported
- **Dynamic binding** - Dynamic binding must be supported. To support overriding, the DBMS must bind method names to logic at run-time – this is known as dynamic binding
- **Complete DML** - The DML must be computationally complete. The DML of the OODBMS should be a general-purpose programming language
- **Extensible set of data types** - The set of data types must be extensible. The user must be able to build new data types from predefined types
- **Data persistence** - Data persistence must be provided. Data must persist after the application is terminated and the user should not need to explicitly initiate persistence
- **Very large databases** - The DBMS must be capable of managing very large databases. An OODBMS should have a number of mechanisms enabling effective management of secondary storage such as indexes
- **Concurrent access** - The DBMS must provide concurrent access to data
- **Recovery facilities** - The DBMS must be able to recover from hardware and software failure
- **Query management** - The DBMS must provide a simple way of querying data

Components of the standard

The major components of the ODMG standard are as follows:

- **The Object Model (OM)** - This defines a common data model to be supported by ODMG-compliant DBMS. It is based upon a data model originally produced by the Object Management Group (OMG).
- **Object Specification Languages** - Two such languages are defined- the object definition language (ODL) and the object interchange format (OIF). ODL is a specification language used to define object types that conform to the object model. OIF is a specification language used to dump the state of an object database to a set of files or load from a set of files into an object database.
- **The Object Query Language (OQL)** - This is a declarative query language for querying and maintaining object databases. It is based upon the structured query language SQL.
- **A number of language bindings (C++, Smalltalk, Java)** - In effect these permit a programmer to read from and write to the same database from different programming languages.

The Object Model

The object model (OM) defines the following constructs for modeling:

- **Objects and Literals** - The basic modeling constructs or primitives are objects and literals

- **Types** - Objects and literals are classified into types. All elements of a given type have the same set of properties and common behavior
- **Properties** - The state of an object is defined by the values associated with its set of properties. The properties of an object may be either an attribute of an object or a relationship between objects
- **Operations** - The behavior of an object is defined by a set of operations (methods) associated with an object. Operations may have a list of input and output parameters, each with a specified type
- **Schemas** - A database is defined by a schema specified in the object definition language (ODL). An object database contains instances of the types defined in a database's schema.

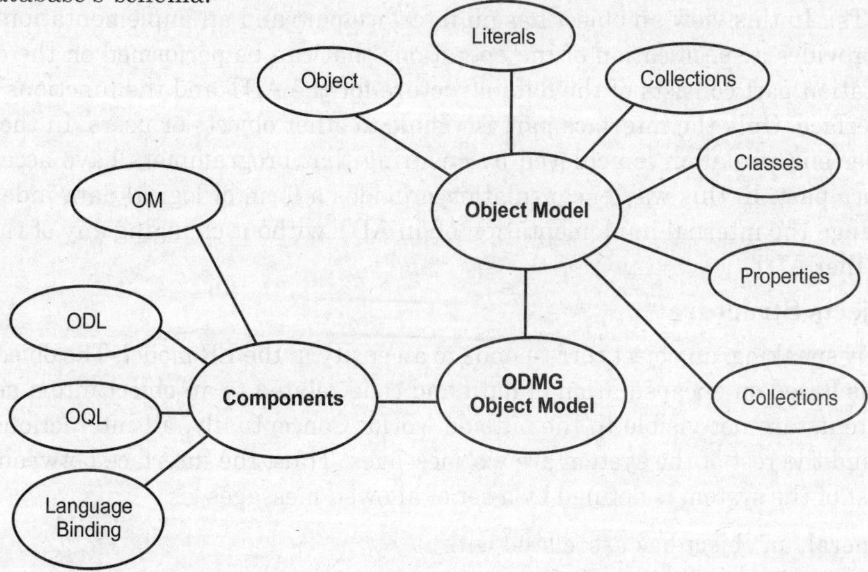

Figure 23.1 Object Oriented Database Management systems (OODBMS)

23.2 OBJECT ORIENTED CONCEPTS

In this section we discuss the main concepts that occur in object-orientation. We start with a brief review of the underlying of the themes of abstraction, encapsulation and information hiding.

23.2.1 Abstraction, Encapsulation and Information hiding

Abstraction is the process of identifying the essential aspects of an entity and ignoring the unimportant properties. In software engineering this means that we concentrate on what an object is and what it does before we decide how it should be implemented. In this way we delay implementation details for as long as possible, thereby avoiding commitments that we may find restrictive at a larger stage. There are two fundamental aspects of abstraction, encapsulation and information hiding.

The concept of **Encapsulation** means that an object contains both the data structure and the set of operations that can be used to manipulate it. The concept of **Information hiding** means that we separate the external aspects of an object from its internal details, which are hidden from the outside world. In this way the internal details of an object can be changed without affecting the applications that use it, provided the external details remain the same. This prevents an application becoming so interdependent that a small change has enormous ripple effects. In other words information hiding provides a form of data independence.

These concepts simplify the construction and maintenance of applications through modularization. An object is a 'black box' that can be constructed and modified independently of the rest of the system, provided the external interface is not changed. There are two views of encapsulation: the object oriented programming language (OOPL) view and the database adaptation of that view. In some OOPLs encapsulation is achieved through Abstract Data Types (ADTs). In this view an object has an interface part and an implementation part. The interface provides a specification of the operations that can be performed on the object; the implementation part consists of the data structure for the ADT and the functions that realize the interface. Only the interface part is visible to other objects or users. In the database view, proper encapsulation is achieved by ensuring that programmers have access only to the interface part. In this way encapsulation provides a form of logical data independence: we can change the internal implementation of an ADT without changing any of the application using that ADT.

23.2.2 Objects Structure

Loosely speaking, an object corresponds to an entity in the ER model. The object oriented paradigm is based on encapsulation of data and code related to an object into a single unit, whose contents are not visible to the outside world. Conceptually, all interactions between an object and the rest of the system are via messages. Thus, the interface between an object and the rest of the system is defined by a set of allowed messages.

In general, an object has associated with it

- A set of **variables** that contain the data for the object; variable corresponds to attributes in the ER model.
- A set of **messages** to which the object responds; each messages may have zero one or more parameters.
- A set of **methods,** each of which is a body of code to implement a message; a method returns a value as the response to the message.

23.2.3 Object Identity

A key part of the definition of an object is unique identify. In an object oriented system, each object is assigned an object identifier when it is created that is:

- System generated
- Unique to that object
- Invariant, in the sense that is cannot be altered during its lifetime. Once the object this OID will not be reused for any other object, even after the object has been deleted

- Independent of the values of its attributes (that is, its state). Two objects could have the same state but would have different identities
- Invisible to the user

23.2.4 Methods

An object encapsulates both data and functions into a self contained package. In object technology, functions are usually called methods. Figure 23.2.4 provides a conceptual representation of an object, with the attribute on the inside protected from the outside by the methods. Methods define the behavior of the object. They can be used to change the object's state by modifying its attribute values, or to query the values of selected attributes. For example, we may have methods to add a new property for rent at a branch, to update a member of staff's salary, or to print out a member of staff's details.

A method consists of a name and a body that performs the behavior associated with the method name. In a object-oriented language, the body consists of a block of code that carries out the required functionality. Messages are the means by which objects communicate. A message is simply a request from one object (the sender) to another object (the receiver) asking the second object to execute one of its methods. The sender and receiver may be the same object.

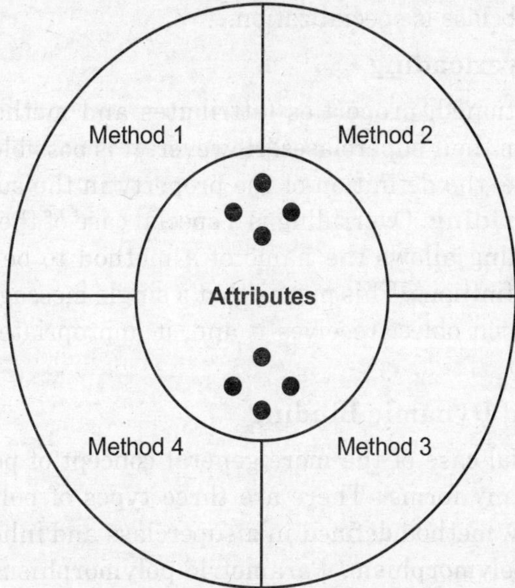

Figure 23.2.4 Object showing attributes and methods

23.2.5 Classes

Classes are blueprints for defining a set of similar objects. Thus, objects that have the same attributes and responds to the same messages can be grouped together to form a class. The attributes and associated methods are defined once for the class rather than separately for each object. For example, all branch objects would be described by a single Branch class. The objects in a class are called instances of the class. Each instance has its own value(s) for each attribute, but shares the same attribute names and methods with other instances of the class.

In some object-oriented systems, a class is also an object and has its own attributes and methods, referred to as class attributes and class methods, respectively. Class attributes describe the general characteristics of the class, such as totals or averages; For example, in the class branch we may have a class attribute for the total number branches. Class methods are used to change or query the state of class attributes. There are also special class methods to create new instances of the class and to destroy those that are no longer required. In an object oriented language, a new instance is normally created by a method called new. Such methods are usually called **Constructors.** Methods for destroying objects and reclaiming the space occupied are typically called **Destructors.** Messages sent to a class method are sent to the class rather than instances of a class, which implies that the class is an instance of a higher level class, called a **Metaclass.**

23.2.6 Subclasses, Superclasses

Some objects may have similar but not identical attributes and methods. If there is a degree of similarity, it would be useful to be able to share the common properties (attributes and methods). **Inheritance** allows one class to be defined as a special case of a more general class. These special cases are known as **Subclasses** and the more general cases are known as **Superclasses.** The process of forming a superclass is referred to as generalization and the process of forming a subclass is specialization.

23.2.7 Overriding and Overloading

As we have just mentioned, properties (attributes and methods) are automatically inherited by subclasses from their superclases. However, it is possible to redefine a property in the subclass. In this case, the definition of the property in the subclass is the one used. This process is called **Overriding.** Overriding is a special case of the more general concepts of **Overloading.** Overloading allows the name of a method to be reused within a class definition or across class definitions. This means that a single message can perform different functions depending on which object receives it and, it appropriate, what parameters are passed to the method.

23.2.8 Polymorphism and Dynamic Binding

Overloading is a special case of the more general concept of polymorphism, from the Greek meaning 'having many forms'. There are three types of polymorphism: operation, inclusion and parametric. A method defined in a superclass and inherited in its subclass is an example of inclusion polymorphism. Parametric polymorphism or genericity as it is sometimes called uses types as parameters in generic type, or class, declarations.

23.3 NEXT GENERATION DATABASE SYSTEM

In the late 1960s and early 1970s, there were two mainstream approaches to constructing DBMSs. The first approach was based on the hierarchical data model, typified by IMS (Information Management System) from IBM. The second approach was based on the network data model, which attempted to create a database standard and resolve some of the difficulties of the hierarchical model, such as its inability to represent complex relationship effectively. Together, these approaches represented the first generation of DBMSs.

In 1970, Codd produced his seminal paper on the relational data model. This paper was very timely and addressed the disadvantages of the former approaches, in particular their lack of data independence. Many experimental relational DBMSs were implemented thereafter, with the first commercial products appearing in the late 1970s and early 1980s. Now there are over a hundred relational DBMSs for both mainframe and PC environments. Relational DBMSs are referred to as second generation DBMSs.

However, as we discussed RDBMSs have their failings, particularly their limited modeling capabilities. There has been much research attempting to address this problem. In 1976, Chen presented the Entity Relationship model that is now widely accepted techniques for database design. In 1979, Codd himself attempted to address some of the failings in his original work with an extended version of the relational model called RM/T (Codd, 1979), and more recently RM/V2 (Codd, 1990). The attempts to provide a data model that represents the 'real world' more closely have been loosely classified as Semantic data modeling.

In response to the increasing complexity of database applications, two 'new' data models have emerged: the Object Oriented Data Model (OODM) and the Object Relational Data Model (ORDM), previously referred to as the Extended Relational Data Model (ERDM). This evolution represents third generation DBMSs, as illustrated in Figure 23.3.

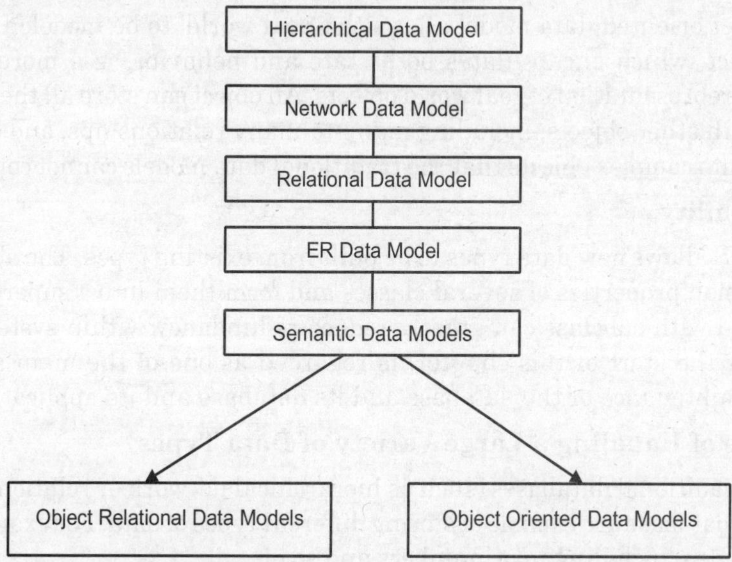

Figure 23.3 Generation of Database System

Object oriented database provide all the facilities associated with object oriented paradigm. It enables us to create classes, organize objects, structure an inheritance hierarchy and call methods of other classes. Besides these, it also provides the facilities associated with standard database systems. However, object oriented database systems have not yet replaced the RDBMS in commercial business applications.

Following are the different approaches for designing an object oriented database:

- Designed to store retrieve and manage objects created by programs written in some object oriented language (OOL) such as C++ or java.

Although a relational database can be used to store and manage objects, it does not understand objects as such. Therefore, a middle layer called object manager or object oriented layer software is required to translate objects into tuples of a relation.

- Designed to provide object oriented facilities to users of non object oriented programming languages (OOPLs) such as C or Pascal.

  The user will create classes, objects, inheritance and so on and the database system will store and manage these objects and classes. This second approach thus turns non-OOPL into OOPLs. A translation layer is required to map the objects by user into objects of the database system.

23.4 ADVANTAGES AND DISADVANTAGES OF OODBMS

OODBMS can provide appropriate solutions for many types of advanced database applications. However, there are also disadvantages. In this section we examine these advantages and disadvantages.

Advantages

- **Enriched Modeling Capabilities**

  The object oriented data model allows the 'real world' to be modeled more closely. The object, which encapsulates both state and behavior, is a more natural and realistic representation of real world objects. An object can store all the relationships it has with other objects, including many-to-many relationships, and objects can be formed into complex objects that the traditional data models cannot cope with easily.

- **Extensibility**

  OODBMS allows new data types to be built from existing types. The ability to factor out common properties of several classes and form them into a superclass that can be shared with subclass can greatly reduce redundancy within system and, as we stated at the start of this chapter, is regarded as one of the main advantages of object maintenance of the database and its database and its applications.

- **Capable of Handling a Large Variety of Data Types**

  Unlike traditional databases (such as hierarchical network or relational), the object oriented database are capable of storing different types of data, For example, pictures, voices, video, including text, numbers and so on.

- **Removal of Impedance Mismatch**

  A single language interface between the Data Manipulation Language (DML) and the programming language overcomes the impedance mismatch. This eliminates many of the inefficiencies that occur in mapping a declarative language such as SQL to an imperative language such as 'C'. Most OODBMS provide a DML that is computationally complete compared with SQL, the standard language of RDBMSs.

- **More Expressive Query Language**

  Navigational access from the object is the most common form of data access in an OODBMS. This is in contract to the associative access of SQL (that is, declarative statements with selection based on one or more predicates). Navigational access is more suitable for handling parts explosion, recursive queries, and so on.

- **Support for Schema Evolution**

  The tight coupling data and applications is an OODBMS makes schema evolution more feasible.

- **Support for Long-duration Transactions**

  Current relational DBMS enforce serializability on concurrent transactions to maintain database consistency. OODBMS use a different protocol to handle the types of long duration transaction that are common in many advanced database application.

- **Applicability to Advanced Database Applications**

  There are many areas where traditional DBMS have not been particularly successful, such as, Computer Aided Design (CAD), Computer Aided Software Engineering (CASE), Office Information Systems (OIS) and Multimedia Systems. The enriched modeling capabilities of OODBMS have made them suitable for these applications.

- **Improved Performance**

  There have been a number of benchmarks that have suggested OODBMS provide significant performance improvements over relational DBMS. The results showed an average 30-old performance improvement for the OODBMS over the RDBMS.

Disadvantages

- **Lack of universal Data Model**

  There is no universally agreed data model for an OODBMS, and most models lack a theoretical foundation. This disadvantage is seen as a significant drawback, and is comparable to pre-relational systems.

- **Lack of Experience**

  In comparison to RDBMS, the use of OODBMS is still relatively limited. This means that we do not yet have the level of experience that we have with traditional systems. OODBMS are still very much geared towards the programmer, rather than the naïve end-user. Also there is a resistance to the acceptance of the technology.

- **Lack of Standard**

  There is a general lack of standard of OODBM. We have already mentioned that there is not universally agreed data model. Similarly, there is no standard object oriented query language.

- **Competition**

  Perhaps one of the significant issues that face OODBMS vendors is the competition posed by the RDBMS and the emerging ORDBMS products. These products have an established user base with significant experience available. SQL is an approved standard and the relational data model has a solid theoretical foundation and relational products have many supporting tools to help both end users and developers.

- **Query Optimization Compromises Encapsulation**

  Query optimization requires an understanding of the underlying implementation to access the database efficiently. However, this compromises the concept of encapsulation.

- **Locking at Object Level may Impact Performance**

  Many OODBMS use locking as the basis for concurrency control protocol. However, if locking is applied at the object level, locking of an inheritance hierarchy may be problematic, as well as impacting performance.

- **Complexity**

  The increased functionality provided by the OODBMS (such as the illusion of a single level storage model, pointer sizzling, long duration transactions, version management and schema evolution) makes the system more complex than that of traditional DBMS. In general, complexity leads to products that are more expensive and more difficult to use.

- **Lack of Support for Views**

  Currently, most OODBMS do not provide a view mechanism, which as we have seen previously, provides many advantages such as data independence, security, reduced complexity and customization.

- **Lack of Support for Security**

  Currently, OODBMS do not provide adequate security mechanisms. The user cannot grant access rights on individual object or classes.

23.5 OBJECT RELATIONAL DATABASE SYSTEMS

Relational DBMS are currently the dominant database technology. The OODBMS has also become the favored system for financial and telecommunications applications. Although the OODBMS market is still small. The OODBMS continues to find new applications areas, such as the World Wide Web. Some industry analysts expect the market for the OODBMS to grow at over 50% per year, a rate faster than the total database market.

However, their sales are unlikely to overtake those of relational systems because of the wealth of businesses that find RDBMS acceptable and because businesses have invested so much money and resources in their development that change is prohibitive.

Until recently, the choice of DBMS seemed to be between the relational DBMS and the object oriented DBMS. However, many vendors of RDBMS products are conscious of the threat and promise of the OODBMS. They agree that traditional relational DBMS are not suited to the advanced application. The most obvious way to remedy the shortcoming of the relational model is to extend the model with these types of feature.

This is the approach that has been taken extended relational DBMS although each has implemented different combinations of features. Thus, there is no single extended relational model; rather, there are a variety of these models, whose characteristics depends upon the way and the degree to which extensions were made. However, all the models do share the same basic relational tables and query language, all incorporate some concepts of 'object' and some have the ability to store methods (or procedures or triggers) as well as data in the database.

In a four quadrant view of the database world, as illustrated in the Figure 23.5, the lower-left quadrant are those applications that process simple data and have no requirement for querying the data.

These types of application, For example standard text processing packages such as WordPerfect and Framemaker, can use underlying operating system to obtain the essential DBMS functionality of persistence. In the lower right quadrant are those applications that process complex data but again have no significant requirements for querying the data. For those types of application, For example computer aided design packages; an OODBMS may be an appropriate choice of DBMS.

In the top left quadrant are those applications that process simple data and also have requirements for complex querying. Many traditional business applications fall into this quadrant and an RDBMS may be the most appropriate DBMS.

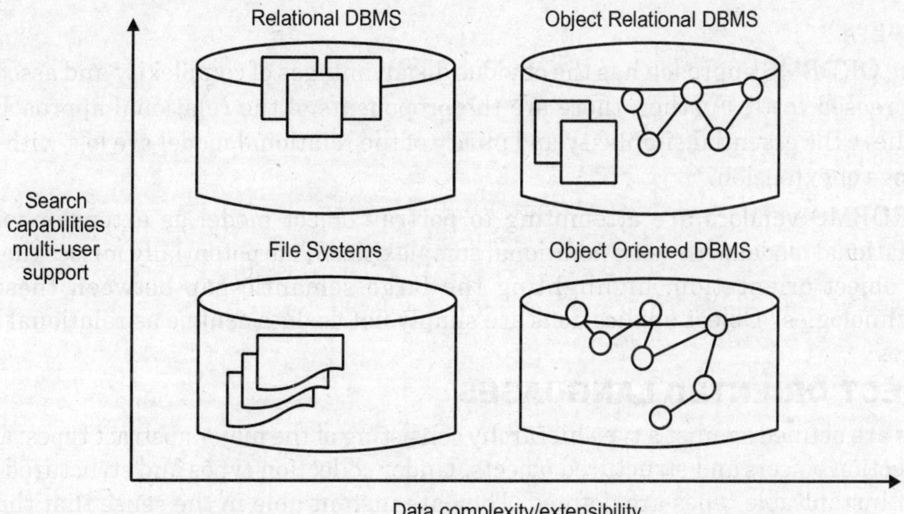

Figure 23.5 Four Quadrant View of Database World

Finally, in the top right quadrant are those applications that process completed data and have complex querying requirements. This represents many of the advanced database applications and for these applications an ORDBMS may be the most appropriate choice of DBMS.

23.6 ADVANTAGES AND DISADVANTAGES OF ORDBMS

ORDBMS can provide appropriate solutions for many types of advanced database applications. However, there are also disadvantages. In this section we examine these advantages and disadvantages.

Advantages

- **Reuse and Sharing**

  The main advantages of extending the relational data model come from reuse and sharing. Reuse comes from the ability to extend the DBMS server to perform standard functionality centrally, rather than have it coded in each application.

- **Increased Productivity**

  ORDBMS provides increased productivity both for the developer and for the end user.

- **Use of Experience in Developing RDBMS**

  Another obvious advantage is that the extended relational approach preserves the significant body of knowledge and experience that has gone into developing relational applications. This is a significant advantage, as many organizations would find it prohibitively expensive to change. If the new functionality is designed appropriately, this approach should allow organizations to take advantage of the new extensions in an evolutionary way without losing the benefits of current database features and functions.

Disadvantages

- The ORDBMS approach has the obvious disadvantages of complexity and associated increased costs. Further, there are the proponents of the relational approach that believe the essential simplicity and purity of the relational model are lost with these types of extension.
- ORDBMS vendors are attempting to portray object model as extensions to the relational model with some additional complexities. This potentially misses the point of object orientation, highlighting the large semantic gap between these two technologies. Object applications are simply not as data centric as relational based ones.

23.7 OBJECT ORIENTED LANGUAGES

Objects are defined against a type hierarchy consisting of the major abstract types: atomic objects, collection objects and structured objects. Under collection types and structured types a number of instant able types are defined. They are instant able in the sense that they are the only types that can be used as base types in the database. Each object has an object identifier and may have a number of names defined for it by users.

23.7.1 Literals

A set of literal types is defined including atomic, structured, collections or null. The value of a literal's properties may not change and hence literals may be used as traditional data types:

- Atomic. These are literals that are not created by applications and typically consist of numbers and character data types such as long, short, char and string
- Structured. These are literals that have a fixed number of elements each of which has a variable name and can contain either a literal value or an object. Structured literals include such data types as date, interval and time.

23.7.2 Collections

Collections may be collection objects or collection literals. The only difference between the two is that collection objects have identity. For instance, we may use a collection object to define the set of students in a school. We may also use a collection literal to define addresses as data structures.

The object model defines five types of collection objects:

- Set– unordered collections that do not allow duplicates
- Bag– unordered collections that allow duplicates
- List– ordered collections that allow duplicates
- Array– one-dimensional arrays of varying length
- Dictionary– unordered sequence of keys and values with no duplicate keys

23.7.3 Types and Classes

The object model distinguishes between types and classes. A type has one specification and one implementation. There are two aspects to a type: a specification and one or more implementations. The specification details the external characteristics of the type: the operations that can be invoked on its instances, the properties that can be accessed and any exceptions that can be raised by specific operations. A type's implementation constitutes the internal details of the type and is determined by a language binding.

The combination of the type specification and one implementation is said to be a class. A class definition is a specification that defines the abstract behavior and abstract state of an object type. The abstract behaviour of an object type is specified in its interface definition. The interface definition specifies its supertypes, its extent and its keys. The set of all instances of a given type is its extent. A key uniquely identifies the instances of an object type.

Example - The class Module defines both the abstract behaviour and abstract state of the Module objects.

CLASS Module {. . .};

23.7.4 Properties

The OM defines two types of property: attributes and relationships. A user accesses and manipulates the state of the instances of some class through its properties.

An attribute is defined on a single object type and takes as its value a literal or an object identifier.

Example

We may define the attributes of the class module as follows:

ATTRIBUTE STRING moduleCode;

ATTRIBUTE STRING moduleName;

ATTRIBUTE SHORT level;

ATTRIBUTE SHORT roll;

All relationships in the object model are binary. In other words, relationships are defined between two types. Each such relationship has a specific cardinality: one-to-one, one-to-many or many-to-many. In the interface definition for a class, traversal paths are defined for each relationship. Traversal paths are declared in pairs, one for each direction of traversal.

23.7.5 Operation

The instances of an object type have behaviour specified in a set of operations. The object type definition defines a signature for the operation which includes the operation name, parameters and type of each parameter, and the types of values returned.

Example - For instance, we might define a signature for an operation relevant to the class Module as below:

```
VOID increaseRoll(IN SHORT amount);
```

This operation increases the roll of a Module instance by a set amount.

The parameters of an operation are listed in rounded brackets. Each parameter has a name and a type. A parameter can also be designated as an input parameter (IN), output parameter (OUT) or both (INOUT). An operation can return an object as its value. If an operation does not return a value, the operation is prefixed with the keyword VOID. The object model specifies built-in operations for adding (FORM) and deleting (DROP) instances of relationships and managing the integrity constraints associated with relationships.

Example - Hence, given the relationships specified for the class Module as above, two further operations will be defined for this class:

```
ATTRIBUTE moduleTaughtBy;
VOID drop_module(IN Module aModule);
VOID form_module(IN Module aModule);
```

23.8 OBJECT DEFINITION LANGUAGE AND OBJECT QUERY LANGUAGE

ODL corresponds to the DDL of a conventional DBMS. It constitutes a language for defining object types in a database. It allows developers to specify the attributes, relationships and operation signatures but does not permit the specification of operations. We have implicitly used parts of ODL in illustrating some of the major constructs of the object model above.

The object query language (OQL) can be used to provide access to an OO data-base. It can also be used directly to maintain data in object databases, although this would normally be achieved through the operations specified against objects in the schema. It uses a syntax closely modeled on SQL2 and can be used as a standalone query language or as an embedded query language in C++, Java or Smalltalk.

23.9 CASE STUDY: SPECIFYING THE ACADEMICS DATABASES IN ODL

Below we specify part of the schema relevant to the academic database in ODL:

```
CLASS Module
(EXTENT Modules; KEY moduleCode)
{
/* Define Attributes */
ATTRIBUTE STRING moduleCode;
ATTRIBUTE STRING moduleName;
```

```
ATTRIBUTE SHORT level;
ATTRIBUTE SHORT roll;
ATTRIBUTE moduleTaughtBy;
ATTRIBUTE modulePresentedOn;
/* Define Relationships */
RELATIONSHIP SET <Lecturer> TaughtBy INVERSE Lecturer::Teaches;
RELATIONSHIP Course PresentedOn INVERSE Course::Presents;
/* Define Operations */
VOID increaseRoll(IN SHORT amount);
}
CLASS Student
(EXTENT Students; KEY sno)
{
/* Define Attributes */
ENUM {male, female} sex;
STRUCT studentAddress {SHORT houseNumber, STRING street, STRING area,
STRING
city, STRING postCode};
STRUCT studentName {STRING fName, STRING lName};
ATTRIBUTE studentAddress termAddress;
ATTRIBUTE studentAddress homeAddress;
ATTRIBUTE studentName sName;
ATTRIBUTE sex studentSex;
ATTRIBUTE SHORT roll;
ATTRIBUTE DATE DOB;
/* Define Relationships */
RELATIONSHIP SET <Module> enrolledOnModule INVERSE Module::HasEnrolled;
RELATIONSHIP SET<Module> assessedOnModule INVERSE Module::HasAssessed;
/* Define Operations */
SHORT studentAge(IN DATE DOB);
}
CLASS UndergraduateStudent:Student
(EXTENT UndergraduateStudents; KEY sno)
{
/* Define Attributes */
ATTRIBUTE SHORT sNo;
```

```
/* Define Relationships */
RELATIONSHIP SET <Course> registeredOnCourse INVERSE Course::HasRegistered
}
CLASS PostStudent:Student
(EXTENT PostgraduateStudents; KEY sno)
{
/* Define Attributes */
ATTRIBUTE SHORT sNo;
/* Define Relationships */
RELATIONSHIP SET<Lecturer> supervisedBy INVERSE Lecturer::Supervises
}
```

In this schema we have four class definitions for object types: Module, Student, Undergraduate Student and Post Student. Undergraduate Student and Post Student are subtypes of the object type Student. For each class an extent (collection of instances) is defined. For instance, the extent of the class Module is modules. Each class also has a key defined. For example, each instance of the class module is distinguished from other instances by the value module Code. The state of each class is defined in terms of a number of attribute definitions. Each class has defined relationships with other classes. The behaviour of each class is defined in terms of operations.

23.10 OBJECT QUERY LANGUAGE

OODBMS also has an in-built query language known as OQL (object query language). The syntax of OQL is SQL-like.

Example

Some OQL queries are provided below:

```
SELECT m.moduleName
FROM m IN module
WHERE level = 1
```

This query extracts the names of all instances in the class module that are level 1.

```
TUPLE(roll: relationalDatabaseSystems.roll, level: relationalDatabaseSystems.level)
```

Here we are extracting the current roll and level of the object named relationalDatabaseSystems.

```
SELECT TUPLE(module: m.moduleName, lecturer: l.staffName)
FROM m IN module, l in lecturer
WHERE l.status = 'PL' AND m.roll > 30
```

This query will retrieve names of Principal Lecturers (PL) that are teaching modules with more than 30 students.

SUMMARY

Object orientation is an approach to software construction that has shown considerable promise for solving some of the classic problems of software development. The underlying behind object technology is that all software should be constructed out of standard, reusable components wherever possible. Traditionally, software engineering and database management have existed as separate disciplines. Database technology has concentrated on the static aspects of information storage, while software engineering has modeled the dynamic aspects of software. With the arrival of the third generation of Database Management Systems, namely **Object Oriented Database Management Systems** (OODBMSs) and Object Relational Database Management Systems (ORDBMSs), the two disciplines have been combined to allow the concurrent modeling of both data and the processing acting upon the data.

Relational DBMS are currently the dominant database technology. The OODBMS has also become the favored system for financial and telecommunications applications. Although the OODBMS market is still small. The OODBMS continues to find new applications areas, such as the World Wide Web. Some industry analysts expect the market for the OODBMS to grow at over 50% per year, a rate faster than the total database market.

Objects are defined against a type hierarchy consisting of the major abstract types: atomic objects, collection objects and structured objects. Under collection types and structured types a number of instant able types are defined. They are instant able in the sense that they are the only types that can be used as base types in the database. Each object has an object identifier and may have a number of names defined for it by users.

EXERCISES

1. Define the OODBMS.
2. What are features of OODBMS?
3. What is an object model?
4. Define the OSL and OQL.
5. Write the short
   - Abstraction
   - Encapsulation
   - Method
   - Class
   - Subclass and Superclass
   - Object Identity
6. What are the advantages and disadvantages of object oriented database?
7. Explain and details with object relational databases system.
8. What do you mean by object oriented language?
9. What is the use of object query language?
10. Write the short note
    - Collections
    - Literals
    - Operations
    - Properties

CHAPTER 24

DATA WAREHOUSES

24.1 INTRODUCTION

A data warehouse is a collection of data designed to support management decision-making. Data warehouses contain a wide variety of data that present a coherent picture of business conditions at a single point in time. Development of a data warehouses include development of systems to extract data from operating systems plus installation of a warehouses database system that provides managers flexible access to the data. The term data warehousing generally refers to combine many different database across an entire enterprise.

Data warehouse is the concept and terminology utilized to describe the forward edge of the MIS (management information system) evolution. Only the simplest organizations today operate without information technology. One of the fundamental tools in the organization's IT strategy is the database.

The database has primarily been directed toward operational (transaction) processing with any analysis or decision-making based on summaries or reports derived from the system. With the development of IT and the increasing needs of the organization, the construction of a database management needs rather than operational concerns is now possible. This new DBMS is called data warehouses.

A number of separate technologies have come together to make it practical to implement Data Warehousing. However it may be developed as a single, consistent store of information with appropriate tools to provide valuable information about a business. Business users at all levels of an organization can work more effectively given a proper understanding of the current status and underlying trends in their areas of responsibility.

While the benefits of the Data Warehouses have been accepted for some years, the notable success mostly have been in large organizations. Historically this has because of the high cost of setting up a data warehouses. The cost is driven by apparent need to use top-of-the range massively parallel computer hardware with the associated high manpower costs to build and manage these complex systems. Some have mistakenly understood data warehouse to be a super database capable of being adapted to present and future organizational needs.

The reality is that there is still the need for a database focused upon the operational (transaction) processing needs of the organization. At the same time, it is important to design and construct a database system (data warehouses), which will answer the growing present, and future managerial needs of the organization. The primary goals of a Data Warehouses are the following

- Provide access to the data of an organization
- Data consistency
- Capacity to separate and combine data
- Inclusion of tools set to query, analyze, and present information
- Publish used data
- Drive business reengineering

The original concept of a data warehouses was devised by IBM as the information warehouses and presented as a solution for processing data held in non-relational systems. The information warehouse was proposed to allow organizations to use their data archives to help them gain a business advantage. However, due to the sheer complexity and performance problems associated with the implementation of such solutions, the early attempts at creating an information warehouses were mostly rejected. Since then, the concept of data warehousing has been raised several times but it is only in recent years that the potential of data warehousing is now seen as a variable and viable solution. The latest and most successful advocate for data warehousing is Bill Inmon, who has earned the title of 'father of data warehousing' due to his active promotion of the concept.

Data warehousing - A subject-oriented, integrated, time-variant and non-volatile collection of data in support of management's decision-making process.

- Subject-oriented as the warehouses is organized around the major subjects of the enterprise (such as customers, products and sales) rather than the major application areas (such as customer invoicing, stock control and product sales). This is reflected in the need to store decision-support data rather than application-oriented data.
- Integrated because of the coming together of source data from different enterprise-wide applications systems. The source data is often inconsistent using, for example, different formats. The integrated data source must be made consistent to present a unified view of the data to the users.
- Time-variant because data in the warehouse is only accurate and valid at some point in time or over some time interval. The time-variance of data warehouse is are shown in the extended time that the data is held, the implicit or explicit association of time with all data, and the fact that the data represent a series of snapshots.
- Non-volatile as the data is not updated in real time but is refreshed from operational systems on a regular basis. New data is always added as a supplement to the database, rather than a replacement. The database continually absorbs this new data, incrementally integrating it with the previous data.

There are numerous definitions of data warehousing, with the earlier definitions focusing on the characteristics of data held in the warehouse.

24.2 CHARACTERISTICS OF DATA WAREHOUSES

To discuss data warehouses and distinguish them from transactional databases calls for an appropriate data model. The multidimensional data model is a good fit for OLAP and decision-support technologies. In contrast to multidatabases, which provide access to disjoint and usually heterogeneous databases, a data warehouse is frequently a store of integrated data from multiple sources, processed for storage in a multidimensional model. Unlike most transactional databases, data warehouses typically support time-series and trend analysis, both of which require more historical data than are generally maintained in transactional databases.

Compared with transactional databases, data warehouses are nonvolatile. That means that information in the data warehouse changes far less often and may be regarded as non-real-time with periodic updating. In transactional systems, transactions are the unit and are the agent of change to the database; by contrast, data warehouse information is much more coarse grained and is refreshed according to a careful choice of refresh policy, usually incremental. Warehouse updates are handled by the warehouse's acquisition component that provides all required preprocessing.

We can also describe data warehousing more generally as "a collection of decision support technologies, aimed at enabling the knowledge worker (executive, manager, and analyst) to make better and faster decisions". Figure 24.2 gives an overview of the conceptual structure of a data warehouse. It shows the entire data warehousing process. This process includes possible cleaning and reformatting of data before its warehousing. At the back end of the process, OLAP, data mining, and DSS may generate new relevant information such as rules; this information is shown in the figure going back into the warehouse. The Figure also shows that data sources may include files.

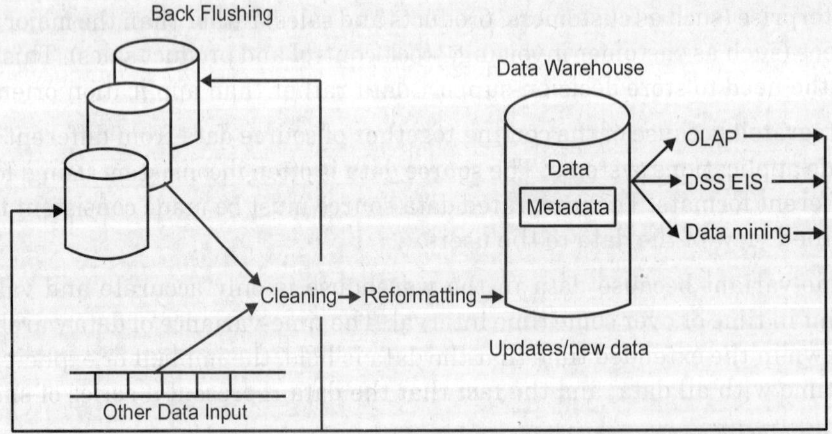

Figure 24.2 Example transactions in Market-Basket Model

Data warehouses have the following distinctive characteristics:

- Multidimensional conceptual view
- Generic dimensionality

- Unlimited dimensions and aggregation levels
- Unrestricted cross-dimensional operations
- Dynamic sparse matrix handling
- Client-server architecture
- Multi-user support
- Accessibility
- Transparency
- Intuitive data manipulation
- Consistent reporting performance
- Flexible reporting

Because they encompass large volumes of data, data warehouses are generally an order of magnitude (sometimes two orders of magnitude) larger than the source databases. The sheer volume of data (likely to be in terabytes) is an issue that has been dealt with through enterprise-wide data warehouses, virtual data warehouses, and data marts:

- Enterprise-wide data warehouses are huge projects requiring massive investment of time and resources.
- Virtual data warehouses provide views of operational databases that are materialized for efficient access.
- Data marts generally are targeted to a subset of the organization, such as a department, and are more tightly focused.

24.3 DATA WAREHOUSES ARCHITECTURE

In this section we present an overview of the architecture and major components of a data warehouse (Anahory and Murray, 1997). The processes, tools and technologies associated with data warehousing are described in more detail in the following sections of this chapter. The typical architecture of data warehouse is shown in Figure 24.3.

24.3.1 Operational Data

The source of data for the data warehouse is supplied from:

1. Mainframe operational data held in first generation hierarchical and network databases. It is estimated that the majority of corporate operational data is held in these systems.
2. Departmental data held in proprietary file systems such as VSAM, RMS, and relational DBMSs such as Informix and Oracle.
3. Private data held on workstations and private servers.
4. External systems such as Internet, commercially available databases, or databases associated with an organization's suppliers or customers.

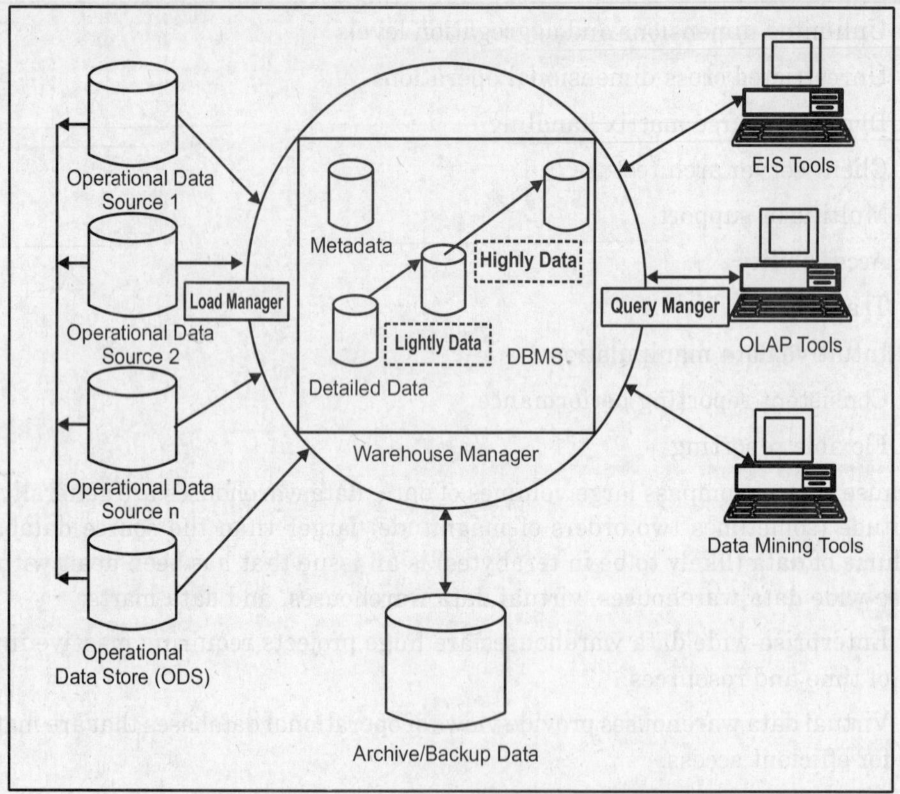

Figure 24.3 Typical Architecture of data warehouse

24.3.2 Operational Data Store

An operational Data Store (ODS) is a repository of current and integrated operational data used for analysis. It is often structured and supplied with data in the same way as the data warehouse, but may in fact act simply as a staging area for data to be moved into the warehouse.

The ODS is often created when legacy operational systems are found to be incapable of achieving reporting requirements. The ODS provides users with the ease of use of a relational database while remaining distant from the decision support functions of the data warehouse.

24.3.3 Load Manager

The load manager (also called the functional component) performs all the operations associated with the extraction and loading of data into the warehouse. The data may be extracted directly from the data sources or more commonly from the operational data store. The operations performed by the load manager may include simple transformations of the data to prepare the data for entry into the warehouse. The size and complexity of this component will vary between data warehouses and may be constructed using a combination of vendor data loading and custom-built programs.

24.3.4 Warehouse Manager

The warehouse manager performs all the operations associated with the management of the data in the warehouse. This component is constructed using vendor data management tools and custom-built programs. The operations performed by the warehouse manager include:

- Analysis of data to ensure consistency
- Transformation and merging of source data from temporary storage into data warehouse tables
- Creation of indexes and views on the base tables
- Generation of denormalizations
- Generation of aggregations
- Backing-up and archiving data

24.3.5 Query Manager

The query manger (also called the backend component) performs all the operations associated with the management of user queries. This component is typically constructed using vendor end-user data access tools, data warehouse monitoring tools, database facilities, and custom-built programs. The complexity of the query manager is determined by the facilities provided by the end-user access tools and the database. The operations performed by this component include directing queries to the appropriate tables and scheduling the execution of queries. In some cases, the query manager also generates query profiles to allow the warehouse manager to determine which indexes and aggregations are appropriate.

24.3.6 Detailed Data

This area of the warehouse stores all the detailed data in the database schema. In most cases, the detailed data is not stored online but is made available by aggregating the data to the next level of detail. However, on a regular basis, detailed data is added to the warehouse to supplement the aggregated.

24.3.7 Lightly and Highly Summarized Data

This area of the warehouse stores all the predefined lightly and highly summarized (aggregated) data generated by the warehouse manager. The area of the warehouse is transient as it will be subject to change on an ongoing basis in order to respond to changing query profiles. The purpose of summary information is to speed up the performance of queries. Although there are increased operational costs associated with initially summarizing the data, this is offset by removing the requirement to continually perform summary operations (such as sorting or grouping) in answering user queries. The summary data is updated continuously as new data is loaded into the warehouse.

24.3.8 Archive/Backup Data

This area of the warehouse stores the detailed and summarized data for the purpose archiving and backup. Even although summary data is generated from detailed data, it may be necessary to backup online summary data if this data is kept beyond the retention period for detailed data. The data is transferred to storage archives such as magnetic tape or optical disk.

24.3.9 Metadata

This area of the warehouse stores all the metadata (data about data) definitions used by all the processes in the warehouse. Metadata is used for a variety of purposes including:

- The extraction and loading processes – metadata is used to map data source to a common view of data within the warehouse
- The warehouse management process – metadata is used to automate the production of summary tables
- As part of the query management process – metadata is used to direct a query to the most appropriate data source.

24.3.10 End-User Access Tools

The principal purpose of data warehousing is to provide information to business users for strategic decision-making. These users interact with the warehouse using end-user access tools. The data warehouse must efficiently support ad hoc and routine analysis. The performance is achieved by pre-planning the requirements for joins, summations and periodic reports by end-users. These tools are divided into five main groups

1. Reporting and query tools
2. Application development tools
3. Executive Information System (EIS) tools
4. Online Analytical Processing tools
5. Data Mining Tools

24.4 DATA WAREHOUSE DATA FLOWS

In this section examine the activities associated with the processing (or flow) of data within a data warehouse. Data warehousing focuses on the management of five primary data flows, namely the inflow, upflow, downflow, outflow and metaflow.

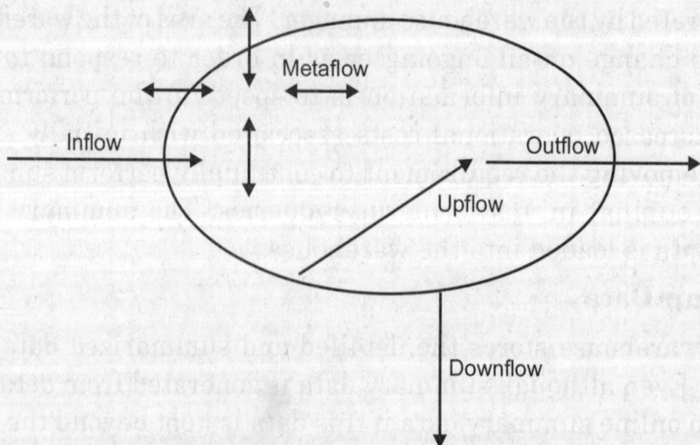

Figure 24.4 Information flows of a data warehouse

- **Inflow** – The processes associated with the extraction, cleansing and loading of the data from the source systems into the data warehouse.
- **Upflow** – The processes associated with adding value to the data in the warehouse through summarizing, packaging and distribution of the data.
- **Downflow** – The processes associated with archiving and backing-up of data in the warehouse.
- **Outflow** – The processes associated with making the data available to the end-users.
- **Metaflow** – The processes associated with the management of the metadata.

24.5 DATA MODELING FOR DATA WAREHOUSES

Multidimensional models take advantage of inherent relationships in data to populate data in multidimensional matrices called data cubes. (These may be called hypercubes if they have more than three dimensions). For data that lend themselves to dimensional formatting, query performance in multidimensional matrices can be much better than in the relational data model. Three examples of dimensions in a corporate data warehouse would be the corporation's fiscal periods, products, and regions.

A standard spreadsheet is a two-dimensional matrix. One example would be a spreadsheet of regional sales by product for a particular time period. Products could be shown as rows, with sales revenues for each region comprising the columns. (Figure 24.5(a) shows this two-dimensional organization). Adding a time dimension, such as an organization's fiscal quarters, would produce a three-dimensional matrix, which could be represented using a data cube.

Figure 24.5(a) Two-Dimensional matrix model

In Figure 24.5(b) there is a three-dimensional data cube that organizes product sales data by fiscal quarters and sales regions. Each cell could contain data for a specific product, specific fiscal quarter, and specific region. By including additional dimensions,

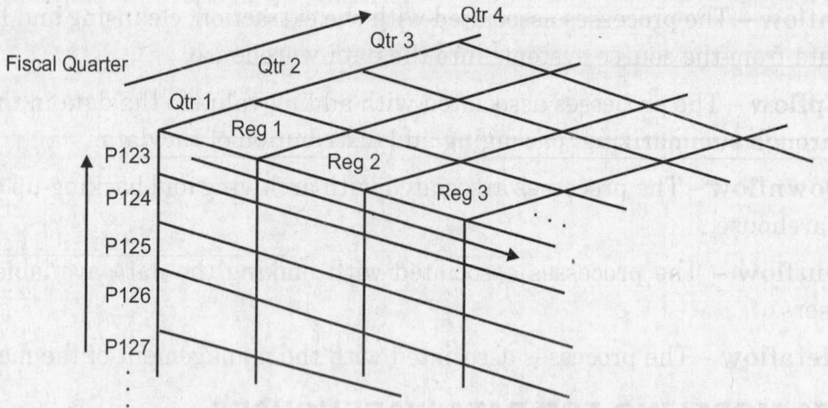

Figure 24.5(b) A Three-Dimensional data cube model

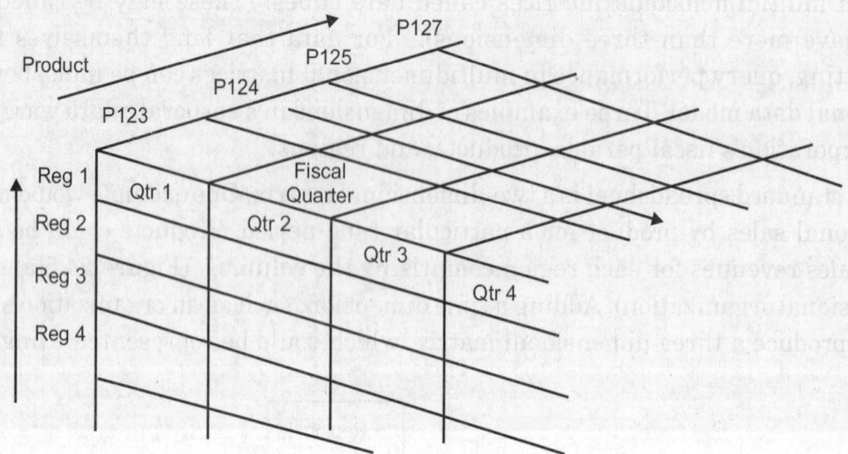

Figure 24.5(c) Pivoted version of the data cube from Figure 24.5(b)

a data hypercube could be produced, although more than three dimensions cannot be easily visualized at all or presented graphically. The data can be queried directly in any combination of dimensions, bypassing complex database queries. Tools exist for viewing data according to the user's choice of dimensions.

Changing from one dimensional hierarchy (orientation) to another is easily accomplished in a data cube by a technique called pivoting (also called rotation). In this technique the data cube can be thought of as rotating to show a different orientation of the axes. For example, you might pivot the data cube to show regional sales revenues as rows, the fiscal quarter revenue totals as columns, and the company's products in the third dimension (Figure 24.5(c)). Hence, this technique is equivalent to having a regional sales table for each product separately, where each table shows quarterly sales for that product region by region.

Multidimensional models lend themselves readily to hierarchical views in what is known as roll-up display and drill-down display. Roll-up display moves up the hierarchy, grouping into larger units along a dimension (e.g., summing weekly data by quarter, or by year). Figure 24.5(d) shows a roll-up display that moves from individual products to a coarser grain of product categories. Shown in Figure 24.5(e), a drill-down display provides the opposite capability, furnishing a finer-grained view, perhaps disaggregating country sales by region and then regional sales by subregion and also breaking up products by styles.

Figure 24.5(d) The roll-up operation

The multidimensional storage model involves two types of tables: dimension tables and fact tables. A **dimension table** consists of tuples of attributes of the dimension. A **fact table** can be thought of as having tuples, one per a recorded fact. This fact contains some measured or observed variable(s) and identifies it (them) with pointers to dimension tables. The fact table contains the data and the dimensions identify each tuple in that data. Figure 24.5(f) contains an example of a fact table that can be viewed from the perspective of multiple dimension tables.

Figure 24.5(e) The drill down operation

Two common multidimensional schemas are the star schema and the snowflake schema. The **star schema** consists of a fact table with a single table for each dimension (Figure 24.5(f)). The **snowflake schema** is a variation on the star schema in which the dimensional tables from a star schema are organized into a hierarchy by normalizing them (Figure 24.5(g)). Some installations are normalizing data warehouses up to the third normal form so that they can access the data warehouse to the finest level of detail. A **fact constellation** is a set of fact tables that share some dimension tables. Figure 24.5(h) shows a fact constellation with two fact tables, business results and business forecast. These share the dimension table called product. Fact constellations limit the possible queries for the warehouse.

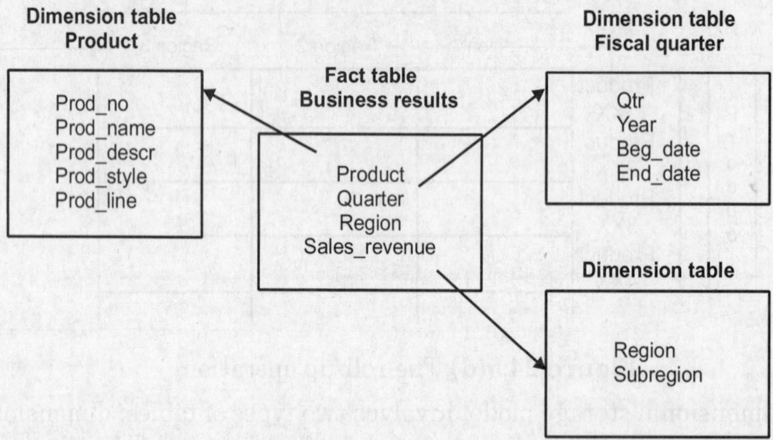

Figure 24.5(f) A star schema with fact and dimensional tables

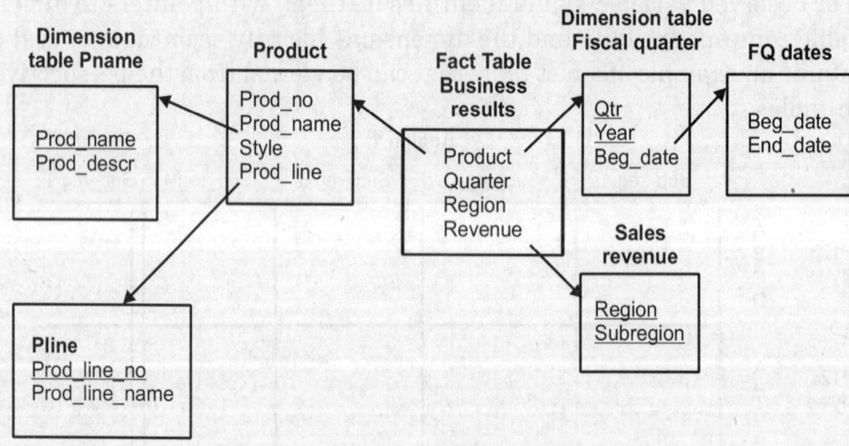

Figure 24.5(g) A snowflake schema

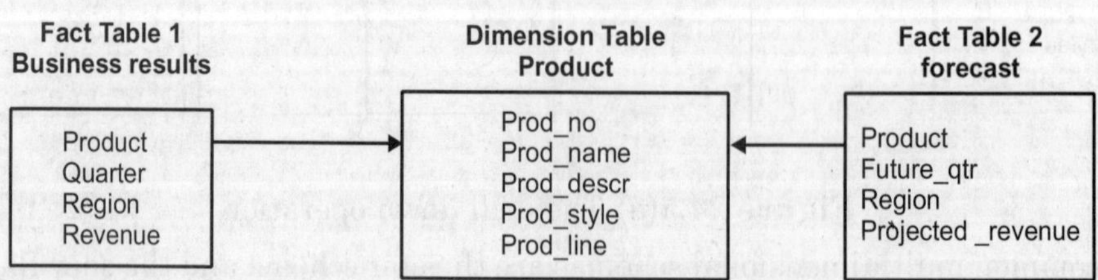

Figure 24.5(h) A fact constellation

Data warehouse storage also utilizes indexing techniques to support high performance access (see Chapter 10 for a discussion of indexing). A technique called **bitmap indexing** constructs a bit vector for each value in a domain (column) being indexed. It works very well for domains of low-cardinality. There is a 1 bit placed in the *J*th position in the vector if the *J*th row contains the value being indexed. For example, imagine an inventory of 100,000 cars with a bitmap index on car size. If there are four car sizes—economy, compact, midsize, and full-size—there will be four bit vectors, each containing 100,000 bits (12.5 K) for a total index size of 50K. Bitmap indexing can provide considerable input/output and storage space advantages in low-cardinality domains. With bit vectors a bitmap index can provide dramatic improvements in comparison, aggregation, and join performance.

In a star schema, dimensional data can be indexed to tuples in the fact table by **join indexing.** Join indexes are traditional indexes to maintain relationships between primary key and foreign key values. They relate the values of a dimension of a star schema to rows in the fact table. For example, consider a sales fact table that has city and fiscal quarter as dimensions. If there is a join index on city, for each city the join index maintains the tuple IDs of tuples containing that city. Join indexes may involve multiple dimensions.

Data warehouse storage can facilitate access to summary data by taking further advantage of the nonvolatility of data warehouses and a degree of predictability of the analyses that will be performed using them. Two approaches have been used: (1) smaller tables including summary data such as quarterly sales or revenue by product line, and (2) encoding of level (e.g., weekly, quarterly, and annual) into existing tables. By comparison, the overhead of creating and maintaining such aggregations would likely be excessive in a volatile, transaction-oriented database.

24.6 TYPICAL FUNCTIONALITY OF A DATA WAREHOUSE

Data warehouses exist to facilitate complex, data-intensive, and frequent ad hoc queries. Accordingly, data warehouses must provide far greater and more efficient query support than is demanded of transactional databases. The data warehouse access component supports enhanced spreadsheet functionality, efficient query processing, structured queries, ad hoc queries, data mining, and materialized views. In particular, enhanced spreadsheet functionality includes support for state-of-the- art spreadsheet applications (e.g., MS Excel) as well as for OLAP applications programs. These offer preprogrammed functionalities such as the following:

- **Roll-up:** Data is summarized with increasing generalization (e.g., weekly to quarterly to annually).
- **Drill-down:** Increasing levels of detail are revealed (the complement of roll-up).
- **Pivot:** Cross tabulation (also referred as rotation) is performed.
- **Slice and dice:** Performing projection operations on the dimensions.
- **Sorting:** Data is sorted by ordinal value.
- **Selection:** Data is available by value or range.
- **Derived (computed) attributes:** Attributes are computed by operations on stored and derived values.

Because data warehouses are free from the restrictions of the transactional environment there is an increased efficiency in query processing. Among the tools and techniques used are: query transformation, index intersection and union, special ROLAP (relational OLAP) and MOLAP (multidimensional OLAP) functions, SQL extensions, advanced join methods, and intelligent scanning (as in piggy-backing multiple queries).

Improved performance has also been attained with parallel processing. Parallel server architectures include symmetric multiprocessor (SMP), cluster, and massively parallel processing (MPP), and combinations of these.

Knowledge workers and decision makers use tools ranging from parametric queries to ad hoc queries to data mining. Thus, the access component of the data warehouse must provide support of structured queries (both parametric and ad hoc). These together make up a managed query environment. Data mining itself uses techniques from statistical analysis and artificial intelligence. Statistical analysis can be performed by advanced spreadsheets, by sophisticated statistical analysis software, or by custom- written programs. Techniques such as lagging, moving averages, and regression analysis are also commonly employed. Artificial intelligence techniques, which may include genetic algorithms and neural networks, are used for classification and are employed to discover knowledge from the data warehouse that may be unexpected or difficult to specify in queries.

24.7 DATA WAREHOUSING TOOLS AND TECHNOLOGIES

in this section we examine the tools and technologies associated with building and managing a data warehouse and, in particular, we focus on the issues associated with the integration of these tools.

24.7.1 Extraction, Cleansing, and Transformation Tools

Selecting the correct extraction, cleansing and transformation tools are critical steps in construction of a data warehouse. There are an increasing number of vendors that are focused on fulfilling the requirements of data warehouse implementations as opposed to simply moving data between hardware platforms. The tasks of capturing data from a source system, cleansing and transformation it and then loading the results into a target system can be carried out either separate products, or by a single integrated solution. Integrated solutions fall into one of the following categories.

- Code generators
- Database data replication tools
- Dynamic transformation engines
- **Code Generators**

  Code generators create customized 3GL/4GL transformation programs based on source and target data definitions. The main issue with this approach is the management of the large number of problems required to support a complex corporate data warehouse. Vendors recognize this issue and some are developing management components employing techniques such as workflow methods and automated scheduling systems.

- **Database Data Replication Tools**

  Database data replication tools employ database triggers or a recovery log to capture changes to a single data source on one system and apply the changes to a copy of the source data located on a different system.

- **Dynamic Transformation Engines**

  Rule-driven dynamic transformation engines capture data from a source system at user-defined intervals, transform the data, and then send and load the results into a target environment. To date, most product support only relational data sources, but products are now emerging that non-relational source files and databases.

24.7.2 Data Warehouse DBMS

There is few integration issues associated with the data warehouse database. Due to the maturity of such products, most relational databases will integrate predictably with other types of software. However, there are issues associated with the potential size of the data warehouse database, parallelism in the database becomes an important issues, as well as the usual issues such as performance, scalability, availability and manageability, which must all the taken into consideration when choosing a DBMS.

Requirement for data warehouse DBMS

The specialized requirements for a relational DBMS suitable for data warehousing are published in a white paper (Red Bricks Systems, 1996) and are listed in Table 24.7.2(a).

Table 24.7.2 (a)

• Load Manager
• Load Processing
• Data Quality Management
• Query Performance
• Terabyte Scalability
• Mass User Scalability
• Networked Data Warehouse
• Warehouse Administration
• Integrated Dimensional Analysis
• Advanced Query functionality

Problems of Data Warehousing

The problems associated with developing and managing a data warehouse are listed in Table 24.7.2(b). (Greenfield, 1996)

Table 24.7.2 (a)

• Underestimation of resources for data loading
• Hidden problems with source systems
• Required data not captured
• Increased end-user demands

• Data homogenization
• High demand for resources
• Data ownership
• High maintenance
• Long-duration projects
• Complexity of integration

24.7.3 Data Warehouse Metadata

There are many issues associated with data warehouse integration, however in this section we focus on the integration of metadata that is 'data about data'. The management of the metadata in the warehouse is an extremely complex and difficult task. Metadata is used for a variety of purpose and the management of metadata is a critical issue in achieving a fully integrated data warehouse.

The major purpose of metadata is to show the pathway back to where the data began, so that the warehouse administrators know the history of any item in the warehouse. However, the problem is that metadata has several functions within the warehouse that relates to the process associated with data transformation and loading, data warehouse management, and query generation.

The metadata associated with data transformation and loading must describe the source data and any changes that were made to the data. For example, for each source filed there should be a unique identifier, original field name, source data type, and original location including the system and object name, along with the destination data type and destination table name. if the field is subject to any transformations such as a simple field type change to a complex set of procedure and functions, this should also be recorded.

The metadata associated with data management describes the data as it is stored in the warehouse. Every object in the database needs to be described including the data in each table, index, and view, and any associated constraints. This information is held in the DBMS system catalog, however, there are additional requirements for the purposes of the warehouse. For example, metadata should also describe any fields associated with aggregations, including a description of the aggregation that was performed. In addition, table range associated with the partition.

The metadata described above is also required by the query manager to generate appropriate queries. In turn, the query manger generates additional metadata about the queries that are run, which can be used to generate s history on all the queries and query profile for each user, group of users or the data warehouse.

Synchronizing Metadata

The major integration issue is how to synchronize the various types of metadata used throughout the data warehouse. The various tools of a data warehouse generate and use their own metadata, and to achieve integration, we require that tools are capable of sharing their metadata. The challenge is to synchronize metadata between products from different vendors using different metadata stores. For example, it is necessary to identify the correct item of metadata at the right level of detail in another product, and then sort out any coding difference between them.

This has to be changes to the metadata (or even meta-metadata), in one product needs to be conveyed to the other product. The task of synchronizing two products is highly complex, and therefore repeating this process for six or more products that make up the data warehouse can be resource intensive. However, integration of the metadata must be achieved.

In the beginning there were two major standards for metadata and modeling in the areas of data warehousing and component-based development proposed by the Meta Data Coalition (MDC) and the Object Management Group (OMG). However, these two industry organizations jointly announced that the MDC would merge into the OMG. As a result, the MDC discontinued operations and work contained in the OMG to integrate the two standards.

The merger of MDC into the OMG marked an agreement of the major data warehousing and metadata vendors to coverage on one standard, incorporating the best of the MDC's Open Information Model (OIM) with the best of the OMG's Common Warehouse Metamodel (CWM). The OMG's CWM builds on various standards, including OMG's UML (Unified Modeling Language), XMI (XMI Metadata Interchange), and MOF (Meta Object Facility),

Oracle, Unisys, Hyperion, Genesis, NCR, USB, and Dimension EDI.

24.8 BENEFITS OF DATA WAREHOUSING

The successful implementation of a data warehouse can bring major benefits to an organization including:

- **Potential high returns on investment** – An organization must commit a huge amount of resources to ensure that successful implementation of a data warehouse and the cost can vary enormously from ₹ 50,000 to over ₹ 10 million due to the variety of technical solutions available. However, a study by the International Data Corporation (IDC) in 1996 reported that average three-year returns on investment (ROI) in data warehousing reached 401%, with over 90% of the companies surveyed achieving over 40% ROI, half the companies achieving over 160% ROI, and a quarter with more than 600% ROI (IDC, 1996).
- **Competitive advantage** – The huge returns on investment for those companies that have successfully implemented a data warehouses is evidence of the enormous competitive advantage that accompanies this technology. The competitive advantage is gained by allowing decision makers access to data that can reveal previously unavailable, unknown and untapped information on, For example, customers, trends, and demands.
- **Increased productivity of corporate decision-makers** – Data warehousing improves the productivity of corporate decision-makers by creating an integrated database of consistent subject-oriented, historical data. It integrates data from multiple incompatible systems into a form that provides one consistent view of the organization. By transforming data meaningful information, a data warehouse allows corporate decision makers to perform more substantive, accurate, and consistent analysis.

SUMMARY

A subject-oriented, integrated, time-variant and non-volatile collection of data in support of management's decision-making process. A data warehouse is data management and data analysis technology. The data warehouse is a distributed data warehouse that is implemented over the web with no central data repository. The major components of a data warehouse include the operational data sources, operational data store, load manager, warehouse manager, query manager, detailed lightly and highly summarized data, archive/backup data, metadata and end user access tools.

Data warehousing focuses on the management of five primary data flows, namely the inflow, upflow, downflow, outflow and metaflow. The potential benefits of data warehousing are high returns on investment, substantial competitive advantage, and increased productivity or corporate decision-makers.

EXERCISES

1. What is a data warehouse?
2. What are the goals of a data warehouse?
3. What are the characteristics of the data in a data warehouse?
4. What is a data warehouse? How does it differ from a database?
5. What is a data cube? How is it used in data warehousing?
6. Define the following terms: star schema, snowflake schema, fact constellation, data marts.
7. Describe the characteristics of a data warehouse. Divide them into functionality of a warehouse and advantages users derive from it.
8. Describe the characteristics and main functions of the following components of a data warehouse:
   - Load manager
   - Warehouse manager
   - Query manager
   - Metadata
   - End-user access tools
9. Define the inflow, outflow, metaflow, upflow and downflow.
10. Describe the specialized requirements of a relational database management system (RDBMS) suitable for use in a data warehouse environment.

■

CHAPTER 25

KNOWLEDGE DISCOVERY IN DATABASES (KDD)

25.1 INTRODUCTION

In the past two decades we have experienced a tremendous increase in electronically available information. A META group survey on data warehouses projects from 1995 revealed that 19 percent of their commercial respondents were beyond the 50 Gigabyte (GB) level and 59 percent were expecting to exceed the same limit in less than a year. Many companies that rely on marketing have come to realize that useful information can be extracted from these huge databases. However this process of extraction has proved to be quite complex and time consuming. In recent years data storage has become cheaper and processing power more advanced making this type of data extraction a tractable goal. More recent applications of knowledge discovery include bio-informatics, biotechnology, medical diagnosis, genetic engineering, fraud detection etc.

25.2 KNOWLEDGE DISCOVERY

Knowledge Discovery is a new field that combines several techniques from computer science and Artificial Intelligence to search for relationships and global patterns in large databases. Knowledge discovery is defined as the non-trivial extraction of implicit, unknown and potentially useful information from data. The basic task of extracting knowledge from data is known as Data Mining, while knowledge discovery covers the entire process from selecting and pre-processing raw data to representing the knowledge. Knowledge discovery uses artificial intelligence, machine learning and neural network techniques to discover new relationships by sifting through as ocean of data to distil fresh answers to unstated questions. The insights from these discovered relationships and trends could result in quantum leaps in understanding the information hidden in the database.

Online data continues to grow at an explosive pace, due to the internet and the widespread use of database technology. This phenomenon has created in immense opportunity and the need for methodologies of Knowledge Discovery in Databases (KDD). An interdisciplinary area, KDD focuses upon building automated techniques for extracting useful knowledge from data. Research in this area draws principally upon methods from statistics, data management, pattern recognition and machine learning to deliver advanced techniques for business intelligence. Key advances in robust and scalable data mining techniques, methods for fast pattern detection in very large databases, text and web mining as well as innovative business-intelligence applications are some of the reasons that fuelled the growth of the KDD discipline.

25.3 KNOWLEDGE DISCOVERY IN DATABASES (KDD)

Knowledge Discovery in Databases (KDD) is the non-trivial extraction of implicit, previously unknown and potentially useful information from the databases. Many scientific and transactional business databases grow at a phenomenal rate. Both, the number and the size of databases are rapidly growing. This growth by far exceeds human capacities to analyze the databases in order to find implicit regularities, rules or clusters hidden in the data. Or in other words, the amount of data being collected in databases today for exceeds our ability to reduce and analyze data without the use of automated analysis techniques. Therefore, knowledge discovery becomes more and more important in databases and knowledge discovery in databases is the field that is evolving to provide automated analysis solutions.

Typical tasks for KDD are the identification of classes (clustering), the prediction of new, unknown objects (classification), and the discovery of associations or derivations in spatial databases. The term 'visual data mining' refers to the emphasis of integrating the user in the KDD process. Since these are challenging tasks, KDD algorithms should be incremental, i.e. when updating the database the algorithm does not have to be applied to the whole database.

Knowledge Discovery in Databases (KDD) is thus the process of discovering valuable information in large volumes of data by using pattern recognition technologies as well as statistical and machine learning techniques. KDD provides a means of extracting previously unknown information from the growing base of accessible data to create competitive advantages for organizations. KDD is often mentioned with Data Warehouses, Data Mining and OLAP.

A Data Warehouses contains large amounts of data in a read-only database where data from several operational systems are integrated, aggregated and historized. **OLAP** (On-Line Analytical Processing) is the multidimensional analysis of data. Existing hypotheses are verified or disproved with queries against the database. OLAP is verification-driven. **Data Mining** is the discovery-driven analysis of databases. KDD addresses the complete business process involving Data Mining and OLAP, i.e. from data collection to the deployment or results.

25.4 BASIC FEATURES OF KDD

Although there are many approaches to KDD, six common and essential elements qualify each as a knowledge discovery technique. The following are basic features that all KDD techniques share:

- All approaches deal with large amounts of data
- Efficiency is required due to volume of data
- Accuracy is an essential element
- All require the of a large of a high-level language
- All approaches use some form of automated learning
- All produce some interesting results

Large amounts of data are required to provide sufficient information to derive additional knowledge. Since large amounts of data are required, processing efficiency is essential. Accuracy is required to assure that discovered knowledge is valid. The results should be presented in a manner that is understandable by humans. One of the major premises of KDD is that the knowledge is discovered using intelligent learning techniques that sift through the data in an automated process. For this technique to be considered useful in terms of knowledge discovery, the discovered knowledge must be interesting; that is, must have potential value to the user.

25.5. ADVANTAGES OF KDD

KDD provides the capability to discover new and meaningful information by using existing data. KDD quickly exceeds the human capacity to analyze large data sets. The amount of data that requires processing and analysis in a large database exceeds human capabilities and the difficulty of accurately transforming raw data into knowledge surpasses the limits of traditional databases. Therefore, the full utilization of stored data depends on the use of knowledge discovery techniques.

The usefulness of future applications of KDD is far-reaching. KDD may be used as a means of information retrieval, in the same manner that intelligent agents perform information retrieval on the web. New patterns or trends in data may be discovered using these techniques. KDD may also be used as a basis for the intelligent interfaces of tomorrow, by adding a knowledge discovery component to a database engine or by integrating KDD with spreadsheets and visualizations.

25.6 PHASES OF KDD

Knowledge discovery also known as data discovery uses data warehouses technology as a starting point. To provide meaningful results, the knowledge discovery software needs extensive and detailed data. The basic steps of knowledge discovery are given below:

- **Selection** – creating possible segmentation criteria for selecting data.
- **Pre-Processing-** normalize, rationalize and cleanse the data.
- **Transformation** – create general representation and tables of metadata.
- **Extraction** – extract patterns from the data warehouses, turning data into knowledge.
- **Interpretation and Evaluation** – evaluate utility of extracted and identified patterns.

The first three steps (selection, pre-processing and transformation) are usually done during the data warehousing stage. The growth step, the extraction of patterns, is performed by applying artificial intelligence or statistical techniques based on initial patterns created from the metadata. Clearly the metadata and knowledge representation activities are important. The interpretation of the results, the fifth step, can be partially automated based on predefined criteria; but for the most part, it is a manual evaluation process. If we could completely define the evaluation criteria, then the process would simply be a database lookup.

25.7 KDD TECHNIQUES

Learning algorithms are in integral part of KDD. Learning techniques may be supervised or unsupervised. In general, supervised learning techniques enjoy a better success rate as defined in terms of usefulness of discovered knowledge. Learning algorithms are complex and generally considered the hardest part of any KDD technique. Machine discovery is one of the earliest fields that have contributed to KDD. While machine discovery relies solely on an autonomous approach to information discovery, KDD typically combines automated approaches with human interaction to assure accurate, useful and understandable results.

There are many different approaches that are classified as KDD techniques. There are quantitative approaches, such as the probabilistic and statistical approaches. There are approaches that utilize visualization techniques. There are classification approaches such as Bayesian classification, inductive logic, data cleaning/pattern discovery and decision tree analysis. Other approaches include deviation and trend analysis, genetic algorithms, neural networks and hybrid approaches that combine two or more techniques. Because of the ways that these techniques can be used and combined, there is a lack of agreement on how these techniques should be categorized. For example, the Bayesian approach may be logically grouped with probabilistic approaches, classification approaches, or visualization approaches. For the sake of organization, each approach described here is included in the group that it seemed to fit best. However, this selection is not intended to imply a strict categorization.

25.8 PROBABILISTIC APPROACH

This family of KDD techniques utilizes graphical representation models to compare different knowledge representations. These models are based on capabilities and data independencies. They are useful for applications involving uncertainty and applications structured such that a probability may be assigned to each "outcomes" or bit of discovered knowledge. Probabilistic techniques may be used in diagnostic systems and in planning and control systems. Automated probabilistic tools are available both commercially and in the public domain.

25.9 STATISTICAL APPROACH

The statistical approach uses rule discovery and is based on data relationships. An inductive learning algorithm can automatically select useful join paths and attributes to construct rules from a database with many relations. This type of induction is used to generalize pattern in the data and to construct rules from the noted patterns. On-Line Analytical Processing (OLAP) is an example of a statistically oriented approach. Automated statistical tools are available both commercially and in the public domain. An example of a statistical application is determining that all transactions in a sales database that start with a specified transaction code are cash sales. The system would note that of all the transactions in the database, only 60% are cash sales. Therefore, the system may accurately conclude that 40% are collectibles.

25.10 CLASSIFICATION APPROACH

Classification is probably the oldest and most widely used of all the KDD approaches. This approach groups data according to similarities or classes. There are many types of classification techniques and numerous automated tools available.

The **Bayesian Approach** to KDD is a graphical model that uses directed arcs exclusively to form a directed acyclic graph. Although the Bayesian approach uses probabilities and a graphical means or representation, it is also considered a type of classification. Bayesian networks are typically used when then uncertainty associated with an outcome can be expressed in terms of a probability. This approach relies on encoded domain knowledge and has been used for diagnostic systems. Other pattern recognition applications, including the Hidden Markov Model, can be modeled using a Bayesian approach. Automated tools are available both commercially and in the public domain.

Pattern Discovery and Data Cleaning is another type of classification that systematically reduces a large database to a few pertinent and informative records. If redundant and uninteresting data is eliminated, the task of discovering patterns in the data is simplified. This approach works on the premise of the old adage, "less is more." The pattern discovery and data cleaning techniques are useful for reducing enormous volumes of application data, such as those encountered when analyzing automated sensor recordings. Once the sensor readings are reduced to a manageable size using a data cleaning technique, the patterns in the data may be more easily recognized. Automated tools using these techniques are available both commercially and in the public domain.

The **Domain Tree Approach** uses production rules, builds a directed acyclical graph based on data premises and classifies data according to its attributes. This method requires that data classes are discrete and predefined. The primary use of this approach is for predictive models that may be appropriate for either classification or regression techniques. Tools for decision tree analysis are available commercially and in the public domain.

25.11 DEVIATION AND TREND ANALYSIS

Pattern detection by filtering important trends is the basis for this KDD approach. Deviation and trend analysis techniques are normally applied to temporal databases. A good application for this type of KDD is the analysis of traffic on large telecommunications networks. AT&T uses such a system to locate and identify circuits that exhibit deviation (faculty behaviour). The sheer volume of data requiring analysis makes an automated technique imperative. Trend-type analysis might also prove useful for astronomical and oceanographic data, as they are time-based and voluminous. Public domain tools are available for this approach.

25.12 OTHER APPROACHES

Neural networks may be used as a method of knowledge discovery. Neural networks are particularly useful for pattern recognition and are sometimes grouped with the classification approaches. There are tools available in the public domain and commercially. Genetic algorithms, also used for classification are similar to neural networks although they are typically considered more powerful. There are tools for the genetic approach available commercially.

- **Statistical Approach** – A hybrid approach to KDD combines more than one approach and is also called a multi-paradigmatic approach. Although implementation may be more difficult, hybrid tools are able to combine the strengths or various approaches. Some of the commonly used methods combine visualization techniques, induction, neural networks and rule-based systems to achieve the desired knowledge discovery. Deductive databases and genetic algorithms have also been used in hybrid approaches. There are hybrid tools available commercially and in the public domain.

SUMMARY

Knowledge Discovery in Databases (KDD) is the non-trivial extraction of implicit, previously unknown and potentially useful information from the databases. Many scientific and transactional business databases grow at a phenomenal rate. Both, the number and the size of databases are rapidly growing. This growth by far exceeds human capacities to analyze the databases in order to find implicit regularities, rules or clusters hidden in the data. KDD is the process of discovering valuable information in large volumes of data by using pattern recognition technologies as well as statistical and machine learning techniques. KDD provides a means of extracting previously unknown information from the growing base of accessible data to create competitive advantages for organizations. All KDD techniques share features like dealing with large amounts of data, high efficiency and accuracy in handling hug volumes of data, necessity of a high-level language, use of automated learning, discovery of interesting and useful information, etc.

There are many different approaches that are classified as KDD techniques. There are quantitative approaches, such as the probabilistic and statistical approaches. There are approaches that utilize visualization techniques. There are classification approaches such as Bayesian classification, inductive logic, and data cleaning/pattern discovery and decision tree analysis. Other approaches include deviation and trend analysis, genetic algorithms, neural networks and hybrid approaches that combine two or more techniques.

KDD is a rapidly expanding field with promise for great applicability. Knowledge discovery seems to be the new database technology for the coming years. The need for automated discovery tools has tools has caused an explosion in the number and type of tools available commercially and it the public domain. It is anticipated that commercial database systems of the future will include KDD capabilities in the form of intelligent database interfaces. Some types of information retrieval may benefit from the use of KDD techniques. Due to the potential applicability of knowledge discovery in so many diverse areas there are growing research opportunities in this field

EXERCISES

1. What is knowledge discovery?
2. Why is knowledge discovery important?
3. What are the techniques used for knowledge discovery?
4. What is knowledge discovery in databases?
5. Why is KDD important and what are its uses?
6. What are the technologies used for KDD?
7. What are the typical tasks for KDD?
8. What do you mean by the terms data warehouses, OLAP and data mining?
9. What are the basic features of KDD?
10. What are the advantages of KDD?
11. What are the different phases of KDD?
12. What are the different KDD techniques?
13. What are the probabilistic KDD approaches?
14. What do you mean by the statistical KDD approach?
15. What is the Bayesian KDD approach?
16. What do you mean by the pattern discovery and data cleaning KDD approach?
17. What do you mean by the decision tree KDD approach?
18. What are the deviation and trend analysis KDD approaches?
19. What are the hybrid KDD approaches?
20. What is the future of KDD?

■

CHAPTER 26

ON-LINE TRANSACTION PROCESSING (OLTP)

26.1 INTRODUCTION

During the past 30 years, companies around the globe have embraced on-line transaction processing (OLTP) as an integral part of doing business. This technology, which has evolved into a huge market while spurring extensive innovation, is particularly vital to business-critical applications conducted by a wide variety of industries, including banking, securities, telecommunications, retail transportation, manufacturing, and health care.

Prior to the development of OLTP systems, companies generally limited the commercial application of computers to automated record-keeping and off-line batch processing. In the 1950s and 1960s, many users found computers to be too expensive and unreliable to connect them directly to their business. Instead, the big mainframe machines were placed in a back room or basement where each night they processed the day's receipts and generated reports for the following morning.

Starting in the early 1970s, different industries began to adopt OLTP strategies by tying their computer systems directly to business transactions. The airline industry was the first to make a massive investment in OLTP technology, spending hundreds of millions of dollars on large mainframes to develop on-line customized reservation systems. This novel approach made booking reservations much more efficient by connecting an airline's most valuable asset-seat inventory-to an on-line system. Nevertheless, any company that decided to run its business electronically rather than on paper took a huge risk. Early OLTP systems were technically difficult to build, expensive to operates, and unreliable, banks, manufactures, and other companies attempted to convert batch mainframe computers by painstakingly programming them to perform jobs they were never designed to do. These pioneers recognized the important benefits of collecting and managing information about customers, inventory, and orders in a timely manner, but also feared losing transactions or access to the completely if a computer failed. To bolster system reliability, therefore, designers typically used two machines together to provide systems redundancy, or backup capability. Much like trying to fit a square peg in a round hole, these contrived OLTP systems were awkward, short-term fixes to important, complex business problems.

Tandem computers incorporated was formed in 1974 to find a better answer. In less than 18 months, the startup company introduced the world's first fault-tolerant computer systems designed specifically to handle OLTP applications for the business-critical market. Called the nonstop system, the machine eliminated the pain from OLTP by offering a technological solution, to industries such as the airlines and the financial intuitions, who were struggling to keep their systems running round-the-clock. In essence, Tandem created a new computer market.

26.2 DESIGNING CRITICAL OLTP FEATURES

From a business point of view, moving from a paper-based to on-line business represented a tremendous leap of faith. System requirements for OLTP were quite different than those for batch processing modes. With so much at stake, OLTP computers needed to combine high availability, a smooth upgrade path, flexible connectivity with other systems, and the ability to maintain the highest possible data integrity.

In the manufacturing industry, for example, the need for higher shop floor efficiency, better responsiveness to customer demands, and cost effective inventory control drove the trend toward OLTP systems. Manufacture typically scheduled their entire production operations by paper, with followed the product-whether a car, computer, or toy-through the factory cycle. Once warehouse inventory was checked out to the shop floor, no efficient way existed to track individual components. This lack of immediate, on-line information from the factory had severe cost consequences; companies routinely ordered too much inventory, did not schedule workers efficiently, and often failed to indentify quality-control problems until after products left and plant.

On-line information allowed manufactures to implement Just-In-Time (JIT) inventory control with bar code tracking. This capability permitted tighter management of raw material purchases and enabled companies to monitor the movement of components as they flowed through production. The key to success was that properly designed OLTP systems minimized the risk and maximized the benefits of replacing paper-based processes with computer-driven applications.

To meet business requirements in a wide range of industries, Tandem designed a number of key fundamental into its systems, which the developers regarded as critical to any true OLTP environment. These included fault tolerance the ensure continuous system availability, linear expandability, distributed databases, networking, data integrity and system security.

First and foremost, computers processing transactions in real time could not fail or corrupt data. Banks routinely send wire transfers worth billions of dollars between corporate accounts and the financial consequences of losing a large transaction due to a system crash would be disastrous. In manufacturing, a large French automobile maker that produces more than twenty lakh vehicles per year calculates it would cost ₹ 200000 each minute the company's production line is down. Simply stated, industries that run their operations on-line need to have their computer systems up and running all the time.

A parallel processing architecture solved this availability problem by providing the first fault-tolerant design, which prevented any single hardware or software malfunction from disrupting system operations. The computer systems divide the workload among loosely coupled processors that perform multiple tasks simultaneously. If a processor fails, its functions are automatically taken over by the other central processing unit.

In addition a fault-tolerant operating system further protects the computer by enabling users to run primary and backup software processes in separate CPUs for all applications. Development of a pioneering requester/server software structure also divided applications into client/server components. The client portion was dedicated to capturing the on-line transaction. While the server handled the database part of the transactions. Introduced in the mid 1970s, this fundamental OLTP concept emerged as an early precursor to the client/server software strategies touted today.

Moving from a batch environment to on-line processing also required linear expandability. In the 1960s, IBM, DEC and other computer manufactures had introduced the model concept, where customers could initially purchase a small computer, then replace it with larger models from a compatible family of products. Although this concept protected business to a certain degree as processing needs grew, pulling out one wheeling in another also caused system downtime and disrupted operations.

With their businesses tied tightly to computer systems in an on-line environment, many companies could not afford the downtime required to bring in a new model. Training and software reprogramming issues presented additional obstacles. Moreover, planners had trouble predicting how fast transaction volumes might grow as customers reacted to on-line services, making it difficult to select which size model to install.

Therefore, enterprises faced a dilemma: if business was good and transaction volumes high, they still might run into problems if an undersized computer could not provide enough power to handle the processing load; if they purchased an oversized system and business volumes did not grow, their service could become too expensive.

The concept of modular expandability for commercial OLTP computing solved this dilemma by enabling companies to add processors and disk storage on-line, without any reprogramming. This also allowed users to increase the size of their system configuration over many years by simply plugging in additional processing capacity. If business increased dramatically, companies could seamlessly upgrade to more powerful computers without disruption to on-line services.

The need for distributed computing represented another important difference between OLTP and batch processing environments. As a network application, OLTP involves many different sources of business transactions. Enterprises therefore need to provide a common view of their service to customers at various network locations, such as automated teller machine (ATM) sites or worldwide branch offices that handle local order entry.

A parallel processing architecture allows centralized or distributed processing. Data can either reside on a single computer or be distributed across multiple systems around the world. This design enables companies to link different transaction locations via a transparent network, where the distributed database appears to all users as a single system. Moreover, the introduction of a fault-tolerant structured query language implementation standard by the American National Standards Institute (ANSI), provided software programmers with the ability to design applications capable of managing highly complex distributed databases.

Today, OLTP has become pervasive throughout the business world. From factories to gas stations to stock exchanges, high-availability on-line computer systems play a key role in capturing and processing transactions, as well as enhancing customer services and enabling industries to offer new products. In the future, OLTP will continue to evolve and promote innovation as banking retail, telecommunications, manufacturing and other industries venture into new areas of endeavour.

26.3 APPLICATION OF OLTP

OLTP systems are being used in many areas like banking, telecommunication, air and railway ticket reservation and so on. In the next few sections we will see the practical applications of OLTP.

26.3.1 OLTP in the Banking System

Prior to destination, the banking industry was not very customer friendly. Open weekdays 10:00 A.M. to 3:00 P.M., most bank branches maintained hours that often it inconvenient for customers to conduct financial transactions. Although increased competition led banks to distinguish their service levels by extending branch hours and offering other incentives, it also resulted in higher staff costs. The need to offer customers better, more diverse services without significantly increasing operating costs drove the banking industry to look for alternative delivery platforms which did not require adding more employees. This key objective marked the advent of automated teller machines.

However, early ATMs were off-line, which required the bank to either take the risk that some customers might withdraw unavailable funds, or place limits on the sessions, thus offsetting the increased convenience of the machines. Card holders could only withdraw up to a predefined cash limit and accounts were settled after hours via batch processing on a mainframe computer. Even through a few financial institutions went through the extensive task of placing their ATMs on-line, the machines typically still remained operational only while the bank was open. The introduction of the nonstop system helped solve this problem. Banks needed reliable, up-to-date, instantaneous information about account balances to offer ATM services and the computers provided the timely transaction data required.

26.3.1.1 Expanding the use of OLTP systems

With the initial success of on-line ATMs as cash disbursement machines, banks moved to expand use of their OLTP systems into areas. Efficient, highly reliable OLTP technology made the evolution painless. In addition, information systems managers were eager to find new uses for the on-line computers to justify spending millions of dollars on a computer system designed for a new one market application. As a result, financial institutions began using OLTP networks to support new type of electronic payment methods, including the wire transfer systems that moved billions of dollars between banks on a daily basis. The high availability, reliability and data security provided by OLTP systems ensured that the funds would not be lost or routed incorrectly. Moreover, banks also developed corporate cash management products for their customers that recognized the need for timely, efficient funds transfer. Home banking systems were introduced, which allowed customers to pay bills, make balance inquiries and transfer funds between different accounts. More recently, new kinds of voice-activated delivery systems such as smart telephones, pager technologies and toll free number call centers have reduced the cost to the point where home banking is more attractive to a wider audience.

26.3.1.2 Redefining OLTP

Today, the banking industry is redefining OLTP. Until recently, OLTP primarily involved on-line credit and debit processing, where the system applied simple logic to business transactions and provided an answer. For example, when a customer used an ATM to withdraw ₹ 2000, the OLTP system checked the account for available funds, dispensed the money, and debited the account. If the account did not contain at least ₹ 2000, the system routinely denied the withdrawal, often resulting in an unhappy customer. With competition increasing throughout the banking industry, institutions must further differentiate their services to attract and maintain customers. In fact, customer service is the primary battleground in finance today. Providing basic transaction processing through an ATM network is no longer enough. Innovative banks instead are seeking a competitive edge by changing their focus from account-oriented transaction processing to information processing, which places greater emphasis on customer service and satisfaction.

The move toward information processing is the next significant step in the evolution from account driven to customer-oriented banking. It enables institutions to consider the sum total of an individual's banking relationship-including how long he or she has been a customer and the amount to money kept in savings, certificates of deposit, or other accounts-when making a decision to dispense cash, approve loans or grant lines or credit. By capturing information on-line, a bank may allow the customer to withdraw ₹ 2000 cash from an ATM even if his or her checking account lacks sufficient funds.

26.3.2 Bringing Stock Exchanges On-line

In addition to playing a key role in the evolution of banking, OLTP has made a dramatic impact on another sector of the finance industry-stock exchanges. In the 1970s many financial markets were notoriously unreliable due to frequent system outages. Computers were primarily used to report the day's trades, but they did not handle transactions on-line. Volume was also very limited; major exchanges traded less than 20 million shares per day on averages. Seeking constant availability the timeliness in reporting trades, the New York Stock Exchange automated with OLTP systems, followed by NASDAQ and scores of the other markets. The payoff has been tremendous; today the combination of OLTP technology and disaster backup sites has all but eliminated computer downtime and reporting delays. With modular expandability, the systems can also easily handle huge trading volumes, which routinely reach more than 200 million shares per day. And although some exchanges still require large amounts of paper to settle trades, a growing number have moved to totally electronic trading, where OLTP computers match a sell request with a buy order or process the entire transaction.

26.3.3 OLTP in Telecommunications

Spurred by increased competition, business critical OLTP systems have proliferated throughout the telecommunication industry. Today, on-line technology is positioned to facilitate and support a wide variety of emerging customer services, ranging from smart phones and private virtual networks to wireless communications and universal numbers.

Much like banking institutions, telephone companies were often slow paced and reluctant to change.

Telephone companies took great care to protect their networks; such provided highly reliable basic service. In many cases, technical managers shunned innovations that required changing the network. Although some telephone companies attempted to automate their cumbersome billing and paper handing functions with batch processing, the system primarily impacted labour requirements rather than the way in which industry conducted its business.

Business critical OLTP systems today are making a tremendous impact throughout the telecommunication industry by providing enhanced network intelligence that facilitates new services and improves productivity. More and more, phone companies are demonstrating how OLTP fundamentals fit hand-in-glove with telecommunications' philosophy and standards. One key example is that telephone companies now routinely serve as billing agents for retailers. OLTP networks provide the physical resources necessary to handle a wide range of electronic transactions, including catalog shopping or ordering home-delivered restaurant meals, which currently account for more than 20 percent of all retail sales. Moreover, consumers can use their touchtone phones to pay monthly bills, including phone service charges. In addition to enhancing customer convenience, this capability benefits the telephone companies and banks by eliminating millions of paper invoices and checks, which reduces costs and enables both industries to serve more customers with fewer people.

During the past several years, improvements in basic network intelligence have also advanced many customer services, including toll free numbers and number translation capabilities. When a caller dials a toll free number, the network quickly translates it into actual business number and routes the call to its proper destination.

SUMMARY

During the past 30 years, companies around the globe have embraced on-line transaction processing (OLTP) as an integral part of doing business. This technology, which has evolved into a huge market while spurring extensive innovation, is particularly vital to business-critical applications conducted by a wide variety of industries, including banking, securities, telecommunications, retail transportation, manufacturing, and health care.

In the manufacturing industry, for example, the need for higher shop floor efficiency, better responsiveness to customer demands, and cost effective inventory control drove the trend toward OLTP systems. Manufacture typically scheduled their entire production operations by paper, with followed the product-whether a car, computer, or toy-through the factory cycle. Once warehouse inventory was checked out to the shop floor, no efficient way existed to track individual components. This lack of immediate, on-line information from the factory had severe cost consequences; companies routinely ordered too much inventory, did not schedule workers efficiently, and often failed to indentify quality-control problems until after products left and plant.

Prior to destination, the banking industry was not very customer friendly. Open weekdays 10:00 A.M. to 3:00 P.M., most bank branches maintained hours that often it inconvenient for customers to conduct financial transactions. Although increased competition led banks to distinguish their service levels by extending branch hours and offering other incentives, it also resulted in higher staff costs. The need to offer customers better, more diverse services without significantly increasing operating costs drove the banking industry to look for alternative delivery platforms which did not require adding more employees. This key objective marked the advent of automated teller machines.

EXERCISES

1. What is on-line transaction processing?
2. Describe the evolution of OLTP.
3. What are the critical features of OLTP systems?
4. What are the practical applications of OLTP?
5. Describe the evolution of OLTP technology in the banking industry.
6. Describe the current use of OLTP technology in the banking industry.
7. How is OLTP helping the stock exchanges?
8. Explain the use of OLTP in the point-of-sale and retail application.
9. Describe the advantage of using OLTP in the telecommunication industry?
10. What are the future trends in OLTP technology?

CHAPTER 27

ON-LINE ANALYTICAL PROCESSING (OLAP)

27.1 INTRODUCTION

OLAP is the term that describes a technology that multi-dimensional view of aggregate data to provide quick access to strategic information for the purposes of advanced analysis. OLAP enables users to gain a deeper understanding and knowledge about various aspects of their corporate data through fast, consistent, intensive access to a wide variety of possible views of the data. OLAP allows the user to view corporate data in such a way that it is a better model of the true dimensionality of the enterprise. While OLAP systems can easily answer 'who?' and 'what?' questions, it is their ability to answer 'what if?' and 'why?' a type question that distinguishes them from general purpose queries tools. OLAP enables decision-making about future actions. A typical OLAP calculation can be more complex than simply aggregating data, for example, 'compare the numbers of properties sold for each type of property in the different regions of Great Britain for each year since 2000'. Hence, the type of analysis available from OLAP range from basic navigation and browsing (referred to as slicing and dicing), to calculation, to more complex analyses such as time series and complex modeling.

The OLAP Council has published an analytical processing benchmark referred to as APB-1. The aim of the APB-1 is to measure a server's overall OLAP performance rather the performance of individual tasks. To ensure the relevance of the APB-1 to actual applications, the operations performed on the database are based on the most common business operations, which include the following:

- Bulk loading of data from internal or external sources
- Incremental loading of data from operational systems
- Aggregation of input level data along hierarchies
- Calculation of new data based on business models
- Time series analysis
- Queries with a high degree of complexity
- Drill down through hierarchies
- Ad–hoc queries
- Multiple online sessions

OLAP applications are also judged on their ability to provide just-in-time (JIT) information, which is regarded as being a core requirement of supporting effective decision making. Accessing a server's ability this requirement is more than measuring processing performance and includes its abilities to model complex business relationship and to respond to changing business requirement.

27.2 OLAP TOOLS

There are many varieties of OLAP tools available in the marketplace. This choice has resulted in some confusion, with much debate regarding what OLAP actually means to a potential buyer and in particular what are the available architectures for OLAP tools. In 1993, E.F. Codd formulated twelve rules as the basis for selecting OLAP tools.

1. Multi-dimensional conceptual view
2. Transparency
3. Accessibility
4. Consistent reporting performance
5. Client server architecture
6. Generic dimensionality
7. Dynamic sparse matrix handing
8. Multi-user support
9. Unrestricted cross-dimensional operations
10. Intuitive data manipulation
11. Flexible reporting
12. Unlimited dimensions and aggregation tools

27.3 CATEGORIES OF OLAP TOOLS

OLAP tools are categorized according to the architecture used to store and process multidimensional data. There are four main categories of OLAP tools as defined by Berson and Smith (1997) and Pendse and Creeth (2002) including:

1. Multi-dimensional OLAP (MOLAP)
2. Relational OLAP (ROLAP)
3. Hybrid OLAP (HOLAP)
4. Desktop OLAP (DOLAP)

27.3.1 Multi-Dimensional OLAP

MOLAP tools use specialized data structure and multi-dimensional database management system to organize, navigate and analyze data. To enhance query performance the data is typically aggregated and stored according to predicated usage. MOLAP data structures use array technology and efficient storage techniques that minimize the disk space requirements through sparse data management. MOLAP tools provide excellent performance when the data is used as designed, and the focus is on data for a specific decision support application. Traditionally, MOLAP tools require a tight coupling of the data application layer and presentation layer. However, recent trends segregate the OLAP from the data structures through the use of published application programming interface (API). The typical architecture for MOLAP tools is shown in Figure 27.3.1.

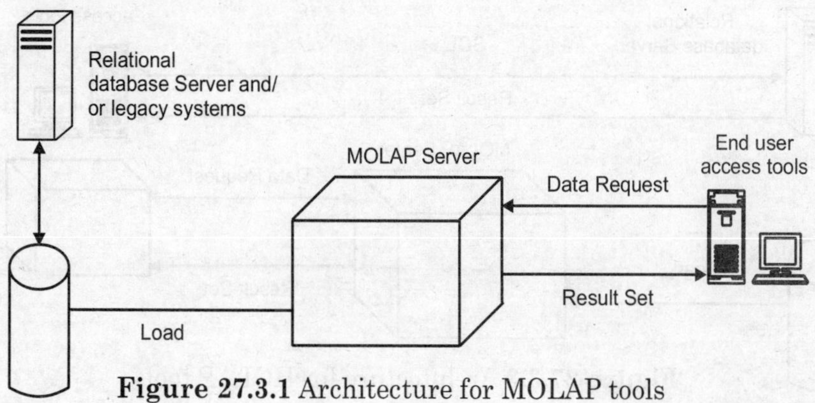

Figure 27.3.1 Architecture for MOLAP tools

27.3.2 Relational OLAP

Relational OLAP is the fastest growing type of OLAP tool. This growth in response to users' demands to analyze ever-increasing amounts of data and due to the realization that users cannot store all the data they require in MOLAP databases. ROLAP supports RDBMS products through the use of a metadata layer, thus avoiding the requirement to create a static multi-dimensional data structure. This facilities the creation of multiple multi-dimensional views of the two dimensional relation. To improve performance, some ROLAP products have enhanced SQL engines to support the complexity of multi-dimensional analysis, while others recommend, or require to support the complexity denormalized database designs such as the star schema. The typical architecture for ROLAP tools is shown in Figure 27.3.2

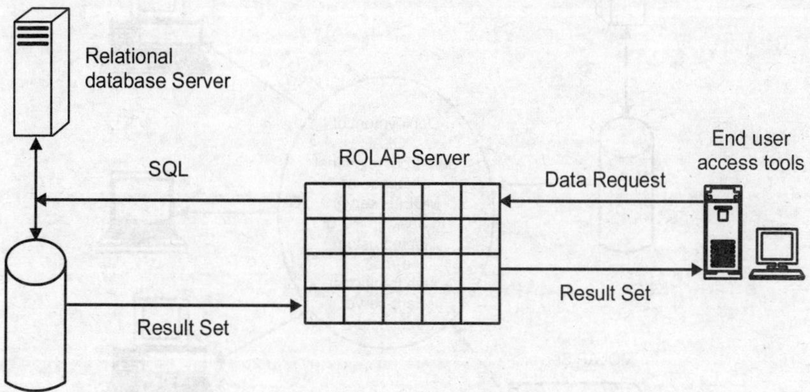

Figure 27.3.2 Architecture for ROLAP tools

27.3.3 Hybrid OLAP

Hybrid OLAP tools provide limited analysis capability, either directly against RDBMS products, or using an intermediate MOLAP server. HOLAP tools deliver selected data directly from the DBMS or via a MOLAP server to the desktop in the form of a data cube, where it is stored analyzed and maintained locally vendors promote this technology as being relatively simple to install and administer with reduced cost and maintenance. The typical architecture for HOLAP tools is shown in Figure 27.3.3.

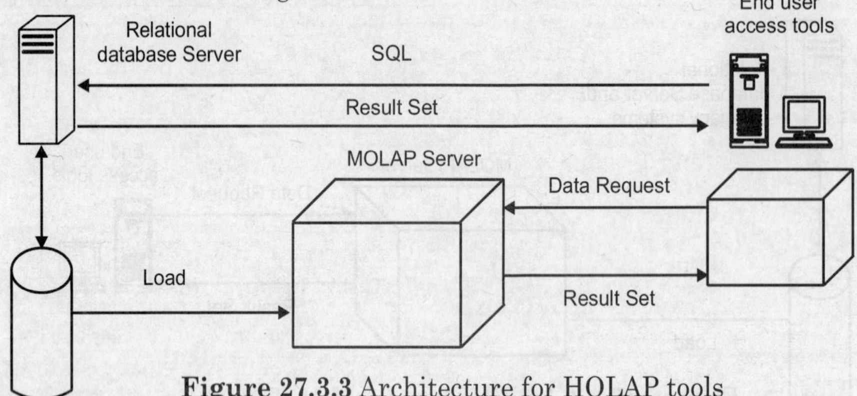

Figure 27.3.3 Architecture for HOLAP tools

27.3.4 Desktop OLAP

An increasingly popular category of OLAP tools is Desktop OLAP. DOLAP tools store the OLAP data in client based files and support multi-dimensional processing using a client multi-dimensional engine. DOLAP requires that relatively small extracts of data are held on client machines. This data may be distributed in advance or on demand. As with multi-dimensional databases on the server, OLAP data may be held on disk or in RAM, however, some DOLAP products allow only read access. Most vendors of DOLAP exploit the power of desktop PC to perform some, if not most, multi-dimensional calculations.

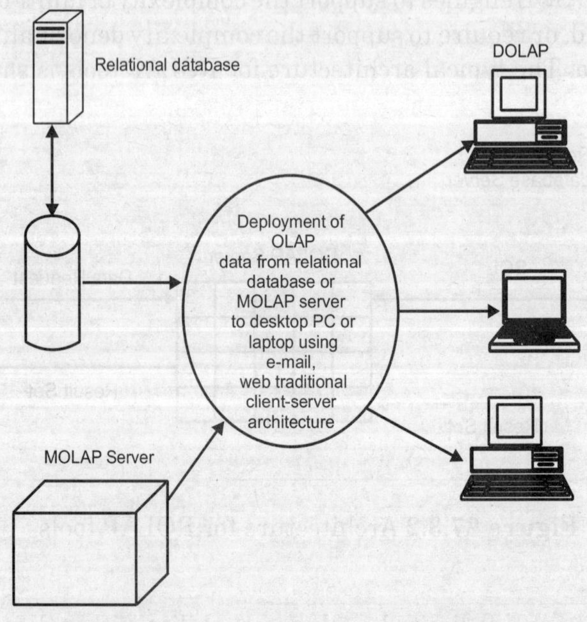

Figure 27.3.4 Architecture for DOLAP tools

The administration of a DOLAP database is typically preformed by a central server or processing routine that prepare data cubes or sets of data for each user. Once the basic processing is done, each user can then access their portion of the data. The typical architecture for DOLAP tools is shown in Figure 27.3.4.

27.4 OLAP APPLICATIONS

There are many examples of OLAP applications in various functional areas as listed Table 27.4.

Table 27.4 Examples of OLAP applications in various functional areas.

Functional Area	Examples of OLAP applications
Finance	Budgeting, activity based costing, financial analysis.
Sales	Sales analysis and sales forecasting
Marketing	Market research analysis, sales forecasting, promotions analysis
Manufacturing	Production planning and defect analysis

As essential requirement of all OLAP applications is ability to provide users with JIT information, which is necessary to make effective decisions about an organization's strategic directions. JIT information is computed data that usually reflects complex relationships and is often calculated on the fly. Analysing and modeling complex relationships are practical only if presence times are consistently short. In addition, because the nature of data relationships may not be known in advance, the data model must be flexible. A truly flexible data model ensures that OLAP systems can respond to changing business requirements as required for effective decision making.

- Multi-dimensional views of data
- Support for complex calculations
- Time intelligence

Multi-dimensional views of data

The ability to represent Multi-dimensional views of corporate data is a core requirement of building a realistic business model. For example, in the case of client server users may require to view property sales data by property type, property location, branch, sales personnel and time. A Multi-dimensional view of data provides the basis for analytical processing through flexible access to corporate data. Furthermore, the underlying database design that provides the Multi-dimensional views of data should treat all dimensions equally. In other words the database design should:

- Not influence the type of operations that are allowable on a given dimension or the rate at which these operations are performed.

- Enable users to analyze data across any dimension at any level of aggregation with equal functionality and ease.
- Support all multi-dimensional views of data in the most intuitive way possible.

Support for complex calculations

OLAP software must provide a range of powerful computational methods such as that required by sales forecasting, which uses trend algorithms such as moving averages and percentage growth. Furthermore, the mechanisms for implementing computational methods should be clear and non-procedural. This should enable users of OLAP to work in a more efficient and self sufficient way. The OLAP council APB-1 performance benchmark contains a representative selection of calculations, both simple (calculation of budgets) and complex (such as forecasting).

Time intelligence

Time intelligence is a key feature of almost any analytical application as performance is almost always judged over time, For example, this month versus last month or this versus the same month last year. The time hierarchy is not always used in the same manner as other hierarchies. For example, a user may require to view, the sales for the month of May or the sales for the first months of 2004. Concepts such as year-to-date and period over period comparisons should be easily defined in an OLAP system.

27.5 OLAP BENEFITS

The benefits that potentially follow the successful implementation of an OLAP application include;

- Increased productivity of business end-users, IT developers, and consequently the entire organization. More controlled and timely access to strategic information can allow more effective decision making.
- Reduced backlog of applications development for IT staff by making end-users self-sufficient enough to make their own schema changes and build their own models.
- Retention of organizational control over the integrity of corporate data as OLAP applications is dependent on data warehouse and OLAP systems to refresh source level data.
- Reduced query drag and network traffic on OLAP systems or on the data warehouse.
- Improved potential revenue and profitability by enabling the organization to respond more quickly to market demands.

27.6 DIFFERENCE BETWEEN OLTP AND OLAP

	OLTP	OLAP
Source of data	Operational data: OLTP are the original source of the data	Consolidation data: OLAP data comes from the various OLAP databases
Purpose of data	To control and run fundamental business tasks	To help with planning problem solving and decision support
What the data reveals	A snapshot of ongoing business process	Multi-dimensional views of various kinds of business activities
Inserts and updates	Short and fast inserts and updates initiated by end users	Periodic long-running batch jobs refresh the data
Queries	Relatively standardized and simple queries returning relatively few records	Often complex queries involving aggregations
Processing speed	Typically very fast	Depends on the amount of data
Space requirements	Can be relatively small if historical data is archived	Larger due to the existence of aggregation structures and history data
Database design	Highly normalized with many tables	Typically denormalized with fewer tables; use of star and/ or snowflake schemas
Backup and recovery	Backup religiously	Instead of regular backup, some environments may consider simply reloading the OLAP data as a recovery method.

SUMMARY

OLAP is the term that describes a technology that multi-dimensional view of aggregate data to provide quick access to strategic information for the purposes of advanced analysis. OLAP is the dynamic synthesis, analysis, and consolidation of large volumes of multi-dimensional data. The key characteristics of OLAP applications include multi-dimensional views of data, support for complex calculations and time intelligence.

OLAP tools are categorized according to the architecture of database providing the data for the purposes of analytical processing. There are four main categories of OLAP tools: Multi-dimensional OLAP, Relational OLAP, Hybrid OLAP, and Desktop OLAP. E.F. Codd formulated twelve rules as the basis for selecting OLAP tools.

EXERCISES

1. Discuss what online analytical processing (OLAP) represents.
2. Describe the architecture, characteristics, and issues associated with each of the following categories of OLAP tools
   - MOLAP
   - ROLAP
   - HOLAP
   - DOLAP
3. Describe OLAP applications and identify the characteristics of such applications.
4. What are benefits of OLAP?
5. Compare OLAP and OLTP.

■

CHAPTER 28

DATA MINING

28.1 INTRODUCTION

Data mining the extraction of hidden predictive information from large databases is a powerful new technology with great potential to help companies focus on the most important information in their data warehouse. Data mining tools predict future trends and behaviours, allowing businesses to make proactive, knowledge-driven decisions. The automated, prospective analyses offered by data mining move beyond the analyses of past events provided by retrospective tools typical of decision support systems. Data mining tools can answer business questions that traditionally were too time consuming to resolve. They scour databases for hidden patterns, finding predictive information that experts may miss because it lies outside their expectations.

Most companies already collect and refine massive quantities of data. Data mining techniques can be implemented rapidly on exiting software and hardware platforms to enhance the value of existing information resources, and can be integrated with new products and systems as they are brought on-line. When implemented on high performance client/server or parallel processing computers, data mining tools can analyze massive databases to deliver answers to questions such as, " which clients are most likely to respond to my next promotional mailing, and why?"

28.2 WHAT IS DATA MINING?

We live in the age of information. The importance of collecting data that reflect your business or scientific activities to achieve competitive advantage is widely recognized now. Powerful systems for collecting data and managing it in large databases are already in the place in most large and mid-range companies. However, the bottleneck of turning this data into your success is the difficulty of extracting knowledge about the system that you study from the collected data. Consider the following questions:

- What goods should be promoted to this customer?
- What is the probability that a certain customer will responds to a planned promotion?
- Can one predict the most profitable securities to buy/sell during the next trading session?

- Will this customer default on a loan or pay back on schedule?
- What medical diagnosis should be assigned to this patient?
- How large the peak loads of a telephone or energy network are going to be?
- Why the facility suddenly starts producing defective goods?

These are all the questions that can probably be answered if information hidden among megabytes of data in your database can be found explicitly and utilized. Modelling the investigated systems and discovering relations that connect variables in a database in the objective of data mining.

The process of extracting valid, previously unknown, comprehensible, and actionable information from large databases and using it to make crucial business decisions.

Modern data mining systems self learn from the previous history of the investigated system, formulating and testing hypotheses about the rules, which this system obeys. When concise and valuable knowledge about the system of interest had been discovered, it can and should be incorporated into some decision support system, which helps the manager to make wise and informed business decisions.

Data mining uses a different model for the creation of information about data. We call this the discovery model. Data mining uses methodologies that can shift through the data in search of frequently occurring patterns, can detect trends, produce generalizations about the data, etc. These tools can discover these types of information with very little (or no) guidance from the user (see Figure 28.2). The discovery of these facts is not a consequence of a haphazard event. A well designed data mining tool is one that is designed and built so that the exploration of the data is done in such a way as to yield as large a number of useful facts about as possible in the shortest amount of time.

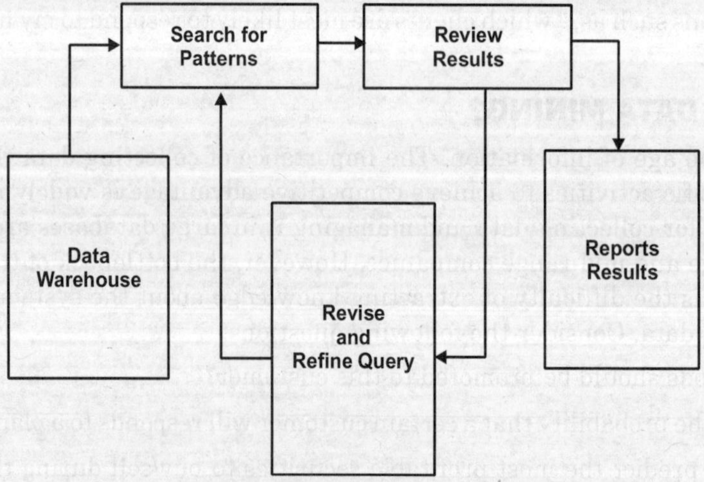

Figure 28.2 Data Mining Process

Comparing the process of finding information in a collection of data to that of mining diamonds in a diamond mine, we can say that verification is like drilling individual holes in a lode with the expectation of finding diamonds. Finding all or many diamonds in this way can be very insufficient. Discovery on the other hand, is similar to scooping out all the material in the lode and dumping it on plain fields so that all the glittering stones are thrown up into the open. Diamonds are then separated from the quartz by further inspection. In data mining, large amounts of data are inspected; facts discovered and brought to the attention of the person doing the mining. Unlike diamonds, which are easily distinguishable from quartz, business judgment must be used to separate the useful facts those that are very useful. Because this last step does not involve sifting through the raw data. Data mining is a more efficient mode of finding useful facts about data.

28.3 DATA MINING TECHNIQUES

There are four operations associated with data mining techniques, which include predictive modeling, database segmentation, link analysis, and deviation detection. Although any of the four major operations can be used for implementing any of the business applications listed in Table 28.3(a), there are certain recognized associations between the applications and the corresponding operations. For example, direct marketing strategies are normally implemented using the database segmentation operation, while fraud detection could be implemented by any of the four operations. Further, many applications work particularly when several operations are used. For example, a common approach to customer profiling is to segment the database first and then apply predicate modeling to the resultant data segment.

Table 28.3(a) Example of data mining applications

1.	**Retail/Marketing**
•	Identifying buying patterns of customers
•	Finding associations among customer demographic characteristics
•	Predicting response to mailing campaigns
•	Market basket analysis
2.	**Banking**
•	Detecting patterns of fraudulent credit card use
•	Identifying loyal customers
•	Predicting customers likely to change their credit card affiliation
•	Determining credit card spending by customer groups
3.	**Insurance**
•	Claims analysis
•	Predicting which customers will buy new policies
4.	**Medicine**
•	Characterizing patient behaviour to predict surgery visits
•	Identifying successful medical therapies for different illnesses

Techniques are specific implementations of the data mining operations. However, each operation has its own strengths and weakness. With this in mind, data mining tools sometimes offer a choice of operations to implement a technique. In Table 28.3(b), we list the main techniques associated with each of the four main data mining operations.

Table 28.3(b) Data mining operations and associated techniques

Operations	Data Mining Techniques
Predictive Modeling	Classification Value prediction
Database segmentation	Demographic clustering Neural clustering
Link analysis	Association discovery Sequential pattern discovery Similar time sequence discovery
Deviation detection	Statistics Visualization

28.3.1 Tasks solved by Data Mining

The main tasks that are solved by a data mining system are the following:

- Predicting – A task of learning a pattern from examples and using the developed model to predicts future values of the targets variable.
- Classification – A task of finding a function that maps an example into one of several discrete classes.
- Detection of relations – A task of searching for the most influential independence between various variables.
- Explicit modeling – A task of finding explicit formulae describing dependencies between various variables.
- Clustering – A task if identifying a finite set of categories or clusters that describe data.
- Deviation Detection – A task of determining the most significant changes in some key measures of data from previous or expected values.

28.3.2 Advantages of Data Mining

Data mining derives its name from the similarities between searching for valuable business information in a large database and mining a mountain for a vein of valuable ore. Both processes require either sifting through an immense amount of material, or intelligently probing it to find exactly where the value resides. Given databases of sufficient size and quality, data mining technology can generate new business opportunities by providing these capabilities:

- Automated prediction of trends and behaviours
- Automated discovery or previously unknown patterns
- Large database could be used

28.4 TECHNOLOGIES USED IN DATA MINING

The most commonly used techniques in data mining are:

- Neural Networks – Non linear predictive models that learn through training and resemble biological neural networks in structure.
- Rule Induction – The extraction of useful if then rules form data based on statistical significance.
- Evolutionary Programming – At present this is the youngest and evidently the most promising branch of data mining. The underlying idea of the method is that the system automatically formulates hypotheses about the dependence of the target variable on other variable in the form of programs expressed in an internal programming language.
- Case-Based Reasoning – The main idea underlying this method is very simple. To forecast a future situation, or to make a correct decision, such systems find the closet past analogs of the present situation and choose the same solution, which was the right one in those situations. That is why this method is also called the nearest neighbour method.
- Decision Tress – Tree-shaped structures that represent sets of decisions. These decisions generate rules for the classification of a data set.
- Genetic Algorithms – Optimization techniques that use processes such as genetic combination, mutation, and natural selection in a design based on the concepts of evolution.

28.5 DATA MINING TOOLS

There are a growing number of commercial data mining tools on the market place. The important features of data mining tools include data preparation, selection of data mining operations (algorithms), product scalability and performance, and facilities for understanding results.

- **Data Preparation**

  Data preparation is the most time-consuming aspect of data mining. Whatever tools can provide to facilitate this process will greatly speed up model development. Some of the functions that a tool may provide to support data preparation include: data cleansing, such as handling missing data; data describing, such as the distribution of values; data transforming, such as performing calculations on existing columns; and data sampling for the creation of training and validation data sets.
- **Selection of data mining operations**

  It is important to understand the characteristics of the operations (algorithms) used by a data mining tool to ensure that they meet the user's requirements. In particular, it is important to establish how the algorithms treat the data types of the response and predictor variable, how fast they train, and how fast they work on new data. (A predictor variable is the column in a database that can be used to build a predictor model, to predict values in another column.)

- **Product scalability and performance**

  Scalability and performance are important considerations when seeking a tool that is capable of dealing with increasing amounts of data in terms of numbers of rows and columns possibly and sophisticated validation controls. The need to provide scalability while maintaining satisfactory performance may require investigations into whether a tool is capable of supporting parallel processing using technologies such as SMP, MPP.

- **Facilities for understanding results**

  A good data mining tool should help the user understand the results by providing measures such as those describing accuracy and significance is useful formats (For example, confusion matrices) by allowing the user to perform sensitivity analysis on the result and by presenting the result in alternative ways (using, For example, visualization techniques). A confusion matrix shows the counts of the actual versus predicted class values. It shows not only how well model predicts, but also presents the details needed to see exactly where things may have gone wrong.

  Sensitivity analysis determines the sensitivity of a predicative model to small fluctuations in predictor value. Through this technique end-users can gauge the effects of noise and environmental change on the accuracy of the model.

  Visualization graphically displays data to facilitate better understanding of its meaning. Graphically capabilities range from simple scatter plots to complex multi-dimensional representations.

SUMMARY

Data mining is the natural evolution of query and reporting tools. Everyone, who creates queries and reports, benefits from having mining capabilities. Data mining is the process of extracting valid, previously unknown, comprehensible and actionable information from large databases and using it to make business decisions. The important characteristics of data mining tools include: data preparation facilities; selection of data mining operations; scalability and performance; and facilities for understanding results.

EXERCISES

1. What is data mining?
2. What are the tasks solved by data mining?
3. What are advantages of data mining?
4. What are the technologies used in data mining?
5. Discuss what data mining tools?
6. Provide example of data mining applications.
7. Explain the data mining process.

■

CHAPTER 29

GEOGRAPHIC INFORMATION SYSTEM

29.1 INTRODUCTION

A geographic information system (GIS) is a computer-based tool for mapping and analyzing things that exist and event that happen on earth. GIS technology integrates common database operations such as query and statistical analysis with the unique visualization and geographic analysis benefits offered by maps. These abilities distinguish GIS from other information systems and make it valuable to a wide range of public and private enterprises for explaining events, predicting outcomes and planning strategies.

The major challenge we face in the world today-overpopulation, pollution, deforestation and natural disasters-have a critical geographic dimension. Whether it is locating a suitable site for a new business or finding the best route for an emergency vehicle most problems also have a geographical component. GIS will give you the power to create maps, integrate information, visualize scenarios, solve complicated problems, present powerful ideas and develop effective solutions like never before. GIS is a tool used by individuals and organizations, businesses seeking innovative ways to solve their problems.

Mapmaking and geographic analysis are not new, but a GIS performs these tasks better and faster than the old manual methods. Before GIS technology came into existence, only a few people and the skills necessary to use geographic information to help with decision-making and problem solving. Today, GIS is a multibillion-dollar industry employing hundreds of thousands of people worldwide. GIS is taught in schools, colleges and universities throughout the world. Professionals in every field are increasingly aware of the advantages of thinking and working geographically.

29.2 COMPONENTS OF GIS

A working GIS integrates five key components: hardware, software, data, people and methods.

29.2.1 Hardware

Hardware is the computer on which a GIS operators. Today, GIS software runs on a wide range of hardware types, from centralized computer servers to desktop computers used in standalone or networked configurations.

29.2.2 Software

GIS software provides the functions and tools needed to store, analyze and display geographic information. Key software components are:

- Tools for the input and manipulation of geographic information
- A database management system (DBMS)
- Tools that supports geographic query, analysis and visualization
- A graphical user interface (GUI) for easy access to tools

29.2.3 Data

Possibly, the most important components of a GIS is the data. Geographic data and related tabular data can be collected in-horse or purchased from a commercial data provider. A GIS will integrate spatial data other data resources and can even use a DBMS, used by most organizations to organize and maintain their data, to mange spatial data.

29.2.4 People

GIS technology is of limited value without the people who manage the system and develop plans for applying it to real-world problems. GIS users range from technical specialists who design and maintain the system to those who use it to help them perform their everyday work.

29.2.5 Methods

A successful GIS operates according to a well-designed plan and business rules, which are the models and operating practices unique to each organization.

29.3 HOW GIS WORKS

GIS stores information about the world as a collection of thematic layers that can be linked together by geography (see Figure 29.3). This simple but extremely powerful and versatile concept has proven invaluable for solving many real-world problems from tracking delivery vehicles, to recording details of planning applications to modelling global atmosphere circulation.

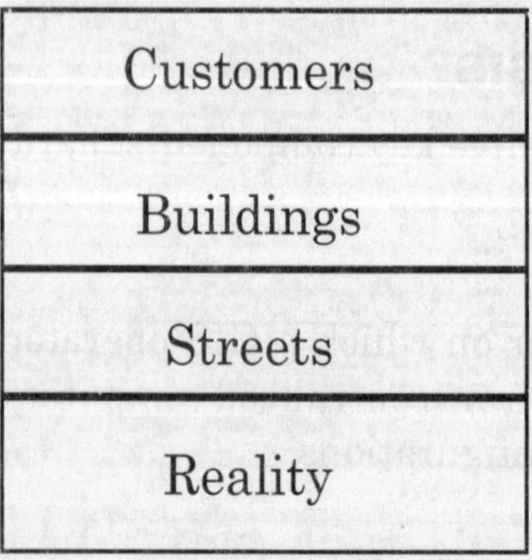

Figure 29.3 How GIS works?

29.4 GEOGRAPHIC REFERENCES

Geographic information contains either an explicit geographic reference such as a latitude and longitude or national grid coordinate, or an implicit reference such as address, postal code, census tract name, forest stand identifier, or road name. An automated process called geo-coding is used to create explicit geographic references (multiple locations) from implicit references (descriptions such as addresses). These geographic references allow you to locate features, such as a business or forest stand and events, such as an earthquake, on the earth's surface for analysis.

29.5 VECTOR AND RASTER MODELS

Geographic information systems works with two fundamentally different types of geographic models-the "vector" model and the "raster" model. In the vector model, information about points, lines and polygons is encoded and stored as a collection of x, y coordinates. The location of a point feature, such as a bore hole, can be described by a single x, y coordinate. Liner features, such as roads and rivers, can be stored as a collection of point coordinates. Polygonal features, such as sales territories and river catchments, can be stored as a closed loop of coordinates.

The vector model is extremely useful for describing discrete features, but less useful for describing continuously varying features such as soil type or accessibility costs for hospitals. The raster model has evolved to model such as continuous features. A raster image comprises a collection of grid cells rather like a scanned map or picture. Both the vector and raster models for storing geographic data have unique advantages and disadvantages. Modern GISs are able to handle both models.

29.6 DATA FOR GIS

If you unfamiliar with map data, think first about how you want to use map data. The following are some of the common map data types:

- **Base Maps** – Include streets and highways; boundaries for census, postal and political areas; rivers and lakes; perks and landmarks; place names; and USGs raster maps.
- **Business Maps and Data** – Include data related to census/demography, consumer products, financial services, health care, real estate, telecommunications, emergency preparedness, crime, advertising, business establishments and transportation.
- **Environmental Maps and Data** – Include data related to the environment, weather, environmental risk, satellite imagery, topography and natural resources.
- **General Reference Maps** – World and country maps and data that can be a foundation for your database.

29.7 GIS AND RELATED TECHNOLOGIES

GISs are closely related to several other types of information systems, but it is the ability to manipulate and analyze geographic data that sets GIS technology apart. Although there are no hard and fast rules about how to classify information systems, the following discussion should help differentiate GIS from desktop mapping, computer aided design (CAD), remote sensing, DBMS and global positioning systems (GPS) technologies.

29.7.1 Desktop Mapping

A desktop mapping system uses the map metaphor to organize data and user interaction. The focus of such systems is the creation of maps: the map is the database. Most desktop mapping systems have more limited data management, spatial analysis and customization capabilities. Desktop mapping systems operate on desktop computers such as PCs, Macintoshes and smaller UNIX workstations.

29.7.2 CAD

CAD systems evolved to create designs and plans of buildings and infrastructure. This activity required that components of fixed characteristics be assembled to create the whole structure. These systems require few rules to specify how components can be assembled and very limited analytical capabilities. CAD systems have been extended to support maps but typically have limited utility for managing and analyzing large geographic databases.

29.7.3 Remote Sensing and GPS

Remote sensing is the art and science of making measurements of the earth using sensors such as cameras carried on airplanes, GPS receivers, or other devices. These sensors collect data in the form of images and provide specialized capabilities for manipulating, analyzing and visualizing those images. Lacking strong geographic data management and analytical operations, they cannot be called true GISs.

29.7.4 Database Management System (DBMS)

Database management systems specialize in the storage and management of all types of data including geographic data. DBMSs are optimized to store and retrieve data and many GISs rely on them for this purpose. They do not have the analytic and visualization tools common to GIS.

29.8 WHAT CAN GIS DO FOR YOU?

GIS can do a lot of things for you and your business. Given below are some examples:

29.8.1 Perform geographic queries and analysis

The ability of GISs to search databases and perform geographic queries has saved many companies literally millions of dollars. GISs have helped reduce costs by:

- Streamlining customer service.
- Reducing land acquisition costs through better analysis.
- Reducing fleet maintenance costs through better logistics.
- Analyzing data quickly.

29.8.2 Improve organizational integration

Many organizations that have implemented s GIS have found that one of its main benefits is improved management of their own organization and resources. Because GISs have the ability to link data sets together to geography, they facilitate interdepartmental information sharing and communication. By creating a shared database, one department can benefit from the work of another – data can be collected once and used many times.

As communication increases among individuals and departments, redundancy is reduced, productivity is enhanced and overall organizational efficiency is improved. Thu, in a utility company the customer and infrastructure databases can be integrated so that when there is planned maintenance; affected customers can be sent a computer-generated letter.

29.8.3 Make better decisions

The old adage "better information leads to better decisions" is as true for GIS as it is for other information systems. A GIS, however, is not an automated decision making system but a tool to query, analyze and map data in support of the decision making process. GIS technology has been used to assist in tasks such as presenting information at a planning inquiries, helping resolve territorial disputes and siting pylons in such a way as to minimize visual intrusion.

GIS can be used to help reach a decision about the location of a new housing development that has minimal environmental impact, is located in a low-risk area, and is close to a population center. The information can be presented succinctly and clearly in the form of a map and accompanying report, allowing decision makers to focus on the real issues rather than trying to understand the data. Because GIS products can be produced quickly, multiple scenarios can be evaluated efficiency and effectively.

29.8.4 Making Maps

Maps have a special place in GIS. The process of making maps with GIS is much more flexible then the traditional manual or automated cartography approaches. It begins with database creation. Existing paper maps can be digitized and computer-compatible information can be translated into the GIS. The GIS based cartographic database can be both continuous and scale free. Maps products can then be created centered on any location, at any scale and showing selected information symbolized effectively to highlight specific characteristics.

The characteristics of atlases and map series can be encoded in computer programs and compared with the database at the final production time. Digital products for use in other GISs can also be derived by simply copying data from the database. In a large organization, topographic databases can be used as reference frameworks by other departments.

29.9 GIS IN EVERYDAY LIFE

In today's global community, the more information you have at your fingertips, the easier it is to make an informed decision. In today's high-tech world, information comes in many different ways, from company reports and statistics from down the hall to digital photos and multimedia from across the world.

Information can be overwhelming and the need for timely decisions calls not only for innovative ways to access accurate, up-to-the minute information, but also tools to help present the information in useful ways.

A geographic information system or GIS allows you to bring all types of data together based on the geographic and locational component of the data.

But unlike a static paper map, GIS can display many layers of information that is useful to you. You will be able to integrate, visualize, manage, solve and present the information in a new way. Relationships between the data will become more apparent and your data will become more valuable.

GIS will give you the power to create maps, integrate information, visualize scenarios, solve complicated problems, present powerful ideas and develop effective solutions like never before. GIS is a tool used by individuals and organizations, schools, governments and businesses seeking innovative ways to solve their problems.

SUMMARY

A geographic information system (GIS) is a computer-based tool for mapping and analyzing things that exist and event that happen on earth. A working GIS integrates five key components: hardware, software, data, people and methods.

GIS stores information about the world as a collection of thematic layers that can be linked together by geography. This simple but extremely powerful and versatile concept has proven invaluable for solving many real-world problems from tracking delivery vehicles, to recording details of planning applications to modelling global atmosphere circulation.

GIS will give you the power to create maps, integrate information, visualize scenarios, solve complicated problems, present powerful ideas and develop effective solutions like never before. GIS is a tool used by individuals and organizations, schools, governments and businesses seeking innovative ways to solve their problems.

EXERCISES

1. What is GIS?
2. What are the components of a GIS?
3. What is the function of GIS software?
4. What is geo-coding?
5. What are vector and raster models?
6. What are the different map data types?
7. How GIS works?
8. What are the technologies related to GIS?
9. What is the difference between GIS and GPS?
10. What is the difference between GIS and CAD?
11. What are benefits of GIS?
12. How GIS can be used to improve organizational integration?
13. How does GIS help in making better decisions?
14. How can GIS used to make better maps?
15. How does GIS help you in your everyday life?

■